WARRIOR

The Autobiography of

ARIEL SHARON

by Ariel Sharon

with David Chanoff

A TOUCHSTONE BOOK
Published by Simon & Schuster
New York   London   Toronto   Sydney   Tokyo   Singapore

To my wife, Lily, who has been with me through
it all and whose love and support have been my
inspiration and strength.

TOUCHSTONE
Rockefeller Center
1230 Avenue of the Americas
New York, NY 10020

Second Touchstone Edition 2001

TOUCHSTONE and colophon are registered
trademarks of Simon & Schuster, Inc.

For information about special discounts for bulk purchases,
please contact Simon & Schuster Special Sales:
1-800-465-6798 or business@simonandschuster.com

Designed by Marybeth KilKelly/Levavi & Levavi
Photos in picture section researched, edited, and arranged by Vincent Virga
Manufactured in the United States of America

10 9 8 7 6 5 4 3 2 1

The Library of Congress has cataloged the Simon & Schuster edition as follows:

Sharon, Ariel.
    Warrior : the autobiography of Ariel Sharon / by Ariel Sharon with David Chanoff.
    p. cm.
    Includes Index.
    1. Sharon, Ariel. 2. Cabinet officers—Israel—Biography. 3. Generals—Israel—
Biography. 4. Israel—History, Military. I. Chanoff, David. II. Title.
DS126.6A42A3 1989
956.9405'092—dc20
[B]
89-6278

ISBN 0-671-60555-0
      0-7432-2566-X (Pbk)

"Terrorist Raids Into Israel 1951–56" from *The Arab-Israeli Conflict: Its History in Maps*
by Martin Gilbert, published by Steimatzky, Israel. Reprinted by permission. (page 87)

Picture Credits: David Rubinger (18); IDF Spokesman (30); Micha Bar-Am/Magnum
(37); Moshe Milner/Sygma (46); Newsphoto Ltd, Tel Aviv (19); Uri Dan (23, 25, 48, 50,
51, 52, 53). Any photos not identified are from the author's collection.

Contents

CONTENTS

Foreword by Uri Dan

On February 6, 2001, the citizens of Israel elected Ariel Sharon as their prime minister. He accepted this position—one which few ever thought he would attain—with spiritual calm, but also with full seriousness, reflecting the single-minded purpose, as Winston Churchill once called it, with which he approached this awesome duty. Because to serve as prime minister of the Jewish state is to assume responsibility for the entire Jewish people, who have achieved their 2,000-year-old dream of reestablishing their homeland.

The people of Israel elected Ariel Sharon at a pivotal moment in their history, a time of critical danger that had seen the country, for the previous four months, dragged into an intolerable war of attrition, accompanied by waves of violence, terrorism, and hateful incitement initiated by Yasser Arafat's Palestinian Authority.

Sharon had promised to restore security and revive the prospects of peace that Israelis so deserve and for which they have longed since their nation was created in 1948. And the people of Israel placed their trust in him, propelling him into office with an unprecedented electoral majority—62.38 percent. It was a tribute to his well-deserved reputation for handling many of the nation's critical struggles and crises, problems that others regarded as "missions impossible."

Yet Sharon understood that in becoming prime minister, he was assuming the toughest assignment of all those he had previously known. After all, he had seen the war clouds gathering in the Israeli skies years before they appeared and had tried his utmost, through the many government and political positions he'd held, to keep those threats from coming to reality.

Since this book first appeared in print, Sharon has faced many difficult challenges, both political and personal. Perhaps none was more painful than the death of his wife, Lily, of whom he wrote in the original dedication of this book, her "love and support have been my inspiration and strength."

And yet, characteristically, he never lost his basic optimism. Though much of the world knows him by the title of this autobiography, he is fundamentally a man of peace. "We can control our destiny," he said in a message to Israelis shortly after his election. "United, I believe, we can win the battle for peace. But it must be a different peace: one with full recognition of the birthrights of Jews in their one and only land; one with security for generations; and one with a united Jerusalem, the eternal, undivided capital of the Jewish people and the State of Israel forever."

Sharon recognized the crisis at hand: It is "not just over security arrangements for Israel," he said, "it is by and large over the inherent right of Jews to exist and live in a Jewish democratic state, the one and only country in the world where we have the right and capability to defend ourselves *by ourselves*, and thus ensure the security of Jews everywhere." It was a desire to make clear this inherent right of existence that led Sharon to make his dramatic visit to Jerusalem's Temple Mount on September 28, 2000—a decision that unexpectedly set into motion the events that led to his remarkable election.

He had been warning of the coming crisis as early as 1990, when, with "a heavy heart," he stunned Prime Minister Yitzhak Shamir by resigning as minister of industry and trade to protest the government's policies. "The matter is one of national principle," he declared. Under Shamir, he charged, "Palestinian terrorism runs unchecked within the whole of *Eretz Israel* [the land of Israel] and causes heavy losses of Jews and of innocent Arabs." As a result, he said, "our capital—the very heart of the Jewish people—has again been split in two." And he could not stand by and acquiesce. "There are times when a man must know when to get up from his seat and start marching," he wrote Shamir. "There are times in the life of a nation, in the lives of people, when they must awaken, arise, and fight with all their might before calamity overtakes them."

Four months later, however, he was back in the cabinet, having in the meantime prevented the Labor Party from toppling Shamir's government. A new crisis was at hand: a critical shortage of housing following a dramatic new wave of immigration from the soon-to-collapse Soviet Union. As minister of housing and construction, Sharon spearheaded the building of 144,000 new apartments and the renovation of 22,000 others within two years, an unheard-of achievement.

But the situation with the Palestinians always took precedence. Just months after the 1991 Gulf War, in which Israel withstood the onslaught of Saddam Hussein's SCUD missiles, Sharon was one of the few voices to oppose Israel's participation in the Madrid Conference. He understood that its real purpose was to force Israel into negotiating with the PLO—at a time when the Palestinian charter still called for the destruction of the Jewish state. And that, he warned, would endanger Israel's security.

To reduce the threat, he stepped up settlement efforts throughout the nation: not just in Judea and Samaria, in Gaza and the Golan Heights, but also in the Galilee—where he was instrumental in creating for the first time a Jewish majority—and the Negev, as well as greater Jerusalem. To hold the security zones, he knew, Jewish settlement there was essential.

Indeed, it is not by accident that the settlements are located where they are. They guard the cradle of the birth of the Jewish people, Judea and Samaria, while simultaneously affording Israel a strategic depth that is vital to its existence. The importance of these security zones has not lessened; indeed, it has become even greater.

But in 1992, the Likud was ousted in national elections by Yitzhak Rabin and the Labor Party. That defeat, he had no doubt, was the result of a short-sighted split within the nationalist camp that failed to appreciate the inherent danger of allowing a left-wing government to come to power. And yet history would repeat itself just seven years later.

It was not easy for Sharon to wage a struggle from the opposition. Yet he had a secret weapon: Contrary to popular myth, his personal ambition was always subordinate to the national interest. For all his interest in becoming prime minister, he was never prepared to abandon his deeply held principles and beliefs—not in regard to the safety of Jews. Which is why, despite his close and special personal relationship with Rabin, from the first he opposed the Oslo Agreements.

It's no exaggeration to say that no one had Rabin's ear on military and security advice more than Sharon. And he warned Rabin, in a frank, face-to-face talk, of Oslo's inherent dangers and the threat of bringing Yasser Arafat back to Gaza and to Israel. But this time, Rabin did not listen. So Sharon went on the stump, in Europe and the United States, warning ominously that peace would prove more and more elusive as terrorism increased. His was a lone voice in the wilderness, but he refused to keep silent. "If I am worried, then you had best also be worried," he cautioned during a hunger strike outside Rabin's office in 1995. Sadly, he was proven right: Suicide bombings and other terrorist attacks have continued incessantly, proving that Arafat had no intention of honoring the agreement he'd signed with Rabin and Peres.

The bitter divide in Israeli society grew to such an extent that it culminated in the most dastardly and abominable deed in the nation's history: the assassination of Prime Minister Rabin by a villainous Jewish assassin in the heart of Tel Aviv in November 1995. Israel was hit by a veritable earthquake that night; such evil was unthinkable in the Middle East's only democracy.

Six months later, the Likud, led by Benjamin (Bibi) Netanyahu, was restored to power by a handful of votes in national elections. Sharon became minister of national infrastructure, a new and powerful position created especially for him. Besides preparing Israel for twenty-first-century needs, he initiated future projects for cooperation with Jordan and the Palestinians, in order to put the peace process onto a viable track by creating a joint economic interest for all the parties. At the same time, Sharon worked to bolster the inexperienced Netanyahu in his struggle against the Palestinian Authority—especially when President Bill Clinton pressed Israel into making withdrawals that endangered security and eliminated Israeli control of sites that are integral to Jewish history, particularly the ancient city of Hebron.

Yet, as a member of the defense cabinet, he also made repeated efforts, in vain, to bring about a gradual withdrawal of Israeli forces from south Lebanon, in a way that would leave the Lebanese army deployed along Israel's northern border. He believed it was essential to end Israel's stay in Lebanon, while ensuring that the Iranian-supported terrorist organization Hezbollah could not threaten Israeli border towns. In the end, Israel did unilaterally withdraw from Lebanon under then–Prime Minister Ehud Barak, in a manner that has aroused new and dangerous hopes in the minds of Israel's enemies. Hezbollah has stationed itself along the border, and the Palestinians drew encouragement from the belief that Israel could be pressured into withdrawals by means of terrorism and violence—of the kind that Arafat renewed in September 2000.

At the same time, Sharon opened his own dialogue with key members of the Palestinian Authority. He met several times with Abu Alla, one of Arafat's assistants, and hosted one of the top Palestinian leaders, Abu Mazen, in his home. Sharon recognized that he could not ignore the new political realities. Understanding that a Palestinian state was inevitable, he focused on reducing the potential security damage and strengthening Jewish settlements in Judea, Samaria, and Gaza.

The peace agreement with Jordan's King Hussein, which had been signed by Rabin in 1994, also influenced a change in Sharon's approach. Until then, he had believed that Israel's conflict with the Palestinians should find its solution through Jordan, whose population was overwhelmingly Palestinian. But peace with Jordan and the Oslo Accords changed the entire situation: Israel could no longer risk the possibility of two Palestinian states coming into being.

This change in Sharon's approach toward Jordan also yielded a special relationship of friendship and trust with King Hussein. Among other areas, they found a common interest in developing water sources for the two desert nations. So strong was the relationship that Netanyahu dispatched Sharon to Jordan to solve a sudden crisis when two Israeli Mossad agents were captured there after failing to liquidate Haled Mashal, head of the terrorist Hamas. After a lengthy late-night conversation with Sharon, the king agreed to release the Israelis and restore diplomatic relations to where they'd previously been.

In October 1998, Netanyahu named Sharon his foreign minister; together, they attended the Clinton-hosted tripartite conference at the Wye Plantation. There, Sharon fought for every inch of ground against Arafat's demands for further Israeli withdrawals. Eventually, with the help of the dying King Hussein, an agreement was reached: Israel would execute a staged withdrawal from 13 percent of Judea and Samaria but only if it was accompanied by Palestinian compliance with its previously agreed-on obligations, including the collection of illegal weapons, the jailing of terrorists, and an end to official hate-filled incitement.

But Netanyahu's government was destined to fall, thanks once again to divisions in the nationalist camp. Ehud Barak won a landslide victory in May 1999 and, when Netanyahu decided to take time out from politics, Sharon was named leader of the opposition. Believing unity imperative in order to meet the challenges of the Wye agreement, he accepted when Barak invited him to join a national-unity government. But the offer was withdrawn, and Barak elected to go it alone, which would lead to his political downfall far more quickly than anyone could imagine.

Sharon's political success was overshadowed by a dark personal tragedy. Shortly before the election, his wife, Lily, was diagnosed with cancer. Now, Lily—who had stood by Arik's side through his toughest times—had to fight for her own life. For the first time, Ariel Sharon could only stand by helplessly. But Lily, true to her nature, did her best to send a message of "business as usual." With astonishing courage and bravery, she endured painful treatments in Tel Aviv and New York. All the while, she did everything in her power to ensure that he would not abandon his political struggle. The Sharons suffered another blow that December when their home on the farm burned down, taking with it all the memories of the warm nest that Lily had provided for the family. Yet it was Lily who, when things looked bleakest, pressed him time after time to continue the fight, to go out in the political fields after the long and heartrending nights he spent at her hospital bedside.

By dint of supreme effort, he rebuilt the Likud as an effective opposition party, fighting Barak's readiness to make further dangerous concessions with stubborn determination.

In March 2000, Lily lost her valiant battle for life. She had lived with dignity, and she died with dignity, surrounded by her entire family, who enveloped her with their love and appreciation. She was laid to rest on Anemone Hill, the hillock on the Sharon farm that she and Arik loved so much. Thousands of people gathered there from all spheres—friends, acquaintences, even total strangers came to console the Sharons that day and during the week of mourning that followed, testifying to their recognition of Lily's unique personality and how she had been inseparable from her husband.

But the loss of Lily did not leave Arik alone: More than ever, his sons, Omri and Gilad, and his daughter-in-law, Inbal, stood loyally by him, giving Sharon their love and total support.

That summer, President Clinton convened the Camp David summit, attended by both Arafat and Barak, who came bearing a package of Israeli concessions of unprecedented proportions. To the astonishment of American and Israeli leaders, Arafat rejected the proposal, in which Barak was demanding a signed document that would recognize the end of the Palestinians' dispute with Israel. Not till later was it learned that it was precisely at this time that Arafat had instructed his armed forces to prepare a campaign of violence and terror aimed at forcing a complete Israeli capitulation.

After the failure of the Camp David summit, Sharon learned, Barak was prepared to offer even further concessions to Arafat. Without consulting with his own cabinet, let alone the Knesset, Barak had offered to turn over 97 percent of the West Bank, uprooting some 100 Jewish settlements. Even more worrisome, Barak—again, acting virtually alone—was going to hand over to the PLO the Old City of Jerusalem and give Arafat control of the Temple Mount. This was nothing less than ceding control of Judaism's holiest site, the very heart and soul of the Jewish people, the center of Jewish hopes, dreams, and prayers during thousands of years of exile.

Once again, Sharon was a voice in the wilderness. Despite his warnings, few appreciated the grave developments, in large part because Barak would never admit that he was still conducting secret negotiations with Arafat through the White House. But when Arafat declared that he could not accept Israeli control of the Western Wall without consulting the world's Muslims— insisting falsely that the Temple Mount had never enjoyed a Jewish presence— Sharon saw his opportunity. Jerusalem, Sharon understood, does not belong only to the state of Israel. It may be the Jewish state's eternal capital, but Jerusalem is the property of the entire Jewish people. Fate has given the modern Jewish state the awesome privilege and responsibility of defending Jerusalem, of liberating and unifying it, as it did in 1967. So, in order to arouse Jewish public opinion that the fate of the Temple Mount was in danger, he undertook to dramatically challenge Barak's concessions.

On September 24, 2000, while in New York, Sharon told the Voice of Israel radio that he intended to visit the Temple Mount that coming Thursday; Israeli public officials had, by and large, avoided any presence in the holiest of Jewish sites. He then informed the appropriate authorities.

One week earlier, against the backdrop of secret talks, the Palestinians had begun a series of terrorist activities in Gaza—a move security officials feared could be the start of a new large-scale campaign. The day before Sharon's trip to Jerusalem, a remote-controlled bomb exploded in Gaza, killing an Israeli officer and wounding another.

On the morning of September 28, Sharon ascended to the Temple Mount, accompanied by several Likud Knesset members. "I have come with a message of peace," he told reporters. "Jews have the right to visit here." But they weren't the only Knesset members there that day: Several Arab representatives from radical anti-Zionist parties had shown up, and they incited Palestinian onlookers to throw stones at Israeli policemen. Still, Sharon's visit might have remained just another internal political move, had Arafat not used it as a convenient pretext for embarking on a campaign of terror and violence.

The following day, at the close of morning prayers on the Temple Mount, Palestinians launched a violent clash with Israeli police and pelted Jewish worshippers at the Western Wall with stones. When security forces opened fire, killing several Palestinians, a new blood libel was born: the accusation, spread by the PLO and picked up by sympathetic journalists, that Sharon's visit to the Temple Mount had directly instigated violence. The Palestinians even labeled their campaign of violence and incitement the "Al-Aqsa intifada" and falsely claimed that Sharon had violated the mosques on the Temple Mount.

In the weeks that followed, even official Palestinian spokesmen eventually abandoned the falsehood and admitted that Arafat had planned a renewal of violence following the collapse of Camp David—long before Sharon had announced his Temple Mount visit. It was Arafat's planned response to the diplomatic stalemate, despite—or perhaps because of—Barak's readiness to make concessions that no prime minister before him would have dared consider. Barak, to his credit, repeatedly defended Sharon's Temple Mount visit.

Arafat pressed his case by demanding an international commission to investigate the "causes" of the ongoing violence; President Clinton gave in, and Barak—against the warnings of Sharon, who feared that Israel would effectively be put on trial—gave his consent. But the commission, headed by former Sen. George Mitchell, did not reach the conclusion that Arafat expected. In its final report, the commission said flatly: "We were provided with no persuasive evidence that the Sharon visit was anything other than an internal political act. . . . The Sharon visit did not cause the 'Al-Aqsa intifada.'" Not that Sharon needed Mitchell's "rehabilitation."

As the situation worsened, Sharon made clear his willingness once again to join a national-unity government. But again, Barak would not follow through, believing that only he could reach an agreement with Arafat to stop the war of attrition. Meanwhile, acts of terrorism against Israelis increased, and all efforts by the United States to halt the violence were flatly rejected, even though Barak—for the first time in Israeli history—agreed to conduct negotiations under fire.

Hoping to score a political coup, Barak abruptly resigned in December 2000, forcing early elections, which he believed he would win handily. But Sharon did not wage the campaign Barak was expecting. He vowed from the start that he would form a national-unity government in order to restore security and promote peace. The campaign was one of Israel's harshest and reached its low point when the Barak camp declared that a vote for Sharon was a vote for war. But as Israelis clearly realized, they had already been in a war for several months.

The results were overwhelming: Sharon was swept into office with a mandate never before seen in Israel. But at the moment of victory, he could hardly celebrate. He'd achieved his greatest political triumph and earned a resounding personal vote of confidence from the nation, but Lily was not there to share it with him. She who'd stood by him through all the trials and tribulations had more right than anyone to savor the well-earned victory. But as he contemplated her absence, he had difficulty holding back the tears that welled up in his eyes.

In swift order, Sharon formed a national-unity government, as he'd promised, not only to achieve unity across the broad spectrum of the Jewish community, but also to reach out to the hearts of those Israeli Arabs prepared to live in peace within the Jewish state. Ultimately, however, he formed a government in order to ensure a return of law and security to Israelis' daily lives.

It is an enormous burden that Sharon has taken on his shoulders. But he recognizes that the Jewish state is at a decisive historical crossroads. He does not believe in a physical separation with the Palestinians; that policy exists only on the left, which holds that Israelis and Arabs cannot live together. Sharon has never thought that way.

Sharon believes that while retaining its strategic assets, such as the Golan Heights, Israel must also preserve its deep-rooted historical links, such as the Cave of the Patriarchs in Hebron, traditional burial place of the biblical forefathers. No country would willingly yield such historical assets. In Washington, crowds stand at the foot of the Lincoln Memorial and Washington Monument, tributes to great leaders of the past two centuries. But in Hebron, says Sharon, you are talking about four thousand years of history, the place where David was crowned king of Israel. Any other nation would see to it that Hebron would be a required chapter in its children's education. Sharon understands that these are our deepest roots; how can you give up something like that?

Strategically, Sharon believes that time does not act against Israel, that the Arab world's ability to launch a military strike will diminish over the next ten to fifteen years. Therefore, it is critical that any solutions be able to stand up over a long period of time. And Sharon's ultimate vision is equally longrange: A new influx of one million immigrants, ensuring that Israel is home to a majority of the world's Jews by 2020; development of the Negev; and renewal of Zionist-value education to reinstill the pioneer generation's legitimate sense of the justice of our struggle and our full right to the land of our fathers.

Sharon has no longing or nostalgia for the past. He is focused on the future. Yet he recognizes that there was a different spirit in the nation's early days, one that enabled his generation to build today's Israel. And at the end of the day, the Zionist revolution is the only one of the twentieth-century's revolutions that succeeded.

Ariel Sharon, prime minister of Israel, knows that if we stand united, we can look to the future with hope. For as he says in this book, when he looks back on all that the people of Israel already have accomplished, it gives him the heart for what remains to be done.

1

An Echo

We had been in "Africa" for several days, on the west side of the Suez Canal. Already it was October 18, 1973. By now the Egyptians had recovered from the surprise of the crossing, an operation Anwar Sadat originally called "a television exercise." At first they had neglected the crossing site, unaware of what our thrust across the canal would come to mean. But now they knew they were facing the imminent encirclement and destruction of their armies, and they were hitting the pontoon bridge with everything they had. Shells buried themselves in the sand with concussive thuds. Now and then a fireball would explode among the men and tanks that were flowing across and spreading south and north behind Egyptian lines. Jets screamed overhead, dropping loads of napalm and high explosives.

We had been fighting since Yom Kippur, almost two straight weeks. Since then no one in the division had gotten any real sleep. Men dozed off in their positions during the occasional lulls or tried to catch an hour or two at night on the warm engines of tanks and armored personnel carriers. The entire previous night I had spent at our forward posts staring into a Starlight scope toward Ismailia, looking for signs of Egyptian movement. Now, despite the shelling, I couldn't keep my eyes open. Wrapping my coat around me, I lay down in the sand next to my command APC. Already half asleep, I felt someone pull a blanket over me. Nearby a voice was shouting something, and I heard a soldier whisper hoarsely, "Be quiet, Arik's tired. Let him sleep." From the edge of a dream the words triggered a distant echo.

A soldier had said it then too, one of the thirty or so I had led out on a raid behind Iraqi lines in the winter of 1948—during the War of Independence. Exhausted from the fighting and the march, we had stumbled back to our camp in the Kfar Saba orange groves, soaked and shivering in the gray morning drizzle. My tent leaked. It had lost its rain cover months ago, and I knew the canvas was as sodden inside as out. Unable to face the idea of crawling inside, I walked over to the packing shed where we stored our weapons and ammunition and collapsed on a broken field cot in the corner. With my heavy British duffel coat pulled up around my ears I was just drifting off when some of the boys clumped into the shed, wanting to talk to me. "Be quiet," I heard my Sergeant Peretz saying, "Arik's tired. Let him sleep." Then too someone had covered me with a blanket or another coat. After twenty-five years I still remembered the tenderness of that gesture. I had felt surrounded by warmth and security, by the protectiveness of a family.

Perhaps these emotions had seemed especially sharp because I had not often experienced the same kind of outward affection from my own family. My father, Samuil, and my mother, Vera, were a different sort of people, not given to displaying their feelings, no matter how strong these might have been. Though they loved my sister, Dita, and me deeply, it was not their way to show it, certainly not through demonstrations of physical affection. They did not wear their hearts on their sleeves. What my parents did exude was strength, determination, and stubbornness. In Kfar Malal, the moshav where they worked their farm and where in 1928 I was born, these were qualities they were famous for. Even among the stiff-necked pioneers who had dragged Kfar Malal's farmland from the barren soil, their own stubbornness set them apart, often far apart.

They were different in other ways too. Most of Kfar Malal's forty or so married couples were Labor Zionists from the Yiddish-speaking ghettos and villages of Eastern Europe. Along with so many others in the second and third waves of immigration, they had come to Israel (Palestine to the world, to them "Eretz Israel"—the Land of Israel) not only to reclaim the Jewish homeland but to build a model socialist society. The co-operative farming village, the moshav, was their vehicle, a place where each family had its own home and land, but where the major decisions about planting, harvesting, and marketing were made in common, a place where communal values prevailed.

At least that was how it was meant to be. But my father did not fit into anybody's mold. Like his neighbors, he was a passionate Zionist. But unlike them, he was no socialist. On the contrary, if anything stood out in his character, it was his individualism. Worse, he made no effort at all to hide his dislike for people he considered too rigidly ideological. In the enclosed social and political world of the moshav, these were volatile qualities. Occasionally the tensions between him and the other moshavniks had positive results. His innovations in planting and cultivating, developed in the face of community opposition, had an impact on farming not only on the moshav but throughout the Jewish settlements. But always the ill fit between my father and his neighbors made for problems, giving a sharper edge to an already hard life.

Like his father before him, Samuil was a Jewish nationalist pure and simple. Except for his Zionism he had no political allegiances whatsoever, not to socialism or communism or anything else. He had grown up in Brest Litovsk, where his father had been a leader in the local Zionist organization. My grandfather's colleague and closest friend was Menachem Begin's father, who was known in our family not as "Begin," but as "Bigun," Russian for "restless" or "driven." Legend had it that the two of them had once broken down the door of a synagogue whose rabbi had refused permission to hold a memorial service there for Theodor Herzl, the founder of the Zionist movement.

Mordechai Scheinerman, my Zionist grandfather had trekked to Israel first in 1910. For two years he had taught school in Rehovot before returning to Russia to try to make arrangements to bring the rest of the family. But although his hopes for a quick return did not materialize, he did manage to instill in my father his deep longing for Eretz Israel. He also worked hard to help Samuil prepare for his own "aliyah"—his ascent to the homeland. An intellectual himself, he sent my father to classical Russian primary and secondary schools where Samuil learned French, German, and Latin. Meanwhile, at home my grandfather taught him Hebrew, Bible, and Zionist philosophy. And when he graduated from high school, my father enrolled in the faculty of agronomy at Tiflis University, where the family had moved to get away from the fighting of World War One. Both my father and grandfather knew that a scientific knowledge of agriculture would be important for someone who was going to be a farmer in the Promised Land.

In Tiflis my father met Vera Schneeroff, a student at the university's medical faculty. Vera was from a family in the Beulorussian district of Mohilov-on-the-Dnieper, the one Jewish family in the little village of Halavenchichi for several generations. Her father was a lumberman, cutting and selling timber from rented woods. Surrounded by Russian peasants, the Schneeroffs had somehow kept their Judaism alive, inviting other Jewish families in to help celebrate the holidays. Theirs was a steadfastness that even their gentile neighbors respected. In 1905 and 1906, when pogroms tore through their region, they were not touched, though perhaps that had as much to do with grandfather's legendary physical strength as with anything else. The Schneeroffs were also fiercely intent on education. Though they lived a hard life, with few luxuries, they saw to it that each of their eight children went through school in the neighboring town. And with the help of their eldest, Joseph, four of them went on to the university.

Perhaps my father recognized in Vera a streak of rock-hard willpower and determination and understood that she would make a good companion in the pioneer's life he was planning. Or perhaps he simply fell in love. Whichever the case, he had found in Vera a young woman of immense personal strength, the kind who would do what had to be done without asking many questions about it, and without any complaints either.

In 1917 the Czar's war against Germany turned into a civil war inside Russia. It took four years before the Revolution got rid of its enemies in Greater Russia and the Ukraine, but by 1921 the Red Army finally turned southward toward the Caucasian cities of Baku and Tiflis. For my parents it was still too soon. My father had just finished his agricultural studies, but my mother was still two years away from the medical degree that was her own great ambition. But there was no help for it. As an active Zionist, my father was sure to be arrested as soon as the communists arrived. Both he and Vera had seen the terrible massacres of Armenians and Turks, and they had no illusions about what the Revolution might bring with it. So with the Red columns closing in, they moved up their plans. In the spring of the year they got married and fled Tiflis, making their way to the Black Sea port of Batum, where they took ship for Israel.

For my father it was a journey that would fulfill his dreams, an "aliyah." But my mother did not share the vision. If Samuil was no socialist, Vera was not even much of a Zionist. While he saw the two of them returning to the homeland, she considered herself not much more than an emigrant. Not that she found anything particularly strange in that. Already her brother Joseph had settled in Istanbul. Another brother, Solomon, was there too. A third brother was studying medicine in Germany, from where he eventually traveled first to Mexico, then to the United States, changing his name from Schneeroff to Montana along the way to ease problems with the immigration people.

Like so many Jewish families of those days, the Schneeroffs were wanderers, shaken from their homes by the upheavals of the times. In the years after the World War the earlier Jewish migration from Eastern Europe and Russia resumed its flow. Almost forty thousand Jewish immigrants arrived in Israel, members of what was called the "Third Aliyah." Following her husband, Vera was one of them, though she had little in common with the inspired Zionists and socialists of that generation. She knew no Hebrew and spoke Russian rather than Yiddish. She knew nothing about crops or soil and was hardly prepared to be a dirt farmer for the rest of her life. She was at home in the genteel world of Russian intellectuals and artists, and she hadn't the vaguest desire to live a communal existence with people she did not know and with whom she had little in common.

More than anything she wanted to finish her medical studies. As they prepared to leave Tiflis, she consoled herself that somehow she would be able to do it, perhaps in Jerusalem or at the American University in Beirut. But in the Caucusus there was no real information about that kind of thing. And when she arrived in the Promised Land, she found it a wilderness, a place for farmers and laborers, not for aspiring medical students. As she moved with my father from the experimental farm at Ben Shemen, where he first found work, to the agricultural school at Mikveh Israel, she began to realize how distant her own dreams had become. It was not in her nature to complain. But the loss scarred her heart.

Meanwhile, my father was trying to decide where to settle down. He heard that the Jezreel Valley kibbutz of Ein Harod had openings for members, but Vera didn't like the idea. It was just as well. For someone of his nature the steamy collective life of a kibbutz would have been a disaster. Then an opportunity came up at Kfar Malal, fifteen miles northeast of Tel Aviv on the coastal Plain of Sharon. Life there would be difficult, but where wasn't it difficult? There was no water or electricity and they would have to live in a tent while they built their own cabin. It would be treacherous too. The village had been destroyed in an Arab raid the year before, then re-established by the moshavniks. But in Kfar Malal they would have their own land, and to my father that was worth anything.

That was how in 1922 Samuil and Vera moved into the moshav. For the first year and a half they lived in the tent and struggled to cultivate the arid slope of land that had been assigned to them as a farm. It took that long for Samuil to construct his "house," two small rooms with a rough lean-to shed for a kitchen. At first my parents lived in one room, a mule and a cow in the other. Inside, the walls were plastered with a mixture of mud, dried manure, and straw. I remember as a child staring at the wall next to my bed, watching the gaps between the studs and the adjoining mud grow wider as time passed. I remember too the ceiling rafters that divided the living space from the attic. Big rats made their homes up there, staring down and waiting to jump on any food that my mother might happen to leave in the kitchen. In the evening I would hear them scurrying around above my head, and looking up, I would see their bare tails curling down below the rafters as they rushed along. When they got too active, it was my job to put the cat up there to do battle. Who won I do not remember. I know the cat survived. My memory is that the tails did too.

Of the two rooms, one was now my parents' bedroom, the other a combined living-dining area and a bedroom for myself and my older sister, Dita. Several years after I was born my father added a third room so that Dita could have at least a taste of privacy. By that time we also had a chicken coop behind the hut and a concrete barn big enough for our horse, a donkey, and two or three cows.

Clearing the new land, planting, and harvesting were brutal work for my parents, especially in the early years before they were hardened to it. Every few days they would haul the water barrel down to the Yarkon River in our horse-drawn wagon, fill it, then haul it back again. My mother milked the cows, cared for the other animals, and worked the fields alongside my father, a bowl of water next to her so she could dip her dry and cracked fingers in a vain effort to keep them moist. At the end of the day the two of them would talk softly together in Russian while my mother washed the dinner dishes in a bucket and my father dried. From my bed on the other side of the room I would listen to them, pretending to be asleep. From the tone as much as from the half-heard words, I sensed that they shared a strong friendship, even if there was not much small talk around the house and even if my mother did not often seem cheerful.

As I grew older, I became aware that though my mother had transformed herself into a veteran farmer, she had never really integrated herself into the world of the moshav. In a special place on the shelf she kept her old surgical scalpel and her student anatomy books, which from time to time she took down and looked through. It seemed to me that she kept inside herself somewhere a different life, separate from the farm—a life where she loved other things and other people. She took out her loneliness and her longing by writing letters—to her parents and friends in Baku and Tiflis, her older sister in Tashkent, her brothers in Paris and Istanbul. On occasion she would even take an entire day off, closing herself in her room and not coming out until dinner. My father called those her "letter days." That meant, "Today you better watch out."

For my father too life on the moshav was a struggle—not just a farmer's struggle against the land and the elements but a struggle to maintain the culture he had been brought up to love. He read books by the great Russian poets and novelists. He painted watercolors of landscapes and friends, played the violin, and sang in a fluid tenor, filling the house with Russian and Zionist songs. Now and then his musician friends would gather for chamber music in the living room (which was also my bedroom), and I would fall asleep to the sounds of their playing.

This rich cultural life was ingrained in my father, and keeping it up while breaking his back on the farm was something like a war with him. He was a man who simply would not allow outside limitations to control his life. But the cultural war was not the only battle he was fighting as I was growing up, nor even the most significant. It was not until I was older that I began to value the music, art, and literature that were part of our household, and to appreciate the struggle it took to sustain them. But I recognized a good deal earlier that my father was also carrying on a running battle with the other moshavniks.

The problem was that the man was by nature unable to compromise. The problem was also that he was an agricultural scientist and, in his own field, a visionary. Nor was he the kind to keep his mouth shut and nurse secret resentments. If he thought something was wrong, he came out and said it. And if he was convinced of his position, he would not give in, not if a majority was against him and not if everyone was against him.

Had he been a private farmer, none of this would have mattered. But on the co-operative moshav it was a different story. He fought about the structure of the co-op, the size of the farms, and the crops to be planted. First he fought. And then when he lost he would refuse to abide by the moshav's dictates. The moshav committee would decide that everyone should plant oranges and lemons; he would insist on experimenting with mandarins and mangoes. The committee would declare that spring was the correct time for potato seeding; he announced that late fall was equally good. He pioneered avocados, calling them the "fruit of the future" when hardly anyone else had heard of them and the idea of devoting good orchard space to their cultivation seemed bizarre. "When you work for something," he told me, "then it's your duty to protect it. A man should protect his property!" And he protected his with a fence around his orchards and a lock on his gate, the only fence and lock in Kfar Malal. It was not so much for security; anyone who wanted could have climbed over the fence. It was the idea of it.

None of this sat well with the other stubborn moshavniks with whom my mother and father co-existed. It was not that relations were hostile. For all the fighting, my parents felt lucky to be where they were; and for as many issues as they fought over, they agreed on that many more. They participated fully in the life of the moshav, stood guard duty with the rest, and went off to help defend other villages when manpower was needed. But there was also a constant tension. I remembered that for years one of their fellow farmers habitually began each of his comments in the community meeting by declaring, "I am not an agronomist, but allow me to say anyway that . . ." And there was, of course, only one agronomist among them.

These tensions and the social isolation that came in their wake were perhaps best summed up in my father's will, which he wrote on his deathbed thirty-fours years after he and my mother settled in the village. Although he would be buried in the moshav cemetery, he would not, he stipulated, be carried there in the village truck. I was to use his own pickup. Neither did he want any funeral speeches from the moshavniks. They should restrict themselves to the traditional prayers. As fate would have it, when it came time to lower him into the ground, it turned out that the plot next to him was occupied by the man who for years had been his chief opponent. But my mother would not allow it. Then and there she decided that the groundskeepers would have to prepare the next space over for him and that she herself would eventually come to lie between the two old antagonists.

All of this had its effect on me as I was growing up. The social tensions did not limit themselves to the adults. In a village of so few families there was no way that the children would not feel them too. I suffered from it, feeling that the friction between my parents and many of their neighbors put a heavy burden on me, that their relationships affected my relationships. I don't know if my friends felt it as strongly as I did, but the effects were obvious. The games we played in the fields and orchards stopped at the doors of their houses. I felt isolated, lonely. I wondered what their homes were like inside. The slights hurt deeply and filled me at times with rushes of turbulent emotion.

Occasional incidents drove the differences home. My friends, I knew, were all treated for the usual scrapes and illnesses at the village clinic, several hundred yards down the road from our house. But we did not go there. I had never been inside and consequently had the greatest curiosity about the place. Instead my parents would take me over to the next village where a woman doctor friend of theirs lived. It was several miles to Dr. Fogel's house, and one had to take a path through the fields to get there. But that was where we went, even in emergencies.

I remember distinctly the shock when I was five years old of being thrown off my beautiful donkey, who had shied at something in the road and had tossed me chin-first onto a rock. With blood flowing from a deep gash, I ran to my mother, who bundled me into her arms and started off on her own run to the neighboring village. In the dusk I saw the lighted windows of the Kfar Malal clinic jog by. Then we were running through the darkening fields where ordinarily one did not venture after sundown. Finally my mother banged on a large gate and Dr. Fogel came out with a lantern in her hands. In its glare I looked up and saw that my mother was covered with blood. I wondered for a moment how she had gotten hurt, then realized the blood was mine. Later that night, after I had been treated and swathed in bandages, we walked home through the same dangerous fields.

Dr. Fogel was Russian-born, and she and my mother were closest friends. On occasion my mother would cook her a dinner of cabbage and borscht, and she and her husband, Vanya, would come over and spend an evening speaking Russian. I would listen from my bed, fascinated both by her character and by the strange and often-told story of how she had come to live in Kfar Saba, the next village over from Kfar Malal. Dr. Fogel was exotic. For one thing, her husband was not Jewish. For another, Dr. Fogel was known among the local Arabs as "Sit Razal," Lady Deer. No one else I knew had an Arab nickname.

Her husband, Vanya Sidorenko, was Ukrainian. He had been an officer with Danekin's Ukrainian Whites during the Russian Revolution, in a regiment that had commandeered Dr. Fogel into service just as she finished medical school. They had been through the entire war together, and at some point the Jewish doctor and the Ukrainian dragoon had fallen in love and gotten married. With the destruction of Danekin's army, they had fled together to Czechoslovakia and then to Palestine, bringing with them Dr. Fogel's ancient father. He still lived with them in a bedroom behind the clinic, though he never spoke—not having forgiven his daughter for marrying a gentile.

Arriving in Palestine, Dr. Fogel heard that the clinic in Kfar Saba was for sale, and she immediately bought it from the former army medic to whom it belonged. (When the narrative reached this point everyone looked over at the bed to make sure I was sleeping.) This medic had had a large Arab clientele, and the story was that his next-door neighbor, an Arab effendi, had had an affair with the medic's wife. When the medic found out, he kept the knowledge to himself until events gave him the opportunity for a horrible revenge. Suffering from a back ailment, the effendi came to him for treatment and allowed the medic to convince him that minor surgery was called for. The surgery was duly performed, and when the effendi woke up he found he was bent almost double, a condition from which he never recovered. Fearing the inevitable consequences, the medic quickly sold off his practice and left for France. There he eventually completed his medical studies and in the course of time became personal physician to the king of Morocco. Lying in my bed listening, it never occurred to me to wonder how much of this might be true. It was all true, and all marvelous.

In any event, it was certainly the case that Dr. Fogel's practice included many Arabs from villages both nearby and farther off. The Arabs loved her. She spoke fluent Arabic, much better than her Hebrew, and she was fearless. During the Arab rebellion that started in 1936, they sometimes traveled days to get her to deliver babies and treat all kinds of emergencies. It was a time when Jews were being ambushed and killed regularly. But in all her travels she was never touched. Her attitude toward the Arabs was special. She told me that during the Revolution she had cared for White Russians who had committed pogroms. "But they needed help, so I took care of them." She was a woman of unusual moral virtue.

Her husband, the blond, blue-eyed Vanya, was another character who stood out from the local population, though not by choice. He wanted badly to contribute to the new settlement. But he was a Ukrainian officer living in a sea of Jews, and they simply would not accept him. He resented that immensely, and like my mother he longed for Russia. They were a strange couple, Vanya and his Lady Deer, eccentrics like my parents and their other close friends—strong individualists who did not mesh well in the new society they found themselves part of.

At some point in my youth I began to understand in an indistinct way what was happening with my parents. It was not that they were rejected by their peers, it was just that they were different. And the differences were nothing to feel ashamed of or resentful about. I could even be proud of them. Not that this slowly dawning realization made my own burdens any easier. But there were compensations—the music, the stories, the unusual personalities who came to visit. There was also the work. Whatever went on in school or with my friends, work was such a constant that everything else seemed unimportant. You could lose yourself in it.

2

Father to the Man

In their seasons the orchards exhale a fragrance of blossoms and the heavy scent of citrus. The odor of oranges and lemons lies over them like a blanket, thicker in the low areas, lighter and more delicate where the land is high. The groves are humid and green and closed in, a separate world that speaks to you in different languages at different times. When you are a child, they are your playground and your most important school. When you are a teenager and a young man, they speak to you of work, but also of yearning and sexual desire. In the moshavim and kibbutzim, where everyone knows everyone else's business, they are the hiding places for secret passions.

As a child I listened to my father talk about the nobility of physical labor. By the time I was old enough to have my own thoughts on the subject, the work itself was in my bones. When I was very young, I would walk behind him in the long furrows of the watermelon field, watching his hoe work the loose red earth so I could drop the seeds in. The hill in front of us seemed endless, and when I got tired we would stop for a moment and look behind so that I could see how much we had accomplished already and take heart for what was left to do.

In our groves my father would treat the trees as individuals—almost, I thought, as if they were human. Some even had special names or titles—"The Wonderful Tree" for its extraordinary bounty, "The Sour Tree" for its strangely acidic fruit. On his maps and record books he would catalogue each tree's pedigree and characteristics, meticulously charting its progress and noting what was to be done with it: more fertilizer or less, more or less water, grafting, pruning, replacement. All these things he talked about as we worked, teaching constantly the need to combine theory with practical experience. By the time he was ready to advocate the cultivation of avocados or mandarins or mangoes, he had already tried them out himself. He knew they could be grown and he knew how to grow them.

By the age of eight or nine I was doing heavier work on my own. In the spring I would take the horse and wagon out to the vineyard and hitch up the plow, the one without the wing so that in turning the earth there would be a minimum of aeration and less moisture lost. But because the plow had no wing it was also slower going. The furrows it made were narrower, and the work seemed to take forever with all the turns up and back across the field. When lunchtime finally came, I would give the horse some water and barley, then sit down in the shade of the wagon to eat my sandwiches and drink the bottle of sweet tea my mother had packed along. Sitting there with my back propped against the wheel, I watched the heat rising in waves from the newly turned soil. Beyond the vineyard fields of wild poppies had sprung to life overnight, turning the rusty spring landscape a fiery red. Hundreds of butterflies flitted through the shimmering air, and crowds of starlings wheeled across the field, attracted by the grubs and insects the plow had turned up.

For a while I would sit motionless against the wagon, caught in a delicious lethargy. Dizzy with fatigue, I felt I could spend the rest of my life in exactly that spot, watching the vineyard put on its amazing display. But inevitably the time would come for the immense effort to get up and water the horse again, then hitch the plow and start trudging behind it in the narrow furrow. No one was there to watch; my father would not care if three dunams or four were plowed that day. Instead it was a battle of will, a test each time to see if I could overcome the paralyzing desire to just sit and rest.

In the winter rainy season I would spend hours in the small barn behind our house, sitting on the cement threshold and listening to the rain beat down on the overhang of the roof. In the barn's enclosed space the animals gave off a pungent warmth that brought with it a feeling of calm and security. When I gave them extra food I'd run my hand through the grain in the feed boxes and take for myself the chunks of carob my father had mixed in. During a violent storm one night my father and I clambered onto the barn roof to tie down the terra-cotta tiles before they blew off. Despite our efforts, almost half the roof tore away. But holding on to the ropes, we managed to save the larger part, salvaging most of the hay underneath. Afterward my father told me about a storm years earlier that hit while he was away somewhere. My mother had saved the house roof by herself, roping it down and anchoring the rope to the wagon. The two of us did all right he said, but it wasn't up to the job Vera had done.

For the farm children the most exciting event of the year came in December, after the long days of sun had turned the oranges a glowing yellow and the sharp citrus smell suffused the air. With the harvest, the itinerant packing crews would arrive in the orchards, led by the chief packer, a man of immense prestige and power. Sitting there in his turtleneck sweater, he was the lord of everything before him. The young women in his crew sat cross-legged on the ground sorting the newly picked oranges by size, their hands flying. Next to them the slightly younger, less experienced girls worked over wooden pallets, wrapping each ripe fruit in tissue paper. They in turn were assisted by the new girls, the fifteen- and sixteen-year-olds eager to imitate the skills of their older sisters. Their eyes were full of admiration for the expert workers, and their frequent quick glances at the packer king told of other emotions too.

From group to group the crew's porters circulated, bringing in empty boxes and carrying full ones away. More important than the porters were the carpenters who built crates out of wooden staves on the long, heavy packing tables, cutting and shaping them with rapid-fire blows of their hammers. Each carpenter had a mouth full of fourpenny nails, and everyone knew that a carpenter's status could be judged by the number of nails he could hold between his lips. But for pride and grandeur, the head carpenter was in a separate class, almost on a level with the packer king himself. This individual used a small ax to top off the full boxes that were placed in front of him and bang them shut, each economical and graceful movement proclaiming his mastery.

All together the sorters, wrappers, apprentices, porters, and carpenters worked like a beautiful machine, but a living machine full of emotions and furtive desires. Each year the chief packer would reassemble his crew, augmenting the veteran workers with apprentice boys and girls. During the season they traveled together from moshav to moshav and village to village, a small and tight-knit community of their own. In their gypsy existence romance flourished, and in each place they stopped the farm children had their ears and eyes wide open, taking in everything, watching for the meaningful look or the occasional touch that suggested things our straightlaced parents never hinted at.

In Kfar Malal the work was a constant, as were the unique joys of farm life. Another constant was tension with the Arabs, whose villages and encampments were interspersed with the Jewish settlements. Kfar Malal had been destroyed in an Arab attack in 1921, the year before my parents joined. It was threatened again during the Arab riots of 1929, the year after I was born. Though other periods were calmer, life never seemed safe. As a child of five I traveled with my mother on the bus from Tel Aviv to Jerusalem for treatment of a chronic eye problem. The entire trip I spent hunched down, peering out the window and scanning the Judean hills for signs of Abu Jilda, a famous terrorist of those days whose specialty was ambushing Jerusalem-bound traffic.

Security was not just an occasional problem but a daily concern for everyone. Each night the moshavniks mounted guard over their fields. From time to time the village would send people off to nearby settlements where conditions had become volatile. My father carried a small pistol with him, and my mother knew how to use it too. Twice my father was ambushed, once riding home from a nearby citrus plantation he was managing in 1936, another time when an irrigation line was sabotaged and a sniper waited for whoever would come to fix it. Both times he escaped unharmed. But many in the Jewish settlements were not so lucky.

By the time I was thirteen, I too was helping to guard the fields, sitting in the dark armed with a club and wearing the engraved Caucasian dagger my father had given to me for my bar mitzvah. Spending the nights alone like that added to the sense of self-sufficiency I was already acquiring. I enjoyed it. I felt in control, a feeling that was not diminished when one night I noticed a movement and, staring into the darkness, recognized my father, obviously checking to see that I was all right. How many nights he spent with me unobserved I don't know. I never told him I had seen him, and he never mentioned the subject.

But despite the background tension and sporadic bloodshed, Jews and Arabs still managed to live with each other, meeting daily in the fields and markets and maintaining relationships that grew normally from their interaction. But in 1936 a new atmosphere took hold. That was the year the Arab Revolt began, bringing with it murder and sabotage. Everyone in the besieged Jewish settlements knew the names of the victims, and talk among the adults was full of dark premonitions. No one had to be reminded of how precarious existence was in the face of organized Arab violence and British government indifference. I remember my mother saying that we had to prepare "to hold." She insisted too that my father teach her to use our rifle, an old German Mauser that was kept buried during the day in a wooden box under the manure pit in the barn. Like the small cache of weapons the moshav had hidden in the new well, the Mauser was "illegal," and its owner subject to imprisonment by the British if they found it. Nevertheless, at night my father dug it out and took it along with him on guard duty.

But though in 1936 the adult talk was grim, I never sensed a trace of fear in it. On the contrary, what filtered through to me was absolute assurance and determination. In these things my parents and the other moshav families were totally at one; all of them were hard people whose lives permitted them no illusions or doubts. They had built their village out of nothing. Through years of backbreaking labor they had taken a malarial wasteland and forced it into productivity. They were people who had refused to tolerate the degrading conditions into which they had been born, who instead had gone out and remade their lives. They were not afraid of anything, and not one of them had a single question about their right to the land.

Even my mother developed a deep identification with the land. She had been no Zionist at all when they first arrived. She felt none of the spiritual attachment to Eretz Israel that had drawn so many, and she was not in love with the socialist principle (which my father also espoused) that physical labor sanctifies existence. But the circumstances of her daily life had taught her the need to make the land productive and livable and to defend what she had achieved. Over time, the land she lived on and worked with her hands had become part of her.

Neither my parents nor their colleagues had any trouble with the idea of living together with the Arabs on an equal basis. Though the moshavniks were zealous nationalists, they were no chauvinists; they were never taken with the idea that they were better than anyone else. My parents believed firmly that the Arabs had full rights in the land; "in the land," they would say, "ba'aretz." Jews and Arabs could be citizens side by side. But they believed without question that only they themselves had rights "over the land," "al ha'aretz." And no one was going to force them out, regardless of terror or anything else.

In my childhood fantasies I dreamed that even if the enemy came, the village would be invulnerable. Later, during the terrible first six months of the War of Independence, I thought that even if the worst happened to the army, once the enemy arrived at the gates of the moshav they would not get through. Years afterward, when I was commanding a division in the 1967 war, I still had the same basic conviction. When the land belongs to you physically, when you know every hill and wadi and orchard, when your family is there, that is when you have power, not just physical power, but spiritual power. Like Antaeus, your strength comes from the land.

In addition to the tensions between Arabs and Jews, I also became aware as I grew up of hostilities among the Jews themselves. Again it was because my parents were up to their necks in controversy with others in the moshav. But this time there was a corrosive bitterness to the feelings that went far beyond the usual aggravation about crops or cultivation techniques. This battle was over Chaim Arlozoroff, a Zionist socialist leader who had been murdered in Tel Aviv. My understanding was that Arlozoroff's death was being blamed on other Jews, Jews who were not followers of the dominant Zionist Labor party, the Mapai. I began to hear the name of Ze'ev Jabotinsky around our house, a man who opposed David Ben-Gurion and his Mapai in the Zionist political world. It was Jabotinsky's men who were being accused of the Arlozoroff murder.

My father was livid. He was not one of this Jabotinsky's followers. On the contrary, like all the other moshavniks he himself was a Mapai party member. But it was intolerable to him that Jews should be accusing other Jews. He could not conceive of the possibility that Jabotinsky's men could have killed Arlozoroff, a young and brilliant Jewish leader—even if they did belong to a different political faction. And he was outraged that the Mapai socialists could bring a false accusation, creating antipathy between Jews for their partisan political ends.

This was not an issue of a moment. It festered for years. The Mapai membership closed ranks behind their leaders, focusing a consuming hatred toward Jabotinsky's "revisionists." It was a hatred that penetrated every corner of the Jewish community, stigmatizing the revisionists as assassins, enemies of the Jewish people, illegitimate Zionists whose methods made them anathema. Like the rest of the country, Kfar Malal was swept by violent emotions.

My father was never one to get out of a hurricane's path for any reason, and here his dearest principles were at issue. First and last he was a Jewish nationalist. The idea of Jews fighting each other while the community as a whole was struggling for existence went against the marrow of his bones. And for this unconscionable development he blamed those who had brought the accusation and were using it to destroy their adversaries. The result was predictable. Like Jabotinsky's followers themselves, he and my mother were branded. For a time the hatred in the village was palpable.

The Arlozoroff murder triggered explosive political emotions. But even in more normal times the moshavniks were caught up in politics, totally involved in the events and movements that infused their world. The talk as I was growing up was about socialism and Zionism and revisionism, and the dozen different factions that made their claims on Jewish allegiance. People scrutinized political developments throughout Europe and endlessly discussed the situation of the Jews in each major center. They watched Russia intensely, arguing into the night about the Bolsheviks and Stalin (whom my parents never called by name, but always referred to as the "Gruzinsky Cham," the Georgian Boor). As I was growing up, the air was always thick with ideas and opinions and debate, and it was in the nature of things that like the other children of these passionate and contentious moshav parents I would be drawn early to the same habits.

In our kitchen was a rough child-sized stool my father had hammered together for me and my sister. Shortly after I learned to read, I got into the habit of sitting on the stool and laying the daily newspaper out in front of me on one of the adult-size chairs, also homemade. As my mother prepared dinner, I would read aloud to her from the paper, articles that in my memory appear to have been mainly about the growing violence of the times and the meaning it had for the Jews. I read about the rise of Hitler's Nazis and about Spain, where there was a civil war and where a group of Israeli Jews had gone to fight in the International Brigades. While I read, I would imagine the Jewish warriors and dream a child's dream of heroism, shrugging off my father's disapproving remarks about Jews fighting in somebody else's cause.

News came through on the radio too, a one-of-a-kind model my inventor uncle Michel had built for us. This radio was a big ungainly contraption with a wire antenna that corkscrewed off into the air. For a while it was one of the few radios in the area, and people came from all over to marvel at it and to listen. But the news was seldom good. We listened to the radio and read the newspapers as the Nazis reoccupied the Rhineland and the Italians attacked Ethiopia. That invasion was brought home when Haile Selassie, the "Lion of Judah," chose Jerusalem for his exile. Then came the German descent on Austria and Hitler's moves against Czechoslovakia. Everywhere it seemed the world was dangerous and filled with hostility, much of it incomprehensible, but all of it very real and very threatening.

For most of the moshav children, life was dominated by the rhythms and demands of the farm. It was a setting where school tended not to be a priority. It certainly was not for me, and I was never more than an ordinary student. My parents used to say that my sister should study, that she had talent. They did not say I had no talent, but there seemed to be an unspoken understanding that I would stay on the farm when I grew up, working it with my father.

Nevertheless, in 1941 at the age of thirteen I went off to high school in Tel Aviv, an hour away on the rickety bus that served the outlying villages. It was still early in the morning when I arrived, and I would walk the mile or so from the central bus station to the school building on Geula Street, not far from the city's beaches. When the last class was over I would stroll through the Bezalel market, or the Carmel market, buy a falafel and a soft drink too if there was enough change in my pocket. Then I would stop by my grandmother's house and talk for a while. In 1925 my father's father had finally managed to bring the rest of his family back with him from Baku, though he himself died a few years after the return. Although by now my grandmother Miriam had been in Israel for almost a decade and a half, she had never learned Hebrew. Instead she spoke to me in Russian, telling me stories of her life in Petrograd, where she had studied to be a midwife; in Brest Litovsk, where she had practiced her profession; and in Baku, where the family had fled during the war. By three or four in the afternoon I would be back home to spend the rest of the afternoon and evening working in the fields, then doing my school assignments.

For me, Tel Aviv was a godsend. After school I loved wandering around the open-air markets with their pungent smells of broiling shashlik and shish kabab, fresh-baked breads, and spicy spinach pies.

People milled around everywhere, some of them intent on getting the daily shopping done, other walking leisurely among stalls piled high with vegetables, meats, fish, poultry, and dry goods. Listening to the sharp bark of the vendors and the hum of the crowd, I would wonder how all these people lived. Without growing potatoes or onions or oranges, what did they do with their lives, and where did they get their money from?

On stormy days I walked instead to the beach to watch the violence of the sky and breakers pounding the shore. Or I would go to visit in the homes of my parents' friends—"good families," as my mother would say, by which she meant people of education and culture. At school I made friends with boys and girls from Tel Aviv and many of the surrounding towns, and I discovered something amazing. They had never heard of my father, of his views about crops, fences, or the Russian Revolution. They hadn't the vaguest notion about the conflicts between my family and the other Kfar Malal families, nor were they in the least interested. They simply treated me as another kid. Along with the rest of the boys, I flirted with girls and sneaked looks through the open windows of the building next to the school, a hotel heavily patronized by Tel Aviv's prostitutes and the British soldiers from whom they made their living.

In almost every way Tel Aviv was a new world, a place where I could leave behind the angry emotions and inner turmoil I so often felt in the village. The change was almost physical, as if a heavy and oppressive burden was falling from my shoulders. I was no longer so disturbed by the turbulence of my feelings or by the confusing sense that my emotions were in control and not I myself. A kind of transformation was taking place, and if I did not understand it completely, I was at least aware that it was happening. I felt I was coming of age.

Though my first years in high school were happy ones personally, life for everyone at that time was carried on against a background of mounting anxiety. By 1940 Hitler's efforts to rearrange the map of Europe were creating a new landscape in the Middle East as well. In June France fell, and with its fall French control over Syria and Lebanon passed to the new Vichy government. Iraq, under British dominion for decades, was shaken by a pro-German coup, and in April of 1941 the Iraqi army revolted against British forces. In the same month the Germans took Greece and Crete, threatening the eastern Mediterranean. Almost simultaneously Rommel's tank army moved into North Africa, striking toward the British lifeline of the Suez Canal. Italian air attacks hit Tel Aviv and Haifa, where the oil tanks went up in flames. From Kfar Malal we watched at night as the glow spread over the horizon.

People hung on each bit of information, feeling as if the world was closing in. Almost everyone had relatives in the overrun countries of Europe, and anguish about their fate competed with fear of a German invasion. If the Germans destroyed the Russians in the Caucasus, the north would be an open door. If they threw the British out of Egypt, there would be nothing to bar their way to the heart of the Jewish community. In 1941 and 1942 annihilation was in the air. It was whispered that if the Nazis broke through, the entire Jewish community would concentrate around Haifa and make a last stand on Mount Carmel.

With Egypt and the Suez Canal threatened, Palestine came alive with troops moving north and south along the ancient routes connecting North Africa and Asia Minor. Israel was again a crossroads. On the coastal road that passed through Kfar Malal we saw convoy after convoy: Free French forces moving up toward the Levant states; Australians and New Zealanders, even Greek troops with mules. In 1942 the Free Poles under General Wladislaw Anders came through Tel Aviv, bringing with them thousands of women and children. At high school we skipped classes to go down to the beach and gawk at the blond Polish girls. We even got into a few fights with the young Polish soldiers over some real or imagined anti-Semitic insult. For a time a Polish unit camped just outside the village, and the moshavniks went out to invite the soldiers into their homes. One officer stopped at our house a number of times, and we got to know him. He and my parents took a liking to each other, and when he came by they would spend time talking and drinking tea, then he and my father would go out into the yard to chop wood.

Among all the allied forces, the Australians and New Zealanders were loved best. They were remembered for what they had done in World War One when they came across the Sinai on their horses—the famous Australian mounted infantry—to attack the Turks in Gaza, Beersheba and Megiddo. Now they had come again from halfway around the world to fight an even more desperate war. When they got leave from the crucial battles in the Western Desert, they would often stop to rest in the Jewish towns and settlements. Many of them were farmers at home, and they missed their own crops and animals, and so sometimes they worked too, as if to satisfy their need for contact with the land. We became friendly with some of these soldiers, one of whom came to stay with us on his leaves. Our whole family called him "Kiwi," which I thought was his name until eventually I discovered it was a nickname for all New Zealanders. Although between his New Zealand accent and our own shaky English we had trouble understanding each other, somehow we managed to get along, and he and my father kept up a correspondence until his death later in the war.

Amidst the bustle and excitement and deep worry, the Jewish community was not simply sitting by and watching. Tens of thousands of young Jewish men and women joined the British forces. And starting in 1941 there was an urgent push by the Jewish Agency to establish an all-Jewish division, a plan the British put off until 1944, when a Jewish Brigade was finally made operational in time for the Italian campaign.

In Palestine, the semi-underground Jewish army—the Haganah— stepped up its training, and at the age of fourteen I was initiated. In an orange grove outside the moshav a group of us lined up, then went one at a time into a small shed where we stood in front of a Bible and a pistol and took an oath of allegiance. The ceremony itself was unimpressive, but the idea of participating in the defense of the community, that meant a great deal.

At first I trained with the boys from the moshav, all Saturday and one night during the week. But before long I was transferred into an elite platoon called the "Signalers," which even had its own secret insignia patch, two small crossed flags. Drawn from various local villages, the Signalers trained near Kfar Malal, learning to use pistols and knives from instructors who were just a few years older than we were. Later members of the Jewish Settlement Police came to teach us other weapons: World War One Lee Enfield rifles, hand grenades, Sten guns, even light machine guns. These Settlement Police were part of a nationwide unit established under British control during the Arab Revolt to help protect both the Jewish settlements and British installations such as the Iraq Petroleum Company pipeline. Licensed to use weapons, the Settlement Police were a first-rate cover under which to train Haganah soldiers and provide instruction with equipment the Haganah itself lacked.

In addition to becoming familiar with small arms, the Signalers learned the terrain. We crisscrossed the entire area, visiting Arab villages and Jewish villages, climbing each hill and exploring every stream and wadi until we knew all the region's features by heart. Since we had no radios, we practiced with semaphore and Morse flags during the day and Lucas lights at night. Later some of the booty General Archibald Wavell had collected from the Italians in North Africa found its way into Palestine, and we mastered an Italian signaling system that made use of cloth squares that could be pulled apart to show red and pushed together to show white. From time to time experts would visit our training sessions, lecturing us about their specialties or about recent developments in the war. On occasion I was sent to short courses on such subjects as the use of field telephones or different types of weapons. It was an intense period, a time when the small Jewish community was tied together before its fate, knowing that the future depended on large forces outside its control but determined to fight for survival in every way it could.

In June of 1945 I was seventeen years old and ready to graduate high school. Adolf Hitler had died in his bunker a month before. The war in Europe was over. In Asia the Japanese empire was on the edge of destruction. But I had no sense that a great traumatic period was drawing to a close. On the contrary, instead of joy and relief, everyone I knew shared a feeling of uneasy expectation. It was as if all the problems that had riven the community had been put on hold by the war. And now they would be coming to claim their place with a vengeance. The unresolved conflicts with the Arabs, the postponed battle with the British Mandatory government, and now the hundreds of thousands of Jewish refugee survivors clamoring to get into Israel. As I prepared to leave for extended military training, I could feel that something was about to happen. Something was knocking at the gate.

3

In the Haganah

The loudest knocking came from the survivors of Europe's Jewish population. It was no secret that during the war the British did everything they could to prevent European Jews from escaping to Palestine. Afraid of the Arab reaction to any increase in Jewish immigration, they had kept strictly to the quotas set by the White Paper of 1939. The results were gruesome. Even those who might have been saved were refused entry. Ships filled with refugees wandered the seas without any place to land. Seven hundred and fifty Jews fleeing Rumania were killed when the *Struma* sank off the Turkish coast, hit by either a torpedo or a mine. Two hundred more died when the *Salvador* sank in the Sea of Marmara. Other refugees who somehow managed to slip through the blockades and land in Israel were rounded up and shipped to concentration camps on the Indian Ocean island of Mauritius and later on Cyprus.

When the *Struma* disaster was reported, thousands of people took to the streets of Tel Aviv. When the British police tried to make arrests, they were met by a storm of resistance. When the Mandatory government decided to deport the refugees who had landed from the *Patria* and the *Atlantic*, a wave of anguish and hatred swept through the community. On the surface, life went on pretty much as usual, but underneath ran a subcurrent of rage and helplessness.

Each time some dramatic refugee incident occurred—and there were plenty of them—the conflict inside the Jewish community flared up. What should be done about the British? Even during the first years of the war, the Stern Group, a militant underground organization, insisted that the British should be held criminally responsible, even though they were fighting the Germans. The Irgun Z'vai Le'umi, a much larger underground led by Menachem Begin, restrained themselves at first. But by late 1943 they too had decided the time had come for open rebellion. Wall posters went up and newspapers circulated urging revolt. The mainstream Zionists believed that during the war against Hitler it was necessary to co-operate with the British, despite their hostility. But the two militant groups advocated—and took—violent action.

In high school some of the students belonged to the militants, others to the mainstream organization. Everyone read the wall posters and leaflets and argued about who was right and what should be done. Everyone knew what the British were doing, and antagonism against them ran deep. But still the regular parties obeyed instructions from the Jewish Agency for restraint and co-operation. But at the same time it was impossible not to watch the Irgun and Stern attacks against the British without being envious of those who were at least taking some kind of action.

In November 1944 it became much harder to just sit and watch. On November 6, two militants assassinated Lord Moyne, the British resident minister in Cairo, who was popularly thought to be behind the British hard line on Jewish refugees. This incident led to a crackdown on militants by the Haganah. Members of the Irgun were hunted down and turned over to the British police in a campaign that came to be known as the "season." I hated it. I could control my envy of the militants and I didn't mind the steps the Jewish Agency took to prevent anti-British activity. Even arresting and punishing the militants seemed reasonable enough. But turning them over to the British? How could Jews turn over other Jews? It seemed criminal, a shameful thing to be associated with.

The "season" lasted for many months, up until the end of the war. It was only after Hitler was dead and the Nazis had finally surrendered that the mainstream Zionists decided to make an arrangement with the rebels. At that point, despite everything, the militant groups and the Haganah began to develop a joint effort. Demands for the establishment of a Jewish state were stepped up, and the continuing British policy of exclusion triggered a series of attacks by the newly co-ordinated resistance movement.

As I prepared to leave for training at a secret Haganah course for squad leaders, an air of tension and menace was building. I had the sense that unknown things lay ahead and that I was going to be part of whatever was taking shape just beyond the horizon.

The squad leaders' course was being held at Kibbutz Ruhama, on the edge of the Negev Desert. To get there I had to take a bus to Kibbutz Negba, itself an isolated outpost, then find an Arab bus going toward Gaza. Getting off at the large Arab village of Breir, I waited in the road, aware of the stares from the men in the cafe and on the street. I had a "nabut" with me, a heavy knobbed club that both Jews and Arabs carried in those days for protection. But it wasn't the nabut that gave me a feeling of security. Even in that place the pride of being Jewish instilled in me a kind of fearlessness. And perhaps I also had the usual youthful sense of invulnerability. But despite the threatening atmosphere nothing happened, and after a time the kibbutz truck came along to pick me out of the road.

Ruhama was at the end of the world, the farthest off, most godforsaken place I had ever seen. The tiny collective farm had been established in 1944 on the site of an earlier settlement that had been burned down by Arabs in the rioting of 1921. Surrounding the few huts and tents and the struggling orchards and fields, a parched moonscape stretched out, dry barren hills and dust giving way in the distance to larger hills and more dust. But while the area might not have been promising farmland, for secret military training it was ideal. Anybody approaching the kibbutz by car or truck could be spotted from miles away by the dust plume rising against the desert sky. There would be plenty of time to hide weapons and if necessary to disappear into one of the numerous ravines and gullies that carved their way through the hills.

Ruhama was scraggly and forbidding, and the kibbutzniks seemed strange too, dressed in ill-fitting shorts and queer Russian caps. But close up they seemed to me like kings and queens. Wherever they had gotten those old clothes from, here they were on their own land. You could see the pride they took in their work and their feeling for what they were accomplishing in a place that made Kfar Malal look like a paradise. And this place had a history too. During the First World War Ruhama had been an important part of NILI, the Jewish intelligence network that provided information to the British on Turkish and German activity. Men like Aaron Aaronsohn, Avshalom Feinberg, and Joseph Lishanski had been associated with this place—Jewish heroes whose stories had been told over and over around my house until they had come to seem an essential part of my upbringing.

As a result, Ruhama had a certain aura about it: a far outpost in the desert, a heroic past, a secret training center for the new Jewish army. But despite the aura, somehow I didn't manage to do very well in the squad leaders' course. Or at any rate, whatever military talent I had wasn't exactly apparent to the instructors. When the two-month course was over, my graduation certificate read not "corporal" but only "probationary corporal," a kind of private first class.

It was a disappointing conclusion. I was sure I was better than that, and I couldn't understand how it was that I hadn't shown it. Not that it made any difference as far as the next step went. Like everyone else, I knew it was just a matter of time before British control was ruptured and all the problems came to a head. And when that happened I would be involved—whether as a corporal or a probationary corporal didn't much matter.

With that in mind, at the end of the course I went back to Kfar Malal to help my father on the farm and decide exactly what I should do. In my own mind the best step would be to join the Palmach, the closest thing the Jewish community had to a standing army. Organized in 1941, the Palmach was originally meant to be a defense force against the Germans while so many Jewish boys and girls were away from home fighting with the British. Based on the kibbutzim, the Palmach combined constant training with agricultural work. In a short time it had become an elite, a three-thousand-strong force with high standards and even higher morale. It was sure to be in the thick of whatever was coming, which was just where I wanted to be too.

But it turned out that my father had other ideas. One day as we were working together in the orange groves, I glanced up and saw him looking at me, his face framed by the branches of a tree. With an expression full of concern he said, "Arik, I want to tell you, anything you decide to do with your life is all right with me. But you have to promise me one thing. Never, never participate in turning Jews over to non-Jews. You must promise me that you will never do that."

He did not mention the Palmach directly; he didn't have to. What he meant was clear enough. The "season" had started up again. And what my father thought of this campaign of Jew against Jew can hardly be described. As the Haganah's strike force, it had been the Palmach that had carried out the hunt. Palmach men had arrested the militants, and Palmach men had turned them over to the British. My father could not stomach the thought of my being connected with that, and though I badly wanted to join, I understood his feelings exactly, and I accepted them.

The result was that instead of joining the Palmach I enrolled in the Jewish Settlement Police. In some ways the JSP was a real police force, protecting the Jewish settlements and patrolling roads and villages. But along with the real Settlement Police, there were also police like myself, Haganah personnel for whom the JSP was nothing more than a handy cover. Although we had British officers, in fact I saw them only when there was an inspection and I had to put on my uniform and report to my station. The rest of the time we spent training in weapons and tactics and instructing those younger than ourselves, exactly as the Settlement Police had taught us when we were in Haganah youth group.

As we trained, conflict between the Jewish community and the Mandatory government grew, erupting in a series of Irgun and Stern Group assaults on British police stations and military posts and Haganah actions against bridges, rail lines, and coast guard stations. Some of these raids were astonishingly successful. Others were not, and numbers of underground fighters were killed or captured.

The trials of these Jewish prisoners affected me deeply. In their fiery courtroom denunciations of British authority they shouted out loud what others only thought. They carried themselves with such defiance and courage—in the courts, then in their cells, and finally on the gallows. Like others, I was transfixed by Matti Shmulevitch, who told his judge, "The idea for which we are all fighting, for which we came to this land, for which I escaped from the detention camp at Latrun, for which I took up arms is to establish the Kingdom of Israel in the land of Israel. This will be done, even if you hang all of Israel's warriors. Because deep inside you know we are not criminals. . . . Deep inside you know that the aspiration of the Jewish nation for freedom will never be suppressed, not by murder, not by torture, not by hanging!"

Along with the rest of the country I followed the saga of Dov Gruner. Painfully wounded in the jaw, he sang "Hatikvah" in the faces of the

British military tribunal that sentenced him to hang, then endured almost a year of suffering in prison before they finally executed him. After Gruner came Meir Feinstein and Moshe Barzani, who blew themselves up with a smuggled grenade the night before their own hanging, and after them came the three Irgun men sentenced to death following the Acre prison breakout.

In the face of events like these I went through my own internal struggle. I was jealous of the militants; I envied their actions and their heroism. But I was also in the Haganah, and I believe that people did not just have the right to go off and do whatever they wanted to, no matter how courageous they might be. When the Irgun threatened to hang two British sergeants if the Acre prisoners were executed, I was part of a Haganah search team sent out to look for the sergeants. When the Jewish prisoners were hanged, we continued to search, tramping through the dunes and brush east of Netanya. But in my heart I didn't want to free the British sergeants. I wanted to avenge the militants' deaths.

Caught between Jewish and Arab nationalism, in 1947 the British Mandatory government made several unsuccessful attempts to negotiate compromise agreements, including a partition proposal that neither the Jews nor Arabs accepted. Then in March of that year they finally threw their hands up in despair and turned the whole problem over to the United Nations.

As the U.N. began its own inquiries, we stepped up our training. I was still living at home, working on the farm as much as I could—especially now that my father was beginning to suffer from the heart problems that would eventually kill him. It was while I was irrigating in our orange grove one day that I looked up and noticed a girl cultivating the vegetable field next to our property. The field belonged to a nearby boarding school for immigrant children, and I often saw people from the school working there. But I had never noticed this particular girl before, and it seemed to me I had never in my life seen anyone so beautiful. Hidden behind the orange trees, I watched her work, my eyes drawn to her face and her light brown braids. I wondered how I could find out who she was, how I could introduce myself to her, and how I could get her to return my feelings. Lost in these reveries, I suddenly found myself knee deep in water from the forgotten irrigation line that was now flooding the ditches and containing dikes I had prepared so carefully.

Arranging a meeting was not so easy. The school kept a close watch over its children, most of whom had gotten out of Europe without their parents. Each night the doors of the place were locked tight. By a stroke of luck, though, I had just then been assigned to train some of the immigrant boys as part of my Haganah duties, so I was able to ask around and eventually to send a message. To my delight, she agreed to see me. Somehow she arranged to get out of the school, and I cut a hole in the wire fence that surrounded the yard so she could sneak through. Her name was Margalit, "Gali." She and her older sister had been sent to Israel from Rumania to join two brothers who had arrived earlier. Her parents and two younger sisters had also survived the war and were hoping to get to Israel themselves later on. She was just sixteen then, still a girl, and very shy. Being with her was intoxicating. She was not exactly my first love, but what I felt now seemed completely different from anything I had felt before. In the evenings we would go out and sit next to the old village well in the middle of the groves, holding hands and talking in the dark. Finally, after several months of secret meetings we made a date to see each other in the daytime, again by the well. But when I got there she was nowhere in sight, and I thought that maybe she hadn't been able to sneak away. Then I noticed her smiling at me from a copse of trees next to the well. It was the first time I had seen her eyes. They were hazel and seemed speckled with gold.

Unfortunately, through the rest of that year our growing attachment to each other was interrupted more and more often as my unit was called up for longer periods. As the U.N. special committee worked to find a solution to the Arab-Jewish conflict, tension between the two communities worsened. Killings and sabotage aimed at the Jewish settlements became more frequent, and we were mobilized on and off. We patrolled constantly, moving through the groves and fields, mostly at night, hoping to make life difficult for the Arab gangs that had started terrorizing the area.

The first operation I actually led took place that autumn. Haganah intelligence suspected the son of a local Bedouin sheikh named Abu Kishik of co-operating with the terrorists. The idea was to punish this individual and warn him against continuing his activities. To do this, it was decided we should confiscate his car, a beautiful red Nash that he loved to drive around the neighborhood and show off. Knowing his habits, I took my squad to a likely spot on a narrow dirt road that ran through one of the orchards. When our lookout shouted that the Nash was coming, we hauled out one of the long orange crating tables, pulling it into position across the road. A moment later the car skidded to a stop and Abu Kishik's son was out the door and running.

I rushed up to the car and jumped in, then saw that he had had the presence of mind to take the keys. In an instant I was after him, running through the groves as fast as I could. I knew those groves like I knew my right hand, and I was fast. But somehow on that occasion Abu Kishik's son ran faster. I must have chased him almost half a mile before I gave it up and ran back to the car. British patrols were in the area, and we had to get the Nash into a hiding place we had prepared in the barn of a nearby Jewish farm. Fortunately, one of the ten or so of us in the squad was something of a mechanic, because the rest were much more familiar with horses and wagons than with gasoline engines. As it was, it seemed to take an eternity before the engine roared into life and we were able to drive the thing off.

By the end of the summer the U.N. commission had finished its work. The only equitable solution, they decided, would be to partition the country and establish two states, one Jewish, one Arab. As the fall lengthened, the U.N. General Assembly meeting in Lake Success, New York, began considering the partition plan. Finally, on November 29, 1947, the vote was taken. That night I happened to be home listening to the radio with my mother and father. As the roll call of U.N. delegates was read off, we counted the votes. When it was over, the tally was thirty-three for, thirteen against, and ten abstentions. The partition plan had won. As far as the United Nations was concerned, the State of Israel was now a reality.

With that announcement the people of Kfar Malal poured out onto the main street dancing and singing, unable to contain what they were feeling. But even then their excitement and happiness was tinged by anxiety. According to the U.N. we were a country, but not a single person believed that the Arabs would accept the partition peacefully. So much blood had been shed already. And now that the British would be moving out, much worse was sure to come. The surrounding Arab countries had already made their intentions plain. They were not going to tolerate a Jewish state in their midst. They would wait only until the

British mandate formally came to an end six months later. Then they would act to tear the new country off the face of the map. The crisis that had been building since the end of World War Two was now at hand.

On December 12 I was mobilized again along with the rest of the Haganah, this time permanently. We were now a full-time army, already deeply engaged in the stepped-up actions that started right after the U.N. resolution. The conflict was now out in the open.

We heard that the Grand Mufti of Jerusalem was back in the Middle East after having spent most of the war in Nazi Germany. From Cairo he had declared a "jihad," a holy war against the Jews. An Arab "Army of Salvation" was operating around Jerusalem and armed groups were in action south of Tel Aviv. Other Arab paramilitary organizations were also on the move, supplemented by Palestinian villagers who co-operated as partisans under their sheikhs.

As the British pulled out in the winter of 1947–48, the war between Arabs and Jews intensified into what started to be called the "Battle of the Roads." Throughout the country Arab forces moved to cut off Jewish settlements and population centers from each other by controlling the roads and bridges that linked them together. Once isolated, the Jewish enclaves could be surrounded, then dealt with piecemeal. Fauzi el Kaukji's Salvation Army attacked Mishmar ha Emek on the Haifa road, Kibbutz Ramat Yohanan east of Haifa, Kfar Szold and Yehiam in the Galilee, and Kibbutz Tirat Tzvi in the Beit Shean Valley. By March the Negev settlements were cut off, as were Jerusalem and the Etzion settlements south of the city.

Around Kfar Malal and its neighboring villages the same pattern of battle took shape. Without the manpower to hold the roads, we concentrated on hit-and-run raids, forcing the Arabs to keep their troops spread out and on the defensive. Since all of us were from the neighborhood, we knew the terrain intimately. In squads of ten and platoons of thirty or thirty-five we hit constantly at roads, bridges, and villages, trying to keep the Arabs from concentrating for assaults on our own settlements.

Operating around the old coastal highway, we raided Arab bases and set ambushes against the superior enemy forces that held the road junctions and strategic strong points. Typically we would leave our camp in the middle of the night, picking our way through the orchards, fields, and wadis and avoiding Arab and British patrols. Leaving men to secure the route back, we would be at our ambush site before first light, waiting for the early-morning traffic between the Arab villages and bases.

By now we had become skilled at finding our way in the darkest nights, and gradually we built the strength and endurance these kinds of operations required. Under the stress of constant action we drew closer to one another and began to operate not just as a military unit but almost as a family.

As the bonds between us grew stronger, I recognized that something personal was happening too. As one action followed the next, I became aware that the others in our platoon had developed confidence in my ability to lead them into these actions, and maybe more important, to get them out. As a result I began to think more about what I was doing and how I was doing it. The knowledge that they were relying on me made me more aware of my own responsibilities, and it gave me a growing confidence in my judgment and skills, far more than I had ever had before.

One landmark on this road to maturity was the attack on Bir Addas during the winter of 1948. Bir Addas was an Arab village close to the heart of the cluster of Jewish settlements that included Kfar Saba, Kfar Malal, and Magdiel. The village was held by troops from Kaukji's Salvation Army, most of them Iraqi irregulars who used the place as a base from which they could launch actions and harass the Jewish settlements with mortar and heavy machine-gun fire. Eventually it was decided that the threat from this place had to be eliminated.

But Bir Addas was fortified and heavily defended, a much harder target than anything we had tried before. Raiding a place like this was no small-scale guerrilla action. It would require a co-ordinated, sustained attack by a battalion-sized force—not the kind of action we had any experience with.

The overall plan developed by the battalion commander, Zvi German, called for a night assault in which Jewish units would circle around the village and attack from the rear. It was a plan that called for close timing and accuracy in getting the soldiers through the fields and into position. When I was told that I had been chosen to lead the column I couldn't have been prouder. The wadi we had to cross was in full flood, and I would have to get all these men with their machine guns and heavy explosives to the right place at the right time. But I felt sure I could do it. I had been fighting here for months, and I knew every square inch of the terrain by heart.

The night of the attack the battalion held a final briefing in the old Magdiel synagogue. After the commanders explained the mission I stood on the platform in front as the soldiers crowded around. As clearly as I could I described the route we would take, the obstacles we would find, the way we would get around to the back side of the village. Outside it was raining heavily. Cracks of thunder interrupted my presentation, and lightning flashes illuminated the walls of the synagogue and the men who huddled inside straining to hear what I was saying.

When the briefing was over we moved outside and formed up in the driving rain. It was a wild night. Every few moments a bolt would turn the blackness into day, silhouetting trees and buildings as the column moved out of Magdiel and into the water-logged fields. Mud clumped onto my boots, making it hard to walk. The soaked wool of my sweater gave off a fusty smell.

It wasn't long before we had reached the barbed wire that divided the Jewish and Arab areas. Then we cut it and walked through. In front of the wadi I pulled the column to a halt, and as the men squatted down I tested out a couple of potential crossing points. When I found one that was only belly deep, we crossed, the men holding their weapons and ammunition up above the rushing water. On the far side we headed east, then turned north toward Bir Addas. Behind me the line of soldiers stretched out, then disappeared into the night.

We had been walking northward for an hour when a runner came up the column panting that the engineers were no longer in the column. They had been bringing up the rear, but now they were gone. And with them were all of our explosives.

As the line pulled to a halt, I told Asher Levy, the lead company commander, that I thought I could find them. The most likely thing was that they had fallen behind and had kept going east when I turned the column north. If I followed the trail back there was a good chance I could pick up their tracks and catch up with them.

When Levy grunted, "Go and do it," I moved back down the line of soldiers, then followed the trail back through the muddy field. Three quarters of a mile to the rear I found the place where we had made the turn. Examining the ground, I could see where the engineers had lost contact and had continued going straight.

I hurried after them, wondering how far they had gone before they realized they were lost and trying to guess what they would do then. But before I knew it I practically tripped over them. Almost immediately they had seen that they were lost and had stopped, squatting on their haunches while they waited for someone to come and get them.

When we got back to the column I took the lead again, shuffling through the mud of the fields that stretched out in back of Bir Addas. Despite the storm and the momentary fright of losing the engineers, I felt in control. Picking my way along, I felt more and more sure that we were going exactly right. The land spoke in a thousand ways—with its ditches and little gullies, its trees and bushes and gradually shifting inclines. Less frequent now, lightning still lit the sky from time to time, flashing on familiar groves and copses that confirmed our direction.

After another hour's march we were near the village, at the exact spot I had been aiming for. The column spread out quickly and quietly, the machine gunners (under a young officer named Israel Tal) setting up their weapons alongside the infantry. From Bir Addas itself there was no sound. The storm that had made the hike so miserable had also masked our approach from the Iraqis and the village home guard.

Then, right on schedule, our machine guns opened up, their hammering breaking through the noise of the storm. Almost immediately answering shots rang out from the village, then picked up in volume until it seemed like a fusillade of shooting was coming back at us. Along with the rest of the platoon I lay there waiting for the order to attack. Bullets began hitting nearby, and now and then someone in the firing line would let out a muffled scream. But no order came, nothing. We didn't know what to do, whether to open fire ourselves, to move forward, or just to wait. As the minutes passed it was obvious that something had happened to the platoon leader. More by instinct than anything else, I got the platoon moving forward, shooting and moving, shooting and moving. Slowly we worked our way toward the trench lines on the outskirts of the village.

But the Iraqis were not running. Instead they were firing back like mad, and the unit that was supposed to take a big stone house that was the primary objective had not been able to get to it. This was early in the war, before the Jewish soldiers had developed a talent for hand-to-hand fighting. By and large both Jews and Arabs took the same general approach to fighting at that time. One side would move into position and open fire, hoping the enemy would withdraw. But if they stood firm and you started taking casualties, then you would withdraw instead.

The Arabs defending Bir Addas obviously had no intention of withdrawing, at least not yet. And since we were attacking from their rear they no doubt felt confused and trapped. But I was sure that if we could just keep the pressure up for a while longer their resistance would start coming apart. Already I could feel a wavering in the volume of fire coming at us. But then, before we had time to tell which way it would develop, our own order came to retreat.

The rain was still coming down as we pulled back from the village outskirts carrying our wounded with us. It was a slow march. The whole way back I kept turning over in my mind what a waste it had been. All the problems we had had getting there, the attack itself, the casualties— all for nothing, a failure that might not have happened if we had just stuck with it a little longer. What was worse, the order had been given by the commander from back in his field headquarters, rather than by somebody on the front line who could tell what was really going on. These thoughts and others like them preoccupied me as I walked on leaden legs back toward Magdiel. I felt half dead from fatigue as we found the break in the barbed wire and marched dejectedly into the village just as dawn broke.

Though the battle had not been a success, the next day there was only silence from Bir Addas instead of the heavy fire we had been experiencing for weeks. The Iraqis, we learned, had withdrawn. Another result of the battle was that I was promoted to platoon commander. A good many of the soldiers I was now leading were from Kfar Malal, boys I had studied with and played with, but whose families had been at odds with mine for ages. But now our relationships had become something else entirely, and when we went back to the village to visit for a few hours or to rest for a day the moshavniks would come out with greetings and blessings. It was more than just acceptance. The village was clasping all of us to its bosom, myself along with the rest.

In the winter of 1947–48 we were in combat almost every day. Ambushes and battles followed each other until they all seemed to run together. Only the high points stood out, the conspicuous or unusual events—the time we surprised the trucks outside Jalgulya, the time we milked the abandoned cows on our way to Kalkilya, the time we drove the Iraqis back at Kfar Saba. Everything seemed muddled. We would fight, take casualties, withdraw, fight again. No one seemed to know if our strategy was working. We lost many of our friends: Peretz Tabakh at Kfar Qara, Ze'ev Gendel near Kalkilya, others at insignificant crossroads and unnamed wadis. With every skirmish and every battle the list of the dead lengthened. We hardly bothered ourselves with thoughts of what would happen when the British were finally gone and the real Arab armies invaded. We all knew we were already fighting for our lives.

One day that March I went home to visit for a few hours. Between Magdiel and Kfar Saba I passed by the defensive positions that were manned day and night by older men from Kfar Malal. I always felt so proud coming back from a raid or ambush at the head of my platoon, especially when I saw my father in the trenches. The truth was that I sometimes even went out of my way to go by the positions. But that afternoon he was not on guard duty. He had been in the trenches all night, I was told, but now he had gone home.

As I walked toward our farm, I saw him working on the slope under a sky heavy with black clouds. High against the clouds tracer bullets arched slow orange pathways, in their last stages of exhausted flight from the Arab villages on the nearby Samarian hills. Beneath this ominous sky my father was preparing the ground for a new plantation. With the war nearing its May crisis this hardly seemed the moment to put energy into a new grove—whose trees wouldn't bear fruit in any event for another four years. Looking at him in amazement, I asked what he thought he was doing. Without interrupting his work, he answered in a sharp voice, "In days of confusion like this everyone should do his best in his own little corner. Do you think this is the time to cry and weep? Just stick to your job." I walked the rest of the way to the house shaking my head and wondering. The man's stubbornness was unbelievable. It could make him tremendously difficult to live with. But it also gave him the kind of will you needed to survive in a land like this.

I was not able to come home again until the afternoon of May 14, the day David Ben-Gurion read out Israel's declaration of independence. But it wasn't the day's historical importance that I was thinking about as I trudged down the main street. What set that day apart was the short pass I had. I would be seeing Gali for the first time in almost two months. That night I was scheduled to lead a raid on the bridge to Kalkilya, a large town through which Arab forces would invade Israel the next day. I already had my plan prepared, and now there was just enough time to get home, give Gali a kiss, and say goodbye.

As I walked toward the children's school where she still lived, I heard a radio turned up loud in the window of somebody's house. Ben-Gurion's voice was coming through the air announcing the establishment of the State of Israel. I heard his words distinctly: "In the land of Israel the Jewish people came into being. In this land their character was shaped." They were beautiful words, sonorous words. But they did not excite me. What he was saying seemed so normal, so natural, not at all like the tension-breaking U.N. announcement from Lake Success in November. It seemed to me that we had really had our independence for the past six months. We had been neck-deep in it and fighting for it since November. The coming night at the bridge to Kalkilya would be no different from all the nights I had already spent doing exactly the same kind of thing.

4

The War of Independence

en-Gurion had declared that Israel would formally come into existence on May 14 at midnight, the moment the British mandate expired. As everyone knew, that moment would also signal an invasion by regular armies of the surrounding Arab nations. Already Syrian and Lebanese forces were gathered in the north, while the Egyptians were poised on the borders of the Sinai. In the center, Jordan's British-officered Arab Legion had been joined by a 10,000-man contingent from the Iraqi army. On May 15 these forces would strike across the borders, linking up with the Arab private armies and irregulars we had already been at war with for months. Before this onslaught, the Jewish community knew it faced not just the elimination of its new state but physical extermination, a "new Mongol massacre," as one of the Arab spokesmen put it.

Five miles to the northeast of Kfar Malal lay the town of Kalkilya, a staging area for Iraqi forces that would attempt to cut the country in two at its narrow waist. On the outskirts of Kalkilya a small bridge crossed a wadi. Under ordinary circumstances the bridge might have been insignificant. But after a hard winter and late rains the wadi floor was still muddy, and so the bridge had become vital to the Iraqi advance. Its destruction would gain vital time.

At the moment Israel's birth became official I was leading my platoon through the night toward this bridge, part of a company-sized assault on key points along the Iraqi invasion route. It was slow going, but I was in no particular hurry. Since we were part of a larger operation, we would have to wait for H-hour anyway, and I did not want to start things off too early.

As we neared the bridge we dropped to our bellies and started crawling. In front of us we could see several guards walking back and forth, unaware of what the night had in store for them. But as we got closer, one of them sensed something was wrong and started to fire. Almost immediately the others joined in.

In a matter of moments a firefight flared up, and the guards retreated toward the nearest houses. With the bridge clear, two demolition people placed the charges and ran the lines back to our positions. From the houses and the orange groves on the side of the road the Iraqi fire picked up. But there was no attack. They knew we were here somewhere, but in the dark they could not tell exactly where or how many we might be.

As we flattened ourselves to the ground, I passed the word not to fire. I wanted to keep them unsettled and guessing until we could destroy the bridge and get out, and I wanted to get that done as fast as I could. I could hear the bullets hitting the ground and ricocheting off stones, and I knew that even after we blew the bridge we would still have three hard miles to go before we got back to our own lines.

It was exactly 1 A.M. when I radioed back that the charges were in place and ready to go. But the beautiful female voice on the other end of the communications set asked if we could wait. The other units we were co-ordinating our attack with were not in position yet. Could we delay it? With the firing from the groves and houses getting more intense, waiting was the last thing I wanted to do. But somehow I couldn't say no to that voice. I thought I knew which of the communications girls it was; I could practically see her. Her voice was soft, full of care and worry. How could I tell her that I was unable to hold on any longer? I couldn't, and I suspect that not many of the other young squad leaders and platoon commanders could have either.

Opposite: Following the Declaration of the State of Israel and the failure of the Palestinian Arabs "to push the Jews into the sea," the Arab armies invaded Palestine. This is how they planned "to erase Israel from the face of the earth." Sharon was a member of the Alexandroni Brigade.

ARAB INVASION, 15 MAY 1948

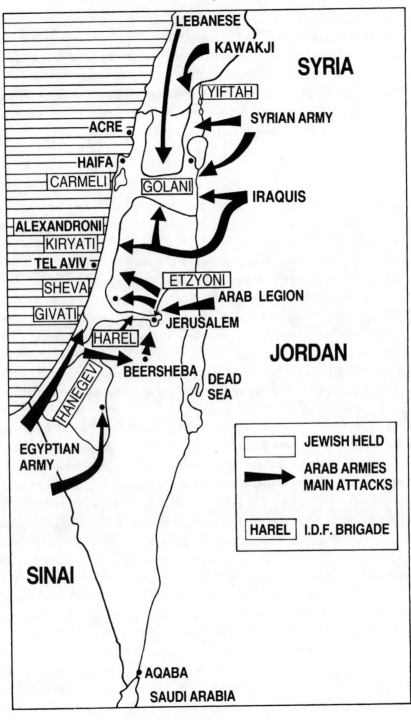

For another half hour or so we waited, watching for the Arabs to attack or try to encircle us. But not knowing it was only a platoon holding their bridge, they decided against doing anything serious and just kept shooting in our general direction. Then the same lovely voice came over the radio. Everything was ready, we could blow the charges. As the bridge collapsed in a roar of TNT, we ran down the road, then took off through the fields behind a small rise in the terrain that gave us cover from the pursuing fire.

For the moment, our units, part of the Alexandroni Brigade, managed to contain the Iraqi thrust across the coastal plain. But in other areas the Jewish positions were precarious. Already the Gush Etzion settlements south of Jerusalem had been overrun and hundreds of defenders killed. The Arabs had also cut the highway connecting Jerusalem and Tel Aviv, blocking the supplies that kept the besieged city alive. From the coast the Jerusalem road wound up into the Judean hills, where Arab villages and strongpoints overlooked the approaches. Without the manpower to take and hold these places, Jewish forces would occupy the ridges long enough to protect one of the lumbering supply convoys with their homemade armored cars. Then they would retreat in front of Arab counterattacks, and the road would be closed again.

By late April nothing was getting through. But on May 14 a Jewish attack took the high ground around the village of Latrun, a key point on the road. For two days the route was clear, but in the confusion of that time no supply convoy had been prepared to make the dash. The delay was crucial. On the sixteenth the Givati Brigade that had opened the road was rushed south to meet the Egyptian army as it crossed into Israel. And as they withdrew, two battalions of Jordan's Arab Legion moved into the Latrun police fort and the small village that dominated the road and the surrounding hills. Once more the lifeline was blocked.

Under pressure from other Jordanian units, the Jewish settlements north of Jerusalem were now abandoned. Inside the city food had virtually run out. With the pipeline destroyed, drinking water was collected in the city's old cisterns and tightly rationed. People lived in basements and trenches, unable to go out on the streets. Each day the defenders in Old Jerusalem's Jewish quarter were driven farther back. No one could guess how long they might hold out, or how long the New City itself might have.

At some point in late May, David Ben-Gurion and the Haganah General Staff made a decision to try and save the city by taking Latrun and pushing a large convoy through. With manpower stretched to the limit everywhere, they gave the operation to a new brigade (the Seventh), made up of units scraped together from other brigades and augmented by two battalions of immigrants just off the boat from the British detention camps in Cyprus. To provide a nucleus, a battalion from the Alexandroni Brigade was attached to the Seventh, a battalion that included my platoon.

From our camp near Netanya we drove toward Latrun in a long convoy of buses. Within an hour we were winding through the streets of Tel Aviv's suburbs. It had been many months since I had seen the city; and with all the fighting we had done, somehow I had the idea that everyone was in the army. But here in Tel Aviv I saw the usual bustle of civilian life going on. Even more surprising were the big wall posters that called on all young men and women to report for service. Apparently there were still some who hadn't joined. Watching the scenes of normal life pass by outside the bus windows was something of a shock to me. But some of the boys took it even more seriously. As I watched, soldiers from the bus in front of us jumped out and commandeered a big car parked on the street, driving it into the line of the convoy as we made our way through the city.

From Tel Aviv we drove to Rehovot, then toward Ekron. Outside the big Arab village of Akir we stopped while someone negotiated with the villagers to let us pass through. Looking back, it seems strange, a Haganah battalion on its way to fight the Arab Legion negotiating with Arab villagers for passage. But then it wasn't strange at all. We had to follow a circuitous route anyway. Ramle and Lod were in Jordanian hands. And here in the middle of the Jewish settlement was this big Arab village filled with armed Arabs. So we had to ask permission to go through. And when they didn't agree to it, we had to take an even more circuitous route, through Kibbutz Na'an, then to Ekron, and finally to Kibbutz Hulda, our staging area for the coming battle.

When we arrived at Hulda it was already past dark. That night we slept fitfully in an open field next to the road, listening to the drone of airplanes as they circled and circled in the dark. We heard one searching for what seemed hours, then we heard a crash and a roar as it exploded. The next morning we were told that two others had made it safely into the nearby Tel Nof airfield.

That day we rested in an olive grove watching the new immigrants train. These were refugees who had tried to get into Israel from Europe but had been stopped by the British and held in the Cyprus detention camps. For years they had rotted in the camps until finally, with the British mandate dissolved, they had been brought out. And now, the moment they arrived, they were being thrown into battle. As I looked at their faces I could not help wondering which of them would not be coming back. It seemed like a double or triple tragedy—they had survived the Holocaust, then the camps, and now they were faced with this. I thought of the biblical injunction that newly married men cannot be called into the army for a year—they have to have time to establish their families. Neither can men who have planted new groves be called—they have to have time to establish their trees. But these poor souls would not have time for any of it. Looking at their faces, I had a vision of those big Tel Aviv wall posters with their message to those Israelis who had still not reported for service.

The next day our own equipment arrived—packs, belts, ammunition, but no canteens. It wasn't something we thought about at the time, though later we would spend many hard hours wishing we had them. Then we were briefed on the operation. The village of Latrun, our first objective, was built around the ruins of an old Crusader castle on the crest of a hill overlooking the Jerusalem road. On the southern slopes of the hill olive groves stretched down to the road, while at the bottom of the western slope sat a big Trappist monastery. A third of a mile farther west was a lower hill dominated by a former British police fortress, also in Jordanian hands.

Our battalion would have the main job of pushing the Jordanians off the heights, then capturing the monastery, and finally taking the police fort to the west. While we were doing this, the other battalions would secure our flanks by occupying the high ground to the east of Latrun— "Artillery Ridge" and "Hill 314." H-hour would be 2400 hours that night. My platoon was designated to lead the attack in across the wheatfields south of Latrun, over the Jerusalem road, then up through the olive groves to the village.

As I studied the map, I saw exactly how I would do it. Covered by the night, I would take the platoon up the left side of the hill, skirt the crown, then hit directly into the middle of the Jordanian positions, taking them by surprise. I knew that by dawn we would have to be in control of the heights, ready to throw back any counterattack. After that it would be a relatively easy matter to take the monastery, which would then be directly beneath our guns—assuming the Arabs would make a fight out of it. (We heard the monks were still living there.) Then we could move on to the police fort, which would by then be completely isolated.

The plan seemed workable, especially when I heard that we would be supported by two 65-mm field guns. I had seen artillery before, during World War Two when the allies moved their batteries up along the coastal road, and also in the movies. But I had never actually been in a battle where we had field guns on our side. It made me wonder for a moment whether there would be anything left for us to do.

But I was also nagged by an almost indefinable worry. Not about the patchwork makeup of our forces or about the Jordanians on top of the hill, but about the terrain. Although I had studied the maps carefully, I didn't feel at home in this place. Instead of the familiar, secure feeling of orange groves, here there were open fields and stony hills. The night air brought with it not the hint of citrus but the somehow disconcerting smell of chickpeas. There was something unknown here, strange fields with their strange crops. What was worse, although I was supposed to lead the attack, the company commander had not taken me along to the forward observation posts. I had never actually seen the ground we would have to cover.

On the night of the twenty-fifth we packed ourselves into buses and drove from the olive grove where we had camped into Kibbutz Hulda. There the buses waited while inside one of the buildings the officers held a last-minute council. As time passed it became apparent that some kind of angry argument was going on. Through the lighted windows we could see the senior officers gesticulating and shouting at each other. While we waited, a nerve-racking half hour turned into an hour, then one hour became two. As the night began to slip by we sat on the buses and worried, beginning to dread what might happen if we were caught in front of the hill by the notoriously sudden Judean daylight, "when morning kisses the night."

An eternity seemed to pass before the buses finally began their short journey. When we climbed down into the field south of Latrun it was already 4 A.M. With another hour's walk in front of us we were five hours behind schedule. A thick predawn fog shrouded the ground as we began to move forward through the standing wheat. In front we heard the boom and screech of Jordanian artillery sending shells over our heads. How they might have picked us up I didn't know, but in the gloom there was little chance of them hitting anything. Then, as I led the column closer to the road, suddenly machine guns opened up in front of us and I sensed rather than saw men dropping suddenly or sliding slowing into the fog. Instantly the soldiers around me stopped and took up positions, letting loose a volley of fire toward the hill. Over the radio I heard our company commander, Asher Levy, reporting that we were under heavy machine-gun fire and taking casualties. From battalion I heard the order to "take the wounded with you and proceed." A moment later one of Asher's runners was next to me saying that instead of heading straight across the road and into the olive groves on the left side of the slope, we should move parallel to the road, to our right, getting around the machine guns rather than walking straight into them. Then we could cut up the right slope of the hill and hit the Jordanians from that side.

Together with Azriel Ratzabi, one of the boys from Kfar Malal, I set up our light mortar and began dropping rounds onto the hill in an attempt to cover the platoon so they could begin moving out. He loaded while I aimed and fired, managing to get off five or six rounds into the Jordanian positions. Suddenly, as Azriel raised himself to drop another round into the tube, he let out a rasping sigh and collapsed next to me. A bullet had hit him in the side and gone completely through both lungs.

As the night turned gray, I began moving the men to the right, near the bank of a small wadi that paralleled the road in front of us. Glancing at my watch, I saw it was already 5 A.M. But though the sky had begun to lighten, the fog still hid us from the Jordanian machine guns raking the field. Here, along the bank of the wadi, we took more casualties—my sergeant, Rami Potash, went down, then quickly somebody else. Others hoisted the wounded onto their shoulders as I headed the platoon toward Bir el Hilu, the sweet-water well that showed on the map a couple hundred yards farther on.

Then, in a moment of startling swiftness, the fog lifted and it was full daylight. We were alone on a stretch of bare ground with the road in front of us and the wheatfield behind, caught in the glare of the morning sun. Although we had been leading two companies toward the hill, now I saw no one else, only the boys in my platoon. The olive grove on Latrun hill looked like it was spitting fire as we hustled toward a shallow gully a hundred yards or so to the right.

A few heartbeats later we had flattened ourselves into the gully, and as I looked around to get my bearings I saw a bullet smash into our one radio, cutting us off from the rest of the battlefield. Lying there on my stomach, I could hear the crump of the Jordanian mortars as they tried to zero in on us. Artillery shells exploded in the wheatfield, which was already smoldering and starting to blaze. Machine-gun slugs cut through the smoke that wafted out of the field on the hot morning wind.

Taking stock, I had no illusions about our situation. We were caught in an open field, saved only by the shallow depression that gave us a degree of protection from the machine-gun and rifle fire pouring down from the Jordanians on the hill. A couple hundred yards in front of us was the Jerusalem road, which I had originally planned to cross under the cover of darkness. Behind were only the burning fields and rocky terraces. There was nothing to do but keep our heads down and wait. Eventually the commanders would realize what had happened and would find a way to get the attack moving again.

Toward the back end of the gully was a little patch of muck where water from an all but dry spring oozed up to form a few black puddles. With no canteens that was the only water, though I couldn't imagine anybody actually drinking it. I wondered briefly what we would do if we had to stay here any length of time. On the bright side, we had a good supply of hand grenades and plenty of ammunition for our Sten guns and Czech rifles. If nothing happens to get the attack moving again, I told the platoon, we'll have to hold out till night. Then we'll be able to get back.

I hoped that soon the commanders would understand what had happened and figure a way to start things up. But somehow it didn't happen. Our radio was smashed and no runners showed up. As the morning passed and the sun baked, the Jordanians kept up their fire, shooting down on us from the hillside. With one person at a time observing, the rest of us lay curled up in the gully, trying to stay out of the line of sight. But now and then someone would change position and get hit in the legs, or raise his head a bit and take a bullet from an Arab rifleman. Every movement brought a volley of shots. Those who were wounded we dragged back to the muddy end, where there was a little more protection. Other than that we just waited, firing off an occasional volley from the light machine gun or dropping a mortar round onto the hill. From our right we heard sounds of more shooting and we guessed that Asher Levy was there with more of the boys. But we couldn't tell for sure, and I didn't want to risk a runner.

We had been in the gully for almost two hours when the Jordanian fire increased its volume and tempo. On the hill in front of us men were moving in our direction, slipping from tree to tree through the olive grove, then ducking behind the stone wall that bordered the far side of the road. Raising my head, I could see them sprinting across the highway firing as they ran, then disappearing into the wadi. Obviously they had decided not to wait until their long-distance shooting took effect. They were going to try a frontal assault.

A few minutes later Arab soldiers were moving toward us from the wadi and from the vineyard in front on our left. A line of them were crawling forward and firing, shouting curses in our direction to give themselves courage. Above the shooting I could hear the screams of "Etbach el Yahud," "Kill the Jews." We waited until they were within thirty or forty yards, then let loose a stream of fire from the machine gun, Sten guns, and rifles. A moment later they were retreating toward the wadi, dragging their casualties with them. Creeping on our stomachs, we pulled our own wounded back to the spring, where the mud was already streaking red. Then we braced ourselves for the next assault.

In the following hours the Jordanians came again and again, each time the same way—moving in, shouting, firing. Each time we drove them back, choking as the stench of cordite mixed with the smoke billowing over us from the fires in the wheatfield. In a quiet moment I heard a drone and looked up at the patches of blue sky that showed through the rifts and windows of smoke. High above us two enemy bombers flashed white and silver against the sky, soaring gracefully like innocent birds and dropping little black bombs on the field below.

By this time I was wondering how we were going to get out. Between the fighting, the sun, and the hot wind coming across the plain, we were dying of thirst. I kept imagining that I was drinking a cold "gazoz," my favorite soft drink, at Whitman's soda fountain in Tel Aviv. I was quickly losing my hopes that something would happen to get us moving, or to get us out. If nothing did happen, our only chance would be to hold out until night could cover our retreat. I kept looking at my watch, but time seemed to have stopped. Thinking it must be broken I wound it again and again until the stem snapped. A biblical verse flitted across my memory, something I had learned years ago. "Shemesh b'Givon dom / V'yareach b'emek Ayalon." "The sun will stop at Givon, the moon at Ayalon." And here we were in the Ayalon Valley, where now it was the sun that seemed to have stopped.

Shortly after the bombers left, a figure appeared through the smoke from the direction of the sweet-water well. It ran toward us jerkily, now and then throwing itself on the ground, then getting up and running again. In a few minutes the figure had made it to the gully and had dived in with us. Only then did I see that it was Mordechai Duchiminer, a young Holocaust survivor who was Asher Levy's favorite runner. Gasping for breath, he told us that the rest of the company was on our right, near the well. But so far they had been unable to move either. He had also come to get our mortar. After lying still a minute, Mordechai grabbed the mortar and looked at me. Then he jumped up and ran off in the direction he had come from, clutching the tube under his arm. Days later I learned that he was killed on the way back.

Around noon the Jordanians on the hill intensified their fire, the usual forerunner of another assault. Raising myself up to see what was happening, I felt something thud into my belly, knocking me back. I heard my mouth say "imah"—mother, and the instant it was out I glanced around to see if anybody had heard. Already blood was seeping through my shirt and from my shorts, where another wound in my thigh had appeared as if by magic. I lay down, still lucid, but feeling my strength ebbing away.

As I rested on the ground, I heard the new Jordanian attack come on—more of the same again, shooting, shouting, but no real drive behind it. Again we forced them back. But this time I could see that the boys were exhausted. Black flies swarmed around, swept in by the hamsin wind. They had been a nuisance all morning, but now their bites seemed almost unbearable. Ants covered the ground, attracted by the blood of the wounded and dead.

While I lay there, two of the "older" men in the platoon crawled up to me, both of them British army veterans in their early twenties. Their eyes looked vacant. "Arik," one of them asked, "how are you going to get us out of this?" I stared at them for a moment, then said sharply, "Look, I've gotten you out of a lot of tight places before. I'll get you out of this too. Just get back and do what I told you." But when they crawled back to their places I heard one say, "Sure he's gotten us out before, but how does he think he's going to get us out of this one?" The remark stung like an insult.

Around one o'clock I felt a change come over the battlefield. From Latrun the Jordanian fire grew fainter, more sporadic. The boom of our own field guns, which we had hardly heard all day, became louder, dominating the noise of battle. I knew something was happening, but it was hard to tell what it was or if we were in any condition to respond to it. Already almost half the platoon was dead and most of the others wounded, some critically. My own wound throbbed. Looking down, I saw that my clothes were soaked with blood from my thighs to my stomach. Though I couldn't tell exactly where I was hit, I had seen enough groin and stomach wounds to make me feel faint. I wondered if I could walk, or even move.

At two the guns stopped. A stillness fell on the field, a strange silence in which nothing moved. At that moment I happened to look back over my shoulder toward Hill 314, a half mile or so behind us on our right. On its brown slopes were Palestinian villagers in kaffiyehs waving their rifles. Now and then they stooped down over black shapes that were just barely distinguishable on the ground. I knew our forces had been on 314, securing the flank of the attack. Instantly I realized what the scene meant. Our people there were gone—dead or withdrawn. The black shapes on the hillside were their casualties; the Arabs stooping over them were looting and mutilating the bodies.

Then I understood the silence. We were alone on the field. The other units had been ordered back. That was what the artillery fire had been for, to cover the retreat. We had not seen them as they pulled out in back of us, and they had not known we were still here, and still alive.

With the Palestinians coming down the hill behind us, there was nothing left but to try to get out. I saw the hopelessness in the men's eyes as I gave the order and pointed out the direction—straight back through the smoke and over the terraces. With any luck, the Jordanians in front would keep their heads down until we were gone. If they didn't, we would all be dead before we could go more than a few steps. But the Arabs on the hillside were moving slowly, going from body to body, oblivious that we were down here. My mouth was as dry as sand as I crawled over to the spring and lowered my lips to the bloody puddle.

Eleven of the wounded could walk. But Simcha Pinchasi, a wonderful boy from Kfar Saba, had been hit badly in both legs and could not move. With a look and a quick nod he indicated that he would cover the withdrawal. All day long he had been firing the light machine gun until he had been wounded and pulled into the back of the gully. "But Arik," he said, "before you go, give me a grenade." I gave it to him, knowing there was no hope whatsoever, not for him and most likely not for the rest of us either. There was no one whom I could ask to carry him, just as there was no one who could carry me. Our eyes caught for a moment, then I turned to go. And as I did I had a momentary image of his parents as they were when I last saw them in their village.

THE FIRST ATTACK ON LATRUN, 26 May 1948

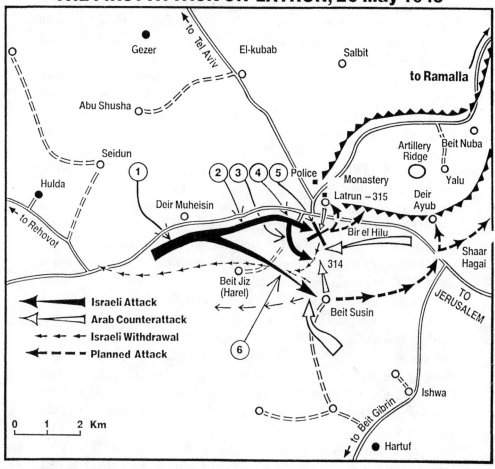

(1) 7th Brigade (including 32nd, 72nd Battalions)
(2) 32nd Battalion (from Alexandroni Brigade)
(3) "A" Company, 32nd Battalion
(4) "B" Company, 32nd Battalion
(5) 1st (Sharon's) Platoon, "B" Company
(6) 72nd Battalion

Latrun, dominating the main bottleneck on the primary road to Jerusalem, was the key
to the survival of Jerusalem. Repeatedly attacked by the IDF, it became the bloodiest
battlefield of the War of Independence. Sharon participated in the first attack and was
badly wounded; his platoon was virtually wiped out.

From the back of the gully I crawled on all fours into the field, unable to get up. I remembered that there was supposed to be a squadron of Jordanian armored cars in the area, and I wondered vaguely if they were out there behind us somewhere. The rocks tore my knees as I made my way along the side of the first terrace behind the gully, but somehow I managed to keep crawling, until I reached the wall to the second. There I stopped, panting for breath. Blood was seeping from my pants, and I knew there was no way I could clamber up onto the second terrace. Looking around, it seemed as if I had entered a scene from hell. Here and there fires blazed in the wheatfield, emitting a pall of choking black smoke that hung low to the ground. Through its slow whirls I caught glimpses of the Palestinians still moving down Hill 314 and into the field, searching for weapons and for the dead and wounded. From all around came the ceaseless drone of the "barkhaches," the miserable black flies that had plagued us all day. On my hands and knees I struggled a few yards farther, then stopped dead when I saw crawling up the slope on my left one of the boys from my platoon.

He was a new boy, just sixteen years old. He had joined us only two days earlier, and somehow I could not remember his name. I stared at him in horror. The bottom of his jaw had been shot up, leaving a mass of gore. At almost the same moment he saw me. Neither of us said a word. He was unable to talk, I was too tired. Then he was crawling next to me, doing his best to keep me moving, pushing me and supporting me over the terrace wall. I tried to tell him to go on, to save himself. But he wouldn't leave.

Together we crawled over one rocky terrace, then another, then another, our hands and knees burned from the charred earth. On the far side of the slopes we met more dazed stragglers. One of them was Moshik Lanzet, the deputy company commander. Moshik hoisted me onto his shoulders and tried to carry me through the burning field toward where we thought our people should be. But he was wounded too, and after a short stumbling walk he almost collapsed, exhausted by the effort. Instead he got his shoulder under my arm, and leaning my weight on him I managed to keep moving.

We walked like that for several miles through the smoke and fire. From time to time other figures stumbled out of the sooty haze, all of them moving in the direction of Hulda. Toward the rear of the valley the air began to clear and I saw our waiting half-tracks loading survivors. Just before I lost consciousness I also saw a jeep driving in and out of the blackened field searching for others who might have been left alive. As it circled and drove close I recognized the girl driving and the boy who sat next to her—Rifka and Shmuel Bogin, a sister and brother, also from Kfar Malal. Then the name of the boy who saved my life came to me, the sixteen-year-old who had been hit in the jaw. It was Yakov Bogin, a cousin of theirs. A moment later, in front of the half-tracks, I passed out.

5

Losses

In my next moment of consciousness I was on a stretcher somewhere, my face covered by a damp towel. Two male voices were talking above me. One of them said, "Here's another one gone. . . . Who is it?" "It's Arik," the second voice answered. "Oh," said the first. "What happened? Where'd he get it?" Just as I passed out again I heard the first one say, "Right in the genitals."

Between clarity and delirium I was taken with the other wounded by ambulance to the nearby village of Ekron, where we stopped for a while next to the old synagogue. There some of the village women came in carrying cans of milk and filling glasses for us. I was so thirsty; but looking down at my abdomen, they wouldn't give me any. I couldn't keep my eyes open and kept lapsing into sleep. But when I was awake I could not keep my mind off my wound.

From Ekron we were driven to the former British army hospital near Rehovot, which by this time was crowded with soldiers wounded in the battle. As I was lying on my stretcher, awake now, but still tired to death, a lovely army nurse came in with a bottle and asked me to urinate in it. When I couldn't, she turned her head and asked someone to bring her a catheter. That was the magic word. As soon as I heard it I asked for the bottle and a moment later felt the flow of urine, a marvelous sensation unaccompanied by any pain. I wondered how that could be. Was it possible I was still in one piece? As the bottle filled, the nurse bent down over me and kissed me softly on the lips. Then again the world went blank.

A short time later I became aware that they were changing my bandages. Then I was in an ambulance along with several others, on our way to the Hadassah hospital in Tel Aviv. The ride went smoothly enough until the ambulance reached the Balfour Street gate to the hospital. Stopping there, we heard air-raid sirens begin to wail, then everyone disappeared—the driver, the nurses, anyone who could walk. Immobilized on the stretcher, I heard the drone of bombers and the pounding of antiaircraft guns. The two planes above Latrun had seemed so distant, as if they were not really part of the battle at all. But now we listened intently as explosions rocked the city, trying to determine if the bombs were coming in our direction.

Once it was over, they carried us into what had been the maternity ward but now housed wounded soldiers. When the doctor came by shortly afterward he examined me, then said with a coarse laugh that if things down there had been a different condition when I was hit I wouldn't have been so lucky. As it was the bullet had plowed through my lower abdomen and come out my upper thigh, the strange trajectory explained by the fact that the Jordanians had been firing down at us. Although I had lost a lot of blood, I would eventually recover.

But as great a relief as it was to know I would be all right, it did nothing to alleviate my feelings about the battle. As I waited for my turn in the operating room, and then as I convalesced, I could not tear my mind away from what had happened. My platoon had been destroyed. Out of thirty-five, fifteen were dead and another eleven wounded. Others were still missing. I knew the news would hit Kfar Malal, Kfar Saba, and Magdiel like a plague. Almost all the boys had come from these settlements and from a few surrounding farms. The losses would send the whole area into mourning.

I had been fighting alongside most of those boys for months, through one hard situation after another. In that time we had grown together; they had become my family, my emotional home—a family I had now lost. Again and again I saw Azriel at the moment he was hit. I saw the look of hopelessness on Simcha Pinchasi's face as he took the grenade from me. These scenes and a dozen others preyed on my mind while I lay in bed and relived the battle.

As if it were a movie, I saw those immigrants speaking to each other in Yiddish while they went through their training next to the olive grove. I saw the commanders shouting at each other through the windows in Kibbutz Hulda while we waited in the buses. I wondered if I might have done something different if I had known the terrain better. Most of all I thought about how we had been left out there alone. Why hadn't one of the commanders been there to see what had happened and get us off the field? As badly hurt as we were, we had driven off one Arab attack after another. The more I thought about it the more I was convinced we could have kept going until nightfall. If only we had not been abandoned. If only someone had been there to make the decision. These were not passing thoughts. They preoccupied me while I lay in bed slowly gathering the strength I would need before they could move me.

Eventually I was well enough to be transferred to Ramat Gan, where Gali came to visit, relieved but still worried. It was the first time we had talked in weeks, though it seemed that a lifetime had passed. It was hard to say when we would be able to see each other again, or under what circumstances. Everything was so uncertain. I knew that before long they would be transferring me again, this time to Tel Hashomer hospital. From there, depending on how long I took to heal, I would find myself back in battle.

Gali was not the only one who came to visit. My parents came too. And so did parents of boys in my platoon, searching for their sons. So little information had gotten out about the battle, and with the primitive communications of those days who could tell how much of it might be accurate. I hardly knew myself who had been left alive. It was so hard to lie there and know that they were standing silently in the room waiting for me to come awake enough to talk to them, and so hard to know that I had survived and their sons hadn't. What could I tell them—about what the Arabs did to the dead and wounded? About what they did to prisoners? These people just stood there, people I had known all my life. In their silence I imagined I could hear them saying that they had given the most precious things they had into my hands. And now where are they, you who are alive? Tell me, they were saying, where are our sons?

I was still convalescing when the first United Nations–sponsored truce went into effect. Everyone knew what a critical time it was. Jerusalem was still cut off, and on its southern outskirts an Egyptian column had linked up with the Jordanians. Meanwhile the main Egyptian column had pushed up along the coast from Gaza to Ashdod, less than twenty miles from Tel Aviv; and from east to west the Egyptians had thrown a cordon across the Negev, isolating Ruhama and its sister settlements.

While the truce lasted, there was a rush to buy arms, though I would only understand what had been accomplished after I returned to my unit and found how many more weapons we now had. During the winter there often hadn't been enough rifles for everyone. The truce time had also been used to reorganize the Israeli forces into something more like a real army, capable of fighting larger-scale actions and moving quickly along the interior lines, which gave it an advantage over the spread-out and unco-ordinated Arab forces.

After almost a month of relative quiet the U.N. Security Council proposed a continuation of the truce. But understanding that every passing day gave Israel's claim to nationhood more credibility, the Arab states rejected the proposal. All across the country fighting broke out again.

By mid-July I was well enough to return to my battalion, which was now holding the Kuleh hills northeast of Lod. Just a few days earlier the Jordanians had launched a counterattack here, overrunning a unit, then massacring the wounded. Twenty-eight bodies had been found, many with their ears missing, some with their genitals cut off and stuffed into their mouths. For days we scoured the area looking for missing pieces, and scattered around the hills we found them: fingers, ears, penises caked into the dusty earth. The tension bothered me, more than it ever had before. Although the wounds still hurt, I knew the problem was more emotional than physical. I caught myself thinking about having been left behind on the field. At night I checked and rechecked to make sure the guards were in position and alert.

The struggle to regain my optimism and confidence was not helped when several weeks after I returned I had an accident in a jeep I was driving. With my company commander in the car, somehow I managed to roll it over on us, breaking some ribs and injuring my spine in the process. When I was released from the hospital this time, I was still in severe pain. I felt like someone who had been badly beaten up

Meanwhile a second truce had been called. But in mid-October this too collapsed, and vicious fighting flared up in the Negev, the Galilee, and around Jerusalem. But by now there was no question about who had the upper hand. In the central and upper Galilee the Lebanese were pushed back, and although the Syrians fought to a stalemate in their bridgehead at Mishmar HaYarden, Fauzi el Kaukji's Arab Liberation Army was destroyed. With the siege of Jerusalem permanently broken now, Israeli forces fought to establish and consolidate the Jerusalem corridor.

In the south, Front Commander Yigal Allon took Beersheba, inflicting the first major defeat on the Egyptians and opening up the encircled Negev. Our objective now was no longer merely to survive but to establish political realities, "facts," as Ben-Gurion was to code-name the final campaign.

By this time I had been appointed reconnaissance officer for our battalion, which was now engaged in a series of clashes against the Iraqis. Then in mid-November we were ordered south against the Egyptians. One of their brigades had been trapped in a pocket between Faluja and Iraq el Manshiyeh, but so far all attempts to dislodge them had been thrown back.

The 4,000 trapped Egyptians were under the command of a Sudanese brigadier named Said Taha Bey, an old warhorse who had received his training in the British army. This Taha Bey was a true hero. Without any real hope of either breaking out or being rescued, his brigade was putting up a fierce resistance, repelling every attack. Despite his position, at first he refused to even talk with any of the Israeli commanders who tried to arrange negotiations. When finally he agreed to meet with Yigal Allon, he rejected Allon's offer to allow his troops to retire with their weapons. According to the story that made the rounds at the time, Taha Bey listened as Allon described the hopelessness of his situation, then told the Israeli commander that he was fighting for the honor of the Egyptian army and would not surrender under any conditions whatsoever.

Despite our complete control over the battlefield, try what we might we could not break through Taha Bey's defenses. Since the end of October, attack after attack had been turned back with serious losses. Finally a major effort was planned for the night of December 27. Our battalion would keep the village of Faluja busy while a second battalion would carry out the main assault on Iraq Manshiyeh. It was a disaster. By the time we were able to disengage we had lost ninety-eight men out of a total of six hundred.

☆　　☆　　☆

Taha Bey never was defeated. Eventually a special agreement was reached with him, and only then did his brigade march home. For the Alexandroni Brigade it was a bitter defeat, especially after the earlier tragedy at Latrun. Of course in the overall scheme, Faluja was only one story. Other Egyptian forces were defeated and surrounded in the Gaza Strip and were only saved by pressure from the Americans (who were pressured by the British). On February 27, 1949, a final cease-fire was signed with the Egyptians, and by early March there was no more fighting anywhere.

With the end of the war and recognition by many of the world's states, Israel had emerged from its traumatic birth as a nation "like other nations." It was a time of victory and rejoicing, a victory I had every right to feel as deeply as anyone. For a year and a half I had fought on the front lines, often behind the front lines, in a bloody and frightening war against a merciless enemy. But strangely, now that all that effort had ended in triumph, in my heart I did not feel much like celebrating. I felt the achievement of the moment; it was impossible not to. But deeper than that I had a sense of frustration and loss. At the age of twenty most of my friends were dead. I had lost so many of them at Latrun and elsewhere. I had participated in a number of daring small-scale victories. I had even commanded in several of them. But I had also been involved in some of the army's most dreadful failures. Above all, I could not get out of my mind the conviction that these operations could have been handled differently, that they could have ended differently. I did not know any more than others about what the future might hold—whether peace or more war. And I had no idea what I myself might be doing. But as the last of the fighting ground to a halt, I was oppressed by feelings of frustration and disappointment, and by nightmares about the things I had seen.

6

Interim

In September of 1949 the Alexandroni Brigade was switched to reserve status and I was assigned as commander of the Golani Brigade's reconnaissance company. The end of the war had left many frontier areas disputed or unclear, and skirmishes with the Egyptians, Jordanians, and Lebanese were a regular fact of life. It was a time for establishing borders and training new recruits in patrolling, intelligence gathering, and night fighting. The job was just down my alley. By now I had completely recovered my health and spirits. Physically exuberant myself, I kept the reconnaissance company on the go constantly, always off the roads and into the swamps and barrens—on both sides of the border—teaching what I always considered the primary lesson: mastery of the terrain.

The Golani Brigade's commander was now Colonel Avraham Yoffe, a large, expansive man whom I quickly came to respect, and as I got to know him well, to love. Born in the lower Galilee, Yoffe was practically a giant. Known to his men as "Yoffe Hagadol" (Yoffe the Big), he had huge shoulders and seemed a head taller than everyone around him. He enjoyed food immensely and had a deep feeling for the country's natural environment, which he knew in astonishing detail. He was an expert on each flower, tree, and bird; and when he eventually retired from the army after serving as commander of the northern and southern fronts, he created and presided over Israel's system of nature preserves.

Yoffe was also an advocate of the same kind of aggressive patrolling and intelligence techniques that I was doing my best to teach, and in mid-1950 he first promoted me to captain, then sent me to the battalion commander's course at Zriffin. He also talked to Benjamin Ghibly about me.

One of Yoffe's many friends, Benjamin Ghibly was chief of military intelligence; and as luck would have it, at that moment he was going through the brigade commanders course, also at Zriffin. When Ghibly invited me to his room for a talk one night, I suspected something was up. As I walked through the barracks, the thought floated across my mind that he might offer me a position as intelligence officer for one of the brigades. By the time I got to his room I had already decided that if he did I would accept on the spot. But to my great surprise, what Ghibly had in mind was not a brigade position, but a job as intelligence officer for the entire Central Command, one of the Israeli army's three regional commands. It was as if somebody had just hoisted me up by the bootstraps.

Central Command headquarters was located in Ramle, in an old military building from World War One. General Zvi Ayalon was the commander, a likable, easygoing individual in his late thirties, whom the rest of the staff nevertheless referred to as "the old man." Ayalon was the kind of straightforward person who gave everyone an immediate feeling of security. With him it was a given that if you did your job conscientiously he would back you to the hilt.

It was an active year. I spent much of the time out visiting the borders and the units that patrolled them, but I also had my first lessons in what a headquarters staff did and how they did it. That year too there was a large-scale military exercise, I believe the first regional command-level exercise the army had ever conducted. It was a complicated affair that included symbolic units as well as real forces and called for sophisticated exercise management techniques that the higher command was not completely at ease with. The aggressor in these war games was Moshe Dayan, commander of the Southern Command; the defender was Zvi Ayalon and the Central Command.

This was the first time I met Dayan, and from the beginning it was obvious he was a different kind of character. In contrast to the friendly and outgoing Ayalon, Dayan rarely so much as said hello to anyone. When we prepared the exercise the headquarters of both sides examined the area, marking out the boundaries and the ground that would be fought over. The tour itself took days, and Ayalon brought his entire staff with him in a convoy that included a kitchen truck and headquarters caravan along with several command cars and jeeps.

Dayan, though, came by himself, driving alone in his jeep and darting all over the terrain, taking in everything and searching constantly, not only for tactical features but for fruit. The man was addicted to fruit of all sorts, figs especially, but also dates and grapes and melons and whatever else he could get his hands on. (Later when I served under him on the northern front I prepared what I called the "Northern Command Fruit Map," showing exactly where the choicest fruits could be had.) But while Dayan was poking his nose into every wadi and grove like a fox, Ayalon's convoy was too cumbersome to get into some of the rougher areas, and by the time the exercise began the Southern Command had a decisive advantage.

When the exercise started, Dayan's troops moved fast. Making good use of his detailed knowledge of the battlefield, they quickly succeeded in penetrating the Central Command defenses and encircling one of our brigades. But though Dayan's plan was bold, it soon was evident that he had not spent enough time on staff work and logistics, and before he could pin down the victory his attacking columns ran out of fuel.

But Ayalon had trouble responding to Dayan's predicament. Although he had proven himself one of the top Haganah commanders, in this exercise it seemed to take him forever to make decisions. In his open, friendly fashion he conducted orders groups that included everyone and lasted hours. Each of the staff officers expressed his point of view, his doubts, and his criticisms; and as intelligence officer I was called on again and again to give the appreciation of the situation—the terrain, the enemy forces, time, space, and all the other factors that go into an intelligence report. And all the while time was passing and conditions on the field were changing. At one point Commander-in-Chief Yigael Yadin came in and yelled, "What are you doing? Why do you keep repeating these things? The situation has changed a dozen times since then!" It was a lesson I remembered very well when I conducted my own orders groups later on.

But meanwhile Dayan was still stuck, and while he was refueling we finally launched a night counterattack against him. Unsure of the route, the brigade commander in charge of this maneuver called for help, and I went to head up the column and find a way over the difficult hills and ravines in our path. Taking command of the reconnaissance and engineering companies, I managed to navigate them through, at some points towing every vehicle up the banks of the steeper wadis. I don't think I saw the brigade leader that entire night, something that taught me another permanent lesson about command and control. When this action was over I knew without a doubt that the real commander is the one out in front. It's only when you are there yourself, seeing everything with your own eyes, that you can make the necessary decisions, and the more complicated and confused a situation is the truer that is. That lesson stuck in 1967 in the Sinai and in 1973 on the canal. If you are on the spot and personally in control, if you are towing them and pushing them with your own hands, only then can you be sure they will move the way you want them to.

By morning I had led the brigade into Kibbutz Bet Kama near Beersheba. That was the end of the exercise; and while we hadn't defeated Dayan, at least we had countered his attack and held him to a standoff.

When the games were over, Dayan treated us to a psychological warfare exercise that summed the whole thing up from his point of view. As talented an artist as he was a writer, he drew up a cartoon that showed a wild young fox (the Southern Command's shoulder patch insignia was a fox) standing triumphantly on top of a toothless half-dead lion (a caricature of the Central Command insignia). Below was written, "Better a live fox than a dying lion." The day the exercise ended a Piper Cub flew over our positions dropping thousands of leaflets adorned by this Dayan original.

Not that Dayan's opinion changed my feelings about what had happened. Regardless of the inconclusive outcome, I felt personally victorious. In effect I had led an entire brigade in a difficult maneuver that had redressed the balance. A few days later, though, my pride in this achievement was deflated some when I was called to General Headquarters and told that it was not an intelligence officer's job to lead a brigade. My place was next to the chief of the command, where I could provide him with regular up-to-date appreciations of the situation. It wasn't a reprimand, but by the time I left the headquarters I had decided that I was not going to make a career in the intelligence branch.

✻   ✻   ✻

Sometime before Avraham Yoffe sent me to the battalion commanders course, I had managed to contract a serious case of malaria. For almost two years the disease kept recurring every two weeks or so, each attack leaving me weaker than the last. With all the high fevers and the large quantities of quinine I ingested, by the end of 1951 I had become very weak. Afraid of the ultimate outcome, the doctors suggested that the only way to get rid of it would be to have a complete change of climate.

As a result I decided to take a two-month leave and go abroad. I had never been out of the country. But I had my Uncle Joseph in Paris; three friends, the young British Jew Cyril Kern (who had volunteered into the Israeli army during the War of Independence), Yitzhak Moda'i (who had distinguished himself as a platoon commander in the battle of Latrun) and Dov Sion in London; and my Aunt Sana in New York—all of whom were happy to show me around. So with my father I went to a clothing store in Tel Aviv, where I bought my first sport jacket and a pair of what were then known in Israel as "half shoes," to distinguish them from the high-top shoes that everyone always wore on the farm.

When I arrived at Orly airport in Paris, my uncle took one look at my outfit and blanched. When we got to his apartment he made me put on one of his elegant suits, claiming that I could simply not walk around Paris dressed in "peasant" clothes like that. Then he took me to a fine tailoring shop where he had me measured for a suit of my own. Watching me squirm while the tailor applied his measuring tape embarrassed him. And when I couldn't think of the answer to the question *"Dans quel coté messieur met'il son équipement?"* he was first speechless with frustration, then furious when after thinking about it a bit I finally said, "In the middle." It had never in my life occurred to me that anybody might think about such things.

The next stop was a glove shop. Uncle Joseph had discovered that I did not own a pair of gloves, another impossibility that had to be remedied if I was to be seen in Paris. But the glove shop was a further embarrassment. When the salesgirl came over to fit the gloves I just stuck out my hand, oblivious of the fitting frame into which the customer was supposed to carefully place his forearm while extending his fingers.

But despite the problems, eventually I was suited up to Uncle Joseph's satisfaction. At that point he supplied me with several carnets of metro and bus tickets, and I began to see Paris. For the next two weeks I went everywhere, sometimes with him but most often by myself. With Joseph I went to the best restaurants and nightclubs, by myself I walked the whole city, marveling at the buildings, the stores, the art museums (which my father had described to me at length), the fashionable women walking down Avenue Victor Hugo and the Champs Elysées. Having read many nineteenth-century French novels, I looked up at the garrets and imagined that they were all inhabited by lovely, naive country girls struggling nightly against their wicked landlords. It was all beautiful and exciting, and such a change from the moshav.

From France I took the Dover–Calais ferry to England to spend some time with my friends there, then flew by Constellation to the United States. My Aunt Sana met me in New York, where the first thing she did was to get me a driver's license so that I could see something of the country. I had a few problems with the English on the written test, but when Sana explained that I was a major in the Israeli army, she apparently touched a soft spot and the examiner let me through.

I walked around New York City much as I had in Paris, with my head up and my eyes opened wide. Then, when Sana left for Palm Beach, I took her car and drove south to Tennessee, Louisiana, and Texas. In New York it was freezing cold and snowing, but the farther south I went the hotter it got. I was awed by the size of the country where one could drive for days and days, even experiencing major changes in climate. The expanses of water and the long bridges and causeways also struck my imagination. They were like nothing I had ever seen before.

By the end of December I was in Palm Beach looking at the Christmas decorations and absorbing the holiday atmosphere. I spent New Year's there lying on the beach, then headed back north, driving up the coast through Georgia, the Carolinas, Virginia, Washington, D.C., and on to New York, taken by the friendliness of the people and the immensity of what I had seen.

By the time I returned to Israel I felt like a man of the world. More important, the malaria seemed to have disappeared and I was ready again for work. My new assignment was as chief of intelligence to the Northern Command, where a short time later Moshe Dayan was appointed commander–in–chief. When Dayan let me know that in his opinion the only worthwhile intelligence officer was one who knew the terrain better than he did himself, I knew we were at least in agreement on essentials. I was always looking for opportunities to go off alone into the countryside, and Dayan's remark seemed to be a green light for the long hikes I loved to take into the mountains and along the borders. It was the beginning of a complicated lifelong relationship between us that was to be marked by deep feelings of respect, but of suspicion too.

One early assignment Dayan gave me suggested in important ways many that would come later. One morning in Nazareth in November 1952 the door to my office opened and Dayan walked in and sat down. He told me the following story: Several weeks earlier two Israeli soldiers on a routine patrol along the border near Kalkilya had mistakenly crossed to the Jordanian side and been captured. The Jordanians had taken them to Amman for interrogation and were now refusing to return them, regardless of persistent Israeli requests through the United Nations. Now, with all the regular channels exhausted, Dayan wanted to know if I thought it might be possible to take some Jordanians as hostages to exchange for the two soldiers.

As soon as he said it I began thinking about how such a thing might be done, but to Dayan I only said that I'd check into it. When he left, I called Shlomo Hefer, one of my officers, to bring a pickup for a drive to the border. I knew a place along the Jordan River that I thought might provide the right opportunity and I wanted to examine it carefully and start laying plans.

We were heading for the old Sheikh Hussein bridge near Kibbutz Ma'oz Chaim east of Beit Shean. This had been one of the bridges the Iraqi forces planned to use in their invasion through Jordan during the War of Independence. It had been destroyed then in a courageous action by an Israeli unit, and since that time the ruins had never been touched. All that remained now were the pillars and a few twisted and corroded steel girders.

Pulling up near the bridge and getting out of the truck, we began examining the other side. A few hundred yards from the weed-covered bank and just barely visible was a small police station, an ideal spot, I thought, to capture some Jordanians. As we stood there under an acacia tree looking across the river, I saw just to the south a squad of three Jordanian soldiers led by a sergeant making their way in our direction through the high reeds. As I watched, I began to think that maybe we would not have to do any planning after all, maybe these were our hostages right here. It could be a rare chance.

With that thought in mind I walked down to the bank and started waving my arms to attract their attention. As they approached, I made my way over one of the rails of the ruined bridge, holding on to an upper girder to keep my balance. Without anything to fear from us (my pistol was in my pocket and all four of them were armed), the Jordanians came to the edge of the bridge to find out what I wanted. I was smiling, talking as fast as I could in Arabic. We were looking, I said, for a cow that had been stolen from the kibbutz. Did they possibly know anything about it?

After a minute or two the tension had disappeared and I invited them to come across the river and sit down with us in the shade of the big acacia, where we could continue our talk more comfortably. When they accepted, I thought that now we were making progress. Sitting under the tree, we talked about farming and other things, all in the friendliest manner. It seemed so natural. Cows and horses were in fact being stolen all the time by Arabs coming across the river, and there was no reason why we might not be down here looking into exactly that kind of incident. Neither was there any particular reason they shouldn't help us if they could.

Knowing that it would be difficult to handle all four of them, I asked the sergeant if he might be so kind as to send one of his men back to ask whether the local police had any information about the cow. By this time I was feeling unhappy about what I had to do, after hosting the sergeant under the tree and all the friendly talk. But when he sent not one man but two, I knew the time had come. The moment their heads disappeared among the reeds on the other side I stood up. Perhaps suspecting something, the sergeant and the one remaining soldier got up too; and as they did, I grabbed the sergeant by the holster he had dangling around his neck, pulling my own pistol at the same instant.

A moment later it was over. While Shlomo held his carbine on them, I took their weapons, then went to get the pickup. With me driving, the two Jordanians sitting next to me, and Shlomo standing on the running board covering them with my pistol, we drove off toward Nazareth.

A half hour later we were back at the base. Locking the Jordanians in the cellar of the headquarters building, I went to report to Dayan but found he was out of the office. Instead of waiting I left him a brief note: "Moshe—The mission is accomplished. The prisoners are in the cellar. Shalom, Arik"

When he found out what had happened Dayan made no attempt to hide his pleasure. He positively relished the idea that someone would do this kind of thing. He especially liked the fact (though he didn't say it directly) that I had not been too meticulous about enticing the Jordanians over the border, and that I had not bothered to ask him for explicit written orders. The fact was, of course, that I had not been meticulous at all, and that I was even ready to set up a trap on the other side of the border. I hadn't exactly felt good about fooling that sergeant, especially after the pleasant talk we had had. But all that was really on my mind was the necessity of grabbing some Jordanians so that we could get our own people back. I had no question that Dayan knew exactly what he was asking for. He certainly didn't believe there would be many Jordanians waiting around to be abducted on our side of the border.

Though new to me, the procedure was vintage Dayan, as I learned soon enough. Typically he would convey his intentions in an ambiguous way, leaving plenty of room for initiative and interpretation. The recipient of the order—me in this case, as in plenty of future cases—would then take it on himself to do whatever he felt had to be done, with the widest freedom of action. If the result was a success, fine. But if it was a failure, well then, the responsibility was not his but yours.

Before two years had gone by, Dayan would be promoted to commander in chief of the Israeli Defense Forces. By that time I would be leading an elite unit created especially to carry out Israel's anti-terrorist policies. Dayan's predilection for ambiguous orders, combined with my own determination to accomplish what I understood was needed, was to make for more than one controversy, and more than one incident with international repercussions too.

In the fall of 1952 I was twenty-four years old. I had been in the army for five years already; but while I knew I had a talent for it, I was not at all sure I wanted to spend the rest of my life as a soldier. Like many in my generation, I had missed a great deal and I felt it keenly. Back in 1947 I had enrolled in the agronomy faculty at the Hebrew University, but the war had intervened. Since then, studies had never been completely out of my mind; and my parents, my mother in particular, were strong on the idea of my going to school. After all those years my mother was still deeply unhappy that her own academic career had been cut short, and she believed that if I had any inclination to go the university I should do it. Although I did not have any specific career in mind, by the fall semester of 1952 I decided that the time had come. Even earlier I had thought about applying to the program in agricultural studies at the University of Colorado, and now I considered law. But in the end I settled on Middle Eastern history at the Hebrew University in Jerusalem.

By this time Gali was also living in Jerusalem. After completing nursing school, she had gone on to specialize as a psychiatric nurse and had gotten a job at a hospital in the Jerusalem suburbs. Although we had known each other for years already and had long ago acknowledged our feelings, this was the first chance we really had to spend long periods of time together. At the age of twenty, Gali had lost the shy demeanor of the girl I had first seen working in the agricultural school's vegetable field and had emerged as an adult with a strong personality and a cool, analytic way of thinking. When I went to the hospital to pick her up, she would be surrounded by the psychiatric patients, some of whom exhibited truly bizarre kinds of behavior. In the middle of it Gali kept a gentle but firm authority, and when she saw my embarrassed awkwardness she would tell me, "Don't treat them as if they were strange, just talk to them as you would to a child." In a short time the feelings I had for her were enhanced by an appreciation for the substantial, graceful person she had become. Before long we found ourselves making plans to get married.

Since neither of us was interested in a formal wedding, on March 29, 1953, we simply went down to the office of an army rabbi I knew and had him perform the ceremony. Then we wired my parents in Kfar Malal, my aunt Sana in New York, and Gali's parents, who had come into the country from Rumania several years after the war and were now living near Haifa.

But finding a place to settle down to married life was not so easy. Gali had been living at the hospital and I was sharing a single room with an army friend who had also belatedly embarked on his studies. With our meager budget, for a while we despaired of ever being able to live together. Eventually, though, we found something within our means—a tiny room with a built-in kitchen in the backyard of a house in Beit Hakerem, one of Jerusalem's lovely residential neighborhoods. The combination toilet-shower was in a kind of shed off the kitchen, with a low roof that forced any occupant to duck down. The place, we learned, was a converted chicken coop, and it was so small that the two of us crowded it. But in the usual manner of newlyweds, we were blind to the inconvenience and thought only about the happiness of being together. And from that perspective the apartment seemed not cramped but cozy and not uncomfortable but picturesque.

The first half of 1953 was a wonderful time. Not only had we finally gotten married, but I was also deeply involved in my studies and absolutely luxuriating in the experience of being a student. I had spent my childhood doing hard work, then I had lost my youth to war. Now for the first time in my life I felt free of burdens and responsibilities. It was a golden moment, unfortunately not the kind of moment that lasts.

Near the middle of July that year I was preparing for an important history exam when my studies were interrupted by a messenger from Colonel Mishael Shacham, chief of the Jerusalem Brigade, to which I was attached as a reserve battalion commander. Would I please come to see him at once.

When I arrived in Shacham's office, he told me that there had just been another in the ongoing stream of terrorist attacks that had been plaguing the country. This time two watchmen had been murdered. As far as he was concerned, Shacham said, there was no alternative but to hit back hard at the gang that had been responsible for these killings and for many previous ones.

The leader of this gang was the notorious Mustafa Samueli, from the village of Nebi Samuel just north of Jerusalem. Unfortunately, Nebi Samuel's location, behind Jordanian lines and on the peak of a high hill, made it an extremely difficult target, and Shacham did not believe any of the standing units were up to the job. Did I think that I and some others I might choose to take with me could get into the village and destroy the gang?

The fact that Shacham had called me about this was an indication of how feeble the IDF—the Israeli Defense Forces—had become since the War of Independence. Going into that war, the Jewish community had had nothing resembling a professional army. The Haganah had been little more than an underground people's militia. Only the returning veterans of the British army and the few thousand men of the Palmach had received regular training. During the war, though, almost the entire male population had served; and by the end of it many of them had acquired first-rate skills. But the IDF was still a people's army, and when the war was over practically everyone had gone home, sure that the armistice agreements would be followed by peace treaties and they would be able to get on with their lives.

At the same time, one of the reservoirs of professional soldiers, the Palmach, no longer existed. During the war, Ben-Gurion had fully integrated the leftist-oriented Palmach into the regular army, eliminating its separate command structure. When the war was over, he went even further, relegating the three Palmach brigades to reserve status. It was a time when many of the Palmach officers ended up resigning from the army to return to their kibbutzim and moshavim.

But beyond the general demobilization and the political infighting, there was another overriding reason for the army's new ineffectiveness. After the war a tidal wave of immigration had engulfed the country. When Ben-Gurion declared independence in 1948 Israel's Jewish population had stood at 600,000. By 1950 it had risen to a million, and by 1953 to a million and a half. Almost all of these new people had arrived destitute, many of them without any utilizable skills. Among them, the immigrants spoke every variety of language. Beyond the fact that they were Jewish they had little in the way of common culture or background. They were refugees and survivors. Many of them had lived through immense personal traumas and were beset by severe residual problems.

All these people had to be clothed and fed and housed. They had to be taught Hebrew and provided with the ability to make a living. They had to be absorbed into the nation. In the years after the war this monumental task was Israel's absolute priority, and accomplishing it took every penny that could be scraped up, both from inside the country and from Jews abroad. The consequence for everybody was austerity, and the military was a prominent victim.

In practical terms all this meant that in the postwar army weapons and ammunition were in short supply and training levels by and large were not good. Beyond that, the IDF was going through a thorough reorganization; it was in effect rebuilt from the ground up. As a result, a great deal of command energy was devoted to structural concerns rather than to the development of basic military skills or specialized training. Without enough officers, attempting to process tens of thousands of immigrants (who often spoke no Hebrew), the army saw its performance level drop catastrophically. Within a few years the battle-hardened wartime force had deteriorated to the point where it was incapable of launching a raid against a terrorist gang living three miles from the nation's capital.

Unfortunately, in those very years of decline this army was being challenged by a growing wave of Palestinian terror from the neighboring Arab countries. Beginning shortly after the war, individuals and small groups from Gaza or the Jordanian-controlled areas west of the Jordan started crossing the borders, mainly to steal and create mischief. But it wasn't long before these spontaneous forays grew more serious. Incidents multiplied. Thievery and vandalism gave way to robbery and murder. By

1950 Israel was faced with systematic infiltration by well-organized gangs of Palestinian terrorists, many of them controlled now by the Egyptian intelligence service.

A reign of terror descended on the country. People were afraid to go out after dark. They were frightened by the explosions and shots they heard at night and horrified by the stories of what had happened to victims of attacks. In 1951, 137 Israelis were murdered by terrorists, almost all civilians, many of them women and children. In 1952, the number rose to 162. Nineteen fifty-three was especially terrible. In that year over three thousand incidents took place, almost ten a day. Again there were over 160 deaths.

As this epidemic grew, Israel took its case to the U.N. and explored other diplomatic channels. At the same time a strong attempt was made to guard the borders better, including the creation of a special border police. But diplomatic efforts proved ineffective, and the borders themselves were long and difficult. With few natural boundaries, they just could not be guarded adequately. When retaliation raids were mounted against terrorist bases, they almost always ended in failure and humiliation. At one place after another—Beit Sira, Beit Awa, Rantis, Idna, Falame, and a dozen more—army units proved unable to locate their targets at night and wandered around aimlessly in the dark. Or if they did manage to find their objectives, they would exchange a few shots with Arab guards, then withdraw. At best they would manage to occupy a few outlying buildings and blow them up before leaving, often carrying casualties back with them.

This impotence was driving Mishael Shacham wild with frustration. It also drove him into thinking of unorthodox alternatives, one of which was the idea that I might be able to find some way to do what the regular units couldn't. As he no doubt expected, I considered it a challenge. So when he asked if I thought I could get into Nebi Samuel and hit Mustafa Samueli and his cutthroats, I said yes. With seven or eight men and the right equipment I was sure I could do it.

In particular I had in mind a number of friends I had served with during the war and afterward. Most of them had left the army, but all had been very good guerrilla fighters, and all of them, I knew, would jump at a chance to get Mustafa Samueli. On Friday I made the calls. By Saturday night we had been briefed by Shacham's intelligence people and were ready to go.

My plan for this operation was simple enough. After dark we would make our way over the steep hills on the Jordanian side of the line, carefully avoiding the several Arab Legion posts in the area. Once in the village, we would locate the gang's house, which intelligence had described for us, blow the door, and break in. With any luck we would catch Samueli and the others by surprise and get them all.

The first part of the operation went exactly as planned. Walking was hard along the ridges and deep ravines that led to the peak of Nebi Samuel, but we found our way easily, circling around the army posts and keeping an eye out for patrols. As we climbed the mountain to the village, no one said a word. But each of us remembered that in 1948 this had been the scene of a major Palmach disaster when they had tried to take Nebi Samuel in an effort to protect Jewish Jerusalem and had been driven off with heavy casualties.

On the peak we slipped by the local militia guards and found the house, just down from the big stone mosque that was said to contain the remains of the prophet Samuel. Only a few candles twinkled in windows here and there as we set the TNT against the heavy door, then crouched down waiting for the explosion.

But here things started to go wrong. Instead of detonating, the charge began to sizzle and burn, starting a small fire but not damaging the door. When we saw this, we managed to lob two grenades into the house. But there was no response; it seemed to be unoccupied. By this time, of course, the neighbors were awake and shots were ringing out from surrounding houses. With surprise gone, there was nothing to do but get out as fast as we could.

In the confusion we managed to disappear down the mountain without attracting more attention. Knowing that the Jordanian posts were alerted, we hurried back through the hills, watching for patrols. By one in the morning we were back on the Israeli side, exhausted and unhappy. It had not been a sterling performance.

In the full report I wrote for Mishael Shacham I concluded that this type of action should only be carried out by professionals, people who were specially trained and experienced in night operations. Only then could we be sure of adequate weaponry, contingency plans, backups, and all the other support necessary to insure success. We needed something different from the usual bumbling army units—and not pickup groups like I had put together. We needed an elite.

After this unhappy experience I went back to my studies, unaware that Shacham had agreed with my conclusions and had written about the matter directly to Ben-Gurion. In his letter Shacham recommended that a highly trained anti-terrorist unit should be created, a force able to strike accurately and effectively at the villages and strongholds the terrorists used as bases for committing their atrocities. Neither did I know that Shacham had recommended that I be appointed commander of this special unit.

7

Commando Unit 101

At the end of July, a couple of weeks after the attempt on Nebi Samuel, I was invited to General Headquarters to meet with Mordechai Makleff, IDF commander-in-chief. Makleff told me that he was going to establish the commando unit Mishael Shacham had recommended and asked if I would be willing to lead it. After a moment I told Makleff that of course I would do it. But I also hoped that at some point I would be able to finish my studies. His response had an edge to it. "I can't make any commitments like that," he said.

On my way home I thought about Makleff's attitude. I was enjoying my student's life so much, and now I was going to be ripped away before I even had a chance to really get used to it. For Gali it would mean facing all over again those worries she had had when we were friends during the War of Independence. When I talked to my parents about it later, I could see that they too were worried, though they only expressed support. They knew, as did I and everyone in those days, that worries and private lives were one thing, security matters were something else. Certain things you simply accepted.

The first problem I faced was finding people for what was being called Unit 101. With the army as demoralized as it was, not many soldiers were volunteering for things like this. There was a general sense that nothing effective could really be done. I knew that I would have to look outside for recruits. I thought immediately of some of the people I had served with over the years who might be interested, and I began drawing up a list of others who had made reputations in the War of Independence. Soon I had launched a search for people who had shown unusual courage or had done extraordinary things. And as I started looking, word spread that something new was starting up. People began to turn up at my door.

Shlomo Baum was the first. He had served with me in the Golani reconnaissance unit under Avraham Yoffe and was one of the group that had gone to Nebi Samuel. Shlomo Hefer volunteered too, the officer who had been with me at the Sheikh Hussein bridge. Another early arrival was Meir Har-Zion, the man Moshe Dayan later called "the finest of our commando soldiers." I had heard about Meir, as had many people. At the age of sixteen he had trekked by himself across the Jordanian desert to the ancient Nabataean city of Petra, traditionally considered the place where Moses struck the rock. He had also crossed by foot from Jerusalem to the Dead Sea, another trip likely to be fatal to any Jew caught by the Bedouin or Jordanians. The man had an almost preternatural feel for terrain and direction. He also seemed possessed by the need to court danger. Har-Zion brought along with him Shimon Kahaner, "Kacha," a friend of his who was destined to become another of 101's legendary fighters. Yitzhak Ghibli also showed up, a former soldier who had joined the Palmach at the age of sixteen. So did Zevele Amit and Yossele Regev, two farmers from Nahalal who knocked on my door one day and told me they were worried about the situation and would like to do something to help.

Slowly they came in, these talented guerrillas, scouts, and nightfighters, drawn by the idea of participating in an elite unit and by the prospect of striking back at the terror gangs. By early September I had gathered twenty people. In another month I had forty-five, the number I considered about right. Unit 101 was never to have more during the five months of its existence, five months that were to have a fundamental impact on the country's effort to rid itself of terrorism.

Establishing a base at Camp Sataf on an isolated mountain not far from Jerusalem, I began to put these extraordinary people through the most grueling and realistic training I could devise. We started out with physical conditioning, weapons training, hand-to-hand fighting, patrol technique, and night navigation. We analyzed the elements involved in night operations and addressed all the problems of approach, execution, contingencies, diversions, and withdrawal. I preached continuously my standard sermon on familiarity with the terrain, the need to develop a sixth sense about a region's vegetation and topography.

But nothing was left to theory. We went on long night patrols across the border that I used to stress the need for physical orientation. From my own experience I knew that all soldiers—even the best—always have a million fears and a million questions. And for the Israeli soldier the blackest fear of all is of being left behind in Arab territory, alone and lost. So going out on patrols, and later on raids, I would always spend time at the beginning crouched down with the men, looking at the lights twinkling in the darkness. I'd point out what they were: Those on the right are such and such a village, to the left is the second village; those back there are the kibbutz, the gray line where the trees are is the border. It was the kind of thing that helped us all feel more secure. It also got people into the habit of taking their bearings constantly, of knowing where they were at all times.

Before long I began to feel that these men could do anything. It was not so much their physical conditioning or their fighting skills. It was their spirit, the immense pride they were developing in themselves and in the unit. Soon I felt we had a group that was ready to strike back. With the failure of diplomacy to stop the terror, the government had been trying to find an answer in a policy of retaliation and deterrence. I believed that we now had the ability to implement that policy.

Inside 101, morale was like nothing I had ever seen before. As the training began paying off, group spirit soared. An unusual camaraderie began to take hold, and a boisterous exuberance that gave the unit its own unique image. At times perhaps the spirit soared a little too high—as happened when some of the group got into a fight once with a military police unit. But the truth was that even then I wasn't displeased. This was a wild group, and I knew they were going to need every ounce of audacity and spirit they could muster for what lay ahead of them.

As Unit 101 gelled I began to turn our long patrols into missions against the Arab gangs operating from what they thought were safe havens in Jordanian villages. Though these were small actions, each one was successful, and the terrorists began to get the feeling that they were no longer invulnerable.

At times the successes were mixed with tragedy and sometimes controversy, as happened at the village of Kibbiya in mid-October. The raid on Kibbiya was mounted in response to a particularly horrendous incident at the town of Yehud, where terrorists murdered a young mother named Susan Kanias and her two infants, one and three years old, while they were asleep. The police investigation indicated that the killers had infiltrated from the direction of Kibbiya, a Palestinian village near the border in an area that was subject to incidents of terror almost every day.

The next day I was called to the Central Command Headquarters in Ramle, where I found the deputy commander of the paratroop battalion in addition to the Central Command Staff and representatives from General Headquarters. The paratroop officer and I were informed that General Headquarters had decided to carry out a retaliatory operation against Kibbiya. The plan called for the paratroopers to attack the village itself, while Unit 101 would create a diversion to draw the Jordanian troops in the area and establish roadblocks to insure that no reinforcements got through.

When the central front commander finished presenting the plan, the paratroop officer was silent for a moment. Then he cleared his throat and said that he didn't believe the paratroopers were well enough prepared for this kind of operation. They were not, he said, sufficiently "fine tuned" for it.

It was a comment that did not sit well with anybody in the room. For myself, I found it unbelievable that someone would try to back out of this. As a result, I interrupted the questions that were beginning to fly around. We were ready to do it, I told them. I would be more than happy to take command of the "unprepared" paratroopers as well as 101. On the spot it was decided to accept my offer and go ahead with the operation. The paratroop officer was instructed to have a company of his men report to Camp Sataf immediately.

That night I spent in camp working up plans and reviewing them with the officers. The following morning I moved the hundred paratroopers and twenty-five 101 men who would be participating into a staging area in the Ben Shemen woods. There among the trees I made the final preparations, briefing the men one last time and making sure they understood the importance of what they were about to do. This raid would be the first major Israeli reaction to Arab terrorism. No one could say whether success would have an effect on the wave of death and sabotage. But passivity and diplomatic complaints were painfully ineffective. Some answer had to be found.

TERRORIST RAIDS INTO ISRAEL 1951 - 1956

Palestinian terrorist groups, or Fedayeen, began systematic raids into Israel from 1950. Towards the end of 1954, the Egyptian Government supervised the formal establishment of Palestinian terrorist groups in the Gaza strip and north-eastern Sinai. Throughout 1955 an increasing number of raids were launched into Israel. From 1951 to 1956, Israeli vehicles were ambushed, farms attacked, fields boobytrapped and roads mined. Fedayeen from Gaza also infiltrated into Jordan, and operated from there. Saudi Arabia, Syria and Lebanon each gave the Fedayeen support and refuge. Local Jordanian-Palestinian Fedayeen were also active operating from the West Bank

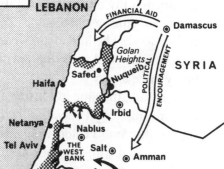

ISRAELI DEATHS AS A RESULT OF FEDAYEEN ATTACKS		
YEAR	FROM	ISRAELI DEAD
1951	JORDAN	111
	EGYPT	26
1952	JORDAN	114
	EGYPT	48
1953	JORDAN	124
	EGYPT	38
1954	JORDAN	117
	EGYPT	50
1955	JORDAN	37
	EGYPT	241
1951-55	SYRIA	55
	LEBANON	6

⊙   Centres of anti-Israel activity

↗   Moral and material support for Fedayeen attacks

➤   Movement of Fedayeen groups

▨   Areas of Fedayeen activity against Israel. With Egyptian encouragement, the Fedayeen also incited demonstrations inside Jordan against the Jordanian regime

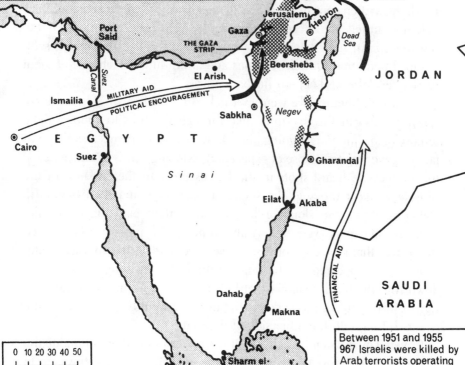

Between 1951 and 1955 967 Israelis were killed by Arab terrorists operating inside Israel's 1949 borders

0 10 20 30 40 50
Miles

© Martin Gilbert

That afternoon as I was going over the plans for the hundredth time, I was given the message that Moshe Dayan wanted to see me before we started out. Standing on the balcony of his office in Ramat Gan, we talked about the operation. "I understand that you are taking this very seriously," he said. I answered that I was indeed. "Look," Moshe went on, "if it turns out to be too difficult, just blow up some of the outbuildings and get out." "No," I replied, "We're taking six hundred kilograms of explosives along. We'll carry out our orders."

The orders were clear. Kibbiya was to be a lesson. I was to inflict as many casualties as I could on the Arab home guard and on whatever Jordanian army reinforcements showed up. I was also to blow up every major building in the town. A political decision had been made at the highest level. The Jordanians were to understand that Jewish blood could no longer be shed with impunity. From this point on there would be a heavy price to pay.

As always, the time just before an action was torturous. This was going to be a complicated operation, with roadblocks, a deception, and a good chance the Arab Legion would be involved. As the men got their gear together, I sat with my back against a pine tree, sweating and trying to finish the written copy of my orders to send back to General Headquarters. When night fell, the deception team under Meir Har-Zion moved out of the woods. An hour later I followed, leading the heavily laden assault group. In addition to their weapons and ammunition each one of them carried ten kilos of TNT on his back.

From Ben Shemen we went by truck to Bet Nabbalah. There we got down and began the five-mile hike through the hills to Kibbiya. The terrain made for rough going, but as we came near the assault point fatigue gave way to a sense of expectancy. Moving across a terrace below the village, we heard shots in the far distance. In the darkness of the hillside we kept moving, the silence broken now and then by a rock clattering down the slope or by the inadvertent clanking of a rifle. Directly above us were the Arab home guard positions; it seemed impossible that they did not suspect we were here. A few moments later Arab figures appeared on the ridge of the hill, dark silhouettes peering down into the black shadows that hid us. In another moment they had started firing, but in the darkness the fusillade went over our heads, the tracers hitting into the other side of the wadi.

Covered by the night, we held our fire and continued our climb up the terraces below them. When we got close enough, I ordered the men to drop their packs and start the assault. Instantly Shlomo Baum took off toward the town with a unit of 101 people. At the same time the paratroop company commander, Aharon Davidi, led two platoons of paratroopers up the hillside directly at the fortified position, followed closely by myself with the reserve platoon. In the firefight in front of the Arab trenches ten of the home guard were killed. Then we moved on toward Kibbiya itself. Just as we arrived, a jeep with two Jordanian soldiers in it wheeled down the main road in our direction, but a burst of fire from the paratroopers killed both of them, sending the jeep to a skidding halt.

In a few more minutes we were in the village proper. As we walked through the streets an eerie silence hung over the place, broken only by the strains of Arab music coming from a radio that had been left playing in an empty cafe. A report came in from one of the roadblocks that hundreds of villagers were streaming by them along the road. Kibbiya seemed completely deserted.

At midnight we began to demolish the village's big stone buildings. Working from the far side of the town inward, soldiers were sent to look through each house to make sure no one was inside; then the charges were placed and set off. We found a young boy cowering in a corner of one of the houses and took him out to safety. Then we heard a cry, and Shlomo Hefer ran into one of the other houses where the TNT fuse had already been lit and emerged with a little girl in his arms. Those two, the boy and the girl, were the only signs of life.

It took several hours before we finished demolishing the houses. Through the roar of the explosions and clouds of dust we could hear the rattle of small-arms fire from the diversionary attack across the hills. When we finally withdrew, we were met at the border by an officer sent by Central Command to get a report on what had happened. I told him that we had destroyed forty-two buildings and inflicted ten to twelve casualties—the home guards in the trenches above the village and the two soldiers in the jeep.

At Camp Sataf I said goodbye to the men and drove home to Jerusalem to sleep. A few hours later I was awake, listening to Jordanian radio. Already they were announcing news of the raid. According to the radio, sixty-nine people had been killed, mostly civilians and many of them women and children. I couldn't believe my ears. As I went back over each step of the operation, I began to understand what must have happened. For years Israeli reprisal raids had never succeeded in doing more than blowing up a few outlying buildings, if that. Expecting the same, some Arab families must have stayed in their houses rather than running away. In those big stone houses where three generations of a family might live together, some could easily have hidden in the cellars and back rooms, keeping quiet when the paratroopers went in to check and yell out a warning. The result was this tragedy that had happened.

But while the civilian deaths were a tragedy, the Kibbiya raid was also a turning point. After so many defeats and demoralizing failures it was now clear that Israeli forces were again capable of finding and hitting targets far behind enemy lines. What this meant to army morale can hardly be exaggerated. The past years had been a time of impotence and frustration, when again and again IDF units had been chased off by Arab militia. But with Kibbiya a new sense of confidence began to take root.

Even more important, Israel's Jews began to feel they were not completely defenseless against the murders and maimings that had by 1953 reached into every corner of the country. For it was not just the border settlements that were being terrorized. Palestinian infiltrators were striking in Lod and Petach Tikva and the suburbs of Tel Aviv. With Israel's tiny dimensions, the heart of the country had been open to them. Now people could feel that the terrorist gangs would think twice before striking, now that they knew for sure they would be hit back. Kibbiya also put the Jordanian and Egyptian governments on notice that if Israel was vulnerable, so were they. From this point on they would be held responsible for the depredations they countenanced and sponsored.

A few days after Kibbiya I was invited to Jerusalem to see Ben-Gurion in his office. It was an exciting moment for me, the first time I had met him. Sitting there by his table, he first asked about some of the details of the raid. Then he wanted to know about me, and about Unit 101. "Where are you from?" he asked. "From Kfar Malal?" Two of his friends lived in Kfar Malal—Lavi and Wohlman, originally from Plonsk, Ben-Gurion's hometown. Did I know them? What about the other 101 boys? Where were they from? Did I think that a unit like this might possibly get out of hand? I told him who they were and what moshavim and kibbutzim they came from. They were the finest boys we had, I said, and there was no chance that they would ever act except under orders.

Then Ben-Gurion said, "It doesn't make any real difference about what will be said about Kibbiya around the world. The important thing is how it will be looked at here in this region. This is going to give us the possibility of living here." I knew that Ben-Gurion was talking about the years in which we had had no answer to give to terrorism, when people in other nations just shook their heads and clucked in sympathy. But now we had an answer, a unit that would force those who wanted us dead to take notice and think again about what they were doing. I couldn't have agreed with him more.

8

"Every Jewish Life"

A t first Moshe Dayan had been opposed to setting up Unit 101. "The army doesn't need any special units," he had said. "Every unit should be able to carry out operations like this." I hadn't agreed. Practically speaking, only a specially trained unit could carry out the kind of retaliation and deterrence operations the situation called for. But beyond that, I believed an elite unit would set an example that the rest of the army would strive to meet. An elite unit would be the prime mover in a race for achievement.

At the end of December 1953 Dayan became commander-in-chief. By that time he had changed his mind. Not only did he see the value of 101 as a model, now he wanted to incorporate that model into the regular army. Specifically, he decided to merge 101 with the paratroop unit.

In fact, the paratroopers already were something of an elite themselves, at least in theory. They were a close-knit group, very physically oriented. They had jump training and paid a lot of attention to athletics. Their teams had won a caseful of sports trophies. They drank together, competed together, and were known for their spirit and verve. Unfortunately, their high morale had never paid off on the battlefield. Despite the unit's bravado, their efforts had been no more successful than those of the army's more ordinary battalions.

Dayan was angry about this; and when it came time to merge the two units, he decided to put them both under my command. Often tactless, Dayan's method of handling the paratrooper chief, Judah Harari, was unnecessarily rough, especially since Harari was personally a courageous man with a long record of service. Harari had assumed that since 101 was being brought into his unit he would retain command. But when Dayan called him in he heard the new commander ask, "How long have you been head of the paratroops?" "Three years," Harari answered. "Well," said Dayan, "that's long enough. I'm turning your command over to Arik." Harari almost had a heart attack.

The results were predictable. When I arrived at the paratroopers' headquarters to take over, there was a rebellion in the works. At the formal ceremony on the parade ground to mark the transfer of command I was greeted by hoots and whistles of derision from the assembled paratroopers. When Harari delivered his final remarks, he began by thanking all the officers who had decided to leave with him. Then he asked them to step forward. Quite a few did.

I knew the situation had to be handled coolly. But somehow my mind went blank and I forgot the parade orders. So instead of making a clear and authoritative statement, I just stood there. Parade-ground rituals had never been my strong point anyway, and I was a little rattled by the whistles and catcalls. But after a moment I regained my composure and ordered a march-by. Then I sent each company to different locations outside of camp so there wouldn't be any unnecessary communication and I went about getting the Harari loyalists transferred as fast as I could.

In the end perhaps half the officers remained with the battalion, including Aharon Davidi, who became my second in command. Just as important, practically all the specialists—the parachute packers and equipment handlers—chose to stay. So I had a good, willing nucleus to build around. I also had a secret weapon, the forty or so people from 101 who had come with me.

Bringing them along had not been easy. Hardly any of the 101 people were regular army types, and they didn't like the idea of merging with the paratroopers in the least. They were sure that all their prestige and free-wheeling camaraderie would go down the drain. But I had managed to convince them, and here they were, with all the fitness, determination, and nightfighting skills they had developed over the previous months.

The next day I began training the paratroopers, using the same techniques I had used with 101. Starting with the officers, I sent them out on long reconnaissance patrols on the other side of the border, hard nighttime patrols that tested their determination and stamina. Ordinarily I'd send them in teams of five, two 101 people and three paratroopers; and at first many of the paratroopers weren't able to keep up. I instituted reports from the reconnaissance teams, requiring everyone who had participated to describe how the patrols had gone and to analyze their own strengths and weaknesses. Within a month the atmosphere of resentment and recrimination had disappeared. The paratroopers started to understand what I was after. They began to see a dramatic improvement in their own abilities, and they began to feel part of something new. In a short time it was hard to distinguish between them and the boys from 101.

In a sense Unit 101 had been a kind of testing ground. Now I began to apply the lessons from 101's experience on a broader scale. I myself looked at each patrol and each action not only for its results but as an opportunity for learning. I tried to instill the idea that there were lessons in everything we did, that we could all learn all the time.

The basic tool for this was the post-action report. After patrols or actions we would bring officers and soldiers together to discuss the operation—all of them, from the youngest to the most experienced. People were tired and weary, so we would give them an hour or two to rest, then call the meetings. In the first stage, officers would meet with their own soldiers while I circulated among the groups. Then there would be a second meeting for the officers, which I would conduct myself. Each one would describe his orders, how he carried them out, what his problems had been, what his solutions were. I hammered at the absolute need for truth and candor. Everyone among us had his weaknesses as well as his strengths, and I wanted to know about them in detail. I wanted to understand each element that went into battlefield behavior, our own as well as our enemy's. I wanted not just the truth, but the truth in detail.

What this meant was that I and the other commanders were able to continually analyze and draw conclusions from the men's experience. It was a permanent development from one operation to the next. We studied every aspect of their behavior, in particular the crisis points. What are the most crucial moments in a soldier's experience, in an officer's experience, in the relationship between them? How do you resolve the problems these crises present?

I made lists of crisis points, then developed training procedures to deal with them. Ambushes, for example. What is the best action to take when you are ambushed? I recalled so vividly a night raid I had led into Samaria in May 1948. On our way back we were walking through a shallow wadi, approaching a bridge that I knew was guarded by Iraqi troops. To avoid them I decided to leave the wadi and circle around. But as I climbed the bank and looked out on the plain my blood froze. There right in front of me were what seemed in the dark to be hundreds of Iraqis. My arms and legs felt paralyzed. I could not move a muscle. Then, staring into the field, I saw that what I had taken for soldiers were nothing more than bundled sheaves of newly harvested barley.

That moment of paralysis had stayed with me, probably because the situation had been so innocent. But I had been caught in one or two lethal ambushes too. I was familiar with the feeling of panic when you are surprised, the confusion as you try to decide what to do and none of your limbs seem to work. In an ambush you experience exactly that. You are walking along, tired, perhaps carrying your wounded or dead. You are unprepared. Your enemy is alert, ready, his finger on the trigger. He is a hunter waiting for the trap to close. All the advantages are his. Then he snaps it shut, hitting you as hard as he can.

In this situation, the last thing he expects is that at the very instant he springs his trap he himself will be assaulted, that in that instant he, the hunter, will become the hunted. So after studying many ambush cases, we concluded that the most effective response is to attack immediately. But this reaction is not something an officer can think about. His first response is confusion and paralysis. So the solution is to take the decision away from him. Train him so well that in this situation he will act reflexively.

And so I made another list, this one a list of occasions for not thinking. We, who were famous for our ability to innovate, made a list of situations where reflex responses were called for. Then we developed training procedures for these situations, and we built them into the paratroopers' training manual.

Constant self-analysis was one aspect of the training. Another was the emphasis on hand-to-hand combat. Like all other soldiers, Arabs have their strengths and weaknesses; and I never in my life underestimated them. In many situations they are excellent fighters. They can shoot well and use artillery well. They are good at fortifications and mines. Once you allow them to fight a battle they are prepared for, a battle they have rehearsed, they will fight courageously. They are quite capable of dying at their posts, and did exactly that on many occasions. But they do not like to be surprised. And they do not like infighting. They don't cope well with the stress of close combat.

To take advantage of this weakness, we trained the paratroopers to avoid firefights. Once you are involved in a firefight, the battle tends to become positional, which favors the Arab's ability to shoot and his qualities as a defensive fighter. Instead we taught the virtues of moving in close, of demoralizing the enemy and playing on his fears. We taught hand-to-hand combat until it was instinctive.

The training went on non-stop, patrol after patrol, and action after action. My goal was to get the paratroopers to the point where they could respond at an instant's notice to any order. Only when we could do that would the political leadership have any real flexibility in its struggle against the terrorization of the nation. If political actions were called for, fine. If military action was called for, the leadership had to know it could be implemented—immediately and successfully.

Dayan summed the situation up best in a speech he gave a year or so after he had merged Unit 101 with the paratroopers. "It is not in our hands," he said, "to guarantee each water line against sabotage, each tree against uprooting. It is not in our hands to prevent the murder of workers in the fields and families in their sleep. But it is in our hands to fix a high price for our blood, so high that the Arab community and the Arab military forces will not be willing to pay it."

But the issue went far beyond simple retaliation. By the early 1950's terrorism had become more than a disturbing phenomenon, it had become an instrument of Arab policy. The fedayeen—Palestinian terror squads —by that time had been co-ordinated by the Egyptian and Jordanian intelligence services. Sometimes they would cross the border from Gaza or Jordanian-held territory at night, carry out their attacks, then return. Other times they would penetrate far inside the country at night, hide during the day, then perform their actions early the next night before making their way back. In this way they could operate twenty miles or more from the border. Even more far-reaching were the squads that crisscrossed the country from Gaza to Jordan and back, hitting anywhere they wanted inside Israel, carrying murder and fear into every corner of the land. The object of this terror was not simply killing and destruction, it was the demoralization of the people through the permanent disruption of normal life. And the tactic was working. One could see the border settlements losing people, the grenade screens going up on house windows. Even to drive from Tel Aviv to Jerusalem it was often necessary to wait until a convoy formed that could be escorted by armed patrols.

The success that these terrorists had over a period of years was what led me to accept the 101 job in the first place. I felt that there must be an answer to the problem, that we were capable of dealing with it. I could not accept the idea that we should be helpless before these people, that we had begun to accept these atrocities as our fate. I was angry that we were allowing ourselves to consider what was happening an inevitable part of our lives.

With Unit 101 and then with the paratroop battalion I had a group of people who came to feel the same way, who cared about these things as deeply as I did. Over the years the Israeli armed forces have fielded many outstanding units, but none I think have had the spirit of these groups. They understood fully the stakes they were fighting for; they were imbued with the need to react. Soldiers were so involved that our mobilization system often wasn't even necessary. If we were ordered to undertake an operation, the unit's recall code would ordinarily be broadcast over the radio: "All citizens in Ramat Gan who were bitten by dogs on Tuesday are urged to report to their local infirmaries," or some equivalent. But paratroopers on leave would not even wait for the code. If they heard on the news that a Jew had been killed by terrorists they would report immediately, expecting that a retaliatory raid was in the works.

And often it was. Because the truth was that in the face of these continuing atrocities I did not take a passive role. As soon as some terrorist incident took place, I would be on the phone to the chief of operations, or to Dayan himself, suggesting action. I would be able to say, "Look, we have already prepared plans for attacks on these several targets. All the reconnaissance is done, all the planning is done. Everyone is briefed. We can hit any of them right now, tonight!"

The result was that the cabinet, which had adopted a policy of retaliation and deterrence, now they had the ability to implement it. They were faced with a fundamental, deadly problem, and now for the first time somebody was saying to them, "Here is the answer." They had doubts, of course. Wouldn't there be casualties? Wouldn't there be international complications? But they had no other solution, and when they saw that these operations were feasible, it gave them confidence and hope.

So the development of the paratroop battalion into an effective anti-terrorist strike force had a substantial impact not just militarily but politically. It injected a radical new element into the equation. And this

Ben-Gurion understood better than anyone. That was why he had asked to see me after the Kibbiya raid, and why he had told me that the raid would "make it possible for us to live here."

Kibbiya, of course, had been a tragedy as well as a turning point. So to avoid the civilian casualties that had taken place there, we began concentrating on strictly military targets, even though the terrorists commonly used towns and villages as bases, shielding themselves behind the civilian population. This signaled a shift in policy as well, away from direct retaliation against the terrorists themselves and toward holding the host governments responsible for terrorism initiated from their territory.

Among other things, the switch to exclusively military targets meant that the raids became increasingly complicated and difficult. More than ever I began to feel the weight of command, especially during the planning stage of an operation. Always I would formulate my basic plan absolutely alone, in seclusion. At those times you are unsure, you wonder if you need more intelligence information, you waver back and forth between alternatives. When should we do it? Exactly what strength forces would we need? How should we strike—from the rear? the flank? the front? And which of my eager commanders had the right qualities to lead this attack? Who should provide support? Who shouldn't go at all? This stage of basic decision making was, I felt, an hour of weakness, and I always believed that if I brought my officers into the process here I might undermine their confidence. I wanted to keep my uncertainties strictly to myself.

Once I had formulated the overall plan I would meet with the staff officers, the operations, intelligence, artillery, personnel, and the other professionals. Explaining the concept, I would leave them to flesh it out into a full-fledged operational plan. When this was done we would call the first orders group, a meeting between the staff officers and the unit leaders and their deputies. Here I would explain the mission and its background and give each of the subordinate commanders his specific objective. Now these officers would go off to make their own plans about how to accomplish their missions. The art here was to give them sufficient guidance without in any way undermining their initiative. To accomplish this, my approach was to circulate among the groups as they were drawing up their plans, listening and making suggestions. I did not want to intrude on their planning in any kind of heavy-handed way, but I did want to give my input early so that I would not have to criticize them at some later stage, after they had their plans fully developed and had invested themselves in them.

When the commanders had finished their work, I would call the second orders group, and each of them would describe exactly what their units were going to do and what their timetables were. These presentations gave everyone a clear picture of the overall action and its individual parts, so they would see how the whole fit together and would know what to expect from each other. Even more important was that in giving his presentation, each of the commanders was also making a commitment. I knew that when a person stands up in front of his peers and tells them what he is going to do, it has a powerful personal effect. Once he has said it out loud and committed himself to it, he will do everything in his power to make sure it gets done.

Finally, with all the planning completed, I would lie down and try to rest or nap. But sleep never came. Instead, a thousand thoughts would rush in: Perhaps I had forgotten this or neglected that. Each step seemed filled with danger, each could lead to disaster. Turning on my cot from side to side, I would race through the entire operation again and again, assaulted by an army of doubts.

But then, when all the units had been briefed by their officers, I would stand out on the porch of the headquarters and watch the preparations. Soldiers would be going and coming, checking their weapons and equipment, loading trucks, talking to each other and their officers. The camp would be a beehive of activity, alive with purpose. Each one knew precisely what his job was, and how he was going to do it. Each had been readied for it by months of the hardest training. I could see the determination in their eyes, and invariably I would feel a surge of assurance. It was a reciprocal process, a flow of confidence from them to me and from me to them. A commander has to inspire his men, but it was always clear to me that they inspire him as well.

Then the time would come to load ourselves into the trucks for the drive to the staging area, where we would form up and begin the march toward our target. Here again the doubts would sometimes come. The weapon would be heavy and the pack would hurt. I would feel the sweat evaporate in the cool evening air, marching along and wondering why I had proposed this particular plan, whether some other wouldn't have been safer, surer.

During many operations I would go through these same stages, oscillating between worry and confidence, and each time the misgivings had to be completely hidden from the eyes of the officers and men. It was almost a relief when we finally arrived at the target and cut the barbed wire. Then there was no more choice, no more time to wonder if the plan was good or not. Then the battle would catch us up in its own momentum.

Starting in 1954, the paratroopers carried out almost every single operation undertaken by the Israeli army. And in one way or another each one of them was successful. One result of this was that I quickly became an object of attention. My first meeting with Ben-Gurion was soon followed by others, and before long I felt comfortable talking with him when important matters came up and comfortable just going to visit him. He told me about his service in the Jewish unit of Great Britain's Royal Fusiliers during World War One and recommended books for me to read, including Thucydides' *Peloponnesian Wars.* I don't know exactly how Ben-Gurion regarded my brashness and strong opinions, but there was no mistaking his affection.

Before long, however, I found that Ben-Gurion's affection was a curse as well as a blessing. At high-level meetings and get-togethers with the room full of generals and staff officers, he would call me up to be next to him. Sitting there, I would watch the generals come up to say hello to the old man and would feel embarrassed to hear him say, "Who are you?" or "What are you doing here?" It was a situation that cried out for tact on my part, but at the age of twenty-six I didn't recognize the need. I was immensely proud of what I was doing, of the paratroopers, the training methods I was developing, the operations I was leading, and I didn't much care who knew it. Without the wisdom to be more careful, I contributed in that period to the birth of jealousies and antagonisms some of which were to last for decades.

But my problems with the military hierarchy were not due simply to Ben-Gurion's friendship. The fact was that the paratroopers were different from every other unit—from their training, to their equipment, to their leadership. And suddenly they were being given every operation, bypassing units led by older, more senior officers who had their own ambitions. Moreover, the paratroopers were commanded by someone who had never even been to officers' school, and who had the brazenness to think that his methods should be adopted by the entire army, someone, to top it all off, who had direct access to both Commander-in-Chief Dayan and Prime Minister Ben-Gurion. The situation might have been especially designed to breed the bitterest feelings.

And these did indeed develop, in spades. Generals complained vehemently to Dayan and Ben-Gurion about all the things that infuriated them. And since I would not keep quiet about the inadequacies I saw in the army's methods, they had plenty to be angry about. I didn't like, for example, the rigid pedagogy of the officers' training courses. I argued that the traditional teaching methods should be reoriented, that officer cadets should be studying more examples, cases, as many descriptions as possible of successful and unsuccessful engagements. These, I said, would give them the "bricks" out of which they could build their battle plans most effectively. Even without having gone through officers' training myself, I had the temerity to preach about these things. And when our paratrooper officers came back from school, I would put them through refresher courses to reorient them to our own system. We developed our own equipment, which we displayed and tried to popularize; and we even published our own instructional material, different from that of the General Headquarters. To publicize our innovations we invited commanders to come and look at what we were doing and to participate in meetings and discussions. Little of this sat well with General Headquarters. But I considered it so important that I kept at it. It was the kind of thing that created almost a kind of running warfare between me and much of the army hierarchy.

Occasionally, my approach also created problems at other levels. By this time Pinchas Lavon had replaced Ben-Gurion as minister of defense. Lavon was a strong advocate of deterrence, but, like a number of other cabinet members, he wanted the policy carried out as quietly as possible. We were, after all, not engaged in active war. And while for us these operations might have been a matter of life or death, the rest of the world did not see them that way. As a result these "peacetime" actions required great care and presented their own political difficulties. Lavon's view was that operations should be strictly limited, that the paratroops should go in, administer a "lesson," then get out quickly with a minimum of fuss. Inexperienced in military matters, he would give specific orders, for example, that "between five and seven" enemy soldiers should be killed in an operation. Then if it turned out that eight or ten were killed there would be problems. Although he felt warmly toward me, he would call me into his office or his home afterward, upset that enemy casualties had been so heavy. I would explain to him that these operations were all highly complex. They involved every kind of contingency and unexpected problem. I would tell him that he could not expect me to start counting enemy casualties in the middle of a battle. Our own soldiers' lives were at stake, and we were going to give them every measure of protection we could. If that meant causing additional enemy casualties, then that is what would happen. And if that wasn't acceptable, then we should either find another target or not take any action at all. And so I regularly found myself in the minister of defense's office involved in heated arguments about the relationship between policy and implementation, his policy and my implementation.

One of the most significant of the paratroop operations—one that turned out to be a watershed in Middle Eastern affairs—was the raid against the Egyptian army headquarters in Gaza on February 28, 1955. Gaza is a strip of arable land along the Mediterranean coast about forty miles south of Tel Aviv. In 1948 this area became home to almost 200,000 Arab war refugees, many of whom had been packed into refugee camps. By the time the war was over these people were in despair. Most of them had originally left their homes at the urging of their leaders, believing they would return as soon as the Jews were destroyed. But now they saw no chance of that. Nor did they see any chance of being resettled in Egypt or any other Arab country, all of which had callously and brutally turned their backs on them. Impoverished, with no hopes for the future, they provided a breeding ground for terrorism.

Despite the successes we had had against a number of Egyptian and Jordanian posts, by 1955 the Gaza fedayeen continued to strike not just in the south but up into the middle of the country. Every week brought its stories of ambushes and murders and minings. A marriage celebration was attacked at Moshav Patish leaving many casualties. A bicyclist was murdered near Rehovot. The incidents came thick and fast. When on February 27 a Jewish orange grove worker was murdered near the Weizmann Institute by a terror squad from Gaza, the government decided to take action. The paratroops would be sent against the main Egyptian base in the strip.

This would be the most difficult operation we had yet undertaken. Gaza was an armed camp full of Egyptian troops and Palestinian fedayeen. On a ridge of hills on Gaza's eastern border the Egyptians had built a series of positions that overlooked both the Israeli settlements in front of them and the strip behind. We would have to penetrate between these positions, secure a corridor for our retreat, and deploy blocking forces to prevent reinforcements reaching the headquarters from the base at Khan Yunis, fifteen miles to the southwest. While we isolated the headquarters camp from the rest of the strip, the assault units would have to move through densely planted orange groves, intersected by thick cactus hedges before we could reach our target. Then the attack would have to proceed quickly, so that we could get out with whatever casualties we suffered before reinforcements could break through our blocking units and cut off our retreat to the border.

A further complication was that teams of U.N. observers constantly patrolled the border region looking for signs of trouble. If they noticed anything unusual they would report to their own people in Gaza and word would get out immediately to the Egyptians. Morover, the U.N. posts would be on high alert. They knew that whenever a Jew was murdered something was likely to happen. Somehow we would have to camouflage our movements from the observers.

By the night of the twenty-seventh, I had developed my plan. The next morning, suffering from a bad cold, I called the officers into my bedroom instead of the briefing room and drew the diagrams on the wall, describing the attack in a hoarse whisper. We would launch the assault from the border kibbutz of Kfar Azah. To throw the U.N. observers off, we would disguise our movements as a battalion day outing, complete with girls, picnicking, and plenty of singing.

After I gave the orders, I went outside to watch the rush of activity. As usual, it gave me a lift to see the briefings going on and the men gathering their equipment and forming up. I watched as they carefully loaded their weapons and ammunition so that they were hidden on the floors of the trucks. I watched the army girls get in, some in their leave uniforms, some in skirts, all of them as bright and cheery as if they really were going off on a picnic. Instead of lining up in convoy fashion, the trucks left one at a time. In each one the girls sat conspicuously, singing army songs and love songs arm in arm with the boys.

An hour later the trucks began to pull into the little woods near Kibbutz Gevim I had picked out as a staging area. There we ate our traditional prebattle meal of rice and meat, and I talked to them about the coming operation. As always, I explained the importance of the action and why it had to be done, trying to share as much as I could about all the details. And as always, the only thing I did not share with them were my thoughts about what would happen if we weren't successful. That anxiety I kept to myself.

When it turned dark, we left the girls and moved out. Silently we made our way to Kfar Azah, where I planned to cut across the border. At the end of the fields there was no line, no fence, just the last plowed furrow to tell us we were in Gaza heading for an opening between two Egyptian positions. After we crossed I stopped the column for a moment. In the troopers' young faces I could read their thoughts. "What will I do if we don't make it?" "What if I'm the only survivor?" Whispering to them in the dark, I pointed out the features of the border, the terrain behind us, the lights of the kibbutzim. And as the orientation took hold I could feel their calm returning, their confidence that they could make it through all right.

When the line started to move again, the scout party spread out in front, led by "Supapo," the company commander who was also one of the paratroopers' most renowned fighters. Suddenly a shout in Arabic broke the silence, then a burst of shooting. In the few seconds it took us to reach the scouts, they had already killed four Egyptian soldiers who had set up an ambush, obviously sent there to close up the gap between the two nearest Egyptian positions. As I came up, Supapo was stepping over the dead Egyptians, planting his foot firmly on the head of one of them as he did. Though usually free of suspicions, seeing him do that gave me a strange twinge of premonition. "Stop that," I hissed. "Leave the dead alone."

Leaving a platoon under Moshe Yanukah to secure the path, we entered an area of thickly planted orange groves. My plan was to move through these groves and across the main Gaza road. Straddling the road a quarter mile to the south were the two main Egyptian camps, a smaller one on the left, the headquarters camp itself a bit farther down on the right. Circling around, we would hit them from the rear. Supapo's unit would destroy the main camp; I would engage the smaller one with the reserve unit. At the same time the third force under Motta Gur[*] would attack the Egyptian forces based at Gaza train station, another quarter mile away west of the main camp.

The groves were heavy with foliage as we made our way through and cut the fence bordering the main road. Orange trees and acacias loomed

---

[*] Gur would in later years become IDF commander-in-chief.

over us, their black shadows swallowing the ribbon of asphalt as it led toward the camps. I watched as Supapo silently crossed into the trees on the far side, leading his men in an arching path that would bring him to the back of his target. In a few moments Motta would be in position next to the train station. From the orange groves I inched forward with my troopers toward a roadside building that would serve as our own jumping-off spot.

Crouching behind a tree, I checked the luminescent dial of my watch. Then the night was suddenly alive with explosions and the crackle of Uzis as Supapo's attack kicked off. Though I couldn't tell at first, Supapo had misjudged his position, and instead of hitting the main camp, he found himself charging at the smaller one. Recognizing his mistake, he decided to rectify it by racing along the highway and breaking through the main gate of the headquarters compound. It was a courageous act, but recklessly dangerous. By this time the Egyptians were scrambling into their positions just a few yards from the road and firing wildly into the dark. Supapo and several of his men were cut down in a hail of bullets.

Realizing what had happened on the road, Uzi Trachtenberg, one of Supapo's officers, cut through the barbed wire at the side of the camp and led the rest of the platoon into the middle of the Egyptians. Inside the compound a fierce firefight raged briefly. But surprised and disoriented, the Egyptians never really had a chance. Those who weren't killed or wounded disappeared into the groves or lay still, hoping to stay unnoticed.

While Supapo's men were silencing the headquarters compound, the reserve platoon blocked the smaller camp, and the third unit pressed home its assault against the train station. Before long it became clear that we were gaining all our objectives. But we were also taking many casualties. As the shooting began to slacken off, I knew we had to move quickly to blow up the buildings, look to our wounded, and get out.

Fire was still coming at us from the Egyptians in the trees as I ordered the withdrawal to begin. One unshakable rule I had instituted was that paratrooper dead and wounded would never be left behind, no matter what. While troopers laid charges in the Egyptian buildings, I had all the casualties brought to the road and loaded into one of the Egyptian trucks. Waiting by the truck, I saw the dead and wounded being carried up and laid gently inside. With the Egyptians still firing, one paratrooper hurried toward us dragging a body by the legs. The dead man's head bounced up and down on the road and in the glare of the fires I recognized Supapo, his face set in a death grimace. For a instant I saw him as he was just an

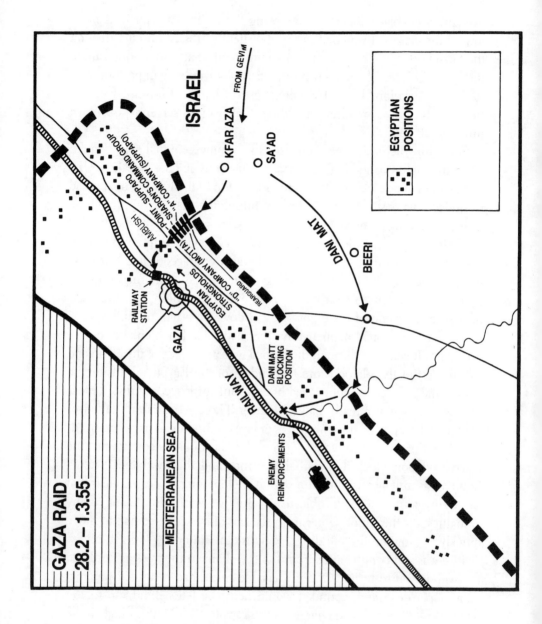

Egyptian-controlled Palestinian infiltrators (Fedayeen) staged a continuous terror campaign from the Gaza Strip. The Gaza Raid (Operation Black Arrow) was launched after a series of deep and murderous raids by the Fedayeen. It was one of the most important of the retaliation raids and had far-reaching political consequences.

hour ago, stepping on the head of the Egyptian he had killed at the ambush site, and I was shaken by a quick chill.

Under increasing Egyptian fire, the truck drove several hundred yards down the road and stopped at the break in the fence where we had come in. Positioning two squads to secure the area and stop any pursuit, I started the men unloading the truck. In teams of four they gently picked up the wounded and the dead, often unable to tell which were which. Soon we ran out of stretchers and had to improvise by tying shirts between two rifles.

A hundred yards into the grove the medical team gave the wounded emergency treatment and bandaged them up for the trip back across the border. In my last briefing I had told everyone that we would not be able to care for the wounded until the assault was finished, that if they were hurt they should just lie quietly and tell someone they needed help. Now, as they were brought in to the medics, the wounded paratroopers seemed almost as silent as the dead. When I asked the first one, a boy with a terrible stomach wound, if he was alive, he whispered, "Yes, but you told us not to cry."

Half an hour passed before the medics had finished doing what they could. While they were working, a message came over the radio from Danny Mat, commander of the blocking force on the Khan Yunis road. A convoy of Egyptian troop trucks had tried to move by them from the south. They had attacked the trucks and inflicted heavy casualties. I told them to stay put until we had crossed the line of border positions. I had the feeling there were Egyptians in the area and that they knew where we were. The half hour seemed to take forever.

When we were finally ready I radioed to headquarters, "We are on our way back. We are very heavy." With a scout party in front and a rear guard behind, the column started through the grove. With us we brought fourteen wounded and six dead, most on stretchers or improvised stretchers, a few making their last trip home on the backs of their friends.

Following our trail back, a half hour later we linked up with the platoon I had left to secure the route. Stopping for a moment, I told Yanukah that Supapo had been killed. Around us no one moved; a dead silence hung over the groves. Then we started eastward again, toward the narrow road that ran between the Egyptian positions and toward the border, just a mile beyond. I passed Zevele Amit and Yoselle Regev in the column, each of them with a body slung fireman fashion across his shoulders. When I asked if they could make it, they answered, "Don't worry, Arik. We're OK." Neither was any longer in the army, but they had insisted on coming along for this raid.

Suddenly a heartstopping clatter of heavy machine-gun fire opened up at the front of the line, followed by the spattering of Uzis. In the din the men moved up, taking positions at the side of the road. From the dark, the Egyptian guns covered the road with a stream of fire. We could not make out exactly where they were, but I knew we must be equally invisible to them. As our own shooting died down, we realized that the machine gunners were firing volleys trying to keep us from crossing—a rapid-fire burst, a pause, another burst. Judging the rhythm, we began sending the men across a few at a time. They ran crouched over, hustling along with the stretchers or shouldering the dead. Moving up with the rear guard, I waited for the right moment, then launched myself into the open, expecting with every step to hear the guns open up.

An instant later I was huddled with the rest of the men in a small wadi on the far side. Two more troopers had been killed running across, their bodies pulled along by others. In the darkness and confusion it was difficult to get a count, but it seemed like everyone was there. Looking around at the boys sprawled out panting along the sandy banks, I felt a rush of admiration for them. Under that murderous fire, with their own lives on the line, they had taken out not just their wounded but their dead too. We counted again and again, trying to make sure that no one had been left. When I was sure we were all accounted for, I radioed to the blocking unit to pull back from the Khan Yunis road. Then I called Kfar Azah to have vehicles waiting at the border. Fire was still spraying across the road behind us as we began to walk toward the plowed fields on the Israeli side.

At Kfar Azah Moshe Dayan was waiting. In a dry voice he asked, "How did it go?" Still hoarse, I told him that we had accomplished the mission but that our own losses were heavy. He looked at me and said, "The living are alive and the dead are dead." Then he turned and left. Gali had come too, driven by Yitzhak Ghibli. She had been listening to the radio net and understood when I had reported that we were "heavy." After our brief moment together she went off to the infirmary to assist the doctors who were tending to the wounded.

In the kibbutz dining room the men sat around exhausted. Many of them were from moshavim and kibbutzim and had been in the army for only six months; I had recruited quite a few in this class myself. This had been their first real action, their baptism. They felt the accomplishment of the moment, as I did, but the satisfaction was mixed with deep sorrow. They had lost their commander, Supapo, whom they had both feared and admired, and they had lost friends. The next day we would all be at the funerals, together with the families of those eight boys, and that would be harder than any operation.

What none of us guessed was that the Gaza operation would have far-reaching consequences. The paratroops had succeeded in penetrating into the heart of the Egyptian military establishment in Gaza. It had been a dramatic demonstration that Israel would not tolerate the continued terrorization of its people, that Egypt was vulnerable despite the strongest measures she could take to shield her forces. The lesson was not lost on Gamal Abdel Nasser. But understanding that he was unable to contain our attacks, he did not move to shut down the terror that had precipitated them. Instead he began looking for allies who could protect him, even while he continued to pursue the destruction of those he saw as his enemies. And the one potential ally that could provide the military and political strength he needed waited in the wings—Russia, a nation whose own dreams of a Middle Eastern foothold were more than a century old.

9

Friends and Enemies

Despite his terse remarks at Kfar Azah, Moshe Dayan had been worried about the raid on Gaza, as he was about many of the paratroop operations. It was no surprise to see him at the border in the middle of the night, anxious to know how things had gone. We often found him waiting for us when we returned from operations.

I knew that other things were worrying him too, the problem of Meir Har-Zion for one. Har-Zion was the fighter who had been perhaps the most talented of all the Unit 101 people. Now he was a captain who commanded the paratroopers' reconnaissance unit, the elite of the elite. By this time his exploits were famous throughout the army.

Several weeks before the Gaza raid, Har-Zion had suffered a devastating personal tragedy. His younger sister, Shoshana, had decided to go with her boyfriend Oded on a hike from the Dead Sea to Jerusalem—overland through Jordanian-controlled territory. It was a trip that Har-Zion himself had made in his teens, despite the danger of being captured by Jordanians or Bedouin nomads. Shoshana and her boyfriend had said goodbye to their friends and disappeared into the desert. That was the last anybody had heard of them. When they didn't show up within a reasonable time, their kibbutz began searching. It was weeks before they discovered that the two young people had indeed been caught by a group of Bedouin and murdered.

Meir and Shoshana Har-Zion had been born on a moshav on the Sharon Plain. Children of divorced parents, they had developed a deep emotional bond with each other. They shared, among other things, a deep love of nature and were addicted to making long treks through the wilderness area. In 1950 on one of these treks they had crossed the Syrian border by mistake and had spent time in a Damascus jail. Alike in many ways, the two had been extremely close. When word came of Shoshana's death, Meir was inconsolable.

Overwhelmed by anger and grief, after a few days he made up his mind that he had to revenge his sister. His plans, as far as they went, were first to quit the army, then as a civilian to track down the Bedouin who had murdered Shoshana. When I heard about this, I tried everything I could to dissuade him. But it was like arguing with a deaf man. "Arik," he told me, "I want you to know I am going to do this. I just cannot rest. I have to do it."

Worried, I had talked to Dayan about it. But Dayan had no more idea what to do than I had. A week before the Gaza raid I had seen Dayan again, this time bringing Meir along. As Dayan, Meir Amit (Dayan's chief of operations), and I talked on the roadside near Rehovot, Har-Zion stood apart. Not knowing what he might say to him, Dayan finally told me, "Look, Arik, make every effort you can to keep him from doing it. But if you can't convince him, then I want you to do everything in your power to make sure he comes back alive."

I already knew that Meir was not in a state to listen to anybody. But I tried again anyway. All I could see was trouble coming out of this, possibly even Meir's death and the death of the four friends who had offered to go with him. It was no use. Meir quit the army, and when he went ahead with his plans I did what I thought was necessary. I gave him weapons. I gave him a command car, and I gave him Yitzhak Ghibli as a driver, the best I had. There was nothing more I could do to try and keep him safe.

That evening Dayan called asking what had happened. There was no mistaking the worry in his voice. "I did what you told me," I said. "I tried to persuade him, but he wouldn't listen. So I gave him some help." "Can we still stop him?" Dayan asked. "No," I answered. "It's too late for that."

Twenty-four hours later Meir and his friends were back. They had succeeded in tracking down a group of Bedouin from the tribe that had murdered Shoshana and her boyfriend. They had caught six of them and had slaughtered five. They left one—an old man—to go back to tell the story.

The entire episode was a throwback to tribal days, the kind of ritual revenge the Bedouin understood perfectly. But the repercussions of what Har-Zion had done were very twentieth century. The Jordanians made a formal complaint to the U.N., and he and his friends were arrested and imprisoned pending an inquiry. These developments made Dayan very nervous indeed. No one could tell what kind of complications might arise. Although Dayan did not know it, I had already decided to cover for him with Ben-Gurion if it became necessary. I had also decided to help get Meir the best legal assistance available. *

All of this was happening in the immediate aftermath of the raid on Gaza, which was having its own volatile impact on the cabinet and had again brought the paratroop battalion onto stage center. Moshe Sharett, who was now prime minister, was especially upset, claiming that Ben-Gurion had told him the operation would be on a smaller scale. As always happened when we had suffered significant losses, Dayan asked me to be at the regular off-the-record meeting with newspaper editors to explain what had happened and why.

By this time the relationship between the two of us was becoming deeply ambivalent, as it was to remain through the rest of Dayan's life. As far as military matters went, I knew that Dayan trusted me implicitly, just as he knew that my appreciation of his own abilities went deep. But he also knew that I was not one of his wholehearted supporters, and that I especially did not like his inability to take public responsibility for his decisions.

The result was that all our interactions became immensely complicated. At times Dayan would display real warmth, other times a sharp edge of alienation. Often both feelings seemed to exist simultaneously. When I was attacked for being overly aggressive he would defend me saying, "I'd rather have spirited horses than lazy bulls." He had a clear vision of the paratroopers' importance in his drive to revive the Israeli army, and he would not allow anyone else to lead the deterrence operations that we both believed were vital. But at the same time he did

---

* In fact I did cover for Dayan with Ben-Gurion, not telling him the entire story until several months later. Meanwhile Meir Har-Zion's lawyer eventually succeeded in winning his client's release, at which point Meir rejoined the paratroops.

things that were calculated to make my life as difficult as it was exciting. That was how in the summer of 1955 I found myself on trial for actions unbecoming an officer right in the middle of a fast-developing military situation that demanded my complete attention.

The charges stemmed from a minor incident more than a year earlier that had not aroused any special notice from anybody. At that time I had sent a group of about eighty paratroopers to take part in the army's course for section leaders. Shortly after they left, I was informed that because of the extensive fieldwork assignments, they would be needing new boots. I had sent the boots immediately, in a command car driven by one of the company quartermasters and his assistant. But when I visited the course two days later, the boots had not yet arrived. While I was standing there wondering what had happened to them, the quartermaster drove up. It turned out that he had decided to spend a couple of days with his girlfriend before making the delivery.

I was livid. I told him and his assistant to unload the boots and get back to the paratrooper base immediately. When we arrived, I ordered them into the stockade. But the quartermaster refused to budge. He wouldn't go, he said, and if I put him there he'd escape. I was so angry I slapped him in the face. A moment later he was in the stockade. But the next day, as promised, he and his friend did escape. When they were brought back, I threw them in the stockade again, this time in handcuffs. The quartermaster was aggrieved by this treatment, and a short time later he made a complaint to the military police about having been slapped and handcuffed.

The complaint had gone through channels and had never amounted to anything. But now, more than a year later, charges were suddenly filed against me, and a three-judge military panel was set up to hear the case, one of whom was a colonel named Chaim Bar-Lev.

The scene that now unfolded would have satisfied the most surreal imagination. Just at that moment the paratroops were involved in an extended series of operations, some on the Syrian border, some against Jordan, some against the Egyptians. It was a time when I found myself constantly on the move, making plans, sharpening training procedures, leading raids, visiting the wounded—overseeing the million and one details these activities brought with them. In the middle of all this I was also on trial in Tel Aviv. I found myself rushing from one border to another, making detours to Tel Aviv to ask for a postponement pending a particular raid, having my request denied, sitting in court for a day, then driving like a wild man back to the battalion in time to lead a complex night action.

By a bizarre coincidence, the courtroom in which the trial was being held was the same one where captured fedayeen were tried. Each time I walked in I would read over the doorway: "Court for Terrorists." By another bizarre chance, the soldier I was accused of mistreating had accidentally shot himself some time earlier and had died without ever imagining that our run-in would become famous. As a result, the lawyers had to content themselves with questioning witnesses.

On the hard bench where I sat, the flowing legal oratory competed for my attention with thoughts of logistical problems and troop movements. Snatches of testimony and argument penetrated the wall of mental privacy I tried to erect: the prosecutor's insinuating voice asking a witness, "Can you tell the court precisely where you were standing at the moment the battalion commanded slapped the departed, may God rest his soul, in the face?" The defense attorney attacking a witness's credibility. "Would you tell the court the name of your friend who deserted to the Syrians?" "Objection, your honor." "Sustained!" "Would you then tell the court how long you have been using drugs?" "Objection." "Denied!" Sometimes I found it fascinating, sometimes I could block it out entirely. Either way, eventually the session would end and my driver and I would be speeding off to wherever the battalion was bivouacked that particular day.

By the end of October the trial had been dragging on for over two months. On the twenty-sixth the paratroopers were camped near the Sea of Galilee, where we had just completed an action against the Syrians. That day we received orders to try to capture some Egyptian soldiers to trade for two of our own people who had been kidnapped in an attack on a new settlement in the Negev near Nizana. According to the orders, we were to assault a fortified Egyptian position in the Sinai and bring back as many POW's as we could get.

That day we moved the two hundred miles from Galilee to the Sinai border and made the final preparations to launch a nighttime attack. But shortly before H-hour we received information that the Egyptians knew we had arrived and were on the alert. As a result the operation was aborted. I hadn't liked the objective anyway. It was too close to the border, and too close to where the kidnappings had taken place. For this kind of thing we needed to choose someplace less likely, where we could be sure of achieving surprise.

The place I had in mind was Kuntilla, an isolated Egyptian outpost seventy miles to the south and eight very rugged miles inside Sinai. Setting up a rendezvous time, I sent the paratroopers to the base at Mishmar Hanegev. Meanwhile I raced back to Tel Aviv to see the deputy chief of operations, Assaf Simchoni, about permitting us to change the target.

I also had to talk to Simchoni about something else. The previous day two MP's had shown up at paratroop headquarters with a court-ordered warrant to search my desk. Exactly what relevant information the panel of judges had thought might be in my desk was impossible to guess. But with all the tension of the developing action, my tolerance for harassment was down to nothing. Something had to give.

Assaf Simchoni was sympathetic. He listened while I told him that I just couldn't keep functioning like this. The pressure was too much, it was too dangerous. I wanted to talk to Dayan, I said, to ask him to postpone the trial until this period was over. Either that or just let me sit in court, and get someone else to carry out the operations. Simchoni agreed but thought it would be better if he took the matter up with Dayan himself.

I walked out of the meeting with a sense of relief. Neither Dayan nor Simchoni ever told me what went on during their subsequent discussion, but whatever Simchoni said, it had quick results. In a matter of days the hearings were postponed. Later the charges were simply dismissed. As suddenly as the trial had materialized it now disappeared.

I presented my plans to General Headquarters at 9 A.M. By eleven I was in Mishmar Hanegev giving officers their orders. They could study the maps and reconnaissance photos on the way to Mizpeh on the Crater of Ramon, a halfway point where we would rendezvous at three. I wanted all the troops there by then, and all the fuel and equipment. I also wanted the officers to have their own plans ready for the second orders group.

At three the Crater of Ramon was deserted except for the two empty huts clinging to its rim. (The two huts have since grown into the town of Mizpeh Ramon.) Wondering what the delay was about, I left one of the troopers who was with me behind to give directions. Then I drove south, crossing the Negev Mountains toward Eilat. I was eager to get to the jump-off point before dark. Wadi Faran led straight from the border across the high Kuntilla plain right to the base of the Egyptian position.

I knew the area, but I hadn't been there for a while and I wanted to get the feel of it again.

By six that evening the paratroop convoy finally arrived at the stone-carpeted barren several miles from the Sinai border. My plan was to drive most of the distance across the hard surface of the plain, then leave the jeeps and command cars and march the rest of the way to the forbidding crag at whose top lay the Egyptian outpost. The usual garrison there was about forty men. With any luck our arrival would be a complete surprise. We would be able to take a good number of prisoners and get back across the border well before dawn.

By now night had fallen. When I consulted with Meir Har-Zion (whose judgment in these things was excellent), he said he did not like the idea of driving across the plain. The previous night a thick fog had blanketed this area. If it came back, we would never find our way. On the other hand, if we went through the wadi we couldn't miss the target, since the rocky crag of the Kuntilla outpost grew right out of the bank. Despite the soft, sandy floor, Har-Zion was sure the wadi was passable. He had driven through it himself the previous year when he took a night patrol out to survey the Egyptian position.

At 7 P.M. we entered Wadi Faran on the Israeli side. Following Har-Zion's advice, we drove along its floor, the vehicles straining for traction on the shifting sand. He had driven it with two scout cars, but now we were an entire convoy. It made a difference we hadn't counted on.

The farther we went, the harder the driving became. Command cars, jeeps, and ambulances got bogged down and had to be manhandled through the sandy wallows. We seemed to be making headway a yard at a time. With the engines laboring, it soon became obvious that we would not have enough fuel for the entire drive. Time became a pressing concern.

At 10 P.M. I made the decision to leave the vehicles and go by foot. Stopping for a few minutes, we held the second orders group, then began to march. With ten miles still to go, I estimated that walking non-stop we would be able to assault by 1 A.M. If everything went right, we could be out by two, which would leave us just enough time to make it back to the border by first light.

At night the desert turned chilly. Leading the two columns of paratroopers, I could feel the cold and fatigue catching up with me. From time to time I walked back along the lines looking at the troopers as they marched. Each face showed a deep exhaustion. These boys had been on the road almost continuously for two straight days without much sleep. Nor had they had time to eat that day. Now they were supposed to march miles through the sand, fight a battle, then march back with any casualties we might have and with prisoners too, all in a space of seven hours. I worried about them, wondering if I hadn't asked too much—and I worried too about how quickly the time was passing. If something unexpected happened at Kuntilla our withdrawal could run into trouble. If we were still in Sinai when daybreak came, we would be naked targets for the Egyptian air force.

With these anxieties crowding in on me, I began to notice a faint glow on the horizon coming from the direction of the Egyptian base. At first I thought it was my imagination or some kind of optical illusion. But as I stared, the light brightened, then dimmed, then brightened again. I couldn't imagine what it might be. Kuntilla was one of the most isolated places in existence. That's why I had chosen it.

After a while the glow lessened, then faded altogether. But it left questions behind. An hour passed, then another. When it seemed that some of the troopers were too tired to take another step, I called a five-minute rest. The instant word was passed the entire column slumped to the ground, falling asleep where they dropped. But in another five minutes they were up and marching again.

A half hour later we were lying in the sand below the rock of Kuntilla. It looked menacing, rearing into the darkness in front of us like some primeval shape. Next to me were Meir Har-Zion and Aharon Davidi. Behind us the paratroopers were all in position, led by their commanders Raful Eytan, Moshe Efron, and Marcel Tobias, men who had been with me through so many operations. In that last minute of tension before the assault I poked Meir in the shoulder and asked him something I had often thought about. "What is it that makes you get up and attack?" I asked. "What makes you do it?" Turning his head, he made a quick gesture toward the men and grunted, "They are watching. They expect me to do it." The next moment we were up and attacking.

The battle was short, the Egyptians so startled they were unable to put up a coherent defense. To add to the confusion, they were just in the process of rotating their garrison. The mysterious glow on the horizon had been the headlights of personnel carriers delivering new troops. So instead of forty Egyptians there were eighty, half of whom knew nothing at all about the base or the surrounding terrain.

When it was over we had twenty-nine prisoners, most of them from the replacement unit that had just arrived. "We aren't involved in this," one had protested when we grabbed him. "We just got here." Of the others, some had been killed in the firefight and the rest managed to run off into the desert. One of the prisoners was the base commander who had hidden for a while, then started calling out in English, "Is there an officer there?" He had only wanted to surrender to a brother officer.

We also found an enormous quantity of weapons and equipment of a type we didn't recognize. We had heard that the Soviets had begun deliveries to Egypt, and at first we thought they were Russian. It wasn't until dawn that we examined them carefully and found they were actually Spanish. While the medics were treating both the Egyptian and Israeli wounded, we piled the machine guns and communications sets on two of the Egyptian trucks, then pushed the rest of the vehicles off the cliff.

Four paratroopers had been hurt in the assault, and two of the wounded were critical. All of the soldiers had been ordered not to shoot if at all possible, but to take prisoners instead. Following these orders, Amnon Avukai had broken into a position and ordered the Egyptians to raise their hands. But as they did, one of them had shot him. Yakov Mizrachi had chased another group into the desert. But when they realized that only one man was following them, one of them had turned quickly and stabbed him before he could fire.

Strapping their stretchers onto one of the trucks, we started the long walk back. Moshe Levy, a platoon leader (Levy was another paratrooper who later became chief of staff), tied the Egyptian commander's hands, then roped him to his belt and walked along next to me. The rest of the prisoners walked in fours with paratroopers guarding them. Earlier I had radioed for fuel to be parachuted near our own vehicles, and now I asked for two light planes to be ready to take the wounded at dawn. But even as I asked for the planes I was afraid we wouldn't need them. Neither Abukai nor Mizrachi looked strong enough to survive the trek back. As we walked, I stopped back at the truck often to see how they were getting along. But before long both of them were in their death agony. They died along the way.

Four hours of non-stop marching later we came out of Wadi Faran and crossed the Israeli border. The sun was just coming up.

* * *

The Kuntilla raid had been launched to take prisoners so that we could bargain for the return of two of our own people. But Kuntilla was hardly unique in that regard. Whenever any Israelis were captured, we never let up in our efforts to get them back. We knew what happened to them in Arab jails, the barbaric conditions, the torture they endured. As a result, if any of our people were taken I never gave either the defense minister or the prime minister a day's rest about it. We planned and carried out operations in Syria, Jordan, Lebanon, and Egypt whose objective was solely to take prisoners. When a company clerk whom I had once allowed to lead a patrol was lured across the border by Egyptians who asked him for a cigarette, we launched operation after operation (code-named Cigarette 1, Cigarette 2, Cigarette 3, and so on) until we had enough Egyptians to get him back. When Yitzhak Ghibli was wounded and captured by the Jordanians, the border came alive with action, prompting the chief U.N. observer, a Canadian general named Barnes, to comment that he had never seen a country that could become so maddened over one sergeant.

And in fact these operations did pose hard moral questions for us. Each one of them cost us casualties; we paid a very dear price in blood to get our people back, often losing more lives in action than we were able to save from Arab prisons. In talks with soldiers and officers these questions were raised and discussed and argued. My own position on it was clear from the beginning. I believed that every single soldier must know with certainty that he would never be left behind in battle, not if he was wounded and not if he was taken prisoner. Each one had to know that if such a thing happened to him his comrades would do everything humanly possible to get him back.

One after another the paratroopers' operations struck home, in Beit Likia, Sabha, Azun, Khan Yunis, and Dir el Ballah, where I was hit in the thigh by a machine-gun slug as I was about to jump into the Egyptian trenches. In 1954 and 1955, then on into 1956, there were some seventy actions altogether, each more difficult and complex than the last.

For me these were crucial years, a time not just of intense activity but of intense learning. Despite the successes, I did not change my opinion that the Arabs could fight well. On the contrary, I became more convinced than ever that the key to beating them was to put them off balance. The trick, the necessity, was not to let them fight their battle but always to do the unexpected. Come at them from the flank, or from the rear, or from all directions at once. Or hit them in the middle and then branch out. "With stratagems you shall wage war," says the Biblical proverb. With stratagems, "tahboulah" in Hebrew. And each time the tahboulah had to be something different, something surprising, something demoralizing.

During these years my ideas about the function of these operations changed too. I came to view the objective not simply as retaliation or even deterrence in the usual sense. It was to create in the Arabs a psychology of defeat, to beat them every time and to beat them so decisively that they would develop the conviction they could never win. This was another reason I objected to the idea of extremely limited surgical strikes. Not only were such operations technically unrealistic, but I came to believe that whenever we were forced to strike, we should do so with the aim of inflicting heavy losses on the enemy troops.

These ideas precipitated bitter controversies about where events were leading. Meir Amit, Dayan's chief of operations, and others too argued that heavy enemy casualties could not possibly be the answer. But as I saw it, our objective had to be to neutralize the Arabs' desire to make war on us, to destroy their will to fight. That, and not retaliation per se, was the ultimate goal of the paratroop raids, a goal that I understood would take a long time to achieve. But with our neighbors bent on harming us to the full extent of their powers, I, for one, could see no other resolution. With our tiny population and limited resources we could never hope to create the kind of balance of power that often allowed enemies to co-exist. The only alternative was to convince the Arabs that war was futile, that aggression would bring them nothing but humiliation and destruction.

10

Storm Before the Storm

By early 1955 the growing pressure from the paratroop raids was edging Egypt toward a crisis. With the continued destruction of his forces and his credibility, Gamal Abdel Nasser had put himself in an untenable situation. But even now he refused to stop the massive terrorism that had created the spiraling military confrontations. Instead his resolution was to look abroad for help. Shortly after the Gaza raid he initiated contacts with the Soviet Union through which he hoped to achieve such massive military superiority that he would be able to deal with Israel exactly as he wished.

In the summer of 1955 Nasser gave an indication of his intentions by closing the Strait of Tiran, Israel's only direct link with the trade routes to East Africa and Asia. Although the strait was an international waterway, there were no significant objections from the community of nations. Then in late September he announced an arms agreement with Czechoslovakia that would bring Egypt large numbers of modern Soviet-made tanks, guns, fighters, bombers, and small arms. With no way of acquiring equivalent weapons (the U.S. and Great Britain had imposed an arms embargo), Israel's ability to defend itself was thrown into doubt.

While there seemed no immediate answer to the new Egyptian arms, the government decided at least to open up the Strait of Tiran by launching a brigade-size operation against Sharm al-Sheikh, the Egyptian base controlling the narrow waterway. The entire paratrooper force would be involved—the active battalion, the reserve battalion, and the various auxiliary units. A non-paratroop battalion would participate as well, along with elements from the navy and air force. This would be by far the largest operation I had ever led.

But when the orders came through from General Headquarters, they contained an extremely unpleasant surprise. Although I was the paratroop commander, it had been decided to bring in a more senior officer to run this particular operation. Colonel Chaim Bar-Lev would soon be arriving with his entire headquarters staff.

Only Moshe Dayan could have arranged such a scene. Bar-Lev was the commander of an infantry brigade that for the last several years had sat around with almost nothing to do, watching from the sidelines as the paratroops carried out a cascade of assignments. What Bar-Lev had thought about this I could only conjecture, something I had had plenty of time to do during the months of my recently postponed trial in which Bar-Lev had been one of my judges—the one, in fact, whose procedural rulings had done most to make the affair so nerve-racking.

Perhaps a different type of person could have accepted this. I couldn't, and I let Dayan know I was planning to resign. His response was to invite me to have lunch with him. In a Rehovot restaurant over humus and salad he talked about how vital this operation was. He would not be willing to undertake it at all without me. Without my experience he just didn't think it could be done. Bar-Lev's appointment was only temporary; there was no intention in the world of having him replace me. On the contrary, as soon as this operation was over I would replace him. Not happy with the prospect of leaving, I allowed myself to be convinced.

Though neither Bar-Lev nor I pretended any love for the other, for the next month and a half we busied ourselves with planning. This was no ordinary operation. Sharm al-Sheikh was 125 miles south of Eilat through virtually impassable desert. And with tensions high over the blockade, the Egyptians would be alert for any signs of military preparation.

As we neared the final stages, it appeared that the Egyptians did suspect something was in the works. Then intelligence confirmed that they had learned we were going to do it. Reinforcements moved into Sharm, and suddenly the feasibility of the thing became doubtful. In the end, despite all the work, the operation was canceled.

Before the cancellation, though, while we were still in the middle of our planning, another crisis had bloomed into life, this one in the north. On December 10, Israeli fishermen on the Sea of Galilee were attacked by Syrian guns, the most recent incident in Syria's ongoing harassment of Israeli fishing in the lake.

In this series of events the artillery attack was the last straw, and with it the government decided to destroy the Syrian positions. That same day I was asked to come to General Headquarters to discuss the operation. It was a strange twist. I was under Bar-Lev's command, but I and not Bar-Lev had been invited to Headquarters. As Dayan described the plan to me, it was evident that this would be a large, complicated operation, calling for many of the same elements we were expecting to use at Sharm: landing craft, artillery, roadblocks in difficult terrain, an airborne communications system. While Dayan laid the concept out, I could not help thinking to myself that this situation was tailor-made to give Bar-Lev a chance to command the brigade in a complicated action, but still a much simpler one than Sharm would be. It would be a first-rate trial run for him.

But Dayan had decided differently. "It will be better," he said, a thin smile playing on his lips, "if you command this. You know the troops, you know the area. You have the experience for it." He might have said virtually the same thing about Sharm al-Sheikh. But maybe this was his way of hinting at an apology. Or perhaps he was playing his own games with Bar-Lev as well as myself. Or maybe it was just that in a crisis—this had to be done quickly—he felt constrained to turn to me.

Whatever his reasons, I didn't argue. When I returned to paratroop headquarters I gathered all the officers around to give them instructions. Not one questioned the turn of events that had mysteriously restored me to command. Later, discussing the operation around the sand table, I noticed Bar-Lev in a corner of the room. His face seemed to betray the whole range of unhappy emotions he was experiencing. And I don't think I succeeded in hiding my feelings any better than he did.

The complications between Dayan and me also generated a few humorous moments, though I cannot recall that I found them funny at the time. One of these had to do with my command car, or what passed for a car. Although I was head of the paratroop brigade (still technically a "unit," though larger now than any of the other brigades), I had not been given the full colonel's rank that was standard for brigade commanders. Instead I was still a lieutenant colonel. The fact that the paratroopers had remained only a "unit" had serious consequences. It meant that we did not have the budget, the logistical support, the intelligence staff, and all the other auxiliary services we needed. It also meant that I had the privilege of a jeep rather than a car. But with all the operations going on in every part of the country, there was a huge amount of driving to do, much of it on dusty unpaved roads, and eventually I was given an ancient Ford. Barely roadworthy anymore, it quickly got the name "Fordel," not quite a Ford.

On the morning of the Galilee operations against the Syrians I had started out early from my headquarters in the south. I had to present my plans to the commander of the northern front in Nazareth, then conduct the final orders group with the paratroop officers, then assemble the brigade. But on the way the Fordel quit, and I found myself on the side of the road with my thumb going up and down trying desperately to hitch a ride. Finally a woman officer in a small pickup truck stopped, someone I had known from the War of Independence. She was happy to give me a lift. I could ride in the back, since between her and her driver there was no room in the cab. But she could not take me to Nazareth; she had her own appointment to keep. There ensued through the cab window an argument about whose appointment should take precedence, a debate I eventually won by swearing mine was an operational matter. In the back of her pickup, wondering if I wouldn't have been smarter just to have stuck with my jeep after all, I arrived late for the orders presentation.

Despite its inauspicious beginning that morning, the Galilee operation was a stunning success. We accomplished all our objectives, inflicting severe casualties on the Syrians and taking thirty prisoners. But there were problems too. Dayan's concept of this raid had gone well beyond the scale that Ben-Gurion had outlined for him. I knew that an unpleasant session

---

Opposite: In December 1955, the attacks from Syrian strongpoints along the eastern shore of the Kinneret Sea on Israeli fishermen became unbearable. The highly successful Kinneret Operation against the Syrians demonstrated the exceptional ability of Sharon's paratroops to execute complex operations against a well-prepared and fortified enemy, anywhere and at very short notice.

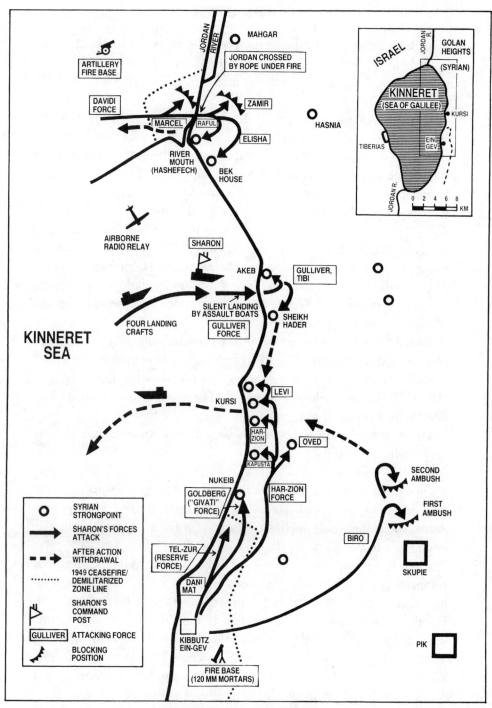

ALEI ZAIT (OLIVE LEAVES) –
THE COMPLEX COMBINED OPERATION THAT STUNNED THE SYRIANS –
DECEMBER 11-12 NIGHT, 1955

with Ben-Gurion was in the works when the following morning Dayan invited me to go with him to Jerusalem to report. That was something he only did when he anticipated the prime minister's anger. He did not like facing Ben-Gurion alone.

On our way there we passed Kfar Tabor, one of the first Jewish settlements in the lower Galilee. This was a place associated in history with the "HaShomer," the early self-defense organization that guarded the farmers against Arab marauders. As we drove by, Dayan and I began to joke that in the future the two of us would be spoken of in the same tones used for the HaShomer. "They'll tell stories about Moshe and Arik," I said, "except that where they protected the people with clubs and shotguns, our weapons were more up to date." "I don't think so," Dayan answered. "There's a big difference between the HaShomer and ourselves. In their day they did everything they possibly could to protect their people, the maximum. We are not nearly on their level; we only do part of what we know we can do."

By the time we arrived at the prime minister's office, Dayan looked very worried. I happened to walk in first; and looking up from his chair, Ben-Gurion caught my eye. "So, Arik," he said slowly, "how did it go?" "I think it was successful," I answered. There was a short silence while Ben-Gurion glowered at us. "Too successful!" he said.

Dayan turned pale. Ben-Gurion was, to my knowledge, the only person who had the ability to frighten him. Most people Dayan despised, and he took no pains to conceal it. But Ben-Gurion he felt a deep respect for; and more than that, he was afraid of him. My own chewing-out went only as far as those two words—"Too successful!" But exactly what ramifications the words might have carried for Dayan—who was directly responsible to Ben-Gurion—I didn't know.

From Jerusalem I drove by myself down to Kfar Malal. One of our company commanders who had been killed in the operation was from near there, and I felt I had to tell his parents myself. But I dreaded it. Usually when someone is killed there is an official notification, the army sends people to the family to convey the news and give them whatever assistance they can. But Yitzhak Ben-Menachem I had known all my life. We had been friends since childhood, so this was clearly my job. Still, I didn't know how I could face his parents; and as I drove, I found myself hoping that somehow they had already been informed. At least then I would not have to be the one to announce it. In a way, perhaps, I felt responsible.

Yitzhak was not only one of my oldest friends, he was one of the brightest, most courageous people I knew. He was also immense, so big and strong that he had been known as "Gulliver" since childhood. He was one of the seven who had gone with me on the Nebi Samuel raid in 1953. But for some reason he had not joined Unit 101, although I had asked him several times. He had not joined the paratroopers either, though he knew I would have welcomed him with open arms.

For several years now there had been a strain in our relationship, though I was never sure exactly why. But just before the Galilee operation I had called him up. We had had a number of company commanders wounded in recent actions and I felt I needed to have someone very good with me. So I told him, "Gulliver, I have a problem. Let's leave everything that happened in the past. I don't know if I have offended you in some way. I have never meant to. But I need you now. Come." And he had. Gulliver took over Company D and led the landing-boat assault across the lake. It was there that he was killed by a Syrian hand grenade.

When I arrived at his house, his parents had just gotten the terrible news a few moments earlier. While I talked to them, his mother cried continuously. "Arik, how did you let him die? You remember how he saved your life. You knew how he loved you. How he stayed behind and saved the wounded." In her grief she was talking about the Battle of Latrun in 1948, when Gulliver had heroically stayed behind with a machine gun covering Asher Levy's retreat with the Second Platoon. It hadn't been my platoon, but that didn't matter. To his mother he had saved the wounded then. He had been ready to sacrifice himself for me and for the others. And now I had let him die. As she talked, she looked at me not with anger but with her eyes full of anguish and disbelief. It was a look I would never forget.

Ben-Gurion may have thought the Galilee operation was excessive. But if he did, it was not because he felt any reluctance about defending ourselves to the best of our ability. Throughout the year he had been confronted with the intensifying terrorist campaign that Nasser was loosing through Gaza. Operated by Egyptian Intelligence, Palestinian squads were raiding the south with ever increasing ferocity. To Ben-Gurion it was clear that the Egyptians had little further interest in even appearing to comply with the armistice agreement that had ended the War of Independence. No doubt he was also thinking hard about the future, specifically about the six or so months that were left before the Egyptian army could assimilate its massive new arsenal. Once that happened, Gaza would be transformed into much more than a base for terror.

Ten days after Galilee I was again called to General Headquarters, where I was told that we were going to launch a major operation in Gaza. The idea was nothing less than to capture the northern part of the strip, destroying the Egyptian army in the whole district. Once again I had been invited to headquarters by myself, without Bar-Lev. Again I heard Dayan telling me, "You know the terrain, you know the troops, you know the commanders. We think you should do it." It was an exact repeat performance. And when I returned to my own headquarters, it had the same effect on Bar-Lev. His face turned the same colors; and as for me, I felt the same vindication.

In planning for this operation I decided to incorporate an amphibious landing and a parachute drop with an overland assault, a comprehensive effort that would envelop the Egyptians from the east, the west, and from above. In the end, though, the operation was canceled while we were already sitting in the half-tracks waiting for H-hour. But the fact that it never happened could not have been any consolation to Bar-Lev. In both of us emotions had been planted that were to help poison the background in the as yet unseen events of 1973.

Nineteen fifty-six was another hard year. Against the ominous background of the Egyptian buildup, the terrorism from Gaza spread and became more intensive, as it also did from the West Bank, controlled by Jordan's King Hussein. The fedayeen grew more daring; and as they did, the number of Jewish dead swelled. The entire southern part of the country up to and including the Tel Aviv suburbs was riddled by the most brutal attacks. One terror squad hand-grenaded a school in Shafir, killing six children, another attacked a group of teenagers near Bet Guvrim, killing seven. An archeological gathering at Ramat Rachel was shot up with four killed and sixteen wounded. A group of workers were murdered on their way to the Dead Sea chemical works in Sodom. Outside of Jerusalem a mother and daughter were raped, then knifed to death and the daughter's arms cut off. When the sun went down, people were afraid to go out. It was dangerous to drive at night.

With this background, Ben-Gurion decided to undertake an ongoing series of actions against Egyptian bases in Gaza and against the Jordanians, whose terror network was linked with theirs. But the Egyptians and Jordanians had also been learning lessons from the encounters of the last several years, and our operations became progressively harder and more complicated, and much heavier in price. The paratroops executed action after action, bearing virtually the entire burden of this mini-war. And while they did, the same internal struggles went on between myself and Dayan.

My driver at that time was Eli Israeli, a wonderful soldier who also served as my battle runner. One night late I heard a knock on the door of the little cottage in Be'er Yakov where Gali and I were living then. With the fedayeen roaming at night, I looked out the window cautiously. It was Eli. He had been at General Headquarters that evening making some deliveries and had happened to overhear a conversation among several of Dayan's staff. They had been laughing, joking about "how Arik will react when he hears he's losing his command." "I would like to see his face," one had said, "when they tell him he has to come to Headquarters as a staff officer."

The next morning I was knocking on Dayan's door. His adjutant came out with word that the commander-in-chief was too busy to see me. "Look," I said, really angry, "what's going on? I heard about what's supposed to happen. If it does, I don't think I can be in the army at all." "Yes." He was gloating. "Maybe there is no room for an officer like you in the Israeli army." I turned and left, making up my mind on the spot that I had to see Ben-Gurion. On my way to Jerusalem I stopped to phone, asking if I could come right away. Ben-Gurion said yes, of course, come.

I was so agitated I couldn't see straight. It was not that I hadn't had plenty of experience in these things already. Over the length of my friendship with Dayan I had become well seasoned. But the way this was done was so cowardly. He had not even been able to call me and say directly that he had decided to replace me. After all those years—1953, '54, '55, '56—the endless raids, battles, being wounded, losing friends. It was a disgrace.

When I got to Ben-Gurion's office I had tears of rage in my eyes. I just couldn't control it. Sitting in his chair, Ben-Gurion listened patiently, then made one of his typically laconic pronouncements, one word this time—"Wait."

"Wait? What should I wait for?"

"Just wait."

"But what for?"

"Listen," he said. "I want to tell you an old Chinese story. About a peasant who made a trip by boat and was drowned at sea. Some fishermen found his body and went to his family asking for a large amount of money before they would give it back.

"So the family went to a monk and said, 'What should we do?'

"The monk said, 'Wait.'

"When the fishermen saw the family would not pay the ransom they too went to the monk and said, 'Look, we have the body, but they won't pay. What should we do?'

"To them the monk also said, 'Wait.'

" 'But what should we wait for?' asked the fishermen.

" 'The family,' said the monk. 'How long can they wait without burying their beloved father? And you, fishermen, how long can you wait with a dead body on your hands? Soon you'll both have a solution.' "

Ben-Gurion started the story deadpan, but by the end he was laughing. It was contagious. I started laughing too. Here was this great man busy with so many things, laughing over these Chinese who couldn't wait. The tension disappeared. I went back with the feeling that he would not let them do it.

A few days later we went out on a raid in Sinai. Coming back. Eli Israeli was so exhausted that my intelligence officer decided to drive. But the road in those days from Nizana on the border to Beersheba was terrible, full of ruts and holes and sharp curves, and the intelligence officer was just as tired as Eli. Around one of the curves he hit a rock and the jeep swerved back and forth between the cliff on one side and the rocks on the other. Then it turned over on us.

Smoke was coming from somewhere, and I was sure the jeep was about to catch fire. But when I tried to get out I found my hand was jammed underneath. I jerked it free, tearing some fingernails off in the process. Eli and the intelligence officer seemed all right, but the radio operator who was with us was trapped underneath. Together we made a superhuman effort to get him out, thinking that any moment we would be in the middle of flames. Finally, with an immense heave, we managed to lift the jeep enough to drag him away.

Eli was in the best shape of anyone, so I sent him to run back to the post at Nizana for help. By the time the ambulance arrived, the rush of adrenaline had long worn off and I knew I had been hurt badly. My upper lip had been cut in two and my hand was crushed. I also had an excruciating pain in my left shoulder, which was obviously broken. When we got to the Beersheba hospital, the doctor examined me, then said that he had just received a call from Southern Command asking if he could do what was needed without putting me to sleep. Would I allow him to do that?

"Why do they want it?" I asked.

"I don't know exactly. There's some kind of problem and they want you at headquarters as soon as possible. It's about something they want to do tonight."

I agreed of course, but I was so exhausted and in so much pain that I couldn't imagine what I might be in condition to do. While the doctor worked on me, Gali arrived to keep me company and see if she could help. As soon as they were finished with the sling for my left arm and all the suturing and bandaging, someone drove me to Southern Command Headquarters, where I found a number of other officers and brigade commanders arriving, some of them directly from the field.

It had been a night of action in Sinai and Gaza. Now General Headquarters wanted another operation for the coming night, this one against the Jordanian army headquarters located in the old British police fort at Daharia. They wanted me to command this raid, and their concept of it was to go in on foot. Could I do it?

None of the field commanders said a word. They just looked at me. Underneath, perhaps I was waiting for one of them to say, "Look, don't you see he can't do it now. We'll do it." But it didn't happen. Finally I said, "You know it's twelve miles from the border. I don't think I can get there and back by foot. But I know the original plan was for a mobile operation. If we can do it that way and I can fix up a half-track with some pillows or something, then I'll go."

While we were in the middle of this discussion, a call came in for me from Chief of Operations Meir Amit at General Headquarters. Amit said that Dayan had asked him to call to let me know that he had reconsidered his decision and that I would remain as commander of the paratroopers after all. "This has nothing to do with tonight's operation," he said. "Moshe just wants you to know that he has changed his mind. . . . But I also want to ask you about the operation. Do you feel up to it?" I told Amit what I had just finished telling the Southern Command—that I would do it in a half-track but not on foot. After a short pause he said, All right, we'll do it that way.

Later while I was planning the raid, I got another call. It had been decided that a mobile raid was not a good idea after all. The operation was being canceled. As soon as I heard this, I had myself driven to the Tel Hashomer hospital, where I checked in and spent the next two weeks in bed.

By the time I was released, contacts between the Israeli, French, and British governments were already under way. England and France were not happy about Nasser's nationalization of the Suez Canal. And we were not happy about his plans for us. A mutuality of interests had opened up.

11

Sinai

A s talk between the French and Israeli governments grew more serious, French military visitors began showing up at the paratroop base. The French had concerns about allying themselves with Israel, and not the least of them had to do with the effectiveness of the IDF. Could Israel be relied on to carry out her part in any joint operation that might take place?

Apparently Dayan's opinion was that if they wanted to know that, they should be looking at the paratroops. There they would meet a group of officers who had had years of combat experience, very tough, very professional men. They would see soldiers with an extremely high level of training and the most wonderful spirit. They would also see, Dayan knew, a semi-secret display of captured weapons and equipment that was tangible evidence of the paratroopers' accomplishments.

Hidden in a small forest on our base was the military hardware that we had taken in battle over the years. I had kept it all—to the vast annoyance of General Headquarters, which was constantly trying to get hold of it themselves. There you could find armored cars, jeeps, mortars, artillery pieces, trucks, an amazing variety of machine guns and small arms, even horses—magnificent Arabian horses that we had taken from forts we had destroyed. I had standing orders that none of those stations should be blown up before the horses were taken out. So whenever we attacked such a place, you could see in the middle of the smoke and confusion of battle these Arabians with terror in their eyes being led off by our troops. (Later, when I spent a year in England, I brought with me pictures of some of these horses. Only half joking, a British officer told me, "If you had only shown us pictures of these horses you saved, you would have won all the sympathy you needed.") The display included equipment with colors and markings of many different units—from Egypt, Syria, and Jordan. You couldn't look at it without thinking, Well, these Jews are capable of doing things.

So the French visitors were sent to us. I remember in particular Colonel Simon (later General Simon), one of the most decorated soldiers in the French army, a man who had lost an eye in battle and whose body was covered with wounds. He came, and I had a beautiful lunch prepared in his honor, to which I invited all the staff officers and battalion and company commanders. We struck up a friendship then that I was able to renew two years later in England, where he had gone to serve as military attaché. Later he told me that he had been hugely impressed by the paratroop base, except for one thing. He had not been able to enjoy the luncheon. When I asked, "Didn't you like the food?" He said, "Yes, the food was wonderful. But you people ate so fast, I didn't have time."

All these things were important. The French came, contacts were made, friendships developed. They liked what they saw. They got the idea that we knew how to handle ourselves, that their equipment would be in good hands (Ben-Gurion was working out an arms deal with them), and that they could rely on us when the action began.

By September and October of 1956 bloodshed between Israel and Egypt had come to seem endless. That year the Egyptian run fedayeen were ambushing car and truck traffic throughout the south. They staged attacks on the region's cities and settlements, in Beersheba, Ashkelon, Zrifin, Beit Dagon, and numerous other places. Despite our counterstrikes, the terrorists' savagery seemed to reach new peaks. At Moshav Shafir, they grenaded a school, killing six children. All this came together with developments around the Suez Canal, which Nasser had now nationalized. The British and French saw in this step a threat to their oil lifelines and were responding in the traditional fashion of their empire days, with what can now be seen as the last gasp of gunboat diplomacy.

Among these storm clouds Ben-Gurion struggled to find an answer to the problem of Israel's security. On all sides he was besieged: Egypt's new arms, the ominous advent of the Soviets, Nasser's aspirations to lead a Pan Arab movement whose goal would be the "liquidation of the Zionist entity" (a favorite phrase in the vocabulary of the Arab leadership), non-stop terrorist activities, our own reprisals, and the casualties we incurred. With it all, no one doubted that we were moving quickly now toward war.

In retrospect, one might ask whether the deterrence policy that Israel pursued for three straight years had failed. Might some other approach have brought peace and security rather than a spiral of violence? At that time I was utterly convinced that there was no alternative. I am even more convinced of that today. The terrorism that assailed us from 1949 on was so destructive that had Israel not taken the steps it did we would have faced drastic consequences, in particular large-scale evacuation of the border areas. So many of the border and desert settlements were populated by newcomers from the destroyed communities of Europe, from towns and cities of Morocco and Yemen, from the mountains of Kurdistan, and from a half dozen other Eastern lands. These were people whose social and family fabric had been devastated by war or by a traumatic migration. They had been transplanted and were struggling to find ways to live in a new and sometimes difficult environment. Vulnerable as they were, unopposed virulent terror would have made their lives unbearable. It would have created mass movement into the center of the country. The outlying settlements, which guarded the nation's periphery, would have been endangered, and with that would have come national demoralization and a ruinous constriction of the nation's economic life.

We could not have chosen other than to defend ourselves vigorously. That path at least provided hope, the confidence that we could exist and flourish even in the face of our neighbors' deadly hatred. And for those neighbors it demonstrated that the Jewish state was a fact that would continue to demand acceptance, no matter how distasteful that prospect might be.

But it was also true that deterrence had not stemmed the violence, and that the actions had become larger and more costly for ourselves as well as for the Arabs. As negotiations with the French and British were entering their last stages, a climactic operation took place that confirmed the need for some more comprehensive solution.

In mid-September three Druze Israelis were murdered by Palestinian terrorists based in Jordan. On October 4 the same group killed five Jewish potash workers near the Dead Sea. Shortly afterward intelligence learned that the gang had been arrested by Jordanians for smuggling and were in jail. Instead of launching a reprisal attack, it was decided to inform King Hussein of the killers' identity and let him take appropriate action. But when the information was passed to him, Hussein's response was to immediately release them from jail. Our restraint had been taken for weakness. Five days later Palestinian terrorists from the neighborhood of Kalkilya murdered and mutilated two orange grove workers in Tel Mond, a few miles from Kfar Malal. In this case the killers had cut off their victims' ears. Many previous victims had also been mutilated in one or another of the standard ways—a traditional symbol in the Middle East not just of hatred but of utter contempt.

In response to this series of incidents we attacked the Jordanian military headquarters in Kalkilya. The raid involved infantry, armor, artillery, and even the air force. When it was over, we had accomplished all our objectives, but eighteen Israeli soldiers had died and another sixty were wounded. The Jordanians' toll was a hundred dead and some two hundred wounded. It had been a pitched battle.

The Kalkilya raid had two sharp consequences. One was that it brought to a head the pressure to move beyond deterrence. That pressure had erupted before—in plans the previous December to take the northern part of Gaza and to seize Sharm al-Sheikh, neither of which had materialized. Now with Kalkilya it became crystal clear that no deterrence operation, no matter how large or successful, would achieve the goal of stopping terrorism. If we wanted the Arab governments to face their responsibility, another route had to be found.

The second consequence was internal. Within the Israeli army Kalkilya triggered an angry debate that was to fire one of the most important (and divisive) discussions that continued right through the Yom Kippur War. In October of 1956 Moshe Dayan and Meir Amit were on one side of this argument. I was on the other.

The Kalkilya military headquarters was located in a massive police fort on the outskirts of the town. Only several hundred yards to the south lay the Kalkilya defensive positions. To the east ran the road to Azun, where the nearest Jordanian reinforcements were stationed. Dominating this road a quarter mile outside of town was the hill position of Zuffin, whose trenches were not occupied at the moment but which could play a key role in any battle on the road. An assault on the police fort was thus a complicated procedure that required a plan to deal with all the elements we would be facing. I had suggested the target to the Central Command. I had also presented a comprehensive plan that included taking the southerly defense positions, setting a blocking force on the road to Azun, and occupying Zuffin Hill to insure against any emergencies on the road. The plan had been approved, except for one element. I would not be permitted to place a force on Zuffin Hill.

The afternoon of the operation I stopped in Kfar Malal to see my parents. From the orchards behind their house the battle scene would be clearly visible that night. I stayed with them half an hour, saying goodbye, telling them not to worry—all the things a son says to his parents at such a time. I especially wanted to reassure my father, who by now had entered the terminal stages of his illness and was extremely weak.

Shortly afterward, when the paratroops were already assembling, I received an order from Central Command informing me that another element of the plan was to be canceled. There was to be no assault on the defensive positions south of the fort. I was not told the reason for this change, as I had not been given a reason for leaving Zuffin unoccupied. It was clear, though, that General Headquarters was trying to limit the scope of the operation.*

I objected as forcefully as I knew how. I argued and railed. I told them in the bluntest terms that they should not interfere. They did not know the target or the terrain as I did. They did not know our units and commanders as I did. They did not know the enemy and what could be expected of him as I did. It was their business to tell me *what* to do. The goal, the target—their job was to define that as carefully as they were able. If they did not want this particular target, fine. They should choose another, or none. But they should not take it on themselves to tell me *how* to do it. When it came to how, there should be as little interference as possible with the commander in the field. My position was then (as it is now) that the upper echelon should intervene only if they are actually on the battlefield, if they know everything intimately, if they are forward where they can see and understand all the elements that affect the

---

* Later I learned that Ben-Gurion and Dayan were afraid that Jordan would invoke its mutual defense treaty with Great Britain if the operation was too extensive. In addition, by this time the Sinai campaign cooperation with the British and French was far advanced. Consequently, any confrontation with the British would have been extremely awkward.

conduct of the battle. It was like shouting in the wind. Central Command would not budge an inch. I am sure they thought me obstinate and ungovernable. But I was sure that what he was doing was wrong and gravely dangerous. Still, when all the arguing was done, I was the one who had to back down and obey the order.

Unfortunately, the battle proved me right. We accomplished all our primary objectives according to plan. But the southerly Arab positions poured a heavy fire onto Motta Gur's battalion as it attacked the headquarters building, causing a number of casualties. Much worse was the experience of the blocking force as it retreated from its holding action against Jordanian reinforcements coming down the Azun road. These reinforcements were from the Arab Legion's Ninth Battalion, which up till a few months earlier had been commanded by Peter Young, a British commando hero famous for his World War Two exploits at Narvik, Dieppe, and other hard battle sites. After the war Young had gone looking for action and, like many of his peers, had found his way to Jordan. Although he was no longer with them, Young had trained the Ninth Battalion well.

When their advance elements were destroyed by the blocking unit, the Ninth sent out a flanking force that managed to get between the Israelis on the road and Kibbutz Eyal, which lay just across the border to the north. It was a crucial move. The Jordanians had guessed that the blocking force would retreat overland toward Eyal after the battle on the road and that they would be able to cut them off. And that was exactly what happened. The 54-man paratroop reconnaissance company fought three separate actions on the Azun road, hitting the Jordanians, withdrawing, then hitting them again and again. But when they left the road and struck north they ran headfirst into the Jordanian flanking force.

As this news came in over the radio, I ordered the reconnaissance company back to the road. By this time most of company's officers were wounded (including the commander, Yehudah Reshef), and there was no way to carry them out. On the road, though, I knew there was a rise where they could hold on while I sent forces in to extricate them. But with no heavy weapons and armed mainly with short-range Uzi subma-chine guns, the reconnaissance company was now in serious trouble. As our artillery ranged in around their position to help keep the Jordanians off, I ordered an armored column I was holding in reserve to move through Kalkilya and up the Azun road to extricate them. But Moshe Dayan, who was with me in my forward command post, refused to allow it. He had doubts about the ability of the armored personnel carriers to get there (they would have to find their way through the town) and wanted me to send Raful Eytan with an infantry battalion instead.

By now the night was already far advanced, and I knew that even while Dayan and I were arguing time was running out; at daybreak we would be confronted by large Jordanian reserve units and thousands of armed villagers. But I insisted on sending the armor. "Moshe," I said finally, "if we don't do this we are going to get their bodies out tomorrow from the U.N. armistice commission." And having said this, I ordered the armored column to move in. Without another word, Dayan turned his back and walked away.

Two hours passed before the armor was able to penetrate to the position on the road, and by that time the reconnaissance company was almost out of ammunition. Under fire from the Jordanians, the Israelis made it onto the half-tracks, which then withdrew back toward Kalkilya. But unfortunately, that was not the end of the story. For by this time elements from the Jordanian Ninth had slipped behind the Israeli forces and occupied the hill positions on Zuffin, exactly where the Central Command had forbidden me to place a unit as part of the overall plan. And now as the armored column withdrew, they came under withering fire from both sides of the road. In an instant Zuffin erupted in a vicious firefight.

As the armored vehicles recovered from the surprise, they swept the hills with fire and were soon able to continue their withdrawal. During the fight, though, one of the half-tracks had been hit badly and put out of commission, but with all the confusion the rest of the column did not realize it was missing until they had cleared the area. At that point an argument broke out between Major Moshe Breuer and Irmi Bardanov, an engineer officer who had gone out with the column. Breuer wanted to drop the wounded off first before returning to Zuffin, while Bardanov insisted they turn around and go back immediately.

This Irmi Bardanov was a forceful and exotic character, famous for his fighting ability and also well known among the cafe society of artists and musicians. Charming and seductive, he was surrounded by women despite his frightening appearance—thick black hair, black beard, bushy black eyebrows, and one eye that was always shut. At the time of the Kalkilya operation he had already left the army and was on separation leave. But when he heard something was up he came searching for me and had been waiting at the gate of the farm when I left my parents' house that afternoon. When he asked to join, I had told him, "Irmi, you've left it already. Don't come." But he had insisted and followed me to the staging area, where later that night I finally gave in and assigned him a job.

That was how he found himself in the lead half-track that night arguing with Major Breuer. What neither of them knew was that back on the hill the soldiers in the crippled half-track (all but one who was wounded) had managed to get out and break through the Jordanian lines, eventually making their way to safety across the border. The end result of their argument was that very quickly both Bardanov and Breuer were racing back toward Zuffin with four of the column's half-tracks. There they rescued the wounded soldier and managed to hitch the disabled vehicle to their own half-track. But while directing his driver on how to turn in the narrow road, Breuer was killed. A minute later Bardanov too was gunned down.

It was early morning before everyone was out, and the results were very heavy indeed. When I could not find Irmi, I finally went over to where we had brought our dead. Lifting the blankets one at a time, I saw many faces I knew. Irmi was lying under the last one, his bad eye wide open in death as it never had been in life. He was one of eighteen we lost that night, with sixty more wounded. The Jordanian death toll was over a hundred. Kalkilya had been more like a pitched battle than a raid.

The review session the paratroop command held on this operation was one of our typical no-holds-barred affairs. Despite the presence of a representative from General Headquarters, I made my thinking very clear about what had gone wrong and why. When Dayan heard about it, he was furious, and he invited me with all my battalion commanders to a meeting at headquarters.

Dayan's idea for this meeting was to reprimand me in front of my officers. With Meir Amit at his side he began to attack me for what I had said. But he was caught by surprise by the massive support I received from all the commanders there. And I was not reticent either. I told them point-blank that they had made a terrible mistake, and that we had paid the price for it. It was a hard, rancorous session, a fitting close perhaps to the years of peacetime operations against the Arabs, years that had also brought warfare of a different kind between myself and many of my colleagues.

*   *   *

As we licked our wounds after Kalkilya, Ben-Gurion, Dayan, and Shimon Peres left for Paris to try to conclude negotiations with the French and British that would bring all three countries into a concerted action against Egypt.

When they returned on October 25, I went to see Ben-Gurion. He told me briefly what had gone on. A deal had been struck by which Israel, France, and Great Britain would each gain their objectives. Ours were in Sinai. We would open the blockaded Strait of Tiran, eliminate the storm of terror from Gaza, and destroy all Nasser's pretensions to leadership, perhaps even bring about his downfall. At the same time the French and British would re-establish their control over the Suez Canal.

The campaign was to be initiated by a carefully co-ordinated ploy. Israel would take action against the Egyptians deep in Sinai, dropping a paratroop battalion close enough to the canal to "threaten" the waterway. At that point Great Britain and France would give an ultimatum to both sides to move their forces away from the canal zone. Israel would agree. Egypt of course would not, and French and British forces would intervene to insure the canal's continued operation. Once the opening phase was over, we would pursue our own objectives by destroying Egypt's forces in the Sinai.

As Ben-Gurion outlined the situation for me, his office was a scene of urgency and excitement. A cabinet meeting had been called and the ministers would be arriving momentarily. Events that would shake our world were now only days away. As I stood there absorbing it, I could almost feel the wings of history brushing the air.

My momentary abstraction was interrupted by a secretary who had come in to tell Ben-Gurion that one of the ministers could not make it on time.

"Why not?"

"Because the minister cannot find his driver."

Ben-Gurion pounded the table and roared at her, "Tell him to take a cab!" Here was the great man, the lion who had established the Jewish people in their homeland. There were the declining empires of England and France mustering their resolve and their armies. We would shortly be involved in the most complicated globally consequential affairs. And in the middle of it all this earthly intrusion—"The minister cannot find his driver!"

On that note I left. The operation would begin on October 29, allowing only four short days to sort out the operational problems we would be facing. For me the chief problem was that we had agreed to begin the war by staging a parachute drop on Mitla Pass, only twenty miles from the canal. The main purpose of this was to give England and France a pretext to intervene, as Dayan put it, so that they could "wash their hands in the waters of purity." It meant that a paratroop battalion would be isolated near the far side of the Sinai until I could link up with them overland with the rest of the brigade.

The paratroop drop would also be followed by Israeli attacks along the major Sinai axes to the north. But if the British and French did not fulfill their part of the bargain by destroying the Egyptian airfields and launching their own assault on the canal cities of Port Said and Port Fuad, the scenario would change dramatically. In that case we would be involved in a very different war from the one we expected, against the undivided strength of the Soviet-armed Egyptian army and the larger and better equipped Egyptian air force.

Although Ben-Gurion had concluded an agreement with the British, he did not trust them. Nor did the rest of us. We remembered the treatment of the Jews during World War Two too well, as we did their 1948 evacuation from Palestine when they turned over the most strategic positions under their control to the Arabs. If they did not implement their part of the plan, the paratroopers would be in a precarious position. "If that happens," Dayan said when he visited my headquarters a day or two before the operation, "it will be a very complicated situation. . . . You'll have to bring back your forces. I'm confident you'll be able to find a solution to that, but you might be the only ones in Sinai."

In order not to arouse Egyptian suspicions, we would attempt to disguise the mobilization of forces as preparation for action against the Jordanians. Such an action would appear quite believable. Kalkilya with its hundreds of casualties was only two weeks behind us, and tensions between Israel and Jordan were still fevered. In addition, Jordan had just signed an agreement placing her army under joint command with Egyptian and Syrian forces. So it would be easy to conceive that we might move forcefully against the Jordanians.

The task of deception was also given to the paratroops. Before we struck across the border, I was to concentrate the brigade near Chatzeva, south of the Dead Sea, giving the impression that we were preparing a strike into Jordan. This I thought was an unnecessary burden on us. Some other unit could have done it equally well, and it would add an extra sixty-five miles to our race to link up with the battalion at Mitla. But we accepted it without complaint. Our standard approach was not to refuse any mission. On the contrary, we always said we could do more than was asked.

I spent the last few days of preparation in our situation room at Tel Nof, a ruin of a building donated to us by the air force. (Since we had only recently been designated a brigade we did not yet have our own headquarters building.) With its crumbling cement walls and high metal roof it was an oven in the summer and a refrigerator in winter; during the rainy season we walked around buckets scattered randomly on the floor to catch leaks. Now my planning staff and I worked continuously. Stretched out along the walls were air photos showing the entire route we would be covering, from the Israeli border to the Mitla Pass, arranged there by an intelligence corporal with a long black braid, Gali's younger sister, Lily. Outside, the companies went through last-minute drills and training. Knowing how much I loved to hear them sing, whenever they got near the headquarters building the choruses would break out. It got so I could recognize them by their favorite songs, Company B leading off with "The Teacher and Miss Rifka," Company C bellowing back "She Saw What the Bull Was Up To." My personal favorite was "The Ballad of Avshalom Adam," about an ex-corporal in Company A. Avshalom Adam was a gifted soldier who could have been a commander of commanders. But he just could not resist the temptation to occasionally liberate a sheep or some chickens from one of the local farmers in order to throw a feast for his friends. Every time that happened, I would take away his corporal's stripes. By the time he earned them back, the temptation would overcome him again. So Company A marched to the rhythm of "Avsha hasn't got it. Avsha hasn't got it. The commander took it. Now Avsha has got it. Now Avsha has got it. The commander gave it back." The paratroops of those years may not have had the poets that had graced the ranks of the earlier Palmach, and they certainly did not have the political orators, but in spirit and ultimate seriousness they were more than a match.

The last night before the border crossing I went to Beersheba to visit Assaf Simchoni, who was now the southern front commander in chief. When I arrived at Southern Command Headquarters it was late already and he wasn't there. Tired, I took off my field pack and, using it as a pillow, fell asleep on the floor. Around midnight someone nudged me awake. In the darkened corridor I made out Simchoni. "Arik, don't sleep there," he said. "I'm going home. Come with me." So I spent that last night in Simchoni's guest room in a bed with nice white sheets, not knowing when I might enjoy such luxury again.

Late the next afternoon, October 29, sixteen DC-3s took off from Tel
Nof with Raful Eytan's battalion of paratroops. Escorted by ten Israeli
Meteor fighters, they were headed for the Mitla Pass, 150 miles behind
Egyptian lines. Originally they had planned to drop on the western end
of the pass, near the canal. But the previous day air reconnaissance had
discovered tents and Egyptian trucks inside the pass, and the plans had
been changed. Now they were to drop on the eastern side, near the
obelisk known as the Parker Memorial, honoring a former British
governor of the Sinai.°

While Raful's battalion was boarding the planes, the rest of the brigade
was assembling at Wadi Faran, the staging area I had used for our raid on
Kuntilla almost exactly one year ago. In the last ten hours they had
crossed the Negev from their camp near the Dead Sea where they had
staged their deception for the Jordanians. Now I planned to move
non-stop across the Sinai. We would take Kuntilla on the run, then the
two other Egyptian bases that barred the road to Mitla. Themed and
Nakhel both were manned by significant Egyptian forces, but I intended
to spend as little time as possible with them. The 395 men with Raful
would be alone in the desert. Somewhere to their north Egyptian forces
might be lurking. Others could well be in the pass behind them. I was
going to cover the 150 miles between us at the maximum speed.

As we crossed the border, a flight of Raful's DC-3s lumbered overhead
in formation, as if to confirm that the war was really on. On the Kuntilla
plain the brigade convoy stretched out, hundreds of vehicles, among
them a company of thirteen French AMX light tanks commanded by Zvi
Dahav. Many of the trucks and half-tracks were also newly provided by
the French. We had pressed them into use despite the fact that they had
arrived without any tools. There was no way to even change a tire.

That evening we took Kuntilla, moving the attacking unit around to
the rear so they could come in out of the setting sun. On the radio we
heard the Israeli military spokesman announcing a "raid to eliminate
terrorist bases in the Sinai," part of the ruse to paint what was happening
as a reprisal rather than the opening moves of a full-fledged war (in fact
there were no terrorist bases in the Sinai). By dawn the next morning we
were in position in front of Themed, a Bedouin oasis that had been
heavily fortified with mine fields and perimeter defenses and was held by

---

° By the day of the attack, General Headquarters knew that the trucks and tents belonged to an
Egyptian maintenance crew. But they had not bothered to return to the original drop order and
had not informed me of the situation.

two companies of Egyptian infantry. We arrived without most of our tanks. Along with almost sixty other vehicles they had broken down in the treacherous dunes and wadis. With no road, there were places where the brigade's tractors had had to tow every single truck and half-track.

But we were there. With the rising sun at our backs this time I sent in a battalion-size attack under Aharon Davidi, who crashed forward in a fast-moving arc of half-tracks, jeeps, and the remaining tanks. Huge whirls of dust clouded the desert from the charging vehicles, illuminated from behind by the bright morning glare. Emerging from the cloud, at the last moment we formed a single line and smashed into the middle of the Egyptian defenses. Themed too fell quickly.

Even before the shooting had stopped, Piper Cubs were landing to take out the wounded, and DC-3s were making parachute drops of fuel and equipment. Since most of the tanker trucks had been left in the wadis on the way to Kuntilla, we received additional fuel with special gratitude. All the while Egyptian fighters were in the air, making it impossible to concentrate the vehicles for refueling and resupply. Practically the whole convoy was scattered among the wadis and ridges, hiding from the searching jets, and venturing out to the fuel supplies only a few at a time.

Except for Motta Gur's battalion. I had fueled them up first, then sent them racing ahead toward Nakhel, another forty miles to the west and a midway point on the road to Mitla. Unlike Kuntilla or Themed, Nakhel looked like an actual settlement—ten or fifteen buildings, including a military post that was headquarters for a battalion of Egyptian frontier police. By late that afternoon the battle of Nakhel was in full swing. Again we mounted a fast, mobile attack, this time with artillery support, and again the end came quickly.

I had left a company behind to secure Themed, and now I left a battalion at Nakhel under Yisrael Cohen. In the back of my mind was the thought that the British and French might not act, and if they didn't I would have to have a protected line of withdrawal out of the desert. The rest of the brigade moved out swiftly, striking westward toward Mitla and Raful's paratroopers, still seventy miles away. But Nakhel had been the last barrier, and now I expected to make better time.

At ten that evening one of our searchlights picked out a big homemade sign by the side of the desert track. It read in Hebrew, "Border Ahead. Stop!" Just beyond, Raful's battalion was waiting, dug into the hard dirt on the flatlands of Mitla's eastern approaches. It had taken us thirty hours to reach them.

That day Raful's paratroops had been hit by Egyptian air strikes and also by some mortar shelling from the pass, where Egyptian motorized infantry had come in through the unguarded western end. During the course of the day, however, Israeli air force attacks on the pass had destroyed the Egyptian convoy. The pilots had described the wreckage and had reported that the pass was now free of any discernible Egyptian presence.

On the basis of this information I decided to move into Mitla Pass at first light. Although Raful had been dropped on the eastern end of the pass, our mission had not been changed. We were to occupy the pass on both ends and hold it. To Southern Command I radioed, "We are proceeding according to plan," requesting them to have air support available at dawn. Then I visited the positions and found a comfortable, small wadi to sleep in. It was hard to believe we were 150 miles inside Sinai. I felt as if I were still on the border.

That morning at three o'clock a cable arrived from General Headquarters saying that they could not provide air support. It was a disturbing message, but I thought that if it wasn't available we would just have to go in without it. Then I fell back asleep.

By 6 A.M. the convoy was formed up and ready to move. But just before we started out another message came in from Headquarters, this one saying that they did not approve my plan to move into the pass and that I should remain where I was. At exactly that moment four Egyptian jet fighters appeared in the sky and made a low sweeping turn above the brigade's drawn-up vehicles. We watched them for a horrified instant as they arranged themselves in attack formation and roared in toward us. By that time the drivers were gunning their vehicles away from the convoy line and everyone else was digging in the sand like madmen, myself along with the rest.

As the Egyptians swooped in for their first run, out of nowhere two Israeli Meteors appeared on their tails, their guns blazing. In a twinkling two of the Egyptian jets were on fire and the other two taking wild evasive action to get away. In another moment a third Egyptian arched toward the ground trailing smoke. The fourth was now a diminishing pinprick in the morning sky.

Soon additional Israeli aircraft were overhead, and as they appeared I felt such security, as if someone from home was stretching out his long arms to keep us safe. The pilots reported that the pass seemed empty, but they also gave me disturbing information that an Egyptian armored brigade was moving toward us from the direction of Bir Gafgafa and was now about forty miles away.

This was critical news. I now had twelve hundred men with me, together with a few field guns, the three AMX light tanks, and several new French recoilless rifles that had been airdropped to Raful. With these it would be impossible to fight off an armored brigade. And we were alone, far behind Egyptian lines with no possible relieving forces to call on. Beyond that, the area where Raful's men had dug in was completely open, a vast tableland that offered no natural defenses against tanks and armored infantry. The only way I could see to defend ourselves was to move into the pass and take up positions there, where the steep cliffs and narrow defiles would give the oncoming Egyptian tanks no room to maneuver.

Again I asked headquarters for permission to move into the pass. But again it was refused. This time I was told that the Southern Command chief of staff would be coming to see the situation firsthand. Soon a light plane arrived with Rechavam Ze'evi aboard. When I went over developments with him and showed him around, he gave me permission to send a reconnaissance into the pass, as long as we did not get involved in any large-scale action. "You can go as deep as possible," he said, "just don't get involved in a battle." He also told me that Dayan himself was planning to visit us that afternoon.

Immediately I put together a unit to go into the pass. My idea was that this unit would move the twenty miles to the western end and hold the position there, preventing Egyptian forces from attacking from that direction. Then the rest of the brigade could move inside, deploying to defend themselves against the armored forces moving down from Bir Gafgafa.

For this job I put the three mobile tanks together with two companies of infantry in half-tracks. I gave Motta Gur, the commander, strict orders not to get involved in any fights. I didn't expect opposition inside Mitla Pass. The jets flying over that morning had seen nothing other than the burned-out trucks. But if anything significant did turn up, he was to break off contact immediately.

Motta left. But within a mile of the entrance the first half-track was slammed by a volley of fire from hidden positions high on the defile walls. The driver was killed instantly and the half-track swerved sideways and stopped. The second half-track moved up and was also hit and stopped.

Had some unit other than the paratroopers been involved, that might have been the end of it. They might have withdrawn to assess the situation without getting themselves further involved. But the paratroopers were trained differently. For long years I had drummed it into them that they could never leave wounded or dead on the field. Never. It was one of the axiomatic lessons that I had preached constantly. The result was that when the half-tracks were hit, their natural reaction was to move forward to get the casualties out. This Motta Gur did, regardless of his orders not to get involved in a battle. And as the paratroopers moved forward to rescue their friends, they found themselves in the middle of a vicious firefight.

It was an act I never blamed Motta for, despite the eventual consequences. I knew it was ingrained in his nature to do this. I also believed it was right. In the short term there are certain actions that may be considered unjustified, and endangering many lives in order to save a few wounded may appear to be such an action. But in the long term such apparently unjustified acts may take on a different meaning. And the welfare of an army is always a long-term consideration. The doctrine that wounded and dead would never be left behind was so instilled into the hearts and minds of our soldiers that they were always willing to do their absolute utmost, because they knew without a trace of doubt that their friends would never leave them.

It was a matter of education, a principle. One should never leave dead. One should never leave wounded. As far as I was concerned, it was a moral principle. Of course it was personal too. I knew what it was like to be left wounded in the field. And I also had had the experience during the paratrooper raid on Dir el Ballah in 1954 of being wounded and taken out. So I had never looked on this coldly as a matter of numbers. There are moral values that have to be kept in an army, and this is one of them.

Motta Gur was on the spot. But he had no question about what to do. He moved in. And as he did he was drawn into battle with an entire Egyptian infantry battalion that had dug themselves into the ledges and caves of the cliff walls and had not been noticed by our planes.

Just as the battle inside the pass was developing, we were hit by attacks from Egyptian jets that strafed and bombed our headquarters area and concentration outside the entrance. These were Vampires, British-made planes that were also used by the Egyptian air force. Egyptian and British markings are also similar: the British use blue, white, and red concentric circles, the Egyptians green, white, and red. I was so distrustful of British motives that even while we were shooting at these planes I was not convinced they were Egyptian.

This was the thirty-first of October. Monitoring the radio, we knew that the British and French had given their planned ultimatum to both Israel and Egypt. Israel had accepted. Egypt, as expected, had not. By now it was past time for the British and French to have moved into action. But as yet they hadn't. At the same time we were getting regular reports from our reconnaissance planes that the Egyptian armor was continuing to move in on us.

It was a precarious situation. We were exposed on the flatland at the end of the pass. Many wounded were already being brought out of the battle. I felt I had to take immediate steps to create a defensive perimeter facing the approaching Egyptian armor and to have the wounded evacuated. With the battle still intensifying in the pass, I sent Raful and Davidi with reinforcements, then started pulling the rest of the brigade into positions on the outskirts of the eastern end. I knew it was not an adequate response to the danger developing from the north, but it would improve our chances.

By late that afternoon we were well into our deployment. While it was going on, I was also involved in heated arguments with the air force about landing planes to evacuate the wounded. But there was no landing strip, and they were afraid the soft sand would not support anything more than Piper Cubs. Bringing in DC-3s would be a tremendous risk. Finally they sent a pilot to make an on-the-spot survey, and in the end they decided to take the risk. Late that afternoon the DC-3 workhorses began arriving, one after another, landing, loading the casualties, then taking off trailing plumes of dust behind them. It seemed like a minor miracle.

Meanwhile, inside the pass the battle was raging. With Motta Gur still pinned down, the reconnaissance unit skirted the cliffs on the right side hoping to come down on the Egyptians from above. But when they got to the ridge, they were hit by a hail of bullets from the caves and hidden ledges on the far side. Unable to identify the source of the fire, they assumed it was coming from below them and stormed down the wall. Here some of them fell to their deaths while others were caught by fire from the positions below as well as from those opposite them.

With this attack halted, the Egyptians continued to pour fire down onto the paratroopers crouching behind whatever cover they could find on the floor of the pass. Still unsure exactly where the enemy positions were, the Israelis held on grimly. At one point in the afternoon a soldier named Yehuda Kendror volunteered to race a jeep through the pass, drawing the Egyptian fire onto himself in an attempt to allow his comrades to identify where the shooting was coming from. Wounded terribly in his run, Kendror somehow managed to crawl back and was evacuated (only to die in the hospital). But even this act of suicidal courage failed to change anything.

Still taking casualties, Motta Gur was unable to withdraw until late afternoon, when Yitzhak Hoffi arrived with two tanks and several half-tracks. Hoffi, my brigade second in command, had been with Motta when the ambush was sprung, but had broken through with a small force and had moved to the western end of the pass, where he had remained throughout the day. Now, under covering fire from the AMX's, the paratroopers were finally able to extricate themselves.

By this time the Egyptian positions had been located, and after nightfall two small units were sent along the cliff walls, the right-side force led by Levi Hofesh, the left by Oded Ladijinsky. Moving slowly along the cliff face, they attacked one Egyptian cave and firing hole after another in hand-to-hand fighting. For two hours the sounds of battle reverberated through the pass before finally giving way around eight o'clock to an ominous silence.

That evening I sat with the commanders inside the pass, all of us weighed down by heavy feelings about the battle and by deep foreboding about what daylight would bring with it from the north. By now we had redeployed our forces. I had also given orders to move sufficient forces into the pass the next morning to clean out the remaining Egyptians so that we would have no pressure behind us. Our only relief as we pondered the situation was that we had at least managed to get our wounded out, over a hundred of them.

When morning came, it was evident that the battle in the pass was over. From the caves and recesses where the Egyptians had been there was no movement. Inside them 260 Egyptian soldiers lay dead. Whatever survivors there might have been had slipped away during the night. But thirty-eight paratroopers had also died, among them Oded Ladijinsky, who had been killed protecting his second in command from a grenade explosion.

From the north too came only silence. The two Piper Cub patrol planes I had with me searched the desert for signs of the Egyptian armored brigade but found nothing. Information came in that during the night they had been ordered to withdraw across the canal to avoid being cut off by the threatened British and French intervention.

In the quiet of that day I felt a terrible fatigue. In deep sadness we buried our dead. I knew most of them personally. Among them were some of our finest soldiers and commanders.

The Battle of Mitla Pass created anger and dissension both within the ranks of the paratroopers and also between myself and General Headquarters, in particular Dayan. The internal criticism was mostly stimulated by Motta Gur, who believed I should have taken personal command of the battle in the pass instead of remaining at the entrance to organize the defense and evacuate the wounded. At the same time, Dayan accused me of disobeying orders by sending a large force into the pass instead of a reconnaissance patrol and of engaging in a battle, although my orders were to avoid any fighting.

After the campaign an inquiry was opened to determine if I had acted according to the orders I received or if I had overstepped the bounds. I believed that no excuses were necessary for what I had done. I had not gone personally to oversee the battle, because my judgment was that the most serious peril to our forces at that time was from the Egyptian armor to the north. In addition, my second in command (Yitzhak Hoffi) and two battalion commanders (Motta and Raful) were already inside the pass. Consequently the greatest need for me was to get the brigade organized into defensive positions. It was for the same reason that I had sent a substantial unit into the pass—not to get involved in a battle but to penetrate to the far end and secure it so that we could deploy deep inside and defend ourselves in what I saw as the coming action.

When the inquiry was completed, Ben-Gurion called me in to see him. "If you had to make the decision right now," he asked, "what would you do?" Outside it was a cold, rainy December day, and foggy condensation coated Ben-Gurion's windows. I told him, "You know, sitting here in your warm room drinking a nice cup of tea, and having all the information, maybe I would have done something different. But that day, I was commanding all those people in that open area, with almost no anti-tank guns, with no news about what the French and British were doing, and with the nearest Israeli forces a hundred miles away. In that situation I was by myself and responsible for all those people. I had to

SINAI CAMPAIGN 1956: THE PARA BRIGADE
THE FIRST TO BATTLE

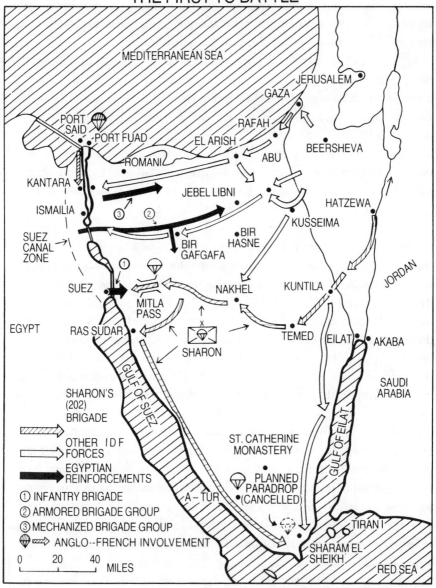

The Sinai Campaign (Operation Kadesh) was a pre-emptive war intended to disrupt the massive Egyptian military buildup against Israel, defeat the Egyptian blockade of the Tiran Straits, and eliminate the growing terrorist and military threats from the Gaza Strip by conquering it. The Suez Canal area was engaged by Anglo-French forces. Sharon's 202 Paratroop Brigade executed the deepest penetration behind the enemy lines.

make the decision, and my judgment then was that we would have to move deep into the pass and do whatever was necessary to defend ourselves."

Ben-Gurion listened to me obviously deep in thought, then concluded the whole thing with one sentence. "I don't feel," he said, "that I'm in a position to judge between two commanders on this issue." Whatever Dayan might have thought when he heard about this, what ran through my mind was that one of these commanders that Ben-Gurion wasn't in a position to judge between was the commander-in-chief of the IDF, the other just a brigade leader. The inquiry board itself was equally inconclusive, and by the end of December the issues were dead, though not, of course, forgotten.

Mitla was not the end of the paratroopers' activities. From the pass we were ordered to send a battalion southeast to the Gulf of Suez to capture the oil refinery town of Ras Sudar, then to proceed down the gulf coast toward Sharm al-Sheikh. At the same time Motta Gur's battalion was dropped on El Tur, farther down the coast. As the paratroopers were approaching from the Suez coast, my old friend and commander Avraham Yoffe was leading the reserve Ninth Infantry Brigade on a murderous march toward Sharm along the Gulf of Aqaba. The two forces were racing each other to the Egyptian strongpoint.

By now the international situation was heating up considerably. Serious pressure was building from the Soviets and the Americans, and although the British and French had landed in Port Said and Port Fuad, they had not yet moved decisively. It was clear that shortly we would be forced into a cease-fire—perhaps before we had gained control of the blockaded Strait of Tiran. On the fourth of November I flew back with the rest of the brigade from Mitla to our base at Tel Nof. We had orders to prepare ourselves for a parachute drop on Sharm al-Sheikh that evening.

We were almost ready to take off when word came that the Ninth Brigade was on the verge of capturing Sharm and that the jump would not be necessary. By 9:30 the next morning we learned that the drive was completed. Yoffe had taken the place and linked up with the paratroopers. With the complete success of other Israeli drives in the northern desert and in Gaza, the entire Sinai was now in our hands. From the time Raful's battalion had dropped on the Parker Memorial to the moment Yoffe's men raised the Israeli flag it had taken less than seven days.

12

Beginnings and Endings

With the order to cancel the jump on Sharm I dropped everything to make a quick visit home. Gali was pregnant by this time, after a number of unhappy years when it had seemed we would be unable to have children. I couldn't wait to see her. I also couldn't wait to see our new home. For the last three years we had been living in a tiny cottage in Beer Ya'akov, too small even to squeeze in the few pieces of furniture we had had in our apartment in Jerusalem. But just before the war we had bought a house in a community for military people near Tel Aviv called Zahala. We had just been in the process of moving when hostilities began; and I had left Gali, two months from term, to complete the job on her own.

We had bought this house from General Chaim Laskov, an extremely modest man whose house reflected his character. Like him it was modest in every way. But modest or not, we couldn't have been happier to at last have a place of our own. My parents, though, did not like it at all. My father especially had hoped we would build a home in Kfar Malal; he had even picked out the right spot in a vineyard he owned a little way from the center of the village. So when he came to Zahala, he looked around disapprovingly and said, "You're making a mistake. This isn't a good place. Why not come back to live on the farm where you belong? You should be living on the land."

By now my father was extremely ill. Already before the war he had been in Tel Hashomer hospital, then when hostilities began he had been evacuated home. On my way from the paratroop base I stopped off briefly to visit him and my mother. We talked for a while, happy to see each other. I knew he took immense pride in the fact that I was the paratroop commander; it was one of the things that had given him the most pleasure over the last few years. He told me he was getting ready to go back into the hospital, and it seemed to me that he suspected it might be for the last time.

I spent the rest of the day with Gali at the new house, then in the evening went to see Ben-Gurion, who had invited me to stop by. When I arrived at his Tel Aviv home, Ben-Gurion was sick in bed with a high fever. He was eager to know how things had gone, but he was also deeply worried. Both the United States and the Soviet Union were applying brutal pressure. That day the Soviets had even warned that they were considering unilateral action against Israel. The United Nations had called for a cease-fire and the rapid withdrawal of Israeli forces. With the taste of victory still fresh, Ben-Gurion was already facing the need to give up what we had accomplished, including the settlement he had established on Gaza's border with Egypt.

It took two months before arrangements were concluded for the Israeli forces in Sinai to be replaced by a multinational U.N. force. During that time the paratroopers roamed the entire territory. We were on every hill, in every wadi, over every mountain and ravine. I wanted each officer to know the place in case we might need that knowledge in the future. Together with the air force we prepared hidden caches of food and water for any downed pilots who might need to survive there. We were on the move constantly. We knew that time was short and that we had to become intimate with the desert. We saw everything and wrote everything down, filing reports together with maps and charts and photographs. It was a monumental survey. I for one was hardly convinced that a U.N. force would provide any solution. We did not know when we might have to come back.

When we were finally forced to leave, I took it very hard. Most of all I could not understand why we withdrew from Gaza and from the settlement Ben-Gurion had established there. The relentless terror from the strip was one of the main problems we had tried to solve with this war. Our overriding goal had been to find a way of forcing Egypt to accept responsibility and put an end to it. And now the Egyptians would be coming back. It was as if we had not solved anything at all.

On December 27, during a meeting of commanders to review the campaign, I got a message that Gali had given birth to a boy. It seemed a miraculous event. Both of us had wanted many children, but two years earlier we had been told we would be unable to conceive. The news had put a cloud over our lives. When she finally did get pregnant, our joy and expectation were heightened by the sadness that had preceded it. Now, at the Jaffa hospital, where I rushed from the meeting, I saw what I thought was an exceptionally handsome child. We were both flushed with happiness.

Three days later my father died. He had been in the hospital since shortly after the war, and I had seen him as often as I could—though with the constant activity in the Sinai and with Gali near delivery it had not been often enough. I had visited him last just the day before, and he had said something that sounded strange but which later meant a great deal more to me. He had been lying in an uncomfortable position when I came in, and I had picked him up in my arms to move him, disconcerted by how weak and light he was. As I did, he said softly, "It's a pity I'm going to die. You still need my help in so many ways."

It had sounded so incongruous. There I was, twenty-eight years old, young and strong, as determined and self-confident as anybody could be. I was the paratroop brigade commander and had been through all these battles. I was at the stage of life where young men think they can do anything, when they are sure that they are immortal and can conquer the world. And here was my father on the edge of death whispering, "You still need my help." When he said it, the words struck me as such a contradiction. But over the years I remembered, and eventually it came to seem that he had been right.

He died on the night of December 31. My mother had been with him almost continuously during the preceding days. But that evening he had felt the touch of something different and had asked her to go home to get his will. So that night she had left him alone. In the early morning hours he realized that he was dying and had called the duty nurse, to whom he whispered his last words—a farewell to my mother.

Altogether I felt I had not known him. In my childhood everyone had been too busy. Then came the War of Independence, then Unit 101 and the paratroops. Since the age of seventeen I had hardly been at home. Perhaps it is normal for children not to fully appreciate their parents until later in life. For me, unfortunately, the first intimations of that truth came with the blow of my father's passing.

Those days seemed crowded with lessons and revelations. Hard years of war had been capped by the climactic Sinai campaign and the euphoria that followed, all of it choked now by the realization that the Egyptians would return to Gaza. I had been in action almost continually since 1947, and now that it was over there was still no rest. During the day I drove myself to finish the vast labor of charting the desert. At night I dreamed terrible dreams of battle and death. Then my beautiful unexpected son was born, even as my father lay dying.

Between my son's birth and my father's death, Ben-Gurion hosted a party for all the ranking commanders who had participated in Sinai. Although Gali and my father were both in the hospital, of course I went. As everyone was gathering, I heard Ben-Gurion's voice calling out, "Is Arik here? Where is he? I want him sitting here with me." There they were, the same words I had heard so often before, the same story starting all over, the same dark looks from the senior commanders. I knew exactly what it would bring. But I enjoyed sitting next to him anyway, watching him during the conversation and the entertainment.

Especially during the entertainment. One of our great actresses was there, Orna Porat, a magnificent woman. As she performed, Ben-Gurion stared at her, his eyes intense. His hand tapped the chair next to his leg in an unconscious, tense rhythm. When she was finished, he called her to come and talk to him, and suddenly I saw for the first time Ben-Gurion as a man of blood and flesh. The great man, interested in all the problems of the world, in philosophy and science, in morals, in global politics, struggling to resolve the needs of the Jews and the passions of the Arabs—in a moment I saw this great man as a human being. He watched her, his hand drumming, drumming, his eyes for no one else, his desire smoldering. Now, when it is known the man had affairs, things are different. But then, in that generation, secrets were kept, the mysteries of life were closely hidden. But here, suddenly, another one had been revealed.

✳   ✳   ✳

I stayed on as paratroop commander until the autumn of 1957, when Dayan asked me to attend staff college in England. "We aren't really interested in their system," he said. "So learning doctrine isn't the most important part of it. What is important is for you to meet the people, learn the language, understand how they think, see what their culture is like and the way they live."

In line with these priorities, Dayan's rule was that during the week Israeli officers had to live at the college in Surrey with their British peers, getting a real taste of their habits and way of life. Meanwhile, wives and families would stay in London, and on weekends they could all enjoy the city's music, art, and theater, experiencing a different dimension of British culture. So in late September we rented a London apartment for Gali and Gur Shmuel, now ten months old and already showing signs of the charm that were to mark his character. Meanwhile, I moved into officers' quarters at the staff college.

Life in the British army was a remarkable experience, as different from the wild and earthy paratroop existence as could be imagined. In the morning I would come awake to the civilized sound of my batman pulling open the window curtains to let in the light. Before I had fully opened my eyes, he was at the side of the bed with a mug of hot tea to soften the trauma of rising. By the time I was actually out of bed he would be mixing hot and cold water in the basin to the proper temperature and laying out my freshly pressed uniform. As I dressed, he would ask if I desired a bath that evening. I think he must have regarded me with a certain curiosity when it turned out I wanted one every evening. It was not a luxury one got to enjoy much in the paratroops. As impeccable and solicitous as my batman was, I was amazed to find that he was very junior in his service, only having been at it twenty-seven years. His most experienced colleague at the college was eighty-five. He served the commandant and remembered distinctly the officers he had waited on during the Boer War.

The whole British experience was strange and new, from the batman and the elegant manners of the British officers to the weekends of music and theater in London. I felt strongly that here was a break with the past, that I was beginning a new stage in my life.

On the whole I was happy about it, but I was concerned too. I had left my command, the source of my strength. I knew I was more on my own now than I had ever been. Then in November I was jolted by the suicide of Nehemia Argov, Ben-Gurion's trusted military adjutant. Although ten years my senior Nehemia and I had been good friends. He had also been my primary channel of contact with Ben-Gurion. Totally loyal to his boss, he knew Ben-Gurion's mind intimately on military matters, and he was one of the few who knew that Ben-Gurion had planned to appoint me commander-in-chief in the near future. With his death, I knew I had lost both a good friend and a strong ally in the battles that were sure to come.

On the other hand, these things were in the future, and I was beginning to find England fascinating. The English were clearly in a state of national decline. They were losing their empire quickly, and they had no distinct national goals to rally around. Their failure at Suez had been a crushing blow which enhanced a growing sense of inferiority, or so it appeared to me as I tried my best to divine the national mood.

Among the things that sustained them was their attachment to tradition. I saw this firsthand, with the batman and the Thursday evening black-tie dinners and the thousand nuances of behavior. I even met Queen Elizabeth briefly. Nineteen fifty-eight was the hundredth anniversary of the staff college, and she was coming to help celebrate. We rehearsed the ceremonies down to the finest details, although I did not absorb enough protocol to keep from making a minor faux pas in her presence. When she asked me, "How do you do?" I forgot that the proper response was simply "Thank you, ma'am," and added, "How do you do, ma'am?" momentarily startling the British officers near me.

But there was also substance to their traditions, not just form. I spent time in the Imperial War Museum looking at the weapons the British had prepared when they were expecting a German invasion in 1940. Behind those shotguns, spears, and clubs you could see courage and an iron determination that seemed almost hereditary. I talked to people who had been at Dunkirk, to officers who had marched in parade formation around the hills attracting a storm of fire onto themselves and away from the evacuation beach. I remembered asking Meir Har-Zion what enabled him to charge into the enemy guns. For him it was the men he was leading. "They expect it," he had said. Obviously the British officers too felt it was expected. It was part of their tradition.

Among the officers and instructors at the college were majors and lieutenant colonels who had risen to high rank during World War Two but in the British fashion had since been reduced back to their former levels. People who years ago had been brigadier generals in France or Italy or the Western Desert were now climbing slowly up the peacetime ladder. And by and large they accepted it with a casual nonchalance.

All this was intriguing, and the studies too had their value. Among the students were people who had served on every World War Two front and who brought a wealth of experience to the discussions. For the required analytical paper I chose the topic "Command Interference in Tactical Battlefield Decisions: British and German Approaches," giving me the chance to pursue my preoccupation with the question of command and control. The basic German model was that command officers should be in the very front. Rommel, for example, wanted to be where he could respond instantly to emergencies or exploit the unexpected opening—where he could intervene personally in tactical decisions. In the Western Desert he was right there with his forward tanks. At the same time his British counterpart Montgomery had painstakingly planned his battles, then had gone to sleep, believing that in essence his job was over. So here was a confrontation between two dramatically different approaches to the question.

The subject was just down my alley, and while I was doing the research it occurred to me to ask Sir Basil Liddell Hart for his thoughts on it. Liddell Hart was the renowned British military analyst whose theories had influenced both British and German doctrine in a variety of areas. I wrote to him at his home near Marlow, introducing myself and telling him I was working on this subject. Could he spare me some time?

I immediately got back a letter inviting me to come and see him. When I did I found him a warm, generous man, quite happy to discuss these issues at length. It was the beginning of a friendship.

To the British officers at the staff college it seemed very strange that an obscure Israeli would be exchanging letters and visits with the revered Liddell Hart. During one of the Thursday black-tie affairs several of them brought it up. "We understand," one said, "that Liddell Hart is a Jew."

"No, why would you think that?"

"Well, how else would you get to see him?"

They weren't trying to be impolite, but somehow it troubled them and got them to thinking about the secret connections that they supposed all Jews had with each other.

"First of all," I said, "Liddell Hart isn't Jewish. He comes from an old English family of border barons. All I did was write a letter and he answered. I'm sure if one of you did the same thing you'd get the same response."

They didn't continue the discussion, but I got the distinct impression they weren't convinced either. Perhaps Liddell Hart did come from an old border family, but he still might have been part Jewish. Underneath there was something that bothered these British military people about Jews, some exotic mystery. Among the staff college students was an officer with the French name of Thierry whose colleagues regarded him as a little out of the norm. "He might," I was told, "be a Jew." During a discussion on the Jewish subject another day one of my British friends expressed the opinion that there must be four or five million Jews in England. When I told him the number was about half a million, he couldn't believe it. How could that be when they seemed to be everywhere?

But though Jews might be a troubling mystery, the staff college officers were friendly and invariably proper. The only racial insult I heard that year was not even directed at Jews but at Arabs. On one occasion Field Marshal Montgomery came to lecture us and delivered his opinion that the Arabs were "ten-minute fighters." I stood up and objected, telling him, "I don't think that's the situation." I knew better than he. And besides, if Montgomery thought they were ten-minute fighters, then maybe he considered us twelve-minute fighters.

By the time the year-long course was finished, I felt I had fulfilled all my expectations. It had been a period of new friends and new experiences, of exposure to different ways of doing things and different habits of thought. I had enjoyed it immensely and had learned a great deal. I left thinking that it had been an important year.

But shortly after we arrived back in Israel, the problems started. First on the agenda was my rank. I was still a lieutenant colonel, although my command of the paratroop brigade should have made me a colonel long ago. Now I was told that the promotion was ready. But it depended on my agreeing to a new appointment as head of the infantry training department, just the sort of staff job I dreaded. With a queasy feeling I realized I was back in the same swamp of maneuvering and infighting I had left a year ago.

After a few months at General Headquarters I was appointed commander of the infantry school. So began four years of what I considered to be exile in the wilderness, years of frustration which despite (or perhaps because of) my desire to command an active unit threatened to draw out indefinitely. I did my best to find a way out, but nothing worked. I even went to see Dayan, who by this time had retired from the army and was serving as minister of agriculture. I found him in his archeological garden behind his house working on one of the antique jars that were a passion with him. As I talked, he raised his head slightly and regarded me from a narrowed eye. "Arik," he said, his voice tired, the eye closing to a slit, "there is no way for you to get out of it. You will have to wait for a crisis to come along. It's only then that they will let you out."

I did what I could with the time. In the infantry school I instituted all the instructional procedures I had developed with the paratroops. I was also made commander of a reserve infantry brigade, which I trained intensively. At the same time I enrolled myself in the school of armor, going through their course from the very beginning as a student, studying tank driving, mechanics, gunnery, and communications. When I finished that, I enrolled in the armor company commanders' course. I also found that I could study law at night at the Hebrew University's Tel Aviv branch. I would have preferred agricultural science, but that faculty required full-time attendance. Law in general had little attraction for me, but constitutional law I found fascinating. (I eventually received my law degree in 1966.)

These things filled up the time, but I was still oppressed by a chronic sense that I was not doing enough. I felt that I was paying a very high rate of interest for the years when I had taken such an active role. One part of me was angry about it. But I also felt, at least after the first year or two, that I couldn't complain. Who else had had the same opportunities, the same experience—the paratroops, armor, infantry, law school? I did the best I could to adjust to the wilderness, even while I kept looking for a way out.

During the spring of 1962 I thought for a moment the chance had come. In one of my periodic requests for reassignment I had asked for the job of IDF chief of operations. Zvi Zur, commander-in-chief at the time, had turned the request down but had offered command of a mechanized brigade instead. But I was holding out for an armored brigade. Tanks were emerging as a crucial element in strategic thinking, and I wanted to get as much experience as I could. For his own reasons Zur had turned this down too, and the result was that I found myself sitting around while he waited for me to give in.

On May 2 all these problems turned suddenly meaningless. That day I had come home early bringing Gur, who had been visiting the base with his kindergarten class. When it got dark I began to worry about Gali, who was usually back by then from her job as supervisory psychiatric nurse at the Ministry of Health in Jerusalem. While I was wondering if something might have happened, my next door neighbor Motti Hod walked in with the terrible news. That morning on the Jerusalem road she was killed in a car crash. She had been driving the little Austin with right-hand steering that we had bought in England and had been hit head-on by a truck. By the time they got her to the hospital, there was nothing more to do.

I was left alone with Gur, who was now five years old. How do you tell a five-year-old child such a thing? He was so tied to her. He trusted her and relied on her so. When I finally brought myself to say it, Gur told me, "No, I don't believe you, Mommy wouldn't leave me." And how do you organize your life? How do you save yourself and your child too? He became so quiet, so withdrawn. I read to him hour after hour, taking the intervals in the stories to explain, to talk about what had happened and what it meant. It was so hard to be alone with him there, waiting for him to come back from wherever it was his mother's death had taken him.

Time passed, and slowly, step by step, Gur began to recover. It was a remarkable experience watching him regain his health, as if his sorrow had reached to the depths and had broken on some inner strength it found there. Lily came to stay with him, Gali's younger sister whom Gur had always loved. She nursed him and mothered him. It was just what he needed. Eventually he even started putting back some of the weight he had lost, and the fragile, hollow look that made me so anxious gradually faded from his eyes. He began to seem more like the boy he had been before.

13

African Interlude

By this time Ben-Gurion had decided that the waiting game between me and the commander-in-chief had gone on long enough, and he pressured Zur to appoint me to an armored unit. Zur did, and I became the commander of another reserve brigade, but at least now it was with tanks.

At the end of 1963 Yitzhak Rabin was selected to replace Zur as commander-in-chief. While his appointment was still in the works, Ben-Gurion talked with Rabin about finding some way to take me out of the deep freeze and allow me to get on with my career. As a result, Rabin offered me the job of Northern Command chief of staff under my expansive old friend Avraham Yoffe. But even as he offered the post, Rabin let me know that this appointment didn't mean that I would ever get to be Northern Command commander, or even that I would ever make general. But still he did it. It was a turning point.

Coming to the Northern Command was like coming home. I had served in the north as company commander and intelligence officer, so I was familiar with the territory and the problems. And Yoffe received me with warmth and friendship. Even after Ben-Gurion's intervention it had required his agreement to arrange the appointment. But we had worked together before, and Yoffe knew that we would feel comfortable with each other. I had first met him as a young reconnaissance officer in his brigade, then we served together as commanders in Sinai. During the Six Day War we were to be colleagues again.

At the beginning of 1964 three main problems faced the Northern Command. The first was Lebanon. Although the PLO had not yet officially declared its existence, already they were beginning to establish their networks, and Beirut was on its way to becoming a center for terror. The Lebanese government, though still unified, had always been weak, and its ineffectuality was an open invitation to the most radical Palestinian terror organizations.

The second problem was the border between Syria and Israel. Here the Syrian army maintained positions on the Golan Heights that looked out over a valley full of kibbutzim and moshavim. It was a complicated border, running unevenly between the two sides and leaving dozens of areas open to dispute. Some of these were an acre, some several acres, a few larger. But there were dozens of them. All these patches of land we were attempting to cultivate, while the Syrians tried to prevent us, shooting down at the farmers and workers with machine-gun and mortar fire at the same time that they bombarded the Hulek Valley's established kibbutzim and moshavim.

Under constant harassment from the Syrians on the heights, we refused to back down from our claim to these disputed parcels. It was not so much that we needed the relatively few acres for agricultural production. It was rather that in those days Israelis shared a nearly universal belief that the only possible way we could survive in the midst of our hostile neighbors was to stand firmly on our rights. The feeling was that we could not afford to back down an inch in the face of those who wanted to annihilate us. So ingrained was this approach that it would have been hard to find someone who opposed making the effort to farm this land. And it was not just a physical effort. It was a heavy economic burden, and it was costly in lives. The end result was that almost each day border clashes erupted over our attempts at farming and their attempts to stop us.

The third major issue was the attempt of the Arab countries to divert the waters of the Jordan River. At an Arab summit conference in Cairo on January 13, 1964, a formal decision was made to build a canal that would channel the waters of the Hasbani and Banias rivers—two of the Jordan's three main tributaries—around Israeli territory and into the Yarmuk in the Kingdom of Jordan. (This was the same conference that initiated the establishment of the PLO, with its covenant calling for the destruction of the State of Israel.)

While the border disputes between Syria and ourselves were of great significance, the matter of water diversion was a stark issue of life and death. A dry country with a critical water shortage, Israel enjoys only a brief winter of rainy weather. Other than that, the three primary sources of water are the Jordan River, various brooks and streams along the coastal plain, and a large aquifer that runs under the coastal plain and extends into Samaria and Judea. Before 1967 a third of the entire water supply came from the Jordan, whose volume was now about to be reduced dramatically.

From our positions along the border we watched as the diversion project got under way. Tractors, earth-moving equipment, and hundreds of heavy trucks were brought into the area and digging began. It was a vast job, requiring the emplacement of huge siphons and culverts to span the wadis. But the Arab engineers and workers went at it with determination and made steady progress. At the end of autumn the land was bone dry and all the digging kicked up man-made dust storms. Along the whole line of work, black and gray dust spewed into the air—except for one hill in the center whose clay soil gave off a dark red powder.

That hill, Tel Hamra, was a matter of chagrin to at least some of us watching the operation. Though insignificant by itself, the difficult topography had made it a critical feature. The canal route would have to be cut right between Tel Hamra and Banias Hill, which adjoined it. Our chagrin stemmed from the fact that Banias Hill had once been within our border. After the War of Independence Banias Hill had been declared a demilitarized zone, which we were permitted to use for a civilian settlement. But somehow the settlement had never worked out. Nobody had paid enough attention to that little hill, nobody had cared about it. And so the settlement was not pushed vigorously, and finally it was aborted. Afterward the army established a small observation post on Banias. But in 1951 the Syrians had captured the observation team there and established their own presence. So we watched, knowing that without Banias the Syrians would have been unable to build the canal and we might have avoided what was likely to turn into a major con-flagration. But by now it was far too late to reclaim what we had once given up.

Two of the three Jordan tributaries ran through Arab territory, the Hasbani in Lebanon and the Banias River in Syria. The third was the

River Dan, and while the source of the Dan was disputed, in this case we had very clearly established our control.

With the water problem growing more tense by the day, we decided to at least remove the source of the Dan from any possible Syrian claims. In that beautiful region where the tribe of the Dan had lived during biblical times, underground springs welled up to form a pond from which the river flowed. It was only the far northern edge of this pond that the Syrians claimed, and to preclude any arguments about who owned the water we decided to build an embankment there that would narrow the pond at that end, clearly enclosing it within Israeli territory.

As we proceeded with this project, the Syrians sat in their tanks watching tensely. In the beginning of November they stopped watching and started shooting. Salvos from their tanks crashed into our bulldozers and dump trucks. We shot back; and a tank, mortar, and machine-gun duel erupted, which we, to our surprise, did not get the better of.

Two days later, on November 3, we began working again, and again the Syrians opened fire. But this time we were better prepared. In the interim Israel Tal had come in and worked with the tank gunners, teaching techniques that eventually allowed them to hit targets up to eleven kilometers away with precise accuracy (ordinary battle range for tanks was about two kilometers). As the Syrians attacked our equipment, we ranged in on their canal project, and this time our shooting was vastly more effective than it had been. Quickly the clash widened. The Syrian guns reached out to the nearby Kibbutz Dan, our planes were called in, and a short, vicious battle flared.

From that time on we did not let them work. Every few days our tanks would hit them at long range, disrupting the canal digging and sending their machinery into flight. Their action against our road builders had provided a provocation. But in fact we could not have sat there much longer just watching the canal make headway. Exactly when the government would have moved against the Syrians, or in what context they would have done so, I do not know. But with their assault in November, Syria started off a round of fighting that gave us the opportunity to put an end to their project. People generally regard June 5, 1967, as the day the Six Day War began. That is the official date. But in reality the Six Day War started two and a half years earlier, on the day Israel decided to act against the diversion of the Jordan. From then on the Syrian border was tense, prepared for the spark the Soviets would provide in the course of time.

*   *   *

Since Gali's death Lily had been a mother to Gur and our relationship had developed into one of deep love and strong friendship which was to profoundly affect the rest of my life. Eventually we had decided to get married. When I was appointed to the Northern Command, we had moved from Zahala to Nahalal, the oldest moshav in the country. Here we got a second-floor apartment in a farmhouse that belonged to Zevele Amit, my close friend who had served in Unit 101 and the paratroopers, and was now working for the Mossad. On this beautiful farm Gur, Lily, and I went through the final stages of recovering from Gali's death. There in August 1964 our family was enlarged with the birth of our son Omri, an alert, robust baby who immediately smiled his way into our hearts. He was the first, we hoped, of many more children, "seven at least," said Lily.

But at the same time we had some concern about how Gur would adjust to his new home. Coming to the countryside from the town life of Zahala he seemed anxious himself. In my family we had always had a prejudice that farm children were superior, and I wondered whether he would be able to fit in with the boys and girls who had grown up in Nahalal. But the worries turned out to be baseless, and Gur quickly made friends and integrated himself into the moshav activities.

Gur seemed to love everything about the farm, but most of all he was enchanted by horses. So for his ninth birthday Lily had the idea of surprising him with one of his own. Secretly we bought a beautiful gray mare and set her up in the barn. When Gur came home from school that day, we sent him out there on some errand, and when he came back his cheeks were glowing. "There's a horse in the barn," he announced in wonder. "Yes," I said, "we know about it. It's your horse."

From that day he rode the mare constantly, through all the fields and orchards and to every corner of the neighborhood. Even before this he had been demonstrating leadership qualities. He had emerged as one of the best students in his class and was extremely popular with all his friends. And now, well now he had a horse too.

It was a wonderful time. We even began to think about buying a farm there ourselves and staying. Once again I caught the smell of the fields, and the feel of living in a community of farmers doing hard physical work. It was something I had been deeply attached to and had hardly realized how much I missed. So even though I had relatively little time to be at home, I found myself enjoying Nahalal immensely.

But I could not say that life at the Northern Command Headquarters was equally enjoyable. After my first year there, Avraham Yoffe retired and was replaced by General David Elazar, later to become commander-in-chief. For me Yoffe's time in command had been blessedly free of sparring and dissension. Avraham Yoffe had been an ultimately secure man, capable and strong, the son of a farming family in Yavniel whose three boys were each as large and stout as tree trunks. He was not a person concerned in any way with jealousy or intrigues. But with the advent of Elazar the atmosphere changed: restrictions, tricks, suspicions—it all came back with a vengeance.

By the end of 1964 I felt I needed to get away from it and decided to take a leave of absence. Besides, the chance had come up to travel to Africa with Yoffe, who now had been appointed head of Israel's nature preserves.

At that time traveling from Israel to Africa was not a simple matter. Israel was closely involved on the continent as part of what was known as the "strategy of the periphery," developing contacts of all sorts with nations lying beyond the Arab ring. But actually getting to these places took some doing. The Egyptians were back in the Sinai, so one could not fly across there. Nor was it easy to find a way through the rest of the contiguous belt of Arab air space.

In the end we flew on a military cargo plane bound to Entebbe, Uganda, with a load of parachute equipment to be used in some demonstration. We took off from Tel Nof, my old base, and passed over Eilat heading south. As night fell, we crossed briefly over Saudi territory in order to get as far as possible from Sharm al-Sheikh, where the Egyptians had a radar station. As we flew over the black Saudi mountains, I stood in the doorway of the cockpit with a cup of coffee warming my hands. Watching the moon rise in front of us gave me an expansive feeling. In that moment it seemed that Israel was not such a small and isolated country after all. Its citizens were working in far-off places, and its planes even had the temerity to fly by night over the lands of its enemies. Then the mountains disappeared into the darkness and we were above the Red Sea watching for the lights of Jedda to come up on our left.

In the early morning we landed in Masawa, Ethiopia, where an Israeli crew was waiting to refuel us. Then we took off again, climbing to get above the Amhara Mountains in whose midst lay Addis Ababa, the Ethiopian capital. There we refueled again and headed southwest toward the Kenyan border, where we ran into a thunderstorm that forced us down low over bush and jungle, almost to treetop level. I had never seen anything like it. Just below the plane the land stretched out, immense and green; and as the plane bumped along, I moved back and forth among the unobstructed windows trying to get a better view.

We entered Uganda over a place called Moroto, then flew on to Entebbe, the plane's final destination. There we picked up a car and began our tour of Uganda, crisscrossing the country from the source of the Nile at Lake Victoria to the magnificent ˜ature preserves at Murchison Falls and Lake George.

After several days of sightseeing we found ourselves back in Moroto, the place we had flown over on our way in. Moroto was as primitive a bush town as I had ever seen, but it had its own strange connection with Zionism and the Jews. In the early years of the century the British had considered giving this region to Theodor Herzl as a Jewish homeland, a concept that fortunately had not found favor with the Zionist movement of those days.

In Moroto, Yoffe and I went to stock up on canned foods and found ourselves queuing up at a little store together with a group of tall Karamojo tribal people. Our queue mates were naked—the men completely, the women wearing only hide loincloths. They carried small three-legged stools so that they could sit down without encountering the biting insects that swarmed on the ground. Though Uganda had magnificently beautiful areas, this was not one of them; and Yoffe and I rolled our eyes at the thought that it might have been an alternative Israel.

From Uganda we crossed into Kenya at Lake Nakuru, a place breathtaking for the countless numbers of flamingos that live there, feeding on the small mollusks and crustaceans in the shallow waters. Thousands of these tall, graceful birds crowded the lake, a shifting living mass of pink and white. When they began moving, it was like watching a cloud come to life.

The highlands of Kenya reminded me of nothing so much as England, very green and dotted with English-style farms left over from the colonial period. But on this trip we were more interested in seeing the wilderness areas, so we drove on toward Tanzania to visit Amboseli and Ngorongoro

Crater, the most wonderful preserve of all, with its huge herds of antelope, graceful impala, and long-necked Gerenuk deer, zebras, gnus, waterbucks, and water buffalo with their wide backs and coarse coats. Among them we could see lionesses hunting and lions striding in to dine first at the kill.

From there we drove southward, just the two of us. For days we saw only animals, around Moshi and Kilimanjaro with its mantle of snow. Yoffe, the great nature lover and expert, was speechless at the profusion of creatures and hardly noticed when I mentioned, only half joking, that it would be nice to have some human company for a change.

After Kilimanjaro we drove back to Kenya, stopping in the Tsavo National Preserve, another one of the great African game parks. Usually in such places visitors spend their nights in hotels or guest houses. But we wanted to stay out in the bush, and in Tsavo we had a chance to do it. Hiring a little hut near one of the watering holes, we ate a dinner out of cans and settled in to watch the animals come down in the evening to drink.

Under the dark red sunset they came, the impalas and gnus and waterbucks, also a herd of zebra snorting nervously. Wild boars trotted arrogantly down to the water's edge, and a family of lions made their appearance, too majestic to pay attention to any of the others. Yoffe and I sat there absolutely still. It was impossible to find a word that might add anything to the scene we had become part of, as if no language was capable of expressing what we felt. Even back in the hut afterward there wasn't a word. We went to sleep that night in utter silence.

Driving out of the park the next day, we saw a commotion stirring among three rhinoceros a little way into the bush. In our little English car we left the road and drove closer where we could get a better look. As we did, a terrible fight broke out between two of them, massive males vying for the favors of the female who stood aside and watched the uproar with less than avid interest. After a few minutes the battle subsided and the female disappeared into the bush with the victorious male. The other one stood there for several minutes, disappointed and angry. Then he turned and began lumbering in our direction. I drove off as fast as the car would go, Yoffe craning his neck to see if he was still coming.

Leaving Tsavo, we drove to Nairobi, from where we intended to cross into Ethiopia. But a tribal revolt near the Somali border forced us to change our plans, and we flew instead. At Addis Ababa we spent some time looking around and planning the next stage of the trip. Haile

Selassie was still emperor then, with unlimited power, and Israel was playing a substantial role in the country. Our military people were there training the Ethiopian army, some of whose officers and NCO's were attending courses in Israel. Our agricultural experts were there too, working with the Ethiopian peasants, while Israeli architects and engineers were helping plan development.

But the connection between the two countries went deeper than co-operation in matters like these. Haile Selassie called himself the Lion of Judah, and the Ethiopians considered themselves descendants of King Solomon and the Queen of Sheba. In the discussions we struck up with them they all talked about this, from the intellectuals, to the court people, to the peasants. The idea seemed ingrained in their sense of themselves.

Another distinguishing characteristic of the country was the combination of elegance and savagery that seemed to co-exist in uneasy balance everywhere we looked. In Ethiopia an ancient civilization was wedded to a primitive wildness in a contrast that was occasionally startling. At one point we were invited to a marriage reception for the newly crowned Ethiopian beauty queen. The affair was elegant in the extreme, attended by strikingly handsome men and exquisite women, all of whom displayed the kind of courtly manners that have to be bred from tradition. Above the lavish buffet tables hung a number of large objects shrouded in white linen, like sculptures waiting to be unveiled. We couldn't imagine what they were or what their purpose was. Then as the guests moved into the buffet room, the waiters suddenly stripped them back to reveal whole quarters of freshly slaughtered cows from which each diner could choose his own cut.

Ethiopia was full of places that I wanted to see. Harar, Gondar, Asmara, Keren—all these names I remembered reading about as a child when the Italians invaded in 1936, then when the British penetrated from the Sudan in 1941 and retook the country in what was perhaps their first victory of the war.

We drove first to Gondar, high on the Ethiopian escarpment. The route through the mountains was a twisting serpentine of a road the Italians had carved out of the sheer walls using forced Ethiopian labor. Hugging the massive walls and peaks, it skirted the edge of perpendicular drops that looked down into chasms of heartstopping depth. The story of this and the other Italian roads told of thousands of workers killed during construction along the dizzying heights. Merely driving these roads made my hands sweat.

Along the rugged mountains and high plateaus we saw hundreds of walkers, tall peasants wearing pants and robes, striding purposefully along with their long walking sticks. We could not imagine where they might be going in this desolate region, or why. The villages and hamlets here were as bleak as the landscape, poverty-stricken collections of huts unalleviated by any trace of either the ancient Ethiopian culture or the Italian influence that marked other areas.

But some of these tribal people of Gondar had a special meaning for us, for they were Jews. Even the language, Amharic, appeared to include words of Hebrew origin. "Amharic" itself—from "am," Hebrew for "people," and "har," "mountain." The robber bands that plagued the mountains they called "shifta," like the Hebrew "shevet," "tribe." We talked with them as much as we could, though our means were frustratingly limited. When they learned that we ourselves were Jews, their eyes showed their emotions—surprise and, so it seemed to me, longing. They wondered about us, trying to make out the connection. What touched me was that here was a Jewish tribe that millennia ago had been cut off from the mainstream of Judaism. Yet still they nurtured their racial memories and they treasured their connection. Years later I was to be involved in their evacuation to Israel. The Red Sea, they believed, was a river upon which they would sail to Jerusalem.

Leaving Gondar, we followed the serpentine toward Asmara, the capital of Eritrea, sharing the road with an occasional giant Fiat tractor-trailer. In this land of no garages, every driver is his own mechanic; and once in a while we would come across one of these Fiat rigs pulled onto a turn-out or side road, its driver working unhurriedly on some repair.

In Uganda and Kenya we had been driving an Austin Mini, but now we had an old VW Beetle provided by the Israeli embassy in Addis Ababa. Halfway along the road from Gondar to Asmara the Beetle decided to break down. When neither Yoffe nor I could fix it, we flagged a truck and tied the car behind its long trailer. Yoffe climbed into the cab with the driver and I stayed in the Beetle to steer.

In the late afternoon light, maneuvering behind the truck was easy enough. But when dark fell it got harder. As an hour passed, then two, I felt sickened by the exhaust fumes. Then the battery started giving out and the headlights dimmed and went out. I couldn't see a thing. The truck swung around curve after curve as I tried to sense how to steer. I pressed the horn to warn Yoffe that I was in trouble. It made a low edgy beep, then died. There was no reaction from the truck, which kept picking up speed as it barreled down the mountain. I fought to suppress a rising panic. Opening the window, I yelled at the top of my lungs into the dust and fumes. No one heard. I couldn't imagine what might have happened to Yoffe. After a while I stopped shouting, thinking that I had better preserve my strength, telling myself over and over to keep calm. On we went, curve after curve, the rope swinging the Beetle out toward where I thought the edge must be. I struggled to keep control, knowing that eventually we had to stop. Down the mountain we drove, into the pitch-dark night, hour after hour.

We had started at around five. By the time the truck pulled to a halt in Asmara it was almost ten. I got out of the Beetle shaking and enervated from the ordeal. As Yoffe opened the cabin door and climbed down, I said, "Avraham, what happened?" His expression was mixed embarrassment and consternation. "Arik, thank God you're all right. I was so tired. I was watching, but then I just fell asleep."

I spent the next day in an Asmara hotel room recuperating from the ordeal. But the day after I was back on my feet, and we drove off to see the city of Keren, about seventy-five miles to the north. Close to the Sudan border, Keren was the site of the first British penetration into Ethiopia in 1941. There Yoffe and I found the battlefield and imagined what the fighting must have looked like, comparing it to the pictures we had in our minds from having read the accounts all those years ago. We located the British military cemetery too, one of the hundreds of burial grounds that mark the course of Great Britain's empire. Among its graves we found those of the Israeli boys who had fought with the Fifty-first Commandos. They, like their British comrades, had never been brought home.

Another trip we made was to the famous walled city of Harar. But after so much driving it was a disappointment. I had expected something like the walls of Jerusalem, but although Harar's walls were ornate and picturesque, they also turned out to be a good deal lower and not nearly so massive. At night we stood on them and watched the hyenas prowling around the outside.

We had also made up our minds to visit what was reputed to be one of the most interesting sights in Ethiopia, the Awash River. This river flows through the Danakil Desert, then abruptly disappears into the sands. At the place it disappears, hot springs and sulphur pools dot the landscape, products, perhaps, of the same geological aberration that swallows the river. The desert around is inhabited by Danakil nomads, primitive camel herders with a reputation for savagery. Tourists are warned away from this area, which is considered too dangerous for ordinary travel.

Only recently a British pilot had made a forced landing in the desert and had been killed there. He had fallen victim to a Danakil tradition according to which the most precious gift a nomad groom can present to his intended bride is the testicles of an enemy. Receiving such a gift, the bride displays them on her forehead to proclaim the honor that has been paid her. The British pilot had been castrated and had hemorrhaged to death, after which the Ethiopian army had inflicted their own cruel punishment on the tribesmen.

But none of this dissuaded Yoffe or me. After all, we had not approached this African trip as tourists. We had read books on the peoples and places we planned to visit and had studied maps, which we both loved, in great detail. We knew exactly where we were going, and we would only be in the desert one brief afternoon anyway. It seemed silly to worry about anything happening. The one concession we made—after a minor argument in which I gave in—was to take along a boy guide from a neighboring village in addition to our Ethiopian driver.

To get to the Awash it was necessary to leave the main road and drive along a dirt track that led the twenty or so miles to the site where the river disappeared. The deeper we penetrated into the bush, the more we saw of the Danakils. All of them went armed, invariably with an old Italian rifle, a spear, and an ornate knife stuck into their belts. The men's hair was coifed with a dressing of dried mud and manure, the eligible bachelors distinguishing themselves by a red coloring. Among the herders looking after their cattle and camels, we saw quite a few of the red dressings.

We were heading for a place where there was a famous hot pond, in which Haile Selassie himself was said to bathe from time to time. The deeper into the desert we drove, the lonelier we felt. When we finally got there, the place seemed deserted. On an old bench by the side of the water we took our clothes off, then we immersed ourselves in the slightly sulphurous pool.

The water was lovely, warm and soothing. But we both felt more than a hint of apprehension. Nobody was in sight, but the sound of camel bells tinkled softly in the distance, and we had the sensation we were being watched by unseen eyes. Just beyond this pool was the place where the river disappeared. It was there, then suddenly it wasn't. Just like that. We floated in the buoyant water and took it all in, trying to register the scene and the experience and at the same time swearing softly at ourselves for having left the embassy in Addis Ababa without weapons.

But except for camel bells in the distance, the landscape was quiet and empty; and after a short time we came out of the water and dressed, happy to be on our way. Driving back, we traced the course of the hidden river and saw still, lustrous ponds dotting what we imagined was its subterranean path.

Around one of the largest of these we came on hundreds of camels drinking. This herd was attended by beautiful, young Danakil women, naked from the waist up. Neither Yoffe nor I could tear our eyes away. But as the car moved slowly by, we were both struck by the thought that exactly these maidens were the potential brides of the red-haired warriors we had seen earlier. "You know, don't you," I said to him, "that there is only one thing these beautiful girls and those red-haired boys need for their engagements to be complete. Only one thing is missing, and you and I have it."

Five minutes later the car coughed and stopped dead. I bolted out one side, Avraham the other. The driver and the village boy stayed inside, huddled down, trying to make themselves invisible. Quickly I began a methodical examination of the engine, opening up the carburetor, then everything else I could think of that might have gone wrong. Soon Danakil warriors were sauntering around, not too close but frankly taking in the scene. In this kind of situation you have to show you are not afraid. So you have to look calm and strong. But not defiant. You can't give any indication that maybe there is something in your car that you are ready to defend, something consequently that they might like to have. While we tried our best to convey the right impression, I did absolutely everything I could think of to the engine—cleaning parts, taking them apart, putting them back together. I worked like mad. But nothing happened. The thing was dead.

Finally I found what was wrong, an electrical part that needed to be replaced, something I simply could not fix. Yoffe and I talked briefly and decided that one of us would have to get back to the village. I would stay behind with the driver—trying to jerry-rig some kind of hookup. Avraham would take the boy and start walking. As they left, I worked feverishly over the engine, but not so feverishly that I didn't notice the driver. He had climbed into the back seat and curled up into a fetal position.

With Yoffe gone, I had no one to talk to. I cursed myself for being such a poor mechanic and I cursed myself doubly for having gotten into this impossibly stupid situation. Here I had been through all these deadly battles in my life, all over, in Jordan, Syria, Egypt. I had fought and been wounded, and all for the highest cause. And now I was going to lose my life for nothing. It was unbelievable.

As I worked, I laid out a plan. I would keep trying to fix the thing until dark, making myself conspicuous. Then when night fell I would take the driver, move away from the car and find a hiding place. I knew they would come at night. Already it was dusk. Then, just as I was waiting for the right moment to move off, I heard the sound of engines in the distance and saw lights, a small convoy racing down the dirt track. As the convoy drew near I jumped out to wave them down. Just in front of me the three trucks lurched to a halt. A man jumped out and barked in English, "What are you doing here? Do you have a gun?"

"No."

"Then what are you doing here?"

"My car's stuck. Who are you?"

They were a local antimalarial team. When I told them I wasn't alone, that I had a friend who was walking toward the village with our guide, they were incredulous. "How can you do something like this?" the team head shouted. "It's unbelievable! We will not find them alive! You cannot do these things." Tying the VW to the third truck, we set off in search of Avraham. My heart was knocking. I couldn't believe I had let him go. We drove on for twenty or twenty-five minutes under the darkening sky. Then, miraculously, we came across a large man and a boy walking very fast in the direction of the village. When we picked him up, Avraham told me that during the whole walk he was kicking himself for his irresponsibility in leaving me behind.

Having seen quite enough of the Danakil Desert, we drove back to Addis Ababa. We had been in Africa for five weeks, and it was time to go home. At the embassy we were told that an Israeli plane would be coming to Djibouti and that we could fly back on that. Meanwhile we could get to Djibouti on one of the old DC-3s that flew the cargo routes around

Ethiopia. When we found a cargo flight that was going our way, it turned out that the entire plane was filled with khat, a kind of chewing marijuana used by almost everyone in the region. Yes, we could go as passengers, but no, there were no passenger seats. We could lie on the khat.

In Djibouti we waited for several days, lolling on the beach and making our last rounds of the bazaars, until the promised flight arrived. I went home loaded down with Masai spears, Danakil knives, and bows and arrows for Gur and jewelry and native crafts for Lily. I brought back with me as well images and experiences of Africa that I would not soon forget.

Arik in a Purim costume at Kfar Malal, the moshav where he was born in 1928.

Arik with his favorite dog, Shpitz, at his home village, Kfar Malal, 1933.

1

2

3

4

Arik with his mother, Vera, and sister, Dita, on a haystack in Kfar Malal.

Arik's father's self-portrait, done in 1949.

5

6

7

1941. In Kfar Malal the work was constant, as were the unique joys of farm life (5). Margalit, Sharon's first wife (6). In June of 1945, Arik was seventeen years old and ready to graduate from high school. He prepared to leave for training at a secret Haganah course for squad leaders being held at Kibbutz Ruhama on the edge of the Negev Desert (7). Winter, 1948. Sharon leading his platoon, most of whom were lost in the War of Independence (8).

8

9

December 12, 1955. Dayan greeting the returning troops on a landing craft returning across the Sea of Galilee from a raid against the Syrian army led by Sharon.

Mordechai Makleff, IDF chief of staff, decided to establish a commando unit and asked Sharon to lead it. Unit 101, which lasted only five months, had a substantial impact on the country's effort to rid itself of terrorism. The men of 101 met with Moshe Dayan in the Negev Desert.

10

11

August 19, 1955. Sharon briefing Parachute Battalion 890 prior to the raid on the Egyptian headquarters in Han-Yunis in the Gaza district.

12

In December 1953, when Dayan became chief of staff, he decided to merge 101 with the paratroop unit. Here the men of 101, indignant at the decision, listen to Sharon reminding them of their very fine record of achievements.

13

October 30, 1955. The paratroop commanders after the raid on Kontilla. From left to right, standing: Meir Har-Zion, Sharon, Dayan, Danny Mat, Moshe Efron, Asaf Simchon; sitting: Ahron Davidi (Arik's deputy), Yaacov Yaacov, Eitan Rafael (Raful).

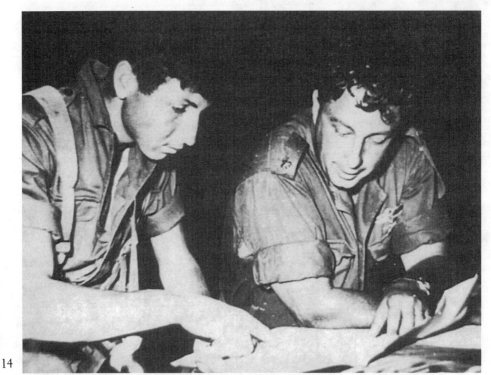

14

1954. With Meir Har-Zion, the man Moshe Dayan later called "the finest of our commando soldiers."

Starting in 1954, the paratroopers carried out almost every single operation undertal by the Israeli army.

15

16

1957. Ben-Gurion often had Arik sit next to him, which provoked the animosity of senior officers.

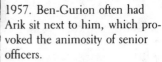

Ben-Gurion and Sharon reviewing the paratroop guard of honor in 1955.

17

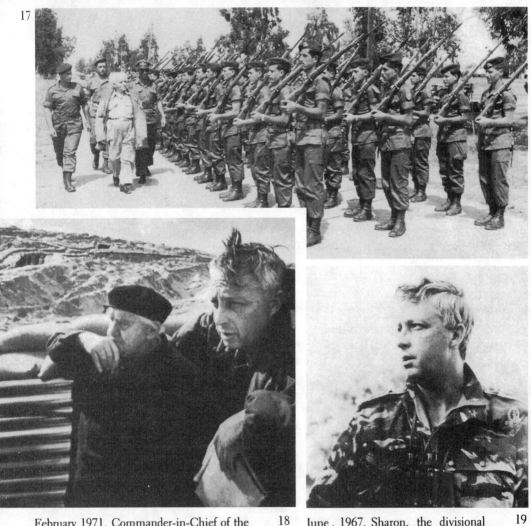

February 1971, Commander-in-Chief of the Southern Command Sharon with David Ben-Gurion on the bank of the Suez Canal.

18

June, 1967. Sharon, the divisional commander, during the Six Day War in the Sinai.

19

20

October 17, 1973, in the afternoon, a few
hours after Sharon was hit (20). October 17,
1973. Dayan's and Sharon's first smiles after
returning from the other side of the Suez (21).
July 15, 1973. Sharon leaving his post as
Commander-in-Chief of the Southern Command (22).

21

22

With Patsy, during the tank battle at
the Suez Canal.

24

25

October 1973, with Chief
Rabbi Shlomo Goren during
the Yom Kippur War (24). October 1973, near the Suez Canal. A lone commander (25).
October 15, 1973, 7:00 A.M.
Sharon giving final orders to
top command officers prior to
the crossing of the Canal (26).

27

26

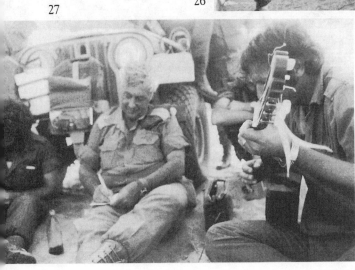

Writing the first letter to
Lily from Egypt after the
cease-fire in October
1973 (27).

29   28

The pontoon bridge that was
completed on October 17 in
the afternoon.

October 16, 1973, 6:00 A.M.
Sharon's division—the First
Tank Platoon—crossing the
Suez Canal.

The great roller bridge across the Suez Canal was assembled with difficulty because
the Seventh Brigade, which had been trained for the job, was then fighting on the
Syrian front.

30

34   1967. Arik with his three sons, baby Gilad, Omri, and Gur (31). October 1929. Arik's   33
father examining a young orchard on his farm (32). January 1975. Arik examining a
young orchard on his farm (33). August 1967. Arik with Gur near the Yarmuk River
on the Israeli/Syrian/Jordanian border (34).

36

35

February 1974. After the Yom Kippur War. Arik is riding his favorite horse, Yardena, on the farm (35). 1972. The camel patrol on standby (36). Security for Sharon was always bound up with the settlements. Here he points to the settlement planned for Judea and Samaria (37). September 1982. Sharon with U.S. Secretary of Defense Caspar Weinberger on a mountain in Samaria east of Kalkilya overlooking the coastal plain, explaining the settlement plan (38).

38

37

39

November 1981. Sharon with Mobuto Sese Seko. A strong antagonism toward Khaddafi was one of the things that brought the two men together.

Sharon being sworn in as Minister of Defense by Menachem Begin in 1981.

40

41

January 17, 1982. Lily and Arik visiting the City of the Suez on the way to Cairo, with the Governor of the Suez and Israel's Ambassador to Egypt, Moshe Sasson.

42

May 1981. With Sadat who
had committed himself to the
peace process because he recognized that only through a negotiated settlement did he have a
chance of regaining the Sinai.

43

Sharon meeting with President Numeiri of the
Sudan, May 13, 1982, and giving him an Uzi sub-
machine gun as an official gift.

November 30, 1981. Sharon
and Weinberger exchanging the
just-executed Strategic Memorandum of Understanding between Israel and the U.S.

44

45

May 1982. Sharon with U.S.
Secretary of State Alexander
Haig, after briefing him on the
terrorist activities from Lebanon.

46   January 19, 1982. In Cairo with President Hosni Mubarak and Kamal Hassan-Ali, Deputy Prime Minister and Foreign Minister of Egypt at the time.

47   With Caspar Weinberger at the Pentagon, November 30, 1981.

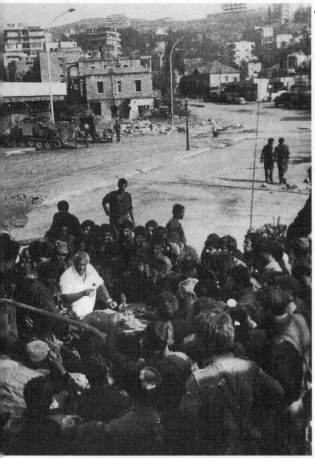

June 24, 1982. On the Beirut-Damascus road, which had just been severed.

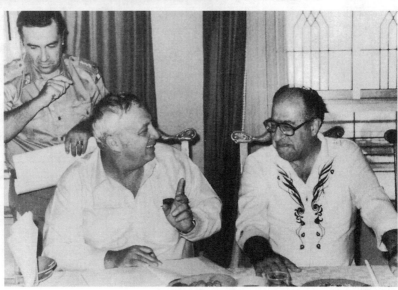

September 1982. Sharon and Philip Habib, with Lebanese officer looking on, celebrating the completion of the PLO terrorist organization's expulsion from Beirut.

50 February 1982. Bashir Gemayel was eager to deepen and specify the long-term relationship the Maronites had maintained with Israel. Shown here during Sharon's secret visit to Beirut five months before the war.

51 August 1983. With Lily, and Pierre Gemayel, father of the murdered President-elect Bashir Gemayel and head of the Phalange in Beirut.

52

January 1985. Sharon on the steps of Foley Square courthouse with his lawyer, Mr. Gould.

53   Arik and Lily in a wheat field.

14

War in the Desert

Coming back to the Northern Command, I found that another chief of staff had been appointed while I was away. I had not been relieved; they had just appointed someone else to share the duty. It was a bizarre situation, unpleasant and delicate, and it make me treasure the year I had worked under Yoffe more than ever.

From then until the fall of 1965 I stepped as lightly as I could through a mine field of bickering and intrigue. Then in October I became a candidate for promotion. At that point I left the Northern Command and went home, expecting my new appointment to come through any day. But Yitzhak Rabin kept putting the decision off, and as he did I just sat at home waiting. I waited for three months. It's a strange time psychologically, as I knew from previous experience. Everybody watches you—your colleagues, your friends, your enemies. They wonder what is going to happen and when it will happen. They wonder how you feel about it. But nobody gets in touch; nobody calls. You are left at home by yourself to brood.

Lily did everything she could to support me during this period, giving me the love and friendship I needed, being a true partner to me. But I still did not find it easy. On the one hand there were a million little things to do. On the other, I didn't have patience for any of them. Every morning

I took Gur's mare and went riding in the mountains of lower Galilee. I rode for days on end, and while I loved being on horseback and exploring, I was also exasperated at the waste of time.

At last Rabin invited me in for a talk—a very blunt talk, as it turned out, with no pulled punches. He let me know precisely how he felt about my performance—the things I had done wrong, my relationship with Northern Command chief Elazar, everything. As he was going through it, I fully expected him to tell me that I would not be receiving a promotion after all, that that was it.

So it was something of a surprise to hear him finish up the litany of my failings by saying that despite the criticisms I was now promoted to major general and appointed as director of military training. At the same time, I would serve as commander of a reserve division.

I was as happy as I was surprised. Lily prepared a small party, and many of our friends from the moshav came to help celebrate. Our apartment in the farmhouse was crowded with people and flowers, a wonderfully warm occasion. Not too long afterward we moved back to the house in Zahala so that I could be closer to my new headquarters. There, six months later our third son, Gilad Yehuda, was born. Our dream of having a large family seemed on its way to being fulfilled.

On the evening of May 14, 1967, I was in Jerusalem watching a military parade, part of the festivities celebrating Israel's nineteenth year of independence. During the parade, word began to spread that large Egyptian forces were moving across the Suez Canal and into Sinai.

It was a surprising development. Up till then, conditions on the Egyptian front had been quite calm. U.N. forces were spread out along the border, and the terrorism from Gaza had been dramatically reduced. Nor was there any conflict between the Egyptian and Israeli armies. For the last five years Nasser's forces had been heavily involved in an inconclusive war in Yemen, where they were supporting a leftist revolution. As a result they had had little energy left for border fights with us.

It was not along the Egyptian front that tension was high, but along the border with Syria, and to a lesser extent with Jordan. Ever since the confrontation in 1964 over the Jordan River diversion, hostilities here had deepened. Palestinian terror squads based in Syria had intensified their attacks on Israeli settlements, most often infiltrating via Jordan and

Lebanon. From their fortifications on the Golan Heights, Syrian artillery regularly pounded the border settlements and Israeli efforts to farm the Huleh Valley. The previous month, an episode of especially heavy shelling had precipitated Israeli air strikes against the gun positions. When Syrian interceptors took to the air, dogfights developed and six Migs were shot down, two of them over the outskirts of Damascus. We knew the Syrians were chafing under their inability to respond to the Israeli attack and that they were talking to Nasser about assistance. We also knew the Soviets were giving false intelligence to both the Syrians and Egyptians about a supposed Israeli buildup along the Syrian frontier, and that they were urging Nasser to take forceful action. But no one had expected the Egyptian dictator to make this particular move.

A day or two after the Egyptian advance I was with my reserve division in the Negev, where we were in charge of the central area of the border. Although we had been mobilized, to this point nothing really had happened. We had been surprised by the Egyptian deployment, but at this moment there seemed to be a kind of stand-off. Their forces were concentrating, but ours were there as well. It did not seem to me a life-threatening situation. We were not, after all, the Israel of 1956, let alone of 1948. We were a different country, no longer in our infancy. We were involved in all those activities around the world; we had contacts, relations; we had experience in solving problems. We were decidedly not an isolated, fragile people whose survival was open to doubt.

I worked my forces day and night. A brigade of armor came into the division to complement the two brigades of infantry. The divisional artillery was activated. I trained the soldiers hard. And not only the soldiers. I trained the officers too. Every morning they were all running and jumping and crawling, going through a rigorous course of physical conditioning. I did everything necessary to get all the reservists into shape. And they responded beautifully—physically and mentally. The division was full of vigor and self-confidence. I had no question at all that if it came to a fight we could handle the Egyptians in front of us.

But almost from the beginning I was aware of a sense of confusion and indecision at General Headquarters. I didn't know what it stemmed from, but I saw the results of it every day in the field. Additional units were attached to my division, then taken back. Other divisions were moving here and there, crossing each other's paths and taking up positions, only to move back from them a day later and take up different ones. You could feel the nervousness and doubt. There was none of the calm seriousness that comes with having deliberate, well-planned goals. The army did not look as if it knew what it was doing.

Meanwhile the Egyptian pressure mounted. On May 19, U Thant, the U.N. secretary general, gave in to Nasser's request that all U.N. forces be removed from the Sinai. On May 22, Nasser declared the Strait of Tiran closed to Israeli shipping, an act that Israel had long ago declared it would regard as a casus belli. By now a hundred thousand Egyptian troops were in the Sinai, along with more than a thousand battle tanks. And still there was no clear government decision about how we should react.

Disturbed by the continued confusion and all the frantic movement, one day I put in a call to Rabin, only to be told that he was sick in bed. Rumor had it that he had suffered a nervous collapse. Several days later Levi Eshkol came to the Southern Command headquarters accompanied by Yigal Allon, the minister of labor who had been the brightest of the Israeli generals during the Independence War. Allon, as everyone knew, expected shortly to be named minister of defense in place of Eshkol, who was at that moment functioning both as prime minister and defense minister. By now Rabin had recovered, and he was there too, as were all the senior commanders on the front. It was a downbeat meeting. The general opinion seemed to be that we could not cope with the entire Egyptian army at once, so we would have to proceed in phases, hoping to limit the scope of confrontation. In Phase A, our goal would be to capture the Gaza Strip and a little to the west of it. That, they were sure, we would be able to do. Once that was accomplished, we would start to negotiate with the Egyptians, pressing them to open the Strait of Tiran in return for their reoccupation of Gaza.

Israel Tal, the commander of the division that faced Gaza and northern Sinai, stood and explained how the operation would be done. Tal was one of the finest generals we had ever had and a world authority on armor, a man who could break a tank down into a thousand parts and reassemble them without pausing. (He would later design the Merkava, Israel's main battle tank.) But when it came to making public presentations, Tal's meticulous devotion to detail did not always serve him well.

This was one of those occasions. Instead of laying the essentials of the plan out for Eshkol, he began describing in technical terms the capabilities and missions of the various tank regiments. "The 334th Regional Tank Unit ('GASHAP' in Hebrew, a military acronym), with modified Shermans, caliber of gun, 76-mm, which has the capability of piercing the armor of the T-34 Soviet tank at such and such a point when the angle of the projectile is forty-five degrees. Also with the Patton M-48 tank . . ." and so on through the entire order of battle. I was sitting very close to Eshkol, and when Tal began talking about the GASHAP, the prime minister leaned over to Yigal Allon and whispered in Yiddish, "Vas ist das Gashap?" When Tal described the 76-mm guns hitting the T-34s, Eshkol's expression grew troubled; and I could hear him muttering, "And what if the T-34s aren't standing at the correct angle?" The longer Tal went on, the more worried Eshkol became.

When Rabin gave me permission to express my view, I tried to be as positive and forceful as possible. I told the prime minister that in my opinion the Israeli army could defeat the Egyptians utterly, there was no doubt of it. I warned against going in phases. After the fighting we would be in a position of political weakness. If the Egyptians did not meet our demands, we would already be under great pressure from the Americans as well as the Soviets. (I vividly recalled Ben-Gurion's plight after the Sinai campaign.) We would not be able to resist and we would become weaker by the day. With the army mobilized, the country would be at a standstill. Going by phases was asking for a disaster, and it was completely unnecessary.

When the meeting was concluded Eshkol said to me privately, "Arik, what you are saying is irresponsible! You are irresponsible!" As he told me after the war, the universal advice he had been getting was that the most we would be capable of was taking Gaza. So with opinions like that on every side, what else could he think? And of course Eshkol did have a terribly difficult decision to make, the most difficult decision. But as he racked himself over what to do, the nation's confidence began to evaporate, and that I felt was the gravest danger of all.

A few days later the impression of Eshkol as a man lacking in strength and decisiveness was confirmed when he addressed the nation in a radio speech. Instead of self-confidence and determination in the face of crisis, Eshkol's speech conveyed hesitancy and doubt. He stammered and tripped over his words; he seemed unsure and confused. By the time he was finished, the crisis of leadership was full blown.

That evening the southern front divisional commanders were asked to come to the operations center in Tel Aviv. The three of us—Israel Tal, Avraham Yoffe (who had been called out of retirement), and I—all felt the seriousness of the moment. But for several weeks now we had been working with our divisions, and none of us had any doubts about their capabilities. With the political echelon so obviously at a loss, we felt as if the burden was on our shoulders. We were three very determined men.

Deep underground in the operations center we met with Eshkol, Yigal Allon, Rabin, and others; and as Eshkol described the situation it was evident he was in a state of depression. He appeared somehow helpless, as if he was looking for someone to support him. When he asked how we saw things, Yoffe, Quartermaster General Matti Peled, and I all spoke strongly and to the same point. Now was the time for us to move, without any more delays. Each day that passed gave the Egyptians more time to deploy their forces and dig themselves in. The Egyptian soldiers were all from the green Nile Delta, and though their country was surrounded by desert, they hated and feared it. But now we were giving them the chance to orient themselves. Every day they became more comfortable with the Sinai, and more knowledgeable about it.

I felt that we had to move now and that it would be a major mistake to go in phases, to first take Gaza, then to stop and talk, for example. With every round of talking and fighting we would find ourselves weaker and under greater pressure to give up what we had accomplished. We all knew how hard it was to make the decision to go to war. But this war was being thrust on us, and our situation was becoming more dangerous by the moment.

Taking every consideration into account, I said that we had no choice but to strike and that right now we were capable of defeating the entire Egyptian army, without any doubt. I was as strong as I could be about it. I spoke about the danger of losing national self-confidence. I spoke about the issue of deterrence, that the psychology of deterrence was something that had taken us years and years to build, but everything we had built could be lost overnight.

The talk went on for hours; it was a serious, grim meeting. Afterward Rabin took us aside and said, "There's only one element that can stand now, and that is the army. That's why our responsibility is so grave. It all depends on us now, all of it."

Though I did not say it aloud, inside I could not blame Eshkol and the other political leaders for their doubts. I thought, rather, that their hesitancy was mostly due to the lack of confidence among so many of the military. For years I had been lecturing officers that they should not expect the political leadership to push them to act. "The political echelon," I would tell them, "has to have the freedom to make choices, to take either political or military steps. Our job is to give them the freedom to decide. They will set the political goals, the strategic goals.

And we have to be in a position to show that these goals can be achieved. That is our duty." And now I felt that the political echelon had lost its self-confidence primarily because the military had not shown the determination that in this hour was so desperately needed.

Just before he left, Eshkol asked me one question: Did I think it would change the situation if he appointed Moshe Dayan minister of defense? The question was no surprise. Already we had heard that Allon had lost support for the job and that Dayan's appointment was virtually certain. And Dayan himself had been visiting the southern front units, though as a private citizen. (In fact his daughter Yael was attached to my division as a military reporter.) "For myself," I told Eshkol, "as a commander who has to lead his soldiers, it doesn't make the slightest difference who the minister of defense is. As far as Dayan is concerned, I appreciate him and his abilities tremendously. But when it comes to how my division will fight, you could invite Beba Idelson [the aged leader of the women's labor union] to be minister of defense. You, or Dayan, or Beba Idelson, it makes no difference." As a matter of fact it was true. Eshkol could have won the war himself; Tal and Yoffe and I would have fought exactly the same way under him as under anyone else.

Afterward we flew back to our divisions with the feeling that it really did depend on us. In the coming days we planned and replanned. The concept changed. Now we were to attack not just in Gaza but all along the front, though still the attack was to go in stages. One division first, then the other two twelve hours later. I argued vehemently against that in what seemed like endless debates. It would be a waste not to attack simultaneously everywhere, to devastate the entire Egyptian army at once.

Day after day there were changes in the order of battle. Units were being taken away from me and given to others. But through it all I strove to make my division a cornerstone of self-confidence. Each time some unit would be taken from us, I would adjust the plan of battle. I never allowed myself to say, "Look, if I do not have such and such a force the job will be impossible." I just adapted the plan. We trained all the time, under very tight discipline. And from day to day I became more sure of our ability, more convinced that we were capable of achieving a truly great victory.

My conviction was reinforced when one day we captured five Egyptians, including an officer, who had crossed the border by accident. They had simply gotten lost. Talking to them, I was impressed by their disorientation. The desert barrens were still strange to them, and daunting.

On Friday, June 2, Yoffe, Tal, and I were again invited to Tel Aviv. This time the entire inner cabinet was there in the operations center, including Dayan, who had just been appointed minister of defense. Sitting to his left, I scribbled a note to him. "Moshe, it seems to me the plan is still to move in phases. In my opinion we should not undertake an operation that will not break the Egyptian main forces. Gaza is not the target!" "Arik," he wrote back, "I've asked Yitzhak to meet this evening to discuss the plans."

During this meeting, various members of the headquarters staff talked, offering several ideas. But again Yoffe, Matti Peled, and I took a strong, united line. Peled got up and again argued lucidly about the need to attack without any more delay, emphasizing that we could not afford to stay mobilized forever. I focused my own remarks on our ability to get the job done and on the need to act decisively to retain our long-term deterrence credibility. As we had talked to Eshkol several days before, now we said the same things to the entire cabinet, and even more firmly.

That evening the field commanders were asked to present our plans to Rabin and his staff with Dayan present. It was like a fresh wind. After so much confusion and so many changes, at last we were able to clarify the overall approach and make the final adjustments. We came away from that meeting knowing that the plans were now clear and as effective as we could make them. From this point on we were ready to move on a moment's notice.

The Sinai's southern triangle is a land of treacherous mountains, sawtooth ridges, and wild dunes. It is in the north that several roads and tracks cut through the desert, leading from the Suez Canal to the Israeli border. The northern half of the Sinai was also the site of all the major Egyptian fortifications and bases, where five of the seven Egyptian divisions had now concentrated. The most significant of these positions were at Rafa and El Arish in northern Sinai and at Abu Agheila and Kusseima, along the central road thirty miles to the south. These were jumping-off points for the anticipated Egyptian attack. They were also heavily fortified defensive bastions complete with mutually supporting infantry, tank, and artillery positions. Behind them deep in the desert lay two Egyptian strike forces. Two other Egyptian divisions waited near Kuntilla in the south, ready to break across the Negev.

Facing this concentration were three Israeli divisions, Tal's, Yoffe's, and mine. Our plan called for a simultaneous strike on the morning of June 5. Israel's air force was to launch a pre-emptive attack on Egypt's airfields. At the same moment Tal's tanks would assault Rafa and El Arish along the coast while I hit Abu Agheila and Kusseima on the central axis. Between us, Yoffe's division would traverse the supposedly impassable sands of Wadi Haridin, isolating the two battlefields and racing toward the Egyptian forces in the interior.

Yoffe's movement would be a special surprise, since it was universally believed that vehicles could not move on the sands in that area. I remembered, though, that when we charted the Sinai after the 1956 campaign we found that tracked movement was possible, despite appearances. In fact the paratroopers had done a survey of precisely this wide east-to-west wadi. After a search through the records, we found it, a report demonstrating that the wadi floor would indeed support mechanized traffic.

In the desert, war is always for control of the roads. That has been true for three thousand years and it is just as true today. For short periods large forces can move through open terrain. But without roads they cannot keep themselves supplied, and without supplies they cannot keep going. A motorized army finds its vehicles breaking down in rugged terrain at a startling rate. (In 1956 I lost ten of my thirteen tanks and sixty trucks to mechanical failures.) Moving across country consumes gigantic amounts of fuel, and in these regions tanker trucks cannot follow. Nor can airdrops supply all of the need. Tracked and multiwheel-drive vehicles have great tactical maneuverability in the desert. But strategically, an army's thrust must follow the roads.

My division's primary task, then, was to open the central axis, the road that led from Beersheba to Ismailia. Blocking our way were the Abu Agheila and Kusseima strongholds, actually two separate but mutually supporting bases held by the Egyptian Second Division. Abu Agheila sat directly on the road, with Kusseima twenty miles to the southeast through broken country. In the Sinai campaign of 1956 Israeli forces had attacked from the south, taking Kusseima first. But they had received a grim welcome at Abu Agheila: three days of bitter fighting at whose end the Egyptians were forced to withdraw only because their water supply ran out.

Although the Egyptian headquarters was at Kusseima, Abu Agheila was the more formidable position. Furthermore, the Ismailia road led right through the Abu Agheila defenses. Were I to take Kusseima first, I would still have to deal with Abu Agheila. But if Abu Agheila fell, we would be in control of the roads behind Kusseima, and the Egyptians would find the position untenable. So there was no question about where to strike. But how to strike was a different story.

Since 1956 the Egyptians had completely rebuilt the Abu Agheila fortifications according to the latest Soviet concepts of linear defense. About fifteen miles from the Israeli border the Ismailia road crossed a long swell of sand known as Um Cataf. There the Egyptians had constructed three parallel trench systems intersecting the road. Anchored in the north by high soft dunes and in the south by jagged ridges and broken foothills, each line was several miles long and each encompassed an array of gun positions, storage depots, and lateral communications trenches. In front of the first line was a thickly laid mine field. With the trench system manned by a full infantry brigade and with its flanks secured on either end by the terrain, this position by itself constituted a major defensive obstacle.

A mile or so behind the trenches the Egyptians kept a mobile reserve of over eighty tanks ready to move in any direction, the sword that complemented their defensive shield. Just to the south of the tanks was their artillery deployment—eighty 122- and 130-mm guns whose range far outmatched my own guns. Perimeter outposts screened this concentration of forces on the approaches to the east and especially in the north, where the flank was guarded by an infantry battalion supported by tanks and artillery in a fortified position which we code-named Oakland.

To destroy Abu Agheila it would be necessary to identify and exploit the position's inherent vulnerability. Here we would be up against good defensive fighters whose numerical strength was not much less than ours and whose firepower was in some ways greater than ours—a far cry from the offensive-defensive ratio of three to one usually considered minimal for an attack against prepared positions. So the plan of battle would have to emphasize concentration of forces, surprise, and maneuver. And the action would have to take place at night, our traditional method of reducing the odds and negating the advantages of prepared fortifications.

In 1956 the Israeli forces had attacked from the south. Now I decided to attack from the north, west, and east. Going around from the north would surprise the Egyptians and would let me get quickly to the roads behind both Abu Agheila and Kusseima. Besides, for political reasons I did not want to be separated from Yoffe's and Tal's divisions. When the inevitable cease-fire was imposed on us, I wanted to have all our areas of advance consolidated.

What I had in mind was a closely co-ordinated attack by separate elements of our forces on the Egyptian trench lines, tanks, and artillery. I wanted these attacks to develop from the north, from the west (at the rear of Abu Agheila), and from the east (at the front of the position) in a continuous unfolding of surprises, each force securing the flank of its neighbor. All together this would make a very complicated operation on the divisional level, but each brigade's specific mission would by itself be simple. Very difficult, but simple. The key to success would be the closest co-operation between the different elements of our forces.

As a result I demanded detailed planning, from myself on the division level and from my subcommanders on their levels. I subsequently have read histories of Israel's wars that have suggested I am a devotee of improvisation, and that it was our ability to improvise that allowed us to defeat the Arabs. One study even called me the "king of improvisation." But the fact is that I was never the king of improvisation, nor the prince, nor the anything of improvisation. Exactly the opposite is true. I was always committed to absolutely detailed planning, planning to the last point and the last position, structuring each of our forces to deal precisely with the problems in front of them.

I emphasized meticulous planning not simply because I thought it was the most effective approach, which it is, but because by taking that approach you enforce on your subordinates the same necessity. They have to learn every detail of the topography, every position, every soldier they will be facing. And once they do that, they will be able to decide rationally—not intuitively—on the steps they have to take. They will make their decisions on the basis of knowledge. Experience had also taught me that if you lay your plans in detail before you are under the stress of fighting, the chances are much greater that you will be able to implement at least the outlines of the plans despite the contingencies of battle.

All of this was especially vital in an operation as complicated as Abu Agheila. Each commander's plan had to be clear so that every other commander would understand what his colleagues were doing—what their objectives were, and how they intended to accomplish them. By the time the order presentations and reviews were completed, they each knew the overall plan in detail, they knew how their own roles fit into the overall concept, they knew what their neighbors were trying to do and where they would be. They also knew that I trusted them to carry out their missions with an absolute minimum of interference. The field assignments were theirs, and my philosophy (as each commander understood) was that they would handle them best.

In my overall approach the first order of business would be to create a deception against Kusseima with a brigade under Uri Baidatz. Then I would isolate the battlefield. In the south a screening force of tanks, half-tracks, and mortars under Arie Amit would block any reinforcements from Kusseima. This force would also give us a lodgement once we were ready to move in that direction. In the north I would launch a reinforced armored battalion, including my best tanks, the British Centurions under Natke Nir, against Oakland, the position that guarded Abu Agheila's northern flank. Once Natke took Oakland, he would then circle around to the rear of Abu Agheila, setting up blocking forces as he went on the road to Jebel Libni, where the Egyptian reserves were. The Centurions would then be in position to assault the base from behind.

Once the field was isolated, we would attack the entire depth of the Egyptian positions simultaneously. That would be the "tahboulah," the shock that would unbalance the defenders. Kuti Adam's infantry brigade would come down on the northern end of the trench lines through the ostensibly secure dunes. At the same time my artillery commander, Yakov Aknin, would concentrate all the division's artillery fire on the trenches just in front of Kuti's attack, making life hell for the defenders as they tried to respond to the unexpected assault. To the right of Kuti's brigade, helicopters would land Danny Mat's paratroop brigade, which would strike into the artillery positions, preventing the Egyptian long-range guns from hitting our own forces. Once the infantry had disrupted the trenches, our tank brigade under Mordechai Zippori would move through the mine fields in a narrow frontal assault. At the same time, Natke's Centurions would hit the Egyptian tanks from behind and come in on the rear of the trenches. And all of this would happen at night, compounding the Egyptians' confusion as they struggled to piece together what was happening to them.

It was a complex plan. But the elements that went into it were ones I had been developing and teaching for many years, starting back in 1953 with the paratroopers—the idea of close combat, nightfighting, surprise paratroop assault, attack from the rear, attack on a narrow front, meticulous planning, the concept of the "tahboulah," the relationship between headquarters and field command. This would be the first time I commanded a division in battle. But all the ideas had matured already; there was nothing new in them. It was simply a matter of putting all the elements together and making them work.

In the evening of June 4, just before we left the assembly area, I wrote a last letter to Lily.

My love,
We all know why we are waiting here, for the third week now. It could happen at any moment. This is something unavoidable, and if we don't do it immediately we will be risking destruction, particularly in light of Iraq's entry into Jordan. You of course know and understand that there is no alternative. You have to keep your spirits up and take care of our three wonderful children, our trio. Are there any like them? They are wonderful, and you are wonderful. But you must take good care of yourself for a few days. You have to understand that the most important thing is that the battle will be in the hands of the most experienced commanders and that's why it's important that I be here. I remember you all always. I love and treasure you all. I will take care of myself because I know about the wonderful things that await me at home. If I don't get in touch by phone tomorrow, please understand that I couldn't. Guard your spirits. We all have to guard our spirits.
Many many many kisses and hugs to you, Gur, Omri, and Gilad.

Arik

That night we moved from the assembly area to the jump-off point on the border. On the sand next to one of the headquarters half-track I caught a couple of hours' sleep, waking up to see the soldiers already cooking breakfast. Lying there on the sand, I listened to the divisional radio nets. Everyone seemed to be talking, there were discussions back and forth among all the Israeli units. Only one net was silent, our own. It was as if we weren't there. Then at eight o'clock the order came that we were waiting for: "Move out."

That morning we took the outposts screening the Egyptian trench lines. I watched as Israeli jets stormed in to the attack, and as fierce anti-aircraft fire rose to meet them. One jet was shot down, and I quickly called the air force off. I wasn't opposed to close air support, but I felt that here it wasn't absolutely necessary, that we had other answers. There was no point in endangering the precious fighters.

By midday we overran the last of the Egyptian eastern outposts. To the south toward Kusseima the screening force had taken up its positions. Meanwhile Natke's reinforced Centurion battalion attacked Oakland, the hinge of the Egyptians' northern flank. Over the radio net I heard he was running into trouble, but he did not ask for help and I didn't intervene. By four o'clock Natke had justified my faith in him. His tanks were inside the position and mopping up.

With the battlefield isolated, the rest of the division began moving up for the main attack. Standing on a low dune, I watched them advance along the old half-ruined British road: tanks, artillery, troops, supplies— all the traffic controlled by the main headquarters which had set itself up at a crucial rise. Kuti Adam's infantry brigade arrived in civilian buses, which let off their passengers and then were towed out of the way to the side. Bus after bus was lined up as far back as I could see.

After a while I went down to the road to watch the procession up close. Zippori's Super Shermans moved up to take positions for their frontal assault. Then Kuti's infantry, two endless lines along the sides of the road, marching into the gritty wind from the dunes. Soon they would leave the road in a wide hook to the north, from where they would be ready to sweep down on the left end of the trench system.

As they passed, I looked into faces suffused by the colors of the dying sun. They saw me in the middle of the road, and it was impossible to miss their expressions of confidence and determination. And, as always, my own mood was buoyed by the sight.

At dark I took up a position with my headquarters vehicles on the dunes near the Egyptian barbed wire and mine field, where I could watch the tank breakthrough. Waiting there for H-hour, a message came in from Southern Command saying that if I delayed the attack until the next day they could provide air support. I thought about it for a few minutes, then radioed back, "No. We'll go in tonight."

At 10 P.M. every artillery piece that I had opened up on the northern end of the trenches. Under its cover Kuti's infantry hit home while at the same moment Danny Mat's paratroopers (who had helicoptered into the northerly dunes earlier) stormed the artillery concentration. Meanwhile Natke had refueled and resupplied his Centurions, and now they came racing at the Egyptian positions from the rear, firing as they came. As one captured Egyptian officer put it afterward, it was like watching a snake of fire uncoiling at them.

In the command post we listened intently to all the nets. On each set an operations officer monitored the flow of battle talk from one of the units—four, five radios going at once. Suddenly I heard that the lead Sherman battalion couldn't find the flail, the special tank designed to open up mine fields. It startled me. Everything was so co-ordinated—we were attacking from the front, from the flank, from the rear, the paratroopers attacking the artillery. It was all working like a Swiss watch. And suddenly this simple thing, the flail was missing. Could I possibly have forgotten it somewhere?

But I also knew that flail or no flail, Sasson, the lead battalion commander of Zippori's tank brigade, would find some way of getting his job done. And he did. In short order the flail was found, but when it was crippled by a mine Sasson went ahead and breached the field using the old hand methods. Then he drove in his attack, a concentrated charge by the Shermans right into the middle of the Egyptian trenches.

With Sasson and the rest of Zippori's brigade attacking along the road moving west, I got a message from Natke, who had broken into the rear of the base heading east. He was being shelled from his front and could not tell whom it was coming from. I ordered Zippori to hold fire, then asked Natke if he was still being attacked. "Yes," came the answer. "Then hit them," I said. "They're Egyptians."[*]

While the fighting was still going on, I received another message from Southern Command, this time asking if one of Yoffe's brigades could use the road for their advance into the interior. I agreed to it, giving orders that only our units to the south of the road could continue firing once Yoffe's tanks had cleared the mine field. So in the middle of the battle we were treated to the remarkable sight of a brigade of tanks moving unscathed right through the two forces locked in combat.

At about 3 or 3:30 A.M. I began to hear over the net the voice of Danny Mat, the paratroop commander, desperately urging the helicopters to come in to evacuate his wounded. From the lead helicopter came

---

[*] A few minutes later Natke's command half-track was hit at very short range by an Egyptian tank, almost blowing off both his legs. Subsequently he underwent eighteen operations, which saved his legs but left him barely able to walk. With irrepressible determination he fought to stay in the army and by 1973 was commanding a tank brigade that played a courageous role in the Yom Kippur War.

repeated requests to mark the landing zone. Fires and explosions were bursting up throughout the whole area; the pilots were unable to distinguish the paratroopers' smoke and burning petrol markers. From where they were circling above the battleground it all looked the same.

By this time my command half-tracks were inside the Egyptian positions. When I heard what was going on, I took a direct hand in orienting the lead pilot, working to establish positions and guide him through the dunes to which Danny Mat had withdrawn after hitting the Egyptian guns. But still unable to read the chaotic scene below him, Eliezer Cohen (nicknamed "Chita"), the helicopter commander, finally devised his own method of locating the paratroopers. With the rest of his squadron hovering above, he set his own chopper down next to one Israeli unit after another and asked directions. By 6:45 A.M. he had found them, and the evacuation began.

Toward ten or eleven in the morning the fighting had mostly died down except for some final mopping up along the miles of trenches. By noon the whole area was quiet, and we found ourselves lying by our tanks and half-tracks, exhausted. But it was an exhaustion accompanied by a sense of self-satisfaction and achievement. We had suffered forty killed and 140 wounded. But the entire Egyptian position was now in our hands.

Our mission had been to open the main axis to our forces in Sinai, and we had now done that. Now I gave instructions to block the road that led from Kusseima west through Bir Hassana to the Mitla and Gidi passes. Already in the early evening we heard explosions from Kusseima. The Egyptians were destroying everything there and moving out as fast as they could.

All that day we waited at Abu Agheila, without orders. In the aftermath of the changes that had been made in the overall Sinai attack plan, General Headquarters had simply neglected to decide what the division's next step should be. Finally we received an order to strike southward across the desert toward Nakhel on the road from Kuntilla to the canal. When the war started, the Egyptian Sixth Division had been stationed near Kuntilla, ready to move into the Negev and sever Eilat from the rest of the country. But with the collapse of Abu Agheila and the abandonment of Kusseima, the Sixth was now withdrawing along the Mitla road, the same road I had driven along in 1956 in my rush to link up with

Eytan's paratroopers in front of the pass. If the Egyptians succeeded in getting to the Mitla Pass before we hit them, they could close off our advance to the canal.

Joining up with the brigade that had staged the deception in front of Kusseima, we now began a race to catch the retreating Egyptians. But problems cropped up immediately. The wadi I planned to follow to the south was still muddy after late-season rains. As we were pulling back from an unsuccessful attempt to maneuver through it, we came under massive Katyusha rocket fire. It was a mess. Our tanks and half-tracks were concentrated in a relatively small area trying to extricate themselves from the mud, and now this rocket bombardment was raining down on us. At one point I had to get up on the hood of my half-track to try and straighten it out, or at least to set an example of calm amid the chaos.

As we pulled ourselves into order, I instructed the brigades to take another route, slightly to the east. But as they were wheeling around, another problem developed. A tank force materialized out of the west, advancing toward us and firing as they came. We identified them immediately as the brigade from Yoffe's division that had passed through Abu Agheila during the battle. Obviously they had continued west, then had turned southward and east, hoping (as we were) to cut off the Egyptians fleeing to the Mitla. Seeing us in the distance, they had assumed we were their prey and had launched themselves at us.

We tried to make radio contact with them to call them off, but for some reason we could not get through. Already an artillery regiment that was directly in their path was being hit. The artillery commander had now lowered his barrels to use his guns as anti-tank weapons, torn between firing on other Israelis or watching passively while his regiment was shredded. I ordered him not to fire, but over the radio his voice pleaded, he was taking casualties, he could not keep his people from defending themselves. I repeated the order, once, twice, "Do not fire!" In the meantime, I sent my operations officer, Yitzhak Ben-Ari, speeding toward the oncoming tanks in a jeep to let them know who we were. His dash into the mouths of the tanks took tremendous courage. But it worked, and we avoided what could have been a disaster.

Shortly afterward we received a huge airdrop of fuel and water, then took up our movement south. On the way I saw a group of soldiers clustered around a prisoner; as I drove up, one of them was hitting the Egyptian. I court-martialed the soldier on the spot, sentencing him to thirty-five days in the stockade. It was the kind of thing that brought my

Opposite: At Kusseima-Abu Ageila sector, the Egyptian 2nd Division had 7 infantry battalions, 140 guns and 130 tanks. Accepted doctrine demands at least 3:1 superiority for the attacks. Sharon's division had 8 infantry battalions, 140 guns, 130 tanks and 78 artillery pieces. Feinting against Kusseima, Sharon attacked Abu Ageila with his whole division. Kuti's infantry penetrated Umm Katef from the north, Sasson's tanks broke in from the east, Mat raided the enemy's artillery, and Natke made a deep penetration to attack the Abu Ageila position from its rear.

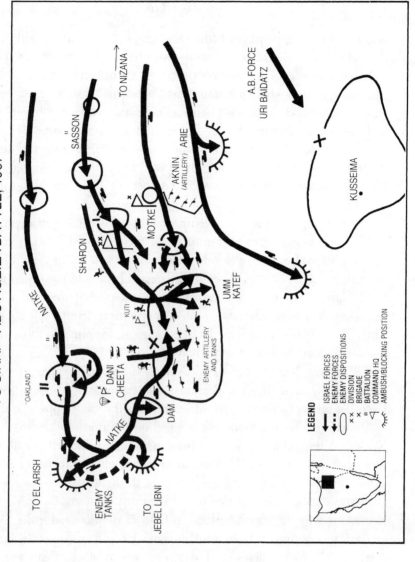

SHARON'S UGDA BREAKING THROUGH THE FORTIFIED GATE
TO SINAI – ABU AGEILA BATTLE, 1967

TO NIZANA

A.B. FORCE
URI BAIDATZ

KUSSEIMA

SASSON

AKNIN ARIE
(ARTILLERY)

MOTKE

SHARON

NATKE

UMM
KATEF

KUTI

"OAKLAND"

DANI
CHEETA

NATKE

ENEMY ARTILLERY
AND TANKS

DAM

TO EL ARISH

ENEMY
TANKS

TO
JEBEL LIBNI

LEGEND

	ISRAEL FORCES
	ENEMY FORCES
	ENEMY DISPOSITIONS
	DIVISION
××	BRIGADE
=	BATTALION
	COMMAND HQ
	AMBUSH/BLOCKING POSITION

anger to a boiling point. In battle you fight and you have to kill. That's the nature of it. But once a man is your prisoner you never touch him.

In the middle of the barren desert we came across an abandoned Egyptian position where a battalion had been just a few hours earlier. As we looked around, three Egyptian soldiers came out from a hiding place and gave themselves up. To my amazement they were crying, "They left us, they left us." I asked them, "Who left you?" "Our officers. They left us here, they just left us." The three of them could have stayed safely hidden, but they were frightened and desperate. They looked to me like orphans.

Moving on, we entered the Kuraya Wadi, a huge desert depression miles wide, the southern beginning of the great El Arish Wadi. Crossing it, you bounce from ridge to ridge, feeling as if you are in the middle of a moonscape. Toward the evening we passed by a wild mountain called Jebel Harim. As we did, I heard on the news that the Old City of Jerusalem had been liberated. Out in that barren desert I felt a sudden surge of conflicting emotions. Disappointment, for one. All those years I had nursed a secret hope that perhaps I would have the privilege of doing that. But I was happy too. Over the airwaves I heard the joyous voices of paratroopers, men that I had known and commanded. So I thought, Even if I am not there myself, at least it was the paratroops who did it.

Sometime after midnight, we stopped on the northern approaches to Nakhel. A few vehicles had hit a mine field, and I decided to call a halt until the next morning. This would give us a chance to refuel and we would be able to examine the situation in daylight.

At sunrise the next morning we picked our way across the mine field, wondering why the Egyptian base in front of us was dead quiet. As we entered the perimeter, we were amazed to find a complete brigade defensive site totally deserted. Everything was in place. Tents were up, self-propelled guns were ready to move, artillery and mortars dug into positions and prepared to fire. Everything was there except the people. Apparently they had seen our approach at night and had just left it all behind. We called it the "ghost brigade."

Outside Nakhel my light reconnaissance helicopter landed with news that the Egyptian armored division was heading toward us from Kuntilla,

---

Opposite is a copy of a map in Arik's own handwriting which was submitted to Southern Command after the battle. It was later published in the Israeli Defense Force book describing the war.

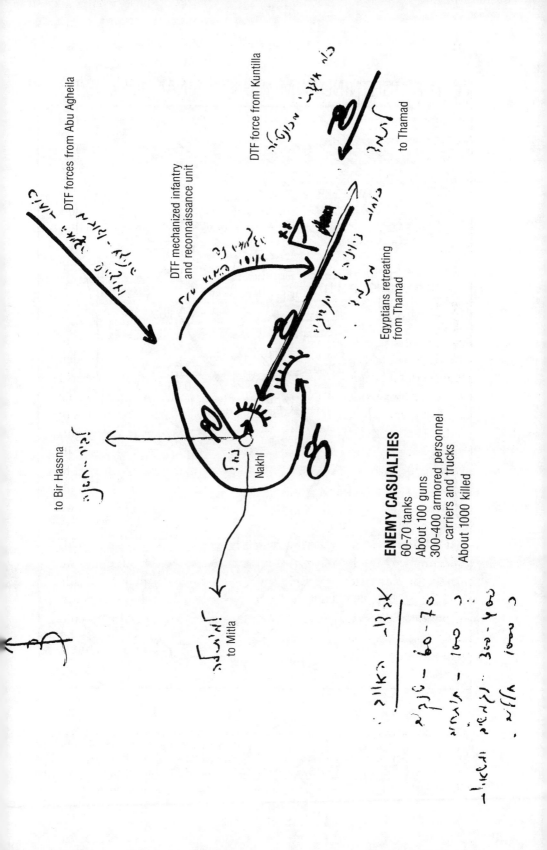

DTF forces from Abu Agheila

DTF force from Kuntilla

DTF mechanized infantry
and reconnaissance unit

to Thamad

to Bir Hassna

Egyptians retreating
from Thamad

Nakhl

to Mitla

ENEMY CASUALTIES
60-70 tanks
About 100 guns
300-400 armored personnel
carriers and trucks
About 1000 killed

THE LIGHTNING CAMPAIGN IN SINAI, JUNE 1967

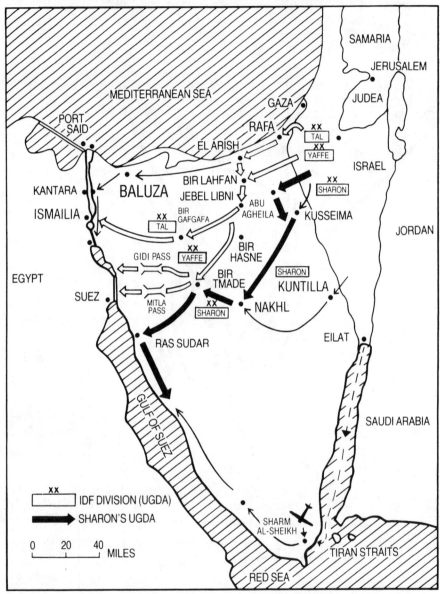

The Six-Day War opened as a preventive war against Egypt and later spread to the Jordanian and Syrian fronts. Egypt was the main enemy and I.D.F. Southern Command forces conquered the Sinai Peninsula for the third time. Sharon was given the mission of breaching and opening the central and main approaches to Sinai.

being chased by an Israeli brigade that had been screening the Negev border and had now come under my command. With a brigade of tanks, a reinforced battalion of half-tracks, and the divisional reconnaissance unit I set an ambush for the fleeing Egyptians. But just as the battle was joined, my command half-track with all the communications equipment in it broke down. We quickly cabled it behind one of the tanks, and I had the unique experience of being towed into battle. Between the tank brigade in front, the half-tracks on the flank, and the pursuing Israeli force behind, the Egyptian Sixth Division entered a terrible killing field. The scene in front of Nakhel was like a valley of death. For miles the desert was covered by ruined tanks and burned-out armored personnel carriers. Bodies littered the ground, and here and there across the scene groups of Egyptians were standing with their hands behind their heads. It wasn't until evening that the destruction came to an end. By then the Sixth Division had ceased to exist.

The next day we moved on to the Mitla Pass, and I found myself in the exact place where the paratroops had fought such a bitter and anxious battle eleven years back. The scene now was indescribable. The entire pass was choked with the wreckage of the Egyptian army. Tanks, artillery, half-tracks—countless hundreds of vehicles smoldered and burned, sending up a black haze that hung like dirty gauze in the clear desert sky. It was impossible to look at that feast of death and not know that the remnants of the Egyptian Sinai force had met their fate right here.

It was now Friday evening, June 9. The entire campaign had taken ninety-six hours. That evening we rested, assessing the situation and binding our wounds. Then on Saturday I was ordered to meet with the southern front commander, Yeshayahu Gavish, at his forward headquarters together with Tal and Yoffe. A small Bell helicopter with two seats and no doors flew me over the desert. Under us the desert was dotted with figures making their way on foot across the sands toward the canal, Egyptians struggling to make their way home after the collapse of their units. Occasional bursts of fire came up at the helicopter, especially as we approached Bir Hassana, where Gavish's headquarters was supposed to be.

But Gavish was not at Bir Hassana, and we quickly took off toward Bir Tmade, farther to the west, where I thought he might have moved. Shortly after the takeoff the pilot told me that he was having a problem with the engine and that we would have to land. We had been flying above the road to stay away from the Egyptian refugees, who were keeping to the dunes and ridges. But as we began to lose altitude, small groups of them began shooting at us, and we traded fire with them.

Landing on the road, I wondered briefly what was going to happen to us. It was too ironic for words. Less than an hour ago I had been secure in the bosom of my division, now I was stranded in the middle of hundreds of desperate armed Egyptians. I felt almost as I had back in the Danakil Desert when the car broke down. But as we crouched down on the road, a large helicopter appeared in the sky. As soon as it appeared, we shot off smoke flares; but at first they seemed not to notice and flew past. Then, in a sudden and beautiful movement, the plane banked and headed toward us.

Before the helicopter had even settled down, the door opened, and who jumped out but my two friends Avraham Yoffe and Israel Tal. I had not seen either of them since the day before the war. We hugged each other in a flood of happiness and released tension, the warmth on my side no doubt at least equal to theirs. In a moment we were all in the big helicopter and on our way, finally, to meet Gavish.

From Gavish's headquarters we flew to Tel Aviv, where Rabin wanted to see us. Somehow Lily had learned that I was coming in and was waiting for me at the airport with Gur. It was a wonderful surprise, despite the fact that we would not have any time together. She drove me to General Headquarters, through streets that had an alien look about them, as if the weeks I had just spent in the Negev and Sinai had disconnected me from civilization. I had not been home for a month now, and the sudden transition caught me off balance. Here were Lily and Gur, bringing with them all the affection of my home and family. But back there camped out around Nakhel were the soldiers with whom I had shared the intensity of war, with all its horrors and burdens and excitement.

Our meeting with Rabin at General Headquarters was full of congratulations and warmth. That day the Golan operation had ended with the complete collapse of the Syrian defense. On every front we had achieved victories that went well beyond the war's initial objectives. Before we left, Rabin appointed me commander of the Sinai, where all the problems of mopping up, caring for prisoners, and setting up an administration were still in front of us. Then Tal, Yoffe, and I flew back, stretching out on the floor of a Superfrelon transport helicopter, our heads propped up on bags of equipment and supplies with which we shared the space. It was dark when we landed at Bir Gafgafa, where Tal disappeared into the night.

Fifteen minutes later we dropped Yoffe off into the arms of his waiting officers. Finally the helicopter put down in Nakhel, where I had established my headquarters. From the sky we had seen scattered pinpricks of light winking up at us, the campfires of the wandering Egyptians. But on the ground in Nakhel the desert seemed black. To me, though, the darkness was like a friend. I looked around at the tents of my division and felt as if I was coming home.

15

Aftermath

Back in Sinai, the first item on the agenda was to collect the thousands of Egyptians who were wandering around the desert, desperate to get back across the canal. It was a dangerous job. These refugees from the shattered Egyptian army had no food or water and no leadership. They were suffering terribly from the summer heat and the sand, and they were tormented by the desert Bedouin who laid ambushes for them and killed them for their weapons. Struggling for survival, they were capable of anything.

Nevertheless we tried our best to capture them and assemble them near Baluza in the northern Sinai, where at least they would not die of exposure or at the hands of the Sinai nomads. We set up holding areas and shared out the water, which was in short supply for everyone. You could see Israeli soldiers and Egyptian prisoners queuing up at taps that gave out only sparse trickles. It would have been easy enough to simply leave the Egyptians to fend for themselves and get back to the canal any way they could. Had we done that, the result would have been the annihilation of a large percentage of the survivors. But almost all of us, myself included, felt strongly that this was not an option we could take in good conscience. None of us had any illusions about the fate of our own families and neighbors had the Egyptians destroyed our forces instead of the other way around. The Jewish people would have suffered a second blood-drenched holocaust. Nor did any of us have illusions about the nature of war. A soldier fights a war for one thing only—to kill the enemy. But afterward, once the enemy is in your hands, his life and well-being are your responsibility. You take care of his wounded the same way you take care of your own wounded. You take care of enemy prisoners the same way you would have him take care of yours. These principles were our general guide in dealing with the Egyptian refugees.

At first we were eager to get as many prisoners as possible in order to trade for the small number of Israelis who had been captured. In the end, though, there were simply too many to handle, and we decided to keep only the officers. The ordinary soldiers we collected and delivered to Kantara on the canal's east bank, from where they were ferried across on boats the Egyptians sent over for them. There was no formal agreement between the two sides on this, just a tacit understanding by which thousands of Arab peasant soldiers were returned unharmed, some of whom had walked a hundred miles through the desert.

But when word got around that we were sending the private soldiers back, all of a sudden it became impossible to distinguish between them and the officers. The officers began to tear off their badges of rank, and since all the Egyptians were filthy and unshaven anyway, they and the enlisted men looked exactly the same. But eventually we found one unmistakable sign by which we could immediately tell who was who. It turned out that the Egyptian officers had on beautiful silken underwear, while the enlisted men wore rough cotton. For the democratic Israelis, this was an amazing discovery, and there was plenty of laughter about it. From that point on the first order to every batch of newly captured Egyptians was to pull down their pants. Those with silk drawers we shipped off to POW camps, those with cotton were sent on to the canal.

In Bir Gafgafa, where I had moved my headquarters, the smell of death tainted the air. The desert wind blew in from the battlefields, and though they were miles and miles away it carried with it the slightly sweet odor of decomposition. The wind also brought swarms of black flies, and I sometimes wondered how far the flies could fly—if they were from the Bir Gafgafa area or if they too had blown in from the battlefields with their as yet unburied dead.

After spending several days in Sinai dealing with some of the immediate problems and looking around at all the places I remembered from the 1956 war and its aftermath, I flew back home. A helicopter had arrived to pick me up and to evacuate an engineer officer who had lost a leg and a hand trying to clear an Egyptian mine field. As I waited to board, the pilot came down from the cockpit to say hello, and as he stretched out his hand in the gathering darkness I saw it was Chita, the squadron leader who had brought the paratroops in at Abu Agheila for their attack on the Egyptian artillery positions, then had made such heroic efforts to evacuate the wounded.

Standing on the tarmac amid the little knot of doctors and medics preparing the wounded engineer for the flight, Chita began crying. As the medical people worked over the engineer, he told me he had just learned that his brother had been killed in the fighting. Even after we crowded into the helicopter, I could still see the pain on his face. Next to me the ashen engineer lay on a stretcher, tubes running into him from various bottles hung on a metal rack. It was not exactly a triumphal return home, but one heavy with reminders of how much the victory had cost.

At Tel Hashomer hospital Lily was waiting to take me back to Zahala and the children for what was to have been my first real rest at home in ages. But the next day Pinchas Sapir, the minister of finance, called, asking me to make an immediate fund-raising and public relations tour to Hong Kong and Australia, with a stop in Iran on the way back. "How soon do you want me to do this?" I asked, not happy about the intrusion. "Yesterday," came the reply.

Before I left, I took a short trip with Lily and Gur to Old Jerusalem, then to Samaria and Judea. All the roads were choked with cars and people, and every place we stopped we were met by an outpouring of love and affection. I had never seen people in such a state of excitement, visiting Jericho, the old cemetery on the Mount of Olives, the Western Wall, all the holiest sites that had been closed to Jews throughout almost twenty years of Jordanian occupation.

But it was a brief visit, just time for a quick look around before my trip abroad. I promised myself, though, that when I returned I'd have time to take the family everywhere. We'd have breakfast in Hebron, lunch in Jerusalem, and dinner in Shechem. Before the war I had been used to taking Gur every once in a while to Mount Zion overlooking Old Jerusalem. I'd point out the sites to him, the destroyed Jewish quarter, the Temple Mount, the Wall. "There," I would say, "those places there, they are not in our hands, but they are ours. They belong to us."

✳   ✳   ✳

After a few too brief days I boarded a TWA 707 bound for Bombay and Hong Kong, the first of the Israeli generals to be sent overseas after the victory. Every place we landed crowds of reporters were waiting, eager to ask a hundred questions about the war, the Israeli army, the Israeli government, the future, and a host of other subjects. Before long the trip began to seem like one interminable press conference. From Hong Kong I took a Qantas jet to Australia. In Sydney, Melbourne, Canberra, Adelaide, and other Australian cities I talked before army officers and Jewish groups. But although I did my best to be personable, I was longing for home. Serving in the army, I had been away from the family for so much of the time, year after year. And now, in this moment of great victory, that was where I wanted to be, at home, sharing the feelings with them. From time to time I managed to call, and each time I did I learned of another old friend or another son of an old friend who had been killed. I was especially saddened by the news of Yair Telzur's death. I had known Yair and his family for fourteen years, ever since he had presented himself as one of the first volunteers for Unit 101. During the war he had commanded my old paratroop battalion. Yair had been killed, Lily told me, by a minefield. It was a bad time to be away.

On the way back I stopped again in Hong Kong, where I stayed at the Peninsula, an elegant colonial-style hotel owned by the Khadouris, a famous family of wealthy Iraqi Jews who had supported Israel for decades. Back in the early 1930s they had donated money to found a Jewish agricultural school in the lower Galilee. Settlers from those impoverished times had been enraged when the British used half the funds to start an Arab school in Tulkarm. For years people had been angry about this piece of British arrogance; though even with only half the resources it should have had, the Khadouri school quickly became famous and counted among its graduates such people as Yigal Allon and Yitzhak Rabin. Now I was able to meet the Khadouri family and take a closer look at Hong Kong than my first stop had allowed. What impressed me most was the sight of crowds of Chinese children on their way to school in the morning, so obviously eager to learn. They seemed to have the same spirit for it that Jewish children had.

From Hong Kong I flew to Tehran, where I spent an emotional twenty-four hours, many of them out walking the streets with our military attaché, Yakov Nimrodi. In the Street of the Carpet Sellers we were recognized and besieged by the bazaar's Jewish merchants. They sat us down on top of a pile of carpets, hundreds of shopkeepers surrounding us and heaping kisses and blessings on us. For the Jews of Iran as for the Jews of Australia and the small Jewish community of Hong Kong, the victory was an inspiration that brought with it an overflow of relief and pride.

Coming home at last, I set out to see Samaria and Judea in earnest, taking Lily and Gur along with me. Crowds of Israelis were still all around, discovering and exploring these places that were so much a part of their heritage, but which since 1948 they had been unable to visit. When they saw me, they would invariably gather around with congratulations, talk, and laughter. At these times I would look into Gur's eyes. Although he never said anything, a proud happiness lit his face as he took in the people's feelings. Watching him, I too felt an immense pride, as if all of this compensated in part for the years when I had never been at home and for all the sorrow that he had gone through. If only, I wished, Omri and Gilad were old enough to breathe in this atmosphere too.

Now that the reserve divisions had been deactivated, I went back to my General Headquarters job as director of military training. I began to study the war intensively, going over each of the battles and each of the battlefields with the individual commanders, refighting the actions with them in an effort to draw as many lessons as possible from their experiences.

I also spent a great deal of time in Samaria and in the Judean desert, looking carefully at these areas in terms of their strategic topography. Then, as director of training, I began to move the various military schools from their old bases into Samaria. In fact I had already begun to do this weeks earlier when I was still with the army in Sinai. As soon as I heard that Samaria and Judea were liberated, I had cabled instructions to the commander of the infantry school to move from the base in Netanya to a captured Jordanian army camp near Shechem. That was the first one I moved. But within a few months I was able to transfer quite a number of them: the infantry school, the engineering school, the military police school, part of the artillery school, the main basic training school for new recruits, the paratrooper recruit school, and others.

Of course the idea of moving the schools was not accepted by everybody, and I had angry discussions on the subject with others at General Headquarters. Bar-Lev, my old rival who had now been named commander-in-chief, was rigidly opposed to moving the basic training facility. "It will cost a million pounds," he said. "Maybe it will," I told him, "but it will be worth a lot more than that." In the end I managed to get it moved.

These were the months just following the war, and I did not at that time have any specific political solution in mind to the problem these territories represented. But I was very clear on certain points. I felt then that in order to secure this part of the country the most important thing was to establish Jewish footholds as fast as possible. The basic fact was that these areas were an integral part of the country that had been captured by the invading Arab armies in 1948. Now we had come back to them.

The idea was not to take Arab agricultural lands; I had no interest at all in productive cultivated areas. We did not want or need them. But I was just as certain that we did need the important road junctions and the high controlling terrain. The hills of Samaria overlooked Israel's narrow coastal plain. I myself had grown up there, in the shadow of Arab towns like Kalkilya, which had served as staging areas for Arab armies and bases for the gangs that for decades had terrorized Jewish farms and villages.

But it did not require either personal experience or military genius to recognize the strategic significance of these territories. The coastal strip they bordered was where two thirds of Israel's population lived. It was here that most of Israel's industrial infrastructure was located, where the three main power stations were, where the only international airport was. All that— the heart of the country—was open and vulnerable to terrorists who could cross the border, carry out their attacks, and return, all in the same night. It was also within easy artillery range of the Samarian high ground. The entire depth of Israel's strategic center was less than what the American army considers tactical depth for a brigade of soldiers. American division commanders habitually think in much larger terms.

The necessity of retaining control here was not connected in my mind with any particular political solution. What I thought was that, regardless of whatever political solution the future might hold, we would have to keep the high controlling terrain—to protect and give depth to the tiny heartland along the coast, to be able to defend ourselves on the line of the River Jordan, and to secure Jerusalem as the capital of the Jewish people forever. That was an indispensable, necessary minimum, and I never considered for a moment that we would relinquish control over territory that was essential to our survival. And those rocky heights and those strategic junctions—they were essential.

The first job, then, was to establish actual control on the ground. I came from a family of what might be called "pragmatic Zionists," people who understood that in a precarious and violent world Jewish existence could not be left to trust or to paper agreements. Survival depended not on faith in someone else's goodwill, but on "facts," actually building on the land and actually defending it. I remember that years later in 1980 and 1981 when I was negotiating with the Egyptians I would occasionally call my mother from Cairo to say hello. And although she knew our conversation was being monitored, she would tell me in her heavy Russian accent, "Do not trust them! Do not trust them! You cannot trust a piece of paper!" In 1967 and 1968 I felt precisely the same way. Whatever kind of agreement we might eventually have, I was going to do everything I could to establish the fact of our strategic control.

And so I moved the schools. As director of military training, by 1968 I managed to occupy almost every single one of the old Jordanian military bases and police outposts outside of the cities. And these were in all the most important strategic locations, because the Jordanians in their occupation of Samaria and Judea had also had strategic considerations and had built their bases accordingly. In some of these places I established a permanent Israeli army presence, and in some of them— because of budgetary restrictions or disagreements in General Headquarters—only a temporary presence. But all of them were occupied.

I also tried to persuade Moshe Dayan to start building accommodations for the families of the officers who were stationed at these bases. The idea appealed to him, but as in many other areas where it would have been necessary to take a strong public position, he refused to make the fight. Transferring the bases was one thing; they were under control of the army, and the moves needed only military approval. But introducing civilian life into Samaria and Judea would have been a great change, and to do that the government would have to go along. So even though Dayan supported the idea, he never took the necessary steps to make it happen.

Yet I knew from our previous experience that the only way to permanently secure the most strategic terrain in our hands was to live on it. The boundaries of the country had always been affected by Jewish settlements and towns that had been built beforehand, and I argued that we must do the same thing here.

When I made these points, people would often say that if we established settlements it would make solutions much more complicated. My response was that the situation was already so complicated that it would be a mistake to give in to simple, easy answers. The circumstances of Israel's life as a nation are just not simple: its coastal strip only a few miles wide, its demographics, its malevolent neighbors, its problems with terrorism—these and the other facts of Israel's life are immensely complicated. Consequently, I believed that we needed to create conditions so that in the future when we found ourselves under pressure, we and everybody else would have no choice but to look for in-depth solutions. Then, in our moment of weakness, we would not be tempted to just give up. We would not be able to say to ourselves: "Look, nothing is there. The easiest thing is just to walk away from it." I thought it had to become impossible to give a fast, easy, clear-cut solution, because no solution of this sort could accord with the reality of Israel's solution.

The first solution that was proposed to deal with the problem of Samaria and Judea was not at all simple. It was the product of the fertile brain of Yigal Allon, who had just missed being appointed minister of defense prior to the war and was now serving as deputy prime minister. Allon was a man of real ability, and as soon as the fighting was over he had gotten to work on a concept he felt could become the basis for agreement with Jordan. It was while he was looking for support for what was to become known as the "Allon Plan" that he invited me to come in and see him.

Allon's basic idea was that Israel should annex a strip of land along the River Jordan from the Valley of Beit Shean in the north to Hebron in the south, leaving a connecting corridor between Jordan and Ramallah. Israel would thus be able to control the Jordan plain so that we could prevent the entrance of Jordanian, Iraqi, or Syrian forces into Samaria and Judea. Meanwhile, the territories would be turned into a kind of demilitarized zone under Jordanian civil administration.

It was an interesting plan; at least it was the first plan, and for that matter it was the only plan. I appreciated Allon for having the courage to come up with something and be willing to push it and fight for it by himself. But in fact Allon's plan had some severe disadvantages. Israel had never managed to block even the previous border against terrorists. The pre-1967 border between Israel and Samaria/Judea was over 300 kilometers long, full of mountainous, brush-covered terrain.

Our small standing army had been unable to secure it, even though for part of the time the Jordanians had not co-operated with the terrorists; on the contrary, after the period of our retaliation raids they even made occasional efforts to stop them. But the Jordanian army had not succeeded, although they had kept up to six army brigades in these areas. I emphasized that to Allon: Even when the Jordanians had troops there, they had never managed to control the terrorists. His plan would make our borders 400 kilometers longer, adding the east and west boundaries of the annexed River Jordan strip to the old border, so that we would now have three borders to guard. Then we would have the Jericho corridor on top of that. If we had never been able to protect the previous borders, how would we protect these?

I had always liked Allon. I respected his intelligence and creativity; but when I looked at the maps where he had sketched out his ideas and saw the border lines proliferating, I could not support him. It seemed to me that even nations that had lived side by side in peace for centuries would find themselves locked in conflict by such an arrangement, let alone Israel and Jordan. It also seemed to me that Allon and others were discounting the potential of terrorism and our vulnerability to it under this plan. Some believed that terrorism from Jordan would now fall off significantly, as it had in Gaza after the 1956 Sinai campaign. But this seemed to me an illusion, although at that time neither I nor anyone else could have predicted the dramatic growth of the terror networks that the Arab nations and the Soviets would stimulate and support during the coming years.

I assume my position on Allon's plan disappointed him to a certain degree, but of course it did nothing to dissuade him from pushing the concept. In the event, the Labor party adopted the plan. They built the settlements and held out the political solution to Jordan's King Hussein. But nothing came of it. Hussein had been directly responsible for precipitating the fighting on the central front by making common cause with Nasser. It was his war that had resulted in Jordan's loss of Samaria and Judea. Nevertheless, Hussein rejected Allon's plan out of hand, even though it would have restored Jordanian civil control. Such a solution was, as he put it, "completely unacceptable."

But neither the uncertainty about the future of Samaria and Judea nor anything else could dampen the euphoria of those days. It was as if the country was collectively celebrating the most joyful period of its existence. Certainly it was the happiest time I had known. There was a feeling that we had finally broken free from the noose that had been around our necks. Up until then everyone had always felt the fragility of this narrow, vulnerable place we lived in. We had existed precariously, under a constant corrosive tension, never knowing when or where the next atrocity would strike, always with a hint of fear about the next inevitable confrontation. I remembered so clearly how I felt the first day or two of the war when the radio announced that the Jordanians had shelled Tel Aviv and that Kiryat Shaul—next to Zahala—had also been hit. When I came home after the war, I saw the shelter and the sandbags that Lily, Gur, and my mother (who had come down from the moshav) had filled and piled up. I saw where the Jordanian shells had hit Tel Aviv. It wasn't massive artillery fire; they hadn't had time for that. But when you realize that they are shelling the place where you live, the place where your children are—and not on the border, but in the very heart of the country—then the understanding comes home of what it means to live on a tiny island amid a sea of enemies.

Now, suddenly, all those worries were gone, and in their place was a vast sense of relief and elation. But even this wasn't all. At the same moment came the most inexpressible feeling of return. Once again we were able to go to all these places, these old places that were so much a part of our identity. People were caught in an overflow of warmth and thanksgiving. It was as if we were all inspired—struck through by emotions compounded of salvation, freedom, and return.

For me personally, the feelings of those days were far more intense than those that had accompanied the end of the War of Independence. Then I had felt that our victory was incomplete. We had saved our lives and established our state, but only at the cost of very heavy losses and an unsure future. Then we had eked out for ourselves a tenuous existence. Now—nineteen years later—the world seemed to have opened up before us.

Although my job at General Headquarters was full-time, there was none of the frantic compulsion of the previous months, and I was able to enjoy the luxury of being at home. Omri, our second child was three; Gilad, our third, was approaching his first birthday. I felt I was making up for lost time with them, and with Lily and Gur too. I began to relax. Memories of my friends who had died were still fresh. But painful as they were, when you know that you have achieved something crucial you feel even terrible losses differently, they taste less bitter in your mouth.

It was a restful, lovely time. Lily and I spent hours riding with Gur, who by now had become a first-class horseman. In the evenings I would go out with him by myself, holding my horse back a little so that I could keep my eyes on him. I felt like the luckiest man alive to have a family life like this, and a son like this. I loved to see him with his friends, so many of whom seemed always to be around. I watched his leadership qualities emerge and assert themselves—unobtrusively but clearly. He was an extraordinarily handsome boy as well, a wonderful child in every respect. It seemed to me that a precious gift had been inexplicably bestowed on me.

In 1967 Rosh Hashana, the Jewish new year, fell on October 4. Like all Jewish holidays, Rosh Hashana begins on the eve of the holiday, and that morning Lily took the car to do some last-minute shopping for presents in Tel Aviv. At 9 A.M. I was sitting on the bed talking with some friends who had phoned to wish us a happy new year. Although it was still early, the phone had been ringing steadily for an hour. While I was talking, Gur came into the bedroom, and I half heard him say that he was going out to play. "I'll be out in the front," he told me, then turned around to leave. Just before he did, he gave me a playful salute, the gesture of a boy who had grown up around the army and who liked military things.

A minute or two later, while I was still talking, I heard a shot ring out from the front of the house. I dropped the phone receiver on the bed and rushed outside to see what had happened. There in the front yard was Gilad in his playpen with Omri standing next to him. Gur was stretched out on the grass with a terrible wound in his eye, his face covered with blood. Next to him lay an old shotgun, an antique that one of my friends had given to him as a present. Omri stood there next to the playpen talking to me. "He told the boy not to point," he said. "Gur told the boy not to point it."

I took Gur up in my arms, looked for our car, then remembered that Lily had it. Standing there, rooted to the spot, I heard myself shouting to our next-door neighbor, Penina, wife of air force commander Motti Hod. Holding Gur close, I walked out to the street, waiting for someone to come, waiting for a car so that I could get him to the clinic.

In a minute or two a car drove up. In another minute I was in the clinic watching the doctor examine him. I had seen so many wounds in my life; no one had to tell me that this one was hopeless. I had known it the moment I looked at him lying on the grass. But despite everything, you clutch at hopes. When the doctor told us to take him to the hospital immediately, we hurried back to the car. I sat in the back seat with Gur on my lap, my shirt soaked with his blood. Ages seemed to pass as we raced to the hospital. And as we did, he died in my arms.

When I got back home, Lily was there. She had tried to call, but with the phone off the hook in the bedroom she hadn't been able to get through. Finally she had called my office, and they had told her what happened. Now, since it was Rosh Hashana eve, all the arrangements had to be decided quickly. In keeping with Jewish law, the funeral would have to be held before sundown.

We both wanted to bury him next to Gali, but there was a problem. When Gali was killed, I had wanted her to lie next to the military cemetery, and her grave was on one of the few pieces of land left in that spot. To make sure we could put Gur next to her, I went out to the cemetery with Shlomo Goren, the chief military rabbi. Together we looked at the place, and at the beautiful flowers in front of the black stone I had brought from the north to be Gali's marker. "There," I told Goren. "I want him there."

Goren was distraught. We had known each other for years, and while I was in shock, hardly thinking or feeling anything, he was overwhelmed. Looking at the grave, he said softly, "She took him back to her."

The funeral started at the Tel Hashomer hospital, where I had brought Gur from the clinic. They had put him in a simple pine coffin, and I asked them to open it for a minute. I looked at him again, then watched as they closed the lid and placed the coffin in a military command car for the procession to the cemetery. He had been a soldier's child; the army had been my life, so it had been his life too. He had loved riding around in command cars and jeeps, and it struck me that the last moment I had seen him alive he had given me that salute. Behind the command car the procession strung out. Although everything was so rushed and there was such short notice, a thousand people seemed to be there. Someone told me that they were announcing it on the radio news.

Standing in front of the grave, I remembered five and a half years ago when we had buried Gali. I had given a brief talk then and it came back to me that I had said, "The only thing I can promise you is that I will take care of Gur." Now I could not shake the thought that I had not kept my promise. At such times one doesn't really think, but this kept coming back to me again and again. I didn't take care of him. I just didn't take care of him.

After the funeral Lily and I went home. For the first time in my life I felt that I was facing something I could not overcome, that I could not live through. I was obsessed by all the things I might have done. If only I had not stayed on the phone, if only I had watched more carefully, if only I had told him more forcefully about guns. A thousand ifs. The hardest times were at night, when sleep was impossible and the scene played and replayed itself in my head. Awake during the nights, Lily and I cried together. During the day there was work, then at home if we did not talk about it we could hold the pain inside. But once we would start to talk, it was impossible to put a barrier to the tears. Neither of us could find any comfort or relief from the terrible grief. There seemed to be no single moment when it was not present. Nothing could soothe it, nothing could lay it to rest.

Always, I thought, it happens like this. Always these tragedies come in the hour of joy. It was right after the Sinai campaign that my father had died, though that passing could not be compared to this. Now I had really come home the victor. We had achieved everything we could have asked, and more. We had resolved all those irresolvable problems that for years had dominated our lives. The hills and mountains of Samaria that had looked down on the orchards of my childhood and on the trenches the Kfar Malal farmers manned in 1947 and 1948, those high places that I knew so well were now in our hands. What a horrible irony that from some village in the Samarian hills a friend had brought this antique shotgun as a gift, a gun that had to be loaded through the barrel with shot and powder, that no one had used for a hundred years. And suddenly this gun had killed the one I loved more than anything in the world.

I found my thoughts invaded by the story from Judges of Jephthah the Gileadite—"Yiftach Ha Giladi"—the warrior who had led the Jews when they were threatened by the Ammonites in the twelfth century B.C. With his enemies already in the field, he had gathered his men for battle. Then, just before leaving, he swore an oath that if God gave him victory when he returned home he would sacrifice the first living thing that came out of the doors of his house. And when he did come home victorious, the first living thing to go out to him was his only child, his beloved daughter. In his moment of victory he was visited by this dreadful tragedy. Worse than that—it was as a result of his victory that his tragedy took place.

✳   ✳   ✳

Somewhere people find the strength to endure. Others had, and eventually Lily and I did also. You think about the good things, the happy moments, the ways your life has been enriched even more than it has been devastated. A year after the accident some of my old soldiers who knew him well established a racing cup for young riders: "In memory of Gur, son of Arik. A wonderful rider, and one who loved horses." Each year it is given at a race in Afula, where Jewish boys and Arab boys compete together. On the first anniversary of his death people came to the cemetery to mourn and to remember—our friends, Lily's and mine, but Gur's friends too. On Rosh Hashana eve some of them still come, twenty years later.

But as the memories are not only ours, I often muse that neither was the loss only ours. He was a child blessed with talents, who had had the fortune to grow up in the lap of history, seeing from the inside so many of the great events of our country's times, meeting and knowing many of its greatest leaders. No one who has lost a child can help but think from time to time of what that child might have developed into, what he or she would have been like as an energetic young adult or as a person gaining stature with years. So it was not just the personal loss we mourned, though of course it was still that more than anything. But we mourned too for the potential, for the contribution that he might have made.

16

The Bar-Lev Line

Despite my long and often bitter personal history with Chaim Bar-Lev, I had supported him to succeed Yitzhak Rabin when Rabin stepped down as chief of staff in January of 1968. It was not exactly that I was so enthusiastic about Bar-Lev, but his rival was Ezer Weizman, and I knew I did not want him in the position. Weizman had been commander of the air force for many years and chief of operations since 1966. He and I had been friends for a long time, and I thought highly of his intelligence and especially of his effectiveness in building the modern Israeli air force. But at the same time I knew he lacked the determination and bulldog tenacity necessary in a chief of staff. I could not forget a scene I had witnessed in the underground Air Force Command Center during a dogfight between Egyptian and Israeli jets. With the Israeli fighters pursuing the Egyptians, Weizman was on the radio ordering his pilots to "Hit them, hit them, hit them!" But then the Egyptian planes suddenly turned to fight, and almost without catching a breath Weizman was yelling, "Come back, come back, come back!" So despite our relationship, I had thrown all the influence I could muster behind Bar-Lev.

But when Bar-Lev did gain the appointment, he and I once again found ourselves locked in a fierce dispute, this time over the questions of how to defend against any Egyptian attempt to cross the Suez Canal. This argument had been brewing since shortly after the war, when the Egyptians began a series of artillery attacks and ambushes against the Israeli troops guarding the water line. Then in early September of 1967 the Arab heads of state met in Khartoum and announced what they called "The Policy of Three Noes": no negotiations with Israel, no recognition of Israel, no peace with Israel.

The immediate practical consequence of Khartoum was the escalation of Nasser's up-till-then intermittent and desultory military efforts. In mid-September Egyptian fire ignited a major artillery battle along the length of the canal. Then on October 21 Egyptian missiles sank the Israeli destroyer *Eilat* while it was patrolling in international waters. Forty-seven crewmen were killed. In retaliation, four days later our artillery ravaged the oil and petrochemical complex around the city of Suez.

After this eruption, hostilities resumed their previous lower level of intensity. But behind the relative quiet, Egypt was busy rebuilding her army and air force with massive infusions of the most up-to-date Soviet equipment. And along with the equipment came Russian advisers, hundreds at first, then thousands. The Soviets, whom Nasser had first brought into the Middle East in 1955, were now becoming deeply involved in Egypt's military effort. By this time the euphoria we had experienced after the war was thoroughly dissipated. No one had any doubt that the Suez would eventually become an active front line.

The team that Bar-Lev eventually assigned to study the problem in 1968 (led by General Avraham Adan) concluded that our response to Egyptian artillery attacks and plans for an offensive should be a series of fortifications built along the bank of the canal. These would, they believed, protect our soldiers from the shelling and provide us with forward observation posts. In an attack they would also help stop the Egyptians on the water line, before they could establish any significant presence in the Sinai. The fortifications would serve a political purpose too in asserting de facto Israeli control of the entire Sinai.

That, at least, was the concept. From the beginning I felt that such a line of fortifications would be a disastrous error. As far as the political aspect of it was concerned, maintaining an Israeli presence at the western edge of the Sinai did not mean we had to sit down along the entire length of the canal. We could carefully choose one or two locations, on the Great Bitter Lake, for example, where we would not be directly under their guns. Much more important, if we built the proposed chain of strongpoints we would be committing ourselves to a static defense. We would be making fixed targets of ourselves three hundred yards from the Egyptian lines. Our positions and movements would be under constant surveillance. Our procedures would become common knowledge. Our patrols and supply convoys would be vulnerable to ambushes, mining, and shelling. In the event of a concerted Egyptian assault the firing ports on the canal would be blocked or destroyed by smoke and fire. Inevitably these positions would be cut off and we would find ourselves making great efforts to relieve them rather than concentrating our strength in the most effective counterattacks.

Besides, I argued, you cannot win a defensive battle on an outer line. Of course we would have no choice if we were defending the Beit Shean kibbutzim or the Western Wall of the Temple or the suburbs of Tel Aviv. But here we were sitting 175 miles from our borders. So in this situation it was our business to fight a defensive battle the way it should be fought—not on a forward line but in depth. And for this the canal was just a tool, an important barrier of course and part of an overall defensive system—but that hardly meant we had to chain ourselves to it.

Specifically, I proposed that we should base our defense on the natural line of hills and dunes that runs parallel to the canal five to eight miles to the east and dominates the canal plain. A second line with our mobile reserves should be established fifteen to twenty miles from the canal, where the mountains begin and the Mitla and Gidi passes cut toward the interior. Between the first line and the canal we should run mobile patrols, keeping on the move constantly and unpredictably so that we would not be sitting ducks for ambushes, snipers, and artillery.

If the Egyptians did try a crossing, we could afford to let them get a mile or two inside the Sinai. Then we would be able to harass them and probe for their weak points at our convenience. Then we would be in position to launch the kind of free-flowing mobile attack we were really good at.

This debate between me and Bar-Lev became harsher and harsher, especially after a large-scale surprise Egyptian artillery attack on September 8, 1968, caused severe casualties. Our relations, never good, now strained toward the breaking point. During one of our regular Monday General Headquarters meetings early in the new year, a particularly acrimonious exchange erupted. For me it wasn't much more than just another in a long string of unpleasant confrontations that always seemed to find me in the distinct, often solitary, minority. But for Bar-Lev it was apparently the last straw. That same evening he called a second meeting, during which he planned to muster his support and put an end to my contentiousness once and for all.

When I walked into the General Headquarters conference room that night, I saw Moshe Dayan sitting there together with his deputy. Alongside them were Bar-Lev and every single one of my most vehement critics. The moment I saw what was going on, I decided that I was not about to wait around docilely like a lamb at the slaughter. If that was what they had in mind, they had better start thinking differently. I would just get up, send them all to hell, and walk out. As I sat down, the tension was so thick you could cut it.

Yeshayahu Gavish, the southern front commander and one of the chief proponents of the Bar-Lev Line, started things off with a wild attack that was personal as well as professional. While he was still speaking, I stood up and said, "I thought we were here to discuss the advantages and disadvantages of the Bar-Lev Line. That's the reason for this meeting and that's what I'm willing to participate in, so that I can tell you again what a dangerous and stupid idea it is. But if you think for a moment that I am going to sit here and be tried by a 'mishpat chaverim,' you're dead wrong."

At that Dayan cut in. "Arik, you've been invited to a General Headquarters meeting. It's not up to you to decide what's going to be discussed."

"Maybe not," I said, "but if you proceed with this, it's going to be without me."

When I sat down, everything was quiet for a moment; then Gavish took up right where he had left off. With that I got up again, announced that I wouldn't take part in it, then walked toward the door. Behind me I heard Dayan's, "Arik, you can't do that. You have to come back. *Come back!*" The door slamming behind me cut off his voice.

As I walked down the corridor, I knew with absolute certainty that I was right and they were wrong, that the Bar-Lev Line was bound to bring us disaster. But it was no pleasure when four years later it did exactly that.

*   *   *

* Literally "trial by friends." "Mishpat chaverim" was a traditional kibbutz and moshav disciplinary technique that had much in common with the group criticism sessions used in Communist countries.

In all of this there was only one general who supported my position and backed me vocally—Israel Tal, my colleague in the Six Day War and our great armor expert. Other than Tal, the entire high command took Bar-Lev's side. With this kind of support, Bar-Lev considered that he might bring the whole discussion to an end, and that he might even be able to get rid of me altogether, at last.

The first indication I had of how the wind was blowing came in a call from an officer at the Personnel Bureau. How, he wanted to know, did I wish to take my accumulated leave? Before I left the service, or perhaps in equivalent pay after I left?

Nonplussed by the apparent innocence of the question, I said, "But I don't have any intention of leaving the army."

"Really? But your contract is up in another month."

"Listen," I told him, "I don't have any plans to leave. Just send me the forms so that I can sign up for another ten years."

So I got the forms and signed up, a formality I had completely forgotten about and to which I suspect few career officers ever give a second thought. But after these preliminaries it came as no great surprise to find that Commander-in-Chief Bar-Lev refused to approve my re-enlistment.

Still I could not believe it. A professional argument is one thing, no matter how bitter. But forcing me out when they so badly needed every bit of advice they could get, even—especially—when it was not what they wanted to hear? Beyond the personal aspect of it, I was immodest enough to believe that the idea was incomprehensibly self-destructive.

I immediately went to see Dayan about it. But Dayan remained true to what had been for so long his standard pattern of conduct: the most courageous man on any battlefield, the least courageous at taking a stand in public. "Bar-Lev doesn't want you," he said. "I don't see how I can interfere in it."

After Dayan I went to talk to Golda Meir, who had succeeded Eshkol as prime minister. But although Golda had never been afraid of a public fight, her answer was essentially the same as Dayan's: "I make it a point never to intervene in matters like this," she told me.

I was at a dead end. With Dayan and Meir unwilling to lend a hand, there was nowhere else to turn. As outrageous as this development was, it was definitely going to happen, and soon. As the inevitability of it dawned on me, I began wondering what I might be able to do afterward.

I was not the kind of person to accept this kind of thing easily, but if they were really going to force me out, then what was I going to do with myself? At the age of forty-one I was not exactly ready for pipe and slippers.

As I thought about it, political life came to seem more and more attractive. I certainly had ideas that I believed should be heard, and 1969 was an election year. At that time I had two good friends in the political world with whom I occasionally talked about such things. One was Pinchas Sapir, the minister of finance and an important Labor party leader, the man who had sent me on tour to Hong Kong and Australia right after the war. He was from Kfar Saba, quite near my parents' farm, and I had known him from childhood.

The other was Joseph Sapir (no relation to Pinchas), the head of the Liberal party. I had known him too since I was young. He had been born into a family of citrus growers in Petach Tikva, also not far from Kfar Saba. The Sapirs had beautiful orchards, and when I was a child I occasionally went with my father to their farm to get graftings for our own trees.

For a number of years already Joseph Sapir had been suggesting that at whatever point I might decide to leave the army I should go into politics. "You want to influence people," he would tell me, "you have your ideas about Israel's borders, about other issues, so eventually you'll have to get into political life. Think about it."

When it became apparent that I could not find any solution to my predicament, I went to see Joseph Sapir. I described the situation and told him that I was ready to take up his suggestion. Since I could not stay in the army, I was interested in going into politics. I had decided that I was ready to join the Liberal party (which some years earlier had become aligned with Menachem Begin's opposition party, Herut).

Joseph Sapir was a good friend with whom I had had this long relationship. But it was not the friendship that led me to the Herut alignment. Nominally I was a member of the Labor party. I had come from a moshav where everybody was Labor, including my parents. But they had been party members with a difference. As far back as I remember they had refused to accept the Labor party line as it was laid down. My father used to say, "No one is above criticism. Never take things for granted." He had always insisted on judging each political figure and each issue on its own terms, regardless of how they fit into the party scheme. His advice, which he dispensed firmly and often, was to accept only what you can accept and oppose what you have to oppose, whatever the line.

That was my background, although up until the time I was promoted to colonel (in 1958), my political views were hardly of concern to anyone. But that changed as soon as I received the promotion. In those days anyone who became a full colonel was expected to join the Labor party. That was simply the way it was done. During all the years of Labor party ascendance, the politicization of the army was considered absolutely normal. It had always been that way, and as far as anyone could tell it always would be. No one questioned it. So when I was promoted, I too became a formally enrolled member.

But by the end of the 1960s the conflict between Labor and the Herut-Liberal bloc over a political solution to the Golan Heights, Samaria and Judea, and the Gaza Strip was already beginning to percolate. By then I too had developed clear ideas about these areas, ideas that were more in line with the emerging Herut-Liberal position.

So I talked to Joseph Sapir and described to him the situation I was in. Sapir treated the question carefully: Was I really out of the army? If I was, if I could not see any way around the impasse with Bar-Lev, then Sapir and I and Menachem Begin should get together to discuss the possibilities.

Though I did not have anything like a close personal relationship with Menachem Begin, I had known him too for quite a while. Our families had been acquainted since the previous century, and of course I had heard the story of my grandmother's presiding over Begin's birth in Brest Litovsk. In my years as a senior officer I had met him and talked to him from time to time, and after the war he had come to visit our forces in Sinai.

From 1948 until 1967, Begin had led the Herut party as Labor's perennial opposition in the Knesset. As the heir of Ze'ev Jabotinsky's Revisionist movement, he, and his party, had been regularly vilified by the majority Labor alignment. Ben-Gurion, in fact, had refused to even call him by name during the years and years of debate, referring to him in the Knesset as "the member sitting next to Dr. Bader." But Begin had persevered in his role of loyal opposition and eventually won himself the legitimacy Ben-Gurion strove to deny him. So much so that when Levi Eshkol put together his national unity government just prior to the Six

Day War, Begin was named minister without portfolio. Now, in 1969, he and his political ally Joseph Sapir were both serving in the cabinet.

My meeting with Begin and Sapir took place in the King David Hotel, in a chilly air-conditioned room whose windows looked out on the walls of the Old City of Jerusalem. It was a cordial meeting. But as the talk went on, I began to feel a cold sweat forming on my back. In later years my relationship with Begin evolved considerably. But during this meeting I was more than a little uncomfortable. Although the discussion was friendly, there was something about the way Begin spoke, and especially the way he looked at me. The man had an extraordinarily powerful presence. And as he spoke, from minute to minute I had more of a feeling that I was getting involved in something I could not control. I am sure the fact that I had been in the army all those years and was now about to plunge into something new and unknown had something to do with this feeling. Although I was used to thinking of myself as confident and secure and so on, in fact the business of suddenly giving up everything I knew couldn't help but be a little unsettling.

But it was mainly Begin himself. He was talking about how I would be included with them in the election, and that if we were successful I would join them in the government, all the things that I had supposed I wanted to hear. But as he spoke, I became more and more aware of the man's strength and determination. Peering through his thick glasses, his eyes seemed to bore into me. I began to picture myself as Pinocchio when he got involved with the cat who wasn't blind and the fox who wasn't lame.

At one point in the discussion I tried to suggest that I would be able to bring some media support with me. Like other generals I had had a substantial amount of press exposure, and with all my battle experiences, and especially now with the Six Day War, almost all of it had been extremely positive. As a result I had made a number of friends among the newspaper editors, and before this King David meeting I had met with some of them. Gershom Shocken, editor of the prestigious daily *Ha'aretz*, had been especially enthusiastic in his support. So I told Begin, innocently and somewhat proudly, that I had talked to Shocken and that he had pledged "all his support." Somehow, when I said this, it had either slipped my mind or perhaps I wasn't even aware that *Ha'aretz* had been consistently and ferociously antagonistic to Begin (as it was later to become toward me). So when I said that Shocken had promised his support, there was a long moment of uncomfortable silence while Begin regarded me with a disconcerting stare. Finally he said slowly and distinctly, "Support? He will give his support? To whom will he give his support?" I felt as if another river of cold sweat had been released on my back.

But despite my growing if intangible misgivings, the discussion proceeded, and eventually we agreed to go ahead together. With that, Mr. Begin in his gallant way called room service and had a good brandy sent up. Then we drank to our understanding. But even as we raised our glasses, I felt that I was locked in and that I was locked in with someone about whom I had inexplicable feelings of apprehension.

Later that evening I drove back from Jerusalem to Zahala. On the way I picked up a soldier hitchhiking by the side of the road, one of the most common sights in Israel. As almost always happens in such situations, within a few minutes we were involved in an intense conversation. Before long I had told him that it looked like I was leaving the army and going into political life. Without paying the slightest deference to my rank or reputation (another common Israeli trait), this young paratrooper began telling me that I was making a terrible mistake, that I shouldn't do it, that I had to stay in the army—on and on in the most passionate tone.

By the time I arrived home, I had been seized by the idea that I didn't know what I was getting into, that I was taking a step into the dangerous unknown. Lily was waiting for me, in bed already. I got in and covered myself up with the blanket. "Lily," I said, "I feel as if I need to be protected." I had already decided that I was not going to go through with it.

But of course now I had gotten myself into a complicated situation. I had already agreed, the cognac had been brought up, we had drunk a toast. I decided that I had to act immediately. First of all I would write a letter to Joseph Sapir explaining why I was retreating. But what could I say? That I knew plenty about warfare but that I didn't feel I could manage a relationship with Mr. Begin?

The next morning's front pages announced, "Sharon Joins Herut-Liberals." With the headlines staring me in the face, I composed a personal letter of apology to Joseph Sapir and a more formal, briefer letter to Begin himself. But at the exact moment that I was feeling such acute embarrassment, fate was already intervening in my personal affairs. While I was writing to Joseph Sapir, the Labor party strongman and finance minister, Pinchas Sapir, was visiting the United States. When he heard about the newspaper headlines, he was livid. Calling Bar-Lev, Sapir asked the military's most prominent Laborite what he thought he was doing (as Sapir himself told me later). In particular, what did Bar-Lev think he was doing to the party? Didn't he know they were in the middle of a difficult election? Hadn't it occurred to him that Sharon might bring a lot of support with him to the Herut-Liberals? Was he crazy? To cap it off, Sapir told Bar-Lev to get busy and find some way of keeping me in the army and out of the hands of the "enemy."

Under this pressure from Sapir, Bar-Lev contrived a solution. First of all, my re-enlistment would be approved. Second, since no appropriate position was open, I would be given special duty. I would be able to travel around the world, touring the United States and other friendly nations, lecturing, visiting their army units and schools, and generally doing whatever I wanted to do. As part of these arrangements the army presented me with an international air ticket that El Al said was the thickest they had ever issued. The only place in the world it didn't allow me to land was Israel.

For the next seven or eight weeks I traveled. I went on a lecture tour of American universities, I saw some American army bases and schools, and I met with American officers. I traveled to Mexico and then the Far East, where I visited Japan and Hong Kong and toured the thirty-eighth parallel in Korea. I stopped back in Israel only once before the elections, at Rosh Hashana to visit Gali's and Gur's graves. Then I took off again.

In November the elections gave a new look to the military as well as the political picture. Once again there was a national unity government that included Menachem Begin and Joseph Sapir. But now Ezer Weizman, who had joined Begin's Herut party, was also in the cabinet. Yeshayahu Gavish was moved from the southern front command onto the General Staff, leaving his former position vacant. In December 1969 I received orders to take over Gavish's command. It was in the middle of the War of Attrition.

17

War of Attrition

At the end of 1969 the War of Attrition was the most serious problem on the southern front, but it was only one of three major concerns. A second was the Jordanian border between the Dead Sea and Eilat. Here, along what was known as the Arava, Saudi Arabian forces had been stationed since the Six Day War; and since then this border had become the site of heavy, ongoing PLO terrorist infiltration. The third problem—I thought of these problems as fronts—was the Gaza district, where the PLO had become increasingly dominant, a development accompanied by the rapid increase of violence, especially against the Arab inhabitants of the strip. Looking at these three very active areas, I was sure the command was going to be a challenge.

By the time I arrived in my new post, the War of Attrition had been going on for more than two years. It was a limited low-level war, and on one hand it posed no mortal danger to Israel. It was, after all, taking place far from the center of the country, which for the first time was living a normal life. The beaches and cafes were crowded, and people were enjoying the luxuries of peace. But at the same time Israeli soldiers along the canal were living very dangerous lives in the forts and bunkers of the Bar-Lev Line.

Regarded historically, the Bar-Lev Line had come into being more by accident than as a result of careful planning. At the end of the Six Day War, Israeli soldiers had arrived on the eastern bank of the canal. Then, a week or two after hostilities ended, they found themselves under fire from the Egyptians on the opposite shore. And once they were under fire, they had naturally enough begun to dig themselves in.

During the war, Moshe Dayan had warned that our forces should not move right down to the banks of the Suez, but instead should stop at a line some miles away. His thinking was that we should stay close enough to stop any Egyptian attempt to recross the canal, but far enough so that normal life in the canal zone could remain undisrupted. In the event, military circumstances at the end of the war forced Dayan to permit troops to move down to the eastern bank. And although he never changed his mind about the wisdom of establishing our permanent lines away from the canal, in fact, once the soldiers were on the bank, he never did order a redeployment.

So it was that without any long-range thinking being done about the situation, our soldiers found themselves on the Suez Canal and under fire. Without cover, units began building shelters for themselves; and as time passed, the defensive works became heavier and more sophisticated. Gradually, step by step, a fortified line had emerged. Then in 1968 heavy, sustained Egyptian shelling crashed down on the Israeli positions, causing serious casualties. By then it had become a matter of prestige, and there was a great deal of talk about how to protect the line. This despite the fact that the line itself had never been planned but had grown up by default.

The first serious in-depth discussion about the concept of defending the Sinai took place at the end of 1968, after we had already sustained many casualties on the canal. It was then that the debate became full blown and the decision was made not only to remain in our lines on the water but to build a series of thirty-two "ma'ozim," strongpoints, each one a miniature fortress capable of standing up to flat trajectory fire. Huge sums of money were poured into a defensive system that included high sand walls along the canal, underground bunkers, tank ramps, supply depots, patrol roads—the entire system meant to insure control of the water.

It was this system that I had argued so persistently against before I became southern front commander and which I continued to argue about after I took command. More than once I was asked if—considering my strong objections to the concept—I shouldn't resign. But in my view resignation wasn't the issue. I considered it my duty to do what I could to influence decisions. But if I failed, it didn't mean I stopped being a soldier. It was still my job to carry out orders and be there and fight, just like everyone else. Not that I was going to stop trying to advance my views either.

So it was that we continued discussing the concept of defense and that I kept up my advocacy of closing as much of the Bar-Lev Line as possible and establishing defensive positions on the hills to the east. At one point in the spring of 1970 I was involved in another meeting on the subject in Bir Gafgafa, which we had made into a major command center. Bar-Lev was there along with some others from the General Staff, as was Moshe Dayan. As usual, my arguments did not prevail. But afterward we all went to inspect one of the fortifications, one opposite Port Taufiq known as "Mezah"—the quay.

These were days of constant heavy shelling. Since vehicles raised plumes of dust, which invariably drew Egyptian artillery fire, we had to leave our command cars some distance from the strongpoint and walk. This was hard on Dayan, who had broken his leg a short time before, jumping from a helicopter, and was dragging it around in a cast. Like most of the strongpoints, Mezah had been built with a heavily walled yard at its back side, and just as we entered this yard the Egyptians started a round of shelling.

As the first shells came whistling in, everyone ran for the underground bunkers, except Dayan, who couldn't run and just threw himself down on the ground. Since I was the area commander, I couldn't very well take shelter myself while the minister of defense was lying out in the open, so I threw myself down next to him. While we were lying there with the shells crashing around us, Dayan turned his head toward me and said, "Arik, this is a bad mistake. You must convince them to change the concept."

I looked back. "Moshe, just an hour ago you heard what these discussions are like. You know I can't convince them. Why don't you just give them an order?"

"No," he said. "I know you'll eventually do it. Just keep at it."

By the time this little exchange was over, the Egyptians had stopped firing. Dayan and I got up, brushed ourselves off, and went in to inspect the bunker and its soldiers.

*   *   *

The fundamental misconception behind the Bar-Lev Line was illustrated by a brief interchange I had with a group of editors who visited the canal a short time after a cease-fire was finally arranged in the summer of 1970. I was describing to them the defense system (though without alluding to my criticism of it) when Mrs. Hanna Zemmer, editor of the Labor newspaper *Davar*, asked, "How would you take action against the Egyptians from here?" "Well," I answered, "we would use planes, artillery, and tanks." "So where are the planes?" she asked. "The planes are at bases in Israel and back in the Sinai." "And where are the artillery and tanks?" "The artillery is about seven miles east of here," I said, "and our tanks are deployed—some five miles back, some twenty miles back."

"So then," asked Mrs. Zemmer, "what are you doing here?"

"Ah, that's exactly what our discussions are about," I told her.

During the three years of the War of Attrition the Egyptians did not shell the strongpoints heavily every day. That wasn't necessary. But if once an hour a shell would fall in the middle of a compound, where people were working, repairing damage, improving the positions, that was enough. Combined with the sporadic barrages and frequent raids and ambushes against our patrols and supply vehicles, the daily pressure took a steady toll of lives.

Interestingly, especially in light of developments during the Lebanon war, there was no attempt whatsoever by opposition parties to make political capital of the hundreds of casualties we were sustaining. (By the time a cease-fire was arranged in August 1970, our battle casualties on the canal numbered 1,366, including 367 killed.) It was clear to everyone that we would be there until we were able to sign a peace agreement. The price we were paying was considered part of the overriding Israeli effort to arrive at a political settlement with Egypt. So even while fierce debates were raging about the tactics of how best to defend Sinai, when it came to the policy of staying put until we had an agreement there was a political consensus that nobody even considered trying to disrupt. And it was that consensus that enabled us to make the tremendous effort that was required.

But as the death roll lengthened, a popular reaction at home started up. Protests against government policy began to grow. High school seniors (whose military service was coming up) wrote a series of letters to Prime Minister Golda Meir that were published in the newspapers and created a powerful impact. A vicious satirical play about the Attrition

War, *The Bathroom Queen*, was performed, then stopped because it was so demoralizing.

But all the while, the soldiers on the canal kept up their spirits. I never heard any criticisms or complaints from the troops, whose feeling generally was that if this kind of sacrifice was needed to enable people at home to live normal lives, then they were ready for it. More than that, hundreds of volunteers came forward for the isolated strongpoints. Officers competed with each other to command these exposed and beleaguered positions.

Under constant harassment, the soldiers who manned the strongpoints were the heroes of this war. But they were not the only heroes. Crews of civilians worked here too, operating the bulldozers and heavy construction equipment with which we tried constantly to build up the defenses. They too were under fire day and night, making a backbreaking effort and demonstrating immense and mostly unsung courage.

One man who visited us regularly was Shlomo Goren, the army chief rabbi. Goren would come and pray with the soldiers in the strongpoints, often staying overnight. When I happened to be present, I would find myself listening to Goren's chanting with one ear and to the incoming artillery rounds with the other. How the orthodox soldiers in the bunkers were able to pray with such peace of mind was always a mystery to me. But of course the death and dying affected Goren too. On one occasion he carefully dug by hand to remove the bodies of several soldiers who had been buried when a special Soviet 152-mm penetrating shell destroyed their bunker. One by one he pulled the bodies out, not allowing anyone else into the area, where sandfalls covered him from time to time and the remaining supports threatened to collapse at any moment. This kind of heroism was unfortunately nothing new to Goren. In 1948 he had gone by himself into the no-man's-land at Latrun to retrieve the Jewish dead from that field. He had brought back the dead too from the overrun Etzion settlements and from other battlefields throughout the country.

Dayan too came to the line often, demonstrating his characteristic bravery. Looking around at all the activity, I would sometimes think about how just a few short months ago I had been on the verge of leaving the military life for the life of a politician. In fact Joseph Sapir and Begin were in the cabinet again, where they had been joined by their new ally, Ezer Weizman, and where I, too, might have joined them. Thinking about it, I decided I was much happier being a general with a portfolio than I ever would have been as a minister without one.

*   *   *

The Egyptians' approach in this War of Attrition was based on the idea that they could create a rate of Israeli casualties that would eventually prove unbearable to an Israeli public always hypersensitive to every single lost life. In response, we did everything we could to demonstrate that Egypt was even more vulnerable than we and that continuing attacks would create unacceptable consequences for themselves. Outgunned by the Egyptian batteries on the canal, we did not limit ourselves to artillery exchanges. In 1969, before I took over command of the front, our forces launched a number of spectacular raids. On July 29 Israeli frogmen stormed and destroyed Green Island, a fortress at the northern end of the Gulf of Suez whose radar and antiaircraft installations controlled that sector's airspace. On September 9 our forces carried out a large-scale raid along the western shore of the Gulf of Suez. Landing craft ferried across Russian-made tanks and armored personnel carriers that we had captured in 1967, and the small column harried the Egyptians for ten hours. Moving down the gulf coast more than thirty miles, they wreaked havoc among the stunned Egyptian forces in the area, inflicting heavy casualties, including an Egyptian general and a top Soviet adviser, also a general. Already a sick man, Gamal Abdel Nasser suffered a heart attack when he learned what had happened.

In an effort to bring the consequences of the War of Attrition even closer to the enemy, in early 1970 the Israeli air force began attacking military targets deep inside Egypt. Very quickly it became clear that the jets could operate with impunity, penetrating the Egyptian air defenses and hitting virtually any target they wanted. But even these strikes did not persuade Nasser, ill as he was, to end the war. Instead he again turned to his Soviet allies, pleading with them for a solution that would enable him to continue drawing Israeli blood while protecting Egypt from the consequences of her actions.

By the early spring of 1970, the Russians had come up with their answer. Large numbers of the most up-to-date SAM-3 antiaircraft missiles were shipped into Egypt along with their Russian operating crews. Our intelligence told us too that advanced Russian-piloted Mig-21J's were also being deployed in large numbers. By June over a hundred of them were in the country, providing Egypt with a formidable, wholly Soviet-run air-defense system. For the first time, Russian military personnel were actively taking part in Middle Eastern combat. We did not announce it, nor did they. But the fact that the new Soviet role was undeclared did not make it any less ominous. Fifteen thousand Soviet missile troops, technicians, advisers, and pilots were now sitting astride Western Europe's traditional lifeline to the Persian Gulf. And for the first time Israel found herself in a face-to-face military confrontation with a superpower.

Up to this point Israeli air strikes had provided a telling answer to Egypt's artillery and commando war on the canal. But with the advent of the Soviets, the picture began to change. Missile sites that had started off covering the Egyptian interior were moved in stages toward the canal. Russian Mig patrols began by protecting Cairo, then slowly expanded their zone of coverage eastward. From the United States there was no significant response, and at first our pilots were ordered to avoid direct confrontations. As time passed, though, we began to feel that we had no alternative but to unambiguously demonstrate our determination. If we allowed Soviet planes and missiles to protect not just the Egyptian interior but also the canal zone, we would have lost any possibility of bringing Nasser's War of Attrition to a halt, or indeed of protecting ourselves.

As a result, we stepped up our bombing of Egyptian emplacements along the canal. Then on June 12 our forces crossed to the west bank above Kantara, destroying Egyptian positions along a two-mile front in an overnight operation. On July 25 and 27, Israeli and Russian pilots skirmished, and on the thirtieth a full-scale dogfight developed in which five Russian-piloted Migs were shot down to no Israeli losses.

The situation was precarious and explosive. We could not allow the front to be placed under a Soviet protective umbrella beneath which the Egyptians could continue their bombardment and their preparations for what Nasser was now calling the "liberation phase" of the war. On the other hand, an intensified, direct confrontation with Soviet forces would create an entirely new set of unpredictable perils which no one was eager to explore.

On August 7 the dilemma was apparently resolved when both Israel and Egypt accepted an American proposal for a standstill cease-fire. The cease-fire came as a relief to everyone concerned. We were suffering daily casualties on the Bar-Lev Line, and the Egyptian canal forces too had incurred extremely heavy losses from the constant battering by Israeli jets, artillery, and tanks.

On August 8 both sides emerged from their bunkers, at first with a nervous hesitation, like animals coming up from their dens into an uncertain daylight. Climbing out of the underground recesses, Israeli soldiers stood on the top of their positions and looked across the canal at the Egyptians, who were standing on top of theirs. The two sides took each other in, staring with curiosity at their counterparts on the opposite bank, who looked surprisingly like normal people.

Nasser's acceptance was something of a surprise, but within hours of the cease-fire the mystery was cleared up. During the past several months the Soviets had been inching their SAM launchers forward, extending the missiles' range toward the canal. This movement had been the primary target of the Israeli air force, which assumed the role of flying artillery in an effort to stop the advance (and had lost considerable numbers of planes in the effort). Now, even as the cease-fire was going into effect, the missile regiments again moved forward. The truce had been accepted by the Russians and Egyptians not with any thought of looking toward a settlement (as the American State Department had supposed), but as a ruse to advance the SAM's quickly, at least temporarily free from Israeli interdiction. It was an astonishingly brazen maneuver.

It was also a decisive moment. Once the missiles were in place, the skies over the canal would be denied to Israeli Phantoms and Skyhawks. Again the Egyptians would be able to hit us hard—and now we would be unable to respond. They could go on making all their preparations without hindrance. In the future if they decided to cross the canal we would be unable to use our air force to stop them. If we refused to confront the situation now, we would be accepting an inevitable slide toward the next war.

With time against us, Southern Command and General Headquarters began immediate discussions of a response. My own recommendation was for strong, decisive action. We should cross the canal near Kantara, destroy all the SAM sites in that region, then withdraw. But we would keep a limited bridgehead on the Egyptian side of the canal. We would make it clear that we did not intend to move beyond the bridgehead; we did not want to renew the general war. But neither were we going to allow any further missile deployment. The concept was well received, found support, and was given General Headquarters approval.

Now for the first time I began to consider the practical aspects of a canal crossing in force. I made a careful study of the most promising crossing sites, especially Kantara in the northern sector and Suez in the south. In each of these places one flank of a crossing force would be protected—in the case of Kantara by impassable swamps, and at Suez by the gulf. With one flank secure, the opportunity for the kind of narrow-front breakthrough I always favored would be maximized.

Of the two sites I liked Kantara best. The lagoons and swamps north and west of Kantara would provide more extensive protection than was available at Suez. Moreover, a west-bank bridgehead in that area would be comparatively easy to defend. To the south of Kantara an arm of the Nile fed into a sweetwater irrigation canal that ran parallel to the shipping canal. With its right flank resting on the swamps, a crossing force could secure its left flank on the sweetwater canal. And once established, a lodgement in the Kantara area would threaten the major part of the Egyptian army, which was positioned to the south. Kantara may not have presented the easiest crossing site, but its overall advantages for the kind of operation we had in mind was undeniable.

In the end, despite the General Headquarters recommendation, the government decided against the crossing operation. We would settle for the cease-fire and allow the missile defenses to come right up to the canal. I was quite concerned about this decision. It was, I believed, a dangerous display of weakness. My feelings on this subject were shared by others; I even received a long letter about it from Menachem Mendel Schneerson, the revered rabbi of the Lubavitcher Hassidic community. After Gur's death in 1967, Rabbi Schneerson had written me a beautiful condolence letter, and since then we had developed a warm relationship.

The rabbi was interested and well versed in a surprising variety of subjects, and now he was deeply worried about the situation on the canal. The Bar-Lev Line he considered a disaster, an outmoded Maginot-like concept which could not be effective "in our time of jets and airmobile forces." But it was the decision not to react to the missiles that had upset him even more, a sign, he thought, of accelerating Israeli weakness that could only have bad results. "In the beginning," he wrote, "it was a matter of our will. But in the end we will be forced. A year or two ago it depended on us." But then, "the government announced to all concerned that Israel was willing to give back the 'occupied territories.' That was a mistake. They should have said 'liberated territories.' So that by itself was a weakness. Then the weakness was enhanced when it became known that the Egyptians had brought up surface-to-air missiles, and we did not react."

Not being involved on the political side myself during that period, I was unable to judge if the decision not to oppose the missiles was unavoidable. But from a military point of view it put us at a bad disadvantage, and three years later was to create devastating problems for us during the initial stage of the Yom Kippur War.

Even though the missiles would remain unopposed, now that the idea of a crossing operation had been broached the army began seriously to consider the details involved in mounting such an operation. One major problem was where to train, a problem we did not solve for another year and a half. A large-scale canal crossing was no simple maneuver; it required practice under realistic conditions. Eventually I found a reasonable site for exercises at the Rueiffa dam that had been built near the Abu Agheila junction by the British governor of Sinai in the 1920s. Here an artificial lake had been created which caught the flow from the great El Arish Wadi during the desert's brief rainy season. In the middle of the desert we worked to deepen the lake and build banks and walls along its shoreline that recreated the canal. Then, with the construction done, we prayed for rain.

Whether in answer to our prayers or for some other reason, that season the weather contrived to produce a beautiful flood. When we held the first large-scale exercise in January 1972, all the leading political and military people came to watch, including Dayan and Golda Meir. For the first time we were able to see what an actual crossing might look like and to include such an operation in our thinking about how to counter an Egyptian attack across the canal.

With the War of Attrition over, in August 1970 our attention turned again to the question of how best to defend the Sinai. And once more the debate between myself and most of the others at General Headquarters heated up. But now, after the experience of this war, Moshe Dayan was talking more and more about leaving the canal altogether. On the one hand, he felt that our continued sitting on the water line might precipitate a new war and would certainly put us under increasing international pressure. The canal had been closed since the war and had caused worldwide shipping problems. On the other, he seemed to believe that if we allowed the Egyptians to open the canal to normal traffic it would give them an incentive to maintain a de facto peace with us.

But despite his obvious sentiments and his talk, Dayan still declined to take a decisive stand. As a result, the issue was not resolved; instead a compromise of sorts was worked out. We would rebuild the Bar-Lev

Line, which had been severely damaged by the Egyptian bombardments, but we would not equip or man all the positions. (In fact, over the next three years I was able to close fourteen of the strongpoints, blocking them with sand.) At the same time we would start work on a chain of fortifications (which I called "ta'ozim"—strongholds, to distinguish them from the "ma'ozim"—strongpoints) along the hill line to the east of the canal.

Here I put command and long-range surveillance posts, underground bunkers, firing positions, bases for forward reserve units, and emplacements for artillery. I also started an immense road-building project, lateral roads running north to south, and east-west roads connecting the canal with the rear areas. I believed that mobile operations would be our best defense, but to conduct mobile operations most efficiently we needed roads on which we could shuttle forces quickly to threatened or tactically important areas. In addition, I was now convinced that if a war started again, we would have to cross the canal in order to bring it to an end. And for that we would need prepared east-to-west approaches.

Altogether it was a gigantic job of road building. And since one could not predict when the situation might alter radically, it was a job I wanted to complete on a crash schedule. Hundreds of trucks and bulldozers were assembled, and hundreds of thousands of cubic yards of crushed stone were hauled into the desert. I set up checkpoints to monitor the traffic, and each night the Command's chief engineer and sector commanders had to report personally on the progress that had been made that day. Before long the entire zone between the canal and the passes was enveloped in a frenzy of construction.

But even as the road system began to take shape, other sections of the southern front were also demanding attention.

18

Two Terrors

From the Dead Sea to the Gulf of Eilat a dry rift known as the Arava Wadi runs along the frontier between Jordan and Israel. A large part of the Arava is below sea level—1,200 feet below in the Dead Sea area—and all of it bakes in the year-round desert sun, interrupted only by the rare winter rainstorm. But this continuation of the Jordan Valley possesses its own special beauty. Dotted with acacia trees and desert bushes, the area is in truth an arable prairie capable of supporting magnificent crops wherever irrigation can be brought in.

Through the Arava runs the main road connecting Israel's industrialized north with Eilat and the eastern Negev, a road that over the years had seen a large quantity of Jewish blood spilled. Terrorists infiltrating across the Jordanian border found the long, isolated highway ideal for laying mines and ambushes; and vehicles bound to and from Eilat were often attacked and their occupants murdered. Scattered along this road were a number of small kibbutzim and moshavim, a tiny line of settlements struggling to open this forbidding wilderness to cultivation, and these too were favorite targets. So were the Dead Sea potash and bromide works, which were within easy mortar range of the border. There was also the oil pipeline that had been laboriously built between the tanker facility at Eilat and Ashkelon on the Mediterranean coast.

With the closing of the Suez in 1967, this had become a major petroleum route, supplying not just Israel, but Western Europe as well, with oil originating in the Persian Gulf and in the Sinai fields we had developed. And this pipeline, of course, also regularly attracted the PLO attention.

The main problem for anyone who proposed to defend this area was that the Arava was a kind of no-man's-land. A few Jordanian army and police units were stationed on the other side of the border, but they were actively supporting the terrorist infiltration. In the unpopulated, trackless mountains of the region near the Dead Sea a brigade of Saudi Arabians kept the border. (The Saudis were a permanent fixture. In 1948 they had fought alongside the Egyptians; in 1967 they had seen action on the Jordanian front. In 1973 they would fight under Syrian command. The world press often referred to them as "moderates"; we did not think of them that way.) But the Saudis cared even less than the Jordanians about sealing the border; indeed, they had no incentive at all to do so.

Not that this would have been an easy job, regardless of whether they had the will to do it. The border itself threaded down the middle of the flat Arava rift. Just west of the boundary—sometimes a few hundred yards, sometimes half a mile—ran the main highway. Twelve or fifteen miles to the east the mountains of Moab and Edom rose out of their foothills. At night the Palestinian terrorist squads would come down from bases in the Jordanian interior. During the daytime they would shelter in the hiding places near the border, then in the evening they would carry out their actions—planting mines, mortaring settlements or the chemical refineries, setting ambushes. Then, their work done, they would have the rest of the night to withdraw back to the mountains. These depredations had been going on for years, until they had almost come to seem a normal element of frontier life.

After I had had a chance to study the terrorists' modus operandi, I decided that the essential element in a workable defense was to take the offense. First of all we had to make it more difficult for them to approach the border. Then, if they did manage to cross, we had to make sure they didn't get back to the safety of the mountains. The only possible way to accomplish this was for us to operate on the desolate Jordanian side of the boundary, where there were no farms and no settlements, only those few lonely Jordanian and Saudi garrisons.

Once I decided on the proper approach, I acted immediately. In something of a throwback to the early paratrooper days, I began sending long-range night patrols out into the mountains of Moab and Edom, establishing listening posts and setting ambushes for the PLO squads. Overnight these veteran terrorists found that their situation had changed dramatically and unpleasantly. Suddenly their secure routes through the wilderness were no longer secure. They became uncertain, unable to move freely, never sure when or where they might be hit, or if perhaps their trail had been picked up by an Israeli patrol. Instead of hunting down their civilian prey with relative impunity, they now discovered that they themselves were being hunted.

These long-range patrols were almost immediately effective. Groups of infiltrators were surprised and killed, and incidences of terrorism decreased sharply. But it was not my intention to simply alleviate the problem and pull back, only to find a month later that the PLO were again raiding the border. They had to understand explicitly that we were there, that we would stay there as long as necessary, and that any attempt to launch operations in this region would be suicidal.

To make this point convincingly I knew that we would have to establish a long-term presence in the mountains. But the difficulty here was that to carry out any kind of extended activity we would first have to move the Saudis out of the Arava and as far back into Jordan as possible. Unless we did that, our patrols would necessarily be hit-and-run affairs. With Saudi troops controlling strategic locations—especially the single road connecting this area to Jordanian forces in the north—our units would be subject to all the dangers and uncertainties of operating behind enemy lines.

Fortunately, we did not have to wait long for an opportunity to confront the Saudis. In March 1970, the PLO hit the Dead Sea works with a mortar attack from Safi, a deserted Jordanian village just east of the salt flats. Safi was a favorite forward base for the terrorists. It was within range of the chemical works and it contained a source of sweet water—one of the very few in the area. In addition, Saudi forces were camped nearby, and their presence gave the PLO a sense of security. There was, they believed, much less chance that we would hit back if it meant getting involved with Saudi regulars.

The Saudis may have thought so too. If they did, both they and the terrorists were surprised on the night of March 20 when I sent our forces in after the mortar attack. The battle in Safi between Israeli units on one side and the PLO and Saudis on the other didn't last long. And when it was over, we were occupying the village.

Early the next morning we began constructing a road linking Safi with the Dead Sea works. Three days later it was completed. Now, with their communications secure, our units settled in for the long run. For the next three months we sat in that village, which also happened to straddle the north-south track on the Jordanian side of the border. With this strategic point firmly in our hands, I lost my concern that either the Jordanians or the Saudis might attempt some action against our operations in the mountains.

As a result, I was able to beef up our patrols and push the observation posts and ambush sites deeper and deeper into the ridges and ravines of the Edomite range. Now any infiltrators who cared to take the chance were forced to start their missions much farther from the frontier, which meant that daylight often caught them on the Arava plain with no place to hide. Meanwhile, along the length of the border I enhanced the barrier zone made up of mine fields, barbed-wire fences, and a ten-yard-wide strip of soft raked sand that showed clearly the footprints of anyone who crossed it.

Some of the terrorists we caught in the mountains, others on the Arava itself. But when we picked up tracks in the barrier zone, there was always a problem. With a 115-mile border to patrol, often the tracks would be hours old by the time we found them. Of course we used helicopters and overland vehicles in our pursuit, but we soon discovered that one especially effective way to follow a trail was on camelback.

With this in mind, I began talking with the Negev Bedouin, and in short order we had several hundred eager volunteers to serve as trackers in our camel corps. They were quite an amazing sight, these camel riders with their yellow kaffiyehs. Nearby, along the Suez Canal, a modern technological war was being waged between radar-operated SAM missiles and F-4 Phantoms packed with the latest electronic gear. And here on another sector of the southern front you could see camel troops patrolling the desert exactly as they did a thousand and two thousand years ago.

Actually, we did make some improvements on the old-style camel patrols. Often our foot or motorized soldiers would find tracks thirty or forty miles from the nearest camel unit. And although the camels were fast, it might take them several hours to reach the spot. So we devised something we called "camels on alert." We trained the camels to ride in command cars—large open jeeps that were standard equipment in our desert units. When a radio report came in that footprints had been discovered, we would rush the command cars to the site, each with a camel riding on its special platform in the back. Then the pursuit would begin. These Bedouin were wonderful trackers with finely honed hunting instincts, often much better at it than their Jewish comrades. Once they picked up a trail, they were relentless.

Between our operations in the mountains, our improved border surveillance, and our trackers, we had soon killed or captured most of the terrorists who had been operating in the Arava. Once this was done, we agreed with the Jordanians to move our forces out of Safi, after gaining their assurance that they would prevent any further PLO attacks in the area. With King Hussein's commitment on this, we withdrew from the village. When we were out, the Jordanians brought in a large armored unit which attacked the empty village with concentrated tank fire. Afterward they announced that the Israelis had been "driven away." It was an amusing piece of military theater which in no way lessened our satisfaction that by the fall of 1970 we had managed to achieve a quiet, peaceful border all the way from the Dead Sea to Eilat.

I was once asked by a newspaper reporter whether there are any differences between Israeli generals and other generals. I answered that when it came to the professional side, generals in first-rate armies are rather alike: They are all well trained, experienced, courageous, and so on. The difference is that Israeli generals have a much broader range of responsibilities than most. An Israeli front commander, for example, ordinarily sees his mission as going far beyond the military realm. His domain includes improving agriculture, developing water resources, assisting local schools, helping with immigration absorption. He is in effect a voluntary regional resource administrator and adviser. For the most part these jobs are not part of his formal duties, but he assumes them anyway. He knows that his manpower and equipment will be in constant demand by a constituency that is made up of all the settlements and municipalities within his military jurisdiction.

In the Arava once I got a call that a freak overnight frost was threatening to destroy the entire off-season tomato crop. That night the command quartermaster gathered every loose tire in the command and distributed them to the settlements so that the farmers could make bonfires in an attempt to save the harvest. That night was memorable, but there was nothing unusual at all about the fact that the front command had been called on to deal with a problem like this, regardless of how heavily engaged we might have been at that moment with the Egyptians or with the PLO.

It was in accord with this wider mission that the very week I took over command of the southern front I asked senior officials from the Ministry of Agriculture and from one of the major water resource companies to come and review with me the comprehensive hydrological survey of the eastern Negev. As a result of that survey I discovered where the main untapped underground sources were, especially along that arid Wadi Arava. Later, once we had resolved the PLO problem there, we were able to open up these sources and use them to establish new settlements and bring a large number of acres under cultivation in tomatoes, melons, and a variety of other off-season fruit and vegetables. It was one of the most satisfying experiences of my tenure as a front commander, and one that still gives me great pride—especially when I drive through the Arava and see how we have converted so much of this once barren and terror-ridden frontier into a garden.

Even as our anti-terrorist operation was taking hold, the PLO in Jordan was rapidly moving that country toward a crisis. There was nothing surprising about King Hussein's support of the terror squads in the barren south. The fact was that by 1970 he was fighting for his life against a PLO that had established itself in the very heart of his country (as it was to do in Lebanon later) and was progressively undermining his ability to govern.

Unable to remove Yasser Arafat's organization because of his perceived need to retain the goodwill of other Arab states, in the summer of 1970 Hussein had reached a crossroads. On June 9 Arafat's people attempted to assassinate him. During the following months tension between the Jordanian army and the PLO intensified, then reached a climax when, on September 1, Palestinians made another attempt on Hussein's life, attacking his motorcade in Amman. Fighting flared, then receded for a moment as Hussein assessed his options and gathered his forces.

On September 17 he struck, assaulting the Palestinian camps north of the capital. The infuriated Jordanian army fought ruthlessly, destroying the PLO fighting units and pouring point-blank fire from massed tanks, artillery, and armored cars into the refugee camps, massacring thousands." In panic the PLO fled for their lives, most into Syria, some hundreds into Israeli territory. Our forces were instructed to let them come in and to arrest them, not to force them back on the pursuing Jordanians, and not to destroy them ourselves—although these were the very terrorists who had carried out who knew how many murderous raids into Israel.

Not content to stand by and watch while the Jordanians destroyed the PLO, on the eighteenth the Syrians began threatening Hussein. By the nineteenth they had deployed their forces along Jordan's northern frontier. Then, on the morning of the twentieth, Syrian tank columns invaded, thrusting toward Irbid and other centers of Palestinian strength.

These events, of course, did not take place in a vacuum. Hussein's attack on the Palestinians and the growing tension between Jordan and Syria had already triggered a series of moves and countermoves by the American government—which maintained close ties with Hussein—and the Soviets—whose clients included the Syrians and the threatened PLO.

As the American ally on the spot, Israel quite naturally played a major role in the developing strategy of President Richard Nixon and especially of his national security adviser, Henry Kissinger. But with the launching of the Syrian tank invasion, Israel was no longer just one important factor in the equation. The Israeli army and air force now became crucial to American policy. Hussein's survival was at stake, and only Israeli forces were positioned to meaningfully threaten the Syrian tank army that had quickly overrun much of northern Jordan.

On September 21 the United States asked Israel to mobilize her forces. This we did, quietly moving strike units into the Beit Shean Valley on the flank of the Syrian columns—not so quietly, however, that the buildup went unobserved in Damascus, or that its significance was at all unclear to the Syrian leadership. Aware that their bluff had been called and unwilling to risk a direct confrontation, the Syrians began to pull back. By the twenty-third the last Syrian tank was gone from Jordan.

Two days later Henry Kissinger sent a note of thanks to the Israeli government:

> According to the latest available information, the forces which invaded
> Jordan have withdrawn to Syria. We believe that the steps Israel took have

---

* To this day no one knows how many Palestinians died in the slaughter, but careful estimates run in the vicinity of seven to eight thousand.

contributed measurably to that withdrawal. We appreciate the prompt and positive Israeli response to our approach. *

The resolution to this crisis was considered a success by the Americans and the Jordanians. Most Israelis were also pleased with the outcome. But I was not one of them. Prior to our decision to mobilize, Israel's options had been closely analyzed by General Headquarters. While most of the senior officers favored complying with the American request, a minority, including myself, believed that Israel should not interfere with events in Jordan.

In my view, Israel was facing two separate dangers, one immediate, one long-term. The immediate danger was that if the Syrians were allowed to defeat Hussein's army, Jordan would become a Palestinian state. In point of fact, Jordan already was a Palestinian state in everything but name. Originally Palestine had included Jordan. The two had only been separated in 1922 by the British, who gave what was then known as Transjordan to their allies, the Hashemite royal family from Saudi Arabia. In 1970, 70 to 80 percent of Jordan's population was Palestinian; its leading political and cultural figures were Palestinian; most of its parliament was Palestinian; its most prominent cabinet members were Palestinian; many of its prime ministers had been Palestinian. If the PLO unseated Hussein, Jordan would formally become a Palestinian political entity.

Such an event would create serious problems: We would then have on our long eastern border a radical Arab state that would likely become a Soviet proxy. And nobody had to tell me what that would mean. We had just then achieved a cease-fire in the War of Attrition with Egypt. It took no effort at all to recall how difficult it had been for us to make decisions during that war, primarily because the Soviets were so deeply involved. How many times had we considered and reconsidered whether or not to attack the SAM missiles with their Soviet advisers? How many doubts had we needed to resolve before engaging Soviet fighters that were in the process of establishing an unacceptable new set of facts over the canal?

Having commanded the southern front during the war just completed and having fought terrorism for so many years, I needed no instruction on the dangers a Palestinian state of Jordan could pose. On the other hand, as I said to the General Staff, we were also facing a long-term danger.

* Henry Kissinger, *White House Years* (Boston: Little, Brown, 1979), p. 631.

And this danger was that the Palestinian issue would weigh heavier and heavier over our heads as the years went by. Though in the short term it might appear that the first danger was more serious, in the long run it was the Palestinian issue that would be our true bane. We should not doubt that for a moment. These clouds would only grow thicker and thicker. So if it had now become possible to resolve the most crucial of these Palestinian problems, through the formal creation of a Palestinian state in Jordan, that is the direction I believed we should move in.

When I made these arguments my colleagues asked with some incredulity, "So, do you think a Palestinian government in Amman will just calmly agree to let us stay on the River Jordan?" I answered that I did not believe for a moment that they would accept our presence there. "But," I said, "at that point the discussion will be about where the border should be. We will be arguing with them about territorial matters. We will no longer be dealing with the issue of Palestinian identity and about their right to a political expression of their identity."

I did not undervalue in the least the arguments on the opposite side, arguments that had to do not just with the Palestinian issue but also with the weighty matter of our relationship with the United States. But Israel's foreign policy needs were matters of survival, whereas in this case America's needs were those of geopolitical advantage. From this perspective, I had not the least uncertainty about which should take precedence.

As a result I argued as hard as I could against Israeli intervention in Jordan. Dayan was also against it. But the majority felt differently, and in the end events took the course they did. Even today I believe this was one of Israel's most crucial mistakes, one whose evil consequences we are continuing to suffer.

The canal and the Arava were two of the three major fronts that occupied the Southern Command. Gaza was the third, and this posed perhaps the most daunting enigma of all. At least on the other fronts the problems were relatively clear-cut. I had, after all, a specific plan for defending the Sinai from the Egyptians, whatever my disagreements with General Headquarters. Clearing the Arava required a certain amount of ingenuity, but on that uninhabited border one could bring more or less uncomplicated military solutions to bear. Gaza was different. Terror in Gaza was a problem that at first seemed to defy analysis.

In 1967, when Israeli forces under Israel Tal took Gaza, the population was about 400,000, almost 200,000 of whom were refugees or children of refugees who had fled Israel during the War of Independence. Although during the Six Day War we had completely broken the Egyptian and Palestinian forces in Gaza, a loose underground collection of terrorist cells survived, hidden among the strip's dense population and its 20,000 acres of thickly grown citrus plantations.

Some of these were leftovers from the old fedayeen organizations of the 1950s that had been under Egyptian command and had done so much to ravage the southern and central areas of Israel proper. But a new generation of terrorists had also made their appearance. Yasser Arafat's PLO was there, and so was George Habash's PFLP (Popular Front for the Liberation of Palestine), separate from the PLO but acting together with it on a tactical level.

By the late 1960s these groups were attempting to imitate the guerrilla warfare style of the Vietcong. They were particularly attracted to Vo Nguyen Giap's theories of national uprising; and modeling themselves on South Vietnam's insurgents, they began to establish a network of local command headquarters. From these headquarters they sent their cadres into the population to recruit and operate small secret cells that were responsible for carrying out acts of violence, "missions" in their terminology. As they controlled their network of cells, the local headquarters were in turn controlled by regional commands that received orders, information, money, and weapons from PLO and PFLP headquarters in Jordan, Lebanon, and Syria. To run the essential supply and communications channels, emissaries and small squads would slip into Gaza from the sea, bringing with them everything from explosives and assassins to experienced commanders, whatever a guerrilla organization might need to survive and to carry out specific operations. And these were directed not only at Jews but also at the local Arab population, which provided most of the victims.

As defense minister, Moshe Dayan was in overall charge of all the administered territories, including Gaza. His priorities in these places were to allow the populations to live normal lives, to give them the benefit of many Israeli public services, to allow them to travel freely, to open up the Israeli marketplace and workplace to them, and generally to improve their opportunities and their standard of living. He did not expect the residents in these areas to outwardly welcome Israeli control. But he believed they would understand the advantages his policies brought them, and he believed that even prior to a political solution the Arabs of these territories could live alongside Israelis on peaceful and relatively co-operative terms.

These were precisely the goals that the terrorists sought to frustrate. As a result, their efforts at first were aimed not so much at hurting Israelis as at intimidating the Arab population; because by and large Dayan's calculations were right. The local Arabs began to experience an economic revolution, and they saw that, despite their dislike of Israeli rule, in a hundred ways their circumstances were improving. They were, in other words, nothing like a fruitful medium for the kind of national uprising Arafat and Habash dreamed of.

The PLO and PFLP's answer was terror. Starting in 1968, Gaza was hit with a growing wave of brutalization, torture, and murder—all of it meant to frighten people away from any co-operation with Israel or any temptation to take advantage of the opportunities that were remaking life in Gaza. From time to time Israeli soldiers or civilians were attacked, but the chief targets were Arabs, ordinary people who had found employment in Israel, who were using Israeli medical services, or who just wanted to live quiet lives and had resisted recruitment by the terrorists. Buses and taxis taking Arab workers to outside jobs were bombed. Families were intimidated and blackmailed. When a rumor started that Arab prostitutes were giving information to Israeli intelligence, the prostitutes were methodically murdered. A skein of violence wrapped itself around life in the district.

Because the object of their campaign was to terrorize the population, the PLO and PFLP death squads used the most horrendous methods of executing their victims. None of us had ever seen anything like the mutilated and tortured bodies that turned up almost every day. It was as if all the stops of cruelty had been drawn.

This intensification of violence created another of the periodic conflicts between Dayan and myself. His position on all this was that we should keep only the most minimal presence in Gaza. What was happening was not our business. We should not interfere. We should not expect our soldiers to police Arab violence against Arabs. Rather than risking Israeli lives, it would be better to "let them kill each other off," as he put it.

It was a position I refused to accept. I told Dayan that if we had taken upon ourselves the government of this area, then we were responsible for the lives of its people, Arab lives as well as Jewish lives. If we refused to carry out this responsibility, if we did not put a stop to the terror, we would find that today's murdered Arabs would become tomorrow's murdered Jews.

My arguments with Dayan over this matter began with my appointment as southern front commander at the end of 1969. From the start I could not accept his reasoning, and at heart I felt I had to do something to resolve the terror there. But though the situation gnawed at me, I simply did not have time to attend to it. The War of Attrition and the problems along the Arava were by themselves almost too much to handle. And when I did look at Gaza, with whatever distracted attention I could spare, the complexity of the problem overwhelmed me. There were so many people there, so many ways for the terrorists to hide in those dense groves or melt into the population, so many targets for them to hit. I couldn't imagine how one might get a handle on it.

By the beginning of 1971 the cease-fire along the canal was in place, the fortification and road-building program was almost complete, and we had managed to calm the Arava. In Gaza, however, violence had mushroomed, and how to approach it was still a bone of contention between Dayan and myself. But on January 2 an incident occurred that galvanized Dayan into action. On that day a family of new Jewish immigrants from England were visiting Gaza—David and Priti Arroyo and their two infants Mark and Abigail. They had just parked their car when a hand grenade was thrown into the back seat and exploded. The two infants were killed instantly, their mother severely wounded.

Shortly after the Arroyo family was attacked, Dayan visited Bir Gafgafa on an inspection. Taking him aside, I told him, "Moshe, if we don't take action now, we are going to lose control there, without any question." Although we had been fighting bitterly about this thing for more than a year, this time there was no argument. Dayan just looked at me and said quietly, "You can start."

That was it, after all the discussions, with all our mutual understanding about how difficult a job this would be, just that: "You can start." Years before, not too long after I had taken over the paratroopers, Dayan had once said to me, "Do you know why you're the one who does all the operations? Because you never ask for written orders. Everyone else wants explicit clarifications. But you never need it in writing. You just do it." Now it was almost twenty years later and absolutely nothing had changed. Anyone other than Dayan would have carefully formulated an order describing what should be done and defining the parameters of the intended action. But from him there was only a signal, the nod of a head. That meant, as it always had, "Do what you want. If you succeed, fine. If it backfires, don't start looking to me for support."

Now, for the first time, I really came to grips with the question of Gaza. This was emphatically not a standard military problem. Among the region's 400,000 inhabitants we would have to find and eliminate seven or eight hundred terrorists, while at the same time doing the least possible harm to the civilian population. One of the things on which I was in complete agreement with Dayan was his policy of allowing Gaza residents to live normal lives. To me this made sense from every point of view: political, practical, and moral. So the problem was to clean out the headquarters and cells without significantly disrupting normal life. I would of course have to use military force; the trick would be to use it with care and precision and to avoid imposing measures that would hurt the innocent along with the guilty.

Having posed the problem in these terms, I found myself without a single decent idea about how to resolve it. Consequently, it was easy to decide that I would have to start by making myself an expert on Gaza. Once I knew the district intimately, I was sure a solution would begin to emerge.

I spent the next two months walking through Gaza's orange groves and refugee camps. I'd get up in the morning, pack a lunch and a canteen of water, take my chief of intelligence and chief of operations, and head off to that day's sector. I did it methodically, walking every square yard of each camp and each grove. Since my childhood I had known that Arab citrus farmers took a different approach than their Jewish counterparts. But now I examined their efforts with new interest. I watched them working the traditional wheel-driven wells, like the ones I remembered from all those years ago. I saw them irrigating and cultivating and harvesting. I noticed that Arab farmers did less pruning, less thinning— less intervention altogether in the natural growth of their trees. As a result, their groves were beautiful but extremely thick and overgrown, very difficult for a squad of soldiers to penetrate, very easy for a squad of terrorists to hide in.

If the orchards were dense with trees, the camps were dense with humanity—so many faces and so impossible to tell face from face let alone terrorist from civilian. Day after day I walked the camps and towns of the district, and in the first few weeks I felt nothing but despair about accomplishing anything here. But then slowly the despair began to dissolve and in its place I saw the outlines of a plan.

We knew that the PLO local command headquarters were hidden in underground bunkers in the groves and in houses within the camps. We also knew that the PLO organization required constant communication and liaison—between the higher commands outside Gaza and the local headquarters as well as between the local headquarters and their networks of cells. Movement was thus the key to survival for them. As our intelligence people began to identify some of the individual terrorists, I felt that with the right kind of effort there was no reason we shouldn't be able to focus on their movements and track down their bunkers and safe houses.

What we needed was the ability to identify who was who and which kind of movements were normal, which were out of the ordinary. But this ability would require a detailed knowledge of everyday life. There was no way for an Israeli soldier to acquire this kind of intimacy (or anything like it) with the whole Gaza district. But I could certainly expect a given squad of soldiers to get to know a small defined sector—the houses and people, the wells, the trees and irrigation systems, whatever was there. By breaking the great problem down into small, concrete divisions they would begin to find their job psychologically manageable. And once they knew by heart the patterns of daily life within their sectors, they would then begin to notice the deviations, the strangers, the unexplained gatherings, the signs of things that did not belong.

With my plans taking shape, I brought in a relatively small number of first-rate infantry units and began to train them for what I called "anti-terrorist guerrilla warfare." First I divided Gaza into small "squares," sometimes a mile by a mile, sometimes a mile by two miles, laying them out so that they divided along natural boundaries and markers. Each square was given a number, and into each square I put a squad of soldiers. "You only have one problem," I would tell them. "This one single square is your only problem. It is your job to know this square inside and out, and it is your job to find and kill every terrorist in it."

With no book and no procedures to draw on, I had to improvise from the ground up and teach as I went along. To make sure that I conveyed my understanding of what had to be done I bypassed the chain of command and talked directly to the junior officers and squad leaders. I would start to explain my ideas to them and I would hear in their questions the same despair that I myself had felt two months earlier. "Yes," they should say. "We are responsible for the square, but exactly how are we supposed to find the terrorists?"

"Your real problem," I would tell them, "is that too many of you are city boys. You don't know the difference between an 'etz limon' and an 'etz rimon,' a lemon tree and a pomegranate. These are the things you have to learn." I remember standing on a small hill facing the lush orange groves of Rashad Ashawa, mayor of Gaza and one of the major landowners (also PLO liaison between Gaza and the outside, though we didn't know it at the time). "What do you see here?" I asked the squad leaders.

"What do you mean? We see an orange grove."

"Look better. What else do you see?"

"Well, there are some palm trees too."

"Yes, but look more closely at the palm trees."

"Well, two of them have their tops cut off. Maybe they are old trees."

"OK," I said. "When we go down into the grove go to those two trees first."

"Why should we do that?"

"Here's why. Because we are putting pressure on the terrorists in the town and in the camps. So we know they are going to hide in the groves. When they leave their old hideouts, they will need to meet someplace. One of them might say, 'Let's meet in Rashad Ashawa's groves.' Somebody else will say, 'OK, but it's a big grove. Exactly where should we meet?' 'Well, let's meet at the palm trees.' 'OK, but there's a bunch of palm trees.' 'Well, we'll meet at the two trees whose tops are cut off.'

"You have to know how these people will think," I told them. "They are moving. They need rendezvous points. They need drops where they can get messages and instructions. They need places where food can be brought to them. They have to use something to mark these places. So what are they going to use? They are going to use something different, something that stands out just a little. That's why if you see two lemon trees in an orange grove, check out the lemon trees. If you see a dead tree among live trees, check that."

Gradually I taught them to think as if they themselves were hunted terrorists and to look at their sectors from that point of view. I taught them to be always on the move, never to sleep in the same place, never to adopt a pattern of patrolling or searching. I urged them to think creatively. The idea was, I told them, to create a new situation for every terrorist every day. I spent seven months, day and night, in Gaza, constantly teaching, constantly on the move myself. And it wasn't long before I began to see results.

As the operation progressed, it went through three distinct phases. In the first phase I brought the military back into the towns and camps, from where Dayan had removed them several months earlier. Inside the camps we started very intensive patrolling, through every neighborhood and every street. Of course the terrorists tried to hit our patrols. But these soldiers were trained precisely, not just in close combat but also in techniques of finding the terrorists.

Every soldier, for example, carried a rope in his belt. They did this because we learned at some point that a favorite PLO trick was to build fake walls in houses and hide in the narrow space between, which they would enter through the ceiling. So if someone threw a grenade and then disappeared inside a house, our soldiers would surround the house, search it, and find nothing. We could have blown up the house, of course, knowing that the terrorist was inside. But we had our policy of not harming the civilian population or their property unnecessarily and we kept to it. That was where the rope came in. With the ropes our soldiers would measure the outside dimensions of the house, then measure the room dimensions. Where the discrepancy was, that was where we would find a secret compartment, often with several terrorists hiding inside. Of course we did not measure every house; selecting houses at random was sufficient. Soon enough word got around that the soldiers were measuring, so the terrorists were forced to get out of these places and find other means of escaping. They were forced to move, and movement was what we wanted. As one terrorist put it in a letter we captured, "The Jews are driving us crazy."

In addition to the ropes, each squad carried a light collapsible ladder. Patrolling in a neighborhood, they might stop in front of a suspected Arab house; and instead of knocking at the locked courtyard door, they would put up their ladder and look in over the wall unannounced. Inside the courtyard the people would glance up and see a soldier looking at them. Most of them would just be surprised, but if the family was harboring a terrorist, both they and the fugitive might easily panic.

Catching the spirit, the soldiers became inventive at these things themselves. They might hide on the roof of a house, just watching. They would perch in trees above favorite luncheon spots of farm workers. A farmer might glance up from his afternoon nap, or from his morning toilet, into the eyes of an Israeli infantryman. In the way of the Middle East, this kind of thing got exaggerated as word spread. One Israeli in a tree quickly became a hundred Israelis in a hundred trees. Before long it seemed like all the trees were crawling with Israelis. Some of the instances were humorous, but the results were deadly serious. The pressure on the terrorists intensified. They could not keep our soldiers out of the camps, and they began to feel they could not hide themselves inside.

As they grew more desperate, armed clashes became increasingly frequent. We suffered casualties ourselves; but the toll of dead terrorists mounted at what was, for them, an alarming rate. This was the second phase. In the first phase we had gone into the camps and flushed them out. Now they were in the open and trying to fight us off. But this effort was futile from the start, and soon the terrorists decided to avoid contact and go into deep hiding, most often in well-camouflaged underground bunkers that they had constructed in the citrus plantations.

Rooting them out of these places was a major job. The bunkers were almost always deep underground and almost invisible, so locating them required a detective's instinct on top of the knowledge I expected each soldier to have of his square. That instinct was almost impossible to teach.

One morning, I remember, there had been an ambush and one of our soldiers was killed. Afterward, walking the grove where it had happened together with the Arab owner, I came across a metal fence post stuck in the ground. When I asked what the post was, he said it marked the boundary between his part of the grove and his brother's. One of our best officers was with me and didn't bat an eye at the answer. But when we were alone I told him, "Look, it's impossible that that post was a marker. The man was born here. He and his brother know every single tree in their groves blindfolded. I haven't worked in my parents' orchards for twenty-five years, but I could go there in the middle of the night tonight and tell you exactly where our trees end and the neighbor's begin."

So we went back and searched the area again. And sure enough, near the post we noticed an inconspicuous trail through the trees where people had been pushing back the lower branches and leaves to get through. Following this trail, we came to a fence and on one of the fence posts was a can. When I saw this I knew we were onto something, and after a short

search we found the telltale ventilation pipe of a bunker poking up next
to a castor tree. A few minutes later the squad that was with us located the
entrance and shot four terrorists.

So now the infantrymen had to become detectives. We began to see on
the grove floors campfires that had been buried. Ordinarily when it is
time for lunch, Arab farm workers will make a fire and sit around boiling
tea and sharing the food each of them has brought from home in a kind
of friendly, communal lunch. So anyone who looks for these things can
see where one of these luncheon campfires was. But in some places we
could see where the same kind of fire had been raked over and the sand
or dirt smoothed out. Why would somebody try to hide such a fire? Only
for one reason, and if we looked around carefully enough we would often
find the ventilation pipe to the bunker whose inhabitants had followed
their customary lunchtime routine.

Hard as it was, with time we trained ourselves until the soldiers knew
hundreds of tricks that helped them locate bunkers. But even that wasn't
enough. To generate more information I decided to introduce soldiers
who could pass themselves off as Arabs. But teaching a Jew to act like an
Arab is a very complicated thing. There are so many special accents,
gestures, expressions. It can be done—and in the past we did do it—but
it takes years. And I did not have the time.

So I decided to establish mixed undercover squads. I put together
groups of four or five, made up of Jews and Arabs—sometimes Bedouin
or Druze, sometimes even captured terrorists who had agreed to co-
operate. We would have two Arabs and two Jews working together, or
three Jews and two Arabs. The Arabs would do all the talking, while the
Jews would wait for any action that developed. Units like this operated all
over the area.

We used every kind of subterfuge. We infiltrated our own "terrorists"
into Gaza on a boat from Lebanon, then chased them with helicopters
and search parties, hoping that eventually the real terrorists would make
contact. And eventually they did. We would stop an Arab cab driver who
might have been speeding, then put our own people in the cab and tour
the camps looking for the armed terrorists who intimidated and shot
Arabs going to work in Israel. We had people selling vegetables in the
market, drinking coffee in the coffeehouses, riding donkeys. Our "terrorists" would sometimes take a suspected PLO man out of his house and
accuse him of co-operating with the Jews. He would say, "No. I've never
co-operated with them. Ask my commander." So we would get the

suspect and the commander too. Often when we did this, the man's family would run to the nearest police or army post screaming that their son or husband had been abducted by the PLO—because they knew that when real PLO people came to get someone that person would never return. At one point our fake terrorists even built bunkers and became bunker dwellers. Our imaginations worked overtime at this sort of thing. We faced the terrorists with new situations constantly, putting them off balance, bringing them out into the open.

But I also used more direct methods. One of the favorite PLO sites for bunkers was next to the thick cactus hedges that ran along the roads and through so many of the Gaza orchards. These hedges can easily be ten feet high and quite thick, with long sharp needles sticking out at every angle. Since the hedges were virtually impenetrable, the terrorists built many of their bunkers so that the ventilation pipes came up right in the middle of them.

As far as I was concerned, I was ready to dig up every last cactus hedge in Gaza in order to get at these bunkers and the terrorists inside them. But here I ran into trouble with the Israeli civilian governor of Gaza, who felt that such a program would be unnecessarily destructive. As a result, whenever I would order some hedge-clearing operation, he would complain to Dayan (the civilian directorate was directly responsible to the minister of defense) and I would get an order to stop.

To me it made no sense. Clearing the hedges did not create real damage in the groves, certainly nothing that affected citrus production. And we were conducting an anti-terrorist operation against the worst kind of murderers, people who cheerfully tortured and killed their own and who were dedicated to doing the same to us. I wasn't happy about damaging the groves even minimally, but in terms of what we were trying to do, the hedges did not enjoy a high priority, at least not to my way of thinking.

As a result, I gave a standing order that battalion commanders who were out looking at some suspected area should always bring a bulldozer along with them. Behind every commander's jeep I wanted to see a bulldozer. Then when they came to a likely spot, they were just to go ahead and dig it up. And this program too was successful. The bulldozers began unearthing bunkers, and the terrorists in other bunkers panicked at the thought of being buried and started to leave. Again they were forced to get out in the open and start searching for other hiding places.

I also took other measures to insure security. The camps were relatively small places but densely crowded. Built in 1949 by the U.N., they housed refugees from the War of Independence whom Egypt had never made any attempt to absorb during nineteen years of occupation.* Over time, families had grown, and as they did they added rooms and sheds until the camps had become choked with buildings and mazes of twisting alleyways no more than three or four feet wide. These crowded alleys provided ideal ground for the terrorists, and now I widened some of them so that we could patrol more efficiently. In doing so, we had to demolish numbers of houses and build or find new living quarters for the inhabitants.

When a special cabinet committee visited me for a briefing on the anti-terrorist effort, I described the various military measures we were taking. I also recommended the establishment of several Jewish settlements, Jewish "fingers," as I called them, to divide the Gaza district. I wanted one between Gaza and Deir el Balah, one between Deir el Balah and Khan Yunis, one between Khan Yunis and Rafah, and another west of Rafah—all of them built, like the Judean and Samarian settlements, on state-owned land. Standing with the cabinet members on a high hill of dunes, I pointed out exactly what I thought we needed. If in the future we wanted in any way to control this area, I told them, we would need to establish a Jewish presence now. Otherwise we would have no motivation to be there during difficult times later on. In addition, it was essential to create a Jewish buffer zone between Gaza and the Sinai to cut off the flow of smuggled weapons and—looking forward to a future settlement with Egypt—to divide the two regions.

The ministers were pleased by the progress that had been made. They also reacted favorably to the idea of establishing settlements. At the same time I put a third proposal in front of them, essentially the same proposal I had made in person to Levi Eshkol after the Six Day Way—which he had rejected. I told them—Yigal Allon, Israel Galili, and the others—just as I had told Eshkol, that I believed it was time to solve the Palestinian refugee problem and that I was prepared to do it.

The essence of my plan was to get rid of the Palestinian refugee camps

---

* Neither Egypt nor Jordan, which controlled camps in Samaria, Judea, and Jordan proper, had taken any steps to resolve the refugee problem, preferring to allow these people to fester in the camps in order to maintain pressure on Israel. Lebanon and Syria, each with its own camps, conducted themselves with the same inhumanity.

altogether. Despite the U.N. subsidies the refugees received and despite the powerful economic and educational uplift the camps experienced after 1967, these places still bred the most serious problems for us and always would. It would be to our great advantage to eliminate them once and for all, and in my view such a thing was quite feasible.

Specifically, of the approximately 160,000 Palestinians in the Gaza camps, I believed we should resettle 70,000 in the established towns of the district, devoting the necessary resources to build new housing for them and to integrate them into the normal life of these places. Another 70,000 refugees I believed we should settle in the same way in the cities and towns of Samaria and Judea. It was possible to do this in a way that would not bring great hardships on these places. We would take pains to provide decent housing, training, and so on, and to integrate the newcomers thoroughly. In all of this we would have one object in mind: to establish normal lives for the refugees, to break the unnatural cycle of impoverishment and despair that had been their lot since 1949.

One more thing I thought we should do. In order to show our goodwill and humane values, I recommended that we take twenty to thirty thousand Gaza refugees, families that had never had any contact with the PLO, families that perhaps had been victims of terror themselves, and settle them inside the pre-1967 boundaries of Israel. We would settle them in Nazareth, Acre, Ramle, and other places, according to the local ability to absorb them. We would have essentially nothing to lose by this gesture and everything to gain. (I did *not*, by the way, believe that these people deserved to come back by right. They had become refugees in a war they themselves had made. They had remained refugees because of the inhumanity of the Arab states in refusing to resettle and absorb them, while at the same time Israel had joyfully welcomed almost a million Jews who fled or were expelled from their own homes in Arab countries.)

The elimination of the camps would be neither easy nor quick; it would take, as I envisioned it, ten years or so. Yet I believed that with the help of other countries and international organizations it would be practical for Israel to do it. With such massive new construction and new jobs, it would even have constituted a major spur to the economy.

Beyond eliminating the camps, I told the cabinet group, the time had come to begin resolving other long-term refugee issues, compensation for property, for example. Israel's traditional position on this subject was that as we had absorbed nearly a million Jewish refugees from Arab countries, so it was the obligation of the Arab world to absorb the Arab refugees.

And since the Jewish as well as the Arab refugees had left all their property behind, any compensation had to be reciprocal. But though Israel's position on this was absolutely fair, I proposed that we go a step beyond it. Even in the absence of any mutual compensation, I believed we could agree to pay the legitimate claims of Arab refugee families once they had permanently settled in other countries. I had no doubt whatsoever that we could establish a long-term fund for this purpose, that however large a sum we would need for this could be raised from a variety of sources, including the immensely supportive overseas Jewish communities.

But as I had not been able to persuade Eshkol to take these steps in 1967 and 1968, neither was I able to persuade Golda Meir's ministers in 1971. My security proposals—widening the camp streets, establishing Jewish settlements—these they approved of wholeheartedly. But solving the refugee problems, and especially resettling some of the refugees in Israel, that they did not want to listen to. I was even called into Dayan's office to hear him explain that my proposal would be a most serious mistake, that it would set a precedent of unilateral concessions and would undermine the government's basic approach to an overall settlement.

I did not dismiss Dayan's reasoning. It was true that the established Israeli position was based on fact and sense, while what I was proposing would indeed be a complicated process that would generate very real problems. Yet these were objectives I was convinced were well worth pursuing, even if the government did not.

My main success in Gaza was that over a period of seven months, from July 1971 to February 1972, we enabled the people in that district to begin living normal lives again. In those seven months we managed to kill 104 terrorists and arrest 742 others, essentially all who had been operating in the district. (The last to die was the terrorist military commander Ziad el Husseini, who committed suicide while hiding in the house of Rashad Ashawa, Gaza's mayor.) And we had accomplished this remarkable feat with an absolute minimum of harm to the civilian population. Specifically, two Gaza civilians had died accidentally in the seven-month-long operation, one a woman who had been used by a terrorist as a shield during a firefight, the other a deaf man who was mistaken for a terrorist and did not hear the warnings shouted at him.

At the same time we succeeded in maintaining the calm that we had worked so hard to achieve. The settlements we built cut off the flow of weapons from Sinai, and we also devised a way of preventing the infiltration of arms into Gaza by sea. With hundreds of fishing boats operating out of the district, this task required a complicated system of registration and controlled embarkation and debarkation checkpoints. It was cumbersome, and it imposed inconveniences on the Arab fishermen, but it did put a stop to the flow of arms that came in through them, and it did allow them to continue their fishing.

Another danger point we successfully dealt with was the potential for confrontations between Israeli soldiers and Arab schoolchildren, a problem that has become so painful over the last few years. I gave the strictest orders that Israeli soldiers were not to enter schools. I did not like the idea, and I refused to allow it. But to make sure that there would be no stoning or other dangerous provocations, I invited all the Arab parents to meetings in the schools where our policy was explained to them. There they were told that they themselves would be held responsible for their children. I would not accept a situation where our soldiers would be stoned by students, just as I would not accept a situation where students would be beaten by soldiers. The parents were told that if a child was caught stoning a soldier, that child's father or eldest brother would be given a jar a water, a loaf of bread, a head covering, some Jordanian money, and a white flag. We would then transport him to the Jordanian border, point out the direction of the nearest Jordanian town, and send him on his way.

In fact we did this. On two separate occasions we deported a small number of people, less than thirty altogether. That was all that was necessary. Soldiers did not beat students, let alone shoot at them, and students did not stone soldiers. On the other hand, when you walked through the streets of Gaza, you often heard parents disciplining their children vigorously. None of them wanted to end up in Jordan, and none of them was going to tolerate a youngster whose behavior put them in such jeopardy.

Overall, I got tremendous satisfaction from our success in Gaza. I felt I had brought quiet to a place that had been suffering the tortures of the damned. (A comparatively long quiet as it turned out. For ten years afterward there was no terrorism in Gaza; it was completely peaceful.) Achieving this had required innovation and imagination. But more than that, it had required the will to fight these people and destroy them. It had also required a struggle against the inertia of the army, the inevitable tendency of any army toward organization and regularity and order— exactly the characteristics that soldiers must shed to become, as I called them, "anti-terror guerrillas," unconventional fighters who could create "a new situation for every terrorist every day."

Until the Yom Kippur War I used to think that the Gaza anti-terror campaign was one of the most significant chapters in my military experience. Certainly it was the most interesting. In a way it brought me back to where I had started, to the small-scale tactics of guerrilla warfare. It showed too that it was possible to find answers to the most complex problems, as unconventional as those answers might have to be. Above all, it proved, to me at least, that terrorism was neither inevitable nor unresolvable, that a population upon whom the worst horrors were being visited could be freed from the hold of the PLO organizations that look on terror as their standard tool of policy.

One day in early February 1972 I was at home watching the news on television when Moshe Dayan came on the screen to make an announcement. I watched as he declared that the steps taken by General Ariel Sharon in Gaza had been highly effective and that the operation had been an outstanding success. As he went on, I felt my surprise turning to suspicion. Dayan, I knew, almost never said a good word about anyone, especially not in public.

Knowing him as I did, I phoned my headquarters to warn them to be on the alert for something unusual. The very next day we received an order transferring jurisdiction of Gaza from the Southern Command to the Central Command. I knew what it was, this message from Moshe. You have done a good job, he was telling me. Be happy about it. You have succeeded in destroying the terrorists and giving these people the chance to live normal lives. But from this point on, we'll let somebody else handle it.

19

Taking Leave

Under cover of the cease-fire, in 1971 and 1972 the Egyptian side of the canal became a beehive of activity. We watched as they constructed more and more bunkers and gun emplacements, as they moved their missiles forward and carved out launching sites for amphibious craft. In some places they built ramparts on their bank that towered well a hundred feet high. Despite our own ramps and fortifications, we knew we were under continuous observation. All our approaches were covered by firing positions on the high Egyptian banks. We felt naked. The shelling and ambushes had ended, but we had the eerie sense that every patrol, every exercise, every move we made toward the canal was being watched and charted.

At the same time Egyptian units trained constantly. Over and over they practiced moving troops and tanks up to the canal bank, deploying equipment, constructing pontoon bridges—rehearsing in detail each separate component of an assault across the canal. Faced with the problem presented by the sloping barrier on our side, they experimented with methods of breaching sand and earth walls, especially with ultra-high-pressure water hoses. South of Kantara, where the canal splits into two branches around El Balah Island, they built replicas of our barrier wall and strongpoints and conducted crossing operations. Hundreds of times we saw them run through the exercises, launching their assault boats, breaching the wall, laying their bridges, moving their units through.

What particularly concerned me in all this was the discipline with which the Egyptians conducted themselves. More officers were present than ever before, and there was no question that their troops were acting purposefully, in accordance with specific training goals. Their movements were marked by determination and initiative, and even the details indicated meticulous planning. I noticed that soldiers training in different areas always wore the right color camouflage uniforms. A transformation had come over the Egyptians since the Six Day War. This was an enemy with a clear mission, concerned about analyzing its problems, finding solutions, and preparing thoroughly for its task. It was no longer the silk underwear army we had broken five years earlier.

Even during the War of Attrition changes had been noticeable. We had discovered then that Egyptian raids and ambushes on our side of the canal were always conducted across from their observation points (this was such a habit that we could even predict probable ambush sites). My own feeling was that the pattern reflected a problem the Egyptians had with lack of initiative. By carrying out actions across from observation posts, the commando squads knew that their performances were being monitored; they could not make up excuses for unnecessary withdrawals or failures.

Procedures like this told me that the Egyptians were facing up to their inadequacies honestly and were taking steps to rectify them. It was an approach I had never seen them take before, and it represented a profound change in their military psychology. Moreover, the change had already had practical results. Although their commando raids had stopped with the cease-fire, we were still finding footprints on our side of the canal. Their people were coming across at night to reconnoiter and examine our positions close up, then slipping back across the canal. This kind of thing demonstrated abilities we could not ignore.

The observations that I and others on my staff were making led to only one conclusion: The Egyptians were seriously preparing to cross the canal. Consequently, when Anwar Sadat announced in his 1972 Ramadan address that "next year I will be blessing you from Sinai," I for one had no doubts about his intentions. (Sadat had become president after Nasser's death two years before.) Unlike many Israelis, I had always considered the Arabs serious people who almost invariably did as they said they would do. Often their time frame was highly imaginative, but eventually their actions followed their words. In this case I had no doubt at all that at some point they would launch an attack.

But this opinion was not widely shared. The Six Day War had generated a popular conception in Israel that the Arabs were not capable of fighting a modern war, that Israel's social, technological, and industrial superiority was so great that they had no hope of closing the gap. But I had never underestimated them and my experience along the canal had reinforced this attitude. Most Israelis, however, continued to believe, as Golda Meir once put it, "The mere thought of the Egyptian army crossing the canal is an insult to intelligence."

Insult to intelligence or not, as the Egyptians trained, we continued our own preparation. We made improvements on two strategic roads running parallel to the canal, one along the ridge line five to eight miles back (the Artillery Road), one twenty miles back (the Lateral Road). These, with the British-built road along the water line (code name Lexicon), gave us adequate north-to-south communications. From the north-south roads I constructed a series of east-west roads which connected the rear areas with the canal. The entire network gave us the ability to move forces swiftly up and down the length of the front and to the canal at any point. They were the prerequisite for conducting the kind of mobile defense I was convinced we would need.

At the same time, we finished building the string of fortifications on the ridges and dunes east of the canal plain. I also continued my personal war against the Bar-Lev Line strongpoints. Although this was a fight I knew I could not win, I did manage to get permission to close down many of them, reducing the number from thirty-two to eighteen. That at least was some improvement, though the concept that the line represented was still very much alive. More than anything I worried that these places would entrap us in a static and piecemeal defense when the Egyptian assault finally came. Of course I had plans in place to evacuate the "ma'ozim" at the first sign of a crossing. But who could tell what my successsor might do? And by the middle of 1972 I knew that my time as commander of the southern front was limited.

In January of 1972 Chaim Bar-Lev retired, and David Elazar replaced him as commander-in-chief. Elazar, known in the army as "Dado," was a man in Bar-Lev's circle. Years earlier they had served together in the

Palmach, and they had been close friends and allies ever since. In the middle of the year Elazar informed me that I would be expected to retire. Although I was only forty-five, retirement at this age had been a custom Moshe Dayan introduced into the army back in 1954. Dayan's idea had been that all officers should retire by their mid-forties, while they were still young enough to begin a second career. He believed that such a system would help revitalize the army, that it would allow room for the advancement of bright younger men into positions of high command, and that it would help insure a continuous infusion of enthusiasm and new ideas.

Dayan's system had remained in effect after his own tenure as commander-in-chief was over, but by the end of the 1960s it had changed. Despite the changes, Elazar made it clear to me that my retirement was expected. I was to be, in fact, one of the last senior officers to leave under the old customs.

Knowing this in advance, I began to think seriously about a second career. Whatever it might be, one thing I knew was that I did not want to work for anybody. Politics was again a possibility. I had had that brief flirtation with Menachem Begin back in 1969, and the political arena was still intriguing. But even more powerful was the idea of going back to a farmer's life. Along with the military, farming was the only pursuit that appealed to me as a vocation, the only other thing I knew I would love to do.

At the same time, I did not want to go back to my family farm on the moshav. That kind of communal social framework held no attraction. What I really wanted was some land of my own, where I could do exactly as I wished. Lily agreed wholeheartedly, though her main concern was to keep me away from the unfortunate circumstances that many retired generals fell into—sitting listlessly around Tel Aviv cafes hoping for a reasonable job offer to come along. For years she had told me, "When you leave the army I want to be able to say to anyone who calls, 'He's in the fields, he'll be back for lunch,' or 'He's riding, he'll be back in the evening.' "

With our minds made up, we began looking for the right spot. After a search that took us to almost every part of the country, we finally found a large farm for sale in the wild, rolling countryside of the northern Negev. To most people I am sure it would have looked like a barren wilderness.

Here and there individual trees pushed themselves out of the parched soil, starved for water but determined to survive. The deep gullies that carved the landscape were bone-dry, but in their vegetation and seamed walls you could see where fierce winter torrents had coursed through them—six, seven, and eight feet deep. It was a land of powerful contrasts, intense and extreme. To me it was beautiful. Years ago this land had been acquired by an Australian Zionist who dreamed that his son would emigrate to Israel as a sheep rancher. But a combination of factors had brought hard times. In the 1950s the region had been subjected to waves of terrorism from Gaza, and its development was curtailed. Then the son and his Israeli wife had decided to move back to Australia. As a result, though the farm was still working, it was poor and badly run-down.

But I found the primitiveness of the place an attraction. In fact, the moment I saw this land I experienced a surge of emotion, for it was just down the road from Kibbutz Ruhama, where twenty-seven years earlier I had started my career as a soldier. I saw the old well out in the fields that our squad used to drink from. There were the same wadis and hills and eroded ravines we had trained in. The whole area looked almost exactly as it had in the summer of 1945. As I walked the land, I felt that it was this place and this place alone that I had to have.

But how to buy it? I had received from my parents the greatest spiritual wealth a child could want, but not a penny of money—they had never had a penny free. My whole adult life I had spent in the army living on the subsistence salary of a career officer. So there were no savings to draw on. And now as I made the round of Israeli banks I found that a private person simply could not get a farm loan. Moshavim and kibbutzim could get loans, but it was not common for individuals to go into farming, and private loans were not to be had.

At this point a friend came to my rescue, a man I had met years earlier in Ramat Gan. Ramat Gan was a town near Tel Aviv that in 1954 had adopted the paratroop brigade. As head of the paratroops then, I had become friendly with the town's founder and mayor, Avraham Krinitzi, a hard-driving individualist who was still a powerhouse of ideas and action when he was killed in a car accident at the age of eighty-five. One of Krinitzi's acquaintances was a businessman and philanthropist by the name of Meshulam Riklis, who had contributed his energy and resources to building a rest and recreation building in Ramat Gan for the paratroopers.

Riklis was an Israeli who had served in the British army during World War Two and subsequently had gone to the United States to study. There he had founded a commercial empire, becoming an almost legendary figure in the world of business. But although he was now an American citizen, Riklis was still very much concerned about Israel and Israeli affairs. When I told him I was leaving the army to become a farmer, he was not happy about it. "I don't think," he said, "that Israel can afford to lose people like you and Ezer Weizman." (He was also friendly with Weizman.) "I don't think people like you should just be dealing with your private affairs and I don't think you should have financial burdens on you. I would like to help you."

The upshot of it was that Riklis offered an interest-free loan of $200,000 to "help you buy the farm." But there was one condition. "I'm doing this," he said, "because it's not my view that you should have to spend the rest of your life as a farmer. Be a farmer. This will give you the security to do it. But also consider how you can continue to make a contribution. I want to give you the possibility of deciding how you can best do that."

Almost immediately a check for $200,000 arrived, and with this money in my pocket I went looking for an additional $400,000 loan to buy the whole farm. When I still found I couldn't raise the money from local sources, I applied to a Chicago bank that had just opened up a branch in Israel. The president of this bank was Samuel Sax, a captain in the U.S. naval reserve as well as a financier with a lively interest in Israel. Sax agreed to provide the funds. As was common in Israel, the loan would be dollar-linked; that is, the amount of the loan would fluctuate according to the exchange rate between the dollar and the Israeli pound. It was a little risky; but grateful and happy, I took it anyway.

All this was going on during my last few months as southern front commander (since I was on the verge of retirement I was authorized to begin making personal arrangements). From time to time I would go to visit the land, and Lily and I would walk through the hills, planning and talking. We took our four horses to stable them there. I could almost feel what it would be like. I was excited about starting something new after all those years in the army. I felt almost as I had when I finished high school, when I was sure that something very different was going to happen, that a decisive change was coming.

*   *   *

The smooth transition I had envisioned from soldier to farmer was suddenly interrupted in May of 1973 when we received intelligence that the Egyptians were about to launch a major cross-canal attack. When the evaluations indicated that this was a serious threat, I moved into Sinai with the forward headquarters. We brought in additional troops, put the finishing touches on our plans, and held exercises, bringing the entire command to a state of readiness. I also concentrated our water-assault equipment in the northern part of the canal, near Baluza—rafts, bridging equipment, heavy engineering gear, everything we would need.

Baluza was about twenty miles east of Kantara, which, together with Ismailia, was one of the two traditional crossing points on the canal. In August 1970, when the Egyptians had broken the cease-fire agreement by moving their missiles forward into the canal zone, I had made detailed plans for a crossing at Kantara. Later I had rehearsed the whole operation; I knew exactly how the thing could be done. If the Egyptians tried to cross now, I planned to surprise them with a crossing of our own.

I also decided to thoroughly prepare a third crossing point, just north of the Great Bitter Lake in the area of Deversoir. We had already built approach roads there adequate to bring in troops and heavy equipment. But our own barrier walls at that point posed a serious problem. While the walls on our side were not as high as those the Egyptians had built, they were very thick, designed both for protection and to prevent amphibious boat assaults. If we wanted to cross the canal here, we would first have to breach our own walls. The question was How?

To solve this problem, I decided to change the structure of the wall at one particular location so that its outward appearance would remain the same, though in actuality it would be thinner and less dense so we could excavate it easily. But now another problem presented itself. If the wall looked exactly the same, how could we mark the thinned-out section properly? Our assault troops would most likely arrive there at night amid all the noise and chaos of artillery fire and all the other unpredictables of battle. How would they know?

So I looked around in that area and saw a place where piles of red bricks were stacked up, meant for some long-ago Egyptian project that had never gotten off the ground. There we reconstructed the wall and also built a large enclosed yard with a hardened floor almost a thousand yards in length and several hundred in breadth with roads going in one side and out the other to facilitate traffic. Since there were ma'ozim on either side, to any outside observer the empty yard looked as if it might be part of these structures or perhaps as if it had been constructed for some unknown purpose never implemented. But in a crossing battle it would serve as a protected staging area for troops, tanks, and other bridging equipment.

As we moved in extra forces and conducted wartime training, the Egyptians watched carefully. Our opinion was then that they understood the thoroughness of our preparations and decided to put off their attack. For the moment at least we had prevented a new Sinai war.

Another result of this emergency was that I brought the matter of the ma'ozim to a head again. At a meeting with Commander-in-Chief David Elazar during the alert, I asked the question: In the event of an all-out Egyptian assault, how should we handle the ma'ozim that were still occupied? Specifically, what orders should we give their garrisons—to fight, or to withdraw?

My own argument was that they should be evacuated immediately. I warned that if we did not evacuate them, we would end up destroying our own forces in trying to protect them. Once the Egyptians crossed the canal, it would be extraordinarily difficult for our tanks to get through to the ma'ozim. In addition, Egyptian firing positions on the high ramparts would cover our approaches. But still we would have no choice except to try and do it. As a result we were likely to suffer heavy losses in an unproductive effort. After this discussion, the decision was taken that in case of an all-out war, the ma'ozim troops would be instructed to withdraw immediately. At the time, I believed I had established this as a principle. But five months later, when the real attack came, these orders were never given.

By the time the emergency wound down, my retirement date was imminent. Among other things, that meant I was subjected to the usual round of parades and celebrations that mark a general's departure. But I did not in the least feel like celebrating. We had just then faced the Egyptians down, and I was worried that before long they would try again. As a result I asked Chief of Staff Elazar if I could extend my stay for a year. Elazar, as I expected, refused. Trodding the well-beaten path, I then appealed to Dayan. But he, as always, declined to intervene, suggesting I speak instead with Prime Minister Golda Meir. She in turn told me that if Elazar did not approve, then the decision was up to the defense minister. She never involved herself personally in such things.

Meir's tone as she told me this was, in fact, a bit ironic. Along with most everyone who knew her, I had great respect for her strength and courage. In many ways she epitomized the proud Jewish woman. But she was also, I knew, a committed party politician, a Labor stalwart for her entire political life. When she asked herself, as she habitually did, "Is this person one of ours?" the answer for me was clearly no. So I was not expecting any favors. But I felt I had to pursue every path anyway.

My last two discussions with Dayan about this situation were on July 10 and on the morning of July 15, just a few hours before the ceremonies in which I would formally hand over command of the southern front to my replacement, General Shmuel Gonen. On the tenth I was still trying to change Dayan's mind. On the fifteenth I was only giving him a warning. I told him then, "Moshe, I believe you are making a grave mistake. If we have a war here, and we might have one, Gonen does not have the experience to handle it."

"Arik," he answered, "we aren't going to have any war this year. Maybe Gonen's not too experienced. But he'll have plenty of time to learn."

A few hours later Lily and the two boys were sitting in the reviewing stand while I inspected a guard of honor. It was a beautiful affair; all the units were represented and all their flags were flying. When it was over, we got into our car and went home to the military apartment in Beersheba where we had been living since my appointment to the Southern Command (though we had already bought the farmland, the house there had long been abandoned and was uninhabitable). That afternoon I signed all the necessary papers. Then I took off my uniform, put on a pair of old trousers and my sandals, and we drove out to see the herd of sheep that was already grazing on the hillsides of the farm.

The next day I went to work on the farm in earnest. The first job was to try to understand all the new agricultural techniques that had come into use over the last quarter of a century. When I left my parents' farm, we had hardly any mechanical equipment at all—we were still using horses to pull a hand-held plow. And though I had kept myself well informed about farming developments, it was one thing to know theoretically about modern methods, quite another to feel comfortable using them.

Still I felt as if I had come home. I picked up a handful of soil, not the red dirt of my childhood but a fine-grained yellow loess. I rubbed it between my fingers, letting the wind take it. Everything looked yellow in the summer heat—the soil, the chaff lying in the fields. It was different, yet at the same time it seemed so familiar. I realized how happy I was, that whatever else I might do, it was this I was really attached to.

Several days later, I had a little going-away party in the garden behind our apartment to which I invited all the senior officers of the command, many of the region's mayors, and some of the Bedouin with whom I had developed close relationships over the past four years. In a brief talk I told them that with one part of me I was sorry to be leaving, since I thought I was still capable of making a contribution to the country's security. It was a sign of things to come that the next morning one of the leading newspapers, commented sarcastically that "There are many who are capable of contributing to the nation's security, not just Ariel Sharon."

A more elaborate party was scheduled too, this one the traditional dinner given by the commander-in-chief for each retiring general. The usual fare at these things included musicians, singers, and a speech by the chief. Then the victim himself was called on to make some appropriate remarks. Just a short while before I had attended air force general Motti Hod's retirement dinner. Hod was my neighbor, a courageous, likable man who had led the air force on its remarkable performance during the Six Day War. It was no pleasure watching him slowly mount the gallows to give his speech. "That is one thing," said Lily, "that I won't let them do to you." Then and there I had decided not to subject myself to the same experience.

So when they asked me when I would like to schedule the dinner, I said I would rather not schedule it at all. They could send the traditional gift clock directly to my home. Instead of a dinner I would simply like to come by at one of the General Headquarters Monday meetings and say goodbye less formally there.

That was arranged, and when I stopped in at the staff meeting, Dayan was there in addition to the regular participants. He himself gave a little speech, full of warm words for many of the things I had managed to do over the years. For all his usual sarcasm, and for all of the conflicts we had had—the most recent just a week or so earlier—Dayan on this morning seemed to be speaking from the heart. It was a sharp reminder to me that the mutual anger we often felt reflected only one dimension of our feelings for each other.

At the end of this meeting I took Dayan aside and told him I would like to be given command of one of the reserve armored divisions. I would feel more comfortable with the Egyptian situation, I told him, if at least I had that. In fact, I was dubious that he would agree, since I knew that arranging it would put him in conflict with David Elazar. But to my surprise Dayan said he would do it, and he did do it, even though it cost him effort and a fight he would rather have avoided. I did not forget it, nor, to tell the truth, would Dayan have let me had I wanted to.

20

The Likud

One of the other perquisities of retirement was an army-sponsored press conference in which an outgoing general could reflect in public on his experiences, his military views, or anything else he might feel like talking about. When the military spokesman asked when I would like to have my conference, I thanked him and said that I didn't want one at all. Or rather, if I did want one I would make my own arrangements.

Meanwhile I was hard at work on the farm, baling husks in the heat of the summer. I am not the only person to have found that farm work stimulates thought. Maybe it is the combination of fresh air and hard but mentally undemanding work that gets the juices flowing. Whatever the reason, sitting on the tractor I found myself absorbed by various ideas of what I might be able to do in the world of politics. Actually becoming a politician myself, perhaps a member of the Knesset, did not seem hugely appealing. I was sure I could get elected without much trouble, but just joining one of the political parties would hardly put me in a position to have any effect on Israeli affairs.

The reason it wouldn't was that, as everyone knew, government in Israel was ossified in a way that made opposition politics hopelessly irrelevant. Since that was the case, I began to wonder if it might not be possible to make some fundamental changes in the system itself. But if something could be done along these lines, what might it be? And how might one do it?

Specifically, the problem was that for forty-five years the Labor party had controlled first the Jewish Agency and then the state. Although Israel was a democracy, in all that time there had never been a practical possibility of unseating them. As a result, one of the most important dimensions of democratic life—a truly competitive political opposition—had never existed in Israel.

Now the results of all those years of one-party dominance were surfacing—as eventually they had to. Political corruption was becoming more frequent and more serious. Angry opposition was growing, especially among the new immigrants from Africa and Asia who resented the stranglehold Labor and its daughter institutions often held over their jobs, their housing, their bank loans, their children's education, and other basic facts of their existence. A proliferation of bureaucratic organizations that paralleled government agencies fed thousands of Labor Alignment functionaries and imposed a heavy burden on almost all the country's economic and social endeavors. One generation had accepted Labor's natural right to order the country's life according to its own socialist vision. Now much of that acceptance was gone. But with almost a dozen small parties fighting each other for votes, there was no politically effective way to channel the unhappiness.

Beyond the domestic disaffection, the War of Attrition had witnessed the first cracks in the consensus on national security. There had been the famous protest letter of the high school students to Golda Meir, and the satirical play *The Bathroom Queen* had been only the first cultural sign of an attack on the time-honored leaders of the political and military worlds. The day seemed to be coming when the substantially monolithic face Israel had always shown the rest of the world would start to crumble. Perhaps that day was already here.

The result of all this rumination was the idea that an alignment of opposition parties might be constructed, a single bloc that would be powerful enough to challenge the Labor party and its allies at the polls. Given the bitter hatreds among the various opposition groups, this was a notion that perhaps no experienced Israeli politician would have considered serious or even sane. My advantage was that I did not have a shred of political experience and so I was blind to the concept's irrationality. On the contrary, the more I thought about it the more I believed that coalition was the only sensible path for the opposition to take.

Once I had fixed on the idea, it also seemed to me that I might be the right person to bring it to life—although looking back on it, that notion was at least as naive as the original concept. Still, such a thing would be a huge challenge, which I loved. And if successful, it would have made a fundamental impact on Israel's political life.

When all this was clear, I decided that rather than presenting the concept privately to Mr. Begin or one of the other opposition leaders, it would make sense simply to hold a news conference and announce it. That would get the idea out to the public in a more dramatic way. If it attracted any media or popular support, I would then be in a stronger position to approach Begin and the others. And if it didn't, then I would know for sure that my thinking was wrong and that there was no grass roots support for what I had in mind.

Toward the end of July I sold two tons of hay. With the proceeds I rented a hall in Tel Aviv's Bet Sokolov Press Building and announced the news conference. A week later I was standing on the podium in front of a full house. It seemed like every newspaper in the country had sent someone. Even without knowing what I was going to say, they had been attracted there, partly, I think, by my maverick reputation and partly because the event itself was unusual. Always before, retired generals had had their conferences arranged by the army and hosted by army spokesmen. If I was doing something different, maybe what I said would be controversial enough to make headlines.

By the time I finished outlining the opposition coalition that I envisioned and explaining why it was necessary, most of them had decided it was definitely news. The next morning's papers announced the proposed coalition. Some opposed it and some favored it, but on all sides it had attracted interest.

The following day Lily and I took the children to the beautiful Haruba Beach between Rafah and El Arish, where the date palms grow right down to the edge of the sea. Lying there on the sand, I was half listening to a radio that some other beachgoer had left on, when I heard my name mentioned. Some political figure was commenting on the press conference, describing my political naiveté in terms that made the whole affair seem pitiful. I was, he declared for everybody to hear, "a political infant."

Lying on the beach in my bathing suit, I suddenly felt a rush of embarrassment. There I was, recognizable to anybody who cared to look, and now I had been exposed as nothing more than a political infant with a stupid idea. I wanted to cover myself up. It was my first real experience with public ridicule, and I felt that everyone on the beach must be staring at me with either pity or scorn. In the army, despite my various disagreements with others, I had always been protected from public exposure. Within the military, of course, your conduct is scrutinized and you are judged constantly; but when it comes to public issues, every officer is covered by a coating of protective feathers. It wasn't that I expected to carry that protection with me into civilian life, but neither was I quite prepared to be the object of outright derision.

Another reason the commentator's words had affected me was that in fact I had no guarantee the idea of a coalition would be taken seriously. It was unclear if a single one of the politicians would deign to sit down and discuss such a thing with a retired general who had no ties with any party and no formal base of electoral support. So there was indeed a chance that I would be revealed as a political naif. On the other hand, it was now three and a half months before the election. I knew that each one of the opposition party leaders would be casting around anxiously for any potential advantage he could find. With even a modicum of voter interest, the coalition idea would seem at least worth talking about. I was betting that they would have to pay attention.

Having convinced myself of this, I began calling on the various party bosses, among them Simcha Ehrlich and Dr. Rimalt of the Liberals (Joseph Sapir had retired), Shmuel Tamir of the Free Center, Yigal Hurevitz of RAFI, Moshe Shamir and Avraham Yoffe of the Land of Israel Movement, and, of course, Menachem Begin. As each one in turn agreed to sit down and talk, I knew that at least my initial reasoning had been correct. To a man they were wary and skeptical. But none of them could afford to simply ignore the idea or to stay aloof from whatever might possibly come of it.

Although I now began negotiating in earnest with the different parties, in fact everyone knew that the key lay in Mr. Begin's hands. While his Herut party had never polled more than 15 percent of the total vote, it was still by far the strongest and best organized of the opposition factions. Herut's 1965 alliance with the Liberals made it that much more powerful. If Begin was willing to accept the smaller parties, they would have to think seriously before saying no. If he wasn't willing to accept them, it wouldn't matter what they said.

✳   ✳   ✳

By this time Begin and I had gotten to know each other somewhat better than we had in 1969. From time to time I saw him at his home in Tel Aviv, and after I became the southern front commander he visited us in the Sinai on occasion. Although he was the head of a party, a cabinet member, and an internationally known political figure, Begin lived the most modest, austere life imaginable. His tiny apartment on the ground floor of a nondescript building was the same place he had lived during his underground days. The furnishings were poor, almost decrepit. Of the few chairs he had there for the convenience of visitors, it was hard to find one without a broken arm or leg. He did his writing and thinking not in a study but at a rickety table next to the wall in the living room. He simply did not pay the slightest attention to his own comforts, let alone to luxuries.

I remember at one point when he was in Beersheba lecturing, Lily and I had invited him to have dinner with us. But at first we had been hesitant about it, because even though we were living in a small military apartment ourselves, still we had paintings and photographs on the walls, vases full of flowers on the tables, and armchairs to sit in. I was afraid that compared to his standards our way of life might appear ostentatious.

Begin's attitude toward material comforts was something he shared with many of the leaders in his generation, Zionists who had neither time for nor interest in their personal well-being. Another thing he had in common with that generation was his admiration for Jewish soldiers. Ben-Gurion, for example, had the same feelings. In a way they were fascinated by the idea of Jewish fighters.

A great deal has been said about Begin's love of military pomp and the show of power. And it is easy to denigrate such things. But to understand how that generation felt one must remember that they grew up in places where the most horrifying things happened regularly to Jews who were helpless to defend themselves. In one of Israeli writer Amos Oz's stories an immigrant from the ghettos sees a picture book about tank battles in the Sinai. He looks at the Jewish tank columns and fantasizes what might have happened had they magically appeared years ago in front of Warsaw or on the Russian steppes. Like this character in the story, Begin and his peers lived through many times when they knew that if only there had been Jewish soldiers many of the tragedies and disasters might not have happened. Or at the very least people would have been able to fight for their lives. I remember Ben-Gurion talking with such emotion about Jewish pilots, Jewish paratroopers, Jewish commanders, as if the very existence of such individuals was a kind of miracle in itself.

To my generation, the idea of Jewish fighting men was perfectly natural. So we looked on a Ben-Gurion's or a Begin's attitudes as anachronistic and romantic. We didn't have any particular emotional attachment to Jewish pilots or Jewish soldiers—although we might admire good Jewish pilots and good Jewish soldiers. But for Begin, as for Ben-Gurion, Jewish fighting men were something special. Such people spoke to something deep in their psyches.

As Begin and I began our discussions about the coalition (which we eventually named "Likud"—Unity), other personal things were in the background too. One was that on the terrible day of Gur's death, Begin had come to the Tel Hashomer hospital, where the funeral procession began. Apparently with all the rush of Rosh Hashana eve and the suddenness of everything, he had arrived late. As the procession began, I saw him from the window of my car standing on the sidewalk, a look of profound grief on his face. He did not see me, and I never mentioned it to him afterward. But it was something I never forgot. Years later when we were involved in our own battles, even when I was absolutely furious at him for one reason or another, that always weighed very heavily in my scales.

I also came to these discussions with Begin loaded down with baggage that went back a good deal further. Politically, I had never been a supporter of either him or the Herut party he headed. Like Herzl and Jabotinsky, Begin belonged to the tradition of "political Zionism." Like them, he was a man who believed in the power of words and legal terms, and consequently he gave a high priority to such things as pronouncements, declarations, and formal agreements. Underneath, the political Zionists believed in achievements as a result of political acts and deeds. This approach was diametrically opposite that taken by "pragmatic Zionism," the tradition to which my family belonged. In pragmatic Zionist circles the idea was to create facts on the ground: reclaim another acre, drain another swamp, acquire another cow. The general attitude was: Don't talk about it, just get it done.

Begin's florid style left me cold. On the other hand, the substance of much of what he was saying I agreed with—his attitude toward the Land of Israel, Jewish rights, Jewish pride, Jewish lives. Those things echoed my own beliefs, even if his manner of expression was not particularly to my liking.

All in all we were perhaps not that strange a couple. But although we may now have known each other a little better than we had in 1969, the events of that summer were still a source of tension. After that Begin knew for certain that I would never accept his leadership blindly. When it came to those things I believed in he would have no stronger, more tenacious backing than mine. But he could never count on me as one of his completely loyal all-out supporters. With that understanding, no doubt he wondered just how comfortable a political ally I would make.

Against this background, the critical moment in our talks came one day when he asked, "Arik, are you going to go along with me all the way in this or not?" When I answered that I would, that was the turning point. From that moment Begin accepted in principle the idea of the Likud.

But while Mr. Begin's agreement was a prerequisite for moving ahead, it was also his relationships with some of the other opposition leaders that presented the greatest obstacles. To succeed, we had to bring together a number of people who had been fighting Begin ferociously for years. Foremost among them was Shmuel Tamir, the head of the Free Center party.

Tamir was a veteran of Begin's "fighting family," the Irgun, a brilliant lawyer who in the early 1950s had been the rising star of the Herut. At that time he caused immense problems for the Israeli establishment (and made his reputation) by prosecuting a several-years-long showcase trial in which he demonstrated that during the Holocaust the Jewish Agency had made insufficient efforts to save the Hungarian Jewish community. His performance then had earned him the eternal hatred of Labor party leaders, including Ben-Gurion, who afterward habitually referred to him as "ocher Yisrael"—defiler of Israel.

Begin, of course, loved him. But Tamir's problem was that his brilliance was complemented by unconcealed ambition and poor timing. Far and away the most talented of the younger generation of Herut politicians, he was Begin's obvious heir. But instead of waiting for the mantle to descend on him, he made the mistake in 1965 of directly challenging Begin for party leadership. Not a man who tolerated even mild opposition from his own, Begin considered Tamir's challenge outright treason.

The end result was that Tamir was suspended by a Herut party court, after which he left to form his own party, the Free Center. Even then the bond that had been forged between Begin and Tamir over so many years was not broken. But what before had been love was now transformed into love-hate. And though the love was still there, the hatred burned.

Consequently, as close as their political views were, bringing Begin back together with Tamir was immensely more difficult than bringing Ben-Gurion together with even his confirmed ideological opponents. The core group of absolutely loyal Herut people who had suffered with Begin in the underground and then in the political wilderness could not bear the idea of accepting an individual like this back into the fold.

But for the Likud to work, Tamir had to be brought aboard. At the same time I also had to bring in a splinter group from Labor led by Yigal Hurevitz, who later became minister of finance and minister of industry. While Tamir's Free Center was on the right, Hurevitz's people were from the left, traditional Herut haters for whom in the old days Begin's name (when it was pronounced at all) was typically followed by the epithet "fascist."

Hurevitz's splinter group was the remnant of the RAFI party established by David Ben-Gurion in 1965 after he was expelled from the Labor party by his old comrades with whom he had been fighting bitterly. In RAFI's first election they won ten seats in the Knesset. But by 1969 some of the RAFI stars had left and Ben-Gurion and Hurevitz managed to gain only four seats. Then in 1970 Ben-Gurion retired from politics for good. RAFI consequently was now a very minor voice but an important one nevertheless. For if RAFI could be brought into the Likud, it would give Begin access to traditional Labor voters.

On the one hand, considering the history between Ben-Gurion's backers and Begin's, such an alliance seemed improbable. On the other, when it came to national issues—borders, peace, security, and so on—RAFI's positions were not that far from Herut's. So despite appearances, I chose to be optimistic. The problem was in getting Begin and the others to see it my way.

That August negotiations were thick between myself and the contending parties. In the morning I'd work in the fields, then take a shower and drive into Tel Aviv to sit down with whoever was on the schedule that day. Occasionally I'd find myself on one side of the table, with twelve or fourteen party stalwarts on the other, all of them wanting something different and all of them talking at once. At times I could not believe I had gotten myself into this voluntarily. More than once I was ready to give the whole idea up. In the early mornings Lily and I would some-times walk around the farm savoring the absolute silence and beauty of the Negev hills. Then I would find myself thinking, Maybe I'm making a mistake. It would be so easy to just live here quietly. Inevitably, however, I would be back in Tel Aviv that afternoon listening to what I considered the most petty intriguing and maneuvering for an extra concession here or an extra seat there.

As the weeks passed, though, I recognized that my standing with Begin was improving. I used to joke that this was due to my feet as much as anything else. Working in the fields in my sandals, a fine black dust would get ingrained in my skin so deeply that even though I showered before going to town my feet would still look black. Sitting next to Begin at the negotiating sessions, I would notice him glancing at my feet (still in sandals) and wondering that someone could come straight off a farm to a political meeting. Golda Meir or Ben-Gurion would have found it entirely normal, but to Begin the idea was exotic.

He also was surprised when he would occasionally call the farm in the morning. We had there a Circassian watchman and gardener by the name of Abu Rashid, an exceptionally clever man, quite old by that time, and a friend of many years. I would ask him to sit by the phone while I was out in the fields and take messages that came in, most of which were about the negotiations. Abu Rashid spoke Hebrew well but with an Arabic accent. Since he could not write Hebrew, he would take down the messages phonetically in Arabic script.

Not infrequently Begin himself would call. Now men from Begin's background might under ordinary circumstances rarely have occasion to speak to an Arab; but when he called my house and asked whom he was speaking to, the Arab voice on the other end would say, "Abu Rashid. You are speaking to Abu Rashid. Who is this?" And then the voice would ask Begin for whatever important message he might have for Arik. Begin of course would leave the message, but this too made him wonder. At one point he asked me, "Who is this Abu Rashid I talk to at your house?" Unable to resist the opening, I answered, "Abu Rashid? Oh, he's my political adviser and press liaison." Begin was pretty sure I was joking, but he still considered it an unusual thing. So I used to say that there were two things that persuaded Begin to go along, my feet and Abu Rashid. As with most jokes, there was an element of truth to it.

Over weeks of hard talks I struggled to convince Begin that he had to accept even his opponents into the coalition, especially Hurevitz and

Tamir. It was, I told him, essential to have Hurevitz in the Likud, and it would be a major mistake to leave Tamir out. "Tamir," I said, "is your own flesh and blood. As long as he is outside, he will drain off some of our supporters. On the other hand, Yigal Hurevitz has to be in, because that will give us a window to a whole new group of supporters. Suddenly Labor voters will be able to see that people from Labor have actually joined you. And that will make it psychologically possible for them to give us their vote."

That was the basic strategy: Bring the Herut together and split Labor. From my point of view it was the overall strategy that was significant, not how many seats we might give to each of the Likud parties—which was what they were fighting about like cats and dogs. But I did recognize that Begin had a responsibility toward all those people who had been with him in the desert for decades. And it was true, these people had really suffered for their loyalty. Regarded as enemies by Labor, they had often had difficulty getting jobs; they had been excluded from government employment; they had been unable to rise to high rank in the army. In almost fifty years of rule, the Labor party had tied up all the strings of social control. So Begin really did owe these loyalists of his a debt that he was intent on paying if once he came to power. He was also worried that if the other parties had too many seats he would not have adequate strength when hard decisions had to be made. And so he was ready to fight his potential partners for the last seat.

I, on the other hand, had no political obligations to anyone. As a result, I had no compunctions about pressing Herut hard for concessions, something that aroused the loyalists to fury. It was Dr. Yochanan Bader who reined them in. Bader was one of the oldest Herut warhorses, a top economist and powerful writer who was a strong and colorful personality in his own right. In one meeting Bader became exasperated with his colleagues' attacks on me and told them, "What are you surprised about? Arik isn't a Liberal and he isn't a Tamir man and he isn't one of us. The only thing he supports is the Likud."

With Bader helping to quiet the ranks, Begin found it easier to agree on an overall strategy and move toward accomplishing it. Up until he began to move, the whole idea had a tentative air about it; and though I didn't realize it, the interparty conflicts were little more than skirmishes. But once the Likud looked like it might become a reality, the parties began fighting each other in earnest about who would get seats, what places on the list of candidates would go to whom, how places in the

government might be shared, what the platform planks would be—
endless meetings and endless acrimony.

Sometimes we would gather at Begin's apartment. But most often we
would meet at the Herut headquarters, where negotiations would go on
far into the night and Shmuel Tamir's beautiful secretary would bring in
food and drinks, but only to his side of the table. At RAFI headquarters
the struggle would be just as intense. But Yigal Hurevitz, with his
collectivist values, would provide ice cream and hot chocolate for
everybody and dish out the ice cream himself.

For seven heated weeks these negotiations went on. To increase the
momentum for an agreement I worked hard with the newspaper people
and managed to get significant backing from them. With editorials
coming out in support of the Likud idea, pressure mounted on the parties
to come to terms, especially as the deadline for the Histadrut elections
approached.

The Histadrut is Israel's workers' association, though in reality it is far
more than that term implies. In fact the organization exerts pervasive
influence on Israeli society through its economic activities (it controls 30
percent of the country's economic life) and its social service network as
well as through its trade union work. Until 1965 the Histadrut was
exclusively associated with the socialist parties. But since then it had
opened itself to the entire political spectrum. Because the vast majority of
Israeli workers are members, the Histadrut's internal elections are an
important testing ground for national elections.

In 1973 Histadrut elections were scheduled for September 11, and
candidate lists had to be submitted three weeks beforehand. By late
August we had reached agreement among Herut, the Liberals, RAFI,
and the Land of Israel party. The only holdout was Shmuel Tamir and
his Free Center. Between Tamir's relentless bargaining and the antipathy
of Begin's diehards, I had just not been able to hammer out a
compromise.

Working frantically, the afternoon before the deadline I presented a
last-ditch proposal for a deal. Herut went along, but still Tamir held out,
wavering about which way to go. From the fourth floor of the Herut
headquarters where we were meeting he called his wife, Ruth, who was
also his political confidante. When she arrived, the two of them together
with several others from his inner circle huddled in a corner whispering.
Time was running out, and upstairs on the fourteenth floor the press
corps was waiting for our announcement.

Suddenly I saw Tamir get up and head for the stairs (one could never be sure how the building's antique elevator might be working). I understood instantly that he had decided to reject the offer and was determined to make his announcement of it first—in his own terms— rather than let me put the Free Center rejection in the context I thought it deserved. Watching Tamir disappear into the stairwell, I realized that I wanted to make the first announcement as badly as he did.

With Tamir half a flight up already, I took off behind him. At every turn in the staircase he glanced behind to see if I was gaining. I was, and somewhere near the fourteenth floor I caught him, though by that time neither of us was exactly running. I felt as if I was about to collapse, and Tamir's panting was so labored I was sure he was already dying. Meanwhile the press was waiting for us just through the stairwell doors.

I managed to catch my breath first. And when I did, I announced that Mr. Tamir was breaking the coalition, out of a short-sighted and self-destructive regard for his own interests, putting it in exactly the terms he was afraid I would use. By the time I was finished, Tamir had recovered, and he made his own announcement about the importance of keeping the Free Center independent. But there was no question that his statement was less effective than it might have been had he beaten me up the stairs.

In fact Tamir almost immediately realized he had miscalculated. The press's reaction was extremely negative, and late that night he reversed himself and decided that he had no alternative but to join. By then it was too late for the Histadrut elections, but there was plenty of time left for Tamir to enroll the Free Center in the Likud for the national elections.

During the weeks when the Likud negotiations were in high gear, I had been asked by several of the leaders to join one of the parties myself. Inevitably that prospect had become an element in the talks. But I had resisted it. In the first place, my idea all along was that creating a Likud coalition was just a first step. The second step would be to transform the coalition into a single unified party. To do that, I thought it would be important for me to remain independent. Secondly, I was not eager to put myself in the position of having to accept party discipline and a party line. Neither of these was a bottom-line position. But in any event I knew beyond a doubt that I was not going to be pressured into joining a party only to find a short time later that the Likud negotiations had not succeeded.

After a good deal of haggling, in the end I agreed to join the Liberals, but only after the Likud coalition had been accepted by all the parties and formalized in an agreement. This happened on September 14, and a week later I was officially inducted into the Liberal fold. At the same time, I was also named as the Likud's campaign manager for elections, now only two months off.

By this time I was well on my way to becoming a bona fide politician. If the Likud negotiations had given me a crash course introduction to the calling, managing the national campaign was like graduate school. Among other things, I was learning why it is that politics is so difficult for people who come to it out of a different world, especially, perhaps, for military people. Many retired career officers try the political life, only to give it up after a brief, unhappy experience. Now I knew why.

Like politics, military life is a constant struggle. But with all the difficulties and bitterness that may develop, at least there are certain rules. In politics there are no rules, no sense of proportion, no sensible hierarchy. An Israeli military man setting foot in this new world has most likely experienced great victories and also terrible defeats. He has had moments of exultation and moments of deepest grief. He knows what it is to be supremely confident, even inspired. But he has also suffered the most abject fear and the deepest horror. He has made decisions about life and death, for himself as well as for others.

This same person enters the political world and finds that he has one mouth to speak with and one hand to vote with, exactly like the man sitting next to him. And that man perhaps has never witnessed or experienced anything profound or anything dramatic in his life. He does not know either the heights or the depths. He has never tested himself or made critical decisions or taken responsibility for his life or the lives of his fellows. And this man—it seems incredible—but this man too has one mouth and one hand.

That is how it looked to me; and that, or something very similar, is how it has looked to every military man who enters politics. It is not that they don't understand democracy; in Israel everybody is nursed on democracy. But that doesn't mean that everybody is able to become a democratic politician. And at the beginning you experience a kind of shock when you understand that in the political arena nothing you have done in your previous life makes any difference. You may be arguing with someone who has never even served in the army. And when his turn comes, he looks you straight in the eye and he says everything that you can say. And he can say it in the rudest manner imaginable. And when it comes to a decision, his vote is worth exactly what yours is.

Needless to say, I kept this kind of feeling very much to myself. But inside I was astonished. Of course many of the party people did have military experience. But many of those who had come up through the political apparatus didn't. And it just made no difference that I had jumped into trenches or been wounded or managed complex battles. None of this counted in the least. I was in a new game in a new arena. So it was not the different circumstances of life that took getting used to. The trick was to overcome that initial sense of astonishment, to force the old mentality to relinquish its hold and to accept a new reality.

I had pretty much accomplished this difficult trick when in early October I received a telephone call from Southern Command. A military alert had been called and they had intelligence information they wanted to show me. Would I please report immediately to my reserve division. It was October 5, a month and four days before the Likud's first national election.

21

Yom Kippur, 1973

he call from Southern Command came on a Friday afternoon in the
middle of a tumult at Likud headquarters. Sabbath was just a few
hours away, and sundown would also mark the beginning of Yom
Kippur, the most solemn day in the Jewish year. Along with everyone else
in the office I was rushing to tie up campaign business and get home for
the beginning of the holiday.

But with that phone call the election suddenly lost its urgency. I
thought for a moment about phoning Begin, but I felt uncomfortable
about disturbing him on Yom Kippur eve. Instead I left instructions with
some of my colleagues, gathered up my papers, and left for home. The
moment I arrived, I called my divisional headquarters to check in, then
rang up my intelligence officer, Yehoshua Saguy, who had served as
chief of intelligence for the entire front when I was commander. Saguy
came over immediately, bringing with him air photographs and other
material. One look was enough. Near the canal the Egyptians had
concentrated all their crossing equipment, a massive deployment that was
quantitatively different from the exercises we had gotten used to watching.
"There's no question," I said. "This time it's war."

Calling southern front headquarters, I asked if any changes had been
made in the plan of response that was in place when I left the command.

"No," I was told, "it's still the same." In essence that meant our tank reserves were supposed to be concentrated no farther than twenty miles from the canal and that the Bar-Lev strongpoints would be evacuated the moment the Egyptian assault began. Perhaps most important, any counterattacks were to be carried out in strength. Tanks would be used in "armored fist," battle groups of battalion size or greater, insuring maximum impact. Satisfied, I called Shmulik Gonen, the southern front commander, to tell him that I was ready and that I considered the intelligence conclusive. War would break out soon.

Since for the moment nothing further was happening, Lily and I decided to try to spend Yom Kippur on the farm with the children. The next morning found us among the beautiful Negev hills, watching the sheep and horses and enjoying the holiday quiet together. At about ten o'clock I noticed cars and trucks on the road, an unusual sight for Yom Kippur, when ordinarily nothing moves. At almost the same time some neighbors from the kibbutz next door came by to tell me that a number of their boys had just received calls to report to their units.

We had just gotten back to the old farmhouse when my own call came in requesting me to report immediately to Southern Command. Wondering if the Egyptians had really moved so soon, I phoned Simcha Ehrlich to let him know that something serious was going on and that I would be in the south for an indefinite time. He would have to find somebody to fill in as campaign manager. Then Lily and the kids drove me to my division, the reserve command that Dayan had given me over David Elazar's vigorous objections.

During the three months since my retirement I had visited the division regularly, and only a short while before I had conducted a training exercise with them. Knowing how competent the headquarters staff was, it was no surprise to find everything in order when I arrived at the base and the mobilization proceeding calmly. With no radio stations broadcasting that day, phone calls were being made to homes and messengers were going out to synagogues, where most people were gathered for prayers. Already a few early arrivals were starting to trickle in.

In the afternoon I left for Southern Command Headquarters, and just as I drove up to the gates, air-raid sirens started to wail. By now I could taste the wartime tension. Soldiers and officers on the headquarters streets looked worried. So many of their faces were familiar from the three and a half years I had spent as commander there that I had a feeling of return. As immersed as I had been in the election campaign, I realized that I still felt far more comfortable with this kind of fighting than with the political battlefield I had just left.

Inside the war room a mass of information was being analyzed. Despite some contradictory reports, one thing was clear. At that very moment a full-blown Egyptian offensive was developing all along the canal. Observation points along the entire length of the front were reporting heavy artillery fire, air strikes, and troops in assault boats storming the banks. As we stood there, word came in that Syria too had launched a massive attack and that tanks were flooding into the Golan. It was a few minutes after two on what should have been a peaceful Yom Kippur afternoon. Somehow Israel had allowed herself to be taken by surprise. War had exploded on two fronts, and for the first time since 1948 the initiative was in the hands of our enemies.

Having seen everything that was necessary, I went back to my division. By now the trickle of reserves had become a stream and the place was bustling. The depots were open, and civilian reservists were busy getting themselves armed and supplied. In the motor pools, tank and truck engines were rumbling while mechanics worked to prepare the vehicles for action. The division was urgently putting itself on a war footing. But still there was a sense of unreality about what was going on, as if people did not quite believe we were really at war. Walking through the depots, I saw soldiers arguing with a quartermaster who was insisting that they fill out every last one of the required forms before he would issue gear or weapons. Tempers flared as the quartermaster physically blocked the doorway to the supply room, intent on defending his stores. Despite the screaming sirens he, like many others, had not yet disconnected himself from the normal peacetime routines.

Meeting with the brigade commanders and headquarters staff, I brought them up to date and checked progress. All of them were working feverishly to put their units on the road. The canal was almost two hundred miles away, and we had to get there as fast as possible. For the moment the entire front was being held only by General Avraham ("Albert") Mandler's regular division with its complement of 294 tanks. Against Mandler the Egyptians had arrayed five infantry divisions, three mechanized divisions, and two armored divisions. Among them they marshaled over 1,400 tanks. Until our division and the other reserve division under Avraham Adan arrived, Mandler would be fighting a defensive battle against very large odds.

With hundreds of tanks in the division, there were two methods of getting to the Sinai. The ideal way would be to use tank transporters, huge low-bed tractor trailers specially designed for this task. But if we did that, it would mean waiting additional hours for the transporters to arrive, hours that might prove crucial. Even more worrisome, I knew that when you send tanks on transporters you lose control over them. With all the rush and confusion, you can never tell when some hard-pressed front commander might get the idea that these particular tanks are needed to resolve a sudden emergency. If I sent them on the transporters, I could easily find my strength dissipating a little at a time, a tank here, a couple of tanks there. I'd never know where they had gone, and I'd never be able to recover them.

That kind of thing cannot happen when tanks are moving together in companies and battalions, with their crews inside and under command of their officers. So even though it would be hard on the tanks mechanically, I decided to save time and make sure I kept control in my hands by sending them under their own power. Consequently I ordered that as each company of tanks became ready, they should move out toward the canal. Their routes were set and rendezvous points marked out. The entire division was instructed to be in the neighborhood of our central sector headquarters at Tasa by the following day, October 7, at noon.

As preparations shifted into high gear, I walked around the base watching the soldiers cleaning and packing equipment; checking tanks, APC's, and jeeps; loading ammunition; energetically doing all those things they were so well trained for. Spirits were high throughout the command as I moved from one group to another exchanging greetings and stopping to talk with soldiers and officers. I knew better than they how massive the Egyptian offensive was and what a serious situation we would face once we got to the canal. But I never dreamed that so very many of those I was talking to would no longer be with us when the war was finally over, two and a half weeks later.

During that same afternoon I talked to General Gonen several times by phone. Because of all the confused information we were getting from the front, I urged him repeatedly to leave his Beersheba headquarters as early as possible and move to Sinai. I believed that he had to put himself in direct contact with our forward troops and see with his own eyes what was happening, that this was the only way he could properly evaluate the situation.

From his replies, however, I got the clear impression that Gonen was not about to take advice, at least not from me. In fact we did have a delicate command situation to deal with. Although Gonen—"Shmulik" to those who knew him—was Commander of the southern front, two of the three division commanders under him were more experienced than he and senior to him. Gonen had previously served under Adan, who was now serving under him. He had served under me as well, and in fact up until three months ago he had commanded the very reserve division I was now commanding. Although Gonen had a fine record as an armored brigade leader (in the Six Day War he had performed with distinction under Israel Tal), I was wary of his lack of higher-level battle experience. Indeed this was the subject of my last debate with Moshe Dayan just prior to my retirement. Against this background, Gonen's sensitivity to advice might have been understandable. But it wasn't a good sign.

When it was clear that our preparations were going smoothly, I went home for an hour to pack the rest of my gear and say goodbye. Then I left for the front, not in my jeep but in a little civilian pickup truck with a big sign on it advertising "Ray of Light Solar Heaters." My jeep was still in the motor pool garage having the communications equipment installed, and I didn't want to wait. So, like many others whose vehicles weren't ready, I simply took one of the hundreds of civilian cars and trucks that had been driven to the base by the reservists and mobilized into the army along with their owners.

The convoy carrying our divisional headquarters into the Sinai included cars, trucks, and vans of every age and description. In the lead was this "Keren Or" pickup, driven by a solar heating installer who may not have known where he was going but must have figured that, considering the company, it was probably in the right direction. Squeezed in between the driver and me was my old friend Zevele Amit. Whenever something big had happened before, Zevele had been out of the country on Mossad work and it would take him a day or two to catch up with me. But this time he was in Israel. As soon as he heard about the mobilization, he had called my home and told Lily, "Just tell Arik to wait for me."

Zevele had arrived at my house two hours later wearing frayed combat fatigues that must have dated from our early days in the paratroop battalion. But he hadn't been able to find any footgear and was still in his street shoes. From the bottom of a closet Lily dug up a pair of my old maroon-colored paratrooper boots, and the outfit was complete. Another close friend, Uri Dan, was also with us. As a leading reporter for the military newspaper, Uri had taken part in most of the earlier paratroop actions. When he eventually left the service, he emerged as one of Israel's top military and political correspondents, covering events all over the world. Now he would be reporting on the war for the correspondents' press pool.

We were on the road for hours, part of a mass movement south—trucks, APC's, and tanks mixed in with cars, buses, and other civilian vehicles, a true people's army. Here and there broken-down tanks were already abandoned on the side of the road. Unable to repair them, their crews had left them where they stopped and hitched rides to the front. As we drove by, I was certain these tanks wouldn't stay abandoned long. My own tankers had crews of mechanics riding behind them. Once they saw an abandoned tank they wouldn't think once, let alone twice, before repairing it on the spot and bringing it along. I wasn't exactly shocked the next day when it turned out we had more tanks on hand than were listed on the roster.

Stopping once or twice to try to hear the radio news above the din of traffic, we arrived in Bir Gafgafa early the next morning, October 7. Bir Gafgafa, the command center for Sinai, had changed remarkably since I first moved my headquarters there after the 1967 war. Then it was just a collection of huts; now it had become a small military town that even boasted several rows of young trees. When I walked into Bir Gafgafa's underground war room, the feeling was momentarily electric. Without a word, the officers who crowded the place stood up, as if for an instant they thought I might have resumed command.

Although we had been in the truck for five or six hours with no communication, I hadn't missed much. A great deal of information was coming in, but much of it was still confused or contradictory. No one could say for sure precisely what was happening on the front line. There was no way of determining where the Egyptians might be making their main thrust, or even if there was a main thrust. Without a clear picture, it was impossible to know what kind of counterattack to plan or exactly how we should best position ourselves.

By this time Gonen had moved from Beersheba to Dveila, a forward command post I had built into a rugged windswept mountain twenty miles to the southwest. I called him there to let him know I had arrived and also to press him again to take a helicopter and look at the front himself. Gonen didn't respond. Clearly he was working under a lot of pressure. Israel's front-line forces had been hit hard, and reports were flooding in from cut-off units and surrounded strongpoints. From his perspective the situation must have seemed like a series of spreading brushfires which he did not have enough forces to stamp out.

As I tried to grasp what was going on, several unpleasant facts became clear. The first was that the air force was not acting effectively. After the 1970 cease-fire the Egyptians had moved those surface-to-air batteries up to the canal. We had not reacted then, and now we were paying a terrible price for it. Second, the Sinai tank force had not been concentrated forward as the reaction plan called for. Instead, of the almost three hundred Israeli tanks, some two hundred had been stationed fifty to sixty miles back from the canal, where they had not been able to respond immediately to the Egyptian crossing.

Worse, the order to evacuate the Bar-Lev strongpoints had never been given. As a result, the Egyptian assault wave had washed over these "ma'ozim," and fierce battles were raging around those that had not been overrun. Part of a reserve infantry brigade from Jerusalem had been manning the line, and ever since the previous afternoon desperate pleas for help had been coming in from the remnants of the garrisons.

In response, platoons of tanks from the forward tank echelon had been sent to support the beleaguered strongpoints. The previous night had witnessed the most courageous efforts by small groups of tanks against the Egyptian forces surrounding the ma'ozim. Advancing toward the canal, the tankers had come under murderous fire from armor and rocket positions on the high Egyptian ramparts overlooking the Israeli side. Those who survived found themselves ambushed on the approaches to the strongpoints by Egyptian tank-killer units armed with RPG's and anti-tank Sagger wire-guided missiles. But still some of them had managed to fight their way through.

One of the most tragic things that happened that night was that the reserve soldiers in the ma'ozim were begging to be brought out, but the tankers could not do it. They had their orders—not to extricate them but only to support the strongpoints and relieve the pressure. Some of the tanks were able to take wounded out. Others simply roared into the Egyptian lines blazing away in a futile attempt to push the enemy back. Suffering terrible losses, the tank crews continued to assault as long as they could. And as second-echelon tanks arrived they too were fed into the carnage.

In attempting to stamp out the fires, the Southern Command was breaking every rule of armored warfare. Instead of using the tanks in large forces as "armored fists," they were frittering them away piecemeal. Instead of taking advantage of the tanks' potential for maneuver and surprise, they were launching them at fixed targets along known approach routes, allowing the Egyptians to anticipate them and organize a deadly reception. Under these circumstances the tankers' efforts were madly courageous but senseless. They were decimated. In the first twenty-four hours we lost two hundred of our three hundred first-line tanks.

As I left Bir Gafgafa for the central sector headquarters at Tasa, most of this was already clear. It was outrageous that those men had been left in the strongpoints in the first place. But sending the tanks to support them in that fashion was a clear sign of panic and of an inability to read the battlefield. Instead of gathering our forces for a hard, fast counterattack, we were wasting them in hopeless small-unit actions. It was an incredible response. No matter how bad the situation looked, the simple fact was that we were 150 miles from our borders. Whatever the appearances, we had time to concentrate our units and really hit the Egyptians a powerful blow. I began to feel that Gonen's headquarters was not comprehending the situation on the ground.

When I got to the Tasa area, I was heartened to see the division's tanks beginning to arrive. By midday most of the units were already concentrating at their rendezvous points. From one of our forward observation posts I had a good look at the barrage of artillery blanketing the front. The Egyptians seemed to be holding shallow bridgeheads all over, but it did not look as if they were yet developing a main attack. It was clear that the weight of the Egyptian forces was still on the west side. But all along the line the Israeli quick reaction units were being pushed back.

I stood on the dunes there, the scene unfolding in front of me. As tanks and APC's withdrew past the observation post, I stopped some of them to talk to the officers and saw something strange on their faces—not fear but bewilderment. Suddenly something was happening to them that had never happened before. These were soldiers who had been brought up on victories—not easy victories maybe, but nevertheless victories. It was a generation that had never lost. Now they were in a state of shock. How could it be that these Egyptians were crossing the canal right in our faces? How was it that *they* were moving forward and *we* were defeated?

As the beaten armored units withdrew, I could not help thinking about the scene on the canal exactly one week earlier. The Saturday before

Yom Kippur I had been here in the Sinai making an election campaign film. Lily, Omri, and Gilad had come with me; and after the filming we had eaten lunch on the canal bank. Across from us the Egyptians were working like crazy, adding height to their already towering ramparts just as they had been doing three months before when I last saw them. Occasionally someone on the other side would make some gesture at us—a greeting from Egypt. Some of our own soldiers were eating with us on the bank, others sat around and talked. Even with all the military preparations, it had seemed so peaceful. But before I left I told the soldiers, "Be careful. It looks quiet now, but everything here can change in an instant." When I said it I hadn't been thinking about a war, only about the periods of quiet before the cease-fire that were sporadically broken by murderous surprise bombardments.

But now it had really broken. Watching from the dunes, I began to get a feel for what had to be done. The Egyptian achievement was already substantial; they had crossed the canal and had beaten back our attempts to fend them off. They were victorious and they were on the move. At this point they had to be pumped up with success. Our own forces were in bad shape—either surrounded in their strongpoints or retreating in confusion. And this was not a generation like mine, which had seen the disasters of the War of Independence and had come back from them. Who could be sure how this army might respond to defeat? Already thousands and thousands of Egyptians were on our side of the canal, their bridgeheads swelling with troops and equipment. My clear sense was that the only way we could break them would be with a major attack, a dramatic and shocking blow by at least two divisions. This should be done quickly, while the bridgeheads were still of manageable size. Every hour that passed allowed them to build and consolidate their strength.

As I envisioned it, this attack should be launched as soon as Avraham Adan's division was in position to act in concert with me, sometime the following day. But even before that, there were other things we could do. Watching what was going on along the front, I was sure it was still possible to rescue our people who were trapped in the Bar-Lev Line. What I wanted to do was launch a concentrated assault at dark on a very narrow front, almost a column attack on specific targets. We could bring the full force of our artillery to bear on either side, drive in with a wedge of tanks, and meet the ma'ozim people, whom we would instruct to break out at the same moment the attack went in. I was convinced that this kind of action would get our people out. It would also disrupt the Egyptian bridgeheads, at least temporarily slowing down their growth.

With this concept clear in my head I went back to the Tasa command post. By two o'clock that afternoon I was talking with Amnon Reshef, the young colonel in command of the forward tank brigade that had suffered so badly. After his bitter night he was dead tired but still calm and able to relate in detail his experiences with the Egyptian infantry. Out of the hundred tanks in his command, he thought that fourteen were still mobile, perhaps twenty.

I also tried to make radio contact with the ma'ozim garrisons, or what was left of them, to check on their condition and see if they could break out on their own. One radio operator in the surrounded Hizayon strongpoint near the Firdan Bridge called my code number repeatedly. "Forty, forty, we recognize your voice. We know you. . . . We know you will get us out of here. Please come to us. Please send us help." A constant stream of talk and pleading from a reserve soldier whose officers had been killed. It was a voice that would continue pleading for the next three days, until the operator was himself killed and the rest of the Hizayon defenders were either killed or captured.

Putting in a call to Gonen, I told him that I believed we could still save those who were alive in the ma'ozim. I said I thought it was not just our military duty to do it, it was our moral duty. But he wouldn't accept it. There was no way to get them out. If we tried, we would lose forces, and we couldn't afford to lose more than we already had. I insisted that I had a way to bring them out, that we had no choice but to make the effort. In the background I could hear that radio operator's voice from Hizayon.

It was an agonizing situation. At strongpoint Hizayon the officers were dead and a number of the soldiers wounded. Purkan, the position opposite Ismailia, was surrounded; but a reserve major there named Meir Weizel was giving calm, clear information about Egyptian movements. Matzmed, at the northern tip of the Great Bitter Lake, was silent. But Lakekan, on the lakeshore to the south, had not yet been attacked, and I instructed them to withdraw at dark.

When Gonen refused to approve a rescue attempt, I called Dayan directly. I described the situation over the phone and brought as much pressure to bear on him as I could. After a long debate Dayan told me that there would be a meeting at seven o'clock that night at Dveila. Permission to launch such an attack could only be granted there. When

I called Gonen back, I told him I would be raising this issue at our meeting. His answer was that I should make the necessary preparations for an attack now, but that I was not to execute it until we were able to discuss it that night. A helicopter would be sent to pick me up.

Meanwhile, the area around Tasa had become very dangerous. Since afternoon we had been seeing Egyptian helicopters come into the zone with commando groups whose object was to sow chaos in our staging areas and command posts. Although we had shot some of these down and had established area security patrols, it was still impossible to tell exactly what was out there. As a result I did not want to use the nearby landing strip. Instead I sent word to Gonen's headquarters that I would be waiting for the copter at a different set of co-ordinates—on the dunes some distance off.

Shortly before the pickup time I left in a jeep with a radio operator and Motti Levy, a regimental sergeant major and friend who had been my driver for some years now. Together we set up the trapeze directional markers, then we lay down on the sand to wait. The rendezvous time came, then went. More time passed, and still no helicopter arrived. It occurred to me that maybe they had made a mistake and had gone to the Tasa strip instead. Despite the danger of moving around, we decided to go and check. With Motti driving, I sat in the jeep straining to see into the dark, my finger tense on the trigger of an AK-47.

But nobody was there either, so we drove back. Meanwhile we were in contact with my headquarters, which had called Southern Command and had been told that the helicopter was on its way. So again we lay down to wait. The night air had turned chilly, but the sand was warm and comfortable from the absorbed heat of the day. We waited there almost two hours before the helicopter showed up.

By the time it did, I was sure that no mistake had been made, that they had delayed sending the helicopter on purpose. Gonen undoubtedly knew I had called Dayan. He also knew for certain that if I was at the meeting I would force them to decide whether or not to rescue the soldiers in those death traps. That would have been a very, very hard discussion indeed. And to avoid it they had let me wait outside on those dunes for hours.

By the time the helicopter put me down on Jebel Um-Hashiba, the mountain into which Dveila was carved, it was ten o'clock. No lights were on and the night was pitch dark. From the west came the thunder of artillery and flashes of light on the horizon. As I stepped toward the darkened gate of the command bunker, I saw two people coming out talking. Moving closer, I recognized Commander-in-Chief David Elazar and Yitzhak Rabin, who had recently flown home from his ambassador's post in Washington.

When Elazar noticed me, he said that the meeting was just over. They had discussed what to do the next day, and the best thing would be for me to go down and find out directly from Gonen what had been decided. I told Elazar that what I had seen that day convinced me that for anything significant to happen we needed a concentrated attack of at least two divisions. "We just can't do that," he said. "The only force we have between this spot and Tel Aviv right now is your division."

When he said this, I told him, "The Egyptians are not heading for Tel Aviv. That's beyond them. Their target is the canal and the ridgeline— five to seven miles. They cannot afford to get beyond their [surface-to-air] missile cover." I tried to emphasize that a concentrated effort now could destroy their entire northern Second Army bridgehead. Then we could turn and destroy their Third Army in the south. As the discussion wound down, Rabin put his hand on my shoulder. "Arik," he said, "we're counting on you to change the situation." With that they shook hands with me and disappeared into the darkness.

Going down into the bunker, I found Gonen and repeated the points I had just made with Elazar. I also recommended that we counterbalance the Egyptian assault by crossing the canal ourselves as soon as possible in the area of Kantara. We should take that decision now and prepare for the crossing by staying as close as we could to the shoreline in that area. Rather brusquely I was told that plans had already been made and could no longer be changed. Adan's division, which was now in place on the northern sector, would be launching a counterattack the next day, October 8. Adan would attack from north to south, parallel to the canal but about two miles east of it to avoid the Sagger missiles from the Egyptian ramparts. Meanwhile my division would concentrate at sunrise northwest of Tasa prepared to attack southeast to northwest to comple- ment Adan's thrust. However, I was not to move until I was given the go-ahead in the morning. As far as the ma'ozim garrisons were con- cerned, nothing special would be done. But in any case, if our attack was successful we would be linking up with them.

I emphasized to Gonen again that we did definitely need a two-division attack at a minimum. But I sensed that the atmosphere was defensive, that there would be no point in pushing the discussion. Instead I took

Gonen aside to where we could talk privately. "Look, Shmulik," I said, "I've left the army already. My life is going in an entirely different direction. I am not coming back to take your place here. The only intention I have is to defeat the Egyptians. Once we've finished with them, I'm gone. Shmulik, you can win this war. You can come out of it a winner. All you have to do is concentrate your forces against them. You don't have an enemy in me. You don't have to deal with me at all. Just deal with the Egyptians." He nodded his understanding and found a few words of agreement. But I wondered.

By 1 A.M. I was back in the Tasa area meeting with my commanders. Outside under jeep and APC lights I explained the situation and went over the maps, telling them that we would move out at four and be in position by sunrise. High above our heads we saw what looked like bolts of fire, Egyptian Frog missiles ripping the sky toward one of our air control centers to the east. I watched them and for a moment saw in my mind's eye the red balls of artillery fire that had come out of the foggy night in front of Latrun twenty-five years earlier.

The reverie lasted only a moment, then I finished the briefing and fell asleep on the spot. While I slept I had the most vivid dream that I was taking part in a huge military exercise in the Sinai. Right in the middle of it I came awake with a start. It was just a few minutes before four. Already APC and tank engines were roaring to life. Still feeling a bit disoriented from the dream, I climbed into my command APC and headed for a forward point near the canal where I would wait for the order from Southern Command.

At daybreak we were on a high point overlooking the canal plain. In front of us in the distance massive clouds of dust marked the start of a large-scale Egyptian effort to push forward out of their bridgeheads. We could make out tanks and infantry moving eastward and could see where our forward units were already engaging them in a desperate attempt to contain the thrust. A hundred yards or so in front of us an explosion lifted swirls of sand into the air. A moment later another shell hit—this one behind us. Somehow Egyptian artillery had gotten our range. The five APC's I used as a mobile command post moved out to another location. But after a couple of minutes the guns were ranging us again. Each time we stopped, incoming shells whistled in at us. Knowing there had to be Egyptian fire-control people nearby, I sent a reconnaissance platoon to comb the dunes. A few minutes later we heard a brief exchange of small-arms fire, and the reconnaissance leader emerged from behind a hillock waving a pair of Soviet-made binoculars he had taken from one of the three Egyptian observers who had managed to penetrate this far into our lines.

A few moments later a message came through Southern Command ordering us *not* to attack. Instead we were to contain the Egyptian advance in our sector and wait for Adan's attack to develop. At that point we would get further orders.

By 8 A.M. the artillery and tank battle we were waging against waves of Egyptians had become more comprehensive. As I understood it, my job was to hold the high ground in our sector, then either support Adan's attack or launch our own attack southward, depending on how Southern Command read the developing battle. Eager to take the offensive, I waited for signs of Adan's forces that were supposed to be moving from north to south parallel to the canal.

At about 9:45 I saw them. But they were not moving along the front several miles to the east of the canal as I had expected. Instead the dust columns were rising in back of us, seven or eight miles from the front. I watched as Adan's tanks pressed southward, passed to our rear, and then turned westward toward the Egyptians. Watching from my observation post on the western slope of Havraga Ridge, I was dismayed by what was happening. Only a relatively small number of tanks were involved, perhaps two battalions charging valiantly into the Egyptian artillery fire. It was not a divisional attack; it was not even a concentrated effort. There was no way it could succeed.

But I did not have much time to worry about it. At 10:45 A.M. I received an order from Southern Command to exploit Adan's success by attacking southward myself. Specifically, I was to move my entire division back to the Lateral Road, ten miles behind us, then proceed southward approximately seventy miles and capture the Egyptian bridges across the canal near the city of Suez. The idea seemed to be that since Adan had now rolled up the Egyptian Second Army, I could smash through the unsuspecting Third Army.

It was unreal. First of all Adan had not rolled up anything. (During the next few hours his attacking units were practically annihilated by the Egyptian tanks and anti-tank infantry.) Second, my division was occupying critical high ground that would cost us dearly to get back if once we gave it up. And if we did not get it back, we could forget about any future assault on the canal in this sector. Third, the idea that we might fight our way through to the canal in the south and find intact Egyptian bridges there was based on the merest wishful thinking. And even if we did, we knew the Egyptian bridges were constructed for the lighter Soviet-made tanks and would not support ours. I could not fathom what headquarters might be imagining.

When I got the order to move south, I called Gonen immediately. In the strongest terms I told him that what he was asking would be a disastrous mistake. "Nothing has been accomplished here," I said. "There is nothing to exploit." I told him what hills we were holding, and what we were doing to contain the Egyptians. I told him the chances of capturing a bridge all the way down at Suez were negligible. I urged him to come to the front and see for himself if he doubted what I was telling him.

The answer was shouted back. If I didn't obey the order I would be dismissed immediately. Immediately! "Then come down here and look yourself," I repeated. "No!" Gonen shouted. "You will be dismissed. I will dismiss you right now!"

I thought about it for a moment, then decided I had no choice except to obey. So I gave my own order for the division to pull back to Tasa and head south. But even as I did, I deviated slightly from Gonen's order. Instead of disengaging completely, I left my divisional reconnaissance unit holding two absolutely critical ridges, one code-named Hamadia, the other Kishuf. These positions were on either side of the Akavish Road, which led to the canal in the region of Deversoir. This was where I had prepared the crossing site five months earlier, with its walled "yard" and its thinned-out ramparts. I was simply not going to hand control of these ridges over to the Egyptians. If I did, not only would we never have a chance of getting to the canal in this prime area, but the approaches to Tasa—the central sector command center—would be left wide open.

Having made arrangements to hold these places, I moved southward at the head of the rest of the division—two hundred tanks and all the divisional APC's, tank trucks, and other equipment. I knew we were making the worst possible mistake, but nevertheless I was intent on moving quickly, as ordered. There was nothing I could do to remedy the situation, and if I had to strike in the south I was going to do it as fast and hard as I could.

Three and a half hours later I was near the Gidi Pass, fifty miles to the south, when a helicopter overflew the column and landed near my APC. A liaison officer from Southern Command climbed out and told me briefly that Adan's attack had failed. There had been no Israeli crossing, as had been mistakenly reported to Southern Command earlier in the day. Not only had we made no impact on the Egyptians, but Adan's division had taken serious losses. Now the Egyptians were moving forward into the area I had left. We were ordered to get back as fast as possible to support Adan and recover as much of the ridgeline as we could.

My inner feelings at that point were simply not describable. If on the surface I appeared normal, it was because I was numbed with rage. It was now October 8. Two days earlier the entire division had been called out of their homes and synagogues. In less than twenty-four hours they had fully mobilized and had driven two hundred miles to the battlefield. It was a remarkable performance, one that no other army in the world could have matched. The previous night they had received their orders and deployed before dawn, ready to fight. And now, on this absolutely crucial day of battle, they had spent their time driving around the desert like idiots. Seething, I swung the column of hundreds of vehicles around and started back.

By early evening we were deployed in front of the hill positions we had left that morning. Kishuf and Hamadia were still in our hands, thanks to the reconnaissance battalion, whose Commander Benzi Carmeli had been killed in the fighting. But the chain of hills to the north of Hamadia had been taken by the Egyptians. That evening we suffered heavy casualties attempting to recapture key positions on the ridgeline. By the time darkness fell, I was in an ugly mood. Around the disputed hills vicious tank battles went on far into the night.

October 8 was the black day of the Israeli Defense Forces, a day that traumatized the army. On the first two days of the war in Sinai, we had suffered defeats. But for those defeats it was easy enough to find scapegoats; poor intelligence, Defense Minister Dayan's miscalculations, the government's errors. October 8, however, belonged to the IDF alone.

The failure stemmed from a combination of major tactical errors and also from an attitude of overconfidence that since the Six Day War had hardened into arrogance. After the victories then, the idea had taken hold that the tank was the ultimate weapon. In every battle zone the Arab infantry had caved in before massed tank charges. Whether Israeli tactics or execution were good or not had not mattered; the tanks had been able to smash through to victory.

The result was that after 1967 the IDF was ovecome by a kind of tank mania. Other combat arms—infantry, armored infantry, and artillery—were neglected. Standard battle doctrines such as ratios of force and concentration of effort were taken less seriously. The commanding idea seemed to be that the business of the Israeli tanks was to charge and the business of the Arab infantry was to run away in horror. Gonen's errors, as Adan analyzed them later, were due to the fact that he did not bother to properly assess the situation but relied instead on his intuition. And his intuition was "based on his previous experience with the Egyptians, whom he held in deep contempt."[*]

But this psychological flaw was not Gonen's alone. That is why it was a profound shock to find on October 8 that the Egyptians did not simply melt away in front of the Israeli tank attack. On the contrary, the soldiers who faced us that day were the first truly modern infantry—equipped and trained to fight and even hunt tanks with their own organic weapons. Adan's Centurion and Patton tanks were hit at long distances by a hail of Sagger missiles and other anti-tank fire. Those that managed to close with the enemy found themselves surrounded by swarms of Egyptians firing Saggers and RPG bazookas. Natke Nir, who led the attack, left eighteen of his twenty-two tanks burning on the field. It was only by incredible courage that he managed to penetrate to within eight hundred yards of the canal before ordering his few survivors to withdraw in reverse gear, firing as they retreated.

For myself, that day was a kind of breaking point. Between Adan and myself we had had sufficient force to eliminate the Egyptian bridgeheads opposite us. These were still relatively weak and unconsolidated—certainly nothing like the powerful defensive positions we encountered when we finally did launch a concerted attack on October 15, seven days later. We needed Gonen or someone from General Headquarters to come forward to physically see the situation and recognize what had to be done. Then we needed a concentrated two-division attack. We got neither. Instead, Adan's assault was poorly co-ordinated and in insufficient force, and I spent my day driving around the countryside. The result was a resounding defeat that lengthened the war by almost two weeks and led to heavy casualties that could have been avoided. After that I scrutinized every single order I received from Southern Command two or three times. I am sure that Avraham Adan and Albert Mandler

[*] Avraham Adan, *The Yom Kippur War* (New York: Richardson and Steirman, 1986), p. 33.

(commander of the southern sector) did the same, though they may have done it more quietly than I.

That evening I called Dayan and told him that a disaster had taken place. He knew it already and understood the reasons for it. Already he had recommended to Commander-in-Chief David Elazar that Gonen and I switch jobs, that Gonen be put at head of the division and myself at Southern Command. Later that night, though, Elazar rejected Dayan's suggestion. Gonen and I would not exchange jobs, nor would Gonen be relieved outright. Instead another commander would be appointed above him to oversee the Southern Command. That commander would be the current minister of trade and industry, retired Commander-in-Chief Chaim Bar-Lev.

Still livid from the day's events, this was the last thing I needed to hear. The single person missing from the stew of intrigue and internal politicking was Bar-Lev. And now I had him on my plate too. I felt like I was in the middle of a "ken tsra'ot," a nest of hornets. It reminded me, I told the people in my APC, of how the Spanish Republic was lost. With all their infighting and backstabbing, the Republicans gave it away. They had spent themselves fighting each other instead of the enemy. At that point it looked to me as if we were heading in the same direction.

22

The Crossing

October 8 had been a disaster, a tankman's nightmare. We had sent in one of our renowned armored charges, and the Egyptians had not only stood up to it, they had destroyed it. With the opportunity for rationalization provided by our eventual victory, it has become popular to say that a farsighted command decision was made that night after a careful analysis of the battlefield. We would assume a static posture while the Egyptians moved the bulk of their armor over the canal, then we would smash their formations up in a defensive battle, after which we would strike across the canal onto the now sparsely defended western side. Unfortunately, that post facto interpretation beautifies what really happened. The truth was that the experience of the eighth left the upper levels of command in a state of shock, without an idea about what to do next except "to hold on."

I was as upset with this as I was with practically every other decision that had been made so far in the war. For me, this was not the time to sit back and allow the Egyptians to build up their bridgeheads and their defenses. Why should we just wait while they brought the rest of their tank army over the canal? Quite the opposite. We should be pushing them, probing for their weak points, looking for openings to exploit. It is no exaggeration to say that by this time my confidence in the ability of either Southern Command or General Headquarters to read the battle-field properly was down to zero.

Nevertheless, in accord with orders I received, in the early morning of October 9 I gave instructions to my three brigade commanders—Amnon Reshef, Haim Erez, and Tuvia Raviv—that we would conduct a holding operation, containing the expected Egyptian advance. But I also expected them to use their initiative. In the kind of mobile defensive battle that tanks fight, they should watch for any opportunity to recover the ridgeline positions we had given up the previous day. That night too I had a long phone conversation with Major Weizel in command at strongpoint Purkan opposite Ismailia. "It's up to you," I told him. "Try to break out tonight and find your way to Hamutal" (a ridgeline hill six miles east of the canal). "I'll have tanks waiting there to pick you up."

Early the next morning several tanks and APC's from Amnon's brigade (with Amnon himself in command) penetrated down Talisman, the east-west road that ran past Hamutal. Already the area was engulfed in battle as Tuvia Raviv's force fought off an attack by Egyptian armor and infantry. In the hail of missiles and gunfire three of Amnon's vehicles were hit. But one tank succeeded in locating and picking up the survivors whom Wiezel had led out with great coolness from Purkan. With all thirty-three of them clinging to its hull, the tank emerged out of the maelstrom looking like something from an alien world. A little to the south, near Hamadia, other elements from Tuvia's brigade ambushed and crushed an assault by the Egyptian Fourteenth Tank Brigade. As the battle developed I sent in local attacks toward Televizia and Machshir in order to stop Egyptian pressure building toward Hamutal and the rear of Hamadia where our artillery was deployed and where Israel Tal's brainchild, the great steel rolling bridge, lay hidden. Farther to the south the reconnaissance regiment probed across the canal plain and found nothing in its path.

As darkness began to fall on the battlefield, the reconnaissance battalion arrived at the Lexicon Road, just a few hundred yards from the banks of the Great Bitter Lake. They had met no opposition. Pushing carefully north-ward, the tanks approached the upper shore of the lake at Deversoir—near the place where the previous May I had prepared the ramparts and the walled "yard" for a canal crossing. Still there were no Egyptians.

Early that evening I knew we had located an open seam between the Egyptian Second Army in the north and the Third army in the south. Here if anywhere was a situation that begged to be exploited. The

Egyptians had not noticed the reconnaissance unit's penetration; the path to the canal beckoned—wide and open.

At 6:30 p.m. I contacted Gonen to tell him that we were on the water. "Shmulik, we are near the canal," I said into the phone. "Shmulik, we can touch the water of the lake." But when Gonen heard where the recon battalion was he blew up. Twenty minutes later I called back. I explained what our main dispositions were, how we were established along the ridgeline after having hurt the Egyptians badly during the day. We were in a position to start bringing assault rafts down from Baluza and preparing the bridging equipment. Right now we could begin organizing for our own crossing. In parallel with Adan's division, we could grab the whole area and push across. Why just sit back and wait for the Egyptians to discover the seam and close it up? In the northern sector we would now have to fight our way to the canal. But here the whole thing was already in the palms of our hands.

This time the response was chilly. I was informed that Southern Command's intelligence had picked up further information about enemy deployment in the sector. The situation did not look promising. They would think about it.

At 7:15 p.m. Uri Ben-Ari, Gonen's deputy, called. They had thought about it. There would be no attack. I was to move the troops away from the water line and pull back generally from the forward positions we had achieved during the day. We were not going to pressure the Egyptians but were to fight a containment battle only. Opportunity or not.

An hour later I was on the phone with General Headquarters trying to get through to Israel Tal—"Talik"—who was deputy commander-in-chief and the only person there who I thought would grasp what was going on. Tal was out, so instead I talked to Dov Sion, a staff officer and old friend. I told Sion that we were near the canal, that we had bitten deeply into the Egyptian bridgehead, and that now we were being told to fall back. I didn't understand the logic of it. If we had had this kind of success yesterday, we would have been jumping for joy. Why not now? What was the point? If I pulled back, the Egyptians would follow and dig in, again. We would just have to do it all over later on, under who knew what circumstances. "Let Talik and the others know what the situation is," I told him. "Tell Talik that I have to talk to him. Tell him I insist on talking to him." I felt like a voice crying in the wilderness.

✶   ✶   ✶

The end result of all my arguments was predictable. In accordance with orders I pulled my troops back from the canal and assumed a purely defensive posture, waiting to see what the Egyptians would do. We waited for the next four days—October 10 through October 13—days characterized by small-scale Egyptian attacks and intermittent attempts to heliport commando units into our rear areas. All along the front we turned back the Egyptian assaults and destroyed the commandos, either knocking out their helicopters or hunting them down after they had landed.

Our own losses were not large. But it was during this waiting period that General Albert Mandler was killed by Egyptian artillery fire that struck his mobile command APC. The shell scored a direct hit while Mandler was talking by radio to Gonen. Mandler had been a first-rate professional commander, and we all felt his loss deeply. He was replaced by Kalman Magen, who until then had been commanding the Kantara sector.

While most of the senior commanders were happy enough to be containing the Egyptians and bleeding their armor, for me these days were immensely frustrating. I emphatically did not think we should be on the defensive. Each day that passed was a mistake. Each day the Egyptian bridgeheads swelled further with armor and infantry. We watched as their tank brigades filled up and as they ceaselessly laid mine fields and strengthened their defensive positions.

The overall concept had firmed up by now: Wait for their tank attack, break it, and only then take the offensive. To my way of thinking this was exactly backwards. The longer we gave the Egyptians to build up and consolidate, the more it would cost us to break through their defenses later on. Beyond that, time was against us. In the north the Syrians had been knocked back from the Golan on October 9. Now they were increasingly desperate, under continuous pressure from the Israeli advance into the Syrian plain. Their gamble had failed. On our front, the Egyptians had already achieved their major goals. They had little incentive to press further—except as a way to relieve the Syrians. I was afraid that an imposed cease-fire was in our future, and not in our distant future.

To me, these different factors led to a single conclusion: Regain the initiative and attack. Not at some future date which might or might not come, but right now. I pressured everyone I could get hold of to take action, the sooner the better. Hit the Egyptians now, disrupt their bridgeheads, push them back, get to the canal. I was convinced we had the forces necessary to put an end to the whole thing. But there was nobody to talk to about it. From Bar-Lev I got the impression that General Headquarters was still afraid of some imaginary Egyptian thrust to Tel Aviv. It was like the 1967 War all over again, no confidence among the senior commanders. Tal was the only one I felt was lending a sympathetic ear, along with Moshe Dayan. But I could rarely get through to Dayan, and he wasn't taking a decisive role anyway. Nor was Tal's influence at headquarters overwhelming. "Listen, Talik," I said to him on the thirteenth, "you must understand. We can take a serious bite of the Egyptians every day. . . . Every day we lose is a pity. Soon we'll have a cease-fire, and we'll be caught here. It's a terrible, terrible shame."

Only years later I learned that on the 12th of October, Commander-in-Chief Elazar decided that the combat power of the IDF, and particularly of the air force, had come too dangerously close to the red line and a cease-fire was required. Kissinger thought that a cease-fire at this disadvantageous stage would diminish the ability of Israel as well as of the United States to be properly positioned for future negotiations. He therefore strongly advocated that the government postpone the cease-fire request to enable the IDF to improve Israel's position. Dayan's position at the government meeting was that if Elazar recommended a cease-fire request then he, Dayan, thought there was no reason why Kissinger should interfere in the government's decision. Nevertheless, Elazar's totally unjustified and erroneous evaluation led the deeply concerned government to ask for the cease-fire. The Egyptians rejected the offer and their two armored divisions, the fourth and twenty-first, were ordered to cross the canal and to deploy in Sinai for a grand-scale attack.

On Sunday, October 14, at 6:20 A.M., massed Egyptian tank forces moved out of the bridgeheads toward our lines. In each sector of the front the Egyptians came on across the sandy canal plain into the sun rising behind the Israeli positions. This grand-scale attack, we learned later, was in response to a Syrian plea to relieve the pressure in the north. Almost a thousand Egyptian tanks rolled forward, most of them Soviet-made T-55s and 62s. In front of Hamadia, Amnon Reshef saw what seemed to him like a river of armor flowing over the desert.

By early afternoon the plain below Amnon and Haim's positions was dotted with bonfires. Between a hundred and a hundred twenty tanks of the Egyptian Twenty-first Armored Division were either flaming like torches or lying dead on the sand. Those that survived retreated back into the defensive positions of the Sixteenth Infantry. Our own losses came to three tanks from Amnon's brigade and two from Haim's.

The same story repeated itself to our north, where Adan's forces stopped the Egyptian Twenty-third Mechanized Division, and to the south, where Kalman Magen repulsed the Third Army's strike toward Mitla Pass. When it was over, almost 250 Egyptian tanks had been destroyed in one of the largest tank battles ever fought. It was a major victory. But it still left the bridgeheads intact, with more than seven hundred tanks sheltering behind infantry defenses bristling with artillery and anti-tank weapons.

Nevertheless, with this blow to the Egyptians the Israeli General Headquarters' psychology of defense became history. At last they decided it was time for us to move. That night approval came to cross the canal. With that I presented my plan to Bar Lev and the headquarters staff had it approved. My division would break through the Egyptian lines, secure a corridor to the canal, and establish a crossing point at Deversoir on the east bank—at precisely the location where the reconnaissance unit had penetrated six days earlier. Meanwhile, rubber assault boats would be brought forward to ferry Danny Mat's paratroop brigade to the west bank. Once the paratroops had secured the area, a pontoon bridge would be laid across the canal and Haim Erez's tank brigade would cross. The great preconstructed rolling bridge would also be towed into place and pushed across.

All this was to happen on the night between the fifteenth and sixteenth. Once the bridge was up, my job would be to keep the corridor open and protect both the east and west bridge sites. Adan's division would then cross into Egypt and strike south down the western shore of the Great Bitter Lake to the city of Suez.

At six in the morning of the fifteenth I convened an orders group at Tasa. But just as Amnon, Haim, Tuvia, Danny Mat, and the others were gathering, Egyptian jets roared over the command center bombing and strafing. Worried about having all the commanders in the same place, I waited to reconvene the meeting until I was sure the area was clear. It was another hour before we were able to assemble again so that I could lay out the plan of battle. Intelligence told us that the seam between the Egyptian Second and Third armies was still open and still apparently unnoticed. On the northern edge of the opening, two east-west roads ran to the water line, roads I had built during the great construction surge in 1970. One, code-named Akavish, connected Tasa with the shore of the Great Bitter Lake. About five miles to the east of the canal another road started and ran parallel to and north of Akavish. This road, code-named Tirtur, had been especially laid out for towing the 600-ton steel roller bridge to the canal. Its terminus on the water line was just above the enclosed yard I had prepared in May as the staging area for a crossing.

These two roads, Akavish and Tirtur, would constitute our corridor to the canal. Along them and along the hard-packed sand to the south we would have to move two divisions and all the crossing equipment. Directly south of Akavish was the undefended seam between the two Egyptian armies, so we had plenty of maneuvering room on that side. But on the northern edge of the seam, Tirtur Road skirted the perimeter of the Second Army bridgehead, and this perimeter was very heavily defended indeed.

Here the Egyptians had established a major fortified base known as "Missouri," whose southwestern anchor was an area we called the "Chinese Farm"—an agricultural station set up with Japanese equipment years earlier. This Chinese Farm, with its interlacing network of dry irrigation ditches, sat on the Tirtur Road and on the junction of Tirtur and Lexicon, the communication road that ran parallel to the canal bank. The deep irrigation ditches and the mounds of dirt thrown up when they were excavated made this a natural defensive site where machine guns and anti-tank weapons could dominate the field. During the days when we had sat on our hands and waited, the Egyptians had developed the network of ditches into a murderous series of interlocking fire zones, the whole fortified area manned by the Sixteenth Infantry Division and the Twenty-first Armored Division, the one we had mauled on the fourteenth.

My plan, as I outlined it to the division's commanders, was to attack at dusk and fight the main battle during the night. Tuvia Raviv's tank brigade would assault Missouri from the east, a head-on thrust that would appear to the Egyptians very much what they expected. But in fact Tuvia's attack would be a diversion, meant to draw their forces and attention. At the same time, Amnon Reshef's brigade would execute a hook to the southwest through the unoccupied gap between the Egyptian armies, then north into the rear of the Egyptian base area. Here his missions were to secure the yard as a crossing site, push the Egyptians northward, and open up Tirtur and Akavish from west to east—that is, from behind. With the roads clear, Danny Mat's paratroop brigade would move into the yard along with the assault boats and cross the canal. Once the paratroop bridgehead was secure, engineers would push the bridges across.

On the divisional level this would be a complex operation, reminiscent in outline of the Abu Agheila battle. Our forces would be attacking at night—from the front, from behind, and from the flank, engaging the whole depth of the Egyptian position at once. But despite the plan's overall complexity, on the brigade level the missions were simple and clear—simple, but very, very hard. Afterward, when I asked the commanders what they had thought when I gave the order, they said it looked like an insanely difficult job, but they were convinced they could do it.

As the officers worked out their own plans, the bridging equipment began moving from the rear areas where it had been concentrated. The great roller bridge was assembled behind Hamadia, and preparations were made to tow it forward using sixteen of Haim Erez's tanks. The towing would be a tedious, delicate process, since the bridge could only move in a straight line and was unable to cope with variations in terrain. The Seventh Brigade had been trained for this job, but unfortunately the Seventh was now fighting on the Syrian front. Other bridging equipment—special rafts that could be floated, then connected together—was having trouble making its way through the traffic jam that was developing on the road from Baluza to Tasa. Even the inflatable boats that Danny Mat's paratroopers were to use in the first crossing wave had not yet arrived at the paratroop staging area.

At about one o'clock that day (the fifteenth) I got a call from Southern Command asking if we needed another day to prepare properly for the attack. Or could we really do it that night? I knew that the organization involved was immense, and in my heart I was not sure we could have the bridges up by the expected time. But at the least I was sure we would be able to establish a bridgehead, so I decided to move ahead anyway. This was the moment we would have surprise on our side. Any delay might allow the Egyptians to guess what was up. Besides, my confidence in those who were giving the orders had not been strengthened during the days of stalemate. Right now we had approval to cross. Tomorrow might be a different story.

However, I did ask Southern Command to take over traffic control on the Baluza–Tasa road. Adan's entire division was moving on this one narrow road, as were the rafts that had to get through to my division for the crossing. Already the road was a mess, and there was nobody from headquarters on the spot to take over and see to it that priorities were sorted out and the flow speeded up. Adan did not have to cross that night. I did; and, incredibly, the rafts had been shunted aside. I also did not yet have the paratroopers with me. They and their rubber boats were out there somewhere in the desert, also jammed into the crawling traffic. But I had great confidence in them. I knew Danny Mat well (Danny had been a paratroop officer since the 1950s and it was he who had led the assault on the Egyptian artillery at Abu Agheila in 1967), and I knew those paratroopers from twenty years back. They would find a way to get through. But still the situation worried me. I could not understand what Southern Command was doing, why they had not taken over the job of co-ordinating the two attacking divisions.

In the late afternoon I moved out with my mobile command APC's. That day happened to be Sukkot, the harvest festival, and as we headed toward the front we passed dozens of jerry-rigged Sukkot huts. Traditionally these huts are made of branches and foliage and are hung with the season's harvest. Often they are elaborate and elegant. But for this Sukkot in the Sinai, ammunition cases and packing crates were the main building material, supplemented by an occasional scraggly bush the soldiers had managed to dig up from the desert.

Just before dark I was south of Akavish near the Great Bitter Lake watching as Amnon's brigade wheeled through the high white dunes on my left. The desert looked so clean and beautiful. It was T. E. Lawrence, I think, who said that the desert is the cleanest place of all, and it is. Over time the white sand covers everything. In the gathering dusk the line of tanks snaked its way along the undulations, weaving in and out of sight like a creature with its own life. Amnon had been fighting since the first day of war; it was his tanks that had suffered so badly in the first reaction to the Egyptian crossing. Now the same unit—the Fourteenth Tank Brigade—was on its way to clear the canal for our own crossing. Leading the Fourteenth was the reconnaissance unit under a young officer named Yoav Brom who had just been called back from his studies in the United States. With Brom in front, Amnon's brigade would sweep in on the Egyptian rear and push out north and east, opening Akavish and Tirtur to the paratroop brigade and assault boats and to the bulldozers and tankdozers we would need to excavate the prepared ramps in the yard.

At 7 P.M. I watched the entire battlefield come alive. From the east the fire and din of Tuvia's attack broke the tension of waiting. Behind me Amnon completed his hook and struck north. Some time later I made out the dark silhouettes of Danny Mat's paratroopers passing in front of me along Akavish. Behind Danny came the rafts, and behind the rafts trundled the big bulldozers. But as we watched, the convoy slowed its progress and seemed to be confused about where to go. With the rest of the command APC's following, I went down to the road and led them toward the yard. From the Chinese Farm, fire lashed out in our direction. But it was not accurate or in sufficient volume to slow us down.

Then suddenly the area around the Tirtur-Lexicon junction erupted in flame. Just before we entered the yard, we saw on our right a fierce battle raging between the reconnaissance unit and Egyptian forces trying to close the road. A few hundred yards away vehicles were exploding and burning as the command APC's passed by at the front of the vulnerable assault rafts. Unnoticed, we entered into the protection of the yard's sand walls. Though we did not know it, behind us the reconnaissance unit was dying in a barrage of Sagger missiles and tank fire.

By 1 A.M. lead elements of the paratroopers had started crossing to the west bank in their rubber assault boats. On the other side of the canal the troopers found the area almost deserted. We had taken the Egyptians utterly by surprise. As they established their beachhead, the paratroopers radioed back the code word Acapulco—Success.

Meanwhile, Amnon Reshef's tank column had continued north until suddenly they found themselves in the rear administrative center of the Egyptian Sixteenth Division. As they did, the area around them was illuminated by thousands of explosions. Egyptian soldiers and vehicles scrambled to get out of the way as tank, artillery, and small-arms fire erupted toward the shadows of the Israeli armor. Over the radio we could hear the quiet, matter-of-fact tones of Amnon's voice as his Pattons wreaked havoc: "The range is forty yards. . . . We are barrel to barrel. . . . We have a direct hit on the divisional command center." By this time Amnon had moved more than five miles north, even though our orders were that a corridor of two and a half miles would be adequate. Now, under intense pressure, he pulled back slowly, shortening lines and concentrating his forces.

Inside the yard the bulldozers had been unable at first to breach the wall, until I pointed out the red bricks that marked the specially thinned area. Now they were digging fiercely at the ramparts, while the engineers had already started wrestling with the bridging equipment. A unit of anti-aircraft machine guns had taken up positions on the walls ready for the air attacks that we knew would come in the morning. Elements of Haim Erez's tank brigade were also crowding into the enclosure, waiting to join the paratroopers on the other side. Akavish was open; it was along that road that the paratroopers, rafts, and tanks had made their way into the yard. But Tirtur—crisscrossed by the Chinese Farm—was still shut tight.

Tirtur was extremely important. It was only along this road that the giant rolling bridge could be towed to the canal, while the extension of Tirtur to the canal bank itself had been especially prepared as a launching site for the bridge. By now we had managed to secure the vital Tirtur-Lexicon junction; but as Amnon's units hammered all night at the Egyptians in the Chinese Farm, it became clear that we simply did not have the strength to dislodge them from Tirtur itself. For the moment, at least, we would have to rely on Akavish to conduit men and armor toward the crossing site.

The morning of October 16 dawned on the most terrible sight I had ever seen. All that night Amnon's brigade, along with several paratrooper elements, the remnants of Yoav Brom's reconnaissance unit, one of Tuvia's battalions and one of Haim Erez's, had been engaged with the better part of two Egyptian divisions. I had listened intently to their reports over the radio net, and the conflagration of the battle had lit the sky just to the north of us. But each of us in the headquarters unit had been directly involved in action, so busy that we had not fully grasped the immensity of the struggle, or its destructiveness. But as the sky brightened, I looked around and saw hundreds and hundreds of burned and twisted vehicles. Fifty Israeli tanks lay shattered on the field. Around them were the hulks of 150 Egyptian tanks plus hundreds of APC's, jeeps, and trucks. Wreckage littered the desert. Here and there Israeli and Egyptian tanks had destroyed each other at a distance of a few meters, barrel to barrel. It was as if a hand-to-hand battle of armor had taken place. And inside those tanks and next to them lay their dead crews. Coming close, you could see Egyptian and Jewish dead lying side by side, soldiers who had jumped from their burning tanks and had died together. No picture could capture the horror of the scene, none could encompass what had happened there. On our side that night we had lost 300 dead and hundreds more wounded. The Egyptian losses were much, much heavier.

As dawn broke, this was the scene we took in just to our north. At almost the same moment another dramatic panorama unfolded before our eyes to the west. Suddenly the bulldozers broke through the last of the ramparts, opening the yard to the canal. And now, directly in front of us across two hundred yards of water was Egypt. We stood there in the opening and stared at the trees and lush green foliage. On our side everything was barren sand and dust. On theirs the palm trees and orchards grew in lush profusion around the Sweet Water Canal. From where we stood it looked like paradise.

During the night we had managed to get Danny Mat's entire paratroop brigade to the western side of the canal. Now they were quickly joined by a number of APC's and twenty-eight of Haim Erez's tanks, which were ferried over on rafts. As soon as they landed, Haim's armor raced westward, destroying the surprised Egyptian units and positions that had the misfortune to be in their path. By nine o'clock they reported they had eliminated five ground-to-air missile sites, tearing a gaping hole in the Egyptian antiaircraft umbrella that had effectively closed this area to Israeli jets. Now they were marauding at will, picking off the last Egyptian units in the area. Nothing stood in their way; the region west of the canal was virtually empty. Haim's voice came over the radio: "We can get to Cairo." From Danny Mat came word that he was experiencing no pressure at all and that paratroop units were proceeding northward along the canal bank rolling up the Egyptian rampart positions.

Since the previous night I had been inside the yard. Now I could not resist the temptation to make a quick visit to "Africa" on one of the rafts that was ferrying tanks. But after checking on the forces there, I came back. The yard was the crucial spot. The fate of our people on the other side depended on whether we could keep it open and working. And the yard was fast becoming a bottleneck, not nearly large enough for the masses of troops, armor, and equipment that were now making their way into it to cross over.

Inside the yard and in the canal opening, engineers were working like mad, directing traffic, widening the breach, getting tanks, men, and supplies onto the rafts and across to the other side. A race was on. The Egyptians were still not aware of what we had done. They were not trying to interdict the crossing, and as yet there was no pressure on the yard itself. Meanwhile, on the far side our forces were having a field day. We could not have asked for a more advantageous situation. Now we had to push everything across that we possibly could, as fast as we could, before the Egyptians recovered their balance. This was the moment we had been waiting for since the war's first shots.

It was right in the middle of this frenzy of activity that an order came through from Southern Command that was so outrageous I at first refused to believe it. All crossing activity, it said, was to cease immediately. Not a single additional tank or man was to be transferred. According to them, we were cut off, surrounded by Egyptian forces.

*   *   *

It was precisely 9 A.M. As I took stock of the situation I knew that Southern Command was once again failing to understand what was happening in the field. Although we had been on the canal twelve hours already, no one had yet come to make a personal assessment. It was true that we had not accomplished all of our objectives that night. But there was absolutely no reason to put the crossing operation on hold. On the contrary, we had surprise with us. Now was exactly the moment to exploit it. On the west side of the canal we had achieved more than expected. Not only had we established a bridgehead, but Haim's tanks were operating twenty miles west of the waterway. Danny Mat was busy cleaning up the ramparts to the north, and we had broken the sector's air defenses. On the east side we had taken control of the yard and the canal bank north and south of it. From the yard the big motorized rafts were operating with complete freedom.

On the minus side, we did not yet have the floating units available to assemble a bridge. They were stuck somewhere in the traffic mess. In the confusion on the roads between my division and Adan's they had been blocked. I knew what efforts my rear headquarters was making to get them through, and I knew all about the conflicts for priority between Adan's people and mine. Inside I was burning that Southern Command had not assigned someone to just take the whole business in hand and clean it up. We were also still fighting to establish the two-and-a-half-mile-wide corridor to the canal prescribed in our orders. But the main road, Akavish, was open, although under intermittent fire. A continual flow of men and matériel was coming down it, and we were just then evacuating hundreds of wounded using the road. Tirtur, however, was still unusable after bloody battles all through the night had failed to push the Egyptians out of the Chinese Farm.

That was the actual situation on the ground. But back at headquarters they saw it differently. All morning long, frantic calls came in over the radio, "You are cut off! You are encircled! You are surrounded!" They were in a panic about the bridgehead's imminent destruction. But I was right there. I did not feel cut off. I was getting supplies, fuel, men, and tanks in. I was getting my wounded out. Akavish was not exactly an open expressway. But it was certainly open.

Meanwhile the assault rafts were working continuously, without any interference whatsoever. Because the fact was that although I had orders not to continue the crossing, I already had men and tanks on the far side who needed supplies and ammunition and reinforcement. And I had wounded and dead over there who had to be taken out. So the rafts were still plying the canal. The Egyptians were in such a state of shock that even now, eight hours after we first crossed, they had hardly realized what had happened to them. They were not attacking the bridgehead, and they were not responding to Haim Erez's tanks that were still moving at will and shooting up everything in sight.

We had now reached the critical point of the battle. A decision had to be made either to exploit the crossing or not. I looked in vain for Gonen or Bar-Lev to come to the yard and assess the situation firsthand. If one of them had come, he would have seen first of all that we were not cut off, that though we did not have a secure two-and-a-half-mile corridor, we did have a corridor and it was usable. Secondly he would have seen that opening the corridor further while at the same time securing and expanding the west-bank beachhead was too heavy for one division. But a few miles behind us an entire fresh division—Adan's—was waiting. Had I been the commander I would have had one division (Adan's or mine; it didn't matter) cross and take responsibility for the west side. The other division I would have kept on the east side to widen and secure the corridor. Had Adan crossed, he could have taken command of the paratroops and Haim's brigade, while giving me one of his brigades. Had I crossed, I could have taken one of Adan's fresh brigades and left him one of mine. There were different ways to do it. But Bar-Lev and Gonen either had to come forward and make the decision themselves or else remain behind and give me the necessary freedom of action. But neither of these things happened.

Instead, since early morning they had been shouting about what a dangerous situation I was in. Again and again they asked me to come to headquarters to discuss what to do. But I told them that the battle we were fighting was so hard that even from the point of view of morale—let alone for command reasons—I would not leave for a minute. Again and again I told them, "You come here! Look at it for yourselves." But they simply would not do it.

Meanwhile the first battalion of Adan's tanks arrived in the yard, unaware that the crossing had been stopped. I was standing there in the opening of the ramp when they drove up—conditions were so tight, with so many vehicles crowded in, that half the people in the command unit were busy with traffic control. As the battalion commander and I were talking, a tank turret opened and a young soldier climbed out, the son of

Hillel Carmeli, my signal officer. Hillel and his son embraced and had time to exchange a word or two before I sent the battalion north to relieve some of the pressure on Amnon.

An hour later a message came that Adan's battalion had been hit and Hillel's son was among the wounded. Immediately I told Hillel to go and see what had happened, but before long he was back. The boy was in critical condition, wounded in the spine and unable to move his legs. He was being evacuated with the other casualties. After telling me this, Hillel climbed back into our APC and silently resumed his job. In the coming days I urged him to take a day or two to visit his son and his wife. But he refused to leave the front, and in fact he did not go until the fighting was over.

Inside our M-113 APC, Hillel's position was on my left, and I watched him all the time, knowing precisely how he felt, and knowing too that his tragedy was not by any means unique. Danny Mat's son was a tank officer in Amnon's brigade, and he too had been wounded. All across the battlefield other fathers were losing sons and sons fathers. Men who had fought in the War of Independence twenty-five years ago were still fighting. And now, a quarter century later, their children were fighting too. It was a phenomenon that gave the war yet another tragic dimension, as if it needed one. I began thinking of it as the war of fathers and sons.

Although we were able to get the wounded evacuated, the dead were another story. We just did not have the resources to make that effort ourselves. In order to evacuate the dead, they first had to be identified, and that by itself was a major job. Somebody had to determine who was an Egyptian, who an Israeli among those boys lying there, almost in each other's arms. I told them on the radio what the situation was and what was needed. But nobody came to do it then, just as nobody came to look at the battlefield. All I seemed to hear over the radio were the constant dire warnings that I was encircled and cut off.

During one of the lulls I told my command group that all the panic reminded me of something that had happened twenty years ago during a field exercise in the Northern Command. A reserve brigade was in defense and an active brigade, commanded by Assaf Simchoni, was on the attack. Simchoni pressed home an aggressive assault and sent a platoon to cut the road behind the defenders. When the defending commander saw that his escape route was blocked, he radioed to the exercise headquarters that he was surrounded. What should he do? From the headquarters Moshe Dayan had shot back, "Maybe you aren't surrounded at all. Maybe it's Simchoni's platoon that's surrounded!"

I certainly didn't feel for a moment that we were the ones who were surrounded. On the contrary, we had cut off the Egyptians. We were in back of them. We were threatening them, not vice versa. We all knew it and felt it. The atmosphere in the command unit was excellent—quiet and optimistic. Even during the most difficult moments feelings of friendship and affection prevailed; there was little anxiety and no panic. After the fighting was over, I told my staff that I was proudest perhaps of the fact that I had never had to shout, rarely even to raise my voice. They had conducted themselves with absolute professionalism and confidence.

I did feel, though, that my own presence right there with the forward troops was essential. You read these days that in modern warfare and especially in future warfare commanders will be wearing white gowns and pressing buttons from high-technology command centers far from the battlefield. But in fact, reality is exactly the reverse. Firepower today is so massive that the battlefield situation can change in an instant. At the canal I saw a company of tanks disappear in less than a minute. An entire battalion was engulfed and destroyed before they had time to report that they were being hit. With events like these there was no substitute for being forward. You could not rely on information given to you through the normal channels—not your intelligence channel, your operations channel, your administrative channel. Nothing. Not because the information was inaccurate but because it was not information in real time. The massiveness of the fire, the numbers of troops engaged, and the swiftness of changes outdated information before it was transmitted. You simply had to be on the spot looking at developments firsthand, as they happened.

But this was not the only reason I felt I had to be forward. I was a divisional commander, making decisions and giving orders that meant life or death. The soldiers and officers I commanded did not necessarily want me to share the exact dangers and hardships they were undergoing. But because their lives were dependent on my orders, I always felt they were more secure knowing that I was right there, seeing their problems with my own eyes, that it was not somebody sending orders and instructions from a distance with no firsthand appreciation of what they were going through. They knew that if I gave them even the hardest orders, involving the gravest danger, that I was doing so on the basis of immediate personal knowledge. And consequently they were willing to do whatever was necessary, despite the risks.

Watching these dynamics reconfirmed for me how immensely difficult it is to be a ranking commander on a modern battlefield. At one and the same time you are busy giving orders, listening to all the important communications nets, and trying to piece together the complicated and rapidly changing jigsaw of events. And while all this is happening, you are also present right there on the battlefield, fighting.

At least this was the way it was on the canal. The enemy was everywhere; by now we were under permanent air attack. Each of our command APC's had three machine guns mounted, and we were shooting constantly. We ourselves managed to shoot down five Egyptian aircraft attacking us. In our position there in the yard (the "death yard" as some began to call it) I often found myself manning a gun; during the war's fifteen days it seemed to me I must have fired as many rounds as I had in my entire previous career as a soldier. Every time I climbed into the APC, I checked the supply of grenades, just in case we might need them. It got to be a kind of reflex action.

October 16 could easily have been the day of our real triumph. But it was not. Instead, after the previous night's immense efforts, the advance was halted. That day and more than that day were wasted. Rather than exploiting our surprise, we were forced to wait. And, as was inevitable, the Egyptians finally understood what a desperate thing had happened to them and they responded. They began to put heavy pressure on Haim Erez's tanks on the west bank, and slowly he was forced to pull inside the paratroopers' defensive perimeter.

All of October 16 we were forbidden to reinforce the west bank bridgehead. That night, exhausted and morose, I went to sleep on the warm engine cover of a tank. Early on the morning of the seventeenth I was awakened by the sound of more self-propelled rafts being towed into the yard. They were a welcome sight. With enough of these rafts on hand, we would now be able to assemble the bridge. Once that was done, we might finally be able to change some minds about getting our forces across fast, even though by this time surprise was no longer with us.

The rafts rumbled slowly into the yard and down toward the rampart opening, where the engineers' already frantic pace began to pick up even more. But just at that moment a tremendous Egyptian artillery barrage brought a curtain of shells crashing down on us. Almost simultaneously Mig fighters swarmed over the yard in an attack that turned the compound into an inferno. With incredible courage, soldiers were standing outside in this storm of fire directing traffic. Columns of vehicles were entering the yard, some of which exploded in the bombardment and had to be pushed out of the way, although with all the tanks and trucks already crowded in, there was hardly room to push them anywhere. Officers from the command APC's were constantly jumping out to help with traffic control. Others worked with the engineers who were assembling and launching the rafts under the same deadly hail. Hundreds of shells seemed to be hitting the area. The chaos was mind-boggling.

At one point I was talking with Zevele Amit, who was helping with traffic control near the launching ramp, when a flight of Egyptian jets swooped in making an "empty run" to line their targets up. As they roared past, Zevele shouted at me to get into the M-113. I jumped in and grabbed one of the machine guns just as the Migs returned for their bombing run. When the planes came in again, the place seemed to explode. The hammering of our fifteen machine guns joined with the perimeter antiaircraft batteries in a deafening racket that was blotted out by the bombs hitting all around us.

In the heat of the action I was aware that casualties were being loaded onto stretchers and taken off toward the medical station. Out of the corner of an eye I noticed that one stretcher had a paratrooper on it. I could tell from the maroon boots that stuck out from under a blanket. But that was just a momentary detail, clearer to me in recollection than it was at the moment. I did not guess that those boots were mine, the pair Lily had given Zevele when we were mobilized.

As more jets came in and the artillery fire intensified, I ordered the five APC's to the other side of the yard. Zevele had been working with the rafts at the opening to the canal, as were my friend Motti and my other two drivers, and it was just there that the shelling was heaviest. As we negotiated our way slowly through the yard, the M-113 was rocked by bomb concussions. Suddenly I felt a smashing pain on my forehead. I had a moment to see blood splattering all over and I heard someone say, "Our friend just bought it." But an instant later my eyes opened and I realized that whatever had hit me was just a glancing blow. Though my head was bleeding heavily, nothing else seemed wrong, so apparently nothing dangerous had happened.

Nevertheless I felt I had to get the command vehicles out of there. The fire was so heavy that our aerials had taken hits and we were in danger of losing radio control. So I ordered them out to the gate area, where just then tanks were rumbling through towing more raft sections. One of these sections was in flames, and as I looked I realized that while inside the yard we were under artillery fire, outside the vehicles were being hit by direct flat-trajectory tank fire. I could not understand exactly what was happening, how there could be enemy tanks so nearby. Through my binoculars I looked toward the road junction just several hundred yards away and was shocked to see an Egyptian counterattack of tanks and supporting infantry coming directly toward us.

It was an absolutely critical moment. These Egyptians were about to close the yard behind us. The only force I had under my hands at that instant was the command APC's, those five M-113s. So our headquarters unit rushed the road juncture. As we did, I called Amnon, who that day was fighting together with Tuvia to stop a co-ordinated Egyptian counterattack by the Sixteenth and Twenty-first Divisions to our north while helping Adan destroy the Egyptian Twenty-fifth Armored Brigade, which was advancing from the south. I asked him to immediately send tanks to the junction.

As we raced ahead, we saw just on our left an M-113 exploding in flames. On our right was a mine field that we ourselves had laid in earlier years. When we approached the burning APC, I was on the outside radio net with Amnon, but since I was standing up I also had the best view of where we were going. So while I was talking to Amnon, I was also shouting directions at the driver, "Driver, to the right." Then when he went too far, almost into the minefield, "To the left, drive to the left." Later I learned that my shouting had raised anxieties in radio operators all along the front. Even at Southern Command, where they were monitoring the net, they thought something serious was happening to me. For a week and a half they had been used to my usual restrained way of relaying orders, and suddenly they were hearing me screaming at the top of my lungs.

In a moment we had gotten to the junction with our machine guns blazing and were able to hold on for the few minutes it took before Amnon's tanks showed up. At that point we backed off and everyone in the five APC's caught his breath. It was our first break since the Egyptian jets had made their targeting run while I was talking to Zevele—a year ago it seemed, though it could scarcely have been fifteen minutes.

I kept puzzling over why our tanks had not been at the junction. What had happened to me? How could I have left that place unguarded? And then I remembered that the previous night I had gotten an order from Southern Command informing me that an attack would be launched to open the Tirtur Road. Since the attack would move from east to west, we had been ordered to move our tanks away so as not to be in the line of fire. Now I realized that no one had informed us during the night that the assault had failed. In fact, this assault was one of the most unbelievably dreadful operations of the war. A battalion of paratroopers had been sent in to take the Chinese Farm without any armor. In effect they had been sent to their deaths in what was little more than a suicide mission. Among the ditches of the Egyptian concentration they were cut to shreds. And when the survivors were finally extricated, we were not told about what had taken place there, and so we had not moved our tanks back to the junction. That was how it had happened.

While I was recalling this train of events, it suddenly dawned on me that neither Zevele nor Motti was in the M-113. Both of them had been sitting next to me in that APC for almost eleven straight days, and their presence had become a kind of mental fixture for me. Then I remembered to my horror that we had left them behind in the inferno in that yard. Worried, I asked around if anyone had seen them. In fact some of the people in the APC already knew that Zevele had been killed in the shelling. But they didn't tell me. They knew we had been intimate friends for twenty years, and they were afraid of the effect it might have on me.

They may have been right. It was not only that we were friends, but as a commander you are so alone. And for me Zevele was so much more than just an effective officer. He was someone I could joke with and talk to, someone who could help me relieve the terrible tension, someone I didn't have to make any effort with or put on any fronts with. So when I asked, one of the other officers there said that Zevele had been wounded and evacuated. I suspected something was wrong. Wounded maybe, but evacuated no. Nobody was being evacuated at that particular moment.

While I was asking around, an orderly bandaged my head, which was pounding like a sledgehammer. At that moment I happened to see "Patsi" Chen. Patsi was a reconnaissance officer, one of the most capable soldiers I had ever seen. His unit had been in charge of providing security against the Egyptian commandos, who since the first days had attempted to land behind our lines and disrupt our rear areas. Now I told him that we had a lot of casualties in the yard and I wanted him to make sure personally that they were evacuated quickly. He should also look for Motti and for Zevele, and let me know when he had found them.

A short time later Motti's voice came over the net. He knew I must be worried, he said. He was badly wounded, but he was alive and just then was being taken out. I felt a great relief. He had been my driver for six years. I knew his wife and two young children and I liked him immensely; it preyed on me that I had left him in that hell in the yard. But from Zevele there was still no word.

A short time later on that hard morning I was ordered to come to a meeting with the upper command at a position in the desert several miles from the canal. In my APC we drove back along Akavish, the road that supposedly had been cut off behind us. When we got to the co-ordinates on the dunes, I saw waiting for me Moshe Dayan, Chaim Bar-Lev, David Elazar, and Avraham Adan. As I approached, nobody said a word—except Dayan, who greeted me with a normal, friendly "Shalom, Arik." I hadn't seen any of them since the fourteenth. Since that day virtually the entire crossing battle had been carried out by my division alone. But now there was not a single word or an outstretched hand. Just silence.

Then Bar-Lev said, very quietly and deliberately, "The distance between what you promised to do and what you have done . . . is very great." At that moment I felt tired to death. After all those terrible battles and casualties, with our dead still on the field where we had been unable to bring them out, when I saw this group of neatly dressed, washed, clean-shaven people, and when I heard that sentence: "The distance between what you have promised to do and what you have done is very great," I knew there was only one thing to do. I had to smack Bar-Lev in the face. I felt I just had to do it.

To this day I do not know how I kept myself from hitting him. Instead, I simply clamped my mouth shut. After a moment more of silence a short discussion took place and they decided to do what they should have done two days earlier. Very soon the pontoon bridge would be completed. Now we could proceed across the canal. My division would hold the yard, secure the corridor, and proceed north on the west bank of the canal toward Ismailia and westward twenty-five to thirty kilometers in the direction of Cairo. Adan and Kalman Magen would cross the bridge and would proceed southward around the shores of the Great Bitter Lake to the rear of the Egyptian Third Army.

It was a brief exchange. When it was over, Gonen, Bar-Lev, and Elazar got into their helicopter and flew off. Adan mounted his APC to go back to his division. I was there alone with Moshe Dayan, who had very obviously not liked the discussion but nevertheless had said nothing. I told him that Zevele (who was from Dayan's moshav) had been

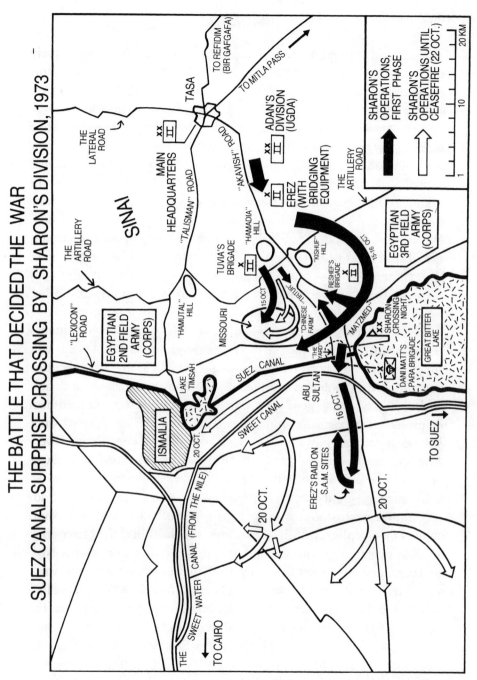

THE BATTLE THAT DECIDED THE WAR
SUEZ CANAL SURPRISE CROSSING BY SHARON'S DIVISION, 1973

The IDF could prevent Arab victory in the Yom Kippur War only by crossing the Suez Canal in order to threaten the Egyptian forces in Sinai from their rear. This mission was given to Sharon's division, which attacked on the night of October 15. Exploiting the unprotected "seam" between the two enemy armies, a paratroop brigade crossed the canal by boat, followed by a tank brigade using rafts. Close by, at the "Chinese Farm" and "Missouri" areas, the rest of Sharon's forces fought the bloodiest battle in the history of the IDF.

wounded and I hoped he was still alive. He asked me about my head. It was, at least, a human interaction.

Dayan had no intention of leaving; he wanted to be taken to the canal and then to the other side. Once inside my APC, he began talking about the urgent need to put troops across. He knew that the rafts had been operating for thirty hours, that the bridge itself was all but finished, and that nobody had crossed other than Danny Mat's paratroops, Haim's original tanks, and some other tanks of Haim's I had spirited across to make up his losses. Dayan was practically beside himself about the lack of movement. "You have to urge them to start crossing," he told me. "We are wasting time!" I had a sudden flashback to our discussion in the yard of that ma'oz during the War of Attrition. "Moshe," I said, "give them an order!"

For the next hour and a half Dayan was with me. Together we crossed to the other side and looked at what was happening in the bridgehead. Apparently after Dayan saw the situation himself, he made up his mind. At four-thirty on the afternoon of the seventeenth the bridge was completed, but still nobody was crossing. Late that afternoon, when he returned to the Southern Command, Dayan issued a direct order to Bar-Lev and Elazar to get forces moving across the canal immediately. But even then it took many hours. It was not until 11:30 P.M. that Adan's units began to cross, almost two days after our original crossing and seven hours after the bridge was completed. For seven hours it had stood there vacant. And even then the tanks that did cross waited until the following morning before launching their assault.

Of course during those two days the Egyptians had time to fully comprehend their predicament. By the time Adan broke out of the bridgehead they had managed to concentrate forces opposite him. And what could have been done so easily on the sixteenth and even on the seventeenth became a hard and costly job on the eighteenth. By then Adan had to fight his way out in a slogging match that would find him just short of his objective when the first cease-fire went into effect four days later.

While Adan was crossing the canal and pushing southward, I was under continuous pressure from Southern Command to widen the corridor on the eastern bank. Specifically, they wanted me to attack and push back the Sixteenth and Twenty-first divisions in their stronghold at Missouri. My constant response was that these divisions were dug in very well, with mine fields and with a tremendous number of RPG's and Saggers, the wire-guided anti-tank missile that was the surprise of this war. I told them that I believed we should not launch an attack there. There was no danger at all to our corridor. (By 1 A.M. on the nineteenth we had the steel roller bridge across.) The Egyptian positions were near Akavish Road, but the road and everything south of it was firmly in our hands for miles. Southern Command's repeated orders were based on nothing more than a wrong reading of the battle map, the kind of thing they had been consistently guilty of all along.

I told them that Tuvia could certainly continue to slice away at Missouri. But there was no need for a major battle there. On the contrary, the most effective thing to do would be to move northward along the west bank of the canal, behind the Egyptian positions. As we moved up behind them toward Ismailia, the Egyptians would be so menaced themselves, they would not even begin to think about threatening our lines of communication.

And in fact we were already doing that. One by one, on the west side the paratroopers were capturing the Egyptian rampart positions. And in each position they captured I had them raise a huge Israeli flag, so the Egyptians on the east bank saw a progressive movement of the Israeli forces cutting them off from behind. The effect was dramatic. As they watched their escape route being closed down, panic began to set in.

But though our forces were in Egypt proper, moving southward, westward, and northward and getting a continuous stream of supplies and reinforcement, still Southern Command kept ordering me to make a major assault on Missouri. I could not understand it. I fought it, I railed against it, I tried in every way I knew to get the order rescinded. It would be a useless gesture, an absolutely needless waste of lives. But at the end I was not able to change it. On the twenty-first I obeyed the order.

The morning of the attack I stood on a rampart on the western bank and watched Tuvia's tanks and APC's rush the Egyptian positions. I saw them penetrate deep into the defenses, and as they did I saw them hit by a torrent of RPG's, Saggers, and tank fire. One after another Tuvia's vehicles stopped and burst into flame. It was a sight that sickened all of us who were watching. We had seen and accepted so much death over the two weeks just past. But every battle we had fought had been necessary. And if your mission is necessary, of course you accept even the worst casualties. But this was meaningless, suicidal. It sickened me then, and I am even more bitter about it now, sixteen years later.

That evening Southern Command ordered me to attack again. This time I redoubled my effort to get the order rescinded. I told them that I was on the spot. I could see exactly what the situation was. There was no need for it at all. If they did not believe me, they should come and see it for themselves. (They had still not come down to the front. Dayan, by contrast, had been visiting us daily in that hell since the seventeenth—the only one who did.) There was no way for a brigade attack to succeed against that position.

The answer was that I should take forces from the western side of the canal. I should actually take troops who were busy with the crucial business on the western side and transfer them back to the east to take part in a battle that should never have been fought in the first place, let alone repeated.

It was generalship of the worst kind. But I am afraid that it was more than just bad generalship. During this period I had proposed that the primary effort on the west side should be to the north in back of the Egyptian Second Army rather than to the south in back of the Third. I knew that Bar-Lev and Elazar considered this proposal self-serving on my part, since it was my own brigades that were positioned for a move in that direction. But in fact there were excellent operational reasons for moving north.

In the first place, three quarters of our forces in the Sinai were facing the northern front. Consequently, we could apply far greater pressure to the Second Army than we could to the Third. Second, the Egyptian reserves were positioned in front of Cairo, from where they could threaten the flank of a southern advance (which they did) but not a northern advance. Third, our air bases were closer to the north and could provide more effective air support. Finally, we had to move north anyway to widen the bridgehead.

To this day I cannot free myself from the feeling that one of the reasons they were pressing me to attack the Sixteenth and Twenty-first divisions on the east side of the canal was not because they considered the corridor too narrow but because they wanted to keep my troops on the eastern side. They would allow me to proceed north, but they did not want me to have sufficient forces to do it effectively. These are hard things to say. But my strong impression then was that the antagonisms of years between myself and those in command (Bar-Lev and Elazar), augmented now by political considerations, played a considerable role in the military decisions that were made at that time. It is an impression the years have not diminished.

When I could not get the order to attack Missouri again rescinded, I finally called Dayan and explained the situation to him. After hearing me out, he instructed Southern Command directly to call the thing off. On the eve of the cease-fire I was thus freed from the necessity of yet another bloody and abortive operation.

After the war these events were to bear very bitter fruit. For me, the memory of that day stayed vivid. Among all the tragic mistakes and all the grim fighting of the Yom Kippur War, it was that attack on Missouri that weighed most heavily on me. I had ordered Tuvia's brigade into battle even though I knew for a fact that many of those soldiers were going to their deaths for nothing. It was something I should never have done, regardless of my own orders. I knew instinctively at the time that it was wrong for me to have obeyed. And later, on reflection, I became sure that morally and legally too I should not have obeyed.

In an interview I gave to the newpaper *Ma'ariv* on January 25, 1974, I said exactly that. I told the interviewer that those who gave the order did not understand the situation on the ground as I did. If they had wanted to override the field commander's tactical decisions, they had an obligation to be there on the spot to assess our forces, the enemy forces, the terrain, morale—everything. I should not have accepted interference in tactical decisions unless my superiors could see the same thing that I was seeing, in the same place I was seeing it. If they had done that and still disagreed with me, then I would accept their decision. But otherwise they should not have interfered and I should not have accepted their interference. Instead I should have disobeyed an order I knew was wrong. I should have disobeyed and accepted a court-martial for my disobedience.

That statement provoked a storm of criticism. As a result of it I was attacked as a person who disobeyed orders, who practically embodied the concept of disobedience. The controversy over this issue became so inflamed that when the Agranat Commission investigated the conduct of the war they directly addressed this charge of insubordination, even though their inquiry was supposed to be limited to the war's first three days.

The result of the commission's inquiry clarified military law. In battle, the commission said, there are very rare cases in which a subordinate is convinced that his superior would not have given a specific order had he known the true facts in the field. But in such a case the subordinate has the right to take every conventional measure to get the order changed. As far as prejudicing discipline is concerned, if an officer submits himself to a court-martial rather than obey an order he is sure is wrong, then he is

SINAI FRONT, 24th OCT. 1973 WHERE THE IDF STOPPED

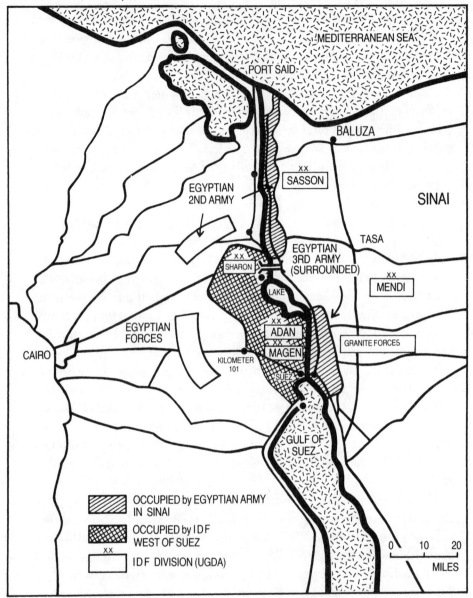

still in accord with military requirements. "Our opinion," the commission concluded, "is that . . . the conception of General Sharon, as he described it, agrees with the demands of military discipline."*

---

*Another issue the Agranat Commission dealt with had to do with an incident that happened on October 8. Abraham Adan claimed that on that day I had been ordered to transfer a tank battalion to his command and that I had refused to do it. After investigation, the Commission also found that there was no basis whatsoever for this charge.

The Agranat Commission fully justified the steps I had taken to avoid carrying out my orders in this situation, up to and including persuading the minister of defense to intervene. After all the controversy, they also justified my instinct that I should not have obeyed even the first order to attack, as long as I was ready to submit to a court-martial for it. But all the justification in the world did not change the fact that what was done was done, that those lives were sacrificed, and that I shared the responsibility for it.

Tuvia mounted his abortive attack on Missouri on October 21. By that time Adan and Kalman Magen had swept around the western shoreline of the Bitter lakes and were on the verge of cutting off the Egyptian Third Army. Six days earlier Sadat had considered the Israeli crossing a "television operation," staged only to make a momentary dramatic effect. Now, with the Third Army almost isolated and with my forces sixty miles from Cairo and at the gates of Ismailia, the Egyptians were in a panic. Their pressure on the Soviets to arrange a quick cease-fire had resulted in an invitation from Leonid Brezhnev for Henry Kissinger to visit Moscow. On the twenty-first—the same day Tuvia attacked Missouri—Kissinger and Brezhnev concluded an agreement. Early the next morning their efforts were embodied in a U.N. Security Council resolution that called on both sides to stop fighting.

The cease-fire went into effect in the evening of October 22 (though continued fighting in the south forced a second resolution two days later). After sixteen days of hell, suddenly it was quiet. Night fell on the desert just south of Ismailia, where we had just fought a fierce battle to take some bridges across the Sweet Water Canal. In the startling silence I called Daliah, Zevele's wife, to tell her what I had known now for several days, that Zevele was dead. It was a bitter, choking moment. When I hung up I walked away from the APC and stood by myself on the bank of an irrigation ditch. I could feel the tears welling up—for Zevele and for all those others. I had seen so many of them with my own eyes, scenes of death unlike those in any of the other wars. The scale of suffering was so much vaster than what I or anyone else had experienced before. For the moment, at least, it was hard to imagine how we might recover from it.

23

Politician and Farmer

Weeks passed. Although there was a cease-fire, I didn't dare leave the front. If I visited somewhere, I would make sure to be away no more than a few hours and never after dark. After all that had happened, I simply did not trust anyone. When it grew dark, I would take my command APC's and move up to the forward tanks, where as often as not we would spend the night. For hours I would sit there staring into the blackness through the Soviet Starlight equipment we had captured from the Egyptians.

At first every night was broken by shelling and small-arms fire, almost as if a new war of attrition was starting up. Meanwhile soldiers were living in the mango trees and citrus plantations of the Sweet Water Canal, digging in and making themselves as comfortable as they could. Before long they had eaten the cattle that wandered ownerless through their positions. When the cattle were gone, they ate the sheep, then the geese and ducks. Most nights I stayed up with them, watching and talking. When morning came, I would fall asleep for a couple of hours, then get up to a day of visiting troops and planning the next move. We were on alert status often, and no one was sure if the war was really over. If it started up again, I was determined to have my plans meticulously worked out.

Going through my routine each day, I thought over and over about how this could have happened to us, this tragedy? How could we have allowed it? Twenty-five years ago, when we were staring at our own extinction in the War of Independence, we had never once lost our self-confidence, not even for a day. How then had we been brought so low now, when we were fighting almost two hundred miles from home? As bad as this war had been, I had never felt we were on the verge of destruction. I knew how precarious our position had been on the Golan, and of course in the Sinai too. But it was still nothing like those first six months of the Independence War. Physical extermination of the nation had not been the issue. So what had happened?

After mulling this question over, I finally came to the conclusion that the reason our morale had been so high in 1948 was that then we were on our way forward. Those hundreds of thousands of Holocaust survivors were still being detained in Europe and in Cyprus, but we knew that we were moving ahead—to independence, to a state, to a decent life for all of us. As fragile as the community's existence had been, everyone was convinced that the war was only a phase, an event on the path toward something better.

Now, I concluded, maybe what had happened was that we did not have any clear idea of what was in front of us. Twenty-six hundred dead was a terrible price to pay in any case. But twenty-six hundred dead when there was no sense of direction, no goals we were aspiring to—that was especially terrible. Of course everyone was vastly relieved that we had emerged from a close situation as victors. But what was there to look forward to? What ideals, what motivation? What sense of national purpose?

Whenever I had to leave, to fly to Bir Gafgafa or Tel Aviv, I would take off from Fayid airfield west of the Bitter lakes. During the first leg of the flight we would stay almost at ground level to avoid Egyptian ground-to-air missiles. Coming back, it was the same thing. We flew in skimming the ground, as if we were making a dash into a camp under siege. Even though our forces were sitting less than sixty miles from Cairo and had a firm lock on the area, still it looked for all the world as if we were the ones who were besieged. After a while I began to see it as a metaphor for Israel's overall situation—victorious but surrounded and constricted. When several months later I came back from a trip abroad, I had the same sharp feeling. As the plane banked sharply toward Ben-Gurion airport, it seemed to me that I was returning to a wary, besieged place, a nation that had been hurt badly and was unsure how to sustain itself. I could not keep out of my mind that wonderful feeling of expansiveness I had experienced just nine years earlier when Avraham Yoffe and I flew over the Red Sea on our way to Africa. The lights of Jedda had come up on our left just beyond the black Arabian mountains, and all of Africa lay in front of us. That had been a striking moment, a memorable moment, full of youth and strength and self-confidence. A very far cry from what I and many others were feeling after the October war.

The Egyptians had planned this war far in advance. They had geared up for it as early as the previous May, and their timing was no doubt determined chiefly by military factors. It is likely that Israel's domestic politics had not played a significant role in their thinking. But they might as well have. For by October a fierce election campaign had been under way, and politics was no longer separable from war.

By October I had been involved in politics to the hilt as the Likud campaign manager. Of course, the moment we were mobilized I had left it behind. But it would not leave me. During the entire war everyone was aware of the political backdrop—even as we were fighting for our lives. And some were more aware than others. For the Labor party I was a good deal more than just a general. I was a general who had made himself political. Not that this was a crime in itself. Chaim Bar-Lev was a cabinet minister. Moshe Dayan, Yitzhak Rabin, and other military people had risen to political heights. But the system had always functioned to insure that leading military people were in the Labor camp. And suddenly here I was, a general and a politician—but on the enemy side.

The result, as I saw it, was a deep ambivalence toward me on the part of my army colleagues, almost all of them Labor people or protégés of Labor people. With many of them I had never had the smoothest professional relationships anyway, and now politics gave their feelings a more vivid color. On the one hand I had a quarter century's worth of military experience and a track record of accomplishment. I knew I was badly needed, and at heart I believe even my antagonists felt the same way. But on the other hand I was, no mistake about it, a political threat.

During the previous elections—in 1969—Labor strongman Pinchas Sapir had attacked then Commander-in-Chief Bar-Lev furiously for putting me in a position where I could run "against us" (as he had put it), against the party that had always ruled the country. This time he was worried about the fact that it was my division that established the bridgeheads and crossed the canal, a division that was already being called "Ugdat ha Likud," the Likud Division. From Labor's perspective, there was every chance I would emerge from this war as a major political headache.

The fact was that I was in a mood to do exactly that. I had been opposed to Labor on a sufficient number of grounds even before the war. Now I felt much more strongly about it. I was angry about the willingness of some top commanders to allow political considerations to interfere with military decisions. Despite my own political convictions, I had made it a principle to strictly avoid involving politics in military affairs. First we had to defeat the Egyptians and Syrians. After that there would be time for our own party struggles. As a result, I was especially angry about the pervasive postwar attempts to denigrate my division's achievements. Nor did I like the fact that at the Geneva talks on an interim withdrawal agreement the Labor government was trying to paint its stance as being the only alternative to more war. I believed Israel was in a position to get much more out of these talks than what we were getting. And it strained credulity to hear the party that had been responsible for this war in the first place (to the extent that Israel's lack of preparation and mistakes had contributed to its outbreak) claiming that only its position and none other would lead to peace. A vote for Labor had somehow, magically, become a vote for peace, while a vote for the Likud, according to them, was a vote for more war.

Personally I felt that Labor's position in Geneva was inadequate. And so was America's. I believed the United States could have taken a substantially stronger approach. The Arab states had declared their oil boycott on October 20, two days before the first cease-fire. The Americans might have said even then: Do you want us to use our influence to stop the Israeli advance—then no embargo please. They might have said at Geneva: Shall we use our influence to induce an Israeli withdrawal from the west bank of the canal—then we expect no further price rises, we want no more oil crises. There was a rich vein to be mined here, a thousand possibilities. But they did not take advantage of it. The only substantial gain the Americans achieved was an improved position in Egypt. But so much more might have been derived from Israeli-American co-operation. Yet neither the Israeli nor the American government pursued the possibilities.

The elections, originally scheduled for October 21 had been put off until December 31. Now that the war was over, the Likud leaders asked me to resume my role as campaign manager. But I still felt uneasy about leaving the front. So I stayed with the division, keeping my mouth shut and watching the race from a distance.

Despite my absence, the Likud did well, increasing its representation in the Knesset from twenty-nine to thirty-nine seats out of one hundred twenty. As a candidate on the Likud list, one of those new seats had gone to me, and by late January the time finally arrived when I had to leave the army to be sworn in as an MK.

My last day with the division was January 20. The parades and farewell ceremonies were touchingly beautiful, but I did not go with an easy heart. Although I knew the deployment on the canal's west bank was temporary and that we would soon be moving out, I was still uncomfortable about leaving the situation in someone else's hands. Besides that, I had lived with these men continuously for three and a half months. The fear and death that had bound us together during the fighting had given way afterward to an overflow of warmth and affection. These feelings of soldiers for each other had always meant a great deal to me, but now there was a special quality to them. None of us had ever lived through such carnage before, so perhaps our feelings were commensurate with the horror we had experienced. But whatever the reason, I found it impossible to go anywhere without constant invitations from the soldiers to sit down and share a cup of tea or coffee or have something to eat. The friendship, the mutual dependence, and the mutual support made for a way of life that was difficult to tear away from. Weeks after I got home I found myself reflexively sharing out my food with Lily and the children and whoever else was around the table.

I wrote my final order of the day in the quiet of my apartment in Beersheba, then carried a boxful of printed copies with me on the short plane ride to the front. In the order I told the division's soldiers that it was they who had taken on themselves the most difficult, most complex, cruelest effort of the war—crossing the Suez Canal. "The crossing was the turning point of the war," I told them. "It was the crossing that brought us victory."

If—despite blunders and mistakes, despite failures and obstacles, despite hysteria and loss of control—we achieved victory, then we should all know that this was the IDF's greatest achievement.

We fought. Hundreds of our best fighters fell in battle, and many more were wounded—but we won. You won. Despite everything. And you did it with devotion and self-sacrifice, with stubbornness and valor . . .

To you soldiers, who are the true heroes of this war, I owe an explanation. The war is over, a stage of discussion with the Egyptians is over, and now I feel the need to fight on another front. It is essential to fight with all our strength to prevent more wars in the future. That is why I am leaving.

I want you to know that I have never before served with fighters like you. You were the finest of them all. I have never before felt the brotherhood of fighting men, and the fellowship that we have had in our division. It has been a warm home that always gave us confidence in our strength and in our abilities.

I leave you today sorrowfully. I wish every one of you a quick return to your own homes. But if we have to come back and resume our fight—I promise that I will be with you.

What I did not say in the order, but believed just as deeply, was that in crossing the canal these men had made peace possible. Had the war ended with the Egyptian crossing, I had not the slightest doubt that the stage would have been set for the next war. As it was, the Israeli crossing would force the Egyptians to cast around for other solutions.

My last order of the day was heartfelt; in a brief space I said what I believed. It was also a spur to controversy. The allusions to blunders, mistakes, and loss of control touched a very sore point, as well they should have. The comment about fighting on another front was a flagrant shot across Labor's bow. It was on the wings of this small conflagration that I left the army for the political battlefield of the Knesset.

Almost as soon as I came back I participated in a major Likud rally against the terms of the interim agreement that had emerged from the Geneva talks. Despite a rainy night, 100,000 people gathered in Kings of Israel Square in Tel Aviv for a mass demonstration of support. When the speeches and cheering were finally over, I tried to get to my car. But as I did, the crowd surged in around me, everyone trying to shake my hands or kiss or embrace. With all the warmth and enthusiasm in the world, a mass of people were slowly bearing me and the few others with me toward the plate-glass windows of a store across from the square. I kept trying to head toward the car, but it was impossible to fight the pressure and flow of the crowd.

Finally, after almost an hour in the crowd's embrace, the police managed to extricate us. By that time I was exhausted physically. But emotionally it had been a powerful experience, a graphic demonstration that in my own right I had the ability to attract support from a large number of people. Here was a new dimension of politics, one I had gotten no taste of during the long weeks when we had hammered out the Likud coalition around tables at the various party headquarters.

Although the new legislative session was under way, the first item on my personal agenda was to move the Likud toward amalgamating its various constituents into one cohesive political party—the second step was one I had always envisioned and which I had already begun to take up with Begin and the others before the war intervened. Toward this end I set up meetings with the Likud leaders, most of whom I had not seen now for four months.

At that point the Likud leadership was in the habit of meeting once a week, alternating between the Herut headquarters (nicknamed "Fortress Ze'ev") and the Liberal party headquarters. Begin's sway over Herut was so pervasive that it even found expression in the Fortress Ze'ev decor, which managed to rival Begin's home in its poverty. On the other hand, the Liberals were wealthy. In their offices one did not perch on flimsy Herut-style cane chairs, one was enveloped in rich, deep armchairs covered with yellow pigskin.

The first meeting I had there was just a few days after returning from the front. That winter in the desert had been unusually hard—so rainy and cold that we had spent months shivering in foxholes and tents. Even after I left, I felt as if the cold had gotten into my bones. Now, at the Liberal headquarters, I was still wearing my fur-lined coat. But although the room was heated and I was surrounded by the velvety yellow pigskin, I was shivering as if I was still out in the desert.

With Begin, Ehrlich, and the others nestled in those luxurious chairs, I began my speech about how it was now time to start the second phase, time to begin the amalgamation we had been discussing since our original talks about forming the Likud. But instead of the serious discussion I had expected, the only response was a kind of weary, half-derisive dismissal. The tone and expressions of the Likud leaders said bluntly what their words attempted to convey with a veneer of politeness: This man, they were saying, he has just come back from the front. What does he really understand about politics anyway? The words were polite, even gentle; but the translation was unmistakable: Why is he bothering us? He has his seat in the Knesset, what more could he possibly want from us?

From that day I knew I was in for a struggle. All the old political leaders felt they had already achieved everything the coalition promised— more seats. This other thing I was talking about—the idea of a unified party—that was an illusion, a child's dream.

While I was being treated with indulgence by the Likud leaders, I was also finding that life as an MK was not something I had bargained for either. I was a member of the Committee on Foreign and Security Affairs and head of the Subcommittee on the Defense Budget. But the day-in, day-out of politicking, the continual smiling and talking and backslapping, was not something I enjoyed. I attended. I participated. But I felt the work and especially the atmosphere as a burden. I couldn't stand the Knesset dining room with all its noise and eternal dealing, and I found myself trying to avoid all the action rather than embracing it.

Avraham Yoffe had been elected to this Knesset too, and he and I would wander the corridors together trying to avoid anyone who needed to be talked with or smiled at. I also found regular refuge in one of the little rooms that had been set aside for resting. The MK I shared this room with was Sheikh Hamad Abu Robeiah, a Bedouin Labor member who had been a close friend of mine for years. Hiding there, the two of us would talk about the desert, the sheep, the fields, the sudden Negev floods—all those things we found so much more congenial than the nerve-racking buzz of politicians.

In December 1974 I received an army appointment as commander of a reserve armored force. Yitzhak Rabin was now prime minister, having replaced Golda Meir after her resignation the previous March, and it was Rabin who had pushed the appointment. The Labor party, however, had fought it; and once it was made, they turned the appointment into a political issue. No one, they argued, should be permitted to hold a field command and a Knesset seat at the same time.

In short order their arguments bore fruit, and the government passed a rule prohibiting a member of the Knesset from at the same time holding a high-level field command. Other MK's were high-ranking reserve staff officers. But since I was the only one with a field command, I felt justified in referring to it as the government's "Anti-Sharon Regulation." There was no question that it had been tailored specifically for me.

Not that I was especially upset about it. On the contrary. By now I had been arguing fruitlessly with the Likud leaders for eleven months, all the while growing more and more depressed about the MK's life I was leading. I was also eager to keep the reserve command. As a result, I didn't find the choice difficult; the new regulation gave me the perfect way out. So without telling either Begin or anyone else in advance, in December 1974 I handed in my resignation from the Knesset, something that seldom happens among the political set. Many people assumed I left in a huff, angry about the anti-Sharon rule. But the truth was that I didn't feel unhappy about it at all. It seemed to me I had thrown off a heavy and unwelcome burden, and the thought of going back to the farm full-time lightened my footsteps.

Very quickly farm work absorbed almost all my energy. I made it a rule always to take full part in the hard physical work; and shortly after I returned, a crisis developed that forced all the farm workers, myself included, onto an especially rigorous schedule. In an attempt to get control of the country's spiraling inflation rate, the government had decided to devalue the Israeli pound 43 percent. Having bought the farm with a dollar-linked bank loan, suddenly I was staring at the loss of everything.

The day after the devaluation announcement was made, I described the situation to our workers over breakfast. All our margins were calculated precisely. Now, with the costs suddenly jumping, we would face collapse—unless we could quickly transform ourselves into an export farm. If we had to pay in dollars, we were going to have to make dollars. But this kind of switchover would take a huge effort on everyone's part. In a way the farm economy was a micro-model of the country's economy. If we wanted to survive, we had to export. The difference was that the country would not fall, regardless of its economic failures, whereas our own demise could happen all too easily.

In response to the crisis we began in a relatively short period to produce and market crops for export. At first it was a tremendous load of work for everyone, but I loved it. I worked with the crews constantly—on the tractors, in the citrus and watermelon fields, in the packing house, everywhere. I quickly found that the technique I had always used in the army—teaching by example—was equally applicable on the farm. With the right kind of modeling the workers showed a real talent for teamwork. Their efficiency was a marvelous thing to watch, and it was that more than anything else that first saved the farm, then turned it profitable.

The close teamwork encompassed all the workers, Jews and Arabs. I used to say that our farm was the only successful Jewish-Arab club in the country. Lily and I would have breakfast with the workers at nine (after several hours of work), then lunch at one, all of us together, Jews and Arabs. The delicious smells from the dishes that Lily and our cook, Kochava, prepared suffused the kitchen and dining room, heightening the feelings of friendship and common effort. On some of the crews Jews were foremen, with Arabs and Jews under them. On others Arabs were foremen, with Jews and Arabs under them. Everyone knew that seniority went to those who showed most ability, that skill and efficiency were the only criteria I cared about. And everyone accepted it. It was very interesting to see how when some new worker would come in, either a Jew or an Arab, all the experienced workers would treat him with equal skepticism until he was able to prove himself.

The high level of cooperation came as no particular surprise. It had always been one of my convictions that Jews and Arabs could live together. Even as a child it never occurred to me that Jews might someday be living in Israel without Arabs, or separated from Arabs. On the contrary, for me it had always seemed perfectly normal for the two people to live and work side by side. That is the nature of life here and it always will be.

During this period I was still in occasional touch with the Likud leaders. My departure from the Knesset had caught them by surprise, and from time to time there were efforts to get me to return. Begin even came out to the farm once. We had breakfast, and I took him around to see the sheep herd, the fields, the horses. To my surprise I found he was fond of horses, a carryover from his World War Two days in the Polish army. I introduced him to the workers, making a point to have him meet Abu Rashid, the old Circassian he had been wondering about earlier. Finally we sat down in a small office off the workers' dining room, and he tried to convince me to come back.

I reminded him of our discussions about the Likud and how important I believed it was to organize the coalition into a single party. My point was simple. "One day," I told him, "when you form a government, the fact that we did not bring all these factions together into a party will make it impossible for you to accomplish your goals. Each one of them will keep open the option to defect and they'll use it against you. You won't be able to keep them in line and you won't be able to get your programs through."

"Look," he said, "come back. We'll do it one day, no question." He wasn't negative about the one-party idea. But it was clear to me that he wasn't ready to take any concrete steps either. So I stayed where I was, working happily in the fields.

*   *   *

After the great effort to reorganize the farm, I divided my time between farm work and my appointment as a reserve commander. This combination of the farmer and the soldier's life seemed to me almost perfect. From the fields I could see Lily driving the tractor, hauling rocks for the beautiful gardens she was creating around the house. I could keep an eye on the boys too, Omri now ten and Gilad eight, as they raced their horses through the wadis and over the hills, then wheeled to gallop back toward me. The physical labor agreed with me. Out on the land I could really work, watching the fields and groves as they changed colors through the long days and catching occasional glimpses of the wild deer that made the farm their home. After the terrible experience of the war and the frenetic life of the Knesset, I finally felt that I had time to relax and think.

The consequences of the war weighed especially heavy on me. During 1974 the Agranat Commission had released its findings in stages, severely criticizing Israel's lack of preparedness and the army's inadequate response to the initial attack. Shmuel Gonen and David Elazar had been dismissed from duty, as had the chief of intelligence and a number of other high-ranking officers. But while the commission analyzed the reasons for our failures, it was the consequences of our victory that concerned me more. We had, I believed, come out of the war trailing a dangerous myth. On October 14 the United States had initiated an air convoy of Galaxy C-5s delivering war matériel. This had been a major psychological asset, the clearest sign to us of American friendship and an equally clear sign to the Soviets that Russian support of her Arab allies would not go unanswered. But for all its real significance, the American airlift was much more a psychological factor than a military necessity. Yet the general conviction was that Israel had desperately needed the emergency resupply to carry on the war, that in effect the United States had saved Israel. And this, fortunately, was just not so.

At the front we had heard that Moshe Dayan had told the Knesset that "the ammunition we receive at night we use in the morning." But everyone involved in the fighting knew that, whatever Dayan thought, this was impossible. After the war I checked into the supply situation carefully. During the two and a half weeks of fighting, Israeli forces had used 25 percent of their small-arms ammunition, 55 percent of their artillery shells, and 48 percent of available tank shells. It was only ammunition for the big 175-mm field guns that had really been depleted, and we had only a small number of these. The anxiety in the political echelon about supplies was induced in part by the fact that our military storehouses were indeed empty. But that was so only because the distribution system had worked almost exactly according to plan. From the first moment of war the supply pipeline had begun funneling ammunition via huge convoys out of the main depots toward the preplanned staging areas and forward dumps. Supplies were not in the storehouses for the excellent reason that they were positioned precisely where they should have been, feeding the front lines.

After the war, with all the visits by American military people and journalists, I had not wanted to discuss any of this. It was an uncomfortable situation. I was deeply grateful to the Americans, but at the same time I was seriously concerned about the constant emphasis on the importance of the airlift for Israel's accomplishments. The impression had been created that Israel was unable to defend herself by herself, that she was wholly reliant on her giant ally. This was an idea that eroded our sense of our own independence and had an especially harmful effect on the American Jewish community.

It was a conception that had the most dangerous and far-reaching implications. As staunch a friend as the United States had been and continued to be, she is still guided, as all nations are, by self-interest. While a commonality of interests as well as emotional factors have bound Israel and the United States, it is to no one's advantage to foster a sense of total Israeli dependency. Israel and Israel's antagonists must both know that Israel is capable of looking out for her own interests, that it is an ally, not a client of the United States, and that its existence has been won and sustained first by the sacrifices of her own people and second by the sacrifices of Jews throughout the world.

Without in any way wishing to diminish the value of American friendship, I have always felt that co-operation between our nations was a two-way street. Israel has already contributed greatly to American goals—which are so deeply intertwined with the fate of the rest of the liberal, democratic world—and there are many substantial areas of Israeli-American co-operation that remain to be explored and realized. It is precisely the mutuality of goals that makes for a stable long-term relationship. And it was in this context that the image of a helpless Israel owing its life to the American airlift was deeply unsettling.

*　　*　　*

In the summer of 1975 Prime Minister Yitzhak Rabin asked me to become his adviser. The position was not one that would take me away from the farm completely, and it would give me a chance to influence decisions to a certain degree. Although Rabin was a lifelong Labor man, he was no party ideologue—not one, like Golda, who would always ask, "Is he one of ours?" Personally we had always gotten along well and had even found a good deal of overlap in our views. It required no struggle at all to accept the offer.

In January 1976, shortly after I began working with Rabin, an important crisis arose. By then Lebanon had been embroiled in an all-out civil war for almost half a year. Although various groups were involved, in essence this was less a civil war than a war between the Lebanese Christians, who were fighting to retain the traditional Lebanese political system, and the PLO, which had step by step built up an independent state within a state in West Beirut and southern Lebanon. From this autonomous base the PLO controlled a worldwide network of terror, striking against international targets as well as at Israeli settlements both near the Lebanese border and deep inside the country.

Now Syria was proposing to intervene directly in this civil war at the invitation of the beleaguered Lebanese central government. Moreover, the United States appeared ready to endorse the Syrian move, apparently hoping it would stabilize the rapidly deteriorating situation. As events thickened, the United States approached Israel to accept the Syrian intervention in return for an understanding on the limits of Syrian deployment.

My recommendation to Rabin was that we should not accept it. I argued that once Syria became the dominant force in Lebanon, we would never see anything like a restoration of Lebanese central authority. Instead, over time Syria would provide a shield behind which the PLO terrorists would become stronger and stronger. Ultimately this would cause us serious damage. It had the potential to precipitate yet another war. In my opinion, I told Rabin, we should express our strongest opposition to any Syrian military intervention whatsoever, even to the point of using the air force if they actually began to move troops across the border. When it was clear that Rabin was going to accept the move anyway, I maintained that at least we should require concessions from Syria in return, specifically recognition of our control of the Golan Heights.

I was not the first adviser to find his advice less than persuasive. American-Israeli talks on the issue proceeded, and the end result was that

Israel acquiesced to the Syrian intervention, believing that Syria would clamp down on the PLO and that, with stability restored, the northern Galilee would be relatively safe.

In the highly complex world of Lebanon, Syria's intervention had a large measure of irony about it. A radical Arab state was intervening on the side of Lebanon's establishment Christians against the PLO and its radical Moslem factional allies. But despite the irony, and despite some initial reverses, Syrian troops eventually exerted their power. They fought the PLO, inflicted heavy casualties, and brought them under control. But by October of 1976 the Syrians had decided that they had more to gain by accepting an accommodation with Yasser Arafat than by eliminating the PLO altogether. The agreement reached on this issue at the Riyadh conference ushered in a golden era for the terrorists in southern Lebanon and problems for Israel that have yet to be resolved.

I stayed with Rabin from June 1975 to February 1976, by which time I decided I had learned everything I was going to and had made all the contributions I could. Rabin and I had begun the association on positive terms, and we ended the same way. It had been a fruitful time, giving me experience at a level which was new to me, forcing me to consider national issues from the point of view of a sitting prime minister, putting me in contact with world leaders. It was with Rabin that I first met Henry Kissinger, who looked at me and growled jovially, "I hear you are the most dangerous man in the Middle East." Thinking of his role in negotiating the cease-fire and interim agreements, I growled back, "No, Mr. Kissinger, I'm not the most dangerous man in the Middle East. You are the most dangerous man in the Middle East."

During this time I had also been able to travel extensively, both outside and inside the country. Again I spent a great deal of time in Samaria and Judea. And being there, I worked out in outline the kind of settlement plan for these areas that I believed was necessary. I knew it was not something which Rabin could ever implement. But who could tell about the future? Nevertheless, it did not occur to me that within a year's time Menachem Begin would be prime minister and that he would appoint me his minister of agriculture and chairman of the Committee on Settlement Policy. At that point the plans I had devised while working for Rabin assumed great importance indeed.

24

Going It Alone

With the approach of the 1977 elections I found my interest in politics stirring again. It was clear to everyone at that time that Israel's political world was in ferment. The public anger that rocked Golda Meir's government after the Yom Kippur War had evolved into a chronic disquiet. People shared a deep-seated sense that Israel was not recovering from the consequences of the war, not spiritually and not economically. As the campaign season drew near, another issue vaulted into prominence, adding fuel to the dissatisfaction: Corruption stories began to fill the newspapers as a number of high-level Labor party figures were first charged, then convicted in highly publicized trials. The war's aftershocks made it clear that something new had to be done, something to get the country going again; it seemed equally clear that Labor was not in a position to do it.

It was against this background that I decided to get back into the political world. The decision was not something I could explain fully. I certainly wasn't longing for the public life. Still, as beautiful and tranquil as the farm was, I was drawn by my concern about Israel's situation. Times were not normal. Changes were coming, and I wanted to have a part in making them.

The question was: How? Simcha Ehrlich, the Liberal leader, was no friend of mine, and by this time my relations with the other party chiefs had become considerably cooler and more distant than they had been. Beyond that, I had been unable to unify the Likud, and that experience had left me with the feeling that I should simply not ally myself with any of the parties involved. But there was also a different option altogether. Thinking the whole thing over, it seemed to me that it might be a good idea to run on my own. If I formed a separate party and did reasonably well in the elections, I might easily find myself in a position to influence affairs.

From the beginning, a number of friends and political allies advised against this move, afraid that I would draw votes away from the Likud and precipitate a Labor win. But on reflection I decided to go ahead and announce my intentions, inviting people to participate in a movement I was calling "Shlomzion"—Peace for Zion. And they came. At the small office I rented in Tel Aviv volunteers arrived by the dozens, more of them than we could find jobs for. An early poll we took indicated that we might get eighteen seats in the Knesset, an astronomically high number and far more than necessary to give us a truly powerful voice.

But shortly after I announced the formation of Shlomzion, another new party declared itself—DASH, the Democratic Movement for Change. Its leader was Yigael Yadin, a well-known archeology professor and former IDF commander-in-chief. He too had seen the handwriting on the wall for the Labor government and had managed to attract support and participation from some of the country's wealthiest and most prominent people. For voters unhappy with the established parties, here was yet another alternative. As time went by, the big party apparatuses too began to move into gear. Like old, heavy machines they needed time to get going. But once they did, their massive organizations mobilized voters and built momentum in a way that no small party could even dream about.

As I worked to elaborate positions on issues and attract support, I found I was learning yet more lessons about political life, this time about the difficulties of independent parties trying to buck an entrenched system. Shlomzion had started fast. But before long all the problems of creating an effective organization, clarifying our platform, gathering allies, and financing the campaign began to exert a constant heavy pressure. As the race progressed, further polls showed us winning eight seats, then six. At that point I had a very careful, very private survey done. The news that came back wasn't good; not six but only two seats seemed to be what we could count on, certainly not more than two.

At first I kept the poll secret from my friends and party workers, sure that it would demoralize them and hoping the numbers might change for the better. But before long a new public poll came out which also gave us two places. All of our people were affected by it, myself as well. I began to feel that maybe I had taken this idea of a separate party as far as it would go and that maybe it would be best if I just quit. Lily had been opposed to the idea of an independent run from the beginning, but when I told her of my worries she said, "Now that you're in it, you simply cannot withdraw." Then she went out to buy mops, pails, and brooms and took the children with her down to our campaign office to start cleaning. When she arrived, the others in the office caught her spirit, and for a few hours a new rejuvenated mood took hold. I joined in too, but whatever outward enthusiasm I managed to muster, inside I was a very unhappy man.

I began to think that perhaps people just do not back these little parties. After all, Ben-Gurion had run on his own in 1969 and gained four places. (Later Moshe Dayan and Ezer Weizman would try. Dayan managed two seats and Ezer three.) But there was little consolation in that thought. Nor was the news any better on the financial front. While the polls were telling the sad story of the decline in voter support, I needed no poll to tell me how serious our money problems were becoming. A yawning deficit had opened up between contributions and the outlay for advertising, transportation, rentals, and the many other expenses of running a campaign.

To try and survive I made two separate fund-raising trips to the United States. But this too was hard. In the States one needs agents, lawyers, advance people; it's a complicated affair. And raising money was not an activity I took to naturally. I remember that at one point a potential contributor from San Francisco contacted our secretary in New York and said that he wanted to make a contribution himself and that he would be able to arrange for me to speak to a group of other interested parties. Could I come out to the west coast? Although I was in the middle of a hectic schedule, I could not reject the opportunity. The next day I gave an early morning press conference in Washington, D.C., then took off across country, making connections in Kansas City. In San Francisco there were more newsmen and another press conference, after which I drove to the hotel where the fund-raising meeting was being held.

When I got there, the room was filled with people who had just begun a sit-down dinner. I recognized my host, who greeted me warmly. But as we ate, I began to understand that although I was the invited speaker of the evening, this affair had not been organized for me but for some other cause. Nevertheless, when dinner was over I gave a speech about the condition Israel was in, what I thought was necessary, what I believed I could do about it, and so on. When I was finished, my host stood up and said, "I believe we should help Mr. Sharon, the hero of the Yom Kippur War. I myself am going to set the example."

With that he gave me an envelope, which I put in my inside jacket pocket. But none of the other guests seemed to be following his lead. When I asked him quietly whether he thought there was something else I should say, he whispered back, "Look, more will be done later, after the meeting." But after the meeting the only thing that happened was that everyone left. Not only that, but I now found that my host had neglected to arrange a hotel room for me and I had no place to sleep.

The only pleasant surprise of the evening was that a man and wife were at the meeting who had been neighbors of ours several years back in Zahala and had subsequently moved to San Francisco. They stayed afterward to talk, then invited me to spend the night at their house. Their home was lovely, and we spent a pleasant few hours reminiscing and bringing each other up to date. But through it all I had a hard time suppressing the desire to close myself in the room and look into the envelope. Finally alone later that night, I opened it with trembling fingers and found inside a check for twenty-five dollars. All I could do was laugh.

But despite other equally unproductive occasions, the two American trips were a salvation. In the United States I met many true friends, some old, some new. Altogether I was able to raise just enough to cover the debts and keep the campaign alive. Nevertheless, I now knew beyond any doubt that I had made a serious error in trying to go this independent route. Like all the candidates, I tried to generate exposure and publicity, but the media seemed to have forgotten my existence. Each day we looked into the papers and listened to the radio and television, but each day there was the same disheartening silence. By now the important thing was no longer victory but survival. I felt that if I did manage to stay alive, political doorways would remain open. But whether we could hang on to those two seats was anyone's guess.

I was now fighting with my back to the wall alongside a small group of close supporters—people who still comprise my closest circle of political allies. The big party machines were chugging away, gaining momentum with each passing day, while each day we were wondering where we would find the strength to keep going. Every day people stopped me on the street to talk, expressing their sympathy and support but telling me also that they could not vote Shlomzion. They were afraid of taking their vote away from the Likud and were unhappy about being faced with this dilemma. Having begun with such enthusiasm, the whole experience had by now turned into a harsh struggle.

During part of this time Menachem Begin was in the hospital, having suffered a heart attack, and about a month before the election I paid a call on him in the Herzliyah's Sharon Hotel, where he was recuperating. In the course of our discussion I brought up the possibility of bringing Shlomzion into the Likud, an idea that struck Begin favorably. He would talk to Yitzhak Shamir about it, he said (Shamir was in charge of the party organization), and work out the necessary arrangements. When I told the Shlomzion people about the deal, some of them were against it; they still had hopes that we would be able to make an impact by ourselves. But I knew they were wrong and that without any doubt this would be our most advantageous path.

Meanwhile, Begin had talked to his own people, as he said he would, and had instructed Shamir to get together with me on the details of the new relationship. But time was now running extremely short; we were right up against the deadline for parties to formally submit their lists of candidates to the Knesset committee on elections.

With the Knesset deadline that evening, Shamir and I sat down together in a cafe on the corner of King George and Dizengoff streets. Obviously less enthusiastic about the merger than Begin was, Shamir now told me that he still had to consult on it with Simcha Ehrlich. Then he disappeared. An hour passed, then two. Shamir did not call, and despite all our efforts we were unable to locate either him or Ehrlich. Neither of them answered the phone, and no one could tell us where they had gone off to. Still in bed, Begin, was furious. "I've been sick," he said. "This is what happens when you're sick." Finally the time just got too close to wait anymore, and I instructed our people to submit the Shlomzion party list separately to the Knesset committee. Begin left the door open, saying, "Arik, I want you to know that we can still do things together in the future." But at the moment it did not seem like much of a consolation.

Two days before the election, newspaper headlines blared out the latest of Begin's election maneuvers. The Likud leader announced that should he become prime minister he would consider two candidates for minister of defense—Ezer Weizman and Arik Sharon. It was a clever move. Although the attempt to bring Shlomzion into the Likud had failed, with this announcement Begin was making a direct appeal to any voter who wanted to see me in government. The message was clear: If you want Arik, vote Likud. By that time Shlomzion had done everything it was capable of doing; this announcement was not going to enhance our vote. Nor was the widespread conception that votes drawn away from the Likud might help give Labor the plurality necessary to form a government.

On May 17 Lily and I went to the polls in Rehovot, where we were living in an apartment while our house on the farm was being built. Rehovot is a well-to-do place, the home of the Weizmann Institute of Science, and the people in Rehovot were mostly Labor voters. (It was the poor who supported Begin.) In the voting line I did not see many friendly faces. Of course no one said anything, but Lily and I figured that we were probably the only ones in the place who were voting for Shlomzion.

Almost all the preliminary polls had pointed to a Likud victory in those elections. But it was still a profound shock to the country when late on election evening the television anchorman announced that the Likud had won, that after twenty-nine years of power Labor was out and Menachem Begin was the new prime minister. Waves of bewilderment and disbelief greeted the announcement. It was almost as if the natural order of things had suddenly been overturned.

As expected, Shlomzion won two seats—two important seats as it turned out, but still only two. People joked that in the end it was mainly the soldiers of my division who had voted for me. But although the campaign had taught me a hard and costly lesson, nevertheless I took pride in having survived at all. Beyond that I also had a parental interest in the Likud victory. I considered that forming the coalition four years earlier had been one of the most difficult yet productive things I had ever done, an accomplishment that had made a major contribution to Israeli democracy. I knew that whatever the immediate shock of seeing a non-Labor government take power, the real importance of the 1977 elections was that they marked the emergence of Israel as a bona fide two-party state.

Early the next morning I called Begin and we resumed the discussion that had been aborted a month earlier. What had been impossible to arrange during the campaign now couldn't have been easier, and within a day Shlomzion had agreed to merge with Herut. At the same time Begin asked me to join the team he had set up to negotiate with the other parties in an attempt to form a governing coalition. Among these smaller elements were the religious parties, and my work with them at that time was the beginning of close long-term relations. Begin also talked to me about becoming minister of defense and told me that he wanted to give me that portfolio. But on this issue he met severe resistance from within Herut, and in the end the appointment went to Ezer.

Failing that, Begin asked if I would take on the ministerial responsibility for secret services and internal security. This was a critical post, but after thinking it over a day or two I decided against it. The idea of being in charge of internal security did not appeal to me. In addition, it was really a co-ordinator's job without the clear-cut policymaking responsibility that I was looking for. Instead, I told Begin, I would like to be named minister of agriculture and head of the cabinet committee on settlements. It was an idea he seemed as pleased with as I was.

On July 15 Begin presented his cabinet to the Knesset to be sworn in. Lily was in the audience gallery with Omri and Gilad, and next to them sat my mother, eighty years old at that time, but still hearty and active. I could see the satisfaction on her face as I took the oath of office. "I, Ariel Sharon, son of Samuil and Vera Sharon, pledge myself as a member of the government to be faithful to the State of Israel and its laws . . ." Standing on the dais, I thought for a long moment about my father—an agronomist, a farmer, a pioneer in his field. I knew exactly how he would have felt had he been alive to see his son named minister of agriculture. And as I looked at my mother, I was sure she was thinking the same thing.

25

Settling the Territories

When I entered the government as minister of agriculture, I felt almost as if I was coming home. Farming was in my blood, and Israel's large agriculture sector presented an array of interesting and difficult problems. These I started dealing with immediately, but at the same time I became deeply engaged with the question of Jewish settlements in Samaria and Judea. This was a subject I had been thinking about actively since right after the Six Day War when I began moving the military schools into old Jordanian army posts. I had walked the entire territory, not once but many times, and had already developed the basics of a settlement plan during the time I spent as Rabin's adviser.

By September 1977, four months after the elections, I was ready to present my proposal. Although I could easily imagine several different political solutions for the territories, it never occurred to me that we would hand them over to Jordan. In the first place, they were not Jordanian, nor had they ever been Jordanian. Carved by the British in 1922 out of what was then Palestine, Jordan was bounded on the west by the River Jordan and had never included any territory on the river's western bank. After the British Mandate ended on May 14, 1948, the Jordanian Legion and other Arab armies had occupied this area, overrunning and forcing the abandonment of Jewish settlements and destroying Jerusalem's old Jewish quarter. British control over this region—historical Samaria and Judea—had thus been succeeded by Jordanian control. And the history of Jordanian control had been marked by the continual shedding of Jewish blood. We had had from the Palestinians of this area two decades of the most vicious terrorism and three wars. The years of murders and mutilations that I and others had spent so much of our lives trying to prevent—these were an unforgettable legacy.

That had been our history with the Jordanians. In 1967 they had made common cause with the Egyptians in an effort to liquidate Israel as a nation, and it was during this war that we had driven them out of Samaria and Judea. To my way of thinking, this background demonstrated in concrete terms—not hypothetical terms, but concrete terms—what to expect from Jordanian control. Under such circumstances, basic intelligence dictated that we act purely on the basis of our own needs. That did not mean that some kind of political accommodation was completely out of the question, but it did mean that first and last we were going to look to our security.

At the cabinet committee meeting on settlements of September 29 I made the first complete presentation of my concept. Referring to a large map of the region I had brought with me, I explained that whatever political solution we eventually agreed upon for these territories, we would in any case be facing three major problems. The first was security for the coastal plain with its population centers, its industrial infrastructure, its power stations and airport.

Defined by the pre-1967 border, this plain was so narrow as to be essentially indefensible. But since 1967 it had lost even the geopolitical integrity it previously had. Israeli territory and West Bank territory were now both completely contiguous and open to each other. There was now no sealed border, no physical boundaries, no barbed wire or other kinds of obstacles. On the Israeli side of the old border (known as the "Green Line") was a concentration of well-to-do Arab towns and villages—Um el Fakhem, Arara, Kfar Qara, Baka el Rarbia, Kalansawa, Taibe, Tira, Jalgulya, and others. Directly across the vanished Green Line in Samaria were other Arab centers—among them Ya'abed, Shweike, Tulkarm, and Kalkilya, whose people were virtually indistinguishable culturally, linguistically, and socially from the Israeli Arabs.

Already people could hardly remember where the Green Line had been. There was no doubt that with time this whole region would become a heavily built up area of hundreds of thousands of Arab inhabitants, some

Israeli citizens, some not, constricting to almost nothing the narrow corridor connecting Israel's central and northern population zones. This would happen naturally and inevitably. As a democracy, Israel would never consider imposing limits on population movement or growth. But some way would have to be found to strengthen the corridor.

Another, bigger problem in this area were the Samarian and Judean hills that dominated the coastal plain. The vital strategic issue here was how to give depth to the coastal plain, and how to keep the dominant terrain in our hands now and in the future so that it could never be used militarily by anyone else. The answer to this, as I saw it, was to build a line of urban, industrial settlements on the ridges overlooking the plain. If we could do this, we would be solving both problems at once.

While I described to the cabinet committee the absolute need to retain strategic terrain, I also stressed that we were not talking about Arab agricultural land. I made it clear that I was not in any way suggesting that we should expropriate productive Arab-owned land. On the contrary, the controlling terrain I was referring to consisted almost wholly of rocky ridges and mountains that were unfit for agricultural use and consequently were unpopulated. Our concern was to make this region defensible, not to dispossess its people.

That was the first problem, to give the coastal plain at least minimal depth and strengthen the corridor. The second problem was the eastern border itself. Israel's neighbors to the east were Jordan, Syria, Iraq, and Saudi Arabia. Each of these countries had fought against us in the War of Independence, the Six Day War, and the Yom Kippur War. Iraq and Syria were especially hard-line antagonists, but there was no doubt that Jordan and Saudi Arabia would also participate in any future conflict, as they had in all the past conflicts. Together these eastern-front states were able to field over four thousand tanks, a thousand combat aircraft, and twenty-five divisions.[*]

Israel's standing forces, on the other hand, were very small, and our reserves needed anywhere from twenty-four to seventy-two hours to mobilize, equip, and bring them to the front. This meant that in any attack our lines had to be held by limited regular forces in conjunction with the civilian communities whose role is to guard borders, secure roads, insure

---

[*] These were the figures in 1977. Currently the Arab eastern-front strength is 12,000 tanks, 1,600 fighters, and 70 divisions. It is worthwhile noting that on this front the Arab armies include roughly the same number of tanks, divisions, and aircraft as NATO deploys against the Warsaw Pact nations on Europe's central front.

communications, and so on. And the fact was that problems of defense were more acute on the eastern front than anywhere else. In the south the Sinai provided a buffer, and in the north our forces controlled the Golan Heights. But in the east there was only the coastal plain, which one could drive across in a matter of minutes, and the Samarian and Judean hills, which extended to the rift of the River Jordan.

Militarily, then, this situation mandated a line of settlements along the Jordan plain from the Beit Shean valley to the Dead Sea. Like all border settlements in Israel, these would be organized for defense, with their own weapons and ammunition, their contingency plans, and their integration into the overall defensive system. The Labor government had recognized this need; and working under the Allon Plan, they had already established twenty settlements on the Jordan. (When the Likud took power, Labor had built twenty-five settlements in all, with two more under construction.)

But ever since Yigal Allon had first described his plan to me back in 1967, I had believed it was inadequate. A thin line of settlements along the Jordan would not provide a viable defense unless the high terrain behind it was also fortified. In addition, the settlements needed secure road communications with the coastal plain. Consequently, I proposed that we thicken the line of settlements on the river and establish other settlements on the high terrain with an eye toward reinforcing this line. Beyond that, I proposed several east-west roads along strategic axes, together with the settlements necessary to guard them.

The other major problem was Jerusalem, specifically how to secure Jerusalem as the permanent capital of the Jewish people. And by this I meant how to really secure it, how to insure a Jewish majority and Jewish control fifty and a hundred years into the future.

Jerusalem had had a continuous Jewish community from biblical times right down to the present. In 1840, the year the first modern census was taken, Jews were the single largest ethnic group in the city. By 1860, the Jewish community had grown larger than the Moslem and Christian communities together, and by 1890 Jews constituted 60 percent of the population. During the War of Independence the Old City's Jews had been either killed, imprisoned, or driven out. Jerusalem's religious sites were sealed off, and the old Jewish quarter razed. Twenty years later the 1967 War had allowed Jews to resettle in the inner city. But the victory had also changed Jerusalem's demographics in other, less predictable ways.

With Israeli control of the West Bank after the Six Day War, Jerusalem had quickly become a magnet for West Bank Arabs. Its employment opportunities, civic amenities, schools, hospitals, and social services made the city the focal point for a steady influx from the Arab towns and villages. In less than ten years Jerusalem's Arab population had doubled, from 65,000 to 130,000.

As Israel could take no steps to change the Arab population pattern around the old Green Line, neither could it take steps to prevent freedom of movement into and around Jerusalem. But if Jerusalem was going to remain Jewish, some kind of solution was required. Pointing out the demographic patterns, I explained to the cabinet that the Jewish core population was at the center of an ever-thickening circle of Arab suburban neighborhoods. Looking at the long-term development of the city, I believed that the answer was to create an outer ring of development around the Arab neighborhoods, a horseshoe that would run about ten to fifteen kilometers outside of the center from Gush Etzion and Efrat in the south to Ma'aleh Adumin in the east to Givat Ze'ev and Bethel in the north. If we could develop a greater Jerusalem along these lines that would eventually include a population of a million people or so, then the city would be secured into the future as the capital of the Jewish people.

The basic tenets underlying my plans were, I believe, quite close to those of the other cabinet members. For all of us Jerusalem was the city that fostered our living civilization for a thousand years and nourished our spiritual life for two thousand more. We were pleased, even honored, to secure the rights of the other great faiths for whom the city was also holy. But we would never, never give up our sovereignty. As for Samaria and Judea, these places were the cradle of the Jewish people, the bone and blood of our nation. We insisted on the right of Jews to settle in the area. And we would not under any circumstances abdicate our responsibility to defend ourselves.

Although our tenets of belief might have been the same, however, I was still not sure when I presented my plans for settlements that the cabinet believed this was something I was really going to do. But as I told them at one point, "I am the only Mapainik in this government. I am not talking here so that I can record my voice in a protocol. Consider it carefully. Because once this is approved, I am going to do it."

Whether in their hearts they believed me or not, the cabinet approved the initial settlement plan on October 2. Once this was done, the next step was to find the exact places for settlements. What we were looking for was high, important terrain and vital road junctions. Though there were many roads in Samaria and Judea, there were hardly any approaches to the mountains. That meant trekking from place to place and climbing with map in hand to decide where each of those settlements would be sited. The days were long and exhausting, clambering up those hills and mountains on foot, usually escorted by Uri Bar-On, my assistant. We climbed, sometimes on our own, sometimes with a group of specialists. And one climb was almost never enough. Because besides examining the place itself, we had to be sure that the land was state-owned. Generally, state-owned areas had belonged to the Turkish government during their 400-year-long occupation, then had passed to the British under their thirty years of occupation, then to the Jordanians during their nineteen years of occupation. Most often state-owned land consisted of swamps or rocks or dunes—almost always it was uninhabitable. But after Mr. Begin formed his government in 1977, the restrictions on using even this land became much more complicated. Before him, the Labor government had taken Arab-owned land, but Mr. Begin took a rigid stand against any expropriation, and that stand became the policy of the government. Consequently, it was not enough to check if the land I wanted to use was state-owned, there was another criterion. This land had also to be untilled and uncultivated. That is, if squatters or neighboring farmers had been using the land without owning it, it would still be untouchable. Beyond that, even if it was untilled, uncultivated land, we had to be able to show that it was not simply productive land that was lying fallow, but that it had not been cultivated for many years. We had to go back to 1945, to the time of the earliest air photographs of the West Bank, to check and recheck the status of those areas we wanted to use.

Begin himself was adamant about these things. But as the settlement process progressed and resistance to the policy grew among Jews who believed we should give up control of these territories, the criteria became even more restrictive. It got to the point where our people were counting individual wheat and barley stalks that might have sprouted on a hillside to be sure that we were not claiming the remnants of a squatter's farm. We also made surveys of the number of sheep and goat droppings per square meter in order to determine if herders had perhaps been using some particular place in a regular, habitual way.

Even as our internal Ministry of Agriculture criteria were growing more stringent, the government was also taking additional measures to insure that no private land would be touched, including the appointment of a distinguished jurist, Mrs. Plia Albeck, specifically to oversee land problems. In practical terms these developments meant that we were now going through a rigorous three-stage process. First we had to find the right strategic places, then ascertain their status, then determine if there was access or if access was blocked by privately owned land. The whole procedure was detailed, time-consuming, and progressively more complicated.

But even under these circumstances the settlement project moved ahead. After a short time, in many places the tractors, bulldozers, backhoes, and compressors were working and roads and utilities were going in. In almost every important strategic location a Jewish settlement was springing up, sometimes only a few tents, sometimes two or three huts, sometimes more. But in every single necessary place something was going in.

The fact that we were able to take these steps was due to a confluence of three factors. The first was political: the 1977 triumph of Begin and the Likud. Historically, Begin's party had been ideologically committed to Eretz Israel, a concept that included the entire Jewish homeland—of which Samaria and Judea were a part. So the Likud victory was the first factor.

The second factor was my own appointment as minister of agriculture. For ten years I had been looking for a way to settle Jews in these places. I had started with the military camps, and had made great (though unsuccessful) efforts to move military wives and children in. I knew these areas intimately, I was committed to establishing a Jewish presence there, and I had over a long period of time defined what I saw as our requirements and had formulated plans for achieving them.

But regardless of how strong the government's will was to implement a settlement plan, it could not have been done without people who were willing to make the sacrifices necessary to live on those barren hills and ridges amidst a hostile local population. The third fortuitous historical factor was that a group of young pioneers had already been formed, ready to do exactly that. It was called "Gush Emunim."

By the 1970s the pioneering spirit that in the past had found its home among the Labor Zionists was fast declining. The drive to return to the homeland and reclaim and work the land that had been instrumental in the Zionist enterprise was simply not any longer the great inspiring ethos it had previously been. But now another stream of ideals had been generated, not from the socialist tradition but from the religious tradition. The people involved named their movement Gush Emunim and they came mostly from one yeshiva in Jerusalem called "Merkaz Harav." The spiritual leader and head of the yeshiva was Rabbi Zvi Yehuda Kook, the son of the revered Rabbi Avraham Isaac Kook, who had been in his day chief rabbi and one of the Jewish people's great spiritual leaders in the century.

The son, Rabbi Zvi Yehuda, was now in his eighties, and it was he who had inspired the young people associated with his yeshiva. The nucleus had started in Kiryat Arba in Hebron, which had been established in 1968. These people made an effort to dig their nails into the mountains of Samaria.

I had had contact with them as early as 1974, while I was still a Knesset member, and I had joined them in their first attempt to settle Samaria, in a place near the Biblical city of Shechem, the modern Nablus. The fact was that I felt a deep identification with them in their effort to establish a Jewish community in the historical Jewish homeland. At the same time I knew that in terms of security for the nation as a whole it was essential to create settlements in these places. So for both national and security reasons I had supported their movement wholeheartedly.

Knowing of my interest, Gush Emunim asked me to help them. I talked to Rabbi Zvi Yehuda about it and quickly accepted when his students asked if I would drive him to the site in Samaria where they and their families would be attempting to build a settlement. On the day of the attempt I drove first to the rabbi's apartment in the Geula section of Jerusalem. The place was tiny—a single room in which every square inch of wall space was covered with books, volume after volume of holy books and commentaries that provided exactly the kind of setting one would expect for this frail old man who had spent his life studying and inspiring in his students a devotion to Zion.

I don't know if Rabbi Zvi Yehuda had ever been to Samaria before that morning, but in him you could see precisely the living spirit that had kept the exiled Jewish people bonded to their homeland for two thousand years. This man and his students knew the Bible by heart. To them the biblical words and places and events were alive. The real landscape they lived in was not where their feet happened to be; it was where their spiritual and intellectual roots had been planted millennia before. During his long life Rabbi Kook had very rarely left Jerusalem. But he knew the rest of his land intimately; the Negev, the Galilee, the Sharon Plain, and the Judean and Samarian hills. To him it was all one.

When we got to the site near Shechem, Rabbi Kook's followers were already busy putting up tents, staking boundaries, stringing barbed wire, and planting trees. Kook joined them and planted a tree himself, slowly and carefully. All the while people were building and singing. There was no missing the spirit of it; the air was alive with the same kind of fellowship and determination that the kibbutzniks had had in earlier and harder times.

Before long, however, army units arrived, and the enthusiasm rapidly gave way to a tense confrontation. The army demanded that the settlers leave, and Rabbi Kook's people just as adamantly refused to go. As tempers rose, I called Rabin on one of the military radio telephones and tried to convince him not to force them out. But as prime minister, Rabin had his own requirements, and he told me that it was impossible for them to remain. A long, difficult negotiation followed, at the end of which I suggested a compromise. The settlers would leave, but instead of going back to Jerusalem they would be allowed to bed down in one of the army bases in Samaria until a final decision was made.

Rabin finally accepted this suggestion, and I explained it to the young men and women who were clustered around. Most of them seemed to be in favor. But when they discussed it with Rabbi Zvi Yehuda, he would not agree. As far as he was concerned, it was simply unacceptable that Jews should not have the right to settle in their land. When I tried to convince him that this would be better than having the army evict them forcibly, that they would not be leaving the area, just moving inside a nearby army camp, that if this was handled right it could be the beginning of settlement in Samaria, he looked at me with his calm eyes and said one word: "No."

With that the issue was settled. Despite the initial willingness of most of the young people to move to a base, now there was no more arguing the point. "If Rabbi Zvi Yehuda says no," they told me, "then it's no!"

That evening a large contingent of troops arrived along with a convoy of buses to take the rabbi and all those young people and their children out. The order was given, the soldiers cut the wire that had been strung, and came into the compound. As they began dragging the settlers out, I saw the old rabbi, a tiny frail man, grasping onto one of the fence posts. In the closing dusk everything seemed confused. The settlers resisted, but passively, digging their hands into the earth and trying to embrace the rocks to keep from being dragged away. Sounds of scuffling and bodies scraping over the ground came from all over, and I saw a group of soldiers closing in on the rabbi. Moving in front of them, I reached the old man first and huddled over him as he hugged the post, trying to protect him from the pushing and shoving. But I felt hands and arms grabbing me and pulling me away. Then there was a loud commotion, and just to my side one huge soldier was throwing other soldiers back into the dark one after the other as if they were rag dolls. After he had manhandled several of them, he leaned over and whispered into my ear, "Arik, I won't let them do this to you."

It took several hours before the army managed to remove all the settlers (including the old rabbi) and load them into the buses. Although they didn't try to force me in with the rest, somehow it didn't seem right that I should just get into my car and drive away, so I too got onto a bus for the ride back to Jerusalem.

That was Gush Emunim. I was acutely aware that without the sudden flow of pioneering nationalism this movement represented, the need to achieve a Jewish presence in Samaria and Judea might well have remained unfulfilled. Beyond that, neither I nor anyone else had a way of judging how long this movement might last. Was it perhaps nothing more than a passing phenomenon, or might it endure and grow? Whichever, it seemed to me that we had arrived at a historical moment and that we had to seize the opportunity.

After November 19, 1977, an additional factor came into play that added immensely to the pressure to get the Samarian and Judean settlements established quickly. On that day President Anwar Sadat stepped out of his plane onto the tarmac of Ben-Gurion airport. That historic step initiated negotiations between Egypt and Israel that a year and a half later culminated in the signing of a peace agreement between the two countries.

The peace negotiations unfolded in fits and starts. From step to step, enthusiasm alternated with anger; and there were times when it seemed that irresolvable differences would put an abrupt end to the whole process. But overall, the momentum toward agreement was unstoppable, and it was this more than anything else that dictated a rapid realization of the settlement plan.

My basic understanding of the situation was that Sadat had committed himself to the peace process because he recognized that only through a negotiated settlement did he have a chance of regaining the Sinai. On a deeper level he—alone among the Arab leaders—had brought himself to realistically assess the cost of four wars against Israel. Reflecting on the immense disruption of Egyptian development that a quarter century of hostilities had brought and looking ahead into Egypt's future with cold objectivity, he had decided that peace with Israel was in the deepest interest of his people. Having made that decision, he was ready to take the dramatic steps necessary to unhitch his country from the policy of endless war that since 1948 had formed Egyptian policy as it had that of virtually all the other Arab states.

To my way of looking at it, Sadat had made a fundamental choice about Egypt's future. Despite his sensitivity to his brother Arabs and his arguments about Arab sovereignty in the West Bank, I did not think he would allow himself to be sidetracked from his basic vision. Specifically, I did not believe that our steps to settle and to insure our vital defenses in Judea and Samaria would adversely affect the negotiations.

On the other hand, it was also clear to me that once a peace treaty was signed Sadat would have little further incentive to understand Israel's needs in the territories. On the contrary, once he had achieved an agreement he would be in a much stronger position to mobilize world opinion and even opinion inside Israel against any settlement effort. And once an agreement was not just signed but implemented too, we would have no leverage with him at all on this subject. It was for this reason that the peace negotiations imposed an inflexible deadline on the realization of the government's plan.

As I put it in one cabinet meeting: "The settlements are not an obstacle to peace. I believe we have to build the settlements now, as long as all of us [Egyptians, Israelis, and Americans] are still interested in the peace process. I believe that Egypt is interested in proceeding on this path, and today we still hold important assets. So we have to act as early as possible. This will not cause any harm to the peace process. But one should talk about it in an open and friendly manner and not try to hide anything. I have explained to Carter and Sadat our reasons for doing this and also what we plan to do in the future. One should handle it this way. These are things people will understand, and we have to stand on them."

The end result was that I moved ahead just as fast as I was able. Despite pressure from those who believed any Israeli settlement activity would disrupt the negotiations, I received permission to establish three settlements a month. Then I really started to push. Despite the winter weather and the harsh circumstances of life awaiting them, the Gush Emunim people were eager to move, and so the process of transforming a concept into a reality began.

Over the next four years I managed to establish sixty-four settlements in Samaria and Judea, some of them hardly more than footholds, little collections of tents or huts, some of them more substantial. With no water or electricity at first, the settlers lived and worked in primitive conditions. The sight of these people washing their babies outside in the cold would bring shivers to my spine. But living near places like Shechem or Shiloh or Bethel, with their rich spiritual and historical associations, held a meaning for them that translated into joy as well as into utter determination.

At the same time, I established fifty-six settlements in the Galilee, where no new Jewish settlements had been planted for years and where the Arab population was fast spreading out into the government-owned lands. Already there were places in the Galilee—in Israel proper—where Jews were stoned and cursed, and to where, consequently, they did not go, places where Israeli Arabs were already talking about autonomy. But by 1981 the Galilee had twenty-two new kibbutzim and moshavim, as well as thirty-four "mitzpim"—watchtower settlements. For the first time the region was covered by Jewish settlements. Over 300,000 dunams of government land were secured, enough for Jewish settlements for the next two hundred years. With the new towns and farms and roads, people now could go from place to place—to work, to school, to shopping centers, to clinics. Normal patterns of life developed in place of the segregated hostility that was beginning to characterize the region.

Even so, as the settlements went up they drew a tide of ridicule from people who believed that these footholds could never sustain themselves, that they were inherently impossible. Newspapers took to calling them "balloon towers and mock towns," as if the settlement plan could only be a figment of the government's imagination. But even among those who agreed about the necessity for settlements there was debate about how to manage the job.

The argument was made by some that settlements should be backed by extensive infrastructures and developmental resources. Once one settlement was firmly established, then we could move on to the next and then the next. My position, however, was that we had to lay the entire skeleton of settlements immediately, even if each one was only rudimentary—in the same way that our parents had originally settled the land. The idea was to secure a presence first and only then to build the settlements up, to secure the state-owned land in these areas for future Jewish settlement. To my way of looking at it, it was essential to take that initial step in one swoop and to make that step as comprehensive as possible—before the sand in the political hourglass ran out.

On November 1, 1979, two years after the first settlements were established, I looked back on what we had done, during one of the many cabinet debates over what resources (if any) should be devoted to Samaria and Judea:

[Then] we put all the skeleton down. Now is the time to strengthen the places we have built. I would like to emphasize that had we not done it the way we did, had we not hurried the way we did . . . now we would not be arguing about whether to strengthen the settlements. We would be arguing about whether to use the land for settlements at all. . . . In the history of Zionism I did not have the privilege to be part of the movement that has now formed this government. But I come from a tradition in Zionism that had this [active] approach for dozens of years. And without denigrating the other tradition, at least in the realm of settlements it has proved itself.

So it is necessary to make decisions, even if it is only to lay a road, or to accomplish the basic preparation for costruction, even if it is only to establish one "balloon tower and mock town." Because I would like to tell you that the first kibbutz on the Golan Heights was a balloon tower. It was built on a corral for stray Syrian cattle. And I would like to tell you that many years ago there was a place called Dardara, east of the Huleh Lake. For years there was only one tower there, in Kibbutz Eyal. At that time I was in the Northern Command, and my weight then was much less than now. But even so, when I climbed that "balloon tower" it shook. Nevertheless that was the only tower we had east of Huleh, and it was directly beneath the Syrian positions on the mountains. Well, that single tower was the reason we managed to keep that area within the boundaries of Israel.

[Interruption] Are you saying that when you brought the settlement plan to the government that was your concept?

Yes, all of it is based upon the same concept.

In fact, my approach to the West Bank had not changed in the least over all the years I had been thinking about it. And, controversial or not, I had made no secret of what it was. My two principles, as I said in interview after interview and debate after debate, were to protect our

population centers and to insure the right of Jews to live in historical
Israel. The settlement policy I proposed and carried out in my term
as minister of agriculture was aimed solely at realizing these two
principles.

But though each step I took in Judea and Samaria was approved and
controlled by the government, I often found myself involved in exasperating complications. Decisions would be made in the cabinet, and I
would move on them. But when the predictable public and press outcry
materialized, I would occasionally find myself facing it alone.

I did not enjoy the media abuse any more than anyone else did. But I
also firmly believed that the policies we were pursuing were vital to Israel's
future safety and security. Consequently I was willing to stand up to the
controversy and invective that swirled around these issues. What affected
me more, what deeply angered me, was the idea that it was I myself who
was sometimes responsible for the government's controversial decisions.

One memorable occasion of this sort had to do with settlements not on
the West Bank but in Sinai. Late in 1977 we began to grapple with the
problem of how to insure that at least the eastern Sinai would remain a
buffer between Israel and Egypt, and it seemed to both myself and others
(especially Dayan, the idea's main advocate) that the only way of securing
the necessary area was the classic one—with settlements.

After considerable debate of this issue, on January 3, 1978, I
recommended to the cabinet that the government enlarge the existing
settlements and establish twenty new ones. On a large map I pinpointed
where we should locate the new settlements and why I believed that once
built they would provide adequate protection against any future Egyptian
threat. When the discussion was concluded, Begin as prime minister put
the formal proposal to a vote. "I propose that the government approve
adding population to existing settlements and adding new settlements
according to the proposal and maps that the minister of agriculture has
brought." Then he announced the vote: "Eight for, three against, one
abstain. The proposal is accepted."

Although we made no public announcements of the new construction,
several days later the story leaked to the press. The reaction was violent.
On January 8, five days after the decision was taken, the cabinet met
again to consider what course to follow, given the storm of criticism.

Begin opened the meeting of the eighth on an ominous note. Now we
had to decide what to do, he said. Today we had to make a decision, then
we would implement it. We would not build new settlements in the

Sinai, only strengthen the existing ones by adding land and population. In that way we would free ourselves from adverse public opinion.

"That," I said, "is a change of our former decision." No, Begin answered, this would be a new decision.

"All this talk about adding people is empty words," I replied. "I would like to make it clear that I did not come on January 3 just to get a decision written into the minutes, for history. I came to get it implemented. Consequently it seems strange to me that someone who was part of the decision thought I wouldn't implement it. But to make sure, I did not give instructions for implementation that day. I waited until we had the formal minutes of the government's decision. Once I got that decision in writing, I informed the people who were going to do the work.

"I don't think there are people around this table who aren't Zionists. But there are some people here who make decisions, and there are some people who implement them. I tried to do it quietly, but I had to apply to the Jewish Agency [for constructions resources], to the Water Authority, and so on.

"I also discussed it with Foreign Minister Dayan—though I am certainly not hiding behind him. But I presented everything to him, just in case I did not understand. But he gave me good advice, to send a letter with a map to the prime minister. I gave that to Mr. Begin on the sixth."

At this Begin interrupted. He had just gotten the map today, he exclaimed.

"You can say," I went on, "that the decision [of the third] was not a good decision. But you cannot say that it was not a decision—or that it was my decision. I wouldn't conjecture how the decision got out. It got out through people here who were against the decision. I certainly never let it out. I would ask the minister of justice to take the appropriate steps against whoever did let this out."

Now, said Begin, only now had he gotten the letter.

At this point Moshe Dayan broke in, saying that he wanted to tell the cabinet members that when he had heard my proposal of the third he had wholeheartedly concurred, and that he had indeed urged me to forward a copy of it to the government.

"I propose," I said, taking up where Dayan left off, "I propose—so there will be no surprises to members of the government in the future— when I propose a decision to the government and the government approves, I will always implement it."

Begin was now growing upset, trying hard to maneuver. He had never seen the maps, he insisted, he had never seen the letter. These points had not been brought to the government before.

I was astonished, so angry that my voice began to rise. "What do you mean?" I asked. "The maps were never presented? This map was presented!" I picked up the map we had worked from on the third. "I am not going to be called a liar," I said, looking directly at Begin. Then, finding the cabinet minutes of the third, I started reading. "What we are proposing is about twenty settlements, including agricultural settlements perhaps thirty."

"In addition to what exists?" asked another minister.

"Yes," I said, "an additional twenty settlements."

Begin was still in a state of agitation. We had not seen any maps with any points on the third. We had only spoken about adding population. Today we were going to make a decision and this was the decision we would make public. If we were asked what our previous decision was, we would say it was secret.

"I would like to state unambiguously," I said, slowly and deliberately, "that there is no basis for what has been said here, that no map was presented to the government. This (I pointed to the map) is the map that was presented."

"No," Begin said, "I meant the map that you sent me."

"That map," I answered, "that was sent to the prime minister is an exact copy of the map presented on the third. The same scale. That is the map that was before the eyes of the government. Adding to the settlements that exist, the establishment of new settlements, everything that was implemented was implemented according to the government resolution. Not one thing beyond the map or beyond the words said in the meeting.

"Mr. Prime Minister, one can change a government resolution. One cannot pretend it doesn't exist. If the government thinks the pressure is so critical that we have to change the resolution, we can do that. The resolution was not sacred. If we are under that pressure, let us change the resolution. I'm the one who has to give the instructions. What should I do right now—give orders to dismantle the water drilling rigs, send back the tractors, stop the pipeline builders? Should I instruct them all to come back?"

"We heard your question," Begin said. "You'll get an answer!"

At this point Dayan made himself heard. He supported the decision of the third, he told them. Maybe most of the members hadn't been paying attention then, but we had indeed all agreed to it. But now we would have to decide not to add to any new settlements. Of course this would be "oral Torah," not "written Torah."

When I asked what I was supposed to do about the workers then, Dayan's opinion was that we should proceed with the work that had already been started. If we were asked about it, the answer was that we were not building any new settlements, only strengthening the present ones. That, anyway, was his personal opinion. We were just preparing, planning, laying pipeline, that was all.

Despite this kind of damaging friction within the cabinet itself and of course the constant heavy pressure from the Israeli and Western press in general, I put every ounce of energy into making the settlement plan a reality. Most of my time I spent in Samaria, Judea, in the Galilee, the Golan Heights, and Gaza, constantly on the move, going from one place to another, watching, encouraging, pushing. I think I must have talked personally with every single bulldozer and backhoe operator working on the projects. I monitored all the plans and looked carefully at each progress report. While all the joking about the "mock towns" was going on, I told the cabinet members that the day would come that I would have to fight with them to cut the ribbons on new streets and plants when those settlements became towns. Personally, I got tremendous satisfaction seeing how everything was moving forward, how drawings on a map were every day becoming more of a reality on the ground. But in quiet moments I also had to reflect that despite all the difficulties within the cabinet, when all was said and done, none of it could have gone forward without the fundamental support of the Prime Minister.

As time went by and the elections of 1981 began to loom on the horizon, I pushed harder than ever. The feeling started to grow that the Likud might find itself out of office, and if Labor did come in I had no doubt they would try to "strangle" the settlements, exactly as they were declaring they would do. Anticipating this, I made the greatest effort I was capable of to drive the work forward, what I called "preparing for the siege." We brought water and electricity into these remote spots, which of course we offered to the Arab villages as well. And most of them accepted it. We accelerated our efforts with the Ministry of Justice to identify all appropriate government-owned land and to allocate it to future settlement. We built roads to connect the settlements with each other and with the main roads. We built the Samaria Crosser connecting the Jordan and the coastal plain.

✻   ✻   ✻

But during the Likud's first term in office these were hardly the only events taking place that were shaping Israel's future. At the same time, Sadat and Begin were creating a relationship between their two nations that was unique in the history of the Israeli-Arab experience. And it was not long before I was involved in that as well.

26

Egyptians and Iraqis

When Anwar Sadat arrived in Israel, he addressed a session of the Knesset. Ezer Weizman had been unable to greet Sadat at the airport. The wheelchair Ezer was confined to after a recent automobile accident made it difficult to get around. But he did not want to miss the speech. When Sadat came into the Knesset, Ezer greeted him, snapping his crutch into a salute in front of him. "I'm saluting you," he said, "because you managed to surprise us in the war." The gesture made a visible impression on the perceptive and clever Sadat. I think he noticed that Weizman was eager to impress him and that here was a man who might possibly be a weak link in the Israeli chain.

From that point on, Sadat insisted on negotiating with Weizman rather than with Foreign Minister Moshe Dayan or with Begin himself. And the fact was that Weizman's positions were consistently softer than Begin's, so much so that the conflict between the two eventually led to Weizman's resignation in 1980. (Ezer had been the most hawkish of hawks, but over the years his foreign policy views moved steadily toward the extreme left, a movement that accelerated sharply after his meetings with Sadat.) After Weizman left his post, I began to carry more and more of the burden of relations myself, eventually becoming the main channel of contact between Begin and Sadat.

By then, of course, I had gotten to know the Egyptians fairly well. On one of their official visits I had even hosted a large group of Egyptian generals led by the defense minister, Kamal Hassan Ali. They had arrived at the farm by helicopter on a winter day, twenty or twenty-five of them altogether. In the living room we toasted each other, and I told them that I had seen them in action in all the wars, that I had met them first during the Independence War, then in the Sinai Campaign, in '67, in the War of Attrition, and in the Yom Kippur War. I had learned, I said, that Egyptians were courageous soldiers who on many occasions had fought until death. I pointed out to them that during the War of Independence Egyptian lines were fifteen miles north of where we were now standing, that this place had been part of the encircled Negev.

After the toasts, Hassan Ali introduced the generals. They were all there, the commander of the Twenty-first Armored Division, the commander of the Sixteenth Infantry Division, the commander and chief of staff of the Second Army. I looked at them closely. I had never seen their faces before, but their voices were all familiar. In 1973 I had listened to them day after day on the radio net. Now they were wearing beautifully tailored uniforms and were raising their glasses to me and the small group of Israeli generals who were also there. But I remembered each one of those voices from the hard days on the canal.

In the aftermath of the Camp David meetings in the U.S., talks between Israel and Egypt on Israel's withdrawal from Sinai and on Palestinian autonomy continued amid suspicions and sporadic deadlocks. In January of 1981 during one of these stalemates I took advantage of a visit by the Egyptian minister of agriculture, Dr. Daoud, to discuss the need for another personal meeting between Begin and Sadat. Daoud, an intelligent and personable former professor, said he would talk to Sadat about it and see what might be done.

Several weeks later Dr. Daoud called from Egypt, but not with any word about a meeting. What he wanted to know was if I could arrange for an Israeli agricultural team to set up a model irrigation system on an Egyptian farm "in a very important place." Could I do it, he asked, within ten days? Although Daoud did not say so directly, I got the distinct impression he was talking about Mit El Kom, Sadat's family farm in his ancestral village. I could not imagine why it had to be done so quickly, but over the phone I did not feel able to ask, so I just said yes. Daoud sounded pleased and asked that I keep everything completely secret.

The next day a small team of Israeli experts left for Egypt to examine the location and decide what would be necessary. I knew that getting there would take them a day. Then they would need a day to study the site and draw up their plans, then a day to return. That would be three days. Preparing the irrigation equipment that was called for might take two more days, and transporting it to Egypt would take another. That would leave only four days for installation and testing, a very tight schedule. I knew we had a good chance of doing it, but why the urgency? Why ten days exactly? Why not two weeks or a month?

When the team arrived in Egypt the next day, they were met by people from the agricultural ministry and taken immediately to Mit El Kom (Daoud had indeed been referring to Sadat's farm). There they were beautifully received, spent the next day planning, then came back. They told me that they had found around Mit El Kom all the ancient, traditional agricultural methods, including yoked oxen walking in circles to power buckets that scooped water into the irrigation ditches. To replace all this the team had planned filtering systems and pumps and pipelines. But something new had been added to the agenda too. In Mit El Kom the Egyptians had asked them not only to construct this irrigation system but to plant a vineyard also. That was one reason it had to be done so quickly. We were already at the very end of the planting season. Once February was over, no seedlings would take. And this vineyard, of course, would also have to be irrigated by an up-to-date drip system.

In record time we got the equipment together, packed it into two big stake trucks, and sent them off to El Arish, the Sinai town that still marked the temporary border. At El Arish our trucks were met by two Egyptian trucks, which unfortunately were flatbeds without stakes. Several hours were consumed making the transfer and getting everything tied down adequately. Then our experts drove across the desert with the equipment, crossed the canal, and drove directly to Sadat's farm.

There they worked almost round the clock for four days. By the tenth day the new vineyard had been planted and the whole system was up and running. On that day Sadat's wife, Jihan, arrived and was tremendously pleased with what had been accomplished. After looking the project over, she thanked the Israeli team profusely, showering them with praise for what they had done.

For some time the project was a closely guarded secret. I told only Begin and Minister of Foreign Affairs Yitzhak Shamir (he had replaced Dayan in 1979), and this was a secret that did not leak out. Then in April 1981, President Sadat invited all the editors of the Egyptian press to Mit El Kom. Showing them around his newly irrigated citrus orchards and his newly planted vineyard, he told them that all this had been done by Israelis—in ten days. "Look at what the Israelis are capable of doing," he said, and went on to describe what he saw as the central importance of Israeli-Egyptian co-operation in agriculture.

When I was in Egypt myself that May, I visited Mit El Kom to see what it looked like and how the system was working. At that point we still had one Israeli expert there who had been on the farm since February making sure the equipment was functioning properly and instructing Sadat's farmers in its operation. I was excited about what we had been able to do there, but it was a little surprising to see that Sadat's fields and plantations now looked almost like an Israeli farm.

During my May trip I also inspected several Egyptian demonstration farms, paying close attention to the innovations they were experimenting with. When I saw Sadat, we discussed the possibilities of agricultural development in Egypt, and Sadat said that he would like us to participate in the effort. Apparently the Mit El Kom project had been more important than I thought. When one of his ministers suggested that once they had the know-how they would be able to do it themselves, Sadat cut him off. "We have the land," he said, "we have the water, and now we have Arik. He will help us do it." As he said this, I remembered the first interchange I had had with him at Ben-Gurion airport. "I tried to catch you at the canal," Sadat had said to me as we shook hands. "Now you have a chance to catch me as a friend," I had replied.

As Sadat finished speaking, he clapped his hands three times, and instantly an aide appeared and bowed. (Sadat always clapped softly—once, then twice more. I could never understand how his aides, standing behind closed doors in the next room, could hear him. Hosni Mubarak, Sadat's successor, has forsaken the traditional method for an electronic buzzer.) A moment later the aide was gone, returning shortly with a big map that he laid open on the floor. Kneeling over the map with me, Sadat pointed out the places where subsurface aquifers had recently been found—mostly near the Sudanese border and in the Western Desert. "These are the areas," he said, "where we would like to develop modern farming." Would I go to see these places and give him my own impression of the problems that developing them would involve. When I nodded that I would, he ordered his private plane to be prepared to take me to the sites the next day.

When he was finished giving instructions and the map was removed, I told Sadat that I would like to speak to him in private for a few minutes. Once the people around him had left I said that Begin had asked me to convey his greetings and to bring up the possibility of an early meeting between the two heads of state. Sadat immediately gave me a positive answer. He too believed an early meeting would be valuable. It would only be necessary to agree on a place. I suggested that either Cairo or Jerusalem would be acceptable to Mr. Begin, and that El Arish, Beersheba, or Sharm al-Sheikh were also possibilities. Sadat said he would consider it and let us know soon.

The following day Lily and I were driven to a nearby air force base along with the small group of staff people I had brought with me. There Sadat's jet was waiting, a sleek Russian-made Antonov. Two young fliers took their seats, and in talking to them I found that they were both jet pilots who had fought in the Yom Kippur War. Both had been active against the canal crossing operation and one of them had taken part in the major Egyptian effort to destroy the bridges on October 18.

As we talked, I was sitting between the two pilots and a little behind them with the map across my knees. When we arrived at the co-ordinates near the Western Desert I asked them to circle around and fly low over the sand. When I had seen everything I wanted, we gained altitude and headed off toward the Sudanese border.

As we flew I understood—I think for the first time—the meaning of peace between our two nations. I was struck by the idea that I, an ex-Israeli general who had battled the Egyptians for twenty-five years, was in the cockpit with two Egyptian pilots who had fought against me in the last war. Here I was with the earphones and microphone on talking to them, telling them to turn this way and that, to fly lower or higher. And where were we going? We were searching for land for food production, to help solve one of Egypt's major problems, producing enough to eat for its growing population. I thought that if I were to look for a real expression of what peace meant, this would be it. An Egyptian airplane, two Egyptian pilots, an Israeli general—looking for arable land. In my eyes that was peace indeed.

That afternoon we landed in Luxor. Looking at the Nile there is a remarkable experience. Everything is quiet and still. It is as if time had stopped. The local inhabitants sit there motionless, squatting torpidly in the heat—a slightly different type of people, not only Arab, but something else too. They looked at us silently as we gazed in the direction of the Valley of the Kings and Queens, where we planned to visit the next day. That evening we saw the famous Temple of Karnak with its looming pillars and its inscriptions telling of the Egyptian punitive expedition the Pharaoh Shishak had sent against Judah and Israel in the time of King Solomon's son Rehoboam. The hieroglyphs told the same story the Bible did, even naming the Israeli towns the Egyptians took. This had happened almost three thousand years ago, and here we were still, Egyptians and Israelis. Suddenly the history of these two people seemed to run together.

We spent the night in Luxor, then flew to Aswan the next morning. When the giant lake appeared below us, I could not take my eyes off it. All that water, all those possibilities. From the plane we could see the desert waste on both sides of the Nile, and I found myself thinking that if we had had all this water we would have irrigated immediately. We had learned a long time ago that with the right system of irrigation and fertilization the neutral sand can grow anything; it provides a wonderful medium for whatever you plant. All that's necessary is the water and the will to do it. And here was all the water anyone could possibly want.

In fact, by this time we had already set up in Egypt two model farms to introduce our techniques and equipment to Egyptian agronomists. (They are still in existence at this writing.) But doing things like that, no matter how potentially productive, was difficult because of the sensitivity in the Arab world. Sadat was a man of great vision and daring, in this regard as in others. But even he had to move slowly and cautiously.

The present minister of agriculture, Josef Wali, has a great appreciation for the possibilities inherent in the transfer of agricultural knowledge. And he more than anyone knows the pervasive importance of agriculture to Egyptian life. While I was minister of agriculture, 60 percent of all Egyptians earned their livelihoods farming; agriculture comprised 70 percent of Egypt's exports, 25 percent of the GNP. In recent years especially, the rapid increase in Egypt's population has created immense strains on the food production system. Every nine months there are a million additional mouths to feed. Yet agricultural production in the Nile Delta—the traditional farming region—is limited. The area itself is confined by the desert and the sea and it is rapidly being built up. Another major problem is that the Egyptians use the mud of the delta for making bricks, as they have for thousands of years. But in so doing they are destroying the most fertile part of their soil.

What they need more than anything is an immense effort to break free of the traditional ways. The Egyptians are wonderful, hardworking farmers whose skills and love of the land have developed over millennia; but they must find a way to go into the desert. As I developed closer relations with them and came to understand their problems better, I tried hard to convince them of this. It was so difficult to stand there in desert sand just a few hundred yards from the Nile and look at the water. I could feel the urge in my hands to lay pipe and start irrigating.

But they have problems, of course, that we do not have. They are tradition-bound because the peasants' way of farming is inseparable from their culture and their social organization. And the patterns they live by have persisted for literally thousands of years. They know how to share water and cultivate in a way consistent with the nature around them, and they love to live amidst the lush greenery of the fertile lands. (One of the reasons we defeated them so quickly in the Six Day War was that with no trees, no greenery, and no water the ordinary Egyptian soldier in Sinai felt lost.) Still, in the last years they have made real efforts in the Western Desert, efforts that will have to progress quickly if they are to even begin meeting their food requirements.

I had wished that Lily and I could spend more time among the Kings and Queens and the beautiful artifacts of the Pharaohs. But we had to get back. In the Israeli cabinet it had already been decided that that Sunday we would launch an air strike on the nearly completed Osirak nuclear reactor near Baghdad. I had arranged in advance with Begin to let him know by four o'clock that Sunday afternoon if there was a chance for a meeting with Sadat or not. If there was, the attack would be postponed.

I was very careful, though, not to say anything specific from Egypt, where we knew the phone lines were monitored. We had decided instead that I would contact Begin from our checkpoint east of El Arish. On the way back Lily and I crossed the canal through the new tunnel the Egyptians had just completed north of Suez, an impressive engineering achievement that Sadat had been eager for me to see. At the El Arish checkpoint, I called Begin with the news that I believed a meeting could take place soon. Hearing this, he indicated that nothing would happen that Sunday.

After a few days the Egyptians let us know that Sharm al-Sheikh would be their preferred site for a meeting and that the two sides should proceed to make the necessary arrangements. But shortly afterward, despite their clear desire for a meeting, for some reason the Egyptians started creating delays and postponements—none of which made any apparent sense. I pushed as well as I could, knowing that time was running very short before we would have to take action against the reactor. But nothing seemed to work, and the preparations moved ahead at a snail's pace.

For several years the Israeli cabinet had been agonizing over Iraq's effort to acquire nuclear weapons. After long in-depth consideration the previous October, the inner cabinet had decided that the Iraqi nuclear facility would have to be destroyed and that a bombing strike would be made before the reactor went "hot"—which was now just a matter of days. But this attack would put Sadat in a very inconvenient position. If we struck before the meeting, he would not be able to come at all. If we struck soon after the meeting, it would look as if he had colluded with us. No matter how it went, he would find himself subjected to another spasm of hatred by the Arab world for his relationship with Israel.

In the end the Israeli-Egyptian summit was set for June 4, 1981, only three days before the scheduled attack. The formal talks and ceremonies were held at one of the modern hotels we had built, and Sadat was in such an expansive mood that he even suggested the Israeli cooks, waiters, and managers who were running the hotel should be able to come back and work there after our withdrawal from the Sinai. In front of reporters from all over the world, Begin and Sadat renewed their commitment to peace between their two nations and gave a new impetus to the realization of the Camp David Accords. Sitting next to me at dinner, the Egyptian foreign minister and former defense minister, Kamal Hassan Ali, leaned over and whispered, "You see, Arik, I was the one who did it. I arranged it so we could meet as close as possible to your elections." (Israeli national elections were scheduled for June 30.) As he said this, his face broke into a broad smile and he laughed. The Egyptians had been playing their own slowdown game in an effort to help Begin win the elections, even as we had tried to speed it up to insulate Sadat.

I nodded up and down, hoping I was showing the appropriate thanks and appreciation. I even felt compelled to join Hassan Ali in a quiet laugh. But I knew that in a very few days I would be back in Cairo doing my best to explain why we had had to do what we did.

*   *   *

Since its birth Israel has lived among countries hostile to its existence. Given the state of belligerence we live with, I have always believed that there are some actions on the part of our neighbors that Israel cannot afford to accept, that should be regarded as "red lines." One of these red lines is the acquisition of nuclear weapons by those states at war with us. I could never understand the people in Israel who talked about the desirability of achieving a "balance of horror" in the Middle East. If Israel and the Arabs both possessed nuclear weapons (so the argument goes) then neither side would be able to initiate an attack, and both sides could reduce conventional forces and cut defense budgets.

In my opinion the concept of a balance of nuclear terror has been very dangerous even for the great powers. But for them at least, for countries like the United States, the Soviet Union, Great Britain, and France, evaluations of dangerous situations are based on caution and logic. Of course, no matter how cautious or logical, mistakes can be made, and if the mistakes involve nuclear weapons the results will be fearful. But among current members of the atomic club the decision-making process itself is careful and conservative.

Here, though, we are speaking of the Middle East, an unstable and volatile region whose leaders include the likes of Saddam Hussein, Hafez al-Assad, and Muammar Qaddafi, men who are accustomed to an entirely different way of thinking. Given the circumstances of our region, I always strenuously opposed the advocates of a Middle Eastern nuclear balance. Such a development, I argued, would limit Israel's ability to defend itself even against minor terrorist raids. In any response we contemplated we would always have to be aware and afraid of the fact that our enemies might make a catastrophic mistake in their evaluations. As a result, we would find ourselves the target of non-stop limited actions, and our hands would be tied. Consequently I knew that among those things we could not afford was the acquisition of nuclear weapons by Arab states.

My view on this subject was shared by Menachem Begin. But in the early years of his government it was not, generally speaking, the view of the inner cabinet. For me, however, the issue was absolutely crucial. And once the Iraqi reactor project was under way and it was clear beyond doubt that its object was to produce atomic weapons, the other ministers were forced to take sides. By early 1980 the inner cabinet knew we were facing the potential for nuclear destruction at the hands of Saddam Hussein, a man whose speeches regularly declared his intention to extirpate what he called "the monstrous Zionist entity."

During the first few months of 1980 the Osirak reactor construction was making fast progress. By then the news that France would furnish Iraq with enriched weapons-grade uranium had become public. As part of his overall nuclear planning, Saddam Hussein had also concluded deals with Niger and Portugal for large quantities of raw uranium to supplement the French deliveries. The problems involved in extracting plutonium from spent uranium fuel rods had already been solved by an agreement with Italy to supply the required high technology. All of the major elements necessary for the manufacture of plutonium bombs were now in place.

Against this background, in April 1980 I had begun a concerted campaign to persuade the cabinet that the reactor had to be destroyed, not damaged by sabotage, but actually destroyed in an outright attack. Sitting in the Knesset cabinet room under the beautiful painting by Reuven Rubin of the olive trees of Safad, I told them, "By any feasible means it is vital that we execute a military operation that will ensure the reactor's destruction." I don't know how many times after that I talked and wrote to Begin about it and pressed my point in cabinet meetings. A few of the others felt as strongly as I did on this subject and also took an active role, including Deputy Prime Minister Simcha Ehrlich, with whom I rarely agreed on anything.

Begin himself understood the issue intimately. He had such a deep feeling for the value of life, and particularly Jewish life. A Polish Jew who had been trapped in Eastern Europe during the first years of World War Two, Begin knew firsthand how real were the threats of extermination the Jewish people had faced in the past and still faced. He was not the man to underestimate the declared intentions of someone like Saddam Hussein. In the end these feelings of his were decisive. They brought him inevitably to decide that the reactor had to be gotten rid of.

For thirteen months inner cabinet deliberations on this subject were kept strictly secret. Not a word was said on the outside. But as preparations for the air strike intensified on the last days before the operation, the great secret leaked out. Labor members outside the government began to pressure Begin to try to prevent him from taking the final step. With information spreading well beyond the small inner circle of decision makers, the situation became extremely dangerous.

A month before the operation Commander-in-Chief Raful Eytan's son, an air force pilot, was killed in a plane crash. At the funeral Ezer Weizman, who had resigned from the government more than a year earlier, began talking to me about the operation, trying to convince me that it was too hazardous, that we had not put sufficient thought into it, and it should not be done. With every word he said I felt the peril. Every word was endangering the pilots and the success of the mission. I told him as quietly as I could, "Ezer, I think you are making a terrible mistake by talking about these things."

Ezer was not the only one who knew. Almost the entire Labor party hierarchy, including Shimon Peres, Yitzhak Rabin, Motta Gur, Israel Galili, Abba Eban, Chaim Bar-Lev, and others had also learned of the details of the operation. In a letter to Begin on May 9, Peres wrote, "I add my voice, and it is not mine alone, to those who tell you not to act, certainly not under the present timing and circumstances."[*]

Despite Labor's opposition, Begin and a majority of the cabinet decided that the operation had to go forward. A new date was set, June 7, 1981, just three days after the upcoming summit. The seventh was a Sunday, the one day of the week we knew the foreign specialists and technicians would be away from the reactor site. At 4 P.M. that day, the F-15 and F-16 pilots took off from their base at Etzion. A half hour later, as they were approaching the border of Iraq, the cabinet met in Begin's residence. Drinking tea and talking quietly, we waited for information, the strain showing on every face, especially Begin's. An hour later the phone rang with the good news from Raful that the attack had been a complete success and that all the planes were on their way home.

After the congratulations were over and everyone had left, I stayed for a moment or two with Begin. Coming up to say goodbye, he put his hand on my shoulder, a rare gesture for him. "Arik," he said, "if it weren't for your persistence I don't know if we would have done it." I could see the relief on his face as he said it, and I was touched by his words. But I knew that though I and others had pushed, the hard decision had been his

[*] Shlomo Nakdimon, *First Strike* (Simon & Schuster, 1987), p. 194.

alone. And I knew it was a decision that had demanded the highest level of personal responsibility and courage.

In Baghdad there was no immediate response to the destruction of the reactor. Syria, Jordan, and Saudi Arabia seemed equally confused, unsure of what had really taken place, and they too remained silent. But as governments in the region and beyond attempted to verify reports and formulate positions, Israel's Labor party had already decided to condemn the bombing as a gravely mistaken act undertaken primarily as an election ploy. Incensed by the charges, Begin retorted, "Would I send Jewish boys to risk death, or captivity, which is worse than death? Would I send our boys into such danger for elections?*

The Labor attack came as a shock to Begin and most of the rest of the cabinet, not because of the specific criticisms but because for thirty-three years Israelis were used to the idea that when it came to security issues and Jewish lives, people backed the government, period. At the time of the Sinai campaign Begin had dropped his role of opposition leader and had supported Ben-Gurion's decision. In 1967 he had accepted Levi Eshkol's invitation to join the national unity government. During the Yom Kippur War, the Begin-led opposition had never once criticized the government, believing that when Jewish lives were on the line unity had to supersede politics as usual.

Now we were all finding out that for Labor, the principle of unity in times of national emergency was not a principle at all. For the first time an operation of magnitude and importance had been carried out by a non-Labor government. And instead of supporting it, or at least maintaining silence, the Labor leaders were denouncing the action, adding fuel to the international diplomatic attack that was at that moment being unleashed against Israel.

Labor's behavior after the reactor strike should have been a flashing red light for all of us. But unfortunately we did not read the handwriting on the wall. Had we done so, perhaps we would have approached the gathering crisis in Lebanon differently. But to our sorrow we did not learn the lesson, and the noise over the destruction of the reactor was quickly subsumed in the larger business of the imminent election.

* Nakdimon, p. 323

27

After Camp David

There was no doubt in anyone's mind that the 1981 elections would be close. From the polls it looked like the Likud coalition had lost some of its support. But more important, Yigael Yadin's Democratic Movement for Change party (which had taken fifteen seats in 1977) had now dissolved, paving the way for a reconstitution of Labor's traditional base. Faced with the prospect of a change in government, I had been pushing the West Bank settlements toward self-sufficiency. Digging water wells, running power lines, building roads, constructing industrial areas, I did everything I could to fortify them against the strangulation policy Labor had promised. Uri Bar-On, my assistant, was a reserve general who had worked tirelessly to bring the settlements into being. Now he and I made plans to move into one of the new settlements with our families, a decision Lily supported wholeheartedly.

But even though the construction workers made excellent progress and the settlers seemed determined to hold on no matter what, I was still deeply worried. Sitting on one of the old Hebrew terraces in the Samarian hills, I would gaze down onto the coastal plain. In front of me to the north I could make out the smokestack of the Hadera power plant. Due west the Tel Aviv power plant was outlined against the sky, while to the south smoke from the Ashdod plant curled upward above the plain.

Between Hadera and Ashdod nestled Israel's heartland. A beautiful sight—but to a military man also a sobering sight. The whole region sat there like a plum that I could grasp in the palm of my hand. If only other Israelis could see it the way I saw it, I thought, and understand it the way I understood it.

At some point that idea began to take root. Indeed, why shouldn't other Israelis see it the way I saw it? One of my assistants at the time, Eli Landau, took the thought up and developed it. Why couldn't we actually bring them here and point out to them the physical reality behind the debate over the territories? Once they had seen it with their own eyes they would understand my position better. All that was necessary was to get them here.

That was how "Sharon Tours" was born, a mass tourist operation that made it easy for large numbers of Israelis to see Samaria and Judea for themselves. Buses with trained guides drove voters up into the mountains, where they could actually look down on their homes and envision for themselves the strategic consequences of giving up the line of western settlements I had built. From there they could travel the twenty miles or so to the Jordan plain and look down at the line of moshavim and kibbutzim that had been built previously under the Allon Plan. They could stand on the biblical heights overlooking the plain and gaze out beyond the River Jordan to the mountains of Gilead and Moab. And they could understand how precarious the rift communities were as defensive positions without the line of eastern settlements I had planted on the dominating high ground behind them. By the time the campaign was over more than 300,000 people had made the trip.

As election day approached, I had a sense of satisfaction that the tours were making at least some difference. No one, I thought, could look at those sights without being affected. Whether or not all the tourists had been converted to my way of thinking I did not know (though I was sure many had been). But there was no doubt that at least 300,000 people would understand it better and think about it more seriously.

With the elections just a few days away, I felt I had done everything for the West Bank settlements that I was capable of doing. But looking back on my four years as minister of agriculture, I had other satisfactions as well. During that time Israel's total agricultural production had increased

15 percent and crop production 21 percent. I had made a tremendous effort to develop the country's agricultural export industry, with the result that foreign sales had risen by an average of 16.5 percent per year, from $359 million in 1977 to $576 million in 1981. (Since 1981 that figure has remained practically unchanged.) At the same time agricultural employment had risen over 5 percent.

I had pushed overseas sales hard, but I had also done my best to strengthen the weaker sectors of Israel's domestic agriculture. In the hard mountainous area of the Galilee, where the soil is poor and the farmers were permanent targets of PLO terrorism from Lebanon, I had increased the production quotas of poultry and eggs—despite the loud objections of the older established producers. In the south I had raised the water quota for the poorer Negev settlements, stimulating agricultural production there.

Overall, the agriculture post was one I had truly loved. I always felt that although I had been a soldier since the War of Independence and was by now an experienced politician, farming was still the one thing I knew best and did best. Farming I understood in my bones; I had brought the feel of it with me from my home and from my childhood.

In addition to strengthening production and marketing I had also made an effort to increase Israeli agricultural assistance programs abroad. The agricultural ministry had been involved overseas for years, and I fostered an even deeper commitment, sending experts to work in various countries, many of which did not even have formal diplomatic relations with Israel.

Over the last thirty years and more Israel had been active in approximately one hundred countries around the world, mostly in agricultural co-operation and assistance, in medicine, and in education. As early as the 1950s Israeli agricultural experts had built moshavim in Burma near the Chinese border and had taught modern farming techniques in Africa. During this period we had sent over 9,000 people abroad. In addition we trained 75,000 foreigners, half of them in Israel, half on site in their own countries.

Israel had, and still has, people with a pioneering spirit, people who were willing to leave their homes and live with peasants in the most remote places. We were not interested in sending experts to sit in offices abroad, but to live and work on the land with native farmers. As a result you could find Israelis in the farthest corners of the globe, in the Majes

Desert in Peru, in the highest farmlands of Nepal, in the poverty-stricken agricultural regions of southern Italy, in dozens of unexpected places, some of which I had managed to visit personally.

To broaden the scope of Israeli aid I developed a government-owned company called "Agridev" whose purpose was to carry out agricultural projects overseas. Agridev worked in tandem with another agriculture ministry company named "Tahal," which for many years had held a strong worldwide position in regional planning and the development of large-scale water and irrigation projects. Tahal was heavily engaged in Nigeria, Mexico, South America, Thailand, and other areas around the world; and now ventures with Tahal and Agridev flourished, with Tahal doing planning and Agridev construction.

These and similar efforts were significant for a variety of reasons in addition to the concrete help they provided in underdeveloped countries. First they were important for the image of Israel in the outside world. Despite what our own preferences might have been, Israel has had the misfortune of serving as one of the world's testing laboratories for weapons. But our expertise was never limited to military affairs, and I always considered it especially important to focus energy and attention on other, more productive areas in which Israel has so much to offer— important for the world's image of Israel but also for the image that Jews have of themselves. Additionally, of course, these projects were significant economically. When you have projects under way and experts working in foreign lands, agricultural inputs generally follow: fertilizers, machinery, agroindustry plants, and so on. Assistance typically generates trade, and trade of course is one of the great stimulators of more comprehensive ties between peoples.

But I also regarded these openings to the outside world from a different point of view altogether. For whatever the reasons, Israel has been blessed with a capable and restless people, a people that seems to be possessed with a nervous energy and a million ideas. They have an irrepressible desire to see things and do things. They want to expand their horizons, but they live in an enclosed place. To the north, the east, the south, their country is sealed in, and so their opportunities might seem constricted.

Agricultural co-operation and everything that came in its wake I considered a step toward alleviating this national problem. The assistance projects and their spinoffs gave people the possibility to go abroad, to do things, then to come back. Paradoxically, the ability to leave made it easier for them to stay in Israel, rather than to look for other potential homes that might beckon with more exciting opportunities. Typically, an Israeli hears about a place he hasn't seen and it bothers him. The Amazon might call, or Peru or Bolivia. But if he has a base, he can go and make a contribution. He can buy the books and study and participate, feeling the satisfaction that he is accomplishing something worthwhile. What, after all, brings Jews to Africa? It isn't the money, it's the excitement. To see the Congo, to talk about it, write about it, those are things that spur them. They simply do not want to sit quietly. They want to plan, to advise, to teach, to do; for better or worse it is a national characteristic. So, I thought you must somehow give them the opportunity.

I was not exempt from this national scourge myself. I loved the trips on planes loaded with flowers and fruit. Once we took a 747 choked with flowers (I almost doubled the export of Israeli flowers). Aside from the crew's places, there were only four seats; every inch of the rest of the plane was thick with blossoms. I got to know the most interesting wholesale markets in Europe—in Paris and Frankfurt and Cologne. I became familiar with the great Grüne Woche agricultural fair in Berlin, and of course the magnificent flower exchange in Aalsmeer, Holland. It was the kind of thing I felt I could do forever.

Nevertheless, on June 30, election night, I was prepared for all of it to come to an end. Ever since January, most of the polls had shown Labor in the lead. Shortly before the thirtieth the Likud seemed to have closed the gap, but everyone knew that it could easily go either way.

When the votes were finally counted, the Likud emerged with forty-eight seats to Labor's forty-seven, giving us the ability to create a governing coalition together with some of the smaller parties. Despite the narrowness of the margin, 1981 was a real triumph, certainly more significant than 1977 when DASH had split the Labor vote. With Yadin and his party now back in the Labor fold, this election had been a true contest, pitting the two opposing political blocs squarely against each other for the first time.

In this head-to-head battle the Likud win was due to several factors. The first was Mr. Begin himself. During this campaign he took upon himself a tremendous burden, speaking non-stop before one huge audience after another, displaying a tireless and effective personal leadership. In addition, the Likud benefited significantly from Yoram

Aridor's economic policy, which stimulated consumer buying. Then of course there were the tours to Samaria and Judea that brought those hundreds of thousands of voters to look down at their homes from the mountain ridges.

Perhaps more important than any of these was the fact that the first four years under Begin had witnessed a second Israeli revolution. The first had been the Zionist movement itself. That revolution had established the nation. Now with Begin at the helm there had been a revolution within the nation, a Sephardic revolution. Since 1977 the Sephardic population had come to feel—for the first time—a kind of rough equality with the Ashkenazi community. Under Begin the government had made tremendous efforts within the developing towns, bringing in industry, building schools and housing, improving health care, roads, and transportation. Suddenly Israel's Sephardis, and the poorer people generally, began to experience benefits and opportunities they had never before had. And they responded. A swell of Sephardi students entered the universities. As time passed, more and more Sephardis rose to become officers and commanders in the army.

But economic and social opportunity was only part of it. For many years the Sephardic segment of the population had been thought of as "b'sar b'hirot," "election meat," and they had been manipulated shamelessly by Labor. From the beginning, Labor leaders had taken a patronizing approach toward them. And while the politicians may have felt that they were providing the fastest, most effective help they could, they had also gone a long way toward destroying the Sephardic immigrants' sense of pride and self-respect.

Among other inequities, the Sephardis had been denied the ability to find a place in the political world. Labor's highly centralized method of allotting power and choosing candidates gave the party old guard their rewards but also kept newcomers out. The Likud's internal elections, however, were open and democratic. As a result, while Labor ossified, new young Likud leaders began to emerge, many of them Sephardi. For the Sephardic community in general this meant that the days of patronization were past. Now they not only had representation, they had a chance to participate fully in the political process. They had helped bring the Likud to power and were an integral part of its fabric.*

*The origins of this association actually went back years. Few Sephardis had achieved positions in the Palmach or Haganah, which were dominated by people from the kibbutzim and moshavim. But the Irgun, which furnished the core of Menachem Begin's Herut party, always

In 1981 they were ready to defend fiercely the gains they had made in the previous years. During the party rallies and marches the noise was deafening. Chants of "Be-Gin, Be-Gin, Be-Gin" or "A-Rik, A-Rik, A-Rik" blotted out everything else. Personally, I was not used to this kind of display, and I was uncomfortable with it. Disturbed, at one of the rallies, I asked one of the people standing next to me why they were all shouting like that. "Look," he said, "we're not calling for anybody, and we're not idolizing anybody. What we're really shouting is 'We are not afraid.' It's more like a battle cry." And it was a battle cry, from the poorest part of the Israeli population, a cry from people who felt that they might lose something they had finally achieved after so many years.

Meanwhile, of course, the peace agreement was signed with Egypt and people generally had started to see Begin in a different light. At first many had been frightened that if the old Irgun chief came into power he would strike out at the country's democratic and socialist institutions and generally live up to Labor's billing of him as a fascist. But when he finally did become prime minister what they found was that this man, for all his forcefulness, was a true liberal.

For these reasons and others the Likud won its second election. And when that happened, it became clear to everybody that 1977 had not been some shocking aberration from which the country would soon recover. The Likud had established itself as a fixture in the Israeli political world. We were now, as the party people put it at the time, "on the map."

Despite my position as one of the leaders of this movement that was now on the map, I still was not exactly an integral part of the political mechanism. The fact that my personal strength did not derive from the party apparatus or from political life in general gave me an independence that kept me something of an outsider. Nevertheless my own relationship with Begin had by that time progressed far beyond the nervous apprehension I had felt during our meeting at the King David Hotel in 1969. On the one hand we were close. By this time we had worked together for years and we held certain basic views in common. On the other, there were conflicts, not personal conflicts but sharp differences about some of the main issues.

Among other things, we had bitter arguments about the settlement

included a large percentage of Sephardis. When the underground fighters were running from the British, they could not hide among the "establishment" population (who might have turned them over). Instead many found shelter in the Sephardi areas. So these relations were shaped right at the beginning.

policy, which I was pushing very hard and which he wanted to moderate for a variety of political and personal reasons. On this subject my position was that once we felt safer from a security point of view, we would have the ability to be more forthcoming in any eventual political settlement. And for me safety was never an abstract thing; it was always bound up with settlements, with holding terrain and hills and strategic positions, and with work, cultivation, and industry—the involvement of people with the land. I was not a great believer in legal terms; I certainly did not believe that Israel could trust its security to international agreements or guarantees.

During my years in government, though, I must say that I learned a great deal about the importance of written agreements and the reasons for their necessity, and this I learned from Mr. Begin. From him I began to better appreciate the tradition of political Zionism as opposed to the pragmatic Zionism I had been born into. I came to understand that our achievements were a combination of the two. I had been bred to the conviction that one cannot accomplish anything through legal agreements unless one has secured the necessities on the ground. But now I had a clearer concept of how the two realities reinforced each other.

Nevertheless it was still axiomatic for me that papers and documents are useless without a reality behind them, while Begin's natural impulse was to reach out to the political agreement. As a result we argued heatedly about different aspects of the settlements, their number, their size, the speed with which we should build them, the nature of the autonomy we would be willing to grant, the precautions we should take before leaving the Sinai. These things were often bones of contention between us and occasionally gave rise to anger and resentment. But beneath the real differences I always appreciated Begin's strengths and his contributions, and I believe my feelings were reciprocated.

That belief was confirmed for me when after the 1981 elections Begin appointed me minister of defense. The appointment came as no surprise; even in 1977 I believe Begin would have named me rather than Ezer Weizman had it been possible for him politically. There was, however, a condition to the appointment. Raful Eytan's tenure as commander-in-chief was up that year, but Begin wanted it understood that Raful would serve for another year before I named someone new. Begin and Eytan had worked closely together since Weizman's resignation, when Begin had taken over the defense portfolio himself. As a result, Eytan had direct contact with the prime minister, a situation Begin wanted to maintain. Under these conditions I knew I would be working in something of a sandwich, but it was not a prospect that bothered me tremendously.

In some ways the work as defense minister carried over from jobs I had already been performing. In particular I became more and more involved in relations with the Egyptians, the two focal points of which were Israel's phased withdrawal from the Sinai and autonomy for the Arabs of Samaria, Judea, and Gaza.

In 1979 I had supported the Camp David Accords because I believed that after all those years of bloodshed we had an obligation to see if there was any possibility for peaceful co-existence. For many reasons Egypt was the most suitable country with which to begin Arab-Israeli peace negotiations. First of all, though Egypt was deeply involved in Arab affairs and in fact could be considered the leader of the Arab bloc, still the Egyptians never completely regarded themselves as Arab. Sadat, for example, would talk in private about the Arabs as if he were someone who did not feel a total identification. "Those Arabs," he would say. Both he and his countrymen thought of themselves as a little separate, a little distinct. In their own eyes they were the inheritors of the great ancient pre-Arab world of kings and pharaohs, Arab, yes, but at the same time something more than Arab.

Second, although Israel and Egypt have a common border, and many problems along this border, still 170 miles of unpopulated desert lay between the Suez Canal and Israel proper. And even this common border lay farther from Israel's population and industrial base than other Arab borders did. Properly demilitarized, the Sinai could provide the security buffer we needed.

Third, Egypt was preoccupied with a series of tremendous internal problems stemming from her rapid population growth. We believed that these problems provided an opportunity for mutual interests to develop. Specifically we knew that there were areas where we could be of real help to the Egyptians and that this could contribute substantially to the development of peaceful and neighborly relations.

When we added to all these elements the fact that Egypt was large enough and strong enough to pursue her own self-interest in the face of pressure from other Arab states, it was clear that any chance of negotiations between Israel and the Arab world lay here if it lay anywhere. This was Begin's analysis, as it was that of others in the cabinet, and this analysis underlay the search for peace he initiated immediately after he first took office. Generally people attributed the Camp David agreement to the initiative of Anwar Sadat. But in fact it did not start with him. It started with Menachem Begin.

At one of Begin's first cabinet meetings in 1977 the new prime minister made it clear that he would make every effort to meet with Arab leaders to try to find some path to peace. Shortly afterwards, Begin paid a state visit to Rumania's Nicholae Ceausescu. In his talks with Ceausescu, he apparently impressed the Rumanian leader with his courage and sincerity, as well as with his commitment to finding a resolution to the Arab-Israeli conflict. Four years later in his Abadin palace, Sadat told me that what really made him decide to come to Jerusalem was the fact that shortly after Begin visited Ceausescu, he himself did. At that meeting Sadat asked Ceausescu what kind of a man Begin was. Ceausescu told him that Mr. Begin seemed like a man who would be "very hard in negotiations." But his strong impression was that once Begin agreed to something he would follow through on his promises exactly.

Sadat also told me that when Begin formed his first government, he (Sadat) had been very worried. It had seemed to him a government that would move Israel toward war. First, Begin's own image in those days was hard enough. Then Begin had named Moshe Dayan as his foreign minister, the man who had defeated the Egyptians twice, as commander-in-chief in '56 and as minister of defense in '67. For his defense minister Begin chose Ezer Weizman, the architect of Israel's surprise air victory in '67, and he had also chosen me, with my own military record. To Sadat, putting such a group of people together, all of them known for their military background and views, was a clear sign that Israel was preparing for war. But when he heard Ceausescu's assessment of Begin, he decided it would be worthwhile to make an effort. He believed, he said, that he could have signed a peace agreement with only two people in Israel: Golda Meir and Menachem Begin. (Sadat's interpretation of Dayan's appointment as foreign minister was especially interesting to me, since I knew Begin's real reasons for the appointment. When I met with Begin directly after the 1977 election, he had told me he would be appointing Dayan despite the great resentment the appointment would cause within the party. He had decided to do it because he felt it would be significant for Israel's image abroad, and also because with Dayan in the government Israel's deterrence capacity would be enhanced. With Dayan, Ezer, and myself the Arabs would be deterred from venturing a new war, Begin thought, and would understand that they had no alternative but to negotiate. Dayan would also be, though Begin did not say it, a shining ornament in the crown of the man who had been scorned by the Israeli establishment for so many years.)

The peace accord that Begin and Sadat agreed to at Camp David stipulated a phased withdrawal of Israeli troops from the Sinai over a three-year period. When the second Begin government took office, all but the last phase of the withdrawal had been accomplished. At that point Israeli forces still held the eastern third of the Sinai, but they were scheduled to complete their evacuation by April 25, 1982, now less than ten months away.

We all knew that this final step would be an extremely dangerous one for us. The Egyptian threat had hovered over Israel for years. Our experience with the Egyptians had been one of constant hostility, from small-scale terrorist attacks to full-blown warfare. Against this background, giving back the territory that protected us from them in return for a promise of peace constituted a profoundly troubling risk.

Long before the Camp David negotiations began, the Israeli concept of how to retain a protective shield in this region was to insist on maintaining a series of Jewish settlements concentrated in the northern Sinai and in a strip approximately fifty kilometers wide along the length of the Sinai border. In accord with this concept we had built over twenty settlements and two major towns, Ophira, next to Sharm al-Sheikh, and Yamit, near the border in the north. However, in his initial secret meetings with Sadat's representatives in Morocco, Moshe Dayan as foreign minister had indicated his willingness to return the whole of Sinai to Egypt. Dayan knew that without giving back sovereignty there was no chance of a peace agreement. (It was because of Dayan's agreement as well as Ceausescu's assessment of Begin that Sadat had gone to Jerusalem.) But he also knew that his offer had gone very far indeed, and he worried about it.

The result was that Dayan had come up with an idea about how to keep at least some sort of control in that area even after it was returned. In essence, we would propose that the fifty-kilometer-wide strip be demilitarized, but that we would have the right to keep a kind of home guard there maintaining communications between the settlements. This is what had brought Dayan and myself to propose thickening the line of settlements in January 1978, the proposal that had drawn such media ire and that precipitated the nasty cabinet confrontation of January 8.

Both of us were sure that a string of isolated frontier settlements would never survive under Egyptian sovereignty. These places would be assailed by the Sinai Bedouin. They would be unable to defend themselves, and the Egyptians would never begin to provide adequate security. Consequently, if we wanted to retain a buffer zone there, we would need to increase the population and create enough additional settlements to generate a normal life and constant communication and movement among the settlements and between the settlements and Israel. If we did not do this, I told Begin and the rest of the cabinet, we would have no practical incentive to keep patrolling these areas. The result would be that we would soon stop patrolling them, and before long we would have no buffer zone. Without additional settlements we would repeat in Sinai our experience on Banias Hill, where our settlement had withered and the Syrians had taken control, and our experience at El Hama, a demilitarized zone southeast of the Sea of Galilee. We had had the right to settle El Hama but had not done it, and when seven men in an Israeli patrol had been killed by the Syrians in an ambush, we had never gone back. There had seemed no good reason to risk more casualties. By the same token, once our patrols in the Sinai started being ambushed by Bedouin or blown up on mines, we would stop sending them—unless there was a vital infrastructure that we had a strong incentive to maintain and defend.

When the Camp David talks got under way, though, the Egyptians made it clear that the very concept of a buffer zone under our control but their sovereignty was entirely unacceptable. Their unyielding position on the issue presented the Begin government with a major sticking point. We would have to make the decision to either abandon the concept or to give up the possibility of achieving peace with Egypt.

As far as I was concerned, there were only two possibilities: Either establish a close-knit belt of strong populated settlements or give up the settlement idea altogether and look for a different concept. There was no question that the settlements we already had there would not be able to survive by themselves and that they would expire under protracted unpleasant conditions. At the same time I felt strongly that we had to try the experiment of peace with Egypt. I knew that abandoning the existing Sinai settlements would bring an outcry from many in Israel, but after thirty years of existing in a state of war, the question of whether we could make peace with an Arab state and then live in peace with them was historic. The opportunity had to be taken, even though the risk was great. It was for this reason—and only because Sinai was not part of the Land of Isreal—that I supported Begin consistently in his negotiating positions and that I voted in favor of the agreement he finally achieved.

But at the same time as I accepted the need to give up the Sinai settlements, I also assumed a firm stance on other points at issue. If we were not to retain a protective buffer, we would have to take every other step possible to assure our security. The Egyptian negotiators complained regularly about my adamance on points they regarded as insignificant. "Why are you so hard," they would ask, "on any possibility of our moving some outpost two or three hundred yards from where it is supposed to be? Why does it make such a difference to you?"

My constant refrain to them was that Israel would always be in an inferior situation vis-à-vis Egypt, and that our inferiority created a host of potentially destructive consequences for us. As I told Kamal Hassan Ali at one point, "According to the agreement you are entitled to keep 240 tanks east of the Suez. Now let's assume that one day we wake up and find three hundred tanks there. For you it is a simple logistical operation, moving sixty tanks from the west side of the canal to the east. But for us, in order to restore the situation we have to be ready to go to war. And that is a difficult decision indeed. Our own people would very rightly say, 'What, you are driving the country to war over fifty or sixty tanks, as strong and well armed as Israel is?' So we would have a problem. Now let's say that a month later there are another fifty or sixty tanks there. For you this was another simple matter of logistics. The result is that you will be sitting in Sinai with your tanks and we will still be sitting on the horns of a dilemma, either to give up our deterrence ability or go to war. We do not want to face that dilemma, and that is why we will not tolerate the slightest deviation from our agreement."

What I did not say to Ali was how vividly I recalled the hesitations of the Eshkol government in May and June of 1967, when we were faced with precisely this problem. Surprised by Egypt's sudden dismissal of the U.N. peacekeeping troops from Sinai and her insertion into the area of large combat forces, both the Israeli government and General Headquarters staff had been afraid to respond quickly and forcefully, reluctant to take the country to war despite the imminent and growing threat. The War of Attrition cease-fire was also on my mind—our indecisiveness when directly afterward the Egyptians had started moving their missiles forward. And in the end, with all the casualties of that war fresh in our memories, we had chosen to do nothing. Always, I thought, the dilemmas and dangers are ours, never yours.

One of these "minor" points of contention that I did not consider minor at all was the delineation of the true Sinai border. This was an issue that had been lying dormant since 1949, and I was determined to resolve it before our final evacuation. As we began to make our preparations for withdrawal, I was bothered by the fact that the boundary line between Israel and Egypt was the only one of Israel's borders not accurately demarcated. The reason for this was that after World War One the British had recognized Palestine's borders with Lebanon, Syria, and Jordan but had never recognized the Palestine-Egypt border. When I started looking into why this was so, I discovered that the Sinai border had been set by an Anglo-Egyptian surveying team in 1906. Obviously the British knew where the border was; they had surveyed it themselves. Why then had they never recognized it?

Late in 1981 I resurveyed the border and discovered exactly why they hadn't. Although the true border had been agreed to by Turkey (which ruled Palestine at the time) and England (which ruled Egypt), when the Anglo-Egyptian team made their survey they had found it advantageous to place a number of specific locations inside Palestine rather that inside Egypt. As a result they had marked the border incorrectly. The fact was that fifteen of the traditional border stones did not lie on the true border. Some were a few dozen yards off, and one actually deviated a mile and a half—all of them east of where they should have been.

Looking closely at those places, it was easy to understand why the British had done what they did. Each one of the mismarked sites had a military significance; most of them were high observation points that enabled whoever occupied them to look deep into Palestine. At the time of the original survey Great Britain had been a virile empire, Turkey the old sick man among the world's rulers. Constantly pressing against what was left of Turkish power, the British had simply decided to take the advantageous terrain for themselves. At Taba, for example, the high ground allowed them to observe Aqaba, then one of the main British targets (the port was taken in 1917 by Lawrence of Arabia). In one of history's minor ironies, after the war the British had moved into Palestine and the Egyptians had taken over Sinai. And now that the British were on the other side of the fence, they refused to accept their own border markers.

Seventy-five years later the consequences of this ploy were that if the true border were observed, Israeli positions would be well placed to observe into Egyptian Sinai, while if the traditional markers were accepted, the Egyptians would be looking deep into Israel. When I insisted on reverting to the true border, the Egyptians refused to accept my position. In 1949, they said, the Israeli army had stopped at the traditional line, and after the Sinai campaign in 1956 we had withdrawn to the same line. What gave us the right to raise this issue now?

As these negotiations continued to be fruitless and the withdrawal date approached, Egyptian suspicions grew that Israel would not after all honor its commitment to leave the Sinai. Despite the agreement at Camp David they knew the importance of what we were giving up, and they suspected we would try to find some way to avoid implementing the final phase. Undoubtedly they did not want to give in on the border issue, but their fear that we might choose not to withdraw at all was a lever I intended to use fully.

I knew, as the Egyptians did not, that we were indeed planning to comply with the agreement, but I argued with Begin that we must use the pressure of the moment to resolve the border problem even if it meant postponing the evacuation for a few days. It is a necessity, I told him, that we not leave anything unresolved, that we settle all the points at issue before we withdraw. Otherwise we would be providing the Egyptians with ready justifications at whatever future date they might decide it was in their interest to undermine relations or minimize them or change them altogether.

Begin understood my position, but he refused to accept it. Being the man he was, he insisted that regardless of the cogency of my argument we were going to go ahead and fulfill the letter of the agreement, including the timing requirements. Although I pressed him hard on this, I got nowhere. The assessment of Begin that Ceausescu had given Sadat had been absolutely accurate—a hard man, he had said, but once he agrees to something he will implement it to the last comma and period.

It could have been that Begin believed the damage any Israeli delay in implementing the accords would cause her in the world would be greater than the potential damage of leaving issues open. But as for me, when I discussed these points I saw in my mind's eye every rock and hill we were talking about. After all those years in the Sinai I could feel in my bones the tactical importance of each of them. As a result I was less inclined than Begin to regard Taba and the others as legal abstractions. I was also less inclined to compromise on them. Nevertheless, when the day came to withdraw, we withdrew.

We did not do it, though, without a great deal of pain. As part of our evacuation we had agreed to turn over to the Egyptians our Sinai settlements, including the towns of Ophira and Yamit. This meant removing the settlers who had been living there, some of them for ten years or even more. Although I understood the necessity for this and had supported the decision, I did not feel at all good about it. The government had made promises to these people when they originally moved in, and I knew what kind of sacrifices the settlers had made to build lives for themselves in the desert. Beyond that, it was one thing to make a decision in the cabinet about evicting them, quite another to personally carry out the eviction. And I was the one who had to carry it out.

(Afterward it was reported in the newspapers that Begin had appointed me minister of defense not because he truly wanted me as minister but because he preferred that I be the one to remove the settlers rather than he himself. Rumors about this became so insistent that afterward Begin felt he had to clarify the situation with me. Speaking privately, he expressed his satisfaction with the way the operation had gone, with no injuries or serious violence despite the crowds and emotional demonstrations. He told me that in spite of the rumors and gossip he had absolutely no intention of replacing me. He had not appointed me for that job, and he was certainly not going to select anyone else now that it was done.)

Removing the settlers was a delicate business in every instance. But it was worst in Yamit. Unlike Ophira, our other Sinai town, Yamit was located on the border. All the other places I was willing to turn over to the Egyptians exactly as we had agreed to do. But not Yamit or the few settlements near it. That, I felt, was too dangerous. Although only a few thousand people presently lived in Yamit, I knew that the infrastructure we had built there—the wells, water installations, electricity, telephones, commercial centers—could serve to transform the place very quickly into a population center of 100,000. All the essentials necessary to make the desert habitable were in place, and I knew that the Egyptians were eager to bring in settlers. I was also convinced that it was important, now and for many years to come, that we would not have Egyptian centers of population near our borders.

The prospect of large numbers of Egyptians living in the desert in hard circumstances with Israeli settlements and villages nearby was not one I thought either Israel or Egypt should want to bring about. Inevitably, even if the Egyptian authorities were careful, some individuals or small gangs would begin to cross the border for mischief and a little stealing. Then it would escalate into violence and the kind of terror we had had so much experience with earlier. The consequence would be regular friction between the Israeli and Egyptian governments, exacerbating exactly those tensions we all hoped the new peace treaty would put to rest.

Consequently I thought it best not to turn Yamit over but to destroy it instead, and I brought this proposal to the government. When the government did not object, I moved ahead to implement it. To the Egyptians I described the serious problems we were having with our settlers. Once we remove them, I explained, they sneak back across the border and we find them there again (which was quite true—the settlers were persistent and ingenious in finding their way back home after they had been evicted). The only way to solve the problem, I told them, is to destroy or move buildings. The small structures in some of the farming settlements near Yamit we could move. But not the more substantial housing and industrial and commercial buildings in the town. As far as Yamit was concerned, I saw no alternative to evacuating the people once and for all, then razing the entire place behind them.

For months I was plagued by the fact that I was going to have to do this. I listened to the settlers who came to argue and plead for their homes, or if not for their homes at least to have the buildings left intact so they might keep the hope of someday returning. On one memorable night several of them made their way through the barbed wire and patrols we were using to seal the settlements off and made their way to my farm, where they argued with me until a little before dawn. No doubt they would have stayed all day as well, except that one of them had to get back to nurse her baby, and all of them had to sneak back to their settlements before light.

But as bad as I felt about it, in the end I removed the settlers and razed Yamit. Ophira and the other places I handed over, not just in habitable condition but in perfect condition. But Yamit I leveled utterly. The affair did not leave a pleasant taste in my mouth. Even now I am occasionally criticized for it, and sometimes I hear myself called "the one who destroyed Yamit." But it is nothing I make any excuses for. An Egyptian town there would have endangered the peace we were all trying to achieve, and what I did was nothing more than what my best judgment told me had to be done.

The Camp David Accords had laid a framework for the return of Sinai to Egypt. (The Gaza district was not to be returned, as it was part of Eretz Israel.) The Accords also outlined a plan to give autonomy to the Palestinians of Judea, Samaria, and Gaza (the plan in its original form was Mr. Begin's). In essence the Camp David plan called for a balance between "the principle of self-government" for the Palestinians and "the legitimate security concerns" of the Israelis. Egypt, Israel, Jordan, and Palestinian representatives would agree on how to elect a Palestinian self-governing body and on what its powers should be. After the self-governing body (the Administrative Council) was elected, a five-year transitional period would ensue, at the end of which Egypt, Israel, Jordan, and the Council would agree on the final status of the territories.

The autonomy plan was not in any way a set of final prescriptions by which to settle the problem of Samaria, Judea, and Gaza. It was, rather, what the Camp David language called it, a "framework" that left the hard issues to be resolved by direct negotiations among the principals. What constituted the "legitimate security concerns" of Israel, what constituted the "legitimate rights of the Palestinian people," how these two concepts might be brought to co-exist—these vital and complex questions the concerned parties were invited to resolve for themselves.

When Begin brought the autonomy plan to the government, many in his Herut party found it insupportable, a betrayal by Begin of the Jewish claim to Eretz Israel. My own reaction was that the plan was loaded with danger. It could easily, I said, become a Balfour Declaration for the Palestinians and might well lead to a second Palestinian state (in addition to Jordan), something no Israeli with any regard for the country's safety could agree to.

On the other hand I did not object to the principles behind the plan. I had no interest in ruling the Arabs of Samaria, Judea, and Gaza; on the contrary, I believed they needed to run their lives with as little Israeli interference as possible. What was necessary was to very carefully identify the risks we would be unable to take, to determine how to avoid them, and to insist on our positions regardless of whatever pressure President Jimmy Carter exerted. We could go along, I thought, as long as we guaranteed the necessary precautions.

In my view it was evident what these precautions were. The primary one I had been working to realize since my first moment in government: to insure that we would keep in our hands the vital strategic terrain and prevent any future possibility that it might fall into someone else's hands. Reiterating arguments I had been making for several years, I said that I did not believe this could be accomplished with military units. Military units can be in one place today, while tomorrow they can be moved somewhere else. They are subject to the shifting policies of every new government. From our historical experience we knew that only settlements could secure a claim to land. As far as Samaria and Judea were concerned, settlements did not mean agricultural settlements. The mountainous and rocky terrain there could not support them. Consequently it would be necessary to build urban sites—residential areas and industrial zones.

So the first precaution was to build settlements that would physically hold the essential ground. But I did not want to build them just to hold the ground. I also felt that the people of Israel had to be motivated to keep this area. So the question was how to create the motivation. Stimulating strong national feelings is one way; but generally speaking, in modern Western societies national feeling plays a decreasing role, and Israel is no exception. But motivation will also take hold, I thought, once Jews actually live in these places. When that happens, an inevitable feeling of mutual responsibility will follow, there will be a need to protect them, and a need to assure that they are doing well.

Holding the high terrain was the first precaution. The second precaution I sought was to insure that only Israel would be responsible for the external and internal security of this area. For almost a hundred years prior to the Six Day War—under the Turks, under the British, under the Jordanians, under the Egyptians in Gaza—the Jewish people had been a target for terror from this area. By and large since the Six Day War we have not been. That doesn't mean that we do not have terror now. But one cannot compare what had gone before with what goes on now. And of course we cannot guess how bad it might have been had we not been there. The fact is that most of the terrorists are caught because we can enter any place any time to search for them. So as far as internal security goes, we must be able to handle it ourselves. In terms of external security, there is simply no question that Israeli forces must be on the River Jordan and on the controlling ridge line behind it.

The third precaution follows from the second. Since we needed to keep the responsibility for internal security, it was my position that we had to insist that no Jordanian soldiers, police, or officials would have any jurisdiction in Samaria or Judea, for the same reason that we would allow no Egyptian jurisdiction in Gaza. The Egyptians professed to be puzzled by my insistence on this point and kept pressing to have at least some police and administrative personnel in Gaza. But I explained to them that as long as we needed to be in charge of internal security, the presence of their officials would be a cause of constant tension. "Let's assume," I would say, "that there is a terrorist attack. Our people will be coming into neighborhoods and searching. Your officials will inevitably try to intervene, and we will just as inevitably push them aside. There will be daily friction. It's not that I would expect you to be happy about our actions or to applaud us if you are on the other side of the border. But at least if you are there, neither of us will be subject to the everyday confrontations. The most important thing is not to ruin our great achievement—peace—by creating a situation where daily small incidents are allowed to sour our relations."

With these three precautions—Israeli settlements on the strategic terrain, Israeli responsibility for internal and external security, and a prohibition against Jordanian police or officials—we could, I argued, accept a five-year transitional period of autonomy for the inhabitants of Samaria, Judea, and Gaza. When I was pressed about a permanent resolution, I answered that I never believed an agreement was something you sign and that is the end of it. There is always development, one always hopes for the best. If, for example, conditions were quiet and there was no terrorism or violence, then it would be in our interest to reduce our military presence. So, I said, first let's put the autonomy plan into effect and allow relations to develop. The Palestinian Arabs can conduct their lives almost without interference. We will proceed with our strategic settlements, but only on state-owned land where we will not disturb them. In those matters that require a common approach, customs, for example, or veterinary standards, we will co-ordinate together. Let's see how it works. At the end of the five transitional years we will have a better view of future directions.

Although I was quite clear in my own mind about the concept of autonomy that would be acceptable to us, I was never satisfied that the cabinet as a whole shared the same sharp definition. For months I kept demanding of Begin that we undertake an in-depth discussion of exactly what we meant, that we should not sign anything whose meaning was at all fuzzy, at least as far as we ourselves were concerned.

But Begin didn't want this discussion. He may have thought that the chances of anything concrete coming of the autonomy plan were not great anyway and that the overriding necessity was to give Sadat a chance to sign the peace agreement. I understood the importance of that well enough, but in my view it was still necessary for us to fully explore among ourselves autonomy in all its aspects. For months Begin and I conducted a harsh debate on this subject; I demanded again and again a comprehensive cabinet review, and he just as persistently kept rejecting it.

I remember one day especially when I came to see him at the prime minister's residence. Begin was ill with the flu at the time, and he asked me to come into his bedroom to talk. As I sat down next to the bed, I noticed his shoes on the floor, newly polished. In the night table cabinet was the shoe brush he had obviously used. The simplicity of the man's life never changed. Even though he had moved out of his little apartment into the official mansion, he still lived this extremely modest existence. He lay there with his head propped up on a pillow and a glass of tea balanced on his chest along with a slice of that black bread. He seemed so weak, I thought that maybe this time I would be able to wear him down. Taking up my argument, I again demanded the cabinet review. I demanded and demanded, and he, as usual, resisted and resisted until somehow with both our temperatures rising the glass of tea overturned on the bed. The man may have looked weak, but he certainly did not act weak, not then and not later. As a result the government never did have the discussion.

In the end the cabinet accepted the idea of an autonomy plan regardless, and the Camp David Accords established a framework for negotiations on making it a reality. But although at Camp David the parties agreed on the language for this framework, in fact there was nothing like an agreement on the underlying issues. Although we ourselves may not have achieved clarity on all the plan's ramifications at Camp David, it was obvious that two distinct lines of thought remained: the Autonomy Plan According to the Arabs and the Autonomy Plan According to the Jews.

For the Arabs, autonomy was a phase that would lead to the creation of a second Palestinian state. The autonomy the Jews were offering (as we said loudly and clearly all along) was specifically for the inhabitants themselves of Samaria, Judea, and Gaza. We had never agreed to hand over any territorial sovereignty. According to the Arabs, either Jordan or the West Bank and Gaza Palestinians would be the legal source of authority for local rule. Our position was that the Israeli civil administrations would be the source authority, even if the administrations were to withdraw physically from the territories.

There were other issues too. The agreement stated that to assure border security Jordan and Israel would participate in "joint patrols." The Arabs took that to mean that both sides would be patrolling together west of the Jordan, whereas our interpretation was that Jordanian patrols east of the river could be co-ordinated with Israeli patrols west of the river. We were certainly not about to allow Jordanian soldiers onto the West Bank. The West Bank police, a "strong local police force," according to the accords was to include "Jordanian citizens." Our understanding of this was that West Bank Arabs, all of whom were Jordanian citizens, would of course compose the West Bank police force. The policemen in Hebron would be from Hebron, and the policemen in Shechem would be from Shechem. But that did not mean that police units from Jordan would be crossing the river.

My position from the beginning was that the two distinct interpretations of the accord language had to be resolved and that the Israeli interpretation had to be accepted. Without this we would run the risk of compromising the precautions I considered essential. But Begin, Dayan, and Weizman (the Israeli team at Camp David) did not see it the same way, believing that the fact of achieving an agreement was worth allowing even major ambiguities to remain. As a result these issues never were clarified.

The Camp David Accords were completed on September 17, 1978, and were subsequently ratified by the Knesset. Although the autonomy talks began almost immediately, it soon became clear that on this subject (as opposed to the Sinai withdrawal) the Egyptians were in no great hurry. They wanted to carry on the autonomy negotiations in such a way that on the day the Sinai was returned, it would look as if we were still in the middle of discussions.

As far as the Egyptians were concerned, the talks could not be allowed to reach a stalemate before that. They could not afford to look as if they were eagerly implementing those sections of the agreement that benefited them but were not showing a decent sense of responsibility toward the Palestinians. But at the same time they knew an untenable situation when they saw one. Jordan and the West Bank Palestinians had caved in to PLO pressure and had chosen not to participate in the negotiations. With the real Arab parties to this agreement sitting on the sidelines, the Egyptians knew their efforts could not result in anything concrete. No matter what version of autonomy they might manage to negotiate, it would never be acceptable, and they would be the scapegoats. Consequently, even though the Egyptians had to look as if they were doing their best not to forsake the Palestinians, they did not want to complete the negotiations and bring even more opprobrium on themselves.

Their answer to this dilemma was to carry on with the negotiations, but slowly and inconclusively. They did this very cleverly. From the outside it seemed as if the talks were progressing. But though meetings went on and discussions took place, in fact nothing substantial happened.

Knowing the dangers of the Camp David framework, we were not overenthusiastic about the negotiations either. But although not eager, we had in fact agreed to the concept of autonomy and we were willing to proceed on resolving the issues and then implementing the plan. But the Egyptians found all sorts of reasons to drag their heels. They did not want to discuss it in Jerusalem or they set agendas that addressed details rather than substantive issues, or they needed extra time for consultation, one thing after another.

But even though no real progress was made I found this a productive period. The negotiations gave us the opportunity to meet regularly with the Egyptians, to talk, to get to know them, to allow them to know us. For me personally it was important, because for the first time I really could have steady contact with Egyptian leaders. So while everyone knew the talks were not going anywhere, still both sides acted as if everything was proceeding normally. It was not until after we returned the Sinai that negotiations actually broke off, leaving the problem of the territories in a state of limbo, continuing to await a resolution.

28

Minister of Defense

In the summer of 1981 the Sinai and autonomy negotiations were the focus of attention. But that did not mean other strategic issues disappeared. For many years Israel had carried on to one degree or another what was called the "strategy of the periphery," an attempt to foster relationships with nations on the borders of the Arab world that encircled us. As part of this strategy we had provided a range of assistance to the Shah's Iran and to various African nations, from agricultural and humanitarian aid to military and intelligence co-operation. I had been involved in these efforts to some extent as minister of agriculture, when I did what I could to further our overseas training and aid projects. Now as defense minister I became much more intimately concerned with questions of Israel's strategic posture.

My overarching goal in this regard was to broaden strategic co-operation between Israel and the United States. Problems created by international terrorism and the Soviet Union's ongoing penetration into the Middle East were of vital concern to both nations and suggested a natural pooling of resources. But I also believed that Israeli-American co-operation could be mutually beneficial on a larger regional stage and even on the global stage. Israel was a country top-heavy with technical know-how and enthusiastic experts. As a small nation with no worldwide ambitions, it was relatively easy for us to offer assistance even in politically sensitive countries for whom direct American aid would constitute an unacceptable geopolitical commitment. What we did not have (as the U.S. did) was the ability to underwrite the costs in these often unstable places. Israeli-American co-operation could be especially effective, I believed, in those strategically important countries where vacuums existed that would inevitably be filled by one power bloc or the other.

These issues were on my mind when I visited Africa in November 1981. My primary objective was to explore bilateral ties between Israel and several African nations. But I also knew I would be discussing strategic aspects of the trip in Washington later on in the month when I hoped to sign the memorandum of strategic co-operation that American and Israeli negotiators had been working on for some time now.

My first stop in Africa was the West African coastal state of Gabon. There I had a series of long talks with President Albert Bongo in an effort to restore the diplomatic relations that Gabon had cut during the Yom Kippur War as a result of Arab pressure. We discussed Israeli exports and assistance, and after very difficult negotiations we signed a memorandum of understanding about co-operation between Israel and Gabon, paving the way for the full restoration of relations that I was looking for.

From there we flew to the Central African Republic to meet with General André Kolingba, who had taken power subsequent to the coup against Emperor Bokassa. Arriving at the Bangui airport, we were received by one of the cabinet ministers, and also by General Shmuel Gonen, who after his personal disaster of the Yom Kippur War had come to this region to prospect for diamonds. This was not the first time I had met Gonen since the war, but it was a shock to see him leading such a life in such a place. He took part of our group on a little tour that included sandwiches at the cottage he lived in, a broken-down place with one bed and a map on the wall of the Central African Republic highlighting its diamond fields. It was a bitter thing seeing this general of the Israeli army alone and in poverty there. The man was after all one of the heroes of the Six Day War, and he was a victim of the Yom Kippur War. Not a completely innocent victim certainly, but a victim nevertheless.

The Central African Republic was a land of immense contrasts, a lush, green country with almost unbelievably rich soil and water in abundance, yet also a land of deathly poverty. Driving through the streets of Bangui, I watched children running after locusts, then impaling them on thin wires until they had enough gathered for a meal. In the very midst of Bangui's poverty rose this palace that Bokassa, emperor for life, had built for himself.

Looking at the huge ramshackle building, I somehow could not get my mind off the kitchen, and I wondered if we would be taken to see it. Bokassa had been a bizarre despot about whom the French press was just then writing the most awful stories, prominent among which were charges that he had been a cannibal and hair-raising descriptions of what had gone on in his kitchen.

But whatever Bokassa had been like personally, General Kolingba turned out to be a frank, intelligent individual, almost painfully modest. His review of the republic's strategic situation focused on Soviet penetration of the region, especially through the Libyan invasion of his northern neighbor, Chad. Sitting together and talking as the lights periodically dimmed and went out, he told me that the republic was in desperate financial straits. Libya, he said, was "knocking at the gates," offering him every possible inducement. He wanted to do whatever he could to keep them out, but he had terrible problems. It was now November, and he did not have the money to pay his army or his government officials at the end of the year. If he could get no other help he would have no choice but to give in to Qaddafi.

When I asked how much he needed, Kolingba answered, "Eight million dollars." I thought to myself that even in Israel every decision we take involves tens of millions of dollars, and here we are sitting in the dark while this man needs eight million to keep the Libyans out of his country. Kolingba went on to openly describe the devastated condition in which he found the country after Bokassa's fall, the poverty, the corruption, the cronyism. "I am trying my best to restore the situation," he said, "to recover from all that." I wondered how something might be done to help him.

My next meetings were in Zaire with President Mobutu Sese Seko, who had successfully contrived to keep together an immensely diverse and incohesive country made up of over two hundred tribal groups. Our first day there we had lunch aboard his yacht floating down the vast Zaire River. Outside the dining-room window a helicopter sat on the yacht's launching pad, while inside the table was loaded with beautiful copper pots containing an array of aromatic foods. Mobutu, a tall, powerful man who wore a kind of African Nehru hat and held a small staff of office in his hand, gestured to the pots on one side of the table and said, "These are for the Jews," meaning that there was nothing unkosher in them. It was a gracious gesture.

Mobutu maintained a dignified air, but after a short time I was convinced that this was a man with whom I could talk about things openly. I had the distinct impression that with him I was in the presence of a leader. We discussed the kind of agricultural assistance Israel might be able to provide, and he expressed interest in military aid as well. "How soon might you want a mission here?" I asked. When he answered, "Three weeks," I told him that they would be landing in exactly twenty-one days from that day. After this our talks went so well that as a special gesture Mobutu invited me to go fishing with him on his private fishing farm. This I understood was a mark of friendship, a signal to everyone that a new era in relations had opened up.

The discussions with Mobutu went smoothly, certainly more smoothly than the hard bargaining with Gabon's Bongo. In a brief time we had decided on the outlines of future co-operation between the two countries, and shortly afterward Mobutu took the first steps toward renewing the ties that had been severed in 1973. Situated in the center of Africa and hugely rich in natural resources, Zaire became the first of the African nations to restore full diplomatic relations with Israel.

From Zaire we went to South Africa, where Lily and I were taken to see the Angola border. There South Africans were fighting a continuous war against Cuban-led guerrilla groups infiltrating from the north. To land there our plane came in very high as helicopters circled, searching the area. When the helicopters were satisfied, we corkscrewed down toward the field in a tight spiral to avoid the danger of ground-to-air missiles, the Russian-supplied SAM 7 Strellas that I had gotten to know well at the canal.

On the ground I saw familiar scenes. Soldiers and their families lived in this border zone at constant risk, their children driven to school in convoys protected by high-built armored cars, which were less vulnerable to mines. I went from unit to unit, and in each place I was briefed and tried to get a feel for the situation. It is not in any way possible to compare Israel with South Africa, and I don't believe that any Jew can support apartheid. But seeing these units trying to close their border against terrorist raids from Angola, you could not ignore their persistence and determination. So even though conditions in the two countries were so vastly different, in some ways life on the Angolan border looked not that much different from life on some of our own borders.

The relief I felt being back in Israel after this protracted trip was short-lived, since I had to leave almost immediately for the United States to finish up and sign the memorandum on strategic co-operation that we had been working on since September. Before I left, however, the cabinet had to give its final approval. Unfortunately, a short time before we were to meet, Mr. Begin had fallen and broken his leg and was now in the Hadassah hospital in Jerusalem. Since we could not postpone the signing, a cabinet meeting was called in the prime minister's hospital room. Tired and in severe pain, Begin conducted the meeting with the ministers ranged around his bed in a semicircle. Whether from the effects of his medication or from the shock of the injury, now and then he dozed off for a few minutes, bringing the discussion to an awkward halt. As the other members shuffled uncomfortably or just waited, I kept looking at my watch, knowing I was already late for my plane.

When we finally did get the memorandum approved, I helicoptered from the hospital directly to Ben-Gurion airport, although still not in time to catch the flight. Instead I flew from Tel Aviv to Paris on a Westwind, a small Israel Aviation Industry jet, arriving there just in time to make connections to New York and then to Washington, where an official reception was waiting.

The idea for a memorandum of strategic co-operation had first been broached by Mr. Begin to President Ronald Reagan during a state visit he made to Washington in September 1981. After receiving a positive response from the president, talks began between Israeli and American negotiating teams, which after three months had now concluded their work.

While signing the memorandum was the formal purpose of this visit, I also took the opportunity to discuss with Secretary of State Alexander Haig, Secretary of Defense Caspar Weinberger, and CIA Director William Casey other issues of mutual interest. I described what I had seen in Africa, including the problems faced by the Central African Republic. I recommended to them that we should try to go into the vacuums that existed in the region and suggested that efforts of this sort would be ideally suited for American-Israeli co-operation.

We also discussed the dangers that Israel was facing in the Middle East that were also dangers to the United States and the rest of the free world, specifically international terrorism and Soviet expansionism. For the first time I raised the problem of the Iran-Iraq war and the Persian Gulf. I emphasized that of course no one could accept the fanatical and extremist ideology of the Ayatollah Khomeini, but that did not negate the importance of Iran as a key country in the region. In light of this long-term reality, I suggested that efforts ought to be made to keep low-profile contacts with Iran, particularly with the military circles there. The kind of catastrophic war the ayatollahs were waging had to eventually bring about profound internal consequences, and when it came to an end the chances were good that a different sort of regime would come to power in Tehran.

Most significant was the potential for a situation that would give the Soviets a foothold in the Persian Gulf. As I saw it, the danger here did not lie in any Soviet invasion. But the Soviets do have a treaty with Iran (signed in 1926 by Riza Shah Pahlavi, the Shah's father) that allows the U.S.S.R. to enter Iran if circumstances develop which constitute a danger to Russia. It was then 1981, and the Iraqis had penetrated into Iran and were on the offensive. Near the Iranian border, in the Caucasus and Afghanistan, the Soviets had fifty divisions concentrated. If the Iraqi penetration continued and Iran found itself really threatened, there was a danger that some of those divisions would find themselves inside Iran, either at Tehran's invitation or through an invocation of the treaty.

To underline the long-term nature of Soviet objectives in this region I brought with me quotations from Stalin's thinking on this subject in 1921 and from Leonid Brezhnev's speech on the same subject fifty-two years later in 1977 in Mogadiscio, Somalia, where he described the grand strategy for defeating the "imperialistic powers" by gaining "control over the two great treasure houses on which the West depends: the energy treasure house of the Persian Gulf and the mineral treasure house of central and southern Africa." I brought with me maps detailing Soviet expansion and spoke at length about the continuing Soviet penetration into Africa, inroads that first began in 1955 as a direct outgrowth of Palestinian terrorism against Israel. I contrasted the Soviet presence in the region in 1955 with what it had become by 1971 and what it was currently. I had had other maps prepared identifying the strategic key points in the Middle East and Africa, and which of them were already either in the hands of the Soviets or under deep Soviet influence.

I discussed the consequences for Israel in the region and in the long run for the West too from continued developments along the same lines. Unlike Europe and Japan, the United States imports only a small fraction of its oil from the Gulf. If persistent pressure eventually provided the Soviet Union with a dominant position there, the United States would have the option of backing away and losing interest. But Europe and Japan do not have the same option. As a result, one future scenario is for a progressive American disinvolvement in the Middle East, her place taken by a Soviet Union sitting on the lifelines of Europe and Japan. The long-term strategic importance of developments in such a direction could hardly be exaggerated. And for the Soviets, of course, there are no elections every four years with their consequent swings in foreign policy. For them, once long-range goals are defined, they tend to remain goals.

In these discussions my hosts described the American ability to react to Soviet military moves in the region. They outlined their response time from the Indian Ocean and indicated that they were considering an effort to establish a closer presence at one of Egypt's Red Sea ports. My response was that a better solution would be to utilize facilities in Israel. It takes forty-eight hours, I told them, to ship oranges and watermelons from Judea, Samaria and Gaza to Saudi Arabia. In an emergency they could move tanks overland to support the Saudis in the same forty-eight hours. And in any kind of confrontation with the Soviets over the Gulf, speed of deployment, not size of forces, would be decisive. The essential factor in such a development would be to confront the other side with the dilemma by inserting forces first. Whatever the balance of forces, the Soviets would not attack even one American company deployed in a danger zone, nor would the United States attack a single Soviet company. The consequences would be far too perilous. For these reasons, I argued, Israel was an ideal strategic partner.

At these meetings I also reviewed the worsening situation in Lebanon, where the Syrian occupation army, to which the United States (and Israel too) had acquiesced in 1976, was applying continual heavy pressure to the militias defending the major Christian enclaves north and east of Beirut. In this crisis of the Lebanese community, only Israel was providing any assistance, while the rest of the free world seemed willing to sit back and watch the Christians' fate unfold.

The Memorandum on Strategic Co-operation itself was quite important. Though not a vehicle for joint Israeli-American activities of the kind I had been recommending to Haig and Weinberger, it did acknowledge explicitly the threat of Soviet-inspired military activity in the region and provided channels for closer military and intelligence co-ordination between the two countries. It read in part, "U.S.–Israeli strategic cooperation is designed against the threat to the peace and security of the region caused by the Soviet Union or Soviet-controlled forces from outside the region introduced into the region."

From my point of view the primary benefit of the agreement was the fact that it tightened bilateral security ties and recognized in formal language the mutually important nature of the relationship. Several of the specific terms also held their own weight. The agreement, for example, provided for the pre-positioning of military equipment in Israel, which enhanced our sense of security about emergency situations. The terms also called for co-operation in defense research and development, another potentially significant advantage for us. On the other side, we undertook to cooperate militarily with the United States in emergency situations and to make available Israeli facilities against the outbreak of any regional conflict in which the U.S. might need the use of them.

I had intended to stay in Washington a day or two beyond the signing to continue my talks at the State Department and Pentagon; but as it turned out, on the day of the signing a no-confidence motion was brought by the Labor party in the Knesset, and I was forced to rush directly back to defend the memorandum.

My concern to continue developing Israel's traditional "peripheral" policy in Africa led on May 13, 1982 to a secret meeting with the Sudanese president, Gaafar al-Nimeiry to discuss strategic issues on the continent. (The meeting had been arranged by Yakov Nimrodi, an old friend who had served in Israel's military intelligence for many years and had then become an international business figure. Nimrodi's dream was to use economic co-operation to create mutual interests between Israel and the Arab nations that might lead toward peace.) I had first met Nimeiry in September after the murder of Anwar Sadat by Moslem extremists. Leaders and heads of state from all around the world came to pay homage to this unusual man, and Israel's large funeral delegation was made up of all the members of the inner cabinet in addition to Prime Minister Begin.

The march behind Sadat's casket was a sad and lengthy affair, even longer for the Israelis than for the others. To avoid violating the Sabbath (the funeral was on a Saturday) we had walked two or three miles from the special accommodations the Egyptians arranged for us to where the procession began. There we joined the other delegations for the walk to Sadat's final resting place.

Once started, the mourners took up their own pace, so that soon the different delegations from all over the world were mixed together, occasionally in combinations that under ordinary circumstances would have been unlikely. Glancing to the side, I found myself next to Nimeiry, a hard-looking Sudanese whose face was lacerated by deep tribal scarifications that gave him a cruel air. Now flying to Africa to meet him, I wondered what kind of man I would find behind that face.

Flying via Kenya, I first saw Kenyan president Daniel Arap Mowi. Like other African nations, Kenya had broken relations with Israel in 1973. But unlike most of the others, they had maintained their contacts.

After discussing matters of mutual interest with President Mowi, I went on to my meeting with Nimeiry. Sitting down with him, Yakov Nimrodi, and Adnan Khashoggi (the Saudi businessman who along with Nimrodi had arranged the meeting), I was surprised to find the Sudanese president soft-spoken and extremely polite. I quickly found he was also knowledge-able and perceptive about developments in his part of the world.

As part of a wide-ranging discussion of the African political scene, Nimeiry described for me current conditions inside his own country as well as on his borders. To Sudan's east lay Ethiopia, its Marxist government fighting a protracted war against Eritrean rebels and heavily beholden to the Soviets. Chad, to Nimeiry's west, was also a troubled place, where the Chadian president, Hissen Habre, was fighting against Libya's Muammar Qaddafi, also supplied by the Soviets.

There was no doubt in Nimeiry's mind, as in mine, that the Libyan efforts to destabilize the Chad government and gain control were part of a Soviet drive to assert dominance down through central Africa, from Libya to Chad, to the Central African Republic (where the Libyans had succeeded in inserting themselves several months earlier) to Congo-Brazzaville, where the Soviets themselves had been dominant for some time already.

Nimeiry, whose country shared borders with Ethiopia, Libya, Chad, and the Central African Republic, was very uncomfortable with the direction of all this activity; and he briefed me on the readiness of the Sudanese army to deal with the various problems. We too had a strong interest in Libyan activity. Of all the Arab countries, Libya was one of the most inveterately hostile toward Israel. With his huge reserves of cash and close ties with the Soviets, Qaddafi was a major supporter of regional and international terror, a supplier of training, arms, and logistical assistance. A shared antagonism toward the Libyan strongman was one of the things that had brought Nimeiry and myself together in the first place.

Another issue on our agenda was a proposal brought by Khashoggi, our host. Khashoggi was in contact with the Shah of Iran's son, who was at that time in exile in Morocco. Along with a number of exiled Iranian generals, the young Riza Pahlavi had developed a master plan to liberate his homeland. His group was in the beginning stages of raising free

Iranian forces that would spearhead a revolution inside Iran against the Ayatollah Khomeini. Their basic plan was to train these soldiers in the Sudan, which was far enough from Iran not to fear providing bases for such overtly hostile activity. The proposal called for financing the liberation forces through the Saudis and equipping them with Israeli arms. After listening to Khashoggi's presentation and clarifying some of the questions the concept raised, we decided to meet in Alexandria the following July to take up the discussion again. It was a meeting that never took place; by then Israel would be deeply involved in Lebanon.

There was one more subject Nimeiry and I discussed that afternoon that closely concerned the Sudan and Israel. This was a subject our government had been following with close and painful attention for the last four years and which concerned me more than all the other points on our agenda. Among the hundreds of thousands of refugees streaming out of the Ethiopian mountains into eastern Sudan was a continuous flow of Falashas, Ethiopian Jews. Even among the starving, homeless fugitives from Ethiopia's civil war and famine these Jews were persecuted outcasts. But unlike the others, they could nurture dreams of a life beyond the grim Sudanese refugee camps. Since 1977 we had been moving them quietly and in small groups to Israel, an extremely hazardous and delicate process, considering the anti-Israeli vehemence of the Ethiopian regime and Sudan's Moslem and Arab allegiances.

Taking up this issue with Nimeiry, I urged him to help make sure these Jewish refugees would be treated carefully and not harmed in any way. Would he, I asked, give us the opportunity to fly them out of Khartoum? This was the first time Israel had been able to broach the subject on this level, and what Nimeiry's response would be I did not know. My worries were aggravated by the fact that a highly complex and secret operation bringing a large number of the refugees out was under way at that very moment. All of the contingencies and organization that had gone into this attempt made the timing impossible to change, and so it had gone forward despite my meeting and the risk of serious embarrassment should something go wrong.

I had been closely involved in the Ethiopian exodus since shortly after my appointment as agriculture minister back in 1977. At that time a group of Ethiopian Jews already in Israel had come to me with a request for help in starting a moshav, and that stimulated a long-standing interest I had

had in this group of people whose bond with Judaism went back thousands of years.

Ethiopian Jews had started to trickle out to Israel as early as the beginning of the century. Eighty years ago Professor Yakov Faitlovich had written a book about them after traveling to Ethiopia to see firsthand these people whose existence was known more in rumor and legend than in fact. Faitlovich had returned to Palestine with the story of this isolated Jewish community that was now living in scattered poverty in their mountain villages, but which during one period had even ruled the Ethiopian kingdom. When I was a child, my imagination had been captured by this book; and when I visited Ethiopia with Avraham Yoffe in 1966, I made it a point to visit the Jewish regions of the country and learn as much about these people as I could.

When I entered the government, the issue of the Ethiopian Jews was still on my mind, and I asked Begin to put it on the cabinet agenda. On September 4, 1977, he did, and the cabinet addressed it formally for the first time. The first problem on the floor was whether we could even consider them to be Jews or not. If so, they would fall under the Law of Return; and we would be obligated to do whatever was possible to help the remnants of this community find a safe haven in Israel. But it was not an easy question. Though all of these people considered themselves Jewish, still they had been separated from any of the known branches of Judaism for so long that the beliefs and ceremonies they observed created questions about the authenticity of their Judaism.

Minister of Interior Dr. Joseph Burg from the National Religious Party was one of those who argued strongly against admitting the Ethiopians. In the first place, he said, we are not even sure if they are Jews. Beyond that there was no doubt, in his opinion, that we would have major difficulties absorbing them, economically, socially, and culturally. There were other serious problems too, including medical questions.

I took exactly the opposite position. I did not, I told the cabinet, consider myself capable of deciding whether they were Jews or not; but I was quite willing to abide by the decision of the Sephardic chief rabbi, Ovadya Josef, who had ruled they were. "If he says yes," I told them, "then for me it's enough. In my eyes they are Jews . . . I know some of them, distinguished soldiers who served in the armed forces, students in the universities. An attempt to demonstrate that Israeli society is unable to absorb them is not the right approach. We have already absorbed people who came from undeveloped areas. And if there are any we have not successfully absorbed, then we don't have to put the blame only on them but also on past Israeli governments, on the Jewish Agency, on other factors, and maybe even on each of us individually."

I said that circumstances in Ethiopia might easily change for the worse. We were speaking here about an area that was in a deteriorating situation, and consequently we could not predict what the fate of that community might be. "They are scattered in fifteen hundred villages," I said. "There are places where they are sitting in quite large concentrations, as there are also places where there are only a few of them. But that should not affect our decision. The issue of disease among them [that Burg had raised] should also not be an issue for discussion here. We bring to Israel every Jew who needs to come to Israel. And I think we will be doing something terrible if there is an existing danger to a group of Jews and we do not give them our hand, even if they are problematic. . . . I saw them in Ethiopia, and I was happy to find that there was a Jewish community there, even though they don't look exactly like ourselves. There are other Jews too who don't look like ourselves. I believe Israel should take this opportunity to bring these people out."

The opportunity I was referring to was that, although by 1977 the Ethiopian revolution had taken place and Haile Selassie, the Lion of Judah, was already dead, the Soviets had not yet become an important factor in Ethiopian affairs. There was at the time a border war going on between Ethiopia and Somalia, and the Ethiopians had recently asked us for military help. As far as I was concerned, we should be open to this request; but we should make the release of the Jewish community a condition for any assistance. "I know we will not succeed in getting 28,000 out. [This was the number of Jews still in Ethiopia according to our information at the time. It turned out to be an underestimate.] But maybe we will get several thousand. And every soul that we can save we must save. . . . We have to bring them, and I will look at it as one of the most important and blessed acts of the government."

I got support on this issue from Finance Minister Yigal Hurevitz and also from Moshe Dayan, although Dayan wanted to give them all health checks before they left. But I told the cabinet that we would not be able to set up screening stations in those Ethiopian villages. And just imagine, I said, if we take some poverty-stricken refugee who has hardly been able to keep body and soul together and has managed somehow to trek out of those mountains, and we tell him he has syphilis and will not be able to come to Israel until he recovers. It will be the worst thing that could possibly happen to this person. Instead we should bring them to Israel and keep whoever is ill in medical quarantine and give them the treatment they need right here.

At this, Dr. Burg interjected loudly that he would never accept such an idea; and Dayan, who was always looking for compromises, said he didn't see that we had to deal with that question immediately. Why couldn't we just make some preliminary checks, see what the situation was, see how many actually wanted to come, see how many of them were healthy, how many ill—then we would know what we were talking about. At this point we could entertain a concrete proposal.

When I refused categorically to accept Dayan's suggestion, Begin said, "I see that this big plan is raising all kinds of questions and problems. Therefore I would like the cabinet to accept the following: First we should decide to approach the matter of bringing the Falashas out positively. Then I would like to be authorized to write a letter to Mengistu [Mengistu Haile Mariam, Ethiopia's president] to ask him to give the approval we want."

That was how the Ethiopian rescue operation started. After the meeting Begin initiated a correspondence with Mengistu that showed promise of resulting in an organized evacuation operation co-ordinated with the Ethiopian government. Unfortunately, a short time later in an interview in France, Dayan inadvertently revealed the secret that Israel was assisting Ethiopia with arms. With that exposure the weapons deal fell apart and progress toward rescuing the Ethiopian Jews came to an abrupt halt.

It was not long afterwards that the furies began to light on Ethiopia. Revolution, counterrevolution, rebellion, and famine joined forces to make large parts of the country uninhabitable by its own people. A mass movement of the displaced began, an army of near naked refugees walking sometimes over six hundred miles through the otherworldly Ethiopian landscape. And among those hundreds of thousands came thousands of Jews heading to the Sudan and, they hoped, toward eventual salvation in Israel.

During seven years, from 1978 to 1984, we were able to bring more than 8,000 of these souls to Israel. Later, in one operation mounted with the help of the United States, we were able to bring out another 8,000. Despite the misgivings, they have been absorbed. The process has not been without problems. Deaths and family separations in Ethiopia and during their lives as refugees have affected them severely. And in Israel itself there have been religious and cultural difficulties. But none of these have prevented the Ethiopian Jews from becoming a positive, productive element in Israeli life, adapting well to an industrial and technological society totally alien to anything in their experience.

In 1982 the evacuation that brought them to us was just beginning to gain momentum. Even now, seven years later, it is too early to tell the entire story.

29

Prelude to Lebanon

Despite its unique history, the Ethiopian exodus was only the most recent in the successive migrations of refugee Jewish communities to Israel. Consequently, although more exotic than most, the Ethiopian Jews and their story were essentially familiar to Israelis, whose nation was built through the absorption of displaced peoples. The other subjects Nimeiry and I took up would also have rung a familiar note with those Israelis who knew the quieter side of their country's traditional foreign policy. There was nothing at all unusual or groundbreaking about my interest in the Sudan and Ethiopia, or in Libya, Chad, or the Central African Republic, nor even about discussions of Riza Pahlavi's plan to liberate Iran.

The fact was that every Israeli government starting with Ben-Gurion's has wrestled with the profound difficulties of existing in isolation amid a sea of enemies. For Begin's predecessors as prime minister and mine as defense minister one answer had always been to look for allies among the peripheral nations. Historically there has been a consensus on the subject. And often daring measures have been taken to outflank the Arab ring, always in the hope that one day the isolation would end and we could devote ourselves to the normal intercourse of neighbors. But in the meantime our preservation demanded that we look beyond the circle for ways to make friends for ourselves and enemies for our enemies.

Even in the years when Israel was a small country facing terrible security and economic problems, when it was absorbing hundreds of thousands of penniless Jewish refugees, even then we took active steps beyond our borders. It was in our interest, we believed, to support the Kurds as they fought for independence from Iraq, one of the most viciously hostile of Israel's enemies. Israeli officers and doctors were on active service then in the Kurdistan mountains, in places so remote the only way to get them was by horseback. It was considered in our interest too to back the Yemenites during their struggle against Nasser's five-year-long invasion of their country in the 1960s. They were, after all, draining the most powerful of all our antagonists.

For the Israeli government in the '60s, Sudan's oppressed Christian minority also seemed worthy of assistance; the Sudan was Egypt's main supporter. Our people and supplies were there too, though they had to make their way hundreds of miles through Africa to do it. We were in various other areas of Africa as well, while in Lebanon there had been traditional contacts with the Maronites, like the Jews a minority people at risk.

My own direct contact with the Lebanon situation came first in 1976, when as Yitzhak Rabin's adviser I had recommended against permitting a Syrian occupation force to enter the country. By then the PLO had established control over parts of southern Lebanon and Beirut and had shredded the political balance through which Lebanese Christians, Shi'ites, Sunnis, and Druze had governed the country for thirty-three years. One result was that terror attacks along Israel's northern border increased in frequency and horror, including an assault on a school in Maalot in which twenty-one children were murdered and sixty-eight wounded and an assault on a school bus at Avivim where nine children were killed and nineteen more injured. Another consequence was the outbreak of civil war, fought primarily between Christians, who wanted to reassert the old national balance, and the PLO, whose "state within a state" could not survive alongside a coherent central government in Beirut.

Intervening in this situation, ostensibly as peacemakers, the Syrians first attacked the PLO and appeared to back the Lebanese Christians and their allies. But before long they were demonstrating that their true interests had nothing to do with an independent Lebanon. (In fact Syria has never recognized Lebanon and continues to formally regard the country as part of Greater Syria.) With the strategic objective of establishing dominance in Lebanon, Syrian tactics changed according to the needs of the moment. Soon they were drawing back from the Christians and linking themselves with the PLO and other Moslem leftist factions. As early as 1976 they had begun sporadic assaults on the Christian militias. On January 21 and 22 they supported a massive PLO attack on the Christian coastal town of Damour. When it was over, many of the Christian inhabitants had been massacred and the rest driven out.

Damour was the bloodiest example of the emerging Lebanese reality. All along the Lebanese coast, from Beirut to Tyre and across a wide swath of southern Lebanon from the Mediterranean to the Bekaa Valley, Syria's reorientation gave the PLO the opportunity to consolidate its control. In effect the PLO was now quickly re-establishing sovereignty over a mini-state virtually contiguous to Israel's northern border.

For Israel the consequences were deadly. Terrorist attacks originating from PLO-held territory increased, and every attempt to respond automatically involved the risk of collision with the Syrians, whose forces in many areas overlapped the PLO units and shielded them. As infiltrations and artillery assaults multiplied and the Galilee became a permanent target, the Rabin government undertook a series of defensive measures. Israel's army took steps to protect the northern Galilee, strengthening defenses and extending additional support to Major Sa'ad Haddad's Christian enclaves in the border area. Rabin and Defense Minister Shimon Peres established contact with Lebanese Christian leaders in the north and created a pipeline for Israeli military assistance. If it was in Israel's interest to help the Kurds six hundred miles away and the Ethiopians over a thousand miles away, no one had any doubts about the need to support the Christians who were fighting for their lives against the PLO on our very doorstep.

This was the situation the Likud government found when it took office in 1977. Although Prime Minister Begin and his new defense minister, Ezer Weizman, continued the Labor government's policies toward Lebanon, they soon realized that they were in the middle of a deteriorating situation. Whatever measures they took, the PLO raids and artillery terror only intensified. The problem was that the kingdom of terror had no address. You could not act against them as you would against a country that cared for its people and would stop aggressive actions if its population was suffering as a consequence. On the contrary, the PLO leaders established their headquarters and arms depots inside camps and cities, taking cover behind the population. Any Palestinian civilian casualties they counted as propaganda victories for themselves.

Unable to effectively defend the Galilee, the Begin government began to plan a ground operation against the PLO in southern Lebanon up to the Litani River, approximately fifteen miles from the border. While stopping short of Syrian lines in the Bekaa, Defense Minister Ezer Weizman and Commander-in-Chief Motta Gur intended with one massive thrust to sweep the Lebanese border area free of terrorists.

On March 11, 1978, a PLO squad from Lebanon eluded Israeli naval patrols and landed on the coast south of Haifa. There they hijacked a tour bus and murdered thirty-nine people, including mothers and children. Triggered by this incident, Israeli forces struck into Lebanon, killing or capturing whatever Palestinian forces they found. After three months of occupation and searching, the "Litani Operation" (as it was called) came to an end and Israeli forces returned behind the border.

Unfortunately, this action provided only a respite for the beleaguered Galilee. The limited goals of the operation, its relatively brief duration, and its restraint in dealing with the major terrorist base at Tyre allowed the PLO to quickly move back into most of the territory it had lost. This result enabled the PLO leadership to view the Litani Operation as an achievement for themselves, proof that even a major Israeli action could do them little permanent harm.

But with the expansion of Haddad's border enclaves into a security strip and the introduction of U.N. units in the wake of Litani, they also changed the emphasis of their operations. Moving away from the concept of small-unit infiltration they began building a heavy concentration of Katyusha rocket launchers and long-range artillery capable of hitting most of the towns and villages in Israel's northern zone. By late 1978 an artillery war against the Galilee's civilian population was upon us.

The lessons of the Litani Operation were not lost on either Defense Minister Weizman or Chief of Staff Gur. They recognized, as did we all, that to effectively deal with the PLO in southern Lebanon something more than a simple retaliation exercise, even a large one would be required. The PLO was entrenched and resilient, with bases and training centers throughout the southern tier, with major troop, weapons, and supply depots in the port cities of Sidon and Tyre, with command centers and more troop concentrations in Beirut. It controlled population centers and a civilian infrastructure and received lavish support from Arab League states, particularly Saudi Arabia. We knew that in Lebanon the PLO and its sister organizations were amassing an arsenal that could shortly make normal life in the upper Galilee impossible. Intelligence told us too that they had intensified training of terrorists who would be launched not just at Israel but at Israeli and Jewish targets around the world.

For the past eight years we had watched Lebanon being dismembered in front of our eyes. And now we could see the results. A neighboring country which had lived at peace with us since 1949 had ceased to exist, and a true kingdom of terror had emerged on our northern doorstep.

Any effective approach to this situation, we knew, would have to look not just at specific local targets but at the entire PLO military and political infrastructure in Lebanon. And this, whether we liked it or not, would force us to take into account the entire Lebanese tangle. Any operation strong enough to deal with the PLO state within a state would almost inevitably also put us in conflict with Syrian occupation forces in the southern Bekaa and in West Beirut, which had become the Palestinian terrorist capital and where most of the planning for their local, regional, and international operations took place. It would also bring us into contact with the Christian north, in Beirut, Junia, and on Mount Lebanon. In 1978 we had tried to restrict ourselves to a local operation. Whatever circumstances might develop in the future, we now had to think in terms of a plan that would affect the overall situation.

Under the guidance of Ezer Weizman the General Headquarters did just that. In 1979 the IDF prepared a plan whose "intent" paragraph stated: "The IDF will occupy south Lebanon up to the Junia-Zahle line [that is, to the Christian enclave north of Beirut], will destroy terrorist forces so as to create a new situation in the area [and], will destroy Syrian and Lebanese forces as may be necessary in executing the mission."[*] We all knew that any implementation of such a plan or any part of it would be determined by future contingencies. In Lebanon we were dealing not only with the terror organizations but with complex factional warfare, with an unpredictable Syrian occupation army; and with a nervous international climate. Yet we also knew that there was no alternative to defending ourselves and that in the end we might have to act decisively.

Nor did Weizman in any way attempt to shy away from that eventuality. Following the attack on the Kibbutz Misgav Am children's

---

[*]In its essentials this was the "Peace for Galilee" plan that was implemented in June 1982.

nursery, he announced at the cabinet meeting of April 8, 1980, that "one has to carry out meaningful operations in the war against the terrorists. . . . In the end we would have to reach a situation whereby we control a large part of Lebanon, starting from Beaufort to relieve Haddad, up to the Zahrani, and to Beirut."

By the middle of 1980 the Christian side of Lebanon's chaotic affairs had begun to sort itself out. Through a combination of violence and political maneuvering the Phalange, one of the three major Christian parties, was asserting its undisputed leadership. The Phalangist patriarch was Pierre Gemayel, who had created the party out of his family base back in the 1930s. But the new driving force was his second son, Bashir. Young, talented, and ambitious, Bashir had begun a campaign in 1978 to gain control of the Christian Front at the expense of the Phalange's chief rivals, Camille Chamoun's National Liberals and Suleiman Franjieh's political family. By July 1980 he had succeeded.

But Bashir Gemayel's pursuit of power was something more than simple warlord politics. Bashir represented the line of Phalangist thought that regarded the Lebanese Christian community as an entity that could best survive by first unifying itself and then by looking beyond the essentially hostile Moslem political world that surrounded it. It was an orientation sensitive to the need for outside alliances, and Bashir was eager to deepen and specify the long-term relationship the Maronites had maintained with Israel.

It was also evident that Bashir Gemayel's unification of the Christian community was not an end in itself. He was not working toward an enclosed and autonomous Christian mini-state, an option some Maronites had always favored. Instead, like his father and other traditionalists, Moslem as well as Christian, he wanted to reconstitute the independent national government that had been buried by the PLO first and then reinterred by the Syrians. In this government the president had traditionally been a Christian and the prime minister a Sunni Moslem. Building a consolidated Christian bloc was a necessary step toward the position Gemayel clearly had his eye on: the Lebanese presidency itself.

Bashir Gemayel's assertion of leadership was a significant development. While Israeli policy had never defined the establishment of a friendly government in Lebanon as a primary goal, nevertheless we always had a strong interest in the kind of government Lebanon would have. Would Lebanon's government invite Syrian forces to stay or insist on their removal? Would it acquiesce to the independent PLO mini-state or work toward establishing its own control? Would the Lebanese government accept a state of war between Israel and those who were using its territory, or would it look for ways to co-exist peacefully with us? On all of these vital subjects Gemayel's rise to power threw a promising light.

In April 1981, two months before the Israeli national elections, the fighting between Lebanon's Christians and the Syrian occupation army flared around the city of Zahle. Zahle was a Christian enclave of about 200,000 people, ten miles east of the Phalangist area of Mount Lebanon and twenty miles east of Beirut. Because the Damascus–Beirut highway running in front of Zahle was in Syrian hands, the Phalangists and their Zahle allies attempted to build a road outside of Syrian control that would link them together.

Fearing any further consolidation of Christian power, the Syrians reacted sharply. Zahle was surrounded and pounded by massive, prolonged artillery bombardments in a siege that was to last for three months. Syrian forces also hit Phalangist positions on top of Mount Sanin, which dominated not just Zahle to the east but also the major Christian port city of Junia to the west. Using assault helicopters, they were able to press home their attack, threatening to overrun the mountaintop defenses. Knowing that once these positions were in Syrian hands the Maronite territorial defenses would be in jeopardy, the Phalangists appealed to Israel for help.

For the most part, our discussion about this situation proceeded on a bipartisan basis. Labor's shadow minister of defense, Chaim Bar-Lev, for example, presented his "defense conception" on April 13, declaring that "We should help the northern Christians not only because we are neighbors and cannot remain impartial to such annihilation by the Syrians . . . What happens there has direct relevance for us not only from the humanitarian aspect . . . If the Christians in the north collapse, there will also be direct implications for the situation in the south."

The end result of our deliberations was that on April 28 Israeli air force jets were sent to shoot down Syrian helicopters taking part in the assault on Mount Sanin. With two of their helicopters destroyed that day, the

Syrians were now on notice that we would not condone any further advance into the Christian area. And though they were able to take the "French Room" fortifications on the mountain's peak, the Syrians never did manage to move forward from there. Our intervention had had its desired effect.

Syrian President Hafez al-Assad's response to the helicopter downings was to escalate the crisis. Ground-to-air missile batteries were deployed in the Bekaa, and Syrian armored forces were introduced there. Inside Syria, longer-range antiaircraft missiles were installed near the border, covering large portions of Lebanese airspace.

The introduction of these missiles dramatically altered the balance between ourselves and the Syrian occupation army that had been the basis of Rabin's agreement in 1976 to allow the Syrians into Lebanon. The missiles gave Syrian forces the ability to intervene against our retaliatory air strikes on PLO positions, and they inhibited the reconnaissance flights over Lebanese territory that we considered essential. These flights allowed us to monitor developments in Lebanon, but they also gave us the ability to "see" inside Syria, providing an important part of our early-warning system against Syrian mobilization. For us this was not an acceptable development.

During the Yom Kippur War the Soviet missile systems had caused us serious fighter losses. Studying the lessons of that experience in the intervening years, we had developed the technical means of dealing with them. By this time we had no doubt about our ability to destroy the missiles with little risk to ourselves.

Making the decision to do exactly that, on April 30 the cabinet gave approval for a raid against the batteries. Bad weather conditions, though, forced its cancellation. As the cabinet reviewed its decision to strike, the Americans sent Philip Habib, a senior State Department diplomat, to attempt to negotiate a resolution. Whether Habib's efforts would bear fruit we did not know, but his presence in the area helped freeze the situation, at least for the moment. If nothing else, it gave us the opportunity to reconsider our course of action.

I was one of those most pleased with the decision to postpone our attack against the missiles. Other more pressing matters were before us at precisely that moment: the Sadat-Begin summit in Sharm al-Sheikh and, most crucial of all, the operation against the Iraqi nuclear reactor. The reactor, I knew, had to be destroyed. But a strike against the missiles first might well put the Arab air forces into a state of alert, making the reactor situation too problematic.

All the while, Labor was creating yet another set of problems. During the election campaign Begin had promised to get rid of the missiles. ("Assad," he had called out at one of the biggest rallies, "Raful and Yanush are waiting for you.") Now they were mocking him viciously for his inactivity, while at the same time they were accusing him of dragging the nation into war. On our side we knew that we were not dragging the nation anyplace but that these things had to be done, that we had no alternative.

Against this complicated backdrop I argued strongly against hitting the Syrians, and eventually my position was accepted. As Begin noted in a cabinet meeting on May 14, "Arik is convinced there should not be a war, and he can appear in public and say so. . . . In my opinion this is very important, especially since there are rumors that Arik is pushing me into war. I have stated that I am not easily pushed."

But even as we attempted to alleviate tensions with the Syrians, the PLO escalated its assault on the Galilee. Perhaps encouraged by our inaction against the missile umbrella, they now initiated an artillery war whose goal was to bring normal life in the northern towns and villages to a halt. Through May and June 1981, the artillery and Katyusha shelling became more ferocious. In mid-July it reached a crescendo. During the week of July 14 to July 21 thirty-three Israeli towns and settlements were hit by over a thousand shells and rockets.

Although the Galilee was dotted with Israeli military camps and installations, the terrorists concentrated exclusively on civilian targets. Typical of the orders that went out from PLO command centers in Tyre, Sidon, and Beirut to artillery batteries in the south is the following from Yasser Arafat:

To Brother El Hadj Ismail [commander of PLO forces, Southern Region]: Greetings and Blessings of the Revolution Be upon You.

The resolution of the General Military Committee is to concentrate on destroying Kiryat Shemona, Metulla, Dan, Sh'ar Yeshuv, Nahariya and its suburbs.

Kiryat Shemona: All elements of the Revolution will take part in hitting this objective. Kiryat Shemona is to be bombarded by "improved Grad" missiles.

Metulla will be shelled by the Palestine Liberation Front and by Saika using 160 mm mortars.

Nahariya and its suburbs will be shelled by the First Battalion using 130 mm artillery.

Dan and Sh'ar Yeshuv will be dealt with by the Eastern Region.

Yasser Arafat
July 18, 1981
1400 hours[*]

In Kiryat Shemona, Metulla, Nahariya, Kibbutz Dan, and a dozen other places people took to the shelters, often living there for days at a time. Hospitals and schools were hit as well as businesses, homes, and fields. Apart from the casualties and destruction, the bombardment created an atmosphere of constant anxiety. Never knowing when or where a rocket or shell might hit, people found it impossible to carry on their daily lives. With the army obviously unable to protect them, thousands of people from the northern Galilee and the Galilee "finger" began to leave their towns and farming villages, moving southward to safety.

In fact the IDF was responding sharply to the PLO's artillery war, returning gunfire and bombing terrorist bases in Beirut as well as southern Lebanon. But the retaliation proved incapable of curbing the assault. By this time the PLO had built an extensive infrastructure in the Southern Lebanon hills. Hidden in tunnels and caves, the guns and Katyushas could be brought out for a quick bombardment, then returned to hiding before Israeli jets were able to locate them. Deployed in this fashion, the PLO artillery was essentially immune. With Israeli countermeasures growing increasingly desperate, on July 16 Commander-in-Chief Eytan proposed to the cabinet a massive and wide-ranging air attack on PLO command positions and military stores throughout Lebanon.

Eytan's proposed operation was, I thought, a necessary one, and I supported it. But I was also sure that even the kind of comprehensive strike he had planned would not bring any resolution to our predicament. The PLO in Lebanon was simply too strong to be seriously affected by limited measures. Whatever we have done, I told the cabinet on July 16, has elicited continued reactions, which at this point are massive. "The complete elimination of the issue can only be brought about if the

---

[*] This is one of hundreds of captured PLO documents assembled in *The Lebanon War: Arab Documents and Sources, Volume A: The Road to the Peace of Galilee War,* ed. R. Avi-Ram (Ma'arachot, 1987), p. 107. Other documents specify targets, assault units, number of shells to be fired, instructional codes, and other details.

terrorists' political-military infrastructure no longer exists. . . . If one wants to speak of a complete solution of this matter—and obviously a further analysis must be made—it should take in the entire area, including Beirut."

There was no doubt in my mind that we could not afford the paralysis of life in northern Israel and the contraction of its population that the PLO's artillery terror was bringing about. Since 1979 the government had had before it the "Oranim Plan" (as it was now called) for a military operation to eliminate the PLO military and political infrastructure in Lebanon. The time had come to put some version of it into effect. To do this a cabinet decision would be necessary. I therefore asked that a full-scale discussion be undertaken immediately.

As the cabinet considered its options, the comprehensive air strikes that Eytan had requested were carried out on PLO areas in Beirut and elsewhere. Now, with the level of violence intensifying, Philip Habib began a series of negotiations aimed at arranging a cease-fire. At the same time, Begin was touring the northern border visiting the underground bomb shelters where people had been living for days on end in sweltering, filthy conditions. Deeply disturbed by what he saw, by the last week in July Begin was ready to accept the American-sponsored border cease-fire.

In the cabinet debates that followed I strenuously opposed the cease-fire, stressing that if we accepted it we would soon find ourselves in a very difficult situation. No doubt the PLO would reduce its activity along the Lebanese border in accord with the letter of the agreement, but at the same time I was sure that would step up their activities elsewhere, sending squads into Israel through Jordan and intensifying terrorism from their cells on the West Bank and in Gaza. They would also be free to undertake actions all over the world, these too orchestrated from their headquarters in Beirut. Meanwhile our hands would be tied by the cease-fire.

Consequently I argued that if we were going to have an agreement it should cover terrorist actions anywhere within Israel, Samaria, Judea and Gaza, and also against Jewish and Israeli targets abroad. Unfortunately I could not convince the government on this matter, and on July 24 Israel undertook to observe a moratorium on actions against the PLO, and the PLO undertook to cease attacks on Israel and on the Haddad zone from Lebanon.

Over the following months this agreement was subject to further clarification, and eventually the Americans agreed that the cease-fire would also apply to all terrorist actions inside Israel. But they did not agree that it would cover Jews and Israelis abroad, and with that the PLO was given carte blanche for murder around the world. As these incidents began to take place, I emphasized again and again to the American representatives that we would eventually have to take steps against these activities.

Though in July both sides were receptive to Habib's diplomacy, the cease-fire was not in any way a resolution of the underlying problem. The PLO's raison d'etre, enshrined in its charter, was "to eliminate the Zionist presence from Palestine." Though they may have been ready for a period of quiet, for them a cease-fire could only be a tactical phase that would help them prepare for the resumption of violence. Unable to accept on our borders a PLO state dedicated to our destruction, we too did not consider that the cease-fire would be permanent.

Although the cease-fire achieved a welcome period of quiet for the Galilee, behind the protection it afforded the PLO undertook a major buildup of modern long-range artillery (mostly acquired from the Soviets through the Syrians and Libyans) and continued to expand its infrastructure of command centers, prepared positions, and ammunition depots. Over the next eleven months the PLO arsenal grew to include approximately ninety 122- and 130-mm cannon and 100 vehicle-mounted Katyusha launchers (with thirty to forty tubes on each vehicle) in addition to large numbers of shorter-range field artillery, 100 tanks, 150 armored personnel carriers, 200 anti-aircraft guns, and 200 anti-tank guns. Although the PLO could deploy only some 15,000 to 20,000 armed regulars, the artillery was the equivalent of normal equipment for four to five full divisions. None of those who knew the figures had any doubt why the terrorists were buying weapons like these in such quantities or about how they intended to use them.

At the same time PLO actions continued in various parts of Israel, the Haddad zone and overseas. Tourists were murdered in Jerusalem. Arabs were assassinated in Judea and Samaria, attacks were staged on a Jewish neighborhood in Antwerp, a Jewish restaurant in Berlin, a synagogue in Vienna. From July 1981 to June 1982 these and other incidents left fifteen dead and 250 wounded. Many other actions were either disrupted by Israeli security people or failed to injure anyone—including an aborted rocket attack on Eilat, bombs placed in buses and phone booths, and an attempt to blow up a kindergarten in Holon.

Under pressure from the Americans to keep the cease-fire, we restrained ourselves, watching as the terrorist incidents multiplied and as more and more batteries were deployed across the border. But it was impossible to see how in the long run we could allow this to continue. Habib and the Americans understood that as well as we did, but they continued to play for time in the hope of devising a diplomatic formula that might achieve a Syrian withdrawal, a removal of the PLO heavy weapons, and conditions for the re-establishment of a viable Lebanese government in the next elections. Given Syria's long-term intentions in Lebanon and the PLO's irreversible desire to destroy Israel, someone other than Habib might have thrown up his hands and started looking for another way. But he kept at it, even as his efforts failed to make headway and as our patience grew increasingly frayed.

One unfortunate consequence of the lack of progress was heightened friction between the Americans and ourselves. In my talks and also in Begin's talks with Habib and with Ambassador Sam Lewis, the discrepancy between American and Israeli views became increasingly evident and increasingly exasperating. In a discussion with Habib in early December I complained bitterly about PLO violations of the cease-fire. What was needed, I said, were free elections and a parliamentary government that could bring Lebanon into the free world and bring about peace with Israel, either formally or informally. But free elections were impossible while the Syrians occupied Beirut and the Christian areas between Zahle and Beirut. As long as they were there, any government in Lebanon would be under Syrian control. The other obstacle was the PLO. Lebanon had become the center of world terrorism, and with 15,000 or more PLO in the country there was no chance for either elections or any kind of stability.

Habib did not disagree with the analysis. But his approach was to first ease the Syrians out through "some mechanism" that would substitute other Arab forces for the Syrians, then to address the Palestinian problem.

To my way of thinking, the American plans were hopeless. Number one, the Syrians were not going to step aside for any other Arab troops (they didn't, of course), and number two, we would not under any circumstances allow still more hostile Arab troops into Lebanon. (It was a terrible mistake to have permitted the Syrians in in the first place.) There was no way to ease either the Syrians or the PLO out painlessly. Nor were we going to stand still eternally for the continuing violence against us.

"The policy of our government is to keep the cease-fire as long as possible," I told Habib. "But if something happens, take it for granted that we will not come back to the situation we had in July. I want to tell you friendly and openly that we will not accept that kind of warfare again . . . This government has decided it cannot have a war of attrition where the targets are children and mothers and old people. So we may face a situation that will develop against our will and against your will, but it will develop. I am not proposing a plan, I am just saying what can be done: a swift, fast move . . . which will cause such heavy casualties to the terrorists that they will not stay there as a political or military factor. . . . This is my personal solution to the problem. It would solve it immediately, and 15,000 armed terrorists would not be there afterwards. Then we will have an entirely different situation. But that is if you really want to solve the problem."

"I want to solve it," Habib answered. "But I want to solve it another way."[*]

In further discussions I tried to persuade Habib how significant an independent and democratic Lebanon would be. "I believe it is in your interest," I told him, "to have another free country here that is part of the free world. I don't see, going from the Soviet border to the Atlantic [across the Middle East and North Africa], that you have one country besides Israel that is a stable democracy. Try to look around. Iran will never be one . . . Syria will never be. Egypt is not a democracy. Libya? You take all these countries—right to the Atlantic. The only one is Israel. The other one that may be is Lebanon. Lebanon could have been the second country in this area. But for that to happen the Syrians must withdraw, at least from a certain part of the country, and the military strength of the terrorists must be reduced if not destroyed completely."[†]

As the PLO continued to acquire and deploy heavy weapons in southern Lebanon, it became apparent that preparation for a real war of attrition was under way. At the same time, I reviewed and refined the military plans drawn up after the Litani Operation. Like every military plan, "Oranim" visualized the most far-reaching objectives possible; in this case the ultimate target was the destruction of the PLO command centers and infrastructure throughout Lebanon, including in Beirut. But also like every military plan, Oranim posited a series of interim objectives, each one logical in itself. I did not at this point know what part if any of this plan the government might at some point approve. But

---

[*] Meeting, November 4, 1981.
[†] Meeting, March 1, 1982.

when the adaptation was completed in November 1981, the objectives of
the overall plan were defined in essence as follows:

1. The main objective is the annihilation of the terrorist threat, i.e.,
the destruction of their military strength as well as their entire infrastructure, including in particular in Beirut.

2. [A second objective is] to neutralize the Syrians through threatening
maneuvers while attempting to avoid real fighting with them.

3. The minimum objective, which should be guaranteed as soon as the
operation begins, is to remove all northern settlements from shelling
range.

4. These operations should be carried out so that Shi'ites, Druze, and
Christians will not be harmed.

5. We have no interest in keeping forces for long periods of time in
areas we would capture. Our success in achieving all the above mentioned
goals will enable us to withdraw.

6. The operation is not aimed at guaranteeing the integrity or the
sovereignty of the government of Lebanon over all its territory. This is a
matter for the Lebanese themselves.

7. Linking up with the Christian zone in the north is the precondition
for attaining all the above mentioned objectives, since that is the only way
to cut off Beirut and the only way to cut the Beirut–Damascus highway
without tackling the main Syrian deployment in the Bekaa.

Although we had now refined our plans, I made it clear to the General
Headquarters staff in a meeting on December 14 at the Defense Ministry
that we still hoped the cease-fire would hold up, and that Oranim was a
contingency plan only. "I want to emphasize," I told the senior officers,
"that we currently have no intention of violating the cease-fire and we have
no intention today of going to war. We want to avoid it." The following
day, December 15, I met with commanders and staff officers of the
northern divisions and repeated what I had told the General Headquarters
staff. We hoped that the cease-fire would hold up. We would only implement Oranim if shelling of the northern settlements was renewed.

But while I wanted them to be precisely aware of the government's
position on the cease-fire, I also wanted to be sure that all the senior and
junior officers knew the entire scope and meaning of all the objectives
incorporated in the full military plan. I kept nothing back at these
meetings. "As far as the [PLO] political arm goes, that is to say their
Beirut command posts, that means we have to reach Beirut. . . . A

second goal is a certain Syrian withdrawal. . . . A third has a more political aspect, the creation of a link between the Christians in the north and Israel so that an elected government can really be established there . . . which would have contacts with the free world . . . [and] a peace agreement or peaceful co-existence with Israel. . . . Civilians should not be hurt." My orders were detailed and clear. So were those of the General Headquarters and the Northern Command. Throughout the army as throughout the cabinet there was not a shadow of doubt about the range of goals we would consider should the cease-fire collapse.

I also wanted to see Lebanon myself, to get as much of a feel as I could for the situation on the ground there and especially to try to understand what, if anything, we could expect from the Lebanese Christian forces in the event of war. I had first met Bashir Gemayel while I was still minister of agriculture during one of his visits to Jerusalem to discuss the assistance we were providing. He had impressed me then as a young man full of self-confidence and determination. He spoke convincingly and with authority, and there was no question he had already demonstrated real leadership ability. Nevertheless I felt that the only way to make an adequate assessment was to visit him on his own ground, to see his people in their homes, to see their families, their forces, their positions, to understand everything I could about the man himself and the condition of his movement.

Begin agreed and authorized the trip. Meanwhile Gemayel had himself invited me to come to Lebanon to meet with him, his father, Pierre Gemayel, and other leaders. The Christian position, he said was becoming increasingly precarious. The Syrian army continued to slice away at their forces, slowly but steadily compressing the Christian-controlled area. It was important, Gemayel said, that someone come to see the situation firsthand.

Eventually we told Gemayel that a "high ranking official" would be arriving in early January 1982. Then we began making arrangements for the trip, a complicated job in itself considering that there was no way to reach the Christian enclave by land and that the entire area was a war zone.

The best and perhaps the only feasible way of going was by helicopter over the Mediterranean. For this we had to bring along rubber boats, lifesaving equipment, emergency landing equipment, and a security team, for myself and for the people accompanying me—including the chief of military intelligence, Yehoshua Saguy, and the deputy commander-in-chief, Moshe Levy. A rescue squad also came along in case we were forced down at sea. Altogether the helicopter was choked with people, rafts, ropes, communication sets, and everything else that might make a dangerous trip uncomfortable as well.

We left Tel Aviv at dark and flew along the coast to Haifa. There the helicopter turned out to sea, skirting the Lebanese coast with its concentrations of antiaircraft guns. We saw the lights of Tyre appear on our right, then those of Sidon. A half hour later Beirut came into sight, and we turned farther out to sea, watching tracer bullets streak through the sky near the city.

Finally we made for Junia, the Christian port city north of Beirut. When we landed on the beach, our liaison people were waiting along with Bashir Gemayel and his top commanders. As I stepped down from the helicopter, he embraced and kissed me in the Arab fashion saying, "I knew you would be the one to come. Even though they didn't tell me, I was sure it would be you."

Looking around to get my bearings, I was surprised to see hundreds of lights bobbing against the blackness of the water. "Those are ships," Bashir told me, "cargo ships." "But there's a war going on. How can you have ships out there like that?" I asked. "Yes," came the reply, "there is a war; but war is one thing, business is something else entirely." I should know, Bashir said, that as bad as it was, the war had never interfered with trade and commercial relations. (The casualties in this war since 1975 had reached 100,000 dead and a quarter of a million wounded—in a country of three million people.) Freighters came, and their cargoes were shipped by truck all over the region—to the Gulf Emirates, to Damascus, to Saudi Arabia, to Jordan. Always they could find an open road or a way through.

From the beach we were taken to a house in Junia where an elaborate dinner had been prepared, then left for a quick tour of Beirut, which I wanted to see before the next morning's heavy schedule of tours and meetings. With Bashir at the wheel and a car full of his security people in front and another behind, we drove into the capital, where the division between the Christian east and Moslem west reminded me immediately of divided Jerusalem before 1967. Signs of war were all around—guarded crossing points, ruined and bullet-riddled buildings, torn metal grates protecting shops and houses. And yet life in the capital seemed normal, or perhaps even livelier than normal. The streets were jammed with cars honking loudly, many of them driven by elegantly dressed young women wearing bright-colored scarves around their necks. Restaurants were doing a booming business, as were the nightclubs whose neon lights illuminated the crowds that filled the sidewalks. We got out and walked around briefly, taking it all in and marveling at such gaiety amid a six-year-long war for survival.

The next day started early with a visit to the headquarters of the Lebanese Christian forces in the northern section of the Beirut port. (The southern section was controlled by Moslem factions and Syrian troops.) One glance at the activity here made it clear why the ports were the object of some of the most deadly fighting in this war of militias. Possession of a port meant revenue; and revenue meant troops, weapons, and control. You could see the excitement among the Christian soldiers here at this surprise visit by an Israeli minister of defense.

From the headquarters we went to several observation posts that enabled us to get a good look into West Beirut. Then we drove up into the mountains, stopping at a little Christian suburb called Beit Mary (the house of Mary), where we climbed to the second floor of a building that gave us a panoramic view of the entire city. All the landmarks and high points stretched out in front of us—the Beirut airport, the port, and to the south a hill with a large building and a somewhat smaller building on it—the Lebanese Ministry of Defense and the presidential residence.

As we took in the scene and compared what we were looking at with our maps, Bashir picked up the discussion that had started the previous night over dinner. "In case there is a war," he asked, "what would you expect of us?" "In that case, the first thing you should do is to defend your borders here. Because you should know that we will not be able to come to your rescue if you are losing ground little by little. So first defend your borders. Second, do you see that hill there, the defense ministry hill? That hill is vital. If there is a war, take that hill. [The hill, called "Yarzah," was vital because on its slopes ran the Beirut–Damascus highway.] Third, Israel will not enter West Beirut. That's the capital, the government, the foreign embassies. Our presence there would cause complex political problems for us. West Beirut is your business and the business of the Lebanese army."*

Our next stop was Mount Sanin, the site of the crucial fighting

* From transcription of meeting by defense ministry note taker.

between the Syrians and Christians the previous July. The mountain was a well-known resort and ski area, a place where years ago wealthy people from Palestine would go for their vacations. I remembered as a child hearing people talk about what you could do if you were rich. If you had money, they said, Palestine was not so bad. You could enjoy your summers in the Lebanese mountains and your winters in Egypt. I had wondered about that and had tried to imagine something other than spending both summers and winters on the farm at Kfar Malal. Now I was looking at what they had meant. The mountain was beautiful, covered by a light dusting of snow, though not enough that year for skiing. At the very top I could make out the so-called French Room, the fortification that had been captured by the Syrians during the action in which we shot down their helicopters.

After that I toured the mountains and the Christian lines, driving with Bashir in his Mercedes with its car telephone, an item we did not have ourselves in those days. We stopped at one village after another, and he described the history and importance of each of them. At each place people recognized him and applauded, calling out his name. He even stopped his car and got out while units of the Lebanese army passed by, the soldiers waving and cheering. The man was obviously known and obviously popular. It was impossible not to be impressed by the prestige and sympathy he enjoyed. We stopped too in his home village of Bikfayeh, where he took me to the cemetery in which his daughter and other members of his family were buried, where he himself would be buried nine months later.

At the end of a long day in the mountains we returned to Bashir's home in the Ashrafiya neighborhood of Beirut. At the door we were met by his beautiful wife, Solange, a strong personality in her own right as I later came to find out. There too were his father, Pierre Gemayel, and Camille Chamoun, the former president of Lebanon, both now old men but still active and mentally sharp.

When you entered a home in Lebanon, you could not avoid the pictures of family members who have been killed during the war. You saw them in Arab Christian homes and Arab Moslem homes; they had all suffered these tragic losses. Among the Christians the deaths had been caused in fighting against the PLO or against Moslem militias or the Syrians or against rival Christian groups. Here the picture that struck me immediately was of an exceptionally beautiful young girl, Bashir and Solange's daughter—the girl whose grave we had visited just an hour earlier. She had been killed by a bomb planted in the family car, an act of revenge by the Suleiman Franjieh organization. Franjieh's own son, Tony, who had had close ties with the Syrians, had been killed together with his wife and child by the Gemayel family a short time earlier. It was impossible not to feel that these people were living in the throes of bloodshed that had been going on—with intervals of truce—for hundreds of years. Everything in Bashir and Solange's home was exquisite, elegant. A magnificent dinner was served, table manners were perfect, the most beautiful French was spoken—and all of it against this backdrop of assassination and death.

Pierre Gemayel, the patriarch, was a tall, slim figure, upright and aristocratic. Chamoun was shorter and heavier, also much more relaxed. I knew that though they were sitting there together like old friends, only a year ago the Gemayel family had attacked and slaughtered Chamoun's militia, eliminating the Chamoun organization as an effective force and bringing their political assets under Phalangist control.

After the coffee was served, we started to deal with the gamut of significant issues. Pierre Gemayel did most of the talking at first, in French, which was translated into Hebrew by one of the Mossad people with me. As he described the losses and bloodshed they had suffered and the help they wanted from us, this stiff old man began to weep silently. I glanced at Camille Chamoun's face and saw that he was upset at the display of emotion. Through clenched lips he muttered to Gemayel in Arabic, "Ma tebke"—Don't cry.

Among the issues Gemayel and Chamoun raised, foremost was their deep concern about the possibility that the Syrians would continue cutting into the Christian enclave. In September, elections were to take place; and they explained the election system, how many votes they needed to have a good chance at the presidency, and where those votes had to come from. They described the population patterns, emphasizing the numbers of Christians in Zahle, under siege by the Syrians, and in the north, living under Syrian control.

One thing they were intensely interested in. Was there any hope that one day Israel would move into Lebanon? They made the point that if the Syrians became involved in a deeper way than they were now, it would be impossible to resist them. I told them, as I had told Bashir earlier in the day, that Israel was trying to avoid war, but that if the terrorist situation continued, we would have to do something. "And if we do come in," I said, "we would come in in order to defend our northern borders. But as a result of that you might have a chance to restore a normal life to Lebanon. But that would depend very much on peace or a peace arrangement between Israel and Lebanon.

At this Camille Chamoun interrupted to say that he did not believe any Lebanese government would be either able or willing to sign a peace agreement with Israel. Their deep contacts and economic interests in the Arab world—the interconnections between Lebanese and other Arab banks, the large numbers of Lebanese working throughout the Middle East, the trade relationships—would prohibit it. If Pierre Gemayel had given me the impression that at some time in the future a peace arrangement might be possible, he, Camille Chamoun would be much more guarded about it.

We also talked at length about the Christians' relations with the other confessional communities, especially the Shi'ites and Druze. My own recommendation was that they make an attempt to strengthen their ties with these other minorities, even suggesting that, if only for symbolic purposes, some of the arms Israel was supplying them be conveyed to the Shi'ites, who were having their own serious problems with the PLO. Though I did not go into details, the fact was that I never considered the Shi'ites as long-term enemies of Israel; and the Druze were not enemies of any kind. The Israeli Druze community had integrated itself into every aspect of our life, from business to the military. Nor did I view the majority Lebanese Sunnis as necessarily or irrevocably hostile. They had co-existed peacefully with us for two decades; there was no reason they couldn't again. The only real enemies I saw there were the PLO terror organizations and their independent kingdom—they and the Syrians who supported and protected them.

Our discussion lasted for several hours, but when it became dark I had to break it off to return to the beach where our helicopter would soon be arriving to ferry us back to Israel. The problem was that even though there was a war going on, the traffic was jammed. Thousands of beautiful expensive cars clogged the roads, slowing us to a crawl as I worried about missing the carefully timed rendezvous.

When I finally arrived home late that night, Lily was waiting up for me. "How did you find the Lebanese?" she asked. "The impression I got," I told her, "was that they are people who kiss ladies' hands—and murder."

☆   ☆   ☆

Shortly after my return I reported on my visit to Begin and the inner cabinet, describing carefully the subjects that had been covered and my impressions of the Christians' strengths and weaknesses. It was against this more detailed understanding of the Phalangists that the Israeli-Christian relationship developed, confirmed next in Begin's talks with Bashir in Jerusalem on February 16, 1982. At that meeting the prime minister reiterated the conditions under which we would enter Lebanon—if terrorist activities continued and if "it becomes clear to the whole world, to the U.S.A., to Europe, and to the Third World that Israel cannot return to the status quo ante of July 1981. If this happens we shall proceed northward as far as possible."

Two weeks after my return from Lebanon I left for another round of talks with Foreign Minister Kamal Hassan Ali in Cairo. We were within months now of the agreed date for transferring control of the Sinai, and all the problems that move involved were now ripening quickly.

Despite all the tensions during this last phase of negotiations with the Egyptians, Hassan Ali and I managed to maintain a friendship that had been building for several years. Meeting in his office in an old Cairo palace, we discussed the state of our evacuation plans and the remaining difficulties. Then I told him about my visit to Beirut. I knew, of course, that he had already heard about it, just as the Syrians and PLO had heard about it. In Lebanon one does not expect to keep secrets. We ourselves knew, for example, that at the same moment Bashir Gemayel was visiting Israel on his previous trip, his brother Amin was sitting down to negotiations with Yasser Arafat.

So I told Hassan Ali about my visit and discussed what I believed the prospects for peace might be. A Jerusalem-Cairo-Beirut connection was, I suggested, not an impossible idea; and if someday such a thing could be realized, it would change the face of the Middle East.

We talked too about terror. We were, I told him, in an extremely difficult situation. I described the circumstances of the cease-fire agreement and the bind it had put us in. Although we had restrained ourselves, the PLO had not. We knew that orders were broadcast from Lebanon for regional actions that individuals and squads were sent out from there on missions all over the world. (Our intelligence estimate was that in 1981 two thousand individuals from terrorist organizations around the world received their training and weapons in Lebanon. Many of them also took refuge there after they had committed their crimes. Documents captured during the war described courses given for terrorists from El Salvador,

Turkey, Bangladesh, Malawi, Haiti, and Ireland, among others.) From the moment of the cease-fire the PLO and its sister groups had intensified their efforts to act against other areas in Israel (they had also continued minelaying in the Haddad strip but at a decreased level), smuggling people and weapons from Lebanon through Syria and into Jordan. The Jordanian policy since 1968 was to allow the terrorists to act inside Israel as long as the border zones themselves remained quiet. East of the Jordan River the Jordanians had succeeded in creating a beautiful agricultural area, and they did not want to endanger this accomplishment. So generally they were able to prevent border incidents and were able to capture terrorists who attempted to create them. But in Samaria and Judea and Gaza and inside Israel the number of PLO actions multiplied, as it also did in Europe.

Consequently we now found ourselves trapped. If we wanted to retaliate by hitting PLO bases in Lebanon, we would be violating the cease-fire agreement. If we decided that we had to react to some incident, the northern settlements would immediately come under heavy shelling and Katyusha fire. What that meant was that the population in the Galilee had become hostages to PLO undertakings elsewhere. At the same time, behind the cover of the cease-fire agreement, the PLO had built up its artillery and rocket forces and constructed tunnel systems and protected emplacements so that now we faced a massive long-range-weapons network across the border.

We cannot accept this way of life, I told Hassan Ali, and we cannot accept these continuing incidents against Israeli and Jewish lives around the world. "You know," he replied, "if they don't stop, break their heads."

At the end of January 1982 a heavily armed PLO squad that had crossed from Lebanon to Jordan and then had penetrated into Israel was captured before it could carry out its mission. To make our position completely clear to the Americans, the cabinet decided to send our director of military intelligence, Yehoshua Saguy, to meet with Secretary Alexander Haig in Washington. There he told the secretary that in the six months of the so-called cease-fire we had suffered over two hundred casualties. We would tolerate no more. Should there be any further incidents, we were prepared to attack the PLO in a major operation that would extend up to the outskirts of Beirut.

By now Haig, Habib, and the other American policymakers knew time was running out fast. Their cease-fire initiative had bought a period in which to find a diplomatic solution to an intolerable situation. But despite the efforts of Philip Habib and Haig himself, they had been unable to do it. Habib's attempt to work out a step-by-step elimination of the causal factors had been frustrated by PLO and Syrian intransigence. Though he still kept up his meetings around the region, further efforts to use Saudi pressure to lever concessions from the Syrians and tie this together with resolutions to the PLO problem and the West Bank autonomy problem were fruitless and increasingly desperate. He had made absolutely no progress in his attempt to have the Syrian missiles removed—an American undertaking at the time of the cease-fire talks in July 1981. And when I remonstrated with him during our March 1, 1982 meeting that a legitimate Lebanese government was impossible as long as the Syrians controlled so much of the country, his answer was that from the beginning he had been working on a process to initiate their withdrawal. "I don't see even the slightest step that was taken," I said. "It was on the agenda," Habib answered, "and nothing happened."

All this created an enervating controversy between ourselves and the Americans. As they attempted to link the regional issues in some sort of master solution, I repeatedly maintained that Lebanon was such a complicated problem itself that it could not be used to solve these other major issues too. The only goals that might be reached here were that 1) the source of terror against Israel and against Jews could be eliminated, 2) the withdrawal of all external forces could be accomplished, and as a result, 3) a stable central government could be formed that would be linked to the free world.

Looking back at this period and at some of the dilatory and unlikely American policies it spawned, Alexander Haig has written that he "had little hope these theatrics would succeed."[*] These were precisely my feelings at the time. What made the situation increasingly dangerous was that with their failure to make any progress toward a solution or to influence the PLO, the Americans were reduced to pressuring us to exercise "restraint." We should take no action, they repeated at the highest levels, unless there was a "clear, internationally recognized provocation."

In March tensions mounted still further following terrorist incidents in Athens and Paris where Israeli offices were attacked, and in Jenin and

---

[*] Alexander Haig, *Caveat* (Macmillan, 1984), p. 334.

THE PLO IN LEBANON
EXPORTER OF INTERNATIONAL TERRORISM

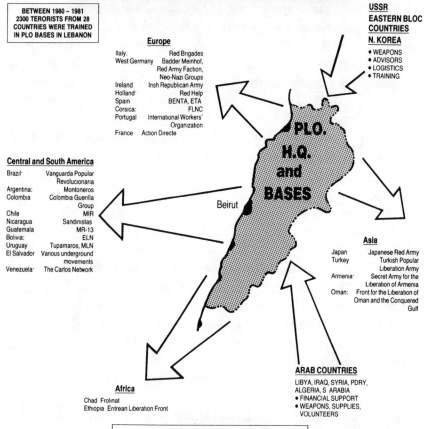

BETWEEN 1980 – 1981 2300 TERORISTS FROM 28 COUNTRIES WERE TRAINED IN PLO BASES IN LEBANON

Europe

Italy.	Red Brigades
West Germany	Badder Meinhof, Red Army Faction, Neo-Nazi Groups
Ireland	Irish Republican Army
Holland·	Red Help
Spain	BENTA, ETA
Corsica:	FLNC
Portugal	International Workers' Organization
France	Action Directe

USSR
EASTERN BLOC COUNTRIES
N. KOREA

- WEAPONS
- ADVISORS
- LOGISTICS
- TRAINING

Central and South America

Brazil·	Vanguarda Popular Revolucionaria
Argentina:	Montoneros
Colombia	Colombia Guerilla Group
Chile	MIR
Nicaragua	Sandinistas
Guatemala	MR-13
Bolivia:	ELN
Uruguay	Tupamaros, MLN
El Salvador	Various underground movements
Venezuela·	The Carlos Network

Beirut

PLO. H.Q. and BASES

Asia

Japan	Japanese Red Army
Turkey	Turkish Popular Liberation Army
Armenia·	Secret Army for the Liberation of Armenia
Oman:	Front for the Liberation of Oman and the Conquered Gulf

Africa

Chad Frolinat
Ethiopia Eritrean Liberation Front

ARAB COUNTRIES

LIBYA, IRAQ, SYRIA, PDRY, ALGERIA, S ARABIA
- FINANCIAL SUPPORT
- WEAPONS, SUPPLIES, VOLUNTEERS

CASUALTIES INFLICTED BY PLO TERRORISM 1965 – 1982 (PRIOR TO OPERATION PEACE FOR GALILEE)

	IN ISRAEL	IN JUDEA, SAMARIA and GAZA	TOTAL
KILLED	689	375	1064
WOUNDED	3799	1872	5671

ABROAD	ISRAELIS and JEWS	FOREIGN NATIONALS	TOTAL
KILLED	60	266	326
WOUNDED	101	667	768

TOTAL	
KILLED	1392
WOUNDED	6439

Gaza where soldiers were killed. Then on April 3 an Israeli embassy official in Paris was gunned down. Three days later the cabinet set up a small committee for security affairs and decided that from this point on we would retaliate, though not every incident would necessarily be considered a casus belli. Three weeks later an Israeli army vehicle in the Haddad buffer zone (covered by the cease-fire agreement) was blown up and two soldiers were killed. After nine months of holding back we struck, sending an air force sortie against PLO bases near Beirut.

On May 4 I met with the Northern Front staff and higher officers down to the level of brigade commander to once more review plans and clarify the government's position. I explained that we would not go to war in order to remove the Syrians from Lebanon, nor would we go to war to establish a legitimate government there, "even if we knew explicitly that we could sign a peace treaty with it. . . . The defined aim," I said, "is the terrorist target." And the solution to the terrorist problem "lies only in an action that will bring about their actual destruction, destruction of the military power, the military command posts, and the political command centers in Beirut. . . . At the end of the day," I told them, "we will get there." This possibility was not news to any of them, since they were all familiar with the Oranim Plan and knew exactly what their expected roles would be.

After a wide-ranging review the officers made their comments and expressed their reservations. Some doubted if we should have any dealings with a government in Lebanon. The divisional commanders thought it unlikely we would be able to avoid clashing with the Syrians and suggested that their expulsion should be an explicit goal. But though there were questions and disagreements of this sort, not a single person present had any doubt about either my position or the government's policy.

On May 7 more mines were laid in the Haddad strip. Israeli planes again attacked PLO targets, which was now followed by a PLO rocket barrage into the northern Galilee. Once more we put our forces on alert (between April 1981 and June 1982 the IDF was called to alert status five times) and war seemed imminent. That day a large bomb was found in a phone booth in Jerusalem. Still we held ourselves in check. Nine days later a member of the PLO Supreme Central Committee announced that "the cease-fire no longer exists. The Palestine Liberation Organization considers itself free to accelerate its activities against Israel anyplace in the world."

On that same day, May 16, the Israeli cabinet met to discuss the situation. Begin started by saying that the time was not yet ripe to present a specific proposal for action, but he did want to examine and consider the plan "Peace for Galilee" (a rechristening of Oranim), whose objective would be to remove the Galilee settlements from firing range (this had always been the minimum objective). Raful Eytan then presented the plan. I seconded Begin's remarks, emphasizing that we did not intend to call for any more half measures such as air strikes, which could lead to further shelling. The response to more terrorist incidents would be the major action we were describing. This, of course, would not be automatic. The prime minister would convene the cabinet and present the plan for final approval and for a decision on timing. Yitzhak Moda'i, minister without portfolio, noted that when the plan was presented previously its objectives were not simply to remove the Galilee from firing range but were "much deeper in Lebanon." Given that there are always unexpected developments on the battlefield, would the cabinet be asked for approval of movements farther north? To this Begin responded that the cabinet could be called to meet at any time such a question came up.

But Moda'i wanted explicit clarification on this point. If we did get to the twenty-five-mile line, might we find ourselves in a position where battlefield developments would force us to move beyond that line? Because if this was a possibility, he wanted it to be made clear right then and there.

"Yes," I told him, "Without any doubt, that might happen. In such an event the ministerial committee for security affairs should meet twice a day . . . This matter will be brought before it. I would not propose to any government, and certainly not one of which I am a member, that it should adopt a resolution and then only convene at the end of the war. . . . With regard to the question Is it possible that there may be a situation where we will have to proceed further north? The answer is yes! . . . To your question if the government will be called to give its approval—that is my opinion and that is my recommendation."

All of the objectives of the complete Oranim plan—from clearing the PLO artillery out of the border area to removing the terrorists from Beirut—had been discussed intensively during the last ten months and even broached to the Americans. But the objective Begin and I were asking the government to take under consideration now was only to clear terrorists out of artillery range, about twenty-five miles from the Galilee border.

But this objective, as everyone knew, was complicated by the fact that PLO batteries in the southern Bekaa Valley were deployed within the Syrian lines. Neither Begin nor I wanted a fight with the Syrians, and we planned to convey that to them. At the same time we knew it was unlikely that they would voluntarily pull back from the southern Bekaa. This was a problem that concerned each of the ministers in the room: Would it be possible to avoid engaging the Syrians? And if it was not possible, to what degree might the conflict spread?

Minister of Housing David Levy looked at the map thoughtfully. It indicated, he said, that we would have an engagement with the Syrians in the Bekaa. To which I responded, "So that the government will not be misled, I want to say that it is very hard to assume there will not be Syrian involvement. Our problem is, Can we succeed in creating a picture for the Syrians that our intention is to do something comparatively limited and that we are not going to threaten Damascus [the Bekaa Valley was an approach route into Syria]? If we can, maybe they will limit their activity. [But] I would not in any circumstances have said to the government that there will be no Syrian activity."

At this point Begin took over the discussion. In his estimation our problem was not one of three or ten miles. Our problem was the interpretation of the cease-fire agreement. The American interpretation was that the cease-fire applied to Israel's fronts with Lebanon, Syria, and Jordan. But if the PLO planted bombs in Jaffa or Ashkelon, the Americans wouldn't be sure if that was a violation or not. And as far as Europe was concerned, according to the American interpretation nothing the PLO did there could be considered a violation. There they had the right to kill Jews.

Israel's interpretation, Begin went on, was different. Ours was that the agreement required a complete halt in terrorist acts. If the agreement applied only to the land of Israel, we would be abandoning Jewish lives and leaders elsewhere. That was why we had to have a complete halt.

At the same time, he said, the terrorists had their own interpretation (the terrorists in Begin's vocabulary being "menuvalim," a word that has no exact English translation but means something near to "malevolent criminals"). As far as they were concerned, the cease-fire applied only to southern Lebanon. The menuvalim were saying that they would keep on attacking us throughout what they called the "occupied homeland."

How, Begin asked, could even men of good will live under a threat like this, particularly from an enemy that was getting ready to implement the threat? The Americans hadn't waited until they were hit by the first Soviet missile from Cuba. President Kennedy had even been willing to get into an atomic confrontation over that issue. And here we were, with missiles and artillery and every other kind of weapon right on our doorstep.

Begin went on to quote the PLO announcement that they would continue their attacks inside Israel. With this announcement, he said, "they are declaring war on the people of Israel, that they will make every trouble, massacre, and assassination of men, women, and children, all over Israel. . . . Every nation," he declared, "would react to that."

At the end of this crucial meeting the cabinet passed a resolution that "Israel would not under any circumstances accept the distorted [cease-fire] interpretation of the terrorist organizations that are directly threatening the lives of Israeli citizens and members of the Jewish people, men, women, and children." With this resolution the government made the basic decision to respond to any further acts of terrorism wherever they occurred.

With the situation between ourselves and the terrorists now just waiting for a spark, I traveled to the United States to meet with Haig and Caspar Weinberger. We had a range of issues to cover, but my primary purpose was to make sure that the United States understood our intentions with total clarity. There were two reasons for this. In the first place I knew that formally putting the United States on notice would create additional pressure on the PLO to bring their activities to a halt. If the United States was sufficiently impressed by our seriousness, we might even yet see some resolution short of war. But even beyond that, whatever might happen, I did not want there to be any surprises between ourselves and our allies.

At a luncheon meeting in the Pentagon I told Weinberger that we understood the sensitive situation but that we had come to the end of the line. We could no longer live under the constant threat of terror. If something happened, we would move "to eliminate the terrorist infrastructure in Lebanon."*

Later that day, I met with Haig and Philip Habib and delivered the same message in even more explicit terms. Almost all the world terror organizations, I told them, are connected with the PLO in Lebanon. We cannot live with the situation; and although it is a dilemma, we cannot see any other way but to clean them out. We aren't looking for war, I said. We don't like the idea of a war, "especially with the Syrians." But "at the same time, we don't want you to be surprised." Habib repeated the

---

* Meeting, May 25, 1982.

point he made many times already, that terrorist attacks against Israelis and Jews in Europe were not included in the cease-fire agreement. But I refused to go along with it. As far as we were concerned, I told him, when these incidents are planned in Lebanon and when the instructions for them originate from Lebanon, we cannot make these kinds of distinctions. In what became a heated discussion, both Habib and Haig stressed that there would have to be an "internationally recognized provocation," and that if Israel took any kind of "disproportionate action" it would create the most severe consequences in the United States. "How many Jews," I asked "have to be killed for it to be to a clear provocation? One Jew? Two Jews? Five? Six? . . . To us it's obvious."

I had not come to Washington to get American approval for whatever we decided to do but to let them know as friends and allies exactly where we stood. By the same token, Haig conveyed to me his position in very blunt terms indeed. And when I left, he followed up with a letter to Begin urging Israel to exercise "complete restraint." Begin's response epitomized the human being he was. "Mr. Secretary," we wrote, "the man has not been born who will ever obtain from me consent to let Jews be killed by a bloodthirsty enemy." It was a proud and defiant reply.

While Lebanon was by far the most pressing issue, it was not the only item on my agenda with Haig. We reviewed at some length the situation in the Persian Gulf and American worries about the spread of Shi'ite radicalism. We also took up the subject of the Lavi, a projected Israeli-built jet fighter that was the subject of possible Israeli-American cooperation.

Caspar Weinberger had certain objections, but we knew for sure that we wanted to build an aircraft that was based on our experience in the Yom Kippur War, when we had faced the most complicated problems of antiaircraft weaponry. We believed that on the basis of this experience we could produce the best so-called second-line aircraft in the world, which would emphasize survivability. This was an especially significant issue for us because of our relatively small number of planes and because of the tenuousness of aircraft sales arrangements. We also believed that it was important for us to have a "lead project," one that would bring us to the highest level of technology and would move all of our technology-based industries forward. An additional consideration was that we would be able to effectively sell different kinds of systems, the avionics for example, once we had incorporated them into our own planes and had had operational experience with them.

Beyond these reasons were the political considerations. I always regarded aircraft as political weapons. Every time somebody wanted to threaten us or pressure us, the first step was to stop selling jets. For many years we had been placed under complete aircraft embargoes by friends. We had been under British and French embargoes. We had been under embargo by the United States for almost twenty years. It was not until 1965 that President Lyndon Johnson first sold us American fighters. And since then we had undergone reassessments and delays and postponements every time we had done something that dissatisfied our allies. Fighters had always been a whip and, considering their significance, a powerful whip.

Another trip I made during this crowded period was to Rumania. Earlier in the spring the Rumanians had quietly approached us about the possibility of a meeting in Rumania to discuss various issues of mutual interest, including technological cooperation. Prime Minister Begin and Foreign Minister Yitzhak Shamir agreed that the meeting should take place, and arrangements were made.

At the Rumanians' request, it was decided that the trip should be conducted quietly, as a family visit. Lily, they knew, had been born in the Rumanian province of Transylvania. What they proposed, then, was that they would invite her to make a visit to her old hometown and that the children and I would accompany her.

It seemed an ideal ruse. On Wednesday, June 2, I went to the Knesset to give a report to the Foreign and Security Affairs Committee. Around midday I left for the airport where a 707 was waiting for me with Lily, Omri, and Gilad already inside.

Landing at the Bucharest airport, we were immediately whisked away in a convoy of cars 150 miles to Brashov, Lily's hometown. Not another car was on the road as our line of official vehicles sped on; the police had blocked off the entire highway. When we got to Brashov, thousands of people lined the streets awaiting the motorcade, but there was not a sound. Wondering, I asked my host what they had told all these people that they were standing there so silently. "Only," he said, "that a delegation is coming."

The next morning we visited the old synagogue where Lily's father used to pray. (She even found the pew he used.) Walking through the street where she was born, Lily wanted to stop into the house of a close non-Jewish girlfriend from her childhood. But with all the security people around, she was reluctant to go in, afraid that somehow it might cause trouble for the family. She did go, however, to the house her family had lived in when World War Two broke out. She remembered that before they left, her mother had hidden a set of silver candlesticks in the attic, candlesticks she had gotten from her own grandmother. These candlesticks had been on Lily's mind for years, and when I told our hosts about them they arranged for her to go into the house to look for them. The attic was full of furniture and old things, the debris of who knew how many generations, all of it covered with a thick carpet of dust. But after an hour and a half of searching she was unable to find them, though they might well be there still.

Back at our hotel that evening after a day of sightseeing, a message came in. The Israeli ambassador to Great Britain, Shlomo Argov, had been shot in the head in an attempted assassination. No other details were available.[*]

With this news I knew that the cabinet would be meeting very soon. But beyond that, at this crucial instant I was largely in the dark.

Preoccupied by developments in Israel, the next day I was driven back to Bucharest, where I was scheduled to visit a car and truck plant and an aircraft factory. With no way of getting more news for the moment, I resigned myself to the visit, which turned out to be surprisingly interesting. At the aircraft factory I learned that the Rumanians had been pioneers in the European air industry. But when the Soviets came into Rumania, they had stripped the plants and deported the engineers and technicians to Russia. For the next twenty years the Rumanians had not dealt with these things at all, and they had lost all of their accumulated expertise. It was only in the 1970s that they had come back to it. Now they were producing French helicopters under license and their own passenger jets. The people who had come with me from the Israeli aircraft industries and the air force were impressed by the professionalism of their work.

That day Rumanian news announced that Israeli jets had bombed southern Lebanon. When I sent a short message recommending that some reserve units be mobilized, the answer came back that it had already been done.

---

[*] One of the assailants was killed by a Scotland yard security officer. In his pocket was found a list of additional targets, including prominent Jews and Israeli representatives in England and other European countries. Shlomo Argov himself did not die but has remained semi-comatose since the shooting.

In the meantime I continued with the visit, meeting first with the minister of heavy industry and then with the minister of defense, going through our agenda as if nothing out of the ordinary was happening. Their main focus was, of course, Israeli technology. But while I had come to discuss technological cooperation, there were other subjects I wanted to explore as well.

Among these the most important was the possibility of using Bucharest instead of Vienna as the transit point for Jews coming out of Russia. Vienna was a problem, one that we thought we might solve by switching transit points. Although many of the Soviet Jews had applied to leave Russia in order to be reunited with their families in Israel, once they got to Austria most of them opted to go directly to the United States instead. This caused repercussions for the emigration process and was also hurtful to Israel, which saw thousands of potential citizens turning away from the country that had been established as a homeland for Diaspora Jews.

It was a difficult situation to get a handle on. One could not, of course, blame the emigrants. They had been living under the Soviets for several generations now, hard enough for anyone but even harder for Jews whose cultural heritage had been systematically destroyed. For the most part they knew little about Judaism and almost nothing about Israel other than what they had read in *Pravda*. Even when they discounted the source, it must have sounded like a terrible place. There was no wonder they had little incentive to come.

One potential resolution we saw to this problem was to bring the Russian Jews directly to Israel from the transit point. At least then they would be able to see the country for themselves before making a decision about where they would live. Afterward if they wanted to leave, fine, they would leave. But many, I thought, would want to stay.

I discussed this with the Rumanians, as well as other subjects that were perhaps more interesting to them, especially their desire to arrange a more favorable trade status for themselves in the West. Before I left I told the minister of defense I would enjoy coming back and visiting some of the interesting places I had not had a chance to see. He answered, smiling, that he was absolutely certain I would be visiting some new, interesting places in the very near future. His estimate, I thought, was undoubtedly correct.

30

Peace for Galilee

That Friday, June 4, while I was visiting and talking in Bucharest, the Israeli cabinet met to decide what action should be taken in response to the shooting of Shlomo Argov. There they were informed that the Abu Nidal group, one of the Palestinian terror organizations, was responsible for the assassination attempt. What we were seeing now was the development of an ongoing effort against our diplomatic corps. "It is inconceivable," Begin said, "that these malevolent criminals should be allowed to strike our ambassadors. We cannot wait for our ambassadors in Athens or Rome to be murdered tomorrow, and it is easier for the terrorists to operate there than in London."

But the Argov shooting was merely the match that ignited the fuse. The real casus belli was the chain of terrorist attacks (290 of them now, of which this was merely the most recent) and the continuing buildup of long-range artillery in southern Lebanon—all of which had taken place during the eleven-month-long supposed cease-fire. On May 16, 1982, the cabinet had made the basic decision to take action against this intolerable situation, though it stipulated then that not every incident would require an all-out response. With that in mind, Prime Minister Begin called not for an invasion but for air strikes against terrorist military targets in southern Lebanon and on the outskirts of Beirut. Even at this stage war was not absolutely inevitable. But the cabinet knew that these strikes would put the decision directly into the hands of Yasser Arafat. If he refrained from responding, we would not attack across the border; and with the stimulus of the emergency perhaps the Americans could even yet work something out. If, on the other hand, the PLO shelled the northern settlements, our answer would be Peace for Galilee.

With all our experience of the PLO, few doubted which Arafat would choose. "Gentlemen," said Begin, "so far as our operation is concerned, after this attack we should be prepared for the maximum." At midday the cabinet approved the air strikes unanimously. Shortly afterward the attacks were driven home against two military targets in the Beirut suburbs and nine others in the south. By five-thirty that afternoon, PLO artillery shells and rockets began to fall on the Galilee towns and villages. The terrorists had unambiguously declared their decision.

The shelling was still under way the following afternoon when we boarded our 707 in Bucharest for the trip home. Over the Medierranean the pilots were briefed to stay away from the Syrian coast to avoid Mig patrols. Veering west, we crossed Crete before turning eastward again toward the Israeli coast. At the airport a ministry official was waiting to brief me on my way to a more thorough review at the General Headquarters complex in Tel Aviv. By nine that evening I was in Jerusalem, where the cabinet had been called together at the prime minister's residence.

Begin opened the meeting by announcing that he was now calling for a decision on the Peace for Galilee operation. Then he turned to me and said, "Mr. Defense Minister, would you be good enough to explain the plan as if the cabinet is hearing it for the first time. We have heard the plan, yet since we must decide on implementing it, we should know every detail."

I then began my presentation, essentially a repetition of what I had told the government on May 16. The operation's objective was to remove the terrorists from firing range of the northern border, approximately twenty-five miles. This included the terrorists who were deployed behind Syrian lines in the Bekaa. However, we explicitly did not intend to hit the Syrians and would do so only if they attacked us. To get them to move back, the army would execute an advance west of the valley, expecting that Syrian forces would retreat to avoid being flanked.

When Deputy Prime Minister Simcha Ehrlich asked whether Beirut would be part of the operation, I answered, "Beirut is out of the picture. . . . The operation does not aim at occupying Beirut but at removing the terrorists—we are today only talking of a distance of twenty-five miles."

At this point Begin interrupted, saying that the cabinet would be monitoring the situation constantly, and that if it became necessary to occupy Beirut the cabinet would take it under consideration and make the decision. Absolutely nothing was going to happen on its own, as it had under previous governments. Today, he went on, what we intended to do was to get the malevolent criminal terrorists out and to destroy their weapons within a range of twenty-five miles. What this operation was going to do once and for all was to secure complete peace for the northern settlements. Within that context, the question of Beirut would remain open.

When Begin then asked the cabinet to approve the operation as it had been presented, Minister Without Portfolio Yitzhak Moda'i took the floor. Looking around at the assembled ministers, he said he wanted to remind them that we, the cabinet, had actually decided to move ahead with the operation ten days earlier, with our promise to the northern settlements that we would not allow them to be shelled. Now we had no way of preventing this other than by implementing the large operation. When Moda'i finished speaking, Minister of Energy Yitzhak Berman added that during the previous day's meeting various ministers had pointed out that the decision to retaliate in fact meant a readiness to undertake the large operation. That perception had been correct, he said, adding that there was nothing new in the proposal that was on the table. It was not something that had suddenly been presented to the cabinet. On the contrary, everyone who opposed the operation had had time to discuss it thoroughly. This was no last-minute thing that the cabinet was being faced with and told to say "amen" to. On the contrary, all those who hadn't seen any logic to the operation—and he himself was one—had already said whatever they had to say.

When the discussion was over, a vote was taken and the resolution passed, with fourteen cabinet members in favor, none opposed, and two abstaining. In addition to approving the military plan as presented, the cabinet resolved that "The Syrian army should not be attacked unless it attacks our own forces," also that "the State of Israel continues to desire a signed peace treaty with an independent Lebanon."

That night I drove down to the farm to catch a few hours of sleep, getting up at four to helicopter to the Northern Command headquarters. There I reviewed the plan with the officers, noting that the government had set the political objective of removing the settlements from artillery range. Consequently, at this point the army only had approval to move up to the Awali River in the west and center and Hasbaiya in the southern Bekaa. Though Hasbaiya was only some eight miles from the border, we would stop at that point to avoid clashing with the Syrians and to give them time to pull back. In accordance with the General Headquarters' Operation Order Number One, the army was also to be prepared to implement the full Oranim Plan, including cutting the Beirut–Damascus highway, linking up with the Christians, and destroying the Syrian occupation forces—if and when government decisions were made to accomplish these objectives.

In the west the plan was quite complicated, encompassing a strike up the coast, an amphibious landing just north of Sidon, and another advance in the center that would eventually link up with the coastal column. Even more complicated was the Syrian front, where we were determined to avoid a confrontation, if possible, and to prevent an all-out war with Syria under any circumstances. If it became necessary to physically push them back to the twenty-five-mile line in the Bekaa, we were ready to do it. But there was not only nothing to be gained from a wider engagement, there was danger in it. We did not want the Syrians attacking our Golan settlements (although they had been reinforced by army units and were prepared to defend themselves). We knew too that the Syrians had been given Soviet Frog and Scud missiles, the Scud having a range that covered all of Israel's main centers of population. In addition, the Soviets were heavily committed to Syria, and we wanted to avoid any Soviet involvement in the developing events. Consequently, even though our assessment was that any fighting limited to Lebanon would not result in an all-out Israeli-Syrian war, we still wanted to avoid any conflict that might unexpectedly get out of hand.

The strategy, then, would be to send Syria a series of unmistakable messages explaining that we did not want to touch them, that the only thing that interested us was the terrorists deployed within their lines. These we wanted removed to a distance of twenty-five miles. What action, if any, we might have to take in the Bekaa would depend on their response. In the meantime we would sit on the Hasbaiya line.

Among the orders I gave just prior to the operation were strict instructions concerning Lebanon's civilian population. To the extent possible, I did not want them harmed. As I put it in my order to the army of June 6, "Behavior toward noncombatants (Shi'ites, Moslems, Druze, Christians):

You must prevent hurting this population. There will be no repeat of what happened in the Litani Operation [in which villages were destroyed]. Officers and commanders of units must implement these instructions."

After the orders review in the north I flew back to Jerusalem for a cabinet meeting, followed by a briefing session with opposition leaders Yitzhak Rabin, Shimon Peres, Chaim Bar-Lev, and Victor Shem Tov (of the left-wing Mapam party), and another with the Knesset Committee on Security and Foreign Affairs. Thus started a grueling schedule that kept up throughout the war. Typically I would begin at night by meeting with the commander-in-chief and the Northern Command staff to go over plans for the following day. In the morning I would visit some of the units in the field, then fly to Jerusalem for meetings with the cabinet and the Knesset Committee on Foreign and Security Affairs. When these were concluded, I would return to the front to get a firsthand account of events and to deal with any problems that had arisen during the course of the day.

On Sunday, June 6, I returned from Jerusalem to the front in time to see the tank columns begin their advance into Lebanon. Along the Lebanese coast in the west, Israeli forces struck toward Tyre, intending to cut off the terrorist forces and headquarters posts in that peninsula city. From Metulla in the center, other units moved toward Nabatiya and Beaufort, the ruined Crusader castle that had housed PLO positions for years. In the east the IDF advanced on Hasbaiya, hoping for quiet from the Syrian positions that lay beyond.

In the west and the center some of the terrorists put up stiff opposition, others fled north toward Beirut, while still others shed their uniforms and melted into the local population. In the Bekaa, developments were ominous. As our forces advanced, they were met by Syrian artillery fire. There were no signs that Syrian forces were contemplating either withdrawing themselves or removing the terrorist units from their deployments. On the contrary, the Syrians started to move southward and westward, putting themselves in better defensive positions to meet our advance. From within their lines, PLO artillery and Katyushas lashed settlements in the Galilee "finger."

In light of these developments, Commander-in-Chief Raful Eytan and I brought the situation to Begin. If events proceeded to unfold as they were, we would be faced with an unacceptable conclusion. The terrorists would be eliminated from the western and central regions, but they would retain the ability to shell the Galilee from the Syrian-controlled southern Bekaa.

We now had two clear options. The Syrians had hit us and caused casualties. They were clearly intending to make a fight of it. We might then simply abandon the idea of avoiding a collision with them and attack their forces immediately. Alternatively, we might try to force them to withdraw by sending the coastal column north, then northeast in toward their rear. Faced with the threat of being flanked, they might very well move backwards. Such a maneuver, however, would necessitate crossing the twenty-five-mile line, and the decision for this would have to be made by the cabinet.

When Raful and I discussed the situation with Begin, he approved our recommendation that we try the flanking maneuver and attempt to get around in back of the Syrians. With that decision made, Begin asked me to present the proposed move to the cabinet that night.

When darkness fell, I flew again to Jerusalem for the second cabinet meeting of the day. There I told the government that the first stage of the operation had proceeded according to the timetable and that I estimated we would clear the terrorists from the twenty-five-mile range within the next twenty-four hours—everywhere but in the Bekaa. There, I explained, the Syrians were not pulling back, nor were they removing the terrorists from their deployments. Using a map to clarify my description of the situation, I then proposed the flanking maneuver which Raful, Begin, and I had agreed on. "Our recommendation," I said, "is not to approach this area [where the Syrian forces were positioned] but to try to move more to the north, where we can threaten to cut them off while not attacking directly."

When I had finished, Housing Minister David Levy noted that this was a change from the original plan and asked if it meant we would have to cross the twenty-five-mile line. "Yes," I answered, "we will be crossing the twenty-five-mile line. . . . We have decided to give the Syrians the option to consider and appreciate that this is not a massive attack on them." At the end of this meeting on the night of Sunday, June 6, the cabinet formally approved the proposal to move north. *

That night I gave instructions to the commander-in-chief for the second day of the operation. He was to continue clearing the coastal road up to Damour, the Christian town whose inhabitants had been massacred and the survivors dispersed by the PLO in 1976. Since then the ruins had been given over as a base for terrorist leader George Habash's People's

---

* Given the fact that this decision meant a change in the original cabinet approval, I presented the issue for discussion again at the following cabinet meeting, June 7. At this meeting the government reconfirmed its decision.

Front for the Liberation of Palestine. From there, a column would cut northeast to the Beirut–Damascus highway, executing a deep flanking movement behind the Syrians. In the center another column would strike north attempting to open another axis along the Syrian flank. Meanwhile, the eastern units would remain stationary on the Hasbaiya line, waiting to see what effect these maneuvers might have.

On Monday, June 7, Philip Habib arrived in Jerusalem on a mission from President Reagan. Among other things, Prime Minister Begin informed him that Israel would not remain in Lebanon indefinitely and that we would consider co-operating with the United States on possible arrangements. Under no circumstances, however, would we return to what Begin called the "cursed status quo ante." "We are ready," he said, "through your good offices, to agree to a renewed cessation of hostilities, but only if it covers all points, including [terrorist attacks] overseas." Other ideas Begin brought up included the creation of a multinational force similar to the one established in the Sinai and the possibility of extending the UNIFIL-controlled area, despite the serious problems we had had with the U.N. troops' procedures. * Meeting later that night, the cabinet asked Begin to have Habib approach Syria's President Assad to demand that shelling from their area onto the Galilee settlements be halted immediately and that the PLO within their lines be removed beyond firing range.

Also on Monday, Begin and I visited Beaufort, the old crusader fortress that had become a symbol of PLO mastery in Southern Lebanon. The previous night Beaufort had fallen to units of the Golani Brigade, one of which had lost six soldiers in its courageous assault. Unfortunately, just prior to our visit we were informed by Raful that there had been no Israeli casualties, and during the press conference in the fortress both Begin and I expressed our happiness that there had been no losses. In so doing we inadvertently caused great pain to the families of the soldiers killed in this battle. The unfortunate rumor also started that we were attempting to cover up casualties, a charge which played a significant part in the anti-government political campaign which developed later.

Other problems developed too on June 7, when the advance along the coastal plain to Tyre and Sidon and the local villages ran into problems. Entrenched in civilian neighborhoods, the terrorists were using the local

---

* UNIFIL troops who caught terrorists attempting to infiltrate the border captured and disarmed them, then returned their prisoners to their own commanders. The confiscated weapons were also returned.

inhabitants as hostages and cover, even putting civilians in the windows and open doorways of buildings from which they were fighting. Because of this, Israeli units were reluctant to use their full firepower in the house-to-house fighting. As a result they found themselves suffering additional casualties and falling behind their timetables.

During a meeting that night at Northern Command Headquarters the problem was brought up. There was one obvious solution to it. Instead of fighting house-to-house, we could use our air force to fly along the main road and destroy whatever buildings were in the way of the advance. That would open the road and save us considerable casualties, but it would also cause a heavy death toll among the civilian population.

This meeting started about 1 A.M. All the divisional commanders were there as well as many of the staff officers. In my military experience, perhaps in anyone's military experience, this was a highly unusual meeting, one in which moral issues, not tactical or strategic ones, dominated the discussion. As the night wore on, the small room we were meeting in became shrouded in cigarette smoke. Despite the crowded discomfort of the place, the discussion was intense and quiet, at times almost whispered. I had known most of these people for years; there was hardly one I hadn't been in battle with. I knew them as professional officers, men who had war in their blood. They knew precisely the price we would pay the next day if we decided not to blast the road open from the air—their soldiers' lives, their officers' lives, perhaps their own lives. As we talked, messages came into the room from the front announcing new developments, adding to the tension. The Israeli army had never consciously and unnecessarily caused civilian casualties; that was a value built into its ethos. What should we do now? Should we pay the price to keep this value, should we make the sacrifices? When we finally finished early in the morning, every single one of the officers present had expressed himself. To a man they recommended that we not use the air force but instead continue house-to-house as we had done that day, in order to harm the Palestinian and Lebanese civilians as little as possible. And after listening to the soul-searching that had gone on for hours, that was the decision I took. I don't know if any other army in the world would have spent a night in the middle of a war, with all the war's problems, discussing such an issue, let alone making such a decision.

The next day, June 8, Israeli forces along the coast rolled past Damour, then headed northeast toward Aley in an effort to cut the Beirut–Damascus highway behind the Syrians. In the center, where our units were moving north on the mountains and ridges to the left of the Bekaa, fighting developed with combined Syrian-PLO units defending the town of Jezin.

At the cabinet meeting on the morning of June 8, I explained the conditions on the battlefield, presenting the ministers with a detailed description of our attempts to reach the crucial Beirut–Damascus highway and requesting permission to open an additional axis of advance to the road to insure supplies to the flanking columns. My purpose in bringing even tactical moves like this to the cabinet was to make sure that everyone knew exactly what was going on and to receive formal approval for each significant step. It was an approach that was beginning to meet with impatience on the part of some of the members.

When Communications Minister Mordechai Zippori declared that the cabinet had already decided it was necessary to approach the Beirut-Damascus road, Yitzhak Moda'i added that consequently we had to open every possible route. He also thought, he said, that we were overdoing the presentation of military matters to the cabinet. It was as if the General Staff or the Northern Command were sitting here being asked for their approval on this axis or that axis. This was no way to manage a war. What difference did it make if we reached our target on two axes or if we opened a third for supply?[*]

But despite the annoyance it might have caused, I continued to insist on giving clear in-depth briefings to the cabinet and on receiving cabinet approval for military moves. For the first time in all of Israel's war experience, cabinet meetings were held every day and sometimes twice a day. For the first time the government set specific goals for the army on an ongoing basis. By contrast, for example, in the Six Day War there was never a government decision to take the Golan Heights. Dayan as minister of defense had simply given that instruction himself on the basis of his own assessment. In the Sinai, even Dayan had not wanted to advance to the canal. But the army had pressured him to do it anyway out of what its field commanders regarded as tactical necessity. And he had given way.

From the beginning I had been determined that the Peace for Galilee operation would not be conducted in the same way, but that the political

---

[*] Although unusual in a war, the habit of keeping the cabinet minutely informed was ingrained during Begin's administration. He himself used to consult with them on every issue, even reading and asking for approval on letters he was writing, as well as reading verbatim letters he received.

echelon would maintain firm direction of the battlefield. As a result I made sure that the cabinet was kept informed of every significant development and potential development. I saw to it that every decision was made in the cabinet and that orders were issued to the army only after the cabinet had deliberated and made up its mind. As I had told the ministers on May 16, meetings would take place not once a day but if necessary twice. Knowing how quickly situations in the field can change, I also appointed a brigadier general as permanent liaison to the cabinet to keep them apprised of important events as they occurred. Cabinet members were also given a special defense ministry phone number that they could call twenty-four hours a day for updates or clarifications. Determined that this war would be understood by all those who were responsible for making decisions, I invited ministers to visit the front at any time and made arrangements to immediately accommodate those who wanted to get a firsthand look at what was happening.

On Tuesday, June 8, the cabinet approved the opening of a third axis of advance northward in our effort to flank the Syrians and force them to withdraw from the lower Bekaa. By this point the maneuver was becoming increasingly urgent. We now had firm intelligence that the Syrian air force had been given instructions to attack Israeli forces moving up the central route. A Syrian tank battalion with accompanying infantry had also been spotted moving southwest into the Jezin area, where the single narrow road created perfect conditions for an effective defense.

At this meeting I recommended that we ask Habib to personally deliver a message to Syrian President Hafez al-Assad informing him that Syrian forces in the Bekaa should withdraw to a line twenty-five miles north of the Galilean border. Begin was in favor of sending a personal message, but he did not agree that we should demand a Syrian withdrawal. Assad would not accede to such a demand, he said, so why make it in the first place? All we could realistically ask for would be a removal of the terrorist artillery, and Assad might even refuse that. But at least there was a chance that he would accept. And if he refused, at least we would have made a very important point with the Americans. Israel would now make a reasonable proposal to have the terrorists retreat. If it was accepted, we would have achieved the goals of the operation. We would have resolved the military problem and we would then be able to begin resolving the political side of the situation.

At the end of this June 8 meeting the cabinet instructed Begin to convey the following four-point proposal to Assad through Philip Habib:

(a) We do not want war with your army.

(b) Instruct your army not to fire on our soldiers. If our soldiers are not hit, they will not attack your army.

(c) Have your army withdraw from west to east and from south to north to the starting point where it was positioned, say, on Saturday, before we commenced our campaign.

(d) Instruct the terrorists to retreat fifteen miles to the north [which would put them twenty-five miles from the border]. If this is done, then the military stage of the operation will have been concluded and the political stage can commence.

That message was given to Habib early on the evening of June 8 and was immediately forwarded to Assad through the U.S. embassy in Damascus. But even while we were deliberating what kind of message would have the best chance of getting the Syrians to pull back from a fight, they themselves continued to take steps in the opposite direction. That day they introduced six additional batteries of SAM-6 missiles into the Bekaa, positioning them to the south of the batteries they already had there. That day too Syrian fighters took to the air against us for the first time, attacking Israeli forces around Sidon. And now intelligence reported that the Syrian strategic reserve, the Third Armored Division with 250 tanks, would soon cross the border into Lebanon.

Very late that night, when it was unmistakable that we were facing the start of a major Syrian buildup, I awoke Begin to convey the latest information and to ask that he convene a cabinet meeting early on the morning of the ninth. By 9 A.M. Begin was telling the assembled ministers that after my call he had immediately phoned U.S. Ambassador Samuel Lewis, asking him to relay a message to the Syrians demanding that they remove the new batteries by 5 A.M. "If he [Assad] does not comply with this request," Begin told the cabinet, "we shall act. The problem is to make a decision about these missiles." By this time Habib himself had flown to Damascus to try to forestall the looming clash between the Syrians and ourselves. But though we did not know it at the time, Assad at first refused to see him, making the American envoy cool his heels for hours. It was a critical juncture. An agreement by the Syrians at that point would have given us all the objectives we had launched the Peace for Galilee operation to achieve. With the terrorists pushed out of the twenty-five-mile belt, we would have been ready, as Begin had said in his four-point message, to begin negotiations.

While Philip Habib waited for Assad, the Israeli cabinet continued to discuss what to do about the Syrians. I proposed that if we did not receive a positive response from Assad, the cabinet should approve an attack on the Syrian missile system. As this was being discussed, an urgent message came in from intelligence that an additional Syrian missile regiment was on its way to Lebanon and that heavy artillery was moving southward from the Syrian city of Homs toward Lebanon. "The Syrians have taken the initiative," it said, "while we are sitting around doing nothing."

In the tense discussion that followed I pushed for a decision on the missiles. But the debate went on. As time passed, I noticed the deputy commander of the air force, Amos Amir, looking nervously at his watch again and again. Better than anyone else there, he knew the technical complexity of the operation and the precise time requirements necessary to launch it. He seemed astonished that in the face of these contingencies the politicians would keep talking. Yitzhak Hoffi, the Mossad chief, noted that we had not gotten an answer from the Syrians and they were not withdrawing and were still bringing missiles up. "In my opinion," he said, "it is necessary to approve the attack." Dr. Burg, minister of interior, argued that the Syrians had now significantly changed the strategic and tactical picture, that we had to give the green light to implement the operation that day, and that we could wait for an answer from the Syrians only until the moment the order goes out. David Levy agreed, declaring that "I am in favor of executing the action and I recommend that it be done as soon as possible." Summing up the discussion, Begin noted that a large majority of the cabinet favored the resolution. But whatever happened, he would inform Lewis that our four points would hold good. Despite the imminent attack on the Syrian missiles, "We do not want war with the Syrians." The final vote was unanimous.

With no Syrian response to our messages except for the new missile deployment and the continued concentration of forces, at 11:45 A.M. on the ninth I instructed the commander-in-chief to destroy the Syrian missiles. At 2 P.M. the attack was launched, making use of all the lessons in anti-missile techniques we had learned in 1973. The result was that by the end of the afternoon all nineteen missile batteries had been eliminated, together with thirty Syrian Migs that had risen to meet the attack. Not a single Israeli plane was lost. It was only after his missiles had been destroyed that Assad received Habib, who had been waiting to see him since that morning.

The destruction of the SAM missiles aroused serious concern in the Soviet Union. Both the previous Israeli experience with these sophisticated Russian antiaircraft missiles and the American experience in Vietnam had attested to the system's effectiveness. But this single sweeping blow had given dramatic evidence that the defenses the Soviets themselves relied on were anything but invulnerable. Shaken by this realization and understanding that the Syrian army was now naked to attack, the Russians began to press the United States to arrange a cease-fire. As a result, on the night of the ninth we came under very heavy pressure ourselves. By 2 A.M. a personal message had arrived from President Reagan demanding that a cease-fire go into effect by 0600 that morning. Our problem was that although we were well on our way to outflanking the Syrians in the Bekaa, they had not yet moved back at all and in fact were allowing the PLO to continue shelling the settlements in the eastern half of the upper Galilee. (Coincidentally, at the same time as we received President Reagan's request for a cease-fire we also received a response from Hafez al-Assad. He could not, he said, decide questions for the PLO.)

When Begin received President Reagan's letter, he called a cabinet meeting to convene at his home at 4 A.M. I demanded at this meeting that we needed several hours to clear the Syrians back to the twenty-five-mile line, since they were neither going to move themselves nor force the terrorists to move. "This is a critical moment for the Syrians and the terrorists," I said, "and that is why a cease-fire request has come. . . . We have witnessed similar occurrences during all the wars to date. Whenever they reach a critical moment, they request a cease-fire. Our achievements here have been extraordinary, and we've paid a high price for them. Therefore we should complete them. For this we require a few more hours, so we can't agree that the cease-fire should take effect now. In principle I support a cease-fire, but that's conditional on an immediate withdrawal by the Syrians—now, not after the cease-fire, when no one will be able to renew firing."

When the meeting reconvened at nine in the morning of June 10, I explained the importance of our being on the Beirut–Damascus road by the time the cease-fire went into effect. With the highway cut, we would be in a very strong position for the coming negotiations. We would by then have completely flanked the Syrians in the Bekaa, which would not only deny them the ability to install a puppet government in the Lebanese fall elections but would also make their sustained military presence in Lebanon untenable. In addition, cutting the road would put us in a position to link up with Christian forces, thus encircling the thousands of terrorists who had fled into the Beirut area. "However," I told the cabinet, "our forces have explicit instructions not to enter Beirut. I stated long ago that we should not take action in Beirut but should leave that to forces of the Lebanese army or government, if they so wish."

In the discussion that followed, the ministers drew their own conclusions regarding what our final dispositions should be now that the cease-fire and negotiations were almost upon us. "What is important," said Haim Korfo, minister of transportation, "is that we will be in a position that gives us superiority in the negotiations and brings about a faster conclusion." Yitzhak Moda'i agreed, declaring that "there can be no doubt, the best negotiating position is to occupy the Beirut–Damascus highway."

Leaving the cabinet meeting, I made a report to the Knesset Committee on Foreign and Security Affairs, as I did almost every day. Just before I got there, they were briefed on the military situation by Chief of Military Intelligence Yehoshua Saguy, and when I walked in I was greeted by dozens of questions. Many of these had to do with Beirut and the terrorist concentration there. I explained carefully that notwithstanding the advice of some of the committee members, the IDF had no intention of entering Beirut, that the city had not been defined as an objective by the cabinet. Yitzhak Rabin supported this position firmly, as he did the effort to take the Beirut–Damascus road. But Motta Gur, the former commander-in-chief who was now a labor MK, argued that it would be a bad mistake to leave the PLO leadership in Beirut, that they would immediately regain their former status once the operation was over.

That day, June 10, Israeli forces broke into the Syrian positions in the Bekaa. By afternoon the Syrians were retreating throughout the valley, and toward evening the Northern Command ordered its forces on all fronts to finish up their operational missions. That evening Begin and I met to discuss the cease-fire. Since it was clear that the day would end with the Syrians pushed back behind the twenty-five-mile line, we decided together that the following day, June 11, we would present a resolution to the cabinet to declare a unilateral cease-fire at midday.

After my meeting with Begin I briefed the IDF command on what would be happening the following day. The army, I told them, had achieved the war's objectives in full, and we would commence a unilateral cease-fire beginning at 1200 hours.* However, they were not to allow any re-establishment of the Syrian surface-to-air missile systems. They were also to take any steps necessary to prevent the deployment of the Syrian Third Armored Division in the Bekaa (this was the Syrian reserve division whose moves we had been watching since the beginning of the campaign). In the twelve hours left before the cease-fire they should destroy any remaining missile batteries, make every effort to reach the Beirut–Damascus highway, and see to it that their final dispositions were made according to tactical considerations.

At the cabinet meeting that morning Begin announced that he, the foreign minister, and the defense minister were in agreement that the government should call a cease-fire to go into effect at noon. He had also received a report from the commander-in-chief concurring with that decision.

Israel wasn't negotiationg with anyone, he said. Not with the Americans, not with the Syrians, and especially not with the malevolent terrorists. The IDF would stop shooting at twelve noon. It would be the initiation of a unilateral cease-fire.

In the discussion that followed, the cabinet examined the proposed cease-fire and clarified exactly what it would mean. Summing up, Begin put it bluntly. "If the terrorists shoot at the IDF, the IDF will smash them. If the Syrians shoot at Israeli soldiers, the same thing will happen." The prime minister also reported that he had talked with Philip Habib earlier in the morning and had informed him that we would be announcing a cease-fire. Habib would immediately relay the message to Assad, including the warning that he should not introduce additional surface-to-air missiles, and that if he attacked us the responsibility would be his. Assad's response was expected by noon.

At the end of the June 11 meeting the cabinet approved the cease-fire resolution. "The IDF," it announced, "has achieved the mission assigned to it in full. . . . As of this hour Israeli forces will cease firing on all fronts in Lebanon, unless they are fired upon."

The ministers decided too that on Sunday, forty-eight hours later, the cabinet would begin preparing the Israeli negotiating positions. The stage was set for an end to the war.

---

* These remarks and those following are contained in the IDF meeting summary.

31

The Expulsion

By the time of the cease-fire the IDF had succeeded in removing all of northern Israel from range of the PLO artillery, a triumph of immense significance itself and one that put us in a good position to achieve even more far-reaching results. But despite the troops' best efforts they had not succeeded in cutting the strategic Beirut–Damascus highway. The advance northward had been slowed in part by the self-imposed restraints the IDF had observed in order to limit civilian casualties along the densely populated coastal strip and by the extremely difficult tank terrain in the center. But serious tactical mistakes and poor staff work had also played a role in the failure. Along the coastal road and in the central sector, tactical errors had led Israeli units into several local ambushes. Problems were also evident in the east where Israeli forces had delayed their initial assault several absolutely critical hours and then had failed to exploit serious Syrian mistakes. One eastern sector tank battalion advanced unknowingly in the middle of a Syrian disposition at the village of Sultan Yakub. By the time they extricated themselves, a number of tanks had been lost and five Israeli soldiers captured. (In subsequent negotiations three Israelis captured in this war were returned in exchange for 1,150 convicted terrorists who were being held in Israeli prisons, many of whom were to become active in the Palestinian uprising five years later.)

One major consequence of the army's failure to keep its planned timetable was that the flanking movement against the Syrians in the northern Bekaa (we had pushed them out of the southern part of the valley) was not completed and Israeli forces were still short of the highway. Another consequence was that many of the terrorists had managed to flee northward in front of the slow advance. Now over 7,000 of them were concentrated in and around Beirut. At Khalde, eight miles south of the city, their southernmost positions faced our advance units. Yet even though they were so nearly in our hands, at twelve noon on June 11 the IDF stopped firing in accord with our own cease-fire declaration.

In the Bekaa Valley, the Israeli silence was answered from Syrian lines, where the volume of fire slackened, then died out. But from the PLO positions south and west of Beirut a brief letup was soon followed by the renewal of heavy shelling and Katyusha fire. For several hours Israeli forces kept quiet while we considered how to respond. As the PLO fire intensified, Prime Minister Begin and I were in the cemetery at Kiryat Shaul at the funeral of Deputy Commander-in-Chief Kuti Adam, who had been killed by terrorists on the coastal road the previous day. Afterward we discussed the situation, then decided to implement the government's resolution in full—we would hit back as hard as we could. At 3 P.M. Raful Eytan gave the order, and once more the battle against the terrorists was in full swing. Two hours later the western sector units were again moving forward.

That night I flew to Junia, the first time I had been to the Christian enclave since the war started. Meeting with Bashir and some of his commanders, I was briefed on where their forces were and I described our dispositions. I did not discuss our intentions with Bashir—indeed at that moment we had no intentions other than to maintain quiet with the Syrians and to continue hitting the terrorists as hard as we could after their violation of the cease-fire. I was, however, interested in finding out what steps Bashir himself planned to take. To this point in the operation we had made it clear to the Phalangists and their allies that we did not want them to assume any kind of active role. We had our own very specific goals, and we had no interest in being drawn into any situations Bashir's forces might create. But at the same time there had been severe criticism in Israel about the lack of activity from Lebanon's Christians.

("In the name of God," said Victor Shem Tov of the left-wing Mapam party, "when are they going to act?") Israel was, after all, fighting their enemies, while they, it seemed, were content to sit back and enjoy the fruits. Even now, with the PLO cooped up around Beirut and under heavy pressure, Bashir and his commanders were less than enthusiastic about doing anything. It was not long before I understood that they were not going to be an active ally in the continuing war against the terrorists.

The night of June 11 and into the following day we pressed forward, one column moving northeast toward Aley, another taking Khalde (just north of which lay Beirut's international airport). With Israeli forces hitting the terrorists hard and threatening to close off the Beirut–Damascus highway—their only escape route from the capital—the PLO on June 12 notified Lebanon's prime minister that they would now accept the cease-fire.

The next day I flew north, intending to get a firsthand report from the forward positions southeast of Beirut. Landing at General Amos Yaron's divisional headquarters, I met with Yaron's chief of staff and was told that the general himself was on the front lines, about forty-five minutes forward. So along with Director of Military Intelligence Yehoshua Saguy, several people on my staff, and Yaron's chief of staff, I got into an APC and went off to look for him.

Climbing along the narrow mountain roads among lines of the paratroop brigade's APC's and tanks, we stopped on occasion to ask for Yaron. Each time the answer was "He should be around here somewhere, maybe just a little forward." The forty-five minutes soon passed, then an hour, then two hours, as we picked our way through the column of armor, watching tensely as the driver maneuvered along the edges of the high Shouf Mountain cliffs. Here and there the burned-out remains of PLO and Syrian tanks and other vehicles and equipment attested to the fighting that had taken place not long before.

For almost four hours we kept moving until we came to the spearhead of the column. With daylight fading, we pulled ahead of the leading tank, but still there was no Yaron. Suddenly on the road in front of us a Lebanese Christian officer appeared, armed with a Kalashnikov. Looking carefully, I thought I recognized him as the man who had commanded the Christian lines in Beirut when I visited in January. As I climbed down from the APC, the officer stared hard, his face showing that he was even more surprised to see me in that place than I was to be there. When I asked what he was doing, he told me that we were in Kfar Shima. We had just entered the Phalangists' forward position.*

The Christian officer was the first person I had met all day who seemed to really know where Yaron was. He would be happy to take me to him. There was just one problem—in the area immediately ahead his troops controlled only a narrow corridor. Beyond the bridge in front of us Syrian positions flanked the road less than two hundred yards away on either side. We would have to go very quietly. In fact it would be much better if we could go in his car instead of in the noisy M-113. But my security people would not agree to that, and so the officer got into the APC with us, obviously anxious.

We approached the bridge slowly, keeping as quiet as we could. But as we did the APC hit a pothole and somebody's rifle went off by accident. The shot rang through the air and we all grasped our weapons, waiting for something to happen. A few moments passed in tense silence, then the APC moved on, arriving soon in a built-up area which we understood was the town of Ba'abde. Around us crowds of people milled through the streets, all of them armed and many of them shooting into the air in the Arab fashion of celebrating what they call the "fantasia."

As we rolled slowly into this scene, my security people became visibly nervous. By now it was dark, and who could tell who was who among the crowd that began to congregate around the APC? When the Lebanese officer tried to climb down, perhaps to ask where the Israeli commander was, one of them grabbed him, insisting that he stay with us in the vehicle. Soon we found ourselves in the center of the town in front of the city hall. And there was Yaron, very surprised by my sudden appearance. But no more so than the town mayor and the local police chief, who also soon arrived at the scene and invited me inside for coffee.

In short order Bashir Gemayel had heard I was in Ba'abde and sent somebody to pick us up and take us to meet him in Beirut. Once again the Lebanese capital was an unbelievable experience, though after my visit in January I wasn't exactly surprised. The restaurants and bars were still full, and the same crowds overflowed the neon-lit sidewalks, while honking cars jammed the streets. There was not a trace of wartime atmosphere. "You know," I said to Bashir, "I thought maybe I would see people rushing off to fight for their country. But look at this." Nobody

---

* Yaron's division had been heading toward Aley but had run into stiff Syrian and PLO terrorist opposition. In response, the lead brigade commander had found this mountain road that had brought him through Kfar Shima into the town of Ba'abde.

was queuing up at induction points, nobody was filling sandbags, nobody was marching off to join units. It was a disturbing sight, especially after having come straight from the Shouf Mountain cliffs littered with the wreckage of war.

Other disturbing thoughts were on my mind as well. Just before the cease-fire my eye had been caught by a headline in one of the newspapers proclaiming that some of the ministers "suspected" the minister of defense. The guns are just about to go silent, I thought, and already the politicians are beginning to growl. With a very hard road still in front of us before a postwar settlement was worked out, I knew that more than anything we would need unity to see it through. And for this prospect the newspaper piece was not a good omen.

The idea that the government might lose its determination and unity at this crucial stage was so upsetting that I had brought the subject up at the cabinet meeting of the eleventh. There should be a very hard reaction from the cabinet or from the prime minister, I said, if the government does not want the achievement, just now in our grasp, to be "ground up." Begin's response was soothing. "This has been one of the greatest actions," he said, "and not only of our nation in its thirty-four years of independence, but throughout the history of our people. . . . Be proud of that. That is my position, and I am sure that is the position of the entire government. These other things are just meaningless noise."

But despite his words, this "meaningless noise" preyed on Begin's mind too, so much so that several days later as he prepared for a visit to the United States he left the cabinet with an admonishment. "There have been whispers of personal hatred," Begin warned, "against the government and especially toward Sharon. Before there was hatred, but now there is something more—jealousy. Only a firm and united stand by the cabinet can oppose this whispering campaign, as well as give comfort to the parents of the dead soldiers. There should be no chink in the wall."[*]

The Ba'abde linkup was the first meeting between Israeli and Christian units. It had been accomplished without fighting by Israeli forces moving up that narrow road that snaked through the Syrian-controlled hill country east of Beirut. With this linkup accomplished, Beirut was cut off. Syrian forces in the city were separated from their compatriots on the

---

[*] Cabinet meeting, June 15, 1982.

highway and in the northern Bekaa, and the terrorists in Beirut had no access to reinforcements or supplies. The city was now under siege, at least in theory.

In fact, though, the corridor that cut the Beirut–Damascus highway and linked the Israeli and Christian forces was only about five hundred yards wide altogether, a tenuous and indefensible position. So narrow was our hold on the road that in Ba'abde our APC's were clustered near the presidential palace, a fact that drove the Americans wild at our supposed arrogance. And now, alive to their peril, the PLO quickly began to organize a reinforcement effort. Almost immediately terrorists from all over began to arrive in the Syrian positions east of the corridor, volunteers from Syria, Libya, Iraq, even Iran, all of them intent on getting into Beirut to join the PLO in their West Beirut redoubts.

With this gathering going on, I knew we had to make every effort to widen our hold on the road, strengthening the barrier between these forces and the PLO in the city. More worrisome were the Syrians. For the moment, the Syrian forces around us were exhausted, a beaten army. But they were still sitting firmly on all the controlling terrain, and with a short respite they could easily regain their strength. Already we were being subjected to infiltration and attacks from the terrorists in the hills. Any Syrian pressure, I knew, would make our position completely untenable.

I knew too that we were facing another grave problem, this one political. Shortly after the cease-fire Philip Habib had started pressing for a separation of forces. On the fifteenth of June he had raised this issue in a meeting that took place in the house of Colonel Johnny Abdou, intelligence chief of the Lebanese army. Yarzah, where this house was located, was a neighborhood of beautiful villas east of Ba'abde where you could look down at the Ministry of Defense and the presidential palace on the hill just below. But inside the house itself there was no electricity, only candlelight. And around it were units of the Lebanese army and the Christian militias, all of them quiet. The Syrian positions, they told me, were just 250 yards away. That was why the lights were off and why the place was so hushed.

When Habib came in, we began our first substantial discussion of future developments, and among other issues the American envoy raised this question of disengagement. He believed, he said, that our forces should withdraw some five kilometers in order to disengage from the Syrians and terrorists and so increase the chances of a cease-fire holding, also to give him something to offer the PLO in the developing negotiations. But the real meaning of a disengagement, I knew, was that we would be removing ourselves from the Beirut–Damascus highway while the Syrians and PLO would be allowed to re-establish the continuity of their forces. A "disengagement" would lift the siege that we had so tenuously established and destroy the achievement that was now in our grasp—the removal of all PLO and Syrian forces from Lebanon, and with them our own withdrawal as well.

I told Habib, of course, that we could not accept any disengagement. But that night I understood we were facing a real danger. I did not know how insistent this American demand might become, but I could already see the scope of it. If we did not have a firm hold on a stretch of the Beirut–Damascus highway much broader than these few hundred yards we were currently sitting on, we could easily find ourselves withdrawing while the Syrians and PLO would be strengthening Beirut, moving troops and supplies in, and preparing to stay forever.

As a result I instructed the IDF to do what it could to improve its positions on the road by slowly expanding eastward, feeling out those places where gains could be made without provoking battle. "We must maintain the cease-fire," I ordered, "and you should only advance in vital places that can be captured without violating it." But within those guidelines, I was intent on achieving the strongest position we could.

By the eighteenth it was obvious that something more than this kind of gradual sneaking forward would be necessary. The cease-fire had never taken hold south and east of Beirut, and in the hills around Ba'abde the Syrians were now bringing up additional forces while they and the international terrorists mixed in with them continued their harassment fire. With Israeli forces stationary, I was worried that the PLO would begin recovering from their shock and start digging in for a protracted battle. Should wide-scale fighting erupt again, the Syrians were in a position to easily overrun our corridor on the highway. With this as background, on the eighteenth I ordered the IDF to prepare an attack eastward down the highway toward the town of Aley. The action, however, would need government approval, and that would have to wait for Prime Minister Begin's return from the United States on the twenty-fourth.

On that day, June 24, I described in detail to Begin and the cabinet our position on the road and my thinking about what our tactical require-ments were. Then I asked for approval of an attack that would once and for all firmly establish our presence there. After a full discussion of the

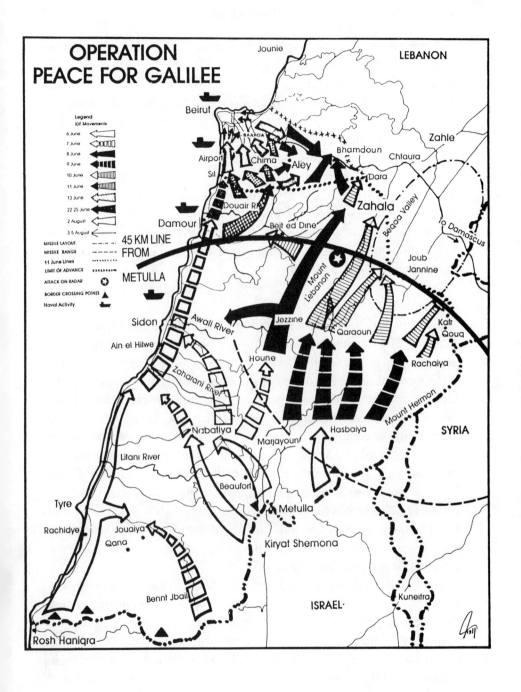

situation, the cabinet accepted my analysis and resolved unanimously in favor of the proposed action.

That same day the attack was launched. When the fighting was over, less than twenty-four hours later, Israeli forces were occupying the Beirut–Damascus highway for a distance of more than twelve miles. The political reality that had been achieved by our original linkup with the Christians was now also an incontrovertible physical reality. Israeli units were sitting in the strategic center of the country, separating Syrian forces in and out of Beirut and eliminating any hope the PLO might have had for relief from the outside. We were now in a position to forcefully pursue our goals in the negotiations that had been under way for two weeks, negotiations that were beginning to show ominous differences between ourselves and the Americans.

These differences had been evident as early as the fifteenth during my meeting with Habib at Johnny Abdou's house. By that time it was absolutely clear that to bring lasting security to our border we had first of all to accomplish the evacuation of all external forces from Lebanon—the terrorist organizations, the Syrians, and of course ourselves. But when I put this position on the table, I heard Habib say, "The withdrawal of external forces cannot be symmetric." "What do you mean it can't be symmetric?" I asked. "Well," he said, "the Syrians have security interests in Lebanon." "What security interests do they have in Lebanon?" I said. "Did Lebanon ever attack Syria? Did they ever threaten Syria? Has Syria suffered from any terrorist activities coming from Lebanon?" The answer to such questions was obvious. But there the American position was anyway, a portentous indication that whatever course they might be traveling, it was not the same as ours.

Habib's thoughts on the PLO were equally unsatisfactory. Maybe what we should do, he said, was not to expel them but to disarm them and turn them into a "political" PLO. A week later, again with the candles burning at Johnny Abdou's house, we were still arguing the same point. "Who has to leave," asked Habib, "all 10,000 [terrorists] or just their leaders?" "All the terrorists," I answered. "We cannot accept that armed terrorists will stay there." "Regarding disarmament," Habib said, hoping he had found an opening, "I agree with you completely." But I would not give in on this issue. It was not disarmament we were talking about, it was expulsion. "They must leave," I told him. "They will be destroyed [if they don't]. We cannot accept that they won't leave. They can be destroyed without going into Beirut itself."

Habib: I know the map. But there are many people and many Shi'ites [in Beirut].

Sharon: Tell them [the terrorists] to leave.

Habib: I think it will be impossible to do what you asked.*

As I soon came to understand, underneath it all was a concept shared by Habib and other state department people—including Morris Draper, Nick Valiotis, and Sam Lewis, ambassador to Israel—that Lebanon might be used as a lever to solve other problems in the Middle East. The Reagan plan was already being developed at that time (though we were not informed of it) that proposed a comprehensive resolution of the "West Bank problem" with the Jordanians and Palestinians. To that end Lebanon might be used as a tool to bring the PLO into the negotiating process. In addition, with the Syrian army beaten, Habib thought that he might move Assad closer to the American side by giving protection to the Syrian position. The fluid Lebanese situation, in which he himself was acting as broker to all sides, thus provided an opportunity to accomplish various desirable ends.

But while weeks passed and the Americans continued their complex and time-consuming maneuvers, the Begin government refused to be sidetracked from its own firm vision. In meeting after meeting with the Americans, my constant theme was that in Lebanon we were dealing with a country that had been torn apart for years already by war, a country whose own problems were so complicated that if we managed to solve just these it would be a remarkable achievement. In particular I was speaking about a long-term solution to the problem of security for Israel's northern border and about bringing Lebanon into a triangle of regional countries—along with Israel and Egypt—with allegiances to the United States and the free world. That possibility seemed to me in those days to be real. I firmly believed then, and I believe now, that it could have been achieved. It was in our grasp. But Philip Habib and his colleagues were moving in a different direction.

And so was Israel's Labor party. Even while the struggle with the Americans was gathering steam, by the last week in June the Begin government was coming under heavy attack from Labor and other leftist-organized groups. The intimations of political opposition that had

* Meeting, June 23, 1982.

already surfaced two weeks earlier were now blossoming into the first large-scale effort in Israeli history to destroy the traditional unity on security issues by making them a subject of domestic politics. Having raised its head briefly after the destruction of the Iraqi reactor, this monster was now shaking itself into vivid life.

In particular, Labor politicians were charging that the government had committed itself to doing nothing beyond pushing the Syrians and terrorists back twenty-five miles. Now, they said, we were unconscionably breaking our word. During the long cabinet meeting of June 27, Begin addressed this issue head-on. He wasn't sorry, he began, about what had been said previously. What had been said was accurate. What wasn't accurate was this opposition charge that the cabinet, and especially two cabinet members, were deceiving people. No one was deceiving anybody. The government hadn't deceived anybody, he hadn't deceived anybody, and Sharon hadn't deceived anybody. Then Begin launched into a brief review of what had happened. He noted that the IDF had stopped shooting on Friday, June 11. But the government had said then that if we were fired upon, we would fire back. Had the enemy also stopped shooting then, everything would have been quiet. From that point the entire struggle would have been political. The IDF would not have moved toward Beirut and there wouldn't have been any more battles with the Syrians.

Right then, Begin went on, Israel would have demanded a political settlement. But, as we knew, the other side had kept firing and we had reciprocated. After that, somebody was going to advance and somebody was going to retreat, and as far as he was concerned it was a good thing the other side did the retreating.

It was for this reason that he was so angry about the charges of deception. It was being made to sound as if we had intentionally set out to deceive people in order to shed the enemy's blood and the blood of our own soldiers. And he didn't have to mention, he said, how he felt in his heart when he heard news of our boys who had been lost. No, these charges were not only a tremendous insult, they were a torture for a legitimate, democratic government. The facts of the situation were plain and they were recorded—we had stood ready to stop all fighting and begin the political process of securing peace for the Galilee. It was the terrorists who said that they would continue to fight, and they had continued. Whatever had happened after that had happened only according to cabinet resolutions. Nothing had gone on by itself, as we all knew had happened during previous wars.

At the same meeting the cabinet discussed in detail how we should best proceed in order to make sure the PLO was removed from Beirut. "Our problem," I said, "is how to find a way that will result in the terrorists leaving Beirut with minimum casualties [for Israeli forces], recognizing that we do have a public situation." As long as there was no significant American negotiating progress (there had been none since the first cease-fire two weeks ago), there were three realistic options. The first was simply for the IDF to enter Beirut and physically destroy them. The second was to bring massive fire to bear on the terrorist-held southern suburbs, from where much of the civilian population had already fled, and to force them to accept our conditions. The third was for the IDF to move into the open ground around two of the most dangerous terrorist-held suburbs, which would give us control of these areas and clearly demonstrate that we meant business. This might not be as effective as shelling the PLO strongholds, but it might be enough to speed up the terrorists' understanding that if they did not agree to leave they would face eventual destruction.

During the hard debate that followed, Begin insisted on the importance of time. He argued that we simply did not have any time left. The United States had vetoed the U.N. resolution calling for our withdrawal. But this would only give us a few days. Those cabinet members who were objecting to the proposal to move on Beirut's suburbs were in fact arguing for a war of attrition. If we didn't act, the PLO would. The people wouldn't stand for it.

There were still, Begin said, seven thousand malevolent criminals in Beirut, and as long as there were we had not secured anything. We needed to force these criminals out of the city. In his estimation, if we took the airport and moved another fifteen hundred yards we would be able to really press them. That was what we needed a decision on, today.

Along with Begin, Foreign Minister Yitzhak Shamir, and Raful Eytan, I had proposed the plan of moving into the airport and the open ground around the suburbs. But when one of the ministers asked what my private thoughts were on the matter, I answered, "My opinion was that we should take the PLO and act against them with all the firepower we have, with all the air force, with all the artillery, and destroy them utterly—I know people don't like that expression—to get them to accept our conditions. That was my opinion. But there was a discussion, and I accept this current plan [that we were proposing], and I fully stand behind it. . . . When a decision has been made, that's the decision."

"It isn't a decision," said Dr. Burg. "It's a proposal."

And it wasn't a decision. A number of ministers were strongly opposed, among them Mordechai Zippori, Yitzhak Berman, and Zevulun Hammer. They knew that the world's television cameras were capturing dramatic images every day of the Israeli army besieging the city. And they, like the rest of us, knew that those cameras would never present the reality of why we were involved in this war—the years of horrific terrorism from Lebanon, the attempted destruction of the Israeli north, the massive PLO buildup of Katyusha rockets and artillery, the utter failure of the American negotiators. As a result they were fearful for Israel's public image, and they believed that additional IDF advances would only tarnish the image more. They were concerned too about the IDF casualties an operation might cause. And so they wanted to avoid action and recommended that we squeeze the political side for all it was worth.

After a long and difficult discussion the cabinet adopted a resolution to carry out a diplomatic effort and await results. The resolution announced that Israel would keep the cease-fire. It also called on the Lebanese army to enter West Beirut and demanded that the fifteen terrorist organizations covered by the PLO umbrella turn over their weapons to the Lebanese army and that all members of those organizations, along with all Syrian forces in Beirut, leave the city under an Israeli safe conduct. Once Beirut was reunified, negotiations would begin on the removal of all remaining foreign forces and on guarantees of Lebanese territorial integrity and peace. Finally, the resolution warned that if the current cease-fire was broken, the government would convene and decide on a course of action.

Three days later, on June 30, Philip Habib delivered a nine-point American proposal on a final settlement that was not very different from our own positions—except in one significant regard. According to the Americans, a "political PLO" would be allowed to remain. Our response was to accept all the American points but this one, which we rejected categorically. At the same time we urged the U.S. to bring the negotiations to a conclusion as quickly as possible. The PLO, we knew, was not yet even thinking about withdrawing.

In fact the PLO's incentives to stay were far greater than their incentives to leave. They could see as well as we that Habib for his own reasons was not pushing for any fast end to the situation. And the lack of any real American pressure encouraged them in their determination to stay put. Beyond that, as the siege of Beirut lengthened, pressure inside Israel itself was growing. Street demonstrations, media attacks, and criticism in the Knesset were building quickly. Partly the pressure came from people who sincerely if naively believed we could put a stop to the war without concluding the situation with the PLO in Beirut. But more important it came from the Labor alignment acting in concert with the Shalom Acshav (Peace Now) group. For Labor it was indeed a dangerous situation. As party leader Shimon Peres put it in one emergency meeting of party leaders, "Contrary to our previous suspicions, the war is a big success. It is about to reach its most important objectives. In a few days—and one cannot escape the facts—an Israeli-Lebanese peace treaty will be signed. This will be *their* second peace treaty. *They* will also succeed in sending Arafat and his terrorists to hell as well as in breaking the PLO [italics mine].* "They," he repeated, as if the war to protect our borders and eliminate the terrorists was being fought in the interest of the Likud, not Israel, as if a peace treaty with Lebanon would have been for the Likud and not for Israel.

Arafat and his friends needed no one to point out how significant Israel's domestic political broils could be to their survival. Documents the IDF found in Beirut after the terrorists' expulsion told the story eloquently. "The most important thing," said a PLO chief in one recorded meeting, "is to increase the demonstrations all over Israel. To do that we have to mobilize all possible means. If the demonstration in Tel Aviv is not repeated, all its effect will be lost."† "Chaim Bar-Lev," reads another, "wants Sharon to be tried. Those ones want to withdraw and to try Sharon. All these things, with God's help, will create pressure on the Israeli government." "Our only hope," says a third, "is in those demonstrations that are taking place in Tel Aviv."

Among the PLO material found were also reports about talks held by Abba Eban and Shimon Peres with Egyptian diplomats, talks in which these Labor party leaders attacked the Begin government ruthlessly. These reports allowed the terrorists to monitor the internal political struggle going on in Israel and to take courage from the divisiveness and enmity that obviously prevailed in the heart of the Israeli establishment.

---

* Quoted by the then-Labor MK Yossi Sarrid, *Ha'aretz*, August 21, 1987.
† This and the following quotations are from captured documents I read in front of the Knesset on September 22, 1982.

Watching the pressure mount on the Israeli government from both inside Israel and outside, Yasser Arafat could easily believe that the more time passed, the more telling this pressure would become. But the PLO also had the most compelling subjective reasons for hanging on as long as humanly possible. Lebanon was, they knew, their best hope, perhaps their last hope to exist as a military force with the ability to strike Israel. If they lost Lebanon, they believed they would essentially be destroyed as an independent movement. But if they could find a way to stay, then anything was possible. Israel, they knew, could not remain in Lebanon for long, nor did it want to. If they could maintain even a base, even a force of cadres, they might in due time be able to reconstitute everything they had had.

And what they had had was not merely a "state within a state." With no effective central Lebanese government, it was an actual state, with many of the institutions of a state: courts, police, jails, a financial system, a welfare system of sorts, a bureaucracy, an army, a reserve militia. In the chaotic and divided world of southern Lebanon they had imposed themselves as masters. They collected "taxes," ran businesses, and charged tolls for road use. They controlled every aspect of life in their regions, attaching people to them through commerce and trade, and ruling over them through intimidation and terror. In Lebanon they had created a center for world terrorism, hosting, training, and providing refuge for terrorist movements from Africa to Central America, from the Indian subcontinent to Asia Minor, from Baader Meinhoff and the Red Brigades to the IRA and the Japanese Red Army.

Operation Peace for Galilee had caught this terrorist state in the process of transforming its army from an organization of guerrilla terrorists into a regular military force, complete with armor, artillery, and communications. In the cities and refugee neighborhoods they had built bunkers under houses and tunnels connecting one area with another. Over the years of war such systems had expanded to become virtual underground cities. In the cliffs and ridges, they had dug underground fortifications and huge tunnels that served as supply depots. In the rugged Lebanese mountains with their few primitive roads and paths and in the thickly grown plantations of the coastal plain, the topography was ideal for defensive fighting. Here a decently trained army could make the cost of any invasion prohibitive. And meanwhile divisions' worth of rockets and long-range artillery could destroy the life of northern Israel. All this the PLO was on its way to accomplishing when Peace for Galilee fell on them. And all this the PLO stood to lose should they be forced out, and so they waited, knowing that time was on their side.

We too knew that time was on their side. But even now I did not believe that the IDF should move into West Beirut, with all the problems and casualties such an operation would bring with it. Instead I pressed for air strikes and heavy artillery fire on the terrorist headquarters and positions in their suburban neighborhoods. I knew that unless the PLO was convinced they would be destroyed, they would never leave. Consequently we had to bring the strongest pressure to bear, forcing them to make the decision. The cabinet, however, did not accept my arguments and opted instead to slowly tighten the siege (I eventually went along with the decision), combining incremental military advances with intermittent shutoffs of electricity and water, and psychological warfare techniques such as leafleting and mock air raids.

By mid-July domestic and international pressure was building ominously, and we were still sitting in front of the city. For all the talk, Habib's negotiations had dragged on for weeks, achieving nothing. "Based on discussions with our friends," Begin declared at the cabinet meeting on July 18, "the director general of the Ministry of Foreign Affairs, the chief of military intelligence, and on the discussions of General Tamir (national security adviser) with Philip Habib in Beirut, I can tell the government . . . that Philip Habib will expel the terrorists from Beirut like he removed the missiles from the Bekaa, no less efficiently and without better results." (Habib had negotiated for ten months without getting the missiles removed.) "Accordingly," Begin went on, "we have to talk about a military operation."

When Begin was finished speaking, I took the floor and said that I had nothing to add to the prime minister's assessment of the American negotiations, that for my part I believed they were only a means of delay. Since there was no movement to be expected on that front, we had to take action. What I was proposing was an operation that would first separate the terrorist-held neighborhoods of Sabra, Shatilla, and Fakahani from the rest of the city. Once this was accomplished, IDF forces would then take the Hippodrome and the Beirut woods area just to the east of these areas.

In the course of the discussion that followed, Chief of Military Intelligence Saguy gave his assessment that the terrorists did not yet feel there was a military threat to the city and that they had no intention of relaxing their grip on West Beirut. They would regard such a step, he said, as the destruction of the Palestinian revolution that had taken such effort to build over the last eighteen years.

For some of the ministers, though, the idea of street fighting was not something they could accept, despite the obvious and overwhelming need to bring the situation to a conclusion. "I prefer air raids," said Minister of Interior Joseph Burg, "to putting our foot soldiers at risk. . . . I am not an anti-humanist, but if it is possible to convince them by occasionally cutting off water, electricity, and fuel supplies, that is better than street battles."

But Prime Minister Begin put the situation in clear perspective. "Gentlemen," he stated, "if we continue to remain at the gates of Beirut as we are doing now, we may bring disaster on ourselves. . . . Do we want to harm the civilian population? But to argue that in case we may hit some civilians we shouldn't do anything—where would such an argument lead us? If we do not enter Beirut, the victory will be the PLO's. Arafat will claim that the PLO is alive, in position, and armed. . . . Gentlemen, we are at a turning point that may lead to a national crisis. Our people will not tolerate weeks and months of an unnecessary mobilization of the army, with extended service, where we are being shot at and our boys are being hurt. We cannot withstand a static war without anything being done for victory."

My own position was as strong as I could make it. It was our business never to allow a terrorist infrastructure that would threaten Israel's security to be built in Lebanon again. But whether or not we would again see one there depended on what happened in Beirut. We had to move ahead and finish it. At the end of the meeting a vote was taken, and the cabinet decided to adopt the proposed plan. At the same time a cabinet committee was instructed to set a date for implementation. A minority group of eight ministers, however, proposed that the IDF produce alternative plans within the following twenty-four hours.

During this absolutely critical time it was evident that many of the members of the government were in the grip of trepidation, that they were making attempts to "leave the wagon." As long as things had been running smoothly, the cabinet had been quite pleased. But now the war was no longer popular. Media attacks had become savage, and demonstrations were rocking the streets. Now the situation had grown a good deal harder. But still it was not the government that was under fire. The attacks were directed at only two people, Mr. Begin and myself. And instead of standing shoulder to shoulder and rebuffing those attacks, some in the cabinet began casting around for ways to get out, ways to separate themselves from the onus of the war.

By late July I understood clearly that this government would have great difficulty carrying on with what had to be done. I had seen the same kind of thing more than once before, in 1956 when the Americans and Russians brought their pressure to bear, then in the waiting period before the Six Day War when the government lost its ability to act. After that war it was said how clever we were then to have waited for the exact moment. But the truth is that it had nothing to do with cleverness. The government of the time just could not find the determination to do what they knew had to be done. I had seen an equivalent collapse during the first days of the Yom Kippur War. And now in Lebanon, when it came down to the hardest point, I watched the same dynamics take over—the weakness, the failure of confidence, the lack of determination. And so they left the two of us, Begin and myself, to carry the burden.

Reflecting on what was happening within the government, I would sometimes turn to my aide-de-camp, Oded Shamir. "Can you imagine what would happen now," I asked at one point, "if we were in a really difficult situation, if the Iraqis were attacking, the Syrians, the Jordanians, if the Egyptians were moving forces into the Sinai? What would happen with this leadership? If they cannot stand up to these problems, which aren't easy but also aren't the kind of problems that cannot be solved? What would happen with them? What would happen with this nation?"

I thought too about Alexander Haig, who had just recently submitted his resignation as secretary of state, in part because he could not stand the way his government was handling this crisis. Haig had been unequivocally opposed to the Peace for Galilee operation. He had told me that bluntly when I met him in Washington in May, and he had given the same message to Begin. But once the war had begun, he understood the circumstances perhaps better than our own government. When Begin went to Washington in mid-June, Haig had told him privately that once you start it, you have to finish it as fast as possible. (When Begin heard that, he sent me a message from Washington with instructions to prepare to go into Beirut itself—although he, like I, still believed the main effort in the city should be carried out by Lebanese forces with the IDF playing only a supporting role. I conveyed this message to the cabinet on June

20.) Only Israeli pressure, Haig insisted to his own president, could produce a situation that would end the fighting.[*]

Haig had understood the atmosphere, and his instincts about getting it done quickly with strong, consistent pressure were right. Because once we were under attack from the Americans, the media, the Labor-organized demonstrations, when we had come to the most difficult part, and had to find a way to get the PLO out of Beirut—then the consensus in the cabinet began to dissolve.

Here, at this very point it began to come apart, when there was no alternative but to finish the mission. It is like when you cut the barbed wire, I thought, when you are lying under the strands and the firing starts. That is the moment of truth for a commander. But governments are faced with the same critical moments on a different echelon, a different field of action, but the same kinds of decisions. At that most crucial moment your natural instinct may be just to lie there or to retreat. But in reality you must take the steps to finish it as fast as possible. And many of the people in this government were not up to making such a decision, to taking on such a responsibility.

As a result the cabinet moved sporadically, tightening the noose around the terrorists in West Beirut but fighting each other bitterly, their unity and determination coming apart. At the same time the diplomatic efforts dragged on inconclusively and the PLO loudly declared their eleven points, insisting that, before they left, a multinational force would have to come in to create a cordon between them and ourselves. They would leave, they said, but first we would have to retreat several kilometers, creating a buffer zone within which the multinational force would be deployed.

While such a plan seemed to make sense to the Americans, I understood it as a desperate maneuver by the terrorists to maintain themselves in the city. We knew that the PLO command had not yet made any decision to leave Beirut. Beyond that, they did not yet have anywhere to go even if they should decide to leave. The Americans were having a frantic time trying to persuade the Arab countries to open their doors to the terrorists. The meaning of it was quite simple. Behind the screen of a multinational force Arafat and his colleagues were sure they could find a variety of ways to stay put. They knew that with American, French, or Italian troops in the way, we would be unable to apply any

[*] *Caveat*, p. 345.

pressure, and they were equally sure that the multinational force itself would never be used to physically expel them. They have no intention of leaving, Begin declared at the August 1 cabinet meeting. If a multinational force comes in and separates us, "the criminals will never leave Beirut."

The debate at this August 1 meeting was heated, as almost all the cabinet debates had become by this time. Arguments raged over how much force to use, whether to restrain ourselves and hope for a diplomatic resolution or to apply real pressure and force the PLO to the wall as fast as we could. In these arguments the use of air power was a central issue. We had bombed the terrorist-held positions heavily; and Begin, I, and others felt we had to continue to do so. Other ministers opposed it bitterly, and American pressure on this subject was growing. Labor had already passed a resolution that there should be no further bombing. It was crucial, Begin argued, echoing my own conviction, to use the airforce, so that we wouldn't have to go in ourselves. But if there was no other choice, the IDF would have to do that, too; if it came down to that he would recommend it. No one should be saying that we wouldn't enter Beirut. That would cause real damage by giving the terrorists an illusion to hold onto while time was at a premium for us. As it was, they thought our army was falling apart. They had heard that one of our colonels had resigned rather than enter West Beirut. They had heard what the opposition was saying. Those were the kinds of things that boosted their morale immensely.

Now Begin proposed that we make our intentions crystal clear to everyone concerned, especially to the Americans who believed that a cease-fire would facilitate Habib's negotiations. We should initiate a cease-fire, the prime minister declared, but it must be absolute and mutual. "We will tell the Americans that we agree to a cease-fire, but it is to be clearly understood that if it is violated once more, there will be no more cease-fires until the malevolent criminals leave Beirut." In other words, should our soldiers be hit at all, we would take whatever steps we could. "Should the terrorists violate the cease-fire," the cabinet resolved at the end of this meeting, "the IDF will respond from land, air, and sea."

The announcement was barely made before this cease-fire too was violated by the terrorists. Our response, in accord with the cabinet resolution of the first, was severe. Over the next several days the IDF moved forward, bringing the entire airport under its control and pushing northward.* With the PLO still undecided about leaving, on August 4 the IDF launched a heavy assault during which I ordered artillery and air attacks on the terrorist neighborhoods.

These attacks had a strong impact on the terrorists. But they also elicited a storm of recrimination within the cabinet and harsh criticism from President Reagan, who transmitted a letter to Begin expressing his anger. In his letter the president attacked Israel for using "disproportionate" artillery and air strikes, for causing the deaths of civilians, and for potentially derailing Habib's negotiations. "The relationship between our two nations," he wrote, "is in the balance."

In Begin's response he reminded the president that Israel's policy was that the cease-fire was to have been complete and mutual. The terrorists had not kept it, and we had responded. He also noted the relationship between military and diplomatic solutions. "We prefer a political solution," the prime minister wrote, "but if the military option had not existed, the political solution of evacuating the terrorists would not exist."

On August 5 the cabinet met and considered the American request that we exercise restraint for several days. In the course of the meeting Foreign Minister Shamir reported on his visit to the United States, including his meetings with American Jewish leaders. He described the administration's anger over our military pressure. But he also noted that in his meeting with Henry Kissinger the former secretary of state had told him that he did not believe diplomatic pressure alone would ever get the PLO out.

"I believe," I told the cabinet, "that we should allow a couple of days' opportunity for serious negotiations. But I will not accept a situation where our soldiers will be unable to defend themselves, not if the president wants it and not if Shultz, Weinberger, or Habib want it. No one has the right to ask something like that of us . . . Still," I said, "if it

---

* Prior to this the airport had been a no man's land between the two sides. On August 1 one of the regular Israeli night patrols had stayed in the area in order to prevent sniping from the PLO patrols which ordinarily infiltrated during the day. When I heard about this the next morning I reported it to the cabinet. Specifically in this context, Prime Minister Begin later answered the housing minister's question about whether he had known of this patrol action in advance, "I can assure you, David [Levy], that I always know, either before or later." On another occasion (August 5) Begin became so exasperated with ministerial questions about the smallest tactical movements that he declared angrily that the campaign had to be carried on, that no country conducted wars in this fashion, with the entire government participating in decisions.

will be possible to conduct negotiations, for several days I'm in favor of it."

We knew from intelligence that our action on the third and fourth had seriously affected the terrorists and had gone some way toward altering their thinking. Intelligence Chief Saguy even reported that many of them had fled into West Beirut, shedding their uniforms and even shaving their trademark beards. But the PLO were still holding tight to their demand that the multinational force come in between us. The Americans knew we did not want this, but they believed that in essence they had achieved an agreement from the PLO to leave. On the other side, our conviction that the multinational force would be used by the PLO as a screen to allow them to stay had not changed. It was a difference that led to a harsh encounter between myself and Philip Habib on August 6, when the American envoy presented his resolution to the problem of how to withdraw foreign forces.

"The French [multinational force troops] will come simultaneously with the beginning of the [PLO] withdrawal. Then we will come," said Habib.

Sharon: "That is contradictory to what you told us."

Habib: "That's correct. . . . I want the package deal to be passed on paper to the Israeli and Lebanese governments and to the Palestinians through the media." (The "package deal" was Habib's term for the arrangements by which all foreign forces would withdraw: PLO, Syrians, and Israelis.)

Sharon (after some discussion): "We do not agree that the MNF will arrive before the last busful of terrorists leaves."

Habib: "I know about that. But you will have to address the president of the United States, because my offer derives from instructions from him."

Sharon: "The French will not come here."

Habib: "When you agree to accept the package deal, you will come and say that I [Habib] promised. Why [should I] tell them in the beginning and then not execute it? It's in instructions from my government."

Sharon: "And I am acting according to instructions from my government. I repeat and emphasize that before the withdrawal of the terrorists and their leaders, we will not agree to a MNF. . . . Why should we offer them a deal when we object to it and you know we do?"

Sharon (after more discussion): "You must understand that after long years of our bloodshed resulting from terror in Lebanon we are not in a position to receive any dictation."

Habib: "It's not a dictation. It's a package deal."

Dictation or not, the "package deal," was not acceptable as long as it called for interposing the multinational force between ourselves and the terrorists. But there was no movement on this issue on the seventh or eighth. And while the diplomatic front remained impacted, PLO fire on our positions kept up, causing us continued casualties. As a result, in accord with the government resolutions to respond to terrorist fire with attacks from "sea, land, and air," on the ninth I began applying military pressure again, which built in intensity over the following days. As the PLO fire still did not stop, finally on August 12 I ordered heavy attacks by the air force on the terrorist-held positions. This assault brought another burst of anger from President Reagan, expressed in a harsh phone call to Prime Minister Begin. The cabinet too was extremely upset and passed a resolution that the air force could no longer be used except by approval of the prime minister and another that the situation in the area should not be altered except by cabinet decision.

It was a day full of tension and anger, most of it directed at me. But I had done what I believed was necessary to bring about a conclusion to this siege that had tragically and unexpectedly lasted since June 25. That night Philip Habib finally used the kind of whip he had had available to him for weeks. He issued an ultimatum to the PLO. The cease-fire that had been called at the end of the day would last only forty-eight hours, he told them. What might happen afterward was anybody's guess. They would have to agree to leave now, without any buffer zones and without the multinational force to protect them. When Habib said this, Arafat knew that the end had come. Faced with what must have seemed the imminent prospect of perishing, he broke. All his temporizing and conditions and deceptions were now things of the past. He would get out, he decided that night, himself and everyone with him. The stage was now set for a final, complete expulsion, which would bring to a close Israel's war against the PLO's kingdom of terror.

32

Closure

The PLO's decision to get out came on the night of August 12. During the preceding two months all of Israel and much of the world had become preoccupied by the particulars of the war, the destruction, the bloodshed, the inevitable tragedies. Beyond the military side of it a political storm had enveloped the Lebanon War that was like nothing else in Israeli history. The Labor alignment had thrown itself into a fierce anti-government struggle, marshaling all its great media strength and international resources, doing everything it could to unseat the government—and all this while Israeli forces were in the field in mid-battle. It was unprecedented and, to anyone with a sense of Israeli political history, unbelievable (the Labor Alignment's left-wing Mapam even distributed leaflets to soldiers in the field excoriating the war effort). *
During the previous months the debate and rage and propaganda that resulted had largely obscured the goals for which we had been fighting.

---

* Some Labor people were candid enough to discuss this phenomenon openly. Writing in the party newspaper *Davar*, Haim Guri, a leading Labor intellectual and one of Israel's best known authors, said, "Now for the first time since 1948 a right wing government went to war. . . . Let's tell the truth. Practically speaking, many among us did not acquiesce to the political change that took place [the Likud's victory in 1977], not for one day have they accepted it. And it is here that the problem lies."

Nevertheless, with Arafat's will finally broken and the terrorist organizations on their way out, it was now possible to begin putting the war into
perspective.

The Lebanon War, like all of Israel's wars, had been a defensive
struggle. Like the Sinai campaign of 1956 and the Six Day War in 1967,
it had taken the form of a pre-emptive strike, an attack against an enemy
that had demonstrated its intentions in the most graphic fashion, with
explicit declarations and bloody actions. It had been a war against our
oldest and cruelest foe, the Palestinian terror movement that had always
rejected our existence and whose avowed raison d'être was (and still is)
our elimination.

In the years since the PLO was founded, from 1965 to 1982, these
terrorists had killed both in Israel and Europe 1,392 people, wounding
and maiming another 6,237.* In the Peace for Galilee operation we had
succeeded in striking at the heart of this enemy. During the course of the
war we had destroyed their infrastructure and now we were expelling
them from the area. At the same time we had also achieved the possibility
of a government coming to power in Lebanon that could create stability
and prevent the re-establishment of the PLO, a government that could
live with us on terms of peace. This had not been our reason for going
to war, but it was nevertheless an achievement that had the farthest-
reaching consequences for Israel's future and for the future of the Middle
East. It presented an opportunity to bring Lebanon together with Egypt
and Israel in a peaceful, Western-oriented association. And it gave the
Arabs of Samaria, Judea, and Gaza the chance to move toward a
negotiated solution with us—free at last from the sinister effect of the
PLO with its assassinations and pervasive threats.

These then were the results of the Lebanon War. Or rather they were
results the war had made possible. How to gather these fruits was the
problem that now confronted us.

The immediate task was to assure that the PLO would in fact leave in
accord with the commitment they had given Habib. This was the subject
of a vexed meeting Begin, Shamir, and I had with Habib and Ambassador
Samuel Lewis on August 15. Already we all knew that Arafat was making
detailed plans to violate the agreement by withdrawing only a part of his
forces. Our intelligence information—from accurate sources—was that
between 2,000 and 2,500 PLO personnel would be planted in West

---

* Israeli Army statistics from the *Israeli Defense Journal.*

Beirut under assumed identities. Forged documents were already being prepared and salaries to cover the next six months were being paid out.

The PLO plan was to send out close to 9,000 people. But of these 9,000, 2,000 to 2,500 would not be real terrorists but civilians or people drawn from other militias, "artificial terrorists," as Begin called them. The remaining 2,500 terrorists would maintain an underground network in Beirut, disrupting Lebanon's political scene and preparing the ground for the redevelopment of a large-scale terrorist presence.

There were several ways we might deal with Arafat's plans, none of them satisfactory. One was to have the Americans require a list of names from the PLO, then check this list against a PLO roster that we might manage to get clandestinely. Another was to have the Americans check the terrorists against our list as they embarked. Alternately, or perhaps in addition, Israeli security people together with American people could search the town after the expulsion and identify those who had stayed.

This last, at least, Habib refused to do. "Bashir will take care of that afterwards," he said. "Bashir told me," I responded, "that the numbers are such that he can't do it." All of us realized that making sure all these people actually departed would be next to impossible. As Ambassador Lewis said, we would need fingerprint records, and even then the lists we got could well be phony. If there was any difference between the Americans and ourselves on this issue, it was our insistence that we at least make a strong effort to find out who was going, while the Americans were willing to leave the problem for the new Lebanese government to deal with. (Elections were scheduled to take place the following week.) But Lewis and Habib were not happy with the situation either. He had been over the problem many times already, Habib told us, and was upset that he could not find an effective solution to it.

The issue was still not resolved when six days later the PLO began boarding ships bound for the eight Arab countries that had at long last agreed to accept them. By the time the operation was completed, 8,856 terrorists had been expelled, together with 6,062 Syrians and their Palestinian auxiliaries. Syria, South Yemen, Tunisia, Yemen, Algeria, Sudan, Jordan, and Iraq were sharing the burden of this dispersal, a burden they had taken on with obvious distaste and reluctance.

Despite the potential problems represented by this PLO core left among the tunnels and weapons stores of West Beirut, this mass expulsion was an event whose importance could hardly be exaggerated. Here was the first step in what I saw as a process that would lead to a peace treaty between ourselves and the new Lebanese government. Hardly less significant, the PLO's defeat and dispersion also meant that the extremism and incessant violence that organization had always stood for would now be badly discredited. We had not fought this war against the Palestinian people; and with the PLO crushed, the possibility of a rational dialogue between ourselves and Palestinians not dedicated to our destruction would be greatly enhanced.

Exactly this was the subject of a meeting I had in Samaria with about thirty Palestinian leaders as the terrorists were boarding their ships in Beirut harbor. I believe, I told them, that we could now open a new era, one in which it would be possible for us to talk with each other and arrive at some mutually satisfactory conclusions. They too expressed themselves frankly. These were not people who were happy about the Israeli presence in Samaria, Judea, and Gaza. But they also understood that as long as the PLO was strong, there could be no negotiations and no peaceful solution either with the Palestinians or with the other Arab peoples. It was an encouraging meeting. By the last week in August it was possible to glimpse the outlines of a new set of relationships between Israel and its neighbors.

On August 23 Bashir Gemayel was elected president by the Lebanese parliament, an event we had expected but could not be sure of. But this good news was darkened a week later when the Americans announced the Reagan Plan, calling in essence for Jordan to act on behalf of the Palestinians in negotiations for territorial concessions on the West Bank and in Gaza. The plan was, as the U.S. State Department knew, a departure from the Camp David agreement that would be unacceptable to Israel. Coming on September 1, the very day the last contingent of terrorists sailed away from Beirut, the announcement was a rude shock. With this timing the Americans were giving the clearest possible signal that Lebanon to them was only a stage in something larger. Their priorities had differed from ours during the long and difficult negotiations while the Israeli army had sat for two and a half months in front of Beirut. And they were still working in a different direction, even while the fate of Lebanon remained to be decided.

At the end of August I was in the United States on an Israeli bond drive. While there I met with Caspar Weinberger and took the opportunity to focus on the significance of Lebanon as a problem by itself and the severe difficulties that had yet to be resolved there. In the course of our discussion I described the situation in Beirut after the expulsion. If Beirut is not unified, I told him, if government authority is not asserted in West Beirut, we will see a return of the previous state of affairs.[*] Stocked with weapons of all sorts, overrun by various Moslem militias, and harboring more than 2,000 hard-core PLO, West Beirut would quickly turn into a base for a new spread of terrorist influence and control. It was a prospect that worried me deeply.

This was one of the subjects President-elect Bashir Gemayel and I took up at his home in Bikfayeh on September 12. By this time I had made so many trips to Lebanon that I had gotten to know the local press, writers, and other intelligentsia and had struck up relationships with a number of gifted and interesting people. With the euphoria that followed the PLO's expulsion, I regularly found myself surrounded by hundreds of joyful well-wishers. The welcomes in Beirut were so effusive that more than once I joked with friends there that if I ever needed political asylum, Lebanon would be my first choice.

The atmosphere in Bikfayeh on the night of the twelfth was especially warm. Around the Gemayel family house, with its old stone walls and graceful arches, Bashir's people seemed especially animated, their faces lit up with pride and admiration for their leader. With the inauguration drawing near, an unmistakable expectancy hung over the house. Something new was about to happen in Lebanon, something hopeful and positive—for the first time since the first civil war of 1975 sparked an apparently endless trail of violence. Bashir and his wife, Solange, were happy and obviously excited about the inauguration; and a feeling of intimacy pervaded the room as Bashir and I sat down to talk over the steps he planned to take as president.

Despite the personal warmth, I knew that the first item of business would be to allay the hard feelings that had developed between Bashir and Menachem Begin at a meeting in Nahariya less than two weeks earlier. The chemistry that night between the older man and the younger had not been good. And although overall prospects for future relations between the two countries were promising, for some reason the discussion in Nahariya had focused on areas of difference, in particular the postwar status of Major Sa'ad Haddad.

Haddad was the Christian officer whose militia had controlled the southern Lebanon border zones since 1978, protecting the local population from the PLO and providing a narrow buffer between the terrorists

---

[*] Meeting, August 27, 1982.

and the Israeli border. In Lebanon's complex factional world, though, Haddad had been associated with one of Bashir's Christian rivals, and relations between the two men were not friendly. Haddad, in fact, had for years now had a court-martial waiting for him in Beirut. That night in Nahariya Begin had made it plain that Israel would not desert a loyal friend, while the newly elected Bashir was in no mood to concede the slightest prerogative of the power he would shortly assume. It had been a tense encounter, and Bashir had left the meeting deeply offended by what he regarded as an attempt by Begin to intrude on Lebanese internal affairs.

Like Begin, I was committed to protecting Haddad, a man who had fought alongside us for years. But I understood Bashir's feelings, and as we sat down to talk in his house on the night of the twelfth I did my best to soothe the residue of anger. Afterward we went on to more substantive issues, first of which was the steps that should be taken to clean the PLO cadres out of West Beirut and create an open, secure city. Neither Bashir nor I had any illusions about his ability to form a stable centralized government as long as a divided capital could provide a breeding ground for a PLO resurgence. It was in both our nations' interests, we agreed, to make sure that West Beirut's stay-behind terrorists were uprooted, a task that could best be handled by the Lebanese government in coordination with our own security services.

Beyond the situation in Beirut, I knew Bashir would be facing other major difficulties. Although his country had been freed from the PLO and Syrian stranglehold, Bashir had not yet even visited Sidon or Tyre or even Jezin. It was a bad sign, I thought. The government had been so impotent for so long that even a man like Bashir was reluctant to go into or through areas where central authority had not been in effect for years. It was clear that tremendous problems lay ahead before the new president would be able to achieve the necessary reorganization of his country.

We discussed these things, and we also discussed future relations between Lebanon and Israel. On this subject too we were walking common ground, even taking into consideration the challenges Bashir faced in consolidating his position as president of Moslem as well as Christian Lebanon. We agreed that direct talks should get under way soon, and we began discussing the nature of the peace treaty we intended to move toward. Knowing that this was a priority, we scheduled a further meeting (in which foreign minister Yitzhak Shamir would participate) for September 15, three days later.

This evening had started late, and the discussion went on until a little past 1 A.M., when Solange came in to invite us to a special dinner she had prepared in honor of the occasion, complete with many of the dishes she knew I loved. When we were finished eating, she and Bashir presented me with a magnificent engraved cherrywood box inside of which nestled a set of ancient Phoenician glass vases. It was an emotional moment. Despite the difficulties we had passed through and those we could foresee, at that instant we shared a feeling that this shattered country might yet regain its health, that after so many hellish years its people might once again live normal human lives. I had seen more than enough to know what that would mean for the Lebanese. Nor did I need anyone to tell me what its significance would be for the Galilee and the rest of Israel.

As I left their house that night, Solange invited Lily, me, and the children to come for an extended visit in the presidential palace after the inauguration. Then Bashir insisted on personally driving me to the beach where the helicopter was waiting. "Don't," I told him. "You have plenty of people around who can drive. You have to be much more careful, especially now. Anything can happen."

The meeting we had scheduled for the fifteenth was not to be, nor was our visit to the presidential palace. Two days later, on September 14, I was driving toward Tel Aviv when I received word on the car radio to telephone the defense ministry as soon as possible. Stopping at an army base along the way, I phoned in and was told that an explosion had taken place in an East Beirut building. Our information was that Bashir Gemayel had been inside.

During that late afternoon and into the evening I consulted with Prime Minister Begin, Commander-in-Chief Raful Eytan, Chief of Military Intelligence Yehoshua Saguy, the head of the Mossad, the head of the security services, and others who were connected with the situation. No one had any firm information on Bashir. His body had not been found, and a dozen reports were circulating that he was alive: He had been seen walking away from the building, he had been wounded in the leg and was being treated at one of Beirut's hospitals, he would appear on television with the outgoing president, Elias Sarkis. The one constant factor through all this confusion, though, was that none of our people had seen him after the explosion. We began to assume the worst.

As it became evident that Bashir had indeed been killed in the blast, our discussions began to focus on the consequences his death would have. Among these, the one critical and imminent problem was West Beirut. Other difficulties—who would form the next government, for example—were certainly significant, but they did not present the looming danger that the situation in West Beirut did.

Now the problems that Habib had wanted to leave to the next government and that Bashir and I had discussed at length only two days before presented themselves in bold relief. West Beirut was an area made up of several neighborhoods, including Sabra, Shatilla, Fakahani, and Burj el-Barajneh. These quarters were often called "refugee camps," bringing to mind concentrations of tents and hovels. But these "camps" were in reality built-up urban neighborhoods of high-rise and low-rise apartments, houses, and stores. That was aboveground. But over the years another city had been built in these places, this one underground. Mazes of tunnels, storehouses, bunkers, meeting rooms, and arsenals, some of them going down several stories, linked the neighborhoods, creating a formidable defensive system.

Throughout the siege, Sabra, Shatilla, and the others had served as the terrorists' headquarters and primary areas of deployment. Consequently it was these places that had been the targets of our shelling and air strikes. (During the entire time only forty of the almost 24,000 buildings in Beirut proper had been hit, each one of them precisely identified as a PLO operations base or as places where PLO Chief Yasser Arafat was likely to be.) As a result these neighborhoods had been badly damaged; they were scattered with piles of rubble and bombed-out buildings, places where live mine fields had been planted along streets and alleys and unexploded bombs lay amid the ruins.

During the siege almost all of the civilian population had left these areas. But now people were streaming back to their old homes. And interspersed among them were somewhere near 2,500 PLO cadres. More than 7,000 other armed members of twenty-seven different left-wing militias were in West Beirut, from the Syrian-controlled Morabitun, which had over a thousand, to tiny factions which might field no more than thirty or forty.

The PLO were there in direct violation of their agreement to evacuate the city. But Arafat had succeeded in violating the agreement in other ways as well. The departing PLO were to have turned over everything but their personal weapons to the Lebanese army before they left. But they had not done that. Instead, some of the heavy weapons had been distributed to their factional allies while other stocks had been hidden. As a result the West Beirut arsenals were still overflowing with machine guns, mortars, anti-tank guns, Katyusha launchers, and artillery pieces. Even tanks had been left behind.

With a strong Lebanese government determined to turn its capital into a unified and secure city, dealing with the problems of West Beirut would have been a difficult and time-consuming job. But it would have essentially been a police action aimed against the PLO and a political campaign to defuse the militias. But with Bashir dead and confusion gripping Lebanon's leaders, there was every likelihood that the terrorists would once again man the defensive positions, marshal the armed militias, and divide the town. Given the chance to organize themselves and make use of their huge stocks of weapons and ammunition, a resurrected terrorist West Beirut might quickly emerge, crippling the ability of some less than determined new government to establish itself and setting the stage for the re-creation of the infrastructure we had just spent three terrible months destroying.

As I discussed the situation with my colleagues on the evening of the fourteenth, this was the appreciation that we arrived at. There are certain moments that are absolutely crucial, that require immediate decisions; and this, I knew, was one of them. Bashir's death had created a critical juncture. If West Beirut were defended, we would be looking at a different and far grimmer future than the one we had envisioned. That possibility had to be precluded and it had to be precluded immediately. As we followed the reports coming in from Beirut, the conviction grew on us—on Raful Eytan, Prime Minister Begin, and myself—that we were at the twelfth hour. Israeli forces, we decided, would have to establish control over West Beirut.

That decision was made shortly after midnight on Wednesday, September 15, eight hours after Bashir's assassination. The IDF would move into West Beirut and establish itself at key points and road junctions, insuring that no coherent terrorist defense of the area could be set up. (This would not be simple. We had relatively few troops in Beirut, so an airlift would have to be organized into Beirut airport to quickly assemble the necessary units.) Israeli troops, however, would not themselves go into the neighborhoods. As far back as June 15 the cabinet had decided to demand that the Christians take a central role in any fighting in Beirut. We did not want our own soldiers taking casualties in street fighting, and the business of going after the terrorists could be handled much more effectively by Arabic-speaking Lebanese familiar with local accents and with the PLO's urban modus operandi. Lebanese troops, then, would be asked to move into West Beirut in conjunction with the IDF. It would be their job to penetrate the neighborhoods and clean out the terrorists.

Early that morning, September 15, I was on my way to Beirut to check on how the plans for this operation were materializing and also to pay my respects to Pierre Gemayel, Bashir's father. Landing at the airport at 8 A.M., I was met by an Israeli intelligence colonel who was to take me (along with Chief of Military Intelligence Saguy, the head of security services, and the deputy head of the Mossad) to our forward command post, which I knew was north of the airport not far from the sports stadium.

Almost immediately I noticed that the car was headed off in a different direction. When I asked the colonel if he knew where he was going, he said, "No problem. I know a shorter way there." Going the shorter way, we drove into Beirut. From the Galerie Samaan checkpoint we saw the smoke of fighting in West Beirut, then crossed into the area. A couple hundred yards farther on we were halted at a barrier manned by Lebanese Christians, then at another controlled by Lebanese army troops. Soon we were on the Boulevard Mazraa, a wide street dividing the terrorist neighborhoods to the south from the rest of West Beirut. "Are you sure you know where we're going?" I asked again. "Yes," came the answer, "we're almost there."

A moment later a Lebanese policeman was standing in front of the car frantically waving his arms for us to stop. We pulled over to the side, then heard him tell us that another two hundred yards down the boulevard we would be in the middle of the terrorist positions. Israelis? There were no Israelis in the vicinity at all.

I don't know who that policeman was or if he knew who was in the car he stopped that day. But I have no doubt that he saved my life along with those of the various high-ranking intelligence and security people with me, including the colonel whose idea this shortcut was. As I shook my head in disbelief, we turned around and retraced our route to the airport, then drove north to Amos Yaron's forward command post, which was located on the top of a heavily damaged building just southwest of Shatilla.

There I met with Raful Eytan, who told me that early that morning he had talked with commanders of the Lebanese forces about participating and had co-ordinated the move into the Sabra and Shatilla neighborhoods with them.[*] They had been instructed to plan the details of their operation with General Amir Drori (commander of the northern front), who was in charge of Israeli forces in Lebanon.

I approved the Commander-in-Chief's arrangements, then called Prime Minister Begin to report the situation and briefly discuss some of the political possibilities, specifically what new nominees for president we might like to see. (Begin knew I would be meeting Pierre Gemayel later in the day.) Then I left the command post to visit the Phalangist headquarters in the port area known as the Karantina. On my way there I noticed that many Christian troops were on the streets. Obviously they had mobilized their reserves, who ordinarily were called out only in emergencies. Overall, the streets looked quiet and under control, the troops guarding them grim-faced but calm.

In the Karantina headquarters the atmosphere was subdued and heavy. Most of the officers there had followed Bashir for many years. They had been with him through very hard times for the Christian community, then they had seen him elected president. Now, suddenly, he was dead, and all the hopes riding with him were in jeopardy. With the Phalangist officers I had a brief discussion of where the political situation stood now that they had lost Bashir, for whom we as well as they had had so many expectations. I also described how critical the tactical situation was in my view. One of the Phalangist chiefs urged that we take control ourselves over all of Beirut. We would do so, I told him, but we needed his support. The IDF would be moving into the focal points and junctions. But it was vital that the Lebanese enter also.

After this general review I drove to Bikfayeh to pay a condolence call on Bashir's father, Pierre, and his brother, Amin, whom I would be meeting for the first time. As we pulled up in front of the father's house, thousands of people were milling around, a crowd which projected a mood of tension as well as mourning. Inside I met Amin (my first meeting with him), who told me that he was aware of the conversation

---

[*] The Lebanese forces were made up of various Christian militias, most importantly the Phalangists. Talks were also under way with the Lebanese army, whose soldiers were drawn from the different confessional communities, including the Christians, and which was under the command of the government. In a state of shock and confusion after the assassination of its president-elect, the government at that point did not appear willing to order its troops in. Some hours later it formally refused to do so.

Bashir and I had had on the twelfth. Then Pierre Gemayel walked in, obviously moved but in full control of himself—much stronger, I thought, than he had seemed when I first met him the previous January. At that moment the old man seemed like a leader who despite the tragedy was holding the reins of power tightly in his hands.

Speaking for the prime minister and the Israeli government, I told him, I wanted to convey our sorrow for what had happened. He should also know that we would give him our full support in the burden of achieving our joint objectives. Bashir's loss was a heavy one, but we had to go on with the work. In particular we had to act immediately to prevent the establishment of a new set of facts during the last days of the present government.

The old man answered with dignity and feeling, expressing his deepest thanks to Israel for all it had done to help Lebanon's Christians, whom everyone else in the world had forsaken. We had, he said, achieved an opportunity to change the shape of Lebanon and the Middle East. Both he and his son Amin were aware of the last talk Bashir and I had had the previous Sunday, and he wanted me to know that he agreed with what had been said there.

With the funeral only a hour or so away, after this brief exchange of sympathy on our side and thanks on the Gemayels' I took my leave and returned to the airport for the flight back to Israel.[*]

The following morning, Thursday, September 16, I met in my office with Raful Eytan, who briefed me on the move into West Beirut. Meanwhile, the Phalangists who would be going into Sabra and Shatilla were at Amir Drori's headquarters, finalizing the co-ordination and completing their preparations. Among other things, they were instructed to be careful in their identification of the PLO terrorists. The mission was only against them. Civilian residents, they were specifically instructed, were not to be harmed.

Early that evening in Beirut the Phalangists entered Sabra and Shatilla. At almost the same time in Jerusalem the cabinet was meeting to consider the new situation that had arisen in Lebanon as a result of Bashir's assassination. In addition to the cabinet members, several high-ranking intelligence, military, and civilian officials were present, including Attorney General Yitzhak Zamir, over twenty people in all. To this group I detailed the immediate dangers in West Beirut and the IDF

---

[*] Minutes of this condolence call were recorded by a Mossad note taker.

operation to take the key points. While I was speaking a note came in that the Phalangists were now fighting inside the neighborhoods, and as I described this development, there was no negative reaction from any one of the assembled people.

The next day was Rosh Hashana eve, the memorial day of Gur's death. As usual on that day, Lily, myself, the boys, and my mother visited the cemetery, where we met the same group of friends who always gathered there, including some of Gur's childhood playmates, grown men and women now. Afterward I left the family and drove to Jerusalem for a meeting at the foreign minister's office with Shamir and Morris Draper. As much as a month earlier the Americans had argued that the Lebanese government should deal with the PLO problem in West Beirut, and now I pressed Draper to use his influence to get them to order the Lebanese army into the Palestinian neighborhoods.

By that night I was back on the farm when at 9 P.M. I received a call from Raful Eytan. He had just returned from Beirut, Eytan told me, and there had been problems. During the operation the Phalangist units had caused civilian deaths. "They went too far," he said. Because of what had happened, the northern front commander, Amir Drori, had called a halt to their part of the operation. Eytan had met with Drori, with other army officers, and with Lebanese Christian officers. All actions had been stopped, no additional Phalangist forces were being allowed into the neighborhoods, and the units inside had been ordered to reorganize and leave the area. They were now calling in their soldiers and would be out by 5 A.M.

Listening to Eytan, several thoughts were going through my mind. Like everyone who has ever experienced house-to-house fighting, I knew that in such actions there is no way to avoid civilian casualties, no matter what precautions are taken. We ourselves had made the greatest precautionary efforts in Sidon, Tyre, and some of the southern refugee camps—to the point of incurring significantly greater casualties among our soldiers—and yet civilians were killed. Knowing too how the PLO fought, using non-combatants as shields, hiding in civilian houses, setting up weapons positions in schools and hospitals, I was not surprised to hear there had been deaths. But they had "gone too far," Eytan had said. So much so that he had terminated the action and ordered the Phalangists out. Something had happened in those neighborhoods that shouldn't have. But it seemed evident that Raful had the situation in hand.

Less than an hour later another call came in, this one from the situation officer at the defense ministry. Information had been received, he reported, that some soldiers from Sa'ad Haddad's southern Christian forces had been found in West Beirut, near the boundary of Shatilla and Burj el-Barajneh. There had been shooting, and Israeli troops had killed two of them.

This report complemented Raful's. Obviously there had been unexpected trouble. What had Haddad's men been doing there anyway? If Israeli forces had actually fired on them, on people we had been working together with for years, then it was clear that the army had taken strenuous measures to put a halt to whatever was happening.

At 11:30 P.M., after I had already gone to bed, I received a third call, this time from an Israeli television journalist by the name of Ron Ben-Yishai. Ben-Yishai told me he had heard that Phalangist soldiers were murdering civilians in Shatilla; he had talked to Israeli officers who had heard from their soldiers that they had seen killings going on. When I asked if he had seen it with his own eyes, Ben-Yishai said he had not, but he had heard it twice, around four in the afternoon, then later in the evening. No, the people he had heard it from had not seen anything personally either, they too had heard about it.

Ben-Yishai was excited, but there was nothing new in what he was telling me. The reports I had gotten from the chief of staff and from the situation desk had said essentially the same thing. Christian forces had been involved in killings. I knew that. I also knew, as Ben-Yishai did not, that Raful and Amir Drori had done what was necessary to put a stop to it.

During the course of the next day it became apparent that something more than a few gratuitous killings had taken place in Sabra and Shatilla. In discussions with Eytan and with the director general of the foreign ministry who had received information from the Americans, I began to understand that the Phalangists had carried out an assault against civilians in the neighborhoods as well as against the terrorists. But even as the media began to break the story that afternoon, it was impossible to determine the extent of what had happened. At six that evening I ordered a detailed report on what by now was ominously being referred to as a massacre.

*　　*　　*

That night and the next day the media spoke of nothing but the killings in Sabra and Shatilla. As the story spread, an outcry began to shake the country, especially at first when the numbers of people killed were wildly exaggerated and when many accounts suggested that Israeli soldiers might have participated in it.˙ We seemed to be living in the middle of a horrible and confusing din in which wild stories, deep moral outrage, and cynical political exploitation of the tragedy by the Labor alignment competed for prominence.

While the public reaction burgeoned, the real story of the IDF's interaction with events was emerging through our own internal analyses. First of all, it was clear that not a single Israeli officer or soldier was involved in what had happened. On the contrary, the Phalangist units that had gone into the camps had been instructed on what was expected of them and explicitly told to avoid harming civilians. There had not been, however, any real anxiety that they would act improperly, no more among the Israeli officers co-ordinating with the Phalangists than among myself, Begin, and Raful, or among the cabinet room full of people who had heard on the night of the sixteenth that the Phalangists had entered Sabra and Shatilla. Phalangist units, after all, had fought under IDF direction in a number of places during the war and had conducted themselves unexceptionably. Bashir, their leader, had been murdered, but not by a Palestinian. The assassin, who had been caught almost immediately, was a Lebanese Christian who turned out to be working for the Damascus-controlled Syrian National Party. As a result, no one had batted an eye at the idea of sending in the Phalangists; certainly no one had in any way anticipated the events that occurred that night.

But while no one from the IDF had been involved in any way, it also became clear that the reporting from the forward command post had been less than perfect. On the night of the sixteenth, Israeli officers in the command post began to suspect that something might not be right from various remarks made by Phalangist officers. One of the Israelis had wired the Northern Command intelligence unit with a report of what he had heard, and Northern Command intelligence had passed the message along to army intelligence in Tel Aviv.

As it came into Tel Aviv, the report included a cover wire noting that

---

* The final Red Cross and Lebanese government figures were 460 dead, including 15 women and 20 children; 328 Palestinian men had been killed, 109 Lebanese, 21 Iranians, 7 Syrians, 3 Pakistanis, and 2 Algerians. Israeli intelligence estimates were somewhat higher.

the material was highly sensitive and concerned the highest levels. Unsure how to handle it, the shift officer had contacted his supervisor to ask if he should call Intelligence Chief Yehoshua Saguy at home. But it was already late and, reluctant to disturb Saguy, the supervisor told the shift officer to hold it until the first morning report. Consequently, Saguy did not see the report until the morning of the seventeenth. And even then it did not seem to him substantial enough to require any special action or any report to me about it.

Meanwhile, at the command post there were more and more rumors that something was wrong in the neighborhoods. With the Israeli officers getting nervous, General Amos Yaron called in the Phalangist liaison and warned him harshly not to allow any atrocities. By the next morning, September 17, there was still no clear indication about what might be going on inside Sabra and Shatilla other than a street battle with the PLO, but when Yaron and Amir Drori met at 11 A.M. they decided to call Raful Eytan and get the Phalangists out. By that afternoon Eytan was in Beirut himself, meeting with both Israeli and Phalangist officers. From the Phalangists he heard only vigorous denials of any atrocities. There was, they said, a hard battle being fought; they were facing stiff resistance and had suffered casualties. They even asked for more help, two bulldozers to level some buildings the PLO was using. Eytan agreed to the bulldozers, but after these talks he made the decision to terminate the operation that night. It was on his return from Lebanon later in the evening that he had called me at the farm.

Although IDF officers had moved cautiously even after they suspected what the Phalangists were doing, to the best of my knowledge and judgment not a single one of them had been involved in any act against civilians. For a short time I considered appointing a formal military inquiry, and I even discussed the possibility with Eytan. That might have short-circuited the political pressure on the government. My old friend Uri Dan pleaded with me time and again to set up a blue ribbon committee to investigate. But despite his entreaties, I refused to do it. I did not want to do anything that might give the impression I was trying to take cover for myself behind the army. As I was soon to realize, that decision was a serious mistake. Despite all my political experience I simply failed to properly assess the potential this tragedy had to be used as a political cause célèbre against the government. Nor did I foresee how the government itself would react when the crisis came on it (an especially glaring oversight given my experience with the cabinet's readiness to step away from responsibility over the construction of settlements back in 1978).

Meanwhile public outrage over what had happened in Sabra and Shatilla continued to swell. All of the anger and frustration that had built up during the long war—that would have dissipated with progress toward peace—now seemed to explode. And the blast of the explosion was centered on myself and on Prime Minister Begin. Buses from the kibbutzim all over the country arrived to feed demonstrations and marches as Labor orchestrated an outpouring of rage. Soon the pressure had focused on convoking a special commission of inquiry to ascertain responsibility for what had taken place.

As I told Begin when he brought the subject up with me, I was not afraid of an inquiry; I had nothing whatsoever to hide. But though I was not concerned personally about an inquiry, still in my mind I was fully aware of the grave national danger such a development would entail. Whatever Begin's own thoughts on this subject might have been, on September 28 he finally acceded to political pressure and demands from the public and media and moved in the cabinet to establish a commission. Supreme Court President Yitzhak Kahan was named to head the commission. Another Supreme Court justice, Aharon Barak, would serve with him, as would Yonah Efrat, a retired general.

As soon as the commission was appointed I instructed the defense ministry people to submit all the documents, papers, and transcripts that were requested. In talking with Chief of Staff Eytan, I said I believed everyone should tell the complete truth and should be totally co-operative. We had, I told him, as I had told Begin, nothing to hide. Not one of us was guilty of anything.

Nevertheless, as the commission started its work I had very bad feelings about the outcome. The public atmosphere was murderous; a cry for blood was in the air that was impossible to ignore. For many the killings were a real moral shock—even though everyone knew that in past years both Palestinians and Arab Christians had committed far more terrible slaughters on each other. Many others saw the political opportunity and grabbed at it with both hands. With some of the war's gains temporarily obscured by the tragedy and others far more distant than they had been before September 14, people were fixated on the costs of the struggle. Blood was needed from the political echelon, someone to bear the blame for what had happened.

Even in the midst of this there were many people—perhaps most, had they been polled—who did not want this commission, who understood the danger of it, not only for Israel but for the Jewish people. But the Labor alignment, the media, the organized sloganeering and demonstrations against "Sharon the Murderer" and "Begin the Murderer," created an undeniable force, not just for appointing the commission but for an assignment of guilt.

I understood well enough what this meant, and from the beginning I told my close friends and colleagues that the end would not be good. Regardless of the facts of the case, the need to find a responsible party or parties and destroy them would be overwhelming.

The atmosphere was impossible to ignore. And so were the private signs I began to pick up. Shortly after the commission had begun its investigation, Aliza Begin, Prime Minister Begin's wife of forty-five years, died. Her funeral was held in the old Jewish cemetery on the Mount of Olives on a bitter cold winter day (a place I knew well because it contained the remains of my great-great-grandfather, who like many Jews in earlier times had come to Jerusalem as an old man to die and be buried). Begin had selected a gravesite for his wife behind the graves of the Irgun's Meir Feinstein and the Stern Group's Moshe Barzani, the two young heroes who had blown themselves up with a grenade in a Jerusalem prison rather than submit to hanging by the British in 1947. As we walked toward the open grave, I happened to turn my head and saw behind me two men in black hats, black ties, and black overcoats walking together and staring at me with the blackest of looks. The eyes belonged to Judge Kahan and Judge Barak.

From the cemetery that day I went directly to the Knesset, where I was scheduled to give a report. Reading from the podium, at one point I looked up into the visitors' gallery directly in front of me and once again saw Judge Kahan and Judge Barak, regarding me with the same intense and unfriendly looks, like two black ravens, I thought. That night, meeting with some of my lawyers and advisers, I told the story of these encounters. The looks in those eyes, I told them, had given me enough indication of what was going to happen—not what might happen, but what would happen.

On a personal level, recognizing that the handwriting was on the wall and that there was nothing I could do about it had a strong calming effect. I found myself working exactly as I had worked before, but with a sense of unusual quiet and focus, as if I were in the still eye of the hurricane. If anything, the pace of work picked up, since once the commission was appointed I knew that time was running out and that the matters I had in hand had to be completed.

When I had last met with Bashir Gemayel, we had made arrangements for me to visit Lebanon together with Foreign Minister Yitzhak Shamir to get the peace negotiations under way. But then had come Bashir's death and on its heels the events in Sabra and Shatilla. Shortly afterward the Lebanese parliament had elected a new president, Amin Gemayel, Bashir's brother. Amin had neither Bashir's leadership abilities nor his clear vision of what had to be done to take Lebanon out of the strife that had destroyed its national life since the advent of the PLO. But despite all that had happened, I felt confident that we could still move toward an Israeli-Lebanese peace agreement, if the United States could be brought to lend its support. In light of the stance the U.S. had taken to this point, I knew such a thing would not be easy. All along, our ally had taken the position that an early peace treaty with Israel was to be avoided, that it would jeopardize Lebanon's position in the Arab world. But I still believed we had a chance for a meaningful agreement, and I was determined to fight for it, both with the Lebanese and with the Americans.

The first step was to meet Amin Gemayel, which Shamir and I did during the last week of September. During the helicopter flight to Beirut, Shamir seemed completely calm, despite the turmoil Lebanon was experiencing and the potential volatility of the capital. My memory is that he slept most of the way. When we landed, some of the Lebanese forces' security people—Bashir's people—picked us up and took us to Amin Gemayel's headquarters at the Beit Mustaqbel building, the "House of the Future." Bashir's people did not like Amin's people, a feeling that was returned in spades. Nor did either side trust the other; and when we arrived at Amin's headquarters, a group of his bodyguards came out and the two groups tensed up, glaring at each other and pointing their weapons.

Shamir and I were standing directly in the middle of the confrontation, and while I was used to this kind of thing, having been to Beirut so many times, Shamir was not. Always interested in seeing how people react to pressure, I glanced at him and saw his face showed absolutely no trace of emotion, let alone fear. The man had complete self-control.

The tension lasted several minutes until a beautiful secretary came out and told the bodyguards that Amin was expecting us and to let us (not Bashir's people) come inside. During the meeting with Amin that followed we talked about developments and about the possibility of going on with our negotiations. I did not sense much enthusiasm on Amin's part, but it was hard to tell. Although Bashir's funeral was so recent, Amin was wearing a beautiful white suit, very sharply tailored. His fingers were weighed down with golden rings, and he was shod in highly polished black snakeskin shoes. Looking at him, I felt we were in for very hard days. When I brought up Sabra and Shatilla, Amin and the people with him looked us straight in the eye and without blinking denied that they had been involved in it. None of them admitted a thing, either then or later. But while we were on the subject, someone behind me leaned over and whispered in my ear. "You Jews, you are crazy. You are a crazy people!"

Despite our doubts about Amin, during late September and early October I proceeded to carefully define the current security issues and to draw up a program for a phased Israeli withdrawal from Lebanon within the framework of an Israeli-Lebanese agreement on security and political normalization. In outline, it called for Israeli forces to maintain their deployment in the heart of the country until the PLO had completely evacuated its personnel (there were still close to 8,000 terrorists in northern Lebanon—a region still occupied by the Syrians—who had been untouched by the war), the Syrians had withdrawn from the Mount Lebanon area, and Israeli POW's and the remains of our dead were returned and MIA's accounted for. Once these conditions were met, the IDF would move back to a line forty-five to fifty kilometers from the border. Meanwhile negotiations would proceed on the evacuation of all foreign forces and a bilateral agreement between Israel and Lebanon on permanent security conditions and the normalization of relations. This position paper was adopted by the cabinet on October 13 and was subsequently presented to Amin Gemayel and simultaneously to Secretary of State George Shultz in Washington.

There was no doubt in my mind that the success of these negotiations would depend largely on the role the Americans chose to take. Possibilities were here to achieve security arrangements and to open a corridor for peace between Israel and Lebanon. But in order to realize these things, the Lebanese government would have to be pushed. Amin Gemayel was not the man his brother was. Without his own coherent view of how to bring Lebanon out of its fragmented condition, he was open to pressure from all sides and ready to say anything to anyone. He possessed precisely those qualities of mind and character that could lead Lebanon straight back to the hell it had been experiencing for years. As I told Philip Habib in one of our meetings that fall, Amin will bring about one of two situations. It is likely he will end up not as president of Lebanon, or president of Beirut, or even president of Ba'abde. He will end up as president of the presidential palace and nothing else, just as his predecessor was. (Until his recent term expired Amin Gemayel was in fact president of the Ba'abde palace.) The other possibility is that he will become president of a united, peaceful country. But that, I told Habib, very much depends on what the American position will be and what direction the United States would give to Amin.[*]

In my view, the American choice was clear. With their help the immediate needs of Lebanon could be achieved: security within the country, the withdrawal of the Syrians (and ourselves), and peace with Israel. But if they continued to try to solve everything, to link progress in Lebanon with their other interests in the region—bringing the Syrians closer to them and resolving the Palestinian question—they would watch the whole thing slip through their fingers. Lebanon had to be pushed, and it had to be pushed fast and hard. That was what was practical, that was the pragmatic course to take right now.

To Habib and other high-level American visitors I emphasized the immense contributions Israel had made to the American strategic posture and to the strategic posture of the free world. If not for Israel, I told them, the Soviets would never have been out of Egypt. If not for ourselves, for our action in the War of Attrition—a thousand days and hundreds and hundreds of our casualties—the Soviets would have been sitting on the Suez Canal to this day. It was Israel's position (at Begin's insistence) that a condition for peace with Egypt was to have American forces stationed in Sinai, not just U.N. forces, and that the Americans would be located in the most sensitive areas. That was our unshakable, non-negotiable demand. And so the American forces are still there. And because they are there, the United States has, in case of need, three first-class air bases in Sinai: Ophir, Etzion, and Etam, three bases that we built. Not that these would be used, except in emergencies. But if the time ever comes when

---

[*] Meeting, November 25, 1982.

you might have to intervene in the Persian Gulf or elsewhere in the region, I told the Americans, you can be sure that no one will help you, not the Saudis, not the Jordanians. But you yourselves will have the ability to act quickly, because these things are in your hands. By the same token, I said to the American ambassadors and generals and congressmen who came to Jerusalem, you now have a foothold in Lebanon, with its port facilities and its airport. Yesterday the Syrians controlled Lebanon, which meant in effect that it was under Soviet control. And now you are there, and you have the possibility of making Lebanon an integral part of the free world.

But the Arabists in the State Department never understood the significance of the concept, and as we fought in the fall and winter of 1982 to salvage an agreement with Lebanon, they, as they had during the war, moved in a different direction.

And so, unfortunately, did the Lebanese Christians. In January, Lily and I visited Beirut as guests of Lebanon's great poet May Mur and her husband, the architect Alfred Mur. As usual the street crowds were wildly enthusiastic. But over the preceding months their government had been far less so. Although negotiations were going on, Amin Gemayel had taken an increasingly anti-Israeli position in public, issuing statements and condemnations that he believed would ingratiate him with the other Arab states. Meeting with the father, Pierre, I said that patience in Israel was growing short. Unless they were able to adopt a favorable position on Israel's role and give it concrete public expression, Israeli opinion could force a troop withdrawal before any arrangements were concluded. Arrangements were of course important to us, but they were no less important to Lebanon. They might easily find themselves on their own. If that happens, I told Pierre Gemayel, as I had earlier told Habib, Amin will find himself president of the palace building and nothing else. If they didn't have the courage now, they might well lose everything. "We didn't come in to save you," I told him. "We came in to save ourselves. But the result has been that you now have a historical opportunity, a chance that might not come again in another fifty years."

As we struggled with the Lebanese and the Americans that fall, the Kahan Commission was slowly but methodically gathering its information and evidence. In the course of time I and others received a "warning" from the commission, a formal announcement that we were under consideration as persons who might be charged. I would soon be called to testify.

The process had now entered its crucial stage. Up to this point the legal adviser to the defense ministry had been handling my case, along with a young lawyer named Dov Weissglas who was doing his reserve service in the ministry. But with the "warning," the attorney general's office informed me that I could no longer use the services of the ministry's legal adviser.

As a result I started looking for a personal attorney. But in the atmosphere of those days finding somebody to handle my affairs proved unexpectedly difficult. Lawyers were reluctant to associate themselves with such a volatile and unpopular case. Eventually I called an old friend, Shmuel Tamir, the former Free Center party leader I had had such problems bringing into the Likud back in 1973, the man I had chased up ten flights of stairs at the Herut building. After Mr. Begin's first government was formed, Tamir had served as minister of justice for a time, then had dropped out of active political life. Now I explained the situation to him and asked if he would take on the defense. Tamir said he would like to think about it and asked me to give him a call in two days.

Two days later I was at his house in Herzliya Pituach, a beautiful place near the beach that I knew well, having been there in times of joy and also sorrow for Tamir and his family. As I sat on his sofa, he told me that he would not be able to defend me. He was thinking of going back into politics, he said. If he took this case, he would have to do it seriously, and that would mean interrogating witnesses at every level of government, from the lower echelons to the very top. And if he did that, it would likely affect his political chances. Consequently he would not be able to take it on. I didn't answer a word when I heard this; I just said thank you, goodbye. Then I left.

After this I lost interest in looking around for anyone else, and the end result was that Dov Weissglas (who had now finished his reserve service) took the case privately, along with an attorney by the name of Zvi Terlow who had been recommended by an official of the Defense Ministry.

The day after I made these arrangements I left for Honduras in Central America. Lily came with me (as she almost always did) on a complicated flight through Amsterdam, Chicago, San Francisco, and Las Vegas, where I was scheduled to give a talk. The next morning our party took off in two small Israeli-made jets for Tegucigalpa, where we were received warmly by the city's Jewish community and by President Cordoba, with whom I reviewed the situation in his region. I was mainly interested in developing co-operation in agriculture. In earlier years Israel had built moshavim in Nicaragua, and it was something that this part of the world remembered. The subject of military assistance came up too, with the Honduran chief of staff. But this was in December already, and nothing was to come of these meetings. The immediate future, at least, was already mortgaged to the Kahan Commission.

As the commission took its testimony, I decided not to interrogate army officers or Mossad people, a few of whom were trying to pretend that they had not known that the Phalangists were being sent into the neighborhoods. I had already made up my mind that if someone from the army was found guilty I would have to resign. As the case progressed, the commission focused on several questions. Were IDF troops involved in any way? Did anyone in the political or military echelons conspire in or know about the massacre? Had anyone acted in a negligent fashion in failing to prevent or stop the massacre?

My personal defense was straightforward. My lawyers argued that I had not been negligent in having failed to stop the massacre. I had been informed on the night of September 17 by Eytan that the Phalangists had "gone too far," but also that the operation had been terminated and the Phalangist forces had been ordered to withdraw. As far as negligence beforehand was concerned, the law in Israel was clear. A person cannot be found negligent, it says, if a "reasonable man" would not have foreseen danger. The simple fact was that no one had foreseen the danger. This situation had dealt a horrible blow to Israel: and had we foreseen it in any way, we never would have sent the Phalangists in. A fair number of high-ranking IDF personnel knew of the intention to use them, and none of them had raised any questions about it. Nor had Begin, Eytan, Saguy, the security chiefs, the heads of the Mossad, the cabinet ministers, or the attorney general, who attended the cabinet meeting of the sixteenth and heard that the Phalangists had entered the neighborhoods. According to Israeli law, my lawyers argued, there had been no expectancy of a problem, and consequently no one could reasonably be accused of negligence.

With these arguments, my lawyers felt the case could not be lost. Not on legal grounds anyway. More cynical than they, I had little hope it could be won. A commission of inquiry in Israel has all the legal powers of a court, but it operates with more latitude than a court. It is not bound by the ordinary rules of law. And this was one case, I was sure, that would be decided on political, not legal grounds.

As the testimony came to an end and the judges began their deliberations, I continued with the defense ministry work, determined to carry
on my functions in a normal fashion but also feeling the need to bring
major pieces of business to a conclusion before the commission issued its
report. Planning we had undertaken to determine the structure of Israel's
defense forces for the 1990s continued uninterrupted (my last meeting on
this subject was held on the morning the report was issued). Negotiations
proceeded in Lebanon, where I visited regularly. I went too to Zaire on
a formal state visit, a direct outgrowth of our initiative the previous year
which had led to Zaire's renewal of diplomatic relations, the first African
nation to do so.

During this visit at the end of January I toured the country with
Mobutu and discussed with him various issues concerning Israeli-African
relations. When he asked me to return at a near date to complete these
discussions, I accepted the invitation. I could come back, I said, on
February 4. Mobutu was somewhat surprised I would be returning so
quickly, though he immediately agreed to the date. What he did not
know (and what I could not tell him) was that the commission's findings
would be coming out on February 7.

I had discovered this by accident. The commission's deliberations were
secret, and they had not announced the date. But I had learned that
another "warned" witness who was represented by a famous and well-
connected lawyer had invited friends to a party on the eighth. So I knew
that he knew at least the date of the report's release.

When I returned from Zaire, I discussed the imminent report with
Begin. As far as I understood, I said, the findings would be coming out
around the seventh. Knowing this government well, I suggested that he
would have to assume a very strong position, because it would be up to
the ministers to accept or reject the commission's findings. Most of them,
I believed, would take any available path to secure their own skins,
regardless of justice and regardless of the ultimate damage to Israel. So
the only way to hold the line against what might well be coming would
be to assert the strongest possible leadership and keep the ministers
focused on the rock-bottom issue—the innocence of the Israeli government and its military. When the findings came out, I told Begin, it would
be a crucial moment. I said that to him directly and hard, and I watched
his reaction. Begin's response was a low rasp. "That will be a very hard
situation," he said. "A very hard situation."

On the fourth I returned to Africa. I was intent on fulfilling the commitments I had undertaken there and on doing everything I could to strengthen Israel's position in that part of the world while I was still able to. This was despite the growing feeling of oppressiveness I was experiencing about the commission report—then due out in three days.

I flew back to Israel on February 5. Without saying anything to anyone, I worked hard during the next two days to wrap up as many items of business as possible. On the evening of the seventh it became known that the commission report had indeed been issued and that Mr. Begin had received a copy of it. But when I called his home, I had difficulty getting him on the line, for the first time in my experience. When he did come on, I said, "I understand you have the report." "Yes," he answered. He was just then consulting on it with one or two people. "Can you tell me what the findings are?" I asked. "No," he said, he had been asked not to talk about them until the next morning. Could I come to see him then? I hung up with very bad feelings about the kind of support I could expect from the prime minister.

By the next morning it was already out. When I met early with Dov Weissglas and Oded Shamir, I found them reading through the report and smiling. It seemed to exonerate me. "We assert," wrote the judges, "that in having the Phalangists enter the camps, no intention existed on the part of anyone who acted on the part of Israel to harm the noncombatant population."

"You had better skip through to the conclusions," I told them.

In its conclusions the commission discussed the roles of Prime Minister Begin and Foreign Minister Shamir as well as my own. It also considered the part played by various army officers and intelligence people including Chief of Staff Raful Eytan, Generals Drori and Yaron, and Director of Military Intelligence Yehoshua Saguy. To one degree or another, each of those under consideration was judged to have had a certain responsibility in the events at Sabra and Shatilla, from Begin, who according to the judges should have taken a more direct interest in the operation; to Eytan, who should have been more active in clarifying what was going on in the neighborhoods after the Phalangists went in and preventing its continuation; to Saguy, who should have known enough to warn beforehand of the potential for atrocities and who should have taken subsequent reports of atrocities more seriously.

As for my own conduct, on the charge that I had been negligent in stopping the bloodshed, the commission decided I had acted properly. But they also concluded that regardless of the fact that so many people had known of the Phalangists entering the neighborhoods without anticipating a massacre, I, as defense minister, should have been more aware of the dangers and should have taken action to preclude them. As a result, according to the commission, I personally bore an "indirect responsibility" for what had happened. The recommendation was that either I should "draw the appropriate personal conclusions" or that the prime minister should consider exercising his authority to "remove a minister from office."

Although I was expecting a conclusion of this sort, I was outraged by the imputation of "indirect responsibility." The concept had no basis in Israeli law. But far more importantly, in my heart I knew that I had never anticipated what had occurred, despite all my familiarity with Lebanese affairs. After the fact, with calm and judicious hindsight, it might have appeared to Judge Kahan and his colleagues that despite the testimony I should have expected it. But the fact was that no one had. Not I and not the others. Or was it perhaps, I thought, that these judges had made a decision that in such a national trauma someone had to be found to bear the blame. Whichever, it was a stigmatization I rejected utterly.

The report came out on February 8, 1983. Two days later a cabinet meeting was called to consider what steps to take. The meeting started in the early evening, but I was unable to get there on time. A demonstration was taking place on the road in front of our farm called by Peace Now and some of the local kibbutzim. The demonstrators seemed to be in a state of mad rage, and it was impossible to predict what might happen. Opposite them, everyone on the farm—Jews and Arabs—were standing by the gate. It was unbelievable to watch it. When they had seen what was developing, the Arab workers had decided not to leave that evening. They stayed and were standing there shoulder to shoulder with Motti Levy and the other Jewish workers, ready to prevent any attempt to come onto the grounds. As the noise of the confrontation rose, I sat inside with Dov and Uri Dan preparing my presentation to the government. It was a while before the police had the situation sufficiently under control so that I felt comfortable leaving the farm in Motti's hands.

As we drove through the front gate, we saw the farm workers lined up and heard the ugly shouts of the crowd through the car windows. An hour's fast driving later we were in Jerusalem, where another demonstration, a huge one, was going on in front of the prime minister's office. This crowd, though, was made up of supporters, people who had come to Jerusalem from all over the country to make their feelings known to the cabinet—which they were now busy doing as loudly as they could. As I stopped for a moment to greet them, I was engulfed by a thousand hands reaching out to shake mine and a thousand expressions of warmth and encouragement. But these supporters were not alone. At the same moment another demonstration came marching through the streets, this one composed of Peace Now people yelling at the top of their lungs, "Sharon Rotzeach (Sharon the murderer), Sharon Rotzeach," their shouts mixing with the "Arik, Arik, Arik" from my supporters.

At the building entrance a flood of blinding camera and television lights switched on, and what seemed like hundreds of reporters and cameramen swarmed around us, their questions and shouts adding to the din. Even inside the cabinet room it was impossible to escape the noise. When I got there, the ministers looked pale and anxious; and as the shouting from the street penetrated into the room, they shut the windows. In a few moments, though, the crowd had shifted around the building, and those shouts of "Arik, Arik" began coming through the windows on that side. When those too were closed, the room quickly grew hot and close. Just a moment before, the ministers had seemed pale, but now sweat began to bead their faces.

Even without the shouting outside and the heat inside, the meeting would have been tense enough. That night the cabinet had to decide either to reject the Kahan report in whole or part or to accept it. Rejecting it would have meant resigning as a government and calling for new elections. That would have brought, I believed, the greatest victory in Likud history. On the other side, accepting it meant in effect forcing my resignation. But it also meant a good deal more than that. It meant confirming a verdict that an Israeli government was guilty of murder. "If you accept the conclusions of the Kahan Commission," I warned them, "you will be branding the mark of Cain on the foreheads of the Jewish people and on the State of Israel with your own hands."

Among the people making that decision were Begin and Shamir, both of whom had themselves been found to have a share of responsibility by the commission. As they and the rest of them sat there in the cabinet room and deliberated, the chants from the street were still audible through the shut windows. Watching the ministers, it was hard to decide which cries from outside were affecting them more—those chanting my name or those demanding my blood. It was, I began to realize, that gigantic spontaneous crowd of Likud supporters that really upset them. It was such an irony, I thought, that these loyal people who had gathered there to help were in effect sealing my fate. The cabinet members did not like hearing those shouts. They hated it. You could see the jealousy and anger in their faces.

Toward the end of the meeting a note was passed to the secretary of the cabinet not to forget in the voting to take into consideration the two ministers who were away. One of these was Professor Yuval Ne'eman of the Tehiya party (who had always been a staunch supporter on national issues), the other Simcha Ehrlich. The answer that came back was "Better sixteen to one against him than seventeen to two." The vote, when it came, was exactly that, sixteen to one against me.

The next day, Friday, I went to see Mr. Begin to tell him I had decided to resign. It was not an easy decision, and at first I had been inclined to force the issue. Begin's response that day did not make it any easier. "When do you want to do it?" he asked. "I'll do it on Monday," I answered. "Why," he said after a pause, "should it take so long?"

That Monday, February 14, I told the staff and workers at the ministry that I had accepted the cabinet's decision. I would resign my office. I emphasized to them that not a single one of us, not a soldier, not a commander, not a person in the political echelon, was involved in those terrible events. I had been singled out, it was true. But as one who had a clear understanding of what had been done and a clear view of his own path and goals, I had the strength to face it.

It was a busy morning, with so many people coming to say goodbye, many of them with flowers, many crying. Lily stood with me there, as she had stood with me through all the years, in days of victory and days of defeat. At one point May Mur unexpectedly made her way through the crowds that blocked the hallways and read one of her beautiful poems. She had come in from Beirut that morning, as had other Lebanese friends. In the square below I could hear preparations for the farewell parade, the same parade that had welcomed me to the post a year and a half before. Together with Lily I went downstairs, then outside, into the parade ground where flags and banners waved in the air and a great crowd had gathered opposite the ministry. Walking there in front of the soldiers,

I looked into their faces. I felt I wanted to remember each one of them, to burn them into my memory.

But despite my intentions, as I walked by them another face appeared in my mind's eye, the face of my father as he was in that orange grove thirty-seven years earlier during the hunting "season" against Menachem Begin's Irgun. Working there in the earth among the trees he had told me, "Arik, you can do anything you want, but one thing you must promise me. Never turn Jews over. Never do it." And now, I said to myself, look what has happened. Those very people who were the victims then, they have handed me over to the mob, they have done it to me.

In the weeks and months that followed, that scene stayed with me. And later, when the emotions of the moment had passed, I found myself one day sitting with Menachem Begin in his office, and I felt the need to tell him what I had experienced that day. "I want to tell you something," I started. "I don't know how you see what has happened. But I want you to know how I feel about it." Then I told him about the parade, about what I had wanted to remember, and about what I did remember. "Menachem," I said, "it was you who handed me over to them. You are the one who did it."

Epilogue

That, of course, was not the end. By early afternoon Lily and I were back on the farm. Strangely, perhaps, I did not feel in the least defeated. What I did feel was a lot of anger. I regarded what had happened as a betrayal, a real betrayal by people who didn't have the strength to stand up for the things they had been discussing for years, people who understood so well what had to be done but had not had the courage of their convictions. When the storm hit, they had started searching for cover, and I had been there to provide what they were looking for. So in the mix of emotions that followed my resignation, anger certainly played its part. But it was not only a personal anger. As I had told them in that cabinet meeting, by accepting the Kahan Commission report they themselves had put the mark of Cain not only on my forehead but on that of the Jewish people and the State of Israel.

Back on the farm these thoughts raced through my head. But I was also aware that a healing calm began to take hold almost immediately. Despite the dramatic and unhappy leavetaking, it seemed so natural to be back on the land again. By the next day I was out in the fields on the tractor, looking down on the crops, on the sheep and lambs, and looking backwards as well to what had happened, trying to get it into perspective. I found myself thinking, not for the first time, about my parents, and about the roots I had been so fortunate to have been raised with. It struck me too as I sat there that I was the only Jewish minister of defense, the only minister of defense, period, who had gone back to his tractor and his farm because of what Christian Arabs had done to Moslem Arabs.

As the days passed, I also thought seriously about leaving the government altogether. Having resigned as defense minister, I was now minister without portfolio. But without a portfolio there was nothing for me to do. Nothing but watch as the cabinet began to scrutinize and review every initiative and every project I had undertaken—the agreement with Zaire's Mobutu and the various agreements I had made with other African leaders among them.

While this was going on, I was completely isolated in the government. Work of any sort was kept out of my hands, even the kinds of projects that are ordinarily given to ministers without portfolio. At times staying on seemed pointless, nothing more than an exercise in enduring whispers and antagonism. And had it not been for my good friend Uri Dan, I might well have quit. Uri had been with me through almost every battle over three decades, since he started covering the paratroopers as a reporter in the 1950s. In all those years his support had been unfailing, but now it was crucial. One especially bad evening he caught me after I had already made the decision to leave, and he argued doggedly against it, refusing to let the matter die.

So had it not been for Uri Dan, perhaps I would have resigned. Instead I stayed. I used to sit in on the cabinet meetings, then go to my office, which was in an unused government building—an empty office in an empty building. There I read the letters I had received, letters that came in that year from all around the world. Over 4,000 of them, from Israel and America, from Poland, Hungary, from dozens of countries, from Jews and non-Jews. Those letters provided inestimable moral support during that period, and I made it a point to answer each one of them. Answering those letters, watching the cabinet, working on the farm— with one thing and another my days were filled and time passed.

What really kept me in the government was the feeling, which Uri had played to, that Israel was just starting to face its problems. When I saw the weakness of the leadership, the hypocrisy, the hatred within Israel among Jews, when I saw the developments throughout the Middle East, I thought that I simply had to stay. As long as I still had a chance to be on guard and to watch what was happening, there seemed no real alternative.

By this time too I was experienced enough to understand that political life is like a big wheel, constantly turning. At times you are up, at times down. But always the wheel keeps moving. And thinking about these things again and again, it seemed to me that even now perhaps the political wheel had not come to a complete halt for me, that though I was somewhere near the bottom, it was still turning. That wheel was moved, I knew, not by opinion, by what people might be thinking at one moment or another, but by the circumstances and problems that surround us, by the changing conditions of our national life.

And being minister without portfolio— Well, at least I was still in the government. I had that, and I also had the opportunity for the first time in years to step back and look around me. It was February—wintertime in the desert. And in the Negev winters are mixed with pain. The clouds blow quickly through the sky, bringing showers here and there—almost always, it seems, on your neighbors' fields, not yours. But you try to be quiet about it, because where rain is concerned complaints are never in order, only thanksgiving. And when the rain comes, as it always does, the land seems to be moving upwards to meet it.

But thanksgiving wasn't only something for the weather. As I worked on the tractor I thought, more than at any other time in my life, of what kind of a home it was that I had to come back to. Lily, Omri, and Gilad were there, as they always had been. But now more than ever I was conscious of the family we had been blessed with, the family that Lily had nurtured over the years. Together we had, as Omri liked to put it, "a home that is a home," "bayit shehu bayit."

I thought about the care with which Lily had raised our children and how she had given this home the warmth of music and flowers and art. Out in the garden and inside the house the flowers blazed—the vivid red of the bougainvillea, the burning red of the amaryllis, the violets of the dahlias and irises. These were things I had always loved, yet now it seemed to me that I had always taken them too much for granted. And as I watched my two sons I seemed to be seeing them too in a slightly different light. It was only a year and half earlier that Lily and I had thought we would be having another child. After years of unsuccessful effort we had been in a fever of excitement about it. But after five months of pregnancy and playing with hopes, the baby had suddenly died. I had had a landslide of work to deal with, to distract me from the shock and sadness, but Lily had borne the brunt of it and it had taken her a long time to recover.

With the loss so recent I now watched Omri and Gilad with different, perhaps even more appreciative eyes. I could see how deep the bond was that they had developed with the land. They had worked on the farm since they were quite young and knew the fields and wadis by heart. I felt so proud of them, proud of the love they had for the country and for the sense of modesty and justice they had both developed. Lily and I had always felt for them not just parental love but also a deep friendship, and in this hour the friendship and trust we shared now seemed more precious than ever.

So I had the opportunity to watch the two boys just as they were in the process of disconnecting themselves from their youth and becoming men. At the same time I was able once again to work hard on the farm, to really focus on it. I always remembered those four years I was on the farm after I had left the army in 1973, difficult years in some ways, but rewarding ones too. So I came back to what I had done then, sharing the daily labor and the daily talk of the shepherds and field workers. And again the work proved tremendously rewarding. Among the successes we managed after I left the defense ministry was a cross between the indigenous Awasi sheep and the imported Merino. The resulting cross-bred ewes combined the Merino's propensity for twins and the Awasi's milk production and excellent maternal behavior. Experimenting with hormones, we developed techniques of inducing three births every two years rather than the usual one a year, an accomplishment I am still proud of. I had time too to actively take part in raising our horses and riding, another pleasure I had missed during the years in the cabinet, one that took me back twenty years to the time we were living in Zevele Amit's farmhouse in Nahalal. Most important of all, Lily and I once again had the chance to spend time together, and that was more healing than anything else could possibly be.

Of course it was not an easy period. Omri had now joined the army and was in the paratrooper basic training course. But the atmosphere created by the Kahan Commission proceedings made it a very hard time for him to serve. Though he never spoke about it, I felt that something wrong was going on. Although I wanted to intervene in my son's struggle because it bothered me, I could not. It was painful, but I believed that there are special situations when you have to let your children confront the realities of life by themselves. Also, knowing my son, I believed that maybe they could break him physically but they could not break him spiritually.

Nor was it easy for Gilad, still in high school. All along the road from

Tel Aviv to the farm and on the roads around the farm itself the graffiti and slogans plastered trees and buildings. "Sharon Rotzeach"—Sharon the Murderer. Cars from the neighboring kibbutzim would not stop to give him a lift. Minor sabotage occurred on the farm. A pall of hatred hung over all of us. But Gilad, like Omri, showed his determination. He never gave in to it in any way.

It was painful watching my family being subjected to the abuse. I never said a word about it. I could see they preferred to struggle with this themselves, and it gave me satisfaction that they had the strength to stand up to all the hostility and the wisdom to keep it in perspective. But it was painful watching them go through this. And it was painful personally too, especially since so much of this feeling came from the kibbutz movement (a constituent of the Labor Alignment). Because, despite the political controversies, the farm side of the country—the kibbutzim and moshavim—was where I was most deeply connected, where my background and my roots were.

But despite the problems, I did not simply sit by and let the aftermath of Sabra and Shatilla play out its course in my life. On the night of February 13, the night before I resigned from the defense post, I received news that the following day's headlines were going to highlight a story about me from the upcoming issue of *Time* magazine. Apparently *Time* was declaring that in my meeting with Pierre and Amin Gemayel just before Bashir's funeral I had discussed "the need for the Phalangists to take revenge for the assassination." This discussion, according to *Time*, was described in the secret appendix to the Kahan Commission report.

It was a plain lie. As a defendant and as a cabinet member I had been permitted to read the appendix—secret because it contained the names of various intelligence officers. I knew that nothing in it referred to any such discussion. I knew that no such discussion had ever taken place and that *Time*, for all its international reputation, was simply printing a fabricated story. That night I decided that I could not sit back and accept such a thing. If the *Time* story turned out to be as it was reported, I would bring suit for libel. There comes a moment, I thought, when you have to turn and fight it. My family was suffering, I was being assaulted and traduced at every corner. I felt like I was being pursued by a pack of wild dogs. The time had come to put an end to it.

The next day's newspapers blazoned the fabrication all over Israel.

Then came the issue of *Time* itself. Over the following months I filed suit in Tel Aviv and in New York, beginning a courtroom battle that was not to end for another two years. At the end of that time the New York jury had decided that the *Time* article was both false and defamatory, and although they were not able to say if *Time* had published the story with actual malicious intent, the jury made a special declaration that "certain *Time* employees had acted negligently and carelessly" in their reporting and verification. In Tel Aviv, where libel does not depend on proving maliciousness along with lying and defaming, the court handed down an immediate judgment against the magazine.

During the year and a half of the trial the political wheel kept turning, and not only for me. In September 1983 Menachem Begin resigned as prime minister. Over the preceding months Begin had grown visibly weaker, no longer the forceful leader he had once been. Along with the other cabinet members I had watched the changes in him. But like most of the others I had seen Begin go through similar episodes in the past and recover from them. So though his resignation was not a surprise, neither had I exactly expected it.

I heard the radio announcement while I was driving. Immediately thoughts about the man and his career came in a flood. Begin had done such tremendous things in his life. The revolt against the British. The way he had held his party together for twenty-nine years, building it step by step until his great personal victory in 1977. The historic achievement of peace with Egypt—in reality more his initiative than Sadat's. The decision to destroy the nuclear reactor in Baghdad, which was perhaps the greatest of all the threats to Israel and to the rest of the Middle East as well. The second election victory in 1981, in which he had taken Labor on head-to-head and defeated them. The great settlement projects in Samaria, Judea, Gaza, and the Galilee. The decision to eliminate the PLO's kingdom of terror in Lebanon. The peripheral strategy in Africa, which he had had the vision to understand and enable. The salvation of so many thousands of Ethiopian Jews (in ways that are still unrevealed). The breakthrough in relations with China that stemmed from Begin's initiative in 1979. The commitment to Jewish honor and Jewish security that was shown in every detail of his interactions with world leaders.

All these were remarkable achievements, done under his leadership. But that was hardly all there was to say about the man. To his lasting merit he presided over the integration of the Sephardic Jews into this country, the third great revolution in Israel after the Zionist movement and the establishment of the state. Within the old Irgun and Herut, Sephardim had always played an equal role. Then in 1977 Begin implemented within the Likud a democratic system of party elections that gave them a strong voice in Israeli national politics for the first time, a reform that took the Labor party fifteen years more to emulate. During his time, conditions in the largely Sephardic developing towns changed completely, with dramatic developments in housing, education, medical care, and industrial investment. And you could see the results. The developing towns began to make a major contribution to the nation, producing young officers, young mayors, young members of the Knesset, and cabinet ministers—all of it built on the democratic system of elections that the Likud adopted under his leadership. It was a pervasive contribution that was the direct consequence of the real liberalism of the man and his party.

So with all the weaknesses and problems, and with all my very mixed personal history with him, when I looked back, Menachem Begin's achievements demanded acknowledgment. And so as I listened to the radio I felt sorrow, tinged, I must admit, with irritation at the undertone of satisfaction that I heard in the commentators' voices. But mostly I felt sorrow that he was gone and especially that he had chosen to go before we had completed the job of establishing security for the northern border. The Lebanon problem was still unresolved, stable security arrangements had not been adopted, the army was not yet withdrawn. These things his resignation had left in the middle. I was certain his leadership would be missed.

With Menachem Begin gone from political life, Yitzhak Shamir took on the mantle as head of the Likud and prime minister. Nineteen eighty-four was an election year, and in the primaries I decided to challenge Shamir and Deputy Prime Minister David Levy. Most of the people I talked to about this step felt it was suicidal, that I could not hope to win more than 5 or at most 10 percent of the vote. I was just barely hanging on to political life as it was, and putting myself at risk in this election was just asking to be pushed over into the grave. Still I felt I had to do it, if only as a protest against those who were in office. To the shock of almost everyone, when the results came in I had won not 10 percent but 42.5 percent (to Shamir's 56 percent). Although I had no foothold in the party apparatus, it was now absolutely clear that at least I had a place with the electorate. The end result was that I took an extremely active role in the 1984 national election campaign appearing as a speaker on almost 180 occasions.

The national elections that year split the country almost down the middle. Although Labor outpolled the Likud, Labor leader Shimon Peres found himself unable to put together a government. In the unsettled period directly following, mutual friends suggested that Peres and I meet secretly to explore the idea of a forming a national unity government in which Labor and the Likud would share power in some manner.

The meeting itself was held in a private house in the Tel Aviv suburbs. On the way there I told my driver and bodyguard whom I would be meeting with, but apparently Mr. Peres had not done the same with his own security people. As a result, when I walked into the front garden, Peres's bodyguard jumped to his feet in something of a panic, sure that some terrible mistake had been made. "Arik," he said, "do you know who is here? Mr. Peres is inside this house!"

Despite the unusual nature of the concept and the difficulties that would be raised by the two parties working together, that night Peres and I found ourselves moving in a positive direction. We discussed the main problems and came up with what seemed to us workable solutions, laying the basis for subsequent negotiations in which a full-scale agreement between the parties was nailed down.

During this entire period I found myself shuttling between Jerusalem and New York, where the *Time* magazine trial was now entering its last stages. One day in the Foley Square courthouse I was given a message to call Mr. Shamir on an urgent matter. A phone was made available in the judges' robing room, and when Mr. Shamir came on the line he immediately began to discuss the list of our appointments to the national unity cabinet. Would I, he asked, be willing to take on the Ministry of Industry and Trade and to serve in the newly established ten-member inner cabinet? Before I accepted, I looked around the room and wondered for a moment at the ironies of life. It was unlikely that the makeup of an Israeli cabinet had ever before been discussed from the robing chambers of an American courthouse. It was certain that no prospective minister had ever been tapped in the middle of a legal struggle like this one. Whatever was ahead for Israel, I was glad I would be part of it.

*   *   *

In the forty years since its birth Israel has transformed itself from a pioneering nation into a normal country, at least on the surface. But this normal country does not have normal problems. No other nation in the world is in our situation. Nowhere else do four million people carry on their lives in the midst of a hundred million hostile people. Because of this, Israel faces non-conventional problems, and to continue to survive we must be able to devise non-conventional solutions.

But such solutions do not come easily. If they are to come at all, they will only come to a nation that has clear national goals for which it is willing to pay the price. Sadly, perhaps disastrously, Israel has lost its goals. We are now a normal country, part of the Western world. And like other peoples of the Western world we are primarily concerned to get on with our lives. As a result, national goals are no longer mentioned. For any country the lack of national ideals or a national vision is a serious problem. But in Israel's unique situation, when there are no goals for which to sacrifice, the very strength you need to live deserts you.

It is for this reason that I often ask myself what kind of special place Israel could be, what kind of goals make sense for this nation. The answer, I believe, grows out of our existence as a Jewish people. Israel should be a country where people are proud of being different, of having something in addition to what other Western democracies have. Certainly, life in Israel will never be easier or more pleasant than, say, life in California. But it can be different, imbued with a special pride.

It should, perhaps, be unnecessary to speak of Jewish pride. After all, Jews have contributed immeasurably to the world. The very basis of Western religion and moral values—the Bible—is a Jewish contribution. Beyond that, this people has contributed vastly in science, in medicine, in literature, in music. They have made so many contributions.

But would you say that the average Israeli citizen is proud of being a Jew? I don't think so. One can be proud only of what one knows, not of what one does not know. And we, unfortunately, do not know. I was born in Israel. I had all my education here from kindergarten through university. But what did I and others of my generation learn in all those years of schooling that might have made us proud of our Jewishness? How much of the Bible did we really learn? How much did we learn about the history of the Land of Israel? How many people here know, for example, that there has been an unbroken continuum of Jewish life in this country since biblical days? Sometimes I talk to people abroad who think that Jews came here after the Holocaust. But even people here often think that Jews came to Israel with the beginning of the Zionist movement, ninety or a hundred years ago. How many know that Jews were the largest community in Jerusalem, going back to the first census in 1840? How many know that in the following years the Jewish community in Jerusalem became larger than all the other communities combined? Who knows the names of villages—Arab villages in this country—where Jews were living until a few hundred years ago? How many people know the number of Jews who never went into exile but lived here continuously, generation after generation? Jews here do not by and large know these things. Nor do they know the greatest creations of Jewish wisdom: the Mishnah and the Talmud. Nor the leading Jewish thinkers: Moses Maimonides, Yehuda Halevi, Ahad Ha'am—among the greatest thinkers the world has produced. You can only be truly proud of something if you know it thoroughly. And such things were not inserted in the hearts of Jews who have come of age here.

A few years ago I was invited to an orthodox kibbutz to speak at the conclusion of Shnat Hashmita—the last year in the biblical seven-year cycle, the traditional year of rest and renewal. At first I could not imagine what I might say to all those learned students and rabbis. What was it that I might be able to tell them? Finally I decided to address them on what I like to think of as a full circle that has taken place over the last hundred years: the development of this country Israel in conjunction with Judaism.

I started by talking about the pioneers of Petach Tikva, the first Zionist settlement. Who were these very earliest pioneers? They were the most orthodox Jews from Jerusalem wearing "shtreimels," the dark fur hats of the Middle Ages. After Petach Tikva came Hibat Zion in the 1880s, also settled by orthodox Jews during the First Aliyah. The Second Aliyah immigrants who arrived prior to World War One were inspired by the social movements fermenting in Europe and especially by the Russian Revolution of 1905. But beneath the veneer they too were yeshiva "buchers"—students who had received their education in the Jewish religious schools of Eastern Europe. After World War One came the Third Aliyah—our parents. And that was a generation of true rebels. But for all their revolutionary fire, they knew in their bones what it meant to be Jewish. They knew their culture; they spoke Hebrew. If I had mastered the richness of this language as my father did, I would be exceptionally proud. So that was a generation of rebels, but rebels with deep roots in Judaism.

The problem started with our generation. Because we were the sons and daughters of rebels, we had no Judaism in our upbringing whatsoever. The result was that our generation in a way lost its roots, the first to have done so. What did we know about Jewish wisdom? What did we know about Jewish contributions to the world or about the Jewish presence here in Israel? Very little. Were we taught to be proud that we were Jews, descendants of those Jews who through the ages had fought to the death for their beliefs? No, we were not taught these things. Instead, with our generation there was an attempt to create not Jews but New Israeli Men and Women. In the process we were disconnected from those earlier generations whose Jewishness was inscribed in their hearts.

And the outside world saw this too. I remember back in the 1950s and '60s when I was traveling abroad I felt the desire by others to consider me not as a Jew but as an Israeli, to draw the distinction. You are an Israeli, they seemed to say. They, those people over there with the strange clothes and strange ways—they are Jews. And in a way it felt easy to be accepted like that. But it was also dangerous. It was a signal that we had lost our Jewishness. And I for one, even then, never believed we would really be able to survive here if we were nothing more than Israelis. For our attachment to the land of Israel, our identity with it, comes through our Jewishness. I am a Jew, I thought then, as I think now. That does not mean I am a religious man. I am not. When it comes to practicing Judaism, there is much I do not know. But I do know for certain that above everything I am a Jew and only afterward an Israeli and the rest.

That is what I talked about at this religious kibbutz. The problems started, I said, in our generation with its loss of roots. And then came another generation—our children, and already another generation has appeared—our children's children. And suddenly the doubts that started with us doubled and redoubled. Is the land ours? Are we completely sure we are not taking something from somebody else? Are we grabbing and stealing and laying claim to something to which we have no right? And as the doubts have thickened, the resolution and purpose have eroded.

But through it all there is something that sustains Jews. Even a non-religious man may say that. Otherwise how could this people have been preserved for thousands of years as they have been, through exile and Diaspora, persecuted and murdered and driven from place to place?

There is something that keeps this nation. So even while we were in a process of deterioration, on the downward slope, suddenly a reaction set in. In 1973 the reaction was in the form of Gush Emunim. For sixteen years I have been watching this movement. And though it is not large, in the course of these years there has been a difference in Israel.

Nowhere else is there an element in this country now where you can come to a moshav or a kibbutz and tell them, "Look, tomorrow morning we need your trucks, your tractors. We need them to help establish a new settlement." That was the great strength of the Jewish community in the 1930s and '40s. Then you could go to any kibbutz and do exactly that. But try it today and see what happens. Yet go to a Gush Emunim community and tell them (as I did many times when I was in charge of the settlement projects in Samaria and in the Galilee) that we need their equipment, their house trailers, that we need to accommodate other families. And without a word these people will leave their houses with their infants and children and all their equipment. They will sleep at their friends' and sacrifice their work and time and get done what has to get done. They embody the spirit that once animated this entire country.

Interestingly, together with this renewal something else has been happening in Israel, something we call "hozrim bitshuva." For whatever reason, the most secular people—some of them kibbutzniks, jet pilots, doctors, artists, paratroopers—will make the decision to become orthodox. Something draws them to their Jewishness, some need to reattach themselves to their roots. And suddenly they grow "peyot," the orthodox sidelocks, and these Israelis find once again that they are Jews first. For the State of Israel, this has not been an unadulterated blessing; some of these converts become extremists, which brings its own serious problems with it. Yet in the main one can make out signs of a new convergence. In a hundred years Zionism and Judaism, together at the beginning, are drawing together again, closing a circle.

Reaffirming the identity between Israel and Judaism seems to me a prerequisite for survival. Not that all Israelis have to become orthodox, but that first of all this country must be a Jewish state and Jews must be proud that it is Jewish and they are Jewish. An example: When Mr. Begin was elected prime minister, he left for the United States on a state visit. At the airport a beautiful leavetaking ceremony was held for him. Flags and banners were flying, Israeli air force jets were flying over, all the dignitaries were there to see him off. After shaking hands with the group that had assembled there, Mr. Begin walked along the line of flags and banners until he came to the national flag, and there he paused and bowed his head.

This was broadcast directly on the radio and then described in the newspapers. And the reporting had an element of sarcasm in it, a touch of mockery about the fact that Mr. Begin had actually bowed his head in front of the flag.

A few years passed, and the peace agreement between Israel and Egypt was signed. Afterward President Sadat went to Santa Caterina Monastery in the southern Sinai for a formal flag-raising ceremony. I wasn't there, but I listened to it on the radio. The announcers described how two tall Egyptian officers were holding swords in their hands and escorting a third officer who was carrying the Egyptian flag. They described how the officers approached President Sadat, and how Sadat bowed and kissed the flag. As they pictured the scene, the announcers' voices were in a state of high excitement. And it sounded very natural. After all, it was a great event for Egypt, and the Egyptian national flag symbolized all that the moment meant. That's how the radio reporters described it, with the dignity and emotion it deserved. And these were exactly the same people who had shown such an edge of cynicism when Mr. Begin bowed to the Israeli flag. And this, if you ask me, is the problem. Not security, not the economy, not whether a peace conference should have an international umbrella, only this. And if we could solve this, we could solve all the rest.

Down the road from my farm sits Kibbutz Ruhama, a great deal larger and more prosperous now than when I first saw it in 1945. Talking with the people there, I tell them that I remember their parents, wearing their funny hats and trousers in a place that was at the end of the world. But nobody, I tell the kibbutzniks, dared to steal a thing from them. Isolated, surrounded by hostile villages, they were only twenty or twenty-five Jews among thousands and thousands of Arabs. But all of the Arabs around had respect for this tiny group. They were newcomers, but they were not strangers. They behaved as if this country had belonged to them for thousands of years, and nobody dared to steal from them or bring sheep to graze in their fields. They walked on every wadi and hill and they knew that they were the owners of this land. They looked odd in those outfits of theirs, but they behaved like kings and queens.

And now you, I tell them, I know you, I know you from the army. You are tall and blue-eyed and blond. You are educated. You know hardware, software, inputs, outputs. You were pilots, battalion commanders, brigade commanders. But look what has happened around here. In the evening while it's still light you are already inside with the perimeter lights playing over the fences. You don't control your land, your property is stolen, others' herds graze on your fields—and you do not react. Look what has happened here in forty-five years, just look what has happened. And that is the problem.

This deterioration did not take place in a year, this loss of our sense of who we are. It happened gradually. Consequently it cannot be corrected by an order or an instruction. We need a long-term plan. In order to have an independent state under the circumstances in which we live, it needs to become Jewish. That is our claim here. But this by itself is a complicated issue. Does Jewish mean orthodox? Most Jews, after all are not orthodox. And where do we turn for an answer? There are not, at the present time in the Jewish world spiritual leaders who are accepted universally— no one whose opinion would be recognized by the majority of the Jewish people. So this is something we have to draw our own conclusions about. And it is complicated. But regardless of its complexity, it is clear to me that the first step toward curing this disease of ours is education. The immediate goal should be that once Israeli youngsters have graduated high school they should have the knowledge to feel proud of themselves as Jews and proud of living in the Jewish State of Israel. That should be primary.

But understanding the historical experience and the historical contributions of the Jews is only a beginning. For the sustaining goals we need are not of the past but of the present and future. Already, of course, the achievement of the Jewish people in Israel has been magnificent. We have built more than a thousand cities, towns, and villages. We have absorbed two million immigrants from 102 countries speaking eighty-two languages, all of whom have learned Hebrew. We have developed one of the world's most advanced farming systems. We have done remarkable things in industry. We have built schools, universities, and hospitals that are models for emulation. In the kibbutzim and moshavim we have pioneered some of history's most dramatic and successful social and economic experiments. We have made our army into one of the world's finest and have won startling military victories. I would add here that had we managed nothing beyond these military triumphs, if ours had turned into a sterile military society, it would be cause for the deepest concern.

But the fact is that at the same time as Israel has been forced to survive with a sword in one hand, it has also managed these tremendous achievements of nation building. We have built the only democracy in our part of the world.

But what else can be done to make Israel different, to provide it with continuing inspiration? If one thinks in terms of fields where Jews have traditionally gained prominence, "Jewish professions," one can, I believe, outline some of the directions in which we might move. Israel could easily become, for example, a world center of science, a world center of music, of medicine, of education. Here are fields in which, for a variety of historical reasons, Jews have excelled, fields in which Israel is known and has already laid down a superb base of achievement. In Rehovot we have our Weizmann Institute of Science, one of the best-known institutions of its kind. But had we devoted the resources to it as a national priority, we might have had not one but two or three Weizmann institutes, or at the least a much larger institute than we now have. We could have done it; we still can do it. We have our Philharmonic Orchestra, one of the finest musical ensembles in the world and probably our most effective ambassador. Israel regularly produces some of the best young musicians, some of the best-known. We might have had two philharmonic orchestras, one traveling, one playing at home. We might have developed an internationally renowned musical conservatory. As national priorities we can still do these things.

Medicine is another area in which our potential goes far beyond our size. We talk a lot about peace, the ways to achieve peace, the terms of peace. But peace is a process; it takes time. One cannot say we are going to have peace, and these are the steps—A, B, C, D. One must speak instead of a process of initiating and sustaining relationships. And one way to give that process momentum is through medicine. It is not widely known that since the Six Day War Arabs from all over the Middle East have come to Israel for medical treatment. They have come from Saudi Arabia, from Iraq, from the Persian Gulf Emirates, from Egypt, from Jordan, even from Libya. Women who for years could not conceive have had their problems resolved here. And when they returned to their homes, all those people who were treated here have carried something in their hearts, something stronger than any written agreement.

During my last meeting with President Sadat in Egypt before he was murdered, he suggested that our two nations should build a monument to peace directly on the border, half in Israel, half in Egypt. But I had a different idea. Why not, I said, build a hospital instead of a monument—an Egyptian–Israeli hospital, half on Egyptian land, half on Israeli, with Israeli and Egyptian doctors, Egyptian and Israeli nurses, where people would be able to come from all over the Middle East for treatment. That would be the best monument we could have, the best symbol of what Israelis and Arabs living at peace might accomplish together.

Despite all our problems we have built beautiful medical centers. We have been so successful at this that we graduate far more doctors than are required for Israel's own needs. As a result doctors (like scientists and musicians) are leaving the country. To many of them it seems there is not adequate room for self-expression here. The country seems too small, and now the world is an open oyster. Doctors in Israel speak the same language as their brothers in the United States. Scientists and musicians speak the same language. Professionally they can go wherever the opportunities and challenges are greatest. The result is that we hear so often the sad refrain "He's an Israeli, but he doesn't live here anymore. He comes here to play, to give concerts, to teach on sabbatical, but he lives in New York." It's sad, because we know that the next generation will no longer be Israelis and they will no longer be coming to play or teach. But if we made it possible for Israelis with strong national roots to combine their careers here and abroad, if we could develop and fund foreign institutional relationships, fellowships, visiting professorships, if the financial means could be found to do that, then we could keep them Israelis.

The kinds of developments I have mentioned are, to be sure, complicated long-term endeavors. But they are within reach, particularly if they are considered not simply for their intrinsic worth but for their value as national goals, as activities from which we can draw inspiration as a nation and in which we can take pride as a nation. They can be done, but they cannot be done in a random fashion. They must be considered as dedicated national targets.

Defining and pursuing a set of national goals of this sort would give the country a sense of direction and identity. It would also help Israel resolve one of its chief problems: how to attract a steady flow of Jewish immigrants. Over the past forty years Israel has been a haven for Jews suffering discrimination and persecution in the places where they have lived. But the bulk of such people—the displaced survivors from Europe, the oppressed minorities from the Arab world—most of these have already immigrated. To continue attracting Jews, Israel must be different; it must provide the incentive of an exciting, unique, inspiring Jewish culture. If Israel is nothing more than a normal country, it will exert little attraction.

So, to survive, Israel must have the internal strength provided by a national vision. It must have a national vision to attract Jewish immigration. It also needs a national vision to achieve its place in the community of nations. Here too Israel has already established a base and a reputation that can be used to carve out a distinct and productive niche among the world's countries and particularly those of the Third World.

We are watching these days as the Third World slowly emerges as a giant on the world stage. And for many of these emerging nations Israel is a tabula rasa. China, India, and others have never had a historical relationship with the Jewish people. There is no background of guilt or hatred or religious passion, none of the historical baggage that informs so many of Israel's connections. What can Israel provide for such nations, what models or solutions can it bring to help with their problems?

In this area I would single out agriculture. In its brief modern history Israel has had a remarkable experience in agricultural development that could help provide answers to the worldwide problems of food production. These problems are not problems of scarcity; the world does not have a shortage of food. It is not as if we are coming down to the end of the century facing a huge and growing food deficit. On the contrary, there are great food surpluses in the world, gluts that have forced down prices and hurt farmers throughout the developed nations. But the surpluses have not helped those areas of the world suffering from famine. The excesses never get to these places. This is not just a logistical problem of how best to transport food. It is a social and cultural problem in the affected areas. People have to learn how to work and produce under new circumstances. Their agricultural economies have to be remade.

It is in precisely this area that Israel has a tremendous wealth of experience to offer. We have managed to take people who had no experience of agriculture whatsoever and turn them into first-class farmers. We have taken agriculturalists used to medieval methods and trained them to successfully manage the most up-to-date farming techniques. We have had aliyahs of Jews who never in their wildest dreams imagined a modern industrial society. And in a short time they were able to integrate themselves as workers in highly sophisticated industries and technologically advanced agriculture. So we have the experience to offer.

In fact, Israel has already been working in the Third World for thirty-five or forty years, in more than a hundred countries, chiefly in agriculture and planning, most often on a co-operative basis. Many of those countries never had any diplomatic relations with Israel. As I mentioned earlier, about 35,000 specialists have come to Israel to learn our systems while we have trained another 35,000 to 40,000 in their own countries.

A recent example. Two years ago I went to Colombia to make a survey of the potential for industrial and agro-industrial co-operation. I signed an agreement. We funded half, they funded half. So now it is being done. Their people are coming to Israel, ours are going there—building relationships, mutual interests, ties. As minister of agriculture I signed agreements with a number of countries, including a cross-section of the world's nations, notably in South America and Africa. There are so many things to do. Right now, for example, I would like to make a common effort with one or more other nations on a major water desalination project. In the past we were the world leaders in this field, perhaps we still are. Solving the problems of desalination has vast significance. Let two countries pool resources on it. It's economically advantageous, it's humanitarian, it's inspiring. A nation has to have a leading project to spur its economy, its technological growth, and above all its vision of itself. But this kind of thing is not a job for any one minister or one man. How can we best contribute to crops, infrastructure, food production, to planning, training, health? A comprehensive national approach is necessary, one that defines foreign agricultural assistance and development as a national priority. One should not be known just for the sword but for the plowshare.

With all Israel's pressing concerns, it is vital that we define our way of contributing to the world, important for both moral and practical reasons—for economic benefits, for our image in the world, for our image in our own eyes. So when I speak of making Israel an interesting country, a different country, these are some of the things that I would like to see done.

Bringing about an Israel of the future that will have the moral strength and national vision to survive is not solely an Israeli project. Because between Israel and the Jewish people abroad there exists an essential interdependence. Israel will not be able to exist and survive in the long term without the Jewish people abroad. But by the same token I do not believe the Jewish people abroad will be able to remain Jews without Israel. It is true that in the past this people has sustained itself without a homeland. But if they were not then in possession of their land, they had waking dreams of it. Every day in their prayers the name of the land was on their lips twenty-one times. The land was the repository of their hopes, their aspirations, their memories of where they came from and where they longed to return. All that kept them together under the terrible circumstances in which they lived, it sustained them as Jews.

But it's a different world now, and the dream has been accomplished. Maybe it has not been accomplished as they wanted it to be accomplished. Maybe they expected more from it. But in essence the goal of 2,000 years has become a reality. And if this goal, Israel, should disappear, it will be a blow that the Jewish people will not be able to recover from. And no doubt they will never be able to accomplish it again.

So there is a mutual responsibility between Jews in Israel and Jews abroad. Israel, as I insist time and again in my trips overseas, is not an Israeli project. It is a worldwide Jewish project. And because Israel is so isolated and faces such grave dangers, a comprehensive effort should be made to organize the great strength of the Jewish people. Thirty years ago I suggested the outlines of such an effort to Ben-Gurion, which I then repeated to Levi Eshkol and Golda Meir and in more detailed form to Yitzhak Rabin when he was prime minister. Speaking in international terms, Jews do not have great financial resources; the real concentrations of wealth in the world are not in Jewish hands. But Jews do have influence and other resources that go far beyond their numbers. Yet nobody really knows anything about this area. Do we have a list of the 1,000 or 2,000 most influential Jews in the world? We don't have anything of this kind. What do we know about Jews who are leading media figures throughout the world, about Jews who are prominent medical or cultural figures? These kinds of data are not assembled. Who are the leading Jewish scientists? Where are they? What are their fields of interest? Do they come to Israel to visit? Do they have relatives here? What about leading physicians? What about people in politics? Who knows how many and who are the Jewish builders and Jewish engineers?

How can we identify these people? How can we discuss things with them, how can we foster our sense of community with them? For the most part they are not connected with the United Jewish Appeal or the other charitable organizations. The charitable groups have never covered more than a narrow area of Jewish life, hardly touching at all on the worlds of media or science or academia. But these people too are conscious of their roots; they have their sympathies and their curiosity. They too want to learn, they too want to teach. What can be done to attract them as partners, to enlist the vast pool of talent and energy they represent in aid of this worldwide Jewish project they are even now connected with, if only in a tangential way?

This of course is only part of the large issue of Israel and the overseas Jewish community, only part of the question of how to rally support and feeling. To do this job comprehensively one must first of all know where the potential backing is. Then it is a matter of generating goals and ideals that animate the sense of Jewish identity and community. Finally, one must provide avenues for its expression. So much can be done along these lines. I would love to be able to come to the Jewish community in, say, Los Angeles or Philadelphia and raise the flag. "We want you to build a town in Israel. See that piece of land, that is your piece of land. Do what you want with it, and do it your way, according to your own concepts of what is fitting. Do it wherever you want—the Galilee, the Judean desert, the Negev, Samaria, anywhere. Take this mountain, take that piece of wilderness. Do something with it. Adopt it."

We in fact did start something of that nature in 1981—the Mediterranean–Dead Sea Canal. We raised a hundred million dollars for it and got it off the ground. The project could have opened up the Negev with lakes and tourism and industry. Unfortunately, in 1984 when the new government came in, the canal was halted. But projects of this sort are feasible and inspiriting. They should be done, and not on a partisan basis. A tremendous effort is required to deal with issues like these. You need to be able to disconnect yourself from the daily problems and crises. You have to define exactly what you are looking for, lay the plans and implement them. Somebody has to take it in hand, perhaps a "minister of overseas affairs," a person in whom this work would be vested as the national priority it deserves to be.

Making Israel into a Jewish nation with a set of commonly recognized goals and a sense of identity and direction is a prerequisite for survival. But though Israel is a Jewish nation it is, of course, not only a Jewish nation. We live here with minorities, with Druze, Bedouin, Circassians, and especially with Arabs, 710,000 Israeli Arabs according to the last census. Our question is one that faces every heterogeneous nation: How do you treat the minorities among you? What should be your approach?

For myself, I begin with the basic conviction that Jews and Arabs can live together. I have repeated that at every opportunity, not for journalists and not for popular consumption, but because I have never believed differently or thought differently, from my childhood on. I am not afraid of Arabs. I feel I can live with them. I believe I understand their problems. I know that we are both inhabitants of this land, and although the state is Jewish, that does not mean that Arabs should not be full citizens in every sense of the word.

That is why I have always regarded it as a mistake to tell Israeli Arabs (as many politicians do when they are looking for votes), "Look, we understand you, you are part of the Palestinian people, the PLO represents part of your aspirations." No, my approach had always been to say, "Look, you are part of Israel, you are citizens, inhabitants. We will always have to live together, you and we, forever. I am not advocating that you forget you are Palestinians. But you are part of this country, part of this democracy that exists here."

To my way of looking at it, this approach is not just a matter of morality, it is a matter of necessity. There are various options among Israelis about what should be done in Samaria, Judea, and Gaza— keeping it the way it is now, granting autonomy, giving them political expression in Amman, annexation, territorial compromise, cantoniza- tion. But for the Israeli Arabs there is only one acceptable possibility, and that is to live together in at least basic harmony. What can we do instead? Give up the Galilee? Then give up the Green Line Arab communities? Then give up part of the Negev? I never saw the major problem as being with the Arabs of Samaria and Judea, but with the Israeli Arabs—who are citizens here but who are not full partners. So the question is How do we bring them to this point, how do we really include them as equals in this country in terms of duties and of rights?

To my way of thinking, the answer has to do with the nature of democracy. First, full rights and full obligations go together, reciprocal parts of one whole. Secondly, laws must be enforced equally for everybody, period. Presently we suffer with a situation where Arab citizens of Israel do not have all the opportunities that should be theirs and do not bear all the obligations that should be theirs. Nor are laws enforced on the Arab community as they are on the rest of Israel.

Arab citizens, for example, pay a disproportionately low share of taxes. Many Arab builders by and large are allowed to ignore the codes that govern everyone else. Minor fees (television and radio fees, for example) are not enforced on Arab homes as they are on Jewish homes. Most importantly, Israeli Arabs do not share the one basic burden that all others do—military service. This is not a relatively minor matter as it is in many other countries. Basic service here takes three years out of a young man's life (women serve two years), four years at the least if the individual becomes an officer. Afterward Israelis serve as reserve soldiers for thirty-five years, and reserve duty means thirty days each year (forty-two for officers) and an additional one day per month—all of which can double in times of tension. Everyone, that is, bears the burden of national service during the prime years of his or her youth and for another month and a half each year through middle age. And military service is a good deal more than just a matter of sharing this substantial burden. When you participate in defending your country, then in an important sense the country becomes yours. If you do not defend it, then it is not fully yours.

I used to appear before the Arab public from time to time, and I remember one day I was invited to speak in one of the largest Israeli Arab towns, Baka el Rarbia. Several hundred Arabs were there, many of them people in their twenties. In a small crowded hall I talked about the future relations between Jews and Arabs. My message was that, knowing the geography and demographics of Israel well, I could not see any possibility of drawing a line that would divide the country in such a way that Jews and Arabs would be able to live separately.

Consequently, I said, Jews and Arabs have to live together in Israel, and I believe they can live together. But exactly on what terms they can live together should be spelled out very clearly. The Arab population does not carry the burden of the duties and obligations. They do not serve in the army, they pay very low taxes. But at the same time because of their voting power they in reality dictate what government Israel will have. And this, I told them, is a wholly unacceptable situation.

We understand what the Arab population here is saying, I told them. They cannot serve in the army, because Israel is fighting their people, or their people are fighting Israel. However, I am looking forward to the day when there will be peace between the Jews and Arabs. And personally I believe that in order to have this peace the Palestinians need a political expression. The fact is that a Palestinian state has existed since 1922, when Great Britain split off 78 percent of Palestine to create Transjordan. Transjordan—Jordan now—is a country where most of the population is Palestinian, most members of parliament are Palestinian, most of the cabinet is Palestinian, and most of the prime ministers have been Palestinian. Jordan is in fact if not in name a Palestinian state with which we should be discussing the future of the inhabitants of Samaria and Judea and the various other problems that exist between us.

"And when that does finally happen," I told them, "and when there is peace, we will have to come to you and talk to you in the frankest way and tell you, Look gentlemen, we are not at war any longer. You are living in this country and enjoying its benefits, you have to share the burdens as well. You will have to serve in the army. Perhaps military service should not start immediately. Perhaps some kind of alternative national service should be made available first. But a national service we can do even now. I agree that you have to be full partners here, but you also have to have all the duties, both."

While I was making these points I could see eyes smoldering in the audience. Then somebody shouted, "And what if we don't want to serve in the army?" "If you don't want to serve in the army," I answered, "then I believe you should live in Israel on exactly the same basis as the 80,000 others, Jews and non-Jews, who reside here but who are not Israeli citizens. They enjoy the social services, the schools, the hospitals, and so on. They can participate in municipal elections. But the one thing they cannot do is vote in the national elections. If they are not Israeli citizens, they cannot decide what government Israel will have."

"So what citizens are we supposed to be then?" somebody else asked. "Be Palestinian citizens, citizens of the Palestinian state residing in Israel. Nobody will harm you, any more than anyone harms other residents here." "And what will happen if we don't like that idea?" "That is up to you," I answered. "Sell your property, go somewhere else, stay here, live as inhabitants. But you cannot dictate what government we will have here unless you bear all the burdens. Equal rights, equal duties."

At that point one young man made himself heard above the din. "What do you mean?" he said. "Why should we just be residents? We were here long before you were." "Where are you from?" I asked. "From Kfar Kara." I knew Kfar Kara well, so I said, "What do you mean, you came earlier than we did? What is your name?" "Masarwa!" he shouted back. "Yes," I said (Masarwa is an Egyptian name, a common one in Kfar Kara), "your family came here from Egypt about 140 years ago. You were brought here by Ibráhim Ali, the Egyptian pasha who settled most of these villages then." At this point the crowd quieted down.

The point, I think, was clear. The two things go together—the rights of citizenship and the responsibilities of citizenship.

A short time ago representatives of a Bedouin town in the Negev came to my office in the ministry, people I have known for years, neighbors. They came with a request to establish some industrial projects in their town. "We're citizens," they said, "Israelis like other Israelis. We'd like help with this." So I said, yes, of course. I will help you exactly as I would help anybody else. I want to provide assistance on this and I will do it. But one thing I would like to say. On Independence Day I happened to drive through your town and I did not see even one Israeli flag flying. Maybe it was there and I just didn't see it. But when I passed through the next Israeli Arab town, well, I didn't see the flag there either, not one flag. Now you come to me and you say, we are equal citizens, you and I. And I say, Of course. But what about the Israeli flags on Independence Day?

This is the kind of problem we should have been dealing with all along, but not on a partisan basis. The issue has nothing to do with parties. When I talk to the Labor people, I tell them, "Look, this is a national problem, an Israeli problem. It makes no difference if it is your government or our government. We must sit together and discuss it. And the common basis of our discussion must be that for Jews and Arabs to live together the laws must be implemented universally—for Arabs as well as for Jews. Justice must be exactly the same for all citizens. If not, the democracy we have, the fair and reasonable guidelines we have devised for our mutual life here, will break apart.

But too often the response is "Can we trust them at all?" I say, "Look, the Druze fought us hard in the beginning of the Independence War. But they have been with us ever since. For years they have served in my commands, many of them: in '56 and '67, during the War of Attrition along the Suez. And many Bedouin too—volunteers fighting in Gaza against the terror, and in the Arava, and in the Yom Kippur War. Various times I have found myself alone in the field with Druze officers and soldiers. They are company commanders, battalion commanders, brigade commanders, division commanders. My sons served under Druze officers. I have been to so many battles with them. Did I ever once start questioning who was Jewish and who was non-Jewish? They were exactly like everyone else. They fought like everyone else, with the same bravery. For forty years already they have been serving in the army, getting their education, bearing their responsibilities. I trust them. That's what happens. If Israel's Arabs were able to integrate themselves in the same way, to bear the same burdens, I would trust them in the same way. That's how I see it."

Admittedly the problem of Israel's Arabs is complicated, far more complicated now that some Israeli Arabs are becoming more and more involved in the current violence and terror. Consequently, to some it may seem easier to simply leave this situation alone and not stir up treacherous political waters. But in fact it requires the most immediate and careful attention. Because this problem is not just complicated, it also is dangerous, even more dangerous than the problems in Samaria and Judea. There at least we have various possible resolutions. But when it comes to Israeli Arabs, there are no alternatives, no options at all. And if a breakdown comes, there are only two possibilities, both of them unacceptable. One is that the Arabs here will eventually face the kind of tragedy their parents brought on themselves in 1948. The other is that the Jews will give up more and more and will concentrate in an ever smaller area until the nation is so constricted it will not have the means to survive.

I do not claim to know all the answers. But I do know that any national solution to these problems has to be grounded in Israel's Declaration of Independence. This is one state, and this one state is a Jewish state, in the same way that France is a French state and Spain is a Spanish state. The anthem of this state is "Hatikvah," the flag is the Star of David. There are not two anthems, there are not two flags. And this Jewish state, they would say, must be one that guarantees full citizenship and asks an equal commitment, for everyone and from everyone.

Peace is another issue on which it is absolutely essential for us to find the broadest possible national consensus. A widely acceptable formula must somehow be found so that Israel can take the initiative in the peace process rather than be relegated to responding to the demands of others. Then, after we had the most nearly bipartisan approach that we could come up with, we should if possible attempt to get American support on substance. At that point, when our own house is in order and our allies are with us, then we can approach the Arab nations.

But regardless of the substance of an Israeli peace plan—or of any peace plan—two prerequisites will have to be in place before progress can be made. The first is that peace must be equally important to both sides, to Arabs as well as Jews. The essence of achieving a negotiated peace is compromise, and compromise by its nature is a two-sided process. As long as the need for peace is asymmetric, one side will be unwilling to compromise, and this is a sure recipe for killing any negotiations.

In general there has not been until now a symmetric desire for peace. It is clear to everyone that Israel, swimming in an Arab sea, would benefit immeasurably from peace. But while the Arab nations' need for peace is no less urgent, this fact has not been acknowledged by Arab leaders and is less apparent to the rest of the world. The result is that Israeli leaders are constantly being asked by journalists, diplomats, heads of state, "What are you willing to give up for peace? What concessions are you willing to make?" But I have never heard anyone ask the Arabs, "What are you willing to give up for peace? Peace is important for you too. What will you give up for it? What are the concessions you are willing to make?" Those questions have always been asked exclusively of Israel.

But the truth is that just as peace is important for Israel it is also important for the Arabs. Egypt, the one Arab nation with which we currently have a peace treaty, is a prime example. Egypt had and still has dire economic problems. They receive grants and other support from the United States, which would not be forthcoming without peace. They have one quiet border, only one, the border with Israel. They have problems and disputes with the Sudan about river water. The Libyan frontier has been troubled for years, troubles that have included skirmishes and local battles. I remember on one of my visits to Egypt when tension was building with Libya and the Egyptians had decided to concentrate troops along the border. Marshal Abu Gazallah, the minister of defense, described the situation to me and said that he was considering moving the Third Army from the area of the canal to the Libyan border. My response was that he could transfer the army without any worries at all. "I can assure you," I said, "that we will not move one soldier from his position." The result was that they transferred their troops and we, of course, did not move an inch. They know, and we know, that their one secure border is the one they share with Israel.

Like Egypt, Jordan has had terrible problems: economic problems, problems with terrorism, problems with their Arab neighbors. At the end of the 1950s, when they were threatened by Iraq, we gave Great Britain the right to overfly Israel with its airlift to Jordan. And the British saved them from the Iraqis. In the fluid Middle East who can predict what might happen once the Iraq-Iran hostilities are over for good and Jordan is faced with a gigantic and idle Iraqi military machine on its eastern border. It is not a prospect King Hussein can be facing with any equanimity. Meanwhile the Jordanians live under a constant threat from Syria. They remember quite well the Syrian invasion in 1970, and they understand exactly what their fate would have been if not for Israeli action at that time. Certainly Hussein would not be there today. Personally, I thought our intervention then was a mistake. But the fact is that we did it, and both the king and the Jordanian state survived. Beyond these events, Hussein knows by heart all the times Israel provided him with information that thwarted attempts on his life. So Jordan too has one really quiet, secure border, the border with Israel. Only there do they have no problems.

The upshot of all this is that when peace is discussed, it must be understood that peace is equally important to both sides. When that is the approach, then both sides realize they have to make concessions, not just one side. And when that happens the chances of actually achieving peace will improve dramatically.

That is the first prerequisite: The search for peace must be symmetric. The second prerequisite is that the peace process cannot be rushed. One cannot stand over such a process with a stopwatch and deadlines, applying pressure to sign and embrace by some particular date. Real problems, problems vital to the life of a nation, can never be dealt with in this way. One might talk about a trend, one might see the development of circumstances conducive to peace or impeding peace. One can take advantage of opportunities and recognize the timeliness of events, but no nation is going to be railroaded into agreements affecting its life.

Israel is hardly alone in this regard. The world has many major problems that have not been resolved. Divided Germany. Divided Korea, Central America, Cambodia, Northern Ireland. But nobody stands there with a stopwatch and asks, When is there going to be a resolution? When are you going to embrace? Take the Panama Canal issue. If the canal treaty had been brought to the United States Senate today, considering developments in that area of the world (this is being written as the contras are suing for peace and as General Noriega is defying the United States), would it not have seemed that the year 2000 was too early? It was hard enough for the Americans to ratify the transfer several years ago. But now that we are actually approaching the year 2000 and we are watching the instability in Central America, would you think for one minute the United States today would have given up control? I doubt it.

Our area too is unstable, traditionally one of the least stable in the world. What will eventually happen in the Persian Gulf is anyone's guess. We do not know what will happen in Syria after Assad or in Iraq after Saddam Hussein or in Iran after Khomeini. What will happen with the Alawis in Syria or the Shi'ites in Lebanon? We live here in the middle of dangerous and fluid situations. It may take another twenty, thirty, fifty years before there is anything like stability in this region. And in such circumstances one must be extremely cautious about taking steps, particularly when those steps affect not just your interests but your survival. So look at our situation exactly the same way you would look at your country, or other places in the world. Extremely complicated situations simply do not respond to deadlines. So this is the second major condition that must be met. Number one: Both sides must want peace and be willing to make concessions for it. And number two: Everyone must understand that it will take time.

Beyond these prerequisites there is at least one further element that must be an integral part of any peace agreement between Israel and the Arab world. The refugee problem must be solved. After forty years we can no longer afford to leave this wound open. By now it should be universally recognized that without solving this problem there is not the slightest possibility of relaxing the Middle East situation. This is not something that can be dealt with after an agreement; it must be accomplished as part of an agreement. So this too is a prerequisite, despite the fact that the surrounding Arab states have never made any effort to relieve the plight of their own Palestinian refugees.

The proportions of the refugee problem are such that its resolution will require co-operation not only by Israel and the Arabs but also by the United States and Europe. But the difficulties, though severe, are not insuperable. Gaza, for example, could be a start. Currently the district is packed with towns, refugee camps, and orange groves, its 550,000 people living in an area of 360 square kilometers. But Gaza does not have to be squalid and overcrowded. With a comprehensive program of planning, rehabilitation, and building it could be transformed into a modern urban industrial area. By way of comparison, greater Tel Aviv, with its airports, industry, universities, and high standard of living, has over a million inhabitants concentrated in 180 square kilometers. Remaking Gaza would be a humanitarian achievement of the first order. The consequences such a project would have for peace in the region can hardly be exaggerated.

Even if the refugee problem is addressed, as it must be, the status of Samaria, Judea, and Gaza will remain one of the most difficult problems facing the parties involved in the Arab-Israeli conflict. This particular conflict, it must be remembered, preceded by many years the Six Day War that brought these areas under Israeli control. But events of the past year have focused world attention on them. Whatever the immediacy of this problem, though, any solution that has a chance of bringing peace instead of increased violence must take account of the realities here, including the bedrock reality, which is Israel's need to live a secure, normal national life.

These disputed areas are part of Palestine, which the Jews have always called Eretz Israel and which was accorded to them as their national homeland in the Balfour Declaration of 1917. In 1922 this land was divided for the first time, with three quarters of Palestine being taken to form Jordan, on the east bank of the Jordan River. With the U.N.'s creation of Israel in 1947 and the subsequent War of Independence, the so-called West Bank was occupied by Jordan and Iraq and Gaza by Egypt. Then in 1967 these areas were freed from Arab occupation. Whatever the political rhetoric, the reality here is that a Palestinian state exists in Jordan with its capital in Amman, and a Jewish state exists in Israel with its capital in Jerusalem.

Then there are Samaria, Judea, and Gaza. The significance of these places to Israel is often expressed in terms of strategic distances. The narrow plain within which most Israelis live has a width of nine miles at Natania; it is eight miles from the Samarian hills to Tel Aviv; three miles from the old demarcation line to Ben-Gurion airport. The corridor to Jerusalem narrows to less than five miles. The distances that provided the parameters for our defense prior to 1967 are substantially less than an easy morning commute in the United States. From the pre-1967 borders, practically the entire country is within artillery range and surface-to-air missile range.

But though all this is true, and grimly serious considering the enmity that surrounds us, the main problem with Samaria and Judea is not the danger of artillery or missiles or tanks. These are dangers in times of war.

More imminent is the kind of war we have experienced from these places in times of peace. And by that I mean terror. One hundred years of terror. And this has nothing to do with our presence in Samaria or Judea or Gaza. Terror was a fact of our lives in the 1960s, '50s, '40s, '30s, and '20s. It was with us during the Turkish occupation, the British occupation, the Jordanian and Egyptian occupations. The maps of these areas, then, that display military features, distances, ranges, topography, and so on are incomplete. To see the real meaning of Samaria, Judea, and Gaza for Israeli security, one would also have to chart the number of raids, murders, and incidents of sabotage that were carried out against the Jewish population by Palestinian Arabs living in those areas—long before 1967.

Consequently, the problem of these territories is not something amenable to an agreement between sovereign states. It is not the kind of problem where a formal solution can be reached and then peace and quiet will automatically follow. In my own approach to these areas I have tried to consider them objectively, outside of the deep emotional and historical feelings that I share with so many other Jews. And looking at them specifically from a security point of view, it is self-evident to me that regardless of what political settlement might be reached, security matters in these areas must be in our hands, internal security as well as external. We have no choice but to take into consideration that even if we reach a peace agreement with Jordan, terror will not cease. In the harsh light of a hundred years of experience, I cannot see any political solution that will put a stop to the terror. Therefore, we have no alternative but to retain responsibility for security here.

Everything starts from that. But with that as a given, we have to ask how the inhabitants of these territories can most fully govern themselves in other regards. How can they best determine the shape of their lives and have a meaningful way of expressing themselves politically?

In my view the logical answer to this is that their political expression must come within the framework of the Palestinian state of Jordan.* We cannot make them Israeli citizens, nor do I think they would want to be.

---

* It should be remembered that King Hussein's Hashemite royal family came from Mecca and was established by the British in Transjordan in 1921. Another branch of the family had been installed by the British in Syria (from where they were expelled), then in Iraq (where they were deposed and murdered 36 years later). Iraq, of course, was Iraq before, during and after the Hashemites, just as Greece was Greece before, during, and after its Danish kings. In exactly the same way, Jordan is Palestinian, regardless of who is on the throne, or whether there is a throne.

And we must say very clearly that concern for our own survival does not permit the establishment of a second Palestinian state on the West Bank. Consequently, the most logical and perhaps the only feasible approach is for the inhabitants of the territories to exercise their political identities as citizens of Jordan, as most of them are now (Arab inhabitants of Judea and Samaria are members of Jordan's parliament and ministers in Jordan's cabinet).

In outline, this would mean close cooperation between Israel and Jordan. We would have to solve several complicated issues. One would be the method of voting and of election to the parliament in Amman. Another would be the issue of taxation. An agreement on the territories would also have to deal with trade issues between Israel and Jordan. Last year, for example, 1.2 million crossings were made between the West Bank and Jordan. Thousands of trucks go from the West Bank and Gaza to Jordan, from where goods are transshipped to Syria, Iraq, the Emirates, and Saudi Arabia—vegetables, fruits, and other products. We would have to establish procedures to continue with this and assist in developing it further. What about the tremendous resources of the Dead Sea? This is a natural area for co-operative industrial and trade development. A railroad serving Jordan and Israel should be built, to the great benefit of all. Jordan, without a Mediterranean outlet, could be accorded use of Ashdod and Haifa, this to be linked with Israeli use of Aqaba. With the West Bank focusing attention on the natural economic community between Israel and Jordan, the two countries might move toward establishing a common market. Who can say how co-operation might develop? The possibilities for mutual assistance in this region are virtually limitless. An agreement by itself is only the beginning of a process. Its real importance is the doors it opens up.

You might say, Look, I've never heard of a solution like that—that people should have their political expression in one country, their security in the hands of another country, and their economic lives integrated with both. But there are a lot of extremely complicated national problems in this world that have not been resolved. And almost always, where competing vital interests and long-term antagonisms make clear-cut resolutions impossible, stalemate, tension, and violence seem to be the rule. But these are just the conditions we are trying to break free of, and people ought to understand that we are dealing, on our side, not simply with problems of national interest but of national survival. This means that resolutions, if they are to come, are likely to be non-conventional. And any resolution will have to be considered with extreme caution.

My generation was fortunate to be born into one of the most dramatic periods in the 3,800-year course of Jewish history. But living in this crucial period also burdens us with a special responsibility for the continuation of Jewish existence. In this generation we must make decisions not only on the basis of our own ease and convenience. We have to look forward, to try to see what circumstances might look like in fifty years, or a hundred, or two hundred. We are living in complicated and dangerous times, for which we must be able to work out appropriate solutions. We cannot rush forward with easy answers.

Withdrawal from the territories is, unfortunately, an easy answer that may satisfy a certain number of people initially but which will inevitably create more violence and a greater threat to our survival than we have faced since the first part of the War of Independence. What will happen if we withdraw is not a matter of conjecture. We have seen it already along the northern border. We did not face all-out war there, only terror—ordinary terror first, then artillery terror. A shell here, a shell there, not more than that, and soon normal life was disrupted. We know exactly what would happen in southern Lebanon if Israeli troops were removed from our security zone there. The shelling would begin again, sporadically at first, then more regularly as the terrorist infrastructure re-established itself.

But here we are not talking about towns and settlements in the northern Galilee. Gaza at this point is our southern security belt. What will we do once we withdraw from Gaza and find, as we inevitably will, that Arafat or his successors have stepped in and that squads of terrorists are again operating from there into Israel, murdering and destroying? What will we do when the Katyusha fire starts hitting Sderot, four miles from the Gaza district, and Ashkelon, nine miles from Gaza, and Kiryat Gat, fourteen miles from Gaza. A Katyusha is nothing more than a metal tube seven feet long, easily transportable, virtually undetectable. The simplest of them has a fifteen-mile range, the more sophisticated can reach twenty-five miles. Will the television pictures showing us shelling Gaza in return be more palatable than those that showed us in front of Beirut, or less upsetting than those of Israeli troops battling West Bank rioters? Or what shall we do if U.N. or multinational forces are positioned around Gaza and there is still terrorism? Shall we hit the Italians, or the British, or the Americans? What will we do when there are raids from Samaria and Judea into Kfar Saba and Petach Tikva and the suburbs of Tel Aviv?

These are the times when we will face the real dilemmas. And how will we react? After all those years and all the fighting and all the struggles, what will we do? Institute a modern version of the paratrooper operations of the 1950s and '60s? Will we go immediately to war? What will happen?

It is a question that hardly needs to be asked. We have already seen what will happen. When the PLO was shelling the northern border, the population started moving away from their homes; thousands of people left their settlements and towns and moved toward the center. But in the center of the country it will be worse. The population who live here have hardly tasted terrorism for a generation. And where are they going to go, to the American embassy? To the roof? To American carriers? What are we going to do? Even those Israelis who want to hand over everything have no answers to such basic questions of our security.

In fact—the fact that the world has been so shockingly unwilling to accept—is that we cannot have different standards applied to our security than the United States or France or any other reasonable nation would apply to its own security. Would an American government stand still for a moment if the American Southwest were being shelled by Mexico? Would France accept endless murders and sabotage from Spain? At NATO meetings, generals anxiously discuss the inadequacy of the West's 500 kilometers of defensive depth against the Soviets, and it makes Israeli planners wonder. I would not suggest that Americans or Western Europeans believe our lives are insignificant, or less significant. Yet so often that is precisely the meaning of the positions they take. We understand very well that we live here in a state of clear and present danger. Against this danger we must have the right to defend ourselves, exactly the same right that the Americans would claim, or the French, or anyone else.

Discussing these things frankly with the Egyptians, as I have so many times on my farm and in Egypt, I tell them that it would be wonderful to be liked by everybody, kissed by everybody, admired by everybody. That would be a fine thing. But we must also take into consideration that we have to exist, we have to develop. We must provide as normal a life as one might have in this region here to millions of people: manufacture, export, import, agriculture, science, art—normal life. Israel is a tiny country. Because we are in the headlines so much, people get the idea that in some ways we are a giant. But Israel from the Mediterranean to the River Jordan is forty-seven miles. From the northern tip of the Galilee to the southern tip of the Negev is 260 miles. Our first job in this small and surrounded place here is to secure life, that is the most important thing. It's like the story I used to be so fond of telling the soldiers. To get the wagon up the hill, first you have to find a stone to put under the wheel. First is that stone. We should be secure, first of all, to enable normal life. Then we have to deal with all the rest.

The great question of our day is whether we, the Jewish people of Israel, can find within us the will to survive as a nation that is necessary to solve the problems confronting us. What should Israel be like in twenty years? What about emigration and immigration? What about the relationships between Israeli Jews and Arabs, between Israel and the Jews of the Diaspora, between Israel and the rest of the world? Somehow these vital problems must be addressed now; they can no longer be left to take their own course. We must be able to determine priorities and set an agenda on basic national issues that are above and beyond party interest. If we fail to do this we risk defaulting in a struggle that we cannot afford to lose.

In some ways Israel's political experience casts a somber shadow on our ability to rise above our own divisiveness. But there is room for optimism too. We are, after all, a people with almost 4,000 years of history linking one generation to the next, a people who despite everything have been able to overcome whatever was inflicted on us both by our enemies and by ourselves. It is the business of our generation to summon up that same genius and insure that our link in this ancient chain remains unbroken. We understand that clearly, all of us do. We also know that in the face of a mountain of problems, our parents and we ourselves have managed the most remarkable achievements. So when I consider how hard it looks now, I think back to when I was a child, working with my father on that arid slope of land, walking behind him to plant the seeds in the earth he had turned with his hoe. When I felt too exhausted to go on, he would stop for a moment to look backwards, to see how much we had already done. And that would always give me heart for what remained.

Index

Acknowledgments

In working with Ariel Sharon on this book I benefited greatly from the cooperation of numerous Israelis who generously shared their memories and understanding. I owe special thanks to the following among them: Oded Shamir, Ariel Sharon's military adjutant during the Lebanon War; Dubi Weissglas, who represented Ariel Sharon during the Kahan Commission proceedings and the *Time* magazine trial; Uri Dan, who shared his knowledge of a number of crucial events to which he was eyewitness. His memoir of the Yom Kippur War (*Sharon's Bridgehead*, E.L Special Edition, Tel Aviv, 1975) was especially helpful in providing a feel for various incidents described in chapter 22. Finally, I would like to express my deepest gratitude to Sara Shema and Rochelle Amera for their help, patience and skill, and to express my gratitude to Raphael Bouganim for his help with translations and for his always stimulating insights into Israeli culture and affairs.

David Chanoff